A Survey of Accounting

What the Numbers Mean

A Survey of Accounting
What the Numbers Mean

Second Edition

by David H. Marshall, MBA, CPA, CMA
Millikin University

IRWIN

Burr Ridge, Illinois
Boston, Massachusetts
Sydney, Australia

© RICHARD D. IRWIN, INC., 1990 and 1993

Sponsoring editor: Jeff Shelstad
Editorial assistant: Branka Rnich
Marketing manager: John Biernat
Project editor: Gladys True
Production manager: Irene H. Sotiroff
Designer: Larry J. Cope
Artist: Kim Meriwether
Compositor: BiComp, Inc.
Typeface: 11/12 Times Roman
Printer: R. R. Donnelley & Sons Company

Library of Congress Cataloging-in-Publication Data

Marshall, David H.
    A survey of accounting : what the numbers mean / by David H. Marshall.—2nd ed.
        p.   cm.
    Includes index.
    ISBN 0-256-11301-7
    1. Accounting. 2. Financial statements. I. Title.
HF5635.M36 1993
657′.3—dc20   92–16798

Printed in the United States of America
  4 5 6 7 8 9 0 DOH 9 8 7 6 5 4 3

The Irwin Series in Undergraduate Accounting

Anderson and Clancy
Cost Accounting

Bernstein
Financial Statement Analysis: Theory, Application and Interpretation
Fifth Edition

Bernstein and Maksy
Cases in Financial Statement Reporting and Analysis

Boockholdt
Accounting Information Systems
Third Edition

Danos and Imhoff
Introduction to Financial Accounting

Deakin and Maher
Cost Accounting
Third Edition

Dyckman, Dukes, and Davis
Intermediate Accounting
Revised Edition

Dyckman, Dukes, and Davis
Intermediate Accounting
Standard Edition

Edwards, Hermanson, and Maher
Principles of Financial and Managerial Accounting
Revised Edition

Engler
Managerial Accounting
Third Edition

Engler and Bernstein
Advanced Accounting
Second Edition

FASB 1992–93 Edition
  Current Text: General Standards
  Current Text: Industry Standards
  Original Pronouncements, Volume I
  Original Pronouncements, Volume II
  Statements of Financial Accounting Concepts

Ferris
Financial Accounting and Corporate Reporting: A Casebook
Third Edition

Garrison
Managerial Accounting
Sixth Edition

Griffin, Williams, Boatsman, and Vickrey
Advanced Accounting
Sixth Edition

Hay and Engstrom
Essentials of Accounting for Governmental and Not-for-Profit Organizations
Third Edition

Hay and Wilson
Accounting for Governmental and Nonprofit Entities
Ninth Edition

Hendriksen and Van Breda
Accounting Theory
Fifth Edition

Hermanson and Edwards
Financial Accounting
Fifth Edition

Hermanson, Edwards, and Maher
Accounting Principles
Fifth Edition

Hermanson, Plunkett, and Turner
Computerized Accounting with Peachtree Complete III

Hermanson, Strawser, and Strawser
Auditing Theory and Practice
Sixth Edition

Hopson, Spradling, and Meyer
Income Tax Fundamentals for 1992 Tax Returns, 1993 Edition

Hoyle
Advanced Accounting
Third Edition

Hutton and Dalton
Two 1992 Individual Tax Return Practice Problems

Hutton and Dalton
1992 Tax Return Practice Problems for Corporations, S Corporations, and Partnerships

Koerber
College Accounting

Larson and Miller
Fundamental Accounting Principles
Thirteenth Edition

Larson and Miller
Financial Accounting
Fifth Edition

Marshall
A Survey of Accounting: What the Numbers Mean
Second Edition

Miller and Redding
The FASB: The People, the Process, and the Politics
Second Edition

Mueller, Gernon, and Meek
Accounting: An international Perspective
Second Edition

Pratt and Kulsrud
Federal Taxation, 1993 Edition

Pratt and Kulsrud
Individual Taxation, 1993 Edition

Pratt, Burns, and Kulsrud
Corporate Partnership, Estate and Gift Taxation, 1993 Edition

Rayburn
Cost Accounting: Using a Cost Management Approach
Fifth Edition

Robertson
Auditing
Seventh Edition

Schroeder and Zlatkovich
Survey of Accounting

Short
Fundamentals of Financial Accounting
Seventh Edition

Smith and Wiggins
Readings and Problems in Accounting Information Systems

Whittington, Pany, Meigs, and Meigs
Principles of Auditing
Tenth Edition

About the Author

David Marshall has been marching to the beat of a different drummer during most of his career. While an undergraduate at Miami University, he developed a career plan that called for achieving partnership status in a public accounting firm, and then at about age 50, retiring to an idyllic campus setting to spew forth accumulated wisdom from the "real world." After three years in the U.S. Navy, his accounting career did begin in public accounting. But, after about three years he accepted an assistant controller position with a publicly held real estate owner, operator, and development firm. Three years later he became controller of a major candy manufacturer. And three years after that he decided to shorten the time originally set for a move to academia. After a year spent earning an MBA from Northwestern University, he was hired to teach accounting at Millikin University in Decatur, Illinois. After four years of teaching, he was named the university's Vice President for Business Affairs. He held that post for three years before returning to the faculty. After all of those three-year stints, he had learned that he really wanted to teach.

Marshall served Millikin University as Professor of Accounting and Chair of the Departments of Accounting and Management Information Systems. He was named Distinguished Faculty Lecturer in 1984, and received the Teaching Excellence and Campus Leadership Award in 1992. One of his teaching principles was that students should work to see the "big picture"; that is, relate course concepts to their application in the business world.

The idea for this text developed from the requirement that Millikin's industrial engineering majors take an accounting course. A traditional financial accounting principles course was available, but Marshall believed that a financial statement user's approach was more appropriate, with coverage of product costing, cost behavior patterns, budgeting, standard costs, and capital budgeting included in the course. After much assistance from colleagues, reviewers, and students, the result of his belief is the book you now have in your hands.

In May 1992, Marshall retired from the faculty of Millikin University, and acepted a post-retirement position as Director of Planned Giving in the Advancement Division. He is still very interested in accounting education, especially the developments resulting from the efforts of the Accounting Education Change Commission.

Preface

The word *accounting* most often conjures up images of tedious figures, thick glasses, and headaches. However, the savvy businessperson realizes that accounting has come to be known as the *language of business* with good reason. Accounting conveys important financial information that is used in the management planning, control, and decision-making processes integral to achieving organizational objectives. Some command of this language is a necessity for those who wish to participate in these processes.

In 1989 the Accounting Education Change Commission was formed "to foster changes in the academic preparation of accountants consistent with the goal of improving their capabilities for successful professional careers." In the exposure draft of Position Statement No. 2, "The First Course in Accounting," the Commission stated:

> The two primary objectives of the first course in accounting are (1) to make clear the ways in which accounting is an information development and communication function that supports economic decision making, and (2) to prepare students to obtain additional knowledge. The knowledge and skills provided by the first course in accounting should facilitate subsequent learning even if the student takes no additional academic work in accounting or directly related disciplines. For example, the course should help those who complete it in performing financial analysis; in deriving information for personal or organizational decisions; and in understanding business, governmental, and other organizational entities.[1]

Typical undergraduate business students are required to complete two entry-level accounting courses covering topics in finan-

---

[1] Accounting Education Change Commission, Exposure Draft of Position Statement No. 2, "The First Course in Accounting" (Torrence, Calif., 1992), p. 3.

cial and managerial accounting. The author of this text believes that over the years, many of the textbooks used in those courses have become increasingly encyclopedic. The result has been the teaching of a great deal of accounting detail without having students obtain a "big picture" of financial statement and accounting information use. One of the objectives of this text is to provide that "big picture" while meeting the objectives for a first course in accounting identified by the Accounting Education Change Commission. When supplemented with appropriate cases and other materials, this text can be used in both the financial and managerial entry-level courses taken by undergraduate business majors. Students who intend to pursue an accounting major will also have to learn the procedures of accounting, which can be taught in courses or with laboratory cases (e.g., practice sets) designed for those students. The majority of students in the entry-level courses will not become accounting majors. This book is aimed at helping them learn how to become effective users of accounting information while providing a solid foundation for those students who will pursue advanced study in accounting.

Many students whose academic interests are not in the business field can also benefit from exposure to accounting. These students, however, often have a restricted curriculum and may simply not be interested in investing two elective courses in acquiring some basic accounting tools. The structure of this book lends itself to a one-semester course that provides a basic understanding of accounting information. Students who could benefit from this approach include undergraduate majors in the following areas:

- Engineering
- Behavioral sciences
- Public administration
- Prelaw programs

Professionals in any of these broad disciplines are likely to be confronted with financial management issues early in their careers. In fact, accounting issues are likely to touch the majority of career paths open to a student today. MBA students who do not have a background in undergraduate business study or feel the need for a refresher course will value the opportunity to gain or revive certain key business skills.

The text takes the reader through the basics: what accounting information is, what it means, and how it is used. Students examine financial statements and discover what they do and do not communicate. This knowledge will help them gain the decision-making and problem-solving abilities so crucial outside the academic environment.

This book is for the benefit of the many who simply want to know "what the numbers mean."

ORGANIZATION

Chapter 1 presents a basic description of accounting and its evolution. Emphasis is placed on developments that have occurred to meet the needs of the users of accounting information and on dispelling the misconception that accounting standards are just a code of rules. The remainder of the text is divided into two major topic areas: financial accounting topics (Chapters 2 through 11) and managerial accounting topics (Chapters 12 through 16).

In presenting these two aspects of accounting, the spiral approach is used. In this teaching method, a general sketch is presented, and each chapter fills in a few of the finishing details until the reader possesses the full picture. The spiral approach is based on the belief that students can better navigate a subject matter if they are given a glimpse of the big picture first. Thus the objectives of the course are clear from the beginning, and the student can keep them in sight throughout the learning process.

Following this model, the first chapter of each section outlines the pertinent fundamental relationships and presents appropriate terminology so that the student is given an overview before exposure to the details. In the following chapters, the fundamentals are elaborated and developed until the picture is sufficiently fleshed out. The focus throughout the presentation is on understanding the meaning of the numbers in financial statements, their relationship to each other, and how they are used in evaluation, planning, and control. In taking the spiral approach, an instructor focuses on the function, not the formation, of the financial statements.

Highlights

The financial accounting portion (Chapters 2 through 11):

- Chapter 2—Getting the big picture

A model of the accounting process and the role of financial statements.

The introduction of a schematic diagram that illustrates the interrelationship of various financial statements and facilitates understanding the effects of various transactions.

- Chapter 3—Introducing basic concepts

Return on investment.

Return on equity.

Liquidity.

• Chapter 4—Understanding the method

The bookkeeping system in general terms.

A powerful transaction analysis scheme featuring the "horizontal model," which builds on the schematic diagram presented in Chapter 2.

Introduction of journal entries and T-accounts with emphasis on the horizontal model as the way to understand the effect of transactions on the balance sheet and income statement.

• Chapters 5 through 10—Examining the specifics

The elements of the balance sheet, income statement, and statement of cash flows in relation to the schematic diagram.

The *unique* and valuable explication of Explanatory Notes in Chapter 10, crucial to understanding financial statements as a whole.

Knowledge of business practices as a foundation for an understanding of accounting for transactions.

• Chapter 11—Using the knowledge

Financial statement analysis: from financial data to decision making.

The managerial accounting portion (Chapters 12–16):

• Chapter 12—Getting the big picture

An introduction to cost accounting systems and cost classifications. Diagrams of cost flow, cost systems, and cost behavior.

• Chapters 13 through 16—Examining the specifics and putting them to use

An in-depth look at the specific uses of cost data in the planning, control, and decision-making processes.

The relationship between cost data and other factors involved in these processes.

NOTABLE FEATURES

Text

• **Business Procedure Capsules** are used throughout the chapters to highlight and discuss various business practices and their financial statement impact. Understanding these business practices facilitates a more complete understanding of financial statements in general.

- **Learning Objectives** guide students conceptually by providing a framework for each chapter.
- **Chapter Summaries and Key Terms and Concepts** promote greater retention of important points and definitions.
- **The 1991 Annual Report of Armstrong World Industries, Inc.,** is presented in Appendix A and is referred to frequently in the financial accounting portion of the text. This real-world example piques student interest and gives students a hands-on experience. In addition, students are asked to obtain their own example of an actual annual report.
- **End-of-chapter Exercises and Problems** illustrate important concepts and applications. Problems that require use of the Armstrong World Industries, Inc., annual report in Appendix A are identified with the logo shown here in the margin. The pencil logo, also shown in the margin, identifies questions requiring written answers.
- **Solutions** to odd-numbered exercises and problems are included in Appendix B in order to reinforce learning and minimize frustration as well as to facilitate the use of the book as a self-study or Continuing Professional Educational resource.

@rmstrong

Supplements

- **Instructor's Manual and Test Bank** featuring teaching/learning objectives, chapter outlines, teaching observations, exercise and problem solutions, quiz/exam questions, and take-home quizzes.
- **Study Guide and Workpapers** (by Wayne McManus) for student use, including several hundred matching, true/false, and multiple choice review questions with answers.
- **Transparency Acetates** (supplied as transparency masters in the first edition) provide instructors with a framework for chapter-by-chapter discussions. Some are figures lifted from the text, others simply organize the material under discussion.
- **Irwin's Computerized Testing Software,** an advanced-feature test generator, allows you to add and edit questions; save and reload tests; create up to 99 different versions of each test; attach graphics to questions; import and export ASCII files; and select questions based on type, level of difficulty, or keyword. This software provides password protection of saved tests and question databases, and can run on a network. Irwin's free customized exam preparation service, Teletest, is also available.

ADDITIONAL NOTES FROM THE AUTHOR

In this text, I have followed a pragmatic approach in explaining the information content and use of financial statements and financial data. Students should be encouraged to read *The Wall Street Journal* and other business publications regularly, and instructors should attempt to call to students' attention current developments relating to the course material.

Users of this text are cautioned that accounting is not a spectator sport and that comprehension of the material does require actually working through the problems. Reviewing solutions without first attempting the problems will significantly dilute the learning process.

I hope the approach and scope of coverage in this text have achieved my identified objectives and, in addition, have adequately filled the user's need. Any ideas for increasing the effectiveness of this text are welcomed.

ACKNOWLEDGMENTS

The first edition of this text had a long gestation period, and I am grateful for the encouragement and support of my colleagues at Millikin University. Dr. C. R. Decker (Grover M. Hermann Professor of Business Policy and former Dean of the Tabor School of Business and Engineering) and R. A. Mannweiler (current Dean of the Tabor School) persevered in challenging me to write. Professor Daniel F. Viele developed Exhibit 2–5. Millikin provided the time I needed to write in the form of an academic leave during the fall of 1985. Without that leave this book would still be just an idea. My thanks also go to Mr. Stuart Koop, Director of the Mueller Computer Center at Millikin while the manuscript was being prepared. He and his staff provided valuable technical assistance in that process.

Mr. Wayne McManus, a onetime colleague at Millikin University, has provided assistance in several respects. His suggestions for improving this text proved almost as beneficial as his creation of the Study Guide and Workpapers.

For several years, Armstrong World Industries, Inc., has provided copies of its annual report for classroom use. This link to reality has been a valuable teaching aid. I am grateful for Armstrong's permission to include its 1991 Annual Report as Appendix A. In addition to the report itself, Armstrong also makes available a "Special Edition" brochure that explains many elements of the annual report. Adopters of this text are encouraged to request annual reports for subsequent years and "Special Edition" brochures from Armstrong World Industries, Inc. The 1991 "Special Edition" brochure, and multiple choice questions and answers supplied by Armstrong World Industries, Inc., have been reproduced in the Instructor's Manual and Test Bank.

Although the approach to the material and the scope of the coverage are the results of my own conclusions, truly new ideas are rare. The authors whose textbooks I have used in the past have influenced many of my ideas for particular accounting and financial management explanations. Likewise, students and colleagues through the years have helped me clarify illustrations and teaching techniques. Many users of the first edition—both teachers and students—have offered comments and constructive criticisms that have been encouraging and helpful. All of this input is greatly appreciated.

In addition, the following persons have provided valuable feedback after reviewing manuscript versions of this text. I am grateful for their supportive comments and constructive criticisms.

Sally Adams, California State University—Chico

Maureen Anderson, University of St. Thomas

Ted Compton, Ohio University

Dave Evans, Johnson County Community College

Keith Howe, Brigham Young University

Zabi Ravaee, Middle Tennessee State University

Paul Schlachter, Florida International University

James Sisson, Oregon State University

David H. Marshall

Contents

Costs for Cost Accounting Purposes. Cost
Accounting Systems—General. Cost Accounting
Systems—Job-Order Costing, Process Costing, and
Hybrid Costing. Cost Accounting Systems—
Absorption Costing and Direct Costing. Relationship
of Cost to Product or Activity. Relationship of Total
Cost to Volume of Activity. Cost Classification
According to a Time-Frame Perspective. Cost
Classifications for Other Analytical Purposes.

Index of Business Procedure Capsules

Chapter 1

Accounting—Present and Past

The objective of this text is to present enough of the fundamentals of accounting to permit the nonaccountant to understand the financial statements of an organization operating in our society, and to understand how financial information can be used in the management planning, control, and decision-making processes. Although usually expressed in the context of profit-seeking business enterprises, most of the material is equally applicable to not-for-profit social service and governmental organizations.

Accounting is sometimes called *the language of business*, and it is appropriate for people who are involved in the economic activities of our society—and that is just about everyone—to know at least enough of this language to be able to make decisions and informed judgments about those economic activities.

LEARNING OBJECTIVES

After studying this chapter, you should understand:

- A definition of accounting.
- Who the users of accounting information are, and why they find accounting information useful.
- Several of the categories of accounting, and the kinds of work that professional accountants in each category perform.
- The development of accounting, from a broad historical perspective.
- That financial statements do not result from following a codified set of hard and fast rules; that there are, in fact, alternative methods of accounting for and reporting similar economic activities.
- That the Financial Accounting Standards Board (FASB) is the current standard-setting body for generally accepted accounting principles.

- The key elements of ethical behavior for a professional accountant.
- The reasons for the FASB's Conceptual Framework project.
- The objectives of financial reporting for business enterprises.

WHAT IS ACCOUNTING?

In a very broad sense, **accounting** is the process of identifying, measuring, and communicating economic information about an organization for the purpose of making decisions and informed judgments. (Accountants frequently use the term *entity* instead of *organization* because it is more inclusive.)

This definition of accounting can be expressed schematically as follows:

Accounting is the process of:

Identifying	Economic information		Decisions/
Measuring	about an entity	> for >	Informed
Communicating			judgments

Who makes these decisions and informed judgments? Users of accounting information include the management of the **entity** or organization, the owners of the organization (who are frequently not involved in the management process), potential investors in and creditors of the organization, employees, and various federal, state, and local governmental agencies that are concerned with regulatory and tax matters. Exhibit 1–1 illustrates some of the uses of accounting information. Pause, and try to think of at least one other decision or informed judgment that each of these users might make from the economic information that could be communicated about an entity.

Accounting is done for just about every kind of organization. Accounting for business firms is what many people think of first, but not-for-profit social service organizations, governmental units, social clubs, political committees, and other groups all require accounting for their economic activities.

Accounting is frequently perceived as something that others do, rather than as the process of providing information that supports decisions and informed judgments. Relatively few people actually become accountants, but almost all people use accounting information. This book has as its principal objective making you an informed user of accounting information; its objective is not to make you an accountant.

EXHIBIT 1–1 Users and Uses of Accounting Information

User	*Decision/Informed Judgment Made*
Management	When performing its functions of planning, directing, and controlling, management makes many decisions and informed judgments. For example, when considering the expansion of a product line, planning involves identifying and measuring costs and benefits; directing involves communicating the strategies selected; and controlling involves identifying, measuring, and communicating the results of the product line expansion during and after its implementation.
Investor	Whether or not to invest in the common stock of the company.
Creditor	How much merchandise to ship to a customer company before receiving payment.
Employee	Whether or not there seem to be long-term job prospects with the company.
SEC (Securities and Exchange Commission)	Whether or not financial statements issued to investors fully disclose all required information.

There are several major classifications of accounting and accountants. The following sections should help you understand these classifications.

Financial Accounting

Financial accounting generally refers to the process that results in the financial statements of an entity. As will be explained in more detail, the financial statements present the financial position of an entity at a point in time, the results of the entity's operations for some period of time, the **cash flow** activities for the same period of time, and other information about the entity's financial resources, obligations, owners' interests, and operations.

Financial accounting has primarily an external orientation: the financial statements are directed to individuals who are not in a position to be aware of the day-to-day financial and operating activities of the entity. Financial accounting also has primarily a historical orientation. Financial statements reflect what has happened in the past, and although readers may want to project past activities and their results into future performance, financial statements are not a clear crystal ball.

Bookkeeping procedures are used to accumulate the results of many of an entity's activities, and these procedures are part of the financial accounting process. Bookkeeping procedures have been thoroughly systematized using manual, mechanical, and computer techniques, and although these procedures support the financial accounting process, they are only a part of the process.

Financial accounting is done by accounting professionals who have generally earned a bachelor of science degree with a major in accounting. The financial accountant is employed by an entity to use her/his expertise, analytical skills, and judgment in the many activities that are necessary for the preparation of financial statements. The title of the chief accounting officer of a corporation, who is usually responsible for both the financial and managerial accounting functions (see below), is **controller**. Sometimes the title *comptroller* (the old English spelling) is used for this position. An individual earns the **Certified Public Accountant (CPA)** professional designation by passing a comprehensive five-part examination taken over a two-and-one-half day period. A uniform exam is given nationally, but it is administered by individual states. Some states require that candidates have some accounting work experience before they can take the exam. CPAs work in all types of organizations. As explained later, a CPA who expresses an auditor's opinion about an entity's financial statements must be licensed by the state in which she/he performs the auditing service.

Managerial Accounting/Cost Accounting

Managerial accounting is concerned with the use of economic and financial information to plan and control many of the activities of the entity, and to support the management decision-making process. **Cost accounting** is a subset of managerial accounting that relates to the determination and accumulation of product, process, or service costs. Managerial accounting and cost accounting have primarily an internal orientation, as opposed to the primarily external orientation of financial accounting. Much of the same data used in or generated by the financial accounting process is used in managerial and cost accounting, but the data are more likely to be used in a future-oriented way, such as in the preparation of budgets.

Managerial accountants and cost accountants are professionals who have usually earned a bachelor of science degree with a major in accounting. Their work frequently involves close coordination with the production, marketing, and finance functions of the entity. The **Certified Management Accountant (CMA)** professional designation is earned by a management accountant/cost accountant who passes a broad four-part examination administered over a two-day period, and who meets certain experience requirements.

Auditing — Public Accounting

Many entities have their financial statements reviewed by an independent third party. In most cases an audit is required by the securities laws if the stock or bonds of a company are owned and traded by investors. **Public accounting** firms and individual CPAs provide this **auditing** service, and constitute an important part of the accounting profession.

The result of the audit is the **independent auditor's report.** The report usually has three relatively brief paragraphs. The first paragraph identifies the financial statements that were audited, explains that the statements are the responsibility of the company's management, and states that the auditor's responsibility is to express an opinion on the financial statements. The second paragraph explains that the audit was conducted "in accordance with **generally accepted auditing standards,**" and describes briefly what those standards require and what work is involved in performing an audit. The third paragraph contains the auditor's opinion, which is usually that the named statements "present fairly in all material respects" the financial position of the entity, and the results of its operations and cash flows for identified periods "in conformance with **generally accepted accounting principles**" during the identified periods. This is an unqualified, or "clean," opinion. Occasionally the opinion will be "qualified" with respect to fair presentation, departure from generally accepted accounting principles, the auditor's inability to perform certain auditing procedures, or the firm's ability to continue as a going concern, and the qualification will be explained. A clean opinion is not a clean bill of health about either the current financial condition of, or the future prospects for, the entity. It is up to the readers to reach their own judgments about these and other matters after studying the financial report, which includes the financial statements and their explanatory footnotes or textual explanations.

Auditors who work in public accounting are professional accountants who have usually earned at least a bachelor of science degree with a major in accounting. The auditor may work for a public accounting firm (a few of these firms have several thousand partners and professional staff) or as an individual practitioner.

Most auditors seek and earn the CPA designation; the firm partner or individual practitioner who actually signs the opinion must be a CPA and be licensed by the state in which she/he practices. To be licensed, the CPA must satisfy the character, education, and experience requirements of the state.

To see an example of the independent auditors' report, refer to page 31 of the 1991 annual report of Armstrong World Industries, Inc., which is reproduced as Appendix A.

Internal Auditing

Organizations with many plants or office locations or activities involving many financial transactions employ professional accountants to do **internal auditing.** In many cases, the internal auditor performs functions much like those of the external auditor/public accountant, but perhaps on a smaller scale, for example, reviewing the financial statements of a single plant. Other internal auditors analyze the operating efficiency of an entity's activities. The qualifications of an internal auditor are similar to those of any other professional accountant. In addition to having the CPA and/or the CMA designation, the internal auditor may also have passed the examination to become a Certified Internal Auditor.

Governmental Accounting

Governmental units have need of the same accounting functions as other entities. Governmental accounting is the performance of professional accounting functions within a governmental unit.

Income Tax Accounting

The growing complexity of federal, state, municipal, and foreign income tax laws has led to a demand for professional accountants who are specialists in this area. These accountants work for corporations, public accounting firms, governmental units, and other kinds of entities. Many income tax accountants have bachelor's degrees and are CPAs; some are attorneys as well.

HOW HAS ACCOUNTING DEVELOPED?

Accounting has developed over time in response to the needs of users of financial statements for financial information. Even though an aura of exactness is conveyed by the numbers in financial statements, there is a great deal of judgment and approximation behind the numbers. There isn't any "Code of Accounting Rules" to be followed indiscriminately, and even though broad generally accepted principles of accounting do exist, different accountants reach different but often equally legitimate conclusions about how to account for a particular transaction or event. A brief review of the history of the development of accounting principles may make this often confusing state of affairs a little easier to understand.

Early History

It is not surprising that evidence of record-keeping of economic events has been found in earliest civilizations. Modern bookkeeping methods have evolved directly from a system that was invented in the 15th century in response to the needs of the mercantile trading practices that developed in that period.

The Industrial Revolution generated the need for large amounts of capital to finance the enterprises that supplanted individual craftsmen. This need resulted in the corporate form of organization marked by absentee owners, or investors, who trusted their money to managers. It followed that investors required reports from the corporation managers showing financial position and results of operations. In mid-19th century England, the independent (external) audit function added credence to financial reports. As British capital was invested in a growing U.S. economy in the late 19th century, British Chartered Accountants and accounting methods came to the United States. However, there was no group authorized to establish financial reporting standards. This led to alternative methods of reporting financial condition and results of operations; this situation resulted in confusion, and, in some cases, outright fraud.

The Accounting Profession in the United States

Accounting professionals in this country organized themselves in the early 1900s, and worked hard to establish certification laws, standardized audit procedures, and other attributes of a profession. However, not until 1932–1934 did the American Institute of Accountants (predecessor of today's American Institute of Certified Public Accountants—AICPA) and the New York Stock Exchange agree on five broad principles of accounting. This was the first formal accounting standard-setting activity. It should be clear that accounting, financial reporting, and auditing weaknesses related to the 1929 stock market crash gave impetus to this effort.

The Securities Act of 1933 and the Securities Exchange Act of 1934 apply to securities offered for sale in interstate commerce. These laws had a significant effect on the standard-setting process, because they gave the **Securities and Exchange Commission** (SEC) the authority to establish accounting principles to be followed by companies whose securities had to be registered with the SEC, and the SEC still has this authority. However, over the years the standard-setting process has been delegated to other organizations. Between 1939 and 1959 the Committee on Accounting Procedure of the American Institute of Accountants issued 51 *Accounting Research Bulletins* that dealt with accounting principles. This work was done without a common conceptual framework for financial reporting. Each bulletin dealt with a specific issue in a relatively narrow context, and alternative methods of reporting the results of similar transactions remained.

In 1959 the Accounting Principles Board (APB) replaced the Committee on Accounting Procedure as the standard-setting body. The APB was an arm of the AICPA, and although it was given resources and directed to engage in more research than its predecessor, its early efforts intensified the controversies that existed, and it did not develop a conceptual underpinning for accounting principles. However, the Board did issue a number of opinions on serious accounting issues.

Financial Accounting Standard Setting at the Present Time

In 1973, as a result of congressional and other criticism of the accounting standard-setting process being performed by an arm of the AICPA, the **Financial Accounting Foundation** was created as a more independent entity. The Foundation established the **Financial Accounting Standards Board** (FASB) to be the authoritative accounting principles standard-setting body. The FASB embarked on a project called the Conceptual Framework of Financial Accounting and Reporting. Through December 1985, six *Statements of Financial Accounting Concepts* had been issued. No additional statements have been issued through April 1992.

Concurrently with its Conceptual Framework project, the FASB has issued **Statements of Financial Accounting Standards** that have established standards of accounting and reporting for particular issues much like its predecessors did. Alternative ways of accounting for and reporting the effects of similar transactions still exist. In many areas, the accountant still must use judgment in selecting between equally acceptable alternatives. Subsequent chapters will describe many of these alternatives because, obviously, in order to make sense of financial statements, one must understand the impact of one alternative relative to another.

The FASB does not set standards in a vacuum. An open, due process procedure is followed. The FASB invites input from any individual or organization who cares to provide ideas and viewpoints about the particular standard under consideration. Among the many professional accounting and financial organizations that regularly present suggestions to the FASB, in addition to the AICPA and the SEC, are the American Accounting Association, the Institute of Management Accountants, the Financial Executives Institute, and the Institute of Chartered Financial Analysts.

The point of this discussion is to emphasize that financial accounting and reporting practices are not codified in a set of rules to be mastered and blindly followed. Financial accounting and reporting have evolved over time in response to the changing needs of society, and they are still evolving. Your objective is to learn enough about the fundamentals of financial accounting and reporting to be neither awed nor confounded by the presentation of financial data.

Standards for Other Types of Accounting

Because managerial accounting/cost accounting is primarily oriented to internal use, and because it is presumed that internal users will know or can find out about the accounting practices being followed, the development of standards has not been as important an issue in this type of accounting. One significant exception occurs in accounting for the cost of work done under government contracts. Over the years various governmental agencies have issued directives prescribing the procedures to be followed by government contractors. During the 1970–1980 period, the **Cost Accounting Standards Board** (CASB) operated as a governmental body to establish standards applicable to government contracts. In 1981 Congress abolished the CASB, although their standards remained in effect. In late 1988, Congress reestablished the CASB as an independent body within the Office of Federal Procurement Policy, and gave it authority to establish cost accounting standards for government contracts in excess of $500,000.

In the auditing/public accounting area, auditing standards are established by the Auditing Standards board, a technical committee of the AICPA. The SEC has had input into this process, and over the years a number of auditing standards and procedures have been issued. One of the most important of these standards requires the auditor to be independent of the client whose financial statements are being audited. Auditors' judgment is still very important in the auditing process, and because of this, although standards and procedures have been issued, critics of the accounting profession have raised questions about the auditing process on several occasions. Congressional committees have held hearings about the role of a company's auditing firm when the company has gone bankrupt shortly after having received an unqualified auditor's opinion, or when the company has been involved in a major fraud. In 1987, the National Commission on Fraudulent Financial Reporting, a private-sector initiative sponsored by several professional associations, including the AICPA, issued recommendations designed to reduce further the already low incidence of fraudulent financial reporting. It is worth repeating here that an unqualified auditor's opinion does not constitute a clean bill of health about either the current financial condition of or the future prospects for the entity. It is up to the readers of the financial statements to reach their own judgments about these and other matters after studying the financial report, which includes the financial statements and their explanatory footnotes or textual explanations.

In 1984 the **Governmental Accounting Standards Board** (GASB) was established to develop guidelines for financial accounting and reporting by state and local governmental units. The GASB operates under the auspices of the Financial Accounting Foundation, which is also the parent organization of the FASB. The GASB will attempt to unify practices of the nation's many state and municipal entities, thus providing investors with a better means of comparing financial data of the issuers of state and municipal securities. In the absence of a GASB standard for a particular activity or transaction occurring in both the public and private sectors, governmental entities will continue to use FASB standards for guidance. Several GASB standards had been issued by the end of 1991.

The United States Internal Revenue Code and related regulations and the various state and local tax laws specify the rules to be followed in determining an entity's income tax liability. Although quite specific and very complicated, the code and regulations provide rules to be followed. In income tax matters, accountants use their judgment and expertise to design transactions so that the entity's overall income tax liability is minimized. In addition, accountants prepare or help prepare tax returns, and may represent clients whose returns are being reviewed or challenged by taxing authorities.

International Accounting Standards

Accounting standards in individual countries have evolved in response to the unique user needs and cultural attributes of each country. Thus in spite of the development of a global marketplace, accounting standards in one country may differ significantly from those in another country. In 1973 the International Accounting Standards Committee (IASC) was formed to create and promote worldwide acceptance and observation of accounting and financial reporting standards. Although now supported by more than 75 nations, the development of uniform standards has been an almost impossible objective to achieve. One of the major challenges relates to a country's interest in protecting its local markets, where participants' interests are frequently quite different from entities involved in a global financial network.

At the present time, the IASC seems to be moving in the direction of seeking methods of providing comparability between financial statements prepared according to one country's own accounting standards and the accounting standards of another country. The IASC is not seeking a single set of uniform accounting standards to be applied to all countries.

The development of a single set of international accounting standards is a long way off and may never be achieved in total. This makes it important to understand the standards of one's own country so that appropriate consideration can be given to financial statements prepared according to another country's standards.

Ethics and the Accounting Profession

One of the characteristics frequently associated with a profession is that those practicing the profession acknowledge the importance of an ethical code. This is especially important in the accounting profession because so much of an accountant's work involves providing information to support the informed judgments and decisions made by users of accounting information.

The American Institute of Certified Public Accountants (AICPA) and the Institute of Management Accounts (IMA) have both published ethics codes. The *Code of Professional Conduct,* most recently revised in 1988, was adopted by the membership of the AICPA. The organization's bylaws state that members shall conform to the rules of the Code or be subject to disciplinary action by the AICPA. Although it doesn't have the same enforcement mechanism, the IMA's *Standards of Ethical Conduct for Management Accountants* calls on management accountants to maintain the highest standards of ethical conduct as they fulfill their obligations to the organizations they serve, their profession, the public, and themselves.

Both codes of conduct identify integrity and objectivity as two of the key elements of ethical behavior for a professional accountant.

Integrity refers to being honest and forthright in dealings and communications with others; **objectivity** refers to impartiality and freedom from conflict of interest. An accountant who lacks integrity and/or objectivity cannot be relied upon to produce complete and relevant information with which to make an informed judgment or decision.

Other elements of ethical behavior include independence, competence, and acceptance of an obligation to serve the best interests of the employer, the client, and the public. **Independence** is related to objectivity and is especially important to the auditor who must be independent in appearance and fact. Competence refers to having the knowledge and professional skills to adequately perform the work assigned. Accountants should recognize that the nature of their work requires an understanding that there is an obligation to serve those who will use the information communicated by them.

In the recent past there have been some highly publicized incidents involving allegations that accountants have violated their ethical codes by being dishonest, biased, and/or incompetent. That some of these allegations have been proved true should not be a condemnation of all accountants. The profession has used these rare circumstances to reaffirm that the public and the profession expect accountants to exhibit a very high level of ethical behavior. In this sense are accountants really any different from those who are involved in any other endeavor?

THE CONCEPTUAL FRAMEWORK

The *Statements of Financial Accounting Concepts* that have been issued by the FASB through 1991 are:

Number	Title	Issue Date
1.	Objectives of Financial Reporting by Business Enterprises	November 1978
2.	Qualitative Characteristics of Accounting Information (Amended by Statement 6)	May 1980
3.	Elements of Financial Statements of Business Enterprises (Replaced by Statement 6)	December 1980
4.	Objectives of Financial Reporting by Nonbusiness Organizations	December 1980
5.	Recognition and Measurement in Financial Statements of Business Enterprises	December 1984
6.	Elements of Financial Statements	December 1985

These statements represent a great deal of effort by the FASB, and the progress made on this project has not come easily. The project has been somewhat controversial because of the concern that trying to define the underlying concepts of accounting may have a significant impact on current generally accepted principles of accounting and may result in major changes to present financial reporting practices. Critics believe that, at the least, this would cause financial statement readers to become confused (or more confused than they are now), and, at the worst, could disrupt financial markets and contractual obligations that are based on present financial reporting practices. The FASB has recognized this concern, and has made the following assertions about the *Concepts Statements:*[1]

> Statements of Financial Accounting Concepts do not establish standards prescribing accounting procedures or disclosure practices for particular items or events, which are issued by the Board as Statements of Financial Accounting Standards. Rather, Statements in this series describe concepts and relations that will underlie future financial accounting standards and practices and in due course serve as a basis for evaluating existing standards and practices.
>
> Establishment of objectives and identification of fundamental concepts will not directly solve accounting and reporting problems. Rather, objectives give direction, and concepts are tools for solving problems.
>
> The Board itself is likely to be the most direct beneficiary of the guidance provided by the Statements in this series. They will guide the Board in developing accounting and reporting standards by providing the Board with a common foundation and basic reasoning on which to consider merits of alternatives.

"Highlights" of Concepts Statement No. 1 — Objectives of Financial Reporting by Business Enterprises

To set the stage more completely for our study of financial accounting, it is appropriate to study the "Highlights" of *Concepts Statement No. 1,* as contained in the Statement. The FASB does caution that these highlights are best understood in the context of the full Statement.[2] The comments in brack-

---

[1] Preface, *FASB Statement of Financial Accounting Concepts No. 6* (Stamford, Conn., 1985). Copyright © the Financial Accounting Standards Board, High Ridge Park, Stamford, Connecticut 06905, U.S.A. Excerpted with permission. Copies of the complete document are available from the FASB.

[2] "Highlights," *FASB Statement of Financial Accounting Concepts No. 1* (Stamford, Conn., 1978). Copyright © the Financial Accounting Standards Board, High Ridge Park, Stamford, Connecticut 06905, U.S.A. Excerpted with permission. Copies of the complete document are available from the FASB.

ets are not part of the Statement; they are this author's explanations:

- Financial reporting is not an end in itself but is intended to provide information that is useful in making business and economic decisions. [Financial reporting must meet the needs of users for information that is relevant to decisions and informed judgments.]
- The objectives of financial reporting are not immutable — they are affected by the economic, legal, political, and social environment in which financial reporting takes place. [Financial accounting standards are still evolving; in April 1992 the FASB issued Standard No. 109, which dealt with accounting for income taxes.]
- The objectives are also affected by the characteristics and limitations of the kind of information that financial reporting can provide.

  The information pertains to business enterprises rather than to industries or to the economy as a whole. [Accounting is done for individual firms, or entities.]

  The information often results from approximate, rather than exact, measures. [Some costs applicable to one year's results of operations may have to be estimated; for example, product warranty costs applicable to 1992 may not be finally determined until 1995.]

  The information largely reflects the financial effects of transactions and events that have already happened. [Financial accounting is historical scorekeeping; it is not future oriented.]

  The information is but one source of information needed by those who make decisions about business enterprises. [A potential employee might want to know about employee turnover rates.]

  The information is provided and used at a cost. [The benefit of the information to the user should exceed the cost of providing it.]

- The objectives in this Statement are those of general purpose external financial reporting by business enterprises. [Reporting for *internal* planning, control, and decision making need not be constrained by financial reporting requirements.]

  The objectives stem primarily from the needs of external users who lack the authority to prescribe the information they want and must rely on the information management communicates to them. [Most users are on the outside looking in. For its own uses, management can prescribe the information it wants.]

  The objectives are directed toward the common interests of many users in the ability of an enterprise to generate favorable cash flows but are phrased using investment and credit decisions as a reference to give them a focus. The objectives are intended to be broad, rather than narrow. [Many users of financial statements want to make a judgment about whether or not they are likely to receive payment of amounts due them by the company.]

The objectives pertain to financial reporting and are not restricted to financial statements. [Financial reporting includes footnotes and other disclosures.]

- The objectives state that:

Financial reporting should provide information that is useful to present and potential investors and creditors and other users in making rational investment, credit, and similar decisions. The information should be comprehensible to those who have a reasonable understanding of business and economic activities and are willing to study the information with reasonable diligence. [The user asks: "Is it likely that I will be paid the amounts due me if I provide goods or services to the firm, or if I invest in the firm?" To answer this question, the user has the responsibility of understanding business practices and financial reporting.]

Financial reporting should provide information to help present and potential investors and creditors and other users in assessing the amounts, timing, and uncertainty of prospective cash receipts from dividends or interest and the proceeds from the sale, redemption, or maturity of securities or loans. Since investors' and creditors' cash flows are related to enterprise cash flows, financial reporting should provide information to help investors, creditors, and others assess the amounts, timing, and uncertainty of prospective net cash inflows to the related enterprise. [Cash has to be received by the company from somewhere before it can be paid out.]

Financial reporting should provide information about the economic resources of an enterprise, the claims to those resources (obligations of the enterprise to transfer resources to other entities and owners' equity), and the effects of transactions, events, and circumstances that change its resources and claims to those resources. [What economic resources does the firm own, how much does it owe, and what caused these amounts to change over time?]

- "Investors" and "creditors" are used broadly and include not only those who have or contemplate having a claim to enterprise resources but also those who advise or represent them. [Financial advisors and consultants base their recommendations on financial reports.]
- Although investment and credit decisions reflect investors' and creditors' expectations about future enterprise performance, those expectations are commonly based at least partly on evaluations of past enterprise performance. [The future is unknown, but it is likely to be influenced by the past.]
- The primary focus of financial reporting is information about earnings and its components. [The user's question is: "How much profit did the firm earn?"]
- Information about enterprise earnings based on accrual accounting generally provides a better indication of an enterprise's present and continuing ability to generate favorable cash flows than information limited to the financial effects of cash receipts and payments. [**Accrual accounting** — to be explained in more detail later — involves accounting for the effect of an economic activity, or transaction, on an entity when the activity has occurred, rather than

when a cash receipt or payment related to the transaction takes place. Thus the company for which you work has a cost for your wages in the month in which you do the work, even though you may not be paid until the next month.]

- Financial reporting is expected to provide information about an enterprise's financial performance during a period and about how management of an enterprise has discharged its stewardship responsibility to owners. [The user asks: "How much was the firm's profit for the year ended December 31, 1992?"]
- Financial accounting is not designed to measure directly the value of a business enterprise, but the information it provides may be helpful to those who wish to estimate its value. [The financial statements of a company don't change just because the market price of its stock changes.]
- Investors, creditors, and others may use reported earnings and information about the elements of financial statements in various ways to assess the prospects for cash flows. They may wish, for example, to evaluate management's performance, estimate "earning power," predict future earnings, assess risk, or to confirm, change, or reject earlier predictions or assessments. Although financial reporting should provide basic information to aid them, they do their own evaluating, estimating, predicting, assessing, confirming, changing, or rejecting. [Each user reads the financial statements of a firm with her/his own judgment and biases.]
- Management knows more about the enterprise and its affairs than investors, creditors, or other "outsiders" and accordingly can often increase the usefulness of financial information by identifying certain events and circumstances and explaining their financial effects on the enterprise. [Footnotes and other disclosures are just as important as the financial statements themselves.]

Objectives of Financial Reporting for Nonbusiness Organizations

At the outset of this chapter it was stated that the material to be presented, although usually to be expressed in the context of profit-seeking business enterprises, would also be applicable to not-for-profit social service and governmental organizations. The FASB's "Highlights" of *Concepts Statement No. 4,* "Objectives of Financial Reporting by Nonbusiness Organizations," states: "Based on its study, the Board believes that the objectives of general purpose external financial reporting for government sponsored entities (for example, hospitals, universities, or utilities) engaged in activities that are not unique to government should be similar to those of business enterprises or other nonbusiness organizations engaged in similar activities."[3] *Statement 6* amended

---

[3] *FASB, Statement of Financial Accounting Concepts No. 4* (Stamford, Conn., 1980). Copyright © the Financial Accounting Standards Board, High Ridge Park, Stamford, Connecticut 06905, U.S.A. Excerpted with permission. Copies of the complete document are available from the FASB.

Statement 2 by affirming that the qualitative characteristics described in *Statement 2* apply to the information about both business enterprises and not-for-profit organizations.

The objectives of financial reporting for nonbusiness organizations focus on providing information for resource providers, rather than investors, as well as providing information about the economic resources, obligations, net resources, and performance of an organization during a period of time. Thus, even though nonbusiness organizations have unique characteristics that distinguish them from profit-oriented businesses, the information characteristics of the financial reporting objectives for each type of organization are similar.

It will be appropriate to remember the gist of the above objectives as individual accounting and financial statement issues are encountered in subsequent chapters, and are related to real-world situations.

SUMMARY

Accounting is the process of identifying, measuring, and communicating economic information about an entity for the purpose of making decisions and informed judgments.

Users of financial statements include management, investors, creditors, employees, and government agencies. Decisions made by users relate, among other things, to entity operations, investment, credit, employment, and compliance with laws. Financial statements support these decisions because they communicate important financial information about the entity.

The major classifications of accounting include financial accounting, managerial accounting/cost accounting, auditing/public accounting, internal auditing, governmental accounting, and income tax accounting.

Accounting has developed over time in response to the needs of users of financial statements for financial information. Financial accounting standards have been established by different organizations over the years. These standards are not a codified set of rules to be blindly followed; alternative methods of accounting for certain activities are used by different entities. At the present time, the Financial Accounting Standards Board is the standard-setting body for financial accounting. Other organizations have been and are involved in establishing standards for cost accounting, auditing, and income tax accounting.

Integrity, objectivity, independence, and competence are several characteristics of ethical behavior for a professional accountant. High standards of ethical conduct are appropriate for all persons, but professional accountants have a special responsibility because so many people make decisions and informed judgments using information provided by the accounting process.

The Financial Accounting Standards Board has issued several *Statements of Financial Accounting Concepts* resulting from a project that has been underway in recent years. These statements describe concepts and relations that will underlie future financial accounting standards and practices, and will in due course serve as a basis for evaluating existing standards and practices.

"Highlights" of the *Concepts Statement* dealing with the objectives of financial reporting provide that financial information should be useful to investor and creditor concerns about the cash flows of the enterprise, the resources and obligations of the enterprise, and the profit of the enterprise. Financial accounting is not designed to measure directly the value of a business enterprise.

The objectives of financial reporting for nonbusiness enterprises are not significantly different from those for business enterprises, except that resource providers, rather than investors, are concerned about performance results, rather than profit.

KEY TERMS AND CONCEPTS

accounting *(p. 2)*   The process of identifying, measuring, and communicating economic information about an organization for the purpose of making decisions and informed judgments.

accrual accounting *(p. 15)*   Accounting that recognizes revenues and expenses as they occur, even though the cash receipt from the revenue or the cash disbursement related to the expense may occur before or after the event that causes revenue or expense recognition.

auditing *(p. 5)*   The process of reviewing the financial statements of an entity by an independent third party with the objective of expressing an opinion about the fairness of the presentation of the entity's financial position, results of operations, and changes in financial position. The practice of auditing is less precisely referred to as "public accounting."

bookkeeping *(p. 4)*   Procedures that are used to keep track of financial transactions and accumulate the results of an entity's financial activities.

cash flow *(p. 3)*   Cash receipts or disbursements of an entity.

Certified Management Accountant *(p. 5)*   A professional designation earned by passing a broad, four-part examination administered over a two-day period, and meeting certain experience requirements. Examination topics include economics and business finance; organization and behavior (including ethical considerations); public reporting standards, auditing, and taxes; internal reporting and analysis; and decision analysis, including modeling and information systems.

Certified Public Accountant *(p. 4)* A professional designation earned by passing a comprehensive five-part examination taken over a two-and-one-half day period. Examination topics include accounting theory and practice, auditing, and business law.

controller *(p. 4)* The job title of the person who is the chief accounting officer of an organization. The controller is usually responsible for both the financial and managerial accounting functions. Sometimes the title is *comptroller*.

cost accounting *(p. 4)* A subset of managerial accounting that relates to the determination and accumulation of product, process, or service costs.

Cost Accounting Standards Board *(p. 9)* A group authorized by the U.S. Congress in 1970 to establish cost standards for government contractors. The CASB was dissolved in 1980, and reestablished in 1988.

entity *(p. 2)* An organization or individual, or a group of organizations or individuals, for which accounting is done.

financial accounting *(p. 3)* Accounting that focuses on reporting financial position at a point in time, and/or results of operations for a period of time.

Financial Accounting Foundation *(p. 8)* An organization composed of people from the public accounting profession, businesses, and the public that is responsible for the funding of and appointing members to the Financial Accounting Standards Board.

Financial Accounting Standards Board *(p. 8)* The body responsible for establishing generally accepted accounting principles.

generally accepted accounting principles *(p. 5)* Pronouncements of the Financial Accounting Standards Board (FASB) and its predecessors that constitute appropriate accounting for various transactions and that are used for reporting financial position and results of operations to investors and creditors.

generally accepted auditing standards *(p. 5)* Standards for auditing that are established by the Auditing Standards Board of the American Institute of Certified Public Accountants.

Governmental Accounting Standards Board *(p. 10)* Established by the Financial Accounting Foundation in 1984 to develop guidelines for financial accounting and reporting by state and local governmental units.

independence *(p. 12)* The personal characteristic of an accountant, especially an auditor, that refers to both appearing and being objective and impartial.

independent auditor's report *(p. 5)* The report accompanying audited financial statements that explains briefly the auditor's responsibility and work done, and includes an opinion about financial statement information being presented fairly in accordance with generally accepted accounting principles.

integrity *(p. 12)* The personal characteristic of honesty, including being forthright in dealings and communications with others.

internal auditing *(p. 6)* The practice of auditing within a company by employees of the company.

managerial accounting *(p. 4)* Accounting that is concerned with the use of economic and financial information to plan and control many of the activities of an entity, and to support the management decision-making process.

objectivity *(p. 12)* The personal characteristic of impartiality, including freedom from conflict of interest.

public accounting *(p. 5)* That segment of the accounting profession that provides professional services to clients. Services include auditing, income tax accounting, and consulting in specific areas.

Securities and Exchange Commission *(p. 8)* A unit of the federal government that is responsible for establishing regulations and assuring full disclosure to investors about companies and their securities that are traded in interstate commerce.

Statements of Financial Accounting Standards *(p. 8)* Pronouncements of the Financial Accounting Standards Board that constitute generally accepted accounting principles.

EXERCISES AND PROBLEMS

1–1. Throughout this course you will be asked to relate the material being studied to actual financial statements. After you complete this course, you will be able to use an organization's financial statements to make decisions and informed judgments about that organization. The purpose of this assignment is to provide the experience of obtaining a company's annual report and to get you a set of financial statements to refer to during the rest of the course.

Required: Obtain the most recently issued annual report of a publicly owned manufacturing or merchandising corporation of your choice. Do not select a bank, insurance company, or other financial institution, or a public utility. It would be appropriate to select a firm that you know something about, or have an interest in. If you don't know the name or title of a specific individual to contact, address your request to the Shareholder Relations Department. Company addresses are available from several sources, including the following reference books in the library:

Standard & Poor's Register of Corporations, Directors and Executives, Vol. 1—Corporations
Moody's Handbook of Common Stocks
Standard & Poor's Corporation Stock Market Encyclopedia
Moody's Industrial Manual

1–2. The accounting profession is frequently in the news, and not always in the most positive light. The purpose of this assignment is to increase your awareness of an issue facing the profession.

Required: Find, read, outline, and prepare to discuss a brief article from a general audience or business audience publication about accounting and/or the accounting profession. The article should have been published within the past 10 months, and should relate to accounting or the accounting profession in general; it should not be about some technical accounting issue. The appropriate topical headings to use in the Business Periodicals Index are Accountants, Accounting, and/or Accounting (specific topic).

1–3. Write a paragraph that describes your perceptions of what accounting is all about and the work that accountants do.

1–4. Write a statement identifying the expectations you have for this course.

1–5. Jim Hall is an accountant for a local manufacturing company. Jim's good friend Mary Hammer has been operating a retail sporting goods store for about a year. The store has been moderately successful, and Mary needs a bank loan to help finance the next stage of her store's growth. She has asked Jim to prepare financial statements that the banker will use to help decide whether or not to grant the loan. Mary has proposed that the fee she will pay for Jim's accounting work should be contingent upon her receiving the loan.

Required:

What factors should Jim consider when making his decision about whether or not to prepare the financial statements for Mary's store?

PART I

Financial Accounting

Chapter 2

Financial Statements and Accounting Concepts/Principles

The financial statements are the product of the financial accounting process. They are the means of communicating economic information about the entity to the individuals who want to make decisions and informed judgments about the entity. There are four principal financial statements, and although each statement has a unique purpose, they are interrelated and all must be considered in order to get a complete financial picture of an entity.

Users cannot understand financial statements without having an understanding of the concepts and principles that relate to the entire financial accounting process. It is also important for users to understand that these concepts and principles are very broad in nature; they do not constitute a fixed set of rules.

LEARNING OBJECTIVES

After studying this chapter, you should understand:

- What transactions are.
- The kind of information reported on each financial statement.
- The name and form of each of the financial statements.
- The way financial statements are related to each other.
- The meaning of each of the captions on the financial statements illustrated in this chapter.
- The accounting equation, and what it means.

- The broad, generally accepted concepts and principles that apply to the accounting process.
- Several limitations of financial statements.
- What a corporation's annual report is, and why it is issued.
- Business procedures related to organizing a business, fiscal year, par value, and parent-subsidiary corporations and consolidated financial statements.

FINANCIAL STATEMENTS

From Transactions to Financial Statements

The financial statements of an entity are the end product of a process that starts with **transactions** between the entity and other organizations and individuals. Transactions are economic interchanges between entities, for example, a sale/purchase, or a receipt of cash by a borrower and the payment of cash by the lender. The flow from transaction to financial statements can be illustrated as follows:

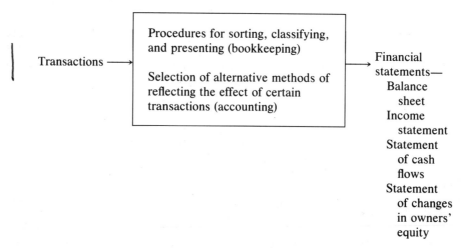

Current generally accepted accounting principles and auditing standards require that the financial statements of an entity for a period should show:

Financial position at the end of the period.

Earnings for the period.

Cash flows during the period.

Investments by and distributions to owners during the period.

• BUSINESS PROCEDURE CAPSULE 1
Organizing a Business

There are three principal forms of business organization: proprietorship, partnership, and corporation.

A **proprietorship** is an activity conducted by an individual. Operating as a proprietorship is the easiest way to get started in a business activity. Other than the possibility of needing a local license, there aren't any formal prerequisites to beginning operations. Besides being easy to start, a proprietorship has the advantage, according to many people, that the owner is her/his own boss. A principal disadvantage of the proprietorship is that the owner's liability for business debts is not limited by the assets of the business. For example, if the business fails, and if, after using all available business assets to pay business debts, the business creditors are still owed money, the owner's personal assets can be claimed by business creditors. Another disadvantage is that the individual proprietor may have difficulty raising the money needed to provide the capital base that will be required if the business is to grow substantially. Because of the ease of getting started, every year many business activities begin as proprietorships.

The **partnership** is essentially a group of proprietors who have banded together. The unlimited liability characteristic of the proprietorship still exists, but with several partners the ability of the firm to raise capital may be improved. Accountants, attorneys, and other professionals frequently operate their firms as partnerships.

Most large businesses, and many new businesses, use the corporate form of organization. The owners of the corporation are called **stockholders.** They have invested funds in the corporation and received shares of **stock** as evidence of their ownership. Stockholders' liability is limited to the amount invested; creditors cannot seek recovery of losses from the personal assets of stockholders. Large amounts of capital can frequently be raised by selling shares of stock to many individuals. It is also possible for all of the stock of a corporation to be owned by a single individual. A stockholder can usually sell her/his shares to other investors, or buy more shares from other stockholders if a change in ownership interest is desired. A **corporation** is formed by having a charter and bylaws prepared and registered with the appropriate office in 1 of the 50 states. The cost of forming a corporation is usually greater than that of starting a proprietorship or forming a partnership.

The financial statements that accomplish the above requirements are, respectively, the:

Balance sheet (or statement of financial position).

Income statement (or statement of earnings, or profit and loss statement).

Statement of cash flows.

Statement of changes in owners' equity (or statement of changes in capital stock and/or statement of changes in retained earnings).

In addition to the financial statements themselves, there will probably be several accompanying footnotes or explanations of the accounting policies, and detailed information about many of the amounts and captions shown on the financial statements. These notes are designed to assist the reader of the financial statements by disclosing as much relevant supplementary information as the company and its auditors deem necessary and appropriate. One of this text's objectives is to permit you to understand these financial statement footnotes. Chapter 10 describes the explanatory notes to the financial statements in detail.

Financial Statements Illustrated

Main Street Store, Inc., was organized as a corporation and began business during September 1992 (see Business Procedure Capsule 1). The company buys clothing and accessories from distributors and manufacturers, and sells these items from a building that is rented. The financial statements of the Main Street Store, Inc., at August 31, 1993, and for the fiscal year (see Business Procedure Capsule 2) ended on that date are presented in Exhibits 2–1 through 2–4.

As you look at these financial statements, you probably have several questions. They will be answered in subsequent chapters when the individual statements and their components are explained in detail. For now, concentrate on the explanations and definitions that are appropriate and inescapable, and notice especially the characteristics of each financial statement.

Explanations and Definitions

The Balance Sheet.   The **balance sheet,** or **statement of financial position,** is like a snapshot. It is a listing of the organization's assets, liabilities, and owners' equity *at a point in time*. The balance sheet is sometimes called the *statement of financial position,* because it summarizes the entity's resources, obligations, and owners' claims. The balance sheet for Main Street Store, Inc., at August 31, 1993, the end of the firm's first year of operations, is illustrated in Exhibit 2–1.

- **BUSINESS PROCEDURE CAPSULE 2**
  Fiscal Year

A firm's **fiscal year** is the annual period used for reporting to owners, the government, and others. Many firms select the calendar year as their fiscal year, but other 12-month periods can also be selected. Some firms select a reporting period ending on a date when inventories will be relatively low, or business activity will be slow, because this facilitates the process of preparing financial statements.

Many firms select fiscal periods that relate to the pace of their business activity. Food retailers, for example, have a weekly operating cycle, and many of these firms select a 52-week fiscal year (with a 53-week fiscal year every five or six years so their year-end remains near the same date every year).

For internal reporting purposes, many firms use periods other than the month (e.g., 13 four-week periods). The firm wants the same number of operating days in each period so that comparisons between the same period of different years can be made without having to consider that there may be a different number of operating days in the respective periods.

EXHIBIT 2–1   Balance Sheet

MAIN STREET STORE, INC.
Balance Sheet
August 31, 1993

Assets		Liabilities and Owners' Equity	
Current assets:		**Current liabilities:**	
Cash	$ 34,000	Short-term debt . .	$20,000
Accounts receivable . .	80,000	Accounts payable .	35,000
Merchandise		Other accrued	
inventory	170,000	liabilities	12,000
Total current assets	$284,000	Total current	
		liabilities . .	$ 67,000
Plant and equipment:		Long-term debt: . . .	50,000
Store equipment	40,000	Total liabilities.	$117,000
Less: Accumulated		Owners' equity . . .	203,000
depreciation.	(4,000)	Total liabilities and	
Total assets	$320,000	owners' equity. . .	$320,000

Notice the two principal sections of the balance sheet that are shown side by side. These are Assets and Liabilities and Owners' Equity. Observe that the dollar total of each side is the same — $320,000. This equality is sometimes referred to as the **accounting equation** or the *balance sheet equation*. It is the equality, or balance, of these two amounts from which the term *balance sheet* is derived.

Now some of those appropriate and inescapable definitions and explanations:

"**Assets** are probable future economic benefits obtained or controlled by a particular entity as a result of past transactions or events."[1] Assets frequently are tangible; they can be seen and handled (e.g., cash or merchandise inventory), or evidence of their existence can be observed (e.g., a customer's acknowledgment of receipt of merchandise and the implied promise to pay the amount due when agreed upon — an account receivable).

"**Liabilities** are probable future sacrifices of economic benefits arising from present obligations of a particular entity to transfer assets or provide services to other entities in the future as a result of past transactions or events."[2] In brief, liabilities are amounts owed to other entities. For example, the accounts payable arose because suppliers shipped merchandise to Main Street Store, Inc., and this merchandise will be paid for at some point in the future. (The supplier has an "ownership right" in the merchandise until it is paid for.)

Owner's equity is the ownership right of the owner(s) of the entity in the assets that remain after deducting the liabilities. (A car or house owner uses this term when referring to her/his **equity** as the market value of the car or house less the loan or mortgage balance.) Owners' equity is sometimes referred to as **net assets.** This can be shown by rearranging the basic accounting equation to:

$$\text{Assets} - \text{Liabilities} = \text{Owners' equity}$$

$$\text{Net assets} = \text{Owners' equity}$$

Another term sometimes used to mean owners' equity is **net worth.** However, this term is misleading because it implies that the net assets are "worth" the amount stated, *but financial statements*

---

[1] FASB, *Statement of Financial Accounting Concepts No. 6,* "Elements of Financial Statements" (Stamford, Conn., 1985), para. 25. Copyright © by the Financial Accounting Standards Board, High Ridge Park, Stamford, Connecticut 06905, U.S.A. Quoted with permission. Copies of the complete document are available from the FASB.

[2] Ibid., para. 35.

prepared according to generally accepted principles of accounting do not purport to show the current market value of the entity's assets, except in a few restricted cases.

Now look at the individual assets and liabilities. Each of these warrants a brief explanation. Each of these items will be discussed in more detail in later chapters. Your task at this point is to achieve a broad understanding of each item, and to make sense of its classification as an asset or liability.

Cash represents cash on hand and in the bank or banks used by Main Street Store, Inc. If the firm had made any temporary cash investment in order to earn interest, these securities would probably be shown as a separate asset.

Accounts Receivable represents amounts due from customers who have purchased merchandise on credit, and who have agreed to pay within a specified period or when billed by Main Street Store, Inc.

Merchandise Inventory represents the cost to Main Street Store, Inc. of the merchandise that it has acquired but not yet sold.

Store Equipment represents the cost to Main Street Store, Inc. of the display cases, racks, shelving, and other equipment that was purchased and installed in the rented building in which it is operating. The building is not shown as an asset because Main Street Store, Inc. does not own it.

Accumulated Depreciation represents the portion of the cost of the store equipment that is estimated to have been used up in the process of operating the business. Note that one-tenth ($4,000/ $40,000) of the cost of the equipment has been depreciated; from this relationship one might assume that the equipment is estimated to have a useful life of 10 years because this is the balance sheet at the end of the firm's first year of operations. **Depreciation** *in accounting is the process of spreading the cost of an asset over its useful life to the entity. It is not an attempt to recognize the economic loss in value of an asset because of its age or use.*

Short-term debt represents a loan, probably from a bank, that will be repaid within a year of the balance sheet date.

Accounts Payable represents amounts owed to suppliers of merchandise that has been acquired and put in inventory.

Other **Accrued Liabilities** represents amounts owed to various creditors, including possibly wages owed to employees for services provided to Main Street Store, Inc., through August 31, 1993, the balance sheet date.

Long-term Debt represents amounts borrowed from banks or others. These amounts will not be repaid for at least a year from the balance sheet date.

Owners' Equity, shown here as a single amount, is explained in more detail later in this chapter in the discussion of the statement of changes in owners' equity.

Notice that in Exhibit 2–1 there is a classification of some assets and liabilities as "current." **Current assets** *are cash and those assets that are likely to be converted to cash or used to benefit the entity within one year,* and **current liabilities** *are those liabilities that are to be paid with cash within one year of the balance sheet date.* In this example, it is expected that the accounts receivable from the customers of Main Street Store, Inc., will be collected within a year, and that the merchandise inventory will be sold within a year of the balance sheet date.' This time-frame classification is important, and, as will be explained later, is used in assessing the entity's ability to pay its obligations when they come due.

To summarize, the balance sheet is a listing of the entity's assets, liabilities, and owners' equity. A balance sheet can be prepared as of any date, but is most frequently prepared as of the end of a fiscal reporting period (e.g., month-end or year-end). The balance sheet as of the end of one period is the balance sheet as of the beginning of the next period. This can be illustrated on a time line as follows:

On the time line, Fiscal 1993 refers to the 12 months during which the entity carried out its economic activities.

Income Statement. The principal purpose of the **income statement,** or **statement of earnings** or **profit and loss statement,** is to answer the question: "Did the entity operate at a **profit** for the period of time under consideration?" The question is answered by first reporting **revenues** from the entity's operating activities (e.g., selling merchandise), and then subtracting the costs and **expenses** incurred in generating those revenues and operating the entity. **Gains** and **losses** are also reported on the income statement. Gains and losses result from nonoperating activities, rather than from the day-to-day operating activities that generate revenues and expenses. The income statement reports results for *a period* of time, in contrast to the balance sheet focus on a single date.

The income statement for Main Street Store, Inc., for the year ended August 31, 1993, is presented in Exhibit 2–2. Notice first

---

EXHIBIT 2–2   Income Statement

MAIN STREET STORE, INC.
Income Statement
For the Year Ended August 31, 1993

Net sales	$1,200,000
Cost of goods sold	850,000
Gross profit	350,000
Selling, general, and administrative expenses	311,000
Earnings from operations	39,000
Interest expense	9,000
Earnings before taxes	30,000
Income taxes	12,000
Net income	$ 18,000
Net income per share of common stock outstanding	$ 1.80

---

that the statement starts with Net sales, and that the various costs and expenses are subtracted to arrive at Net income in total and per share of common stock outstanding. **Net income** is the "profit" for the period; if costs and expenses exceed **net sales,** a net loss results. The reasons for reporting net income or net loss per share of common stock outstanding, and the calculation of this amount, will be explained in Chapter 9.

Now look at the individual captions on the income statement. Each warrants a brief explanation, which will be expanded in subsequent chapters. Your task at this point is to make sense of how each item influences the determination of net income.

Net sales represents the amount of sales of merchandise to customers, less the amount of sales originally recorded but that were canceled because the merchandise was subsequently returned by customers for one reason or another (wrong size, spouse didn't want it, and so on). The sales amount is frequently called *sales revenue,* or just *revenue.* Revenue results from selling a product or service to a customer.

Cost of goods sold means what it says. This is shown as a separate expense because of its significance, and because of the desire to show gross profit as a separate item.

Gross profit, the difference between net sales and cost of goods sold, is shown as a separate item because it is significant to both management and the nonmanagement reader of the income statement. Sometimes gross profit is referred to using the alternative term *gross margin*. The uses made of this amount will be explained in subsequent chapters.

Selling, general, and administrative expenses represents the operating expenses of the entity. In some income statements, these expenses will not be lumped together as in Exhibit 2–2, but will be reported separately for each of several operating expense categories.

Earnings from operations represents one of the most important measures of the firm's activities. Earnings from operations (or operating income) can be related to the assets available to management to obtain a useful measure of management's performance. A method of doing this is explained in Chapter 3.

Interest expense represents the cost of using borrowed funds. This item is reported separately because it is a function of how assets are financed, not how assets are used.

Income taxes is shown after all of the other income statement items have been reported because income taxes are a function of the firm's earnings before taxes.

Net income per share of common stock outstanding is reported as a separate item at the bottom of the income statement because of its significance in evaluating the market value of a share of common stock. This measure will be explained in more detail in Chapter 9.

To review, the income statement summarizes the entity's income (or loss) producing activities *for a period of time*. Transactions that affect the income statement will also affect the balance sheet. For example, a sale made for cash increases the sales revenue of the income statement and increases cash, an asset on the balance sheet. Likewise, wages earned by employees during the last week of the current year to be paid early in the next year are an expense of the current year. These wages will be deducted from revenues in the income statement, and are considered a liability reported on the balance sheet at the end of the year. Thus the income statement is a link between the balance sheets at the beginning and end of the year. How the link is made is explained in the next section, which describes the statement of changes in owners' equity. The time line presented earlier can be expanded as follows:

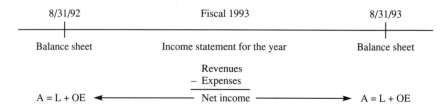

The Statement of Changes in Owners' Equity. The **statement of changes in owners' equity,** or **statement of changes in capital stock** or **statement of changes in retained earnings,** like the income statement, has a *period of time* orientation. This statement shows the detail of owners' equity, and explains the changes that occurred in the components of owners' equity during the year.

Exhibit 2–3 illustrates this statement for Main Street Store, Inc., for the year ended August 31, 1993. Remember that the year ended August 31, 1993, is Main Street Store's first year of operations, so the beginning-of-the-year balances are zero. On subsequent years' statements the beginning-of-the-year amount is the ending balance from the prior year.

Notice that in Exhibit 2–3 Owners' Equity is made up of two principal components: **Paid-In Capital** and **Retained Earnings.** These items are briefly explained here, and are discussed in more detail in Chapter 8.

Paid-In Capital represents the amount invested in the entity by the owners, in this case, the stockholders. When the stock issued to the owners has a **par value** (see Business Procedure Capsule 3), there will usually be two categories of paid-in capital, one describing some data about the stock, and the other representing the difference between the total owners' investment and the amount of owners' investment represented by the stock.

EXHIBIT 2–3   Statement of Changes in Owners' Equity

MAIN STREET STORE, INC.
Statement of Changes in Owners' Equity
For the Year Ended August 31, 1993

Paid-in capital:

Beginning balance	$ –0–
Common stock, par value, $10; 50,000 shares authorized,	
10,000 shares issued and outstanding	100,000
Additional paid-in capital	90,000
Balance, August 31, 1993	190,000

Retained earnings:

Beginning balance	$ –0–
Net income for the year	18,000 •
Less: Cash dividends of $.50 per share	(5,000)
Balance, August 31, 1993	$ 13,000
Total owners' equity	$203,000

From Previous Exhibit

Common Stock reflects the number of shares authorized by the corporation's charter, the number of shares that have been issued to stockholders, and the number of shares that are still held by the stockholders. When the common stock has a par value or stated value, the amount shown for common stock in the financial statements will always be the par value or stated value multiplied by the number of shares issued. If the common stock does not have a par value or stated value, the amount shown for common stock on the financial statements will be the amount invested by the owners.

Additional Paid-In Capital is the difference between the total amount invested by the owners and the par value or stated value of the stock. (If no-par-value stock without a stated value is issued to the owners, there won't be any additional paid-in capital because the total amount paid in, or invested, by the owners will be shown opposite the common stock caption.)

Retained earnings is the second principal category of owners' equity, and it represents the cumulative net income of the entity that has been retained for use in the business. **Dividends** are distributions of earnings that have been made to the owners, so these reduce retained earnings. If retained earnings has a negative balance, because cumulative losses and dividends have exceeded cumulative net income, this part of owners' equity is referred to as *deficit*.

Note that in Exhibit 2–3 the Net Income for the Year of $18,000 added to Retained Earnings is the amount of Net Income reported in Exhibit 2–2. The Retained Earnings section of the statement of changes in owners' equity is where the link between the balance sheet and income statement, which was mentioned earlier, is made. The time line model is thus expanded and modified to:

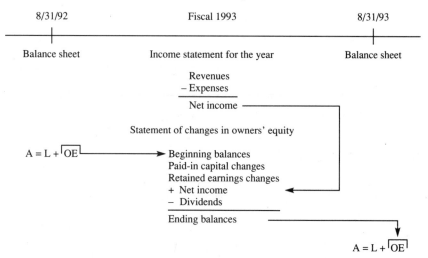

> • **BUSINESS PROCEDURE CAPSULE 3**
> **Par Value**
>
> Par value is a relic from the past that has, for all practical purposes, lost its significance. The par value of common stock is an arbitrary value assigned when the corporation is organized. Par value bears no relationship to the fair market value of a share of stock (except that a corporation may not issue its stock for less than par value). Because of investor confusion about the significance of par value, most states now permit corporations to issue no-par-value stock. Some state laws permit a firm to assign a stated value to its no-par-value stock, in which case the stated value operates as a par value. Incorporators who assign a stated value to a no-par-value stock instead of using a par value have their own reasons for following this confusing practice.

Notice that the Total Owners' Equity reported on Exhibit 2–3 agrees with Owners' Equity shown on the balance sheet, Exhibit 2–1. Most balance sheets include the amount of common stock, additional paid-in capital, and retained earnings in the owners' equity section of the balance sheet. Changes that occur in these components of owners' equity are likely to be shown in a separate statement so users of the financial statements can learn what caused these important balance sheet elements to change.

The Statement of Cash Flows.   The purpose of the **statement of cash flows** is to identify the sources and uses of cash during the year. This objective is accomplished by reporting the changes in all of the other balance sheet items. Because of the equality that exists between assets and liabilities plus owners' equity, the total of the changes in every other asset and each liability and element of owners' equity will equal the change in cash. The statement of cash flows is described in detail in Chapter 9. For now, make sense of the three principal activity groups that cause cash to change, and see how the amounts on this statement relate to the balance sheet in Exhibit 2–1.

The statement of cash flows for Main Street Store, Inc., for the year ended August 31, 1993, is illustrated in Exhibit 2–4. Notice that this statement, like the income statement and statement of changes in owners' equity, is for a *period of time*. Notice also the three activity categories: operating activities, investing activities, and financing activities.

EXHIBIT 2–4   Statement of Cash Flows

MAIN STREET STORE, INC.
Statement of Cash Flows
For the Year Ended August 31, 1993

Cash flows from operating activities:

Net income	$ 18,000
Add (deduct) items not affecting cash:	
Depreciation expense	4,000
Increase in accounts receivable.	(80,000)
Increase in merchandise inventory	(170,000)
Increase in current liabilities	67,000
Net cash used by operating activities	$(161,000)

Cash flows from investing activities:

Cash paid for store equipment	$ (40,000)

Cash flows from financing activities:

Cash received from issue of long-term debt	$ 50,000
Cash received from sale of common stock	190,000
Payment of cash dividend on common stock	(5,000)
Net cash provided by financing activities	$ 235,000
Net increase in cash for the year	$ 34,000

Cash flows from operating activities are shown first, and Net Income is the starting point for this measure of cash generation. Using net income also directly relates the income statement to the statement of cash flows. Check out this link between the two financial statements (Exhibits 2–2 and 2–4). Next, items that affected net income but that did not affect cash are considered.

Depreciation expense is added back to net income because even though it was deducted as an expense in determining net income, *depreciation expense did not require the use of cash*. Remember — depreciation in accounting is the process of spreading the cost of an asset over its estimated useful life.

The increase in accounts receivable is deducted because this reflects sales revenues, included in net income, that have not yet been collected in cash.

The increase in merchandise inventory is deducted because cash was spent to acquire the increase in inventory.

The increase in current liabilities is added because cash has not yet been paid for the products and services that have been received during the current fiscal period.

Cash flows from investing activities shows the cash used to purchase long-lived assets. You should find the increase in store equipment in the balance sheet (Exhibit 2–1), which shows the cost of the store equipment owned at August 31, 1993. Since this is the first year of the firm's operations, the equipment purchase required the use of $40,000 during the year.

Cash flows from financing activities include amounts raised from the sale of long-term debt and common stock, and dividends paid on common stock. You should find each of these financing amounts in the balance sheet (Exhibit 2–1) or the statement of changes in owners' equity (Exhibit 2–3). For example, the $190,000 received from the sale of stock is shown on the statement of changes in owners' equity (Exhibit 2–3) as the increase in paid-in capital during the year.

The net increase in cash for the year of $34,000 is the amount of cash in the August 31, 1993, balance sheet. Check this out. This should make sense because the firm started in business during September 1992, so it had no cash to begin with.

The statement of cash flows results in an expansion and modification of the time-line model that can be seen in the diagram that follows.

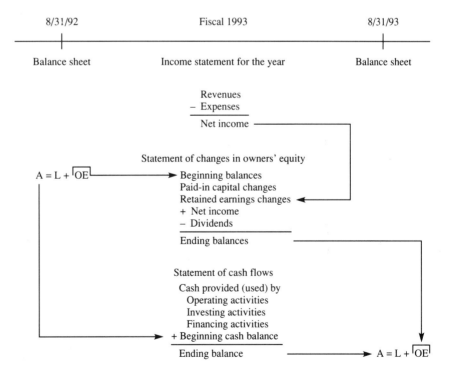

Comparative Statements in Subsequent Years

The financial statements presented above for Main Street Store, Inc., show data as of August 31, 1993, and for the year then ended. Because this was the first year of the firm's operations, comparative financial statements are not possible. In subsequent years, however, comparative statements for the current and prior year should be presented so that users of the data can more easily spot changes in the firm's financial position and in its results of operations. Some companies present data for two prior years in their financial statements. Most companies will include selected data from their balance sheets and income statements for at least 5 years, and sometimes for up to 25 years, as supplementary information in their annual report to stockholders.

Illustration of Financial Statement Relationships

Exhibit 2–5 uses the financial statements of Main Street Store, Inc., to illustrate the financial statement relationships just discussed. Note that in Exhibit 2–5 amounts are shown in thousands of dollars, and that the August 31, 1992, balance sheet has no amounts. That is because Main Street Store, Inc., started business in September 1992. As you study this exhibit, note especially that net income for the year was an increase in retained earnings, and is one of the reasons retained earnings changed during the year.

In subsequent chapters, the relationship between the balance sheet and income statement will be presented using the following diagram:

Balance sheet	Income statement
Assets = Liabilities + Owners' equity ←	Net income = Revenues − Expenses

The arrow from Net income in the income statement to Owners' equity in the balance sheet is to indicate that net income affects retained earnings, which is a component of owners' equity.

The following examples also illustrate the relationships within and between the principal financial statements.

Using the August 31, 1993, Main Street Store, Inc., data for assets and liabilities in the balance sheet equation of A = L + OE, owners' equity at August 31, 1993, can be calculated:

$$A = L + OE$$
$$\$320 = \$117 + OE$$
$$\$203 = OE$$

EXHIBIT 2–5

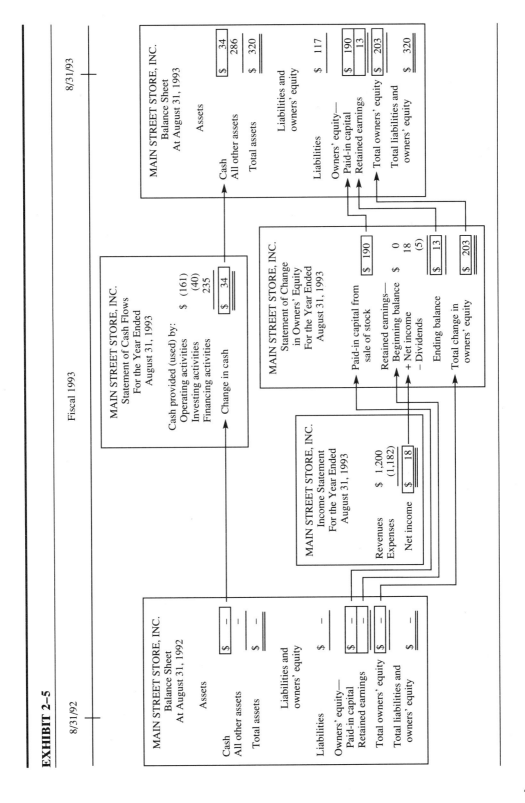

8/31/92   Fiscal 1993   8/31/93

MAIN STREET STORE, INC.
Balance Sheet
At August 31, 1992

Assets

Cash $ —
All other assets   —
Total assets $ —

Liabilities and
owners' equity

Liabilities $ —
Owners' equity—
Paid-in capital $ —
Retained earnings   —
Total owners' equity $ —
Total liabilities and
owners' equity $ —

MAIN STREET STORE, INC.
Income Statement
For the Year Ended
August 31, 1993

Revenues $ 1,200
Expenses   (1,182)
Net income $ 18

MAIN STREET STORE, INC.
Statement of Cash Flows
For the Year Ended
August 31, 1993

Cash provided (used) by:
Operating activities $ (161)
Investing activities   (40)
Financing activities   235
Change in cash $ 34

MAIN STREET STORE, INC.
Statement of Change
in Owners' Equity
For the Year Ended
August 31, 1993

Paid-in capital from
sale of stock $ 190
Retained earnings—
Beginning balance $ 0
+ Net income   18
– Dividends   (5)
Ending balance $ 13
Total change in
owners' equity $ 203

MAIN STREET STORE, INC.
Balance Sheet
At August 31, 1993

Assets

Cash $ 34
All other assets   286
Total assets $ 320

Liabilities and
owners' equity

Liabilities $ 117
Owners' equity—
Paid-in capital $ 190
Retained earnings   13
Total owners' equity $ 203
Total liabilities and
owners' equity $ 320

Remember, another term for owners' equity is *net assets*. This is shown clearly in the above calculation, as owners' equity is the difference between assets and liabilities.

Now suppose that during the year ended August 31, *1994*, total assets increase $10, and total liabilities decrease $3. What was owners' equity at the end of the year? There are two ways of solving the problem. First, look at just the changes in the elements of the balance sheet equation:

$$A = L + OE$$

$$\text{Change:} \quad +10 = -3 + \text{?}$$

It is clear that for the equation to stay in balance, owners' equity must have increased $13. Since owners' equity was $203 at the beginning of the year, it must have been $216 at the end of the year.

The second approach to solving the problem is to calculate the amount of assets and liabilities at the end of the year, and then solve for owners' equity at the end of the year, as follows:

$$A \quad = \quad L \quad + \quad OE$$

	A	=	L	+	OE
Beginning	320	=	117	+	203
Change:	+10	=	−3	+	?
End	330	=	114	+	?

The ending owners' equity or net assets is $330 − $114 = $216. And, since ending owners' equity is $216, it increased $13 during the year from August 31, 1993, to August 31, 1994.

Assume that during the year ended August 31, 1994, the owners invested an additional $8 in the firm, and that dividends of $6 were declared. How much net income did the firm have for the year ended August 31, 1994? Recall that net income is one of the items that affects the retained earnings component of owners' equity. What else affects retained earnings? That's right—dividends. Since owners' equity increased from $203 to $216 during the year, and the items causing that change were net income, dividends, and the additional investment by the owners, the amount of net income can be calculated as follows:

Owners' equity, beginning of year	$203
Increase in paid-in capital from	
additional investment by owners	8
Net income	?
Dividends	−6
Owners' equity, end of year	$216

Solving for the unknown, net income is equal to $11.

An alternative solution to determine net income for the year involves focusing on just the *changes* in owners' equity during the year, as follows:

Increase in paid-in capital from additional investment by owners	8
Net income	?
Dividends	−6
Change in owners' equity for the year	$13

Again, solving for the unknown, net income is equal to $11.

The important points to remember here are:

1. The balance sheet shows the amount of assets, liabilities, and owners' equity at a point in time.
2. The balance sheet equation must always be in balance.
3. The income statement shows net income for a period of time.
4. The retained earnings component of owners' equity changes over a period of time as a result of the firm's net income (or loss) and dividends for that period of time.

ACCOUNTING CONCEPTS AND PRINCIPLES

In order to understand the kinds of decisions and informed judgments that can be made from the financial statements, it is appropriate to have an understanding of some of the broad concepts and principles of accounting that have become generally accepted for financial accounting and reporting purposes. Again, it is important to recognize that these concepts and principles are more like practices that have been generally agreed upon over a period of time than hard and fast rules or basic laws such as those encountered in the physical sciences.

These concepts and principles can be related to the basic model of the flow of data from transactions to financial statements illustrated earlier, as shown at the top of page 44.

Concepts/Principles Related to the Entire Model

The basic accounting equation described earlier in this chapter is the mechanical key to the entire financial accounting process because the equation must be in balance after every transaction has been recorded in the accounting records. The method for recording transactions and maintaining this balance will be illustrated in Chapter 4.

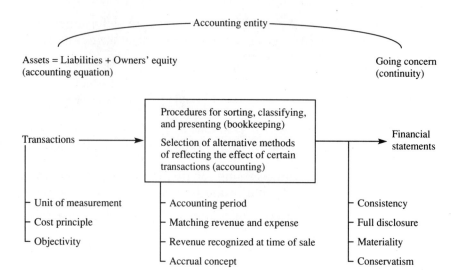

Accounting entity refers to the entity for which the financial statements are being prepared. The entity can be a proprietorship, partnership, corporation, or even a group of corporations (see Business Procedure Capsule 4—Parent and Subsidiary Corporations). The entity for which the accounting is being done is defined by the accountant, and even though the entities may be related (e.g., an individual and the business she owns), the accounting is done for the defined entity.

The **going concern concept** refers to the presumption that the entity will continue to operate in the future—that it is not being liquidated. This continuity assumption is necessary because the amounts shown on the balance sheet for various assets do not reflect the liquidation value of those assets.

Concepts/Principles Related to Transactions

In the United States, the dollar is the unit of measurement for all transactions. No adjustment is made for changes in the purchasing power of the dollar. No attempt is made to reflect qualitative economic factors in the measurement of transactions.

The *cost principle* refers to the fact that transactions are recorded at their cost to the entity as measured in dollars. For example, if a parcel of land were purchased by a firm for $8,600 even though an appraisal showed the land to be worth $10,000, the purchase transaction would be reflected in the accounting records, and the financial statements would report the land at its cost of $8,600. If the land is still owned and being used 15 years later, even though

---

• **BUSINESS PROCEDURE CAPSULE 4**
Parent and Subsidiary Corporations

Because of the advantages of the corporate form of organization, it is not
unusual for a new corporation that wants to expand its operations to form a
corporation to carry out its plans. In such a case the original corporation
owns all of the stock of the new corporation; it has become the "parent" of
a "**subsidiary.**" One parent may have several subsidiaries, and the subsidiaries themselves may be parents of subsidiaries. It is not necessary for the
parent to own 100% of the stock of another corporation for the parent/
subsidiary relationship to exist. If one corporation owns more than half of
the stock of another, it is presumed that the majority owner can exercise
enough control to create a parent/subsidiary relationship. When a subsidiary is not wholly owned, the other stockholders of the subsidiary are referred to as *minority* stockholders.

   In most instances, the financial statements issued by the parent corporation will include the assets, liabilities, equity, revenues, expenses, and gains
and losses of the subsidiaries. Financial statements that reflect the financial
position, results of operations, and cash flows of a parent and one or more
subsidiaries are called *consolidated* financial statements.

---

its market value has increased to $80,000, it continues to be re-
ported in the balance sheet at its original cost of $8,600.

   Objectivity refers to accountants' desire to have a given transaction recorded in the same way in all situations. This objective is
facilitated by using the dollar as the unit of measurement, and by
applying the cost principle. However, as previously stressed, there
are transactions for which the exercise of professional judgment
could result in alternative recording results. These alternatives will
be illustrated in subsequent chapters.

Concepts/Principles Related to Bookkeeping Procedures and the Accounting Process

These concepts/principles relate to the accounting period, that is,
the period of time selected for reporting results of operations and
changes in financial position. Financial position will be reported at
the end of this period of time (and the balance sheet at the beginning of the period will probably be included with the financial statements).

   Matching revenue and expense is necessary if the results of the
firm's operations are to reflect accurately its economic activities

during the period. The **matching concept** does not mean that revenues and expenses for a period are equal. Revenue is not earned without effort (businesses do not receive birthday gifts), and expenses are the measure of the economic efforts exerted to generate revenues. A fair presentation of the results of a firm's operations during a period of time requires that all expenses incurred in generating that period's revenues be deducted from the revenues earned. This results in an accurate measure of the net income or net loss for the period. This seems like common sense, but, as we shall see, there are alternative methods of determining some of the expenses to be recognized in any given period. This concept of matching revenue and expense is very important, and will be referred to again and again as accounting practices are discussed in the following chapters.

Revenue is recognized at the time of sale, that is, when title to the product being sold passes from the seller to the buyer, or when the services involved in the transaction have been performed. Passing of legal ownership (title) is the critical event, not the cash payment from buyer to seller.

Accrual accounting utilizes the **accrual concept,** and results in recognizing revenue at the point of sale and recognizing expenses as they are incurred, even though the cash receipt or payment occurs at another time or in another accounting period. Thus, many activities of the firm will involve two transactions: one that recognizes the revenue or expense, and the other that reflects the receipt or payment of cash. It is the use of accrual procedures that accomplishes much of the matching of revenues and expenses because most transactions between business firms (and between many firms and individuals) involve purchase/sale at one point in time, and cash payment/receipt at some other point in time.

The financial statement user primarily relies on these concepts and principles related to the accounting period when making judgments and informed decisions about an entity's financial position and results of operations.

Concepts/Principles Related to Financial Statements

Consistency in financial reporting is essential if meaningful trend comparisons are to be made using an entity's financial statements for several years. Thus it is inappropriate for the accountant to change from one generally accepted alternative of accounting for a particular type of transaction to another generally accepted method, unless both the fact that the change has been made, and the effect of the change on the financial statements, are explicitly described in the financial statements or the accompanying notes and explanations.

Full disclosure means that the financial statements and notes or explanations should include all necessary information to prevent a reasonably astute user of the financial statements from being misled. This is a tall order, and one that the Securities and Exchange Commission has helped to define over the years. This requirement for full disclosure is one reason that the notes and explanations are usually considered to be an integral part of the financial statements.

Materiality means that absolute exactness, even if that idea could be defined, is not necessary in the amounts shown in the financial statements. Because of the numerous estimates involved in accounting, amounts reported in financial statements may be approximate, but they will not be "wrong" enough to be misleading. The financial statements of publicly owned corporations usually show amounts rounded to the nearest thousand, hundred thousand, or even million dollars. This rounding does not impair the information content of the financial statements, and probably makes them easier to read. A management concept related to materiality is the cost/benefit relationship. Just as a manager would not spend $500 to get $300 worth of information, the incremental benefit of increased accuracy in accounting estimates is frequently not worth the cost of achieving the increased accuracy.

Conservatism in accounting relates to making judgments and estimates that result in lower profits and asset valuation estimates rather than higher profits and asset valuation estimates. Accountants try to avoid wishful thinking or pie-in-the-sky estimates that could result in overstating profits for a current period. This is not to say that accountants always look at issues from a gloom and doom viewpoint; rather they seek to be realistic.

Limitations of Financial Statements

Financial statements report quantitative economic data; they do not reflect qualitative economic variables. Thus the value to the firm of a management team, or of the morale of the work force, is not included as a balance sheet asset because it cannot be objectively measured. Such qualitative attributes of the firm are frequently relevant to the decisions and informed judgments that the financial statement user is making, but they are not communicated in the financial statements.

As already emphasized, the cost principle requires assets to be recorded at their original cost. The balance sheet does not show the current market value or the replacement cost of the assets. Some assets are reported at the lower of their cost or market value, and in some cases market value may be reported parenthetically, but asset values are not increased to reflect current value. For example, the trademark of a firm has virtually no cost; its value has developed over the years as the firm has successfully met customers' needs. Thus trademarks are excluded from the balance sheet listing of assets.

Estimates are used in many areas of accounting, and when the estimate is made, about the only fact known is that the estimate is probably not equal to the "true" amount. It is hoped that the estimate is near the "true" amount (the concept of materiality); it usually is. For example, recognizing depreciation expense involves estimating both the useful life to the entity of the asset being depreciated, and the probable salvage value of the asset to the entity when it is disposed of. The original cost minus the salvage value is the amount to be depreciated or recognized as expense over the asset's life. Estimates must be made to determine pension expense, warranty costs, and numerous other expense and revenue items to be reflected in the current year's income statement because they reflect the economic activity of the current year. These estimates also affect balance sheet accounts. So even though the balance sheet balances to the penny, do not be misled by this aura of exactness. Accountants do their best to make their estimates as accurate as possible, but estimates are still estimates.

The principle of consistency suggests that an entity should not change from one generally accepted method of accounting for a particular item to another generally accepted method of accounting for the same item. However, it is quite possible that two firms operating in the same industry may follow different methods. This means that comparability between firms may not be appropriate, or if comparisons are made, the effects of any differences between the accounting methods followed by the firms must be understood.

Related to the use of the original cost principle is the fact that financial statements are not adjusted to show the impact of inflation. Land acquired by a firm 50 years ago is still reported at its original cost, even though it may have a significantly higher current value because of inflation. Likewise, depreciation expense and the cost of goods sold — both significant expense elements of the income statement of many firms — reflect original cost, not replacement cost. This weakness is not significant when the rate of inflation is low, but the usefulness of financial statements is seriously impaired when the inflation rate rises to double digits. In 1980 the FASB began to require that large, publicly owned companies report certain data to show some of the impacts of changing prices as supplementary information in the footnotes to the financial statements. In 1986 the FASB discontinued the requirement that this information be presented, but it encouraged further supplementary disclosures of the effects of inflation and changes in specific prices. This is a very controversial issue that will become more important if the rate of inflation rises significantly in the future.

Financial statements do not reflect **opportunity cost,** which is an economic concept relating to income not earned because an opportunity to earn income was not pursued. For example, if an individual or organization maintains a checking account balance that is $300 more than that required to avoid any service charges, the opportunity cost associated with that $300 is the interest that could otherwise be earned on the money if it had been invested. Financial accounting does not give formal recognition to opportunity cost; however, financial managers should be aware of the concept as they plan the utilization of the firm's resources.

THE CORPORATION'S ANNUAL REPORT

The **annual report** is the document distributed to shareowners that contains the reporting firm's financial statements for the fiscal year, together with the report of the external auditor's examination of the financial statements. The annual report document can be as simple as a transmittal letter from the president or chairman of the board of directors along with the financial statements, or as fancy as a glossy, 100-page booklet that showcases the firm's products, services, and personnel, as well as its financial results.

In addition to the financial statements described above, and the explanatory comments (or footnotes or financial review) described more fully in Chapter 10, some other financial data are usually included in the annual report. Highlights for the year, including total revenues and net income, net income per share of common stock outstanding, and dividends paid during the year, are reported inside the front cover or on the first page of the report. Most firms also include a historical summary of certain financial data for at least the past five years. This summary is usually located near the back of the annual report.

Appendix A at the back of this text is the 1991 Annual Report of Armstrong World Industries, Inc. You should review this appendix now to see a good example of an annual report. Find the financial statements in the report to see the end product of the financial reporting process. Many of the specific elements of these financial statements will be studied in subsequent chapters.

SUMMARY

Financial statements are used to communicate economic information for decisions and informed judgments.

The bookkeeping and accounting processes result in an entity's numerous transactions with other entities being reflected in the financial statements. The financial statements presented by an entity are the balance sheet, income statement, statement of changes in owners' equity, and statement of cash flows.

The balance sheet is a listing of the entity's assets, liabilities, and owners' equity at a point in time. Assets are probable future economic benefits (things or claims against others) controlled by the entity. Liabilities are amounts owed by the entity. The owners' equity of an entity is the difference between its assets and liabilities. This relationship is known as the *accounting equation.* Current assets are cash and those assets likely to be converted to cash or used to benefit the entity within one year of the balance sheet date, such as accounts receivable and inventories. Current liabilities are expected to be paid within one year of the balance sheet date. The balance sheet as of the end of a fiscal period is also the balance sheet at the beginning of the next fiscal period.

The income statement reports the results of the entity's operating activities for a period of time. Revenues are reported first, and costs and expenses are subtracted to arrive at net income or net loss for the period.

The statement of changes in owners' equity describes changes in paid-in capital and retained earnings during the period. Retained earnings is increased by the amount of net income and decreased by dividends to stockholders (and by any net loss for the period). It is through retained earnings that the income statement is linked to the balance sheet.

The statement of cash flows summarizes the impact on cash of the entity's operating activities, investing activities, and financing activities during the period. The bottom line of this financial statement is the change in cash from the amount shown in the balance sheet at the beginning of the period (e.g., fiscal year) to that shown in the balance sheet at the end of the period.

Financial statements are usually presented on a comparative basis so users can easily spot significant changes in an entity's financial position (balance sheet) and results of operations (income statement).

The financial statements are interrelated. Net income for the period (from the income statement) is added to retained earnings, a part of owners' equity (in the balance sheet). The statement of changes in owners' equity explains the difference between the amounts of owners' equity at the beginning and the end of the fiscal period. The statement of cash flows explains the change in the amount of cash from the beginning to the end of the fiscal period.

Accounting concepts and principles reflect generally accepted practices that have evolved over time. They can be related to a schematic model of the flow of data from transactions to the financial statements. Pertaining to the entire model are the accounting entity concept, the accounting equation, and the going concern concept.

Transactions are recorded in currency units without regard to purchasing power change. Thus, transactions are recorded at an objectively determinable original cost amount.

The concepts and principles for the accounting period involve recognizing revenue when a sale of a product or service is made, and then relating to that revenue all of the costs and expenses incurred in generating the revenue of the period. This matching of revenues and expenses is a crucial and fundamental concept to understand if accounting itself is to be understood. The accrual concept is used to implement the matching concept by recognizing revenues when earned and expenses when incurred, regardless of whether cash is received or paid in the same fiscal period.

The concepts of consistency, full disclosure, materiality, and conservatism relate primarily to financial statement presentation.

There are limitations to the information presented in financial statements. These limitations are related to the concepts and principles that have become generally accepted. Thus, subjective qualitative factors, current values, the impact of inflation, and opportunity cost are not usually reflected in financial statements. In addition, many financial statement amounts involve estimates. Permissible alternative accounting practices may mean that interfirm comparisons are not appropriate.

Corporations and other organizations include financial statements in an annual report that is made available to stockholders, employees, potential investors, and others interested in the entity. Refer to the financial statements in the Armstrong World Industries, Inc., annual report in Appendix A, and refer to the financial statements of other annual report(s) you have, to see how the material discussed in this chapter is applied to real companies.

KEY TERMS AND CONCEPTS

account payable *(p. 31)*   A liability representing an amount payable to another entity, usually because of the purchase of merchandise or service on credit.

account receivable *(p. 31)*   An asset representing a claim against another entity, usually arising from selling goods or services on credit.

accounting equation *(p. 30)*   Assets = Liabilities + Owners' equity. The fundamental relationship represented by the balance sheet, and the foundation of the bookkeeping process.

accrual accounting *(p. 46)*   Accounting that recognizes revenues and expenses as they occur, even though the cash receipt from the revenue or the cash disbursement related to the expense may occur before or after the event that causes revenue or expense recognition.

accrual concept *(p. 46)*   See *accrual accounting.*

accrued liabilities *(p. 31)*   Amounts that are owed by an entity on the balance sheet date.

accumulated depreciation *(p. 31)*   The sum of the depreciation expense that has been recognized over time. Accumulated depreciation is a contra asset that is subtracted from the cost of the asset on the balance sheet.

additional paid-in capital *(p. 36)*   The excess of the amount received from the sale of par value stock over the par value of the shares sold.

annual report *(p. 49)*   A document distributed to shareowners that contains the financial statements for the fiscal year of the reporting firm, together with the report of the external auditor's examination of the financial statements.

assets *(p. 30)*   Probable future economic benefits obtained or controlled by an entity as a result of past transactions or events.

balance sheet *(p. 28)*   The financial statement that is a listing of the entity's assets, liabilities, and owners' equity at a point in time. Sometimes this statement is called the *statement of financial position.*

cash *(p. 31)*   An asset on the balance sheet that represents the amount of cash on hand and balances in bank accounts maintained by the entity.

common stock *(p. 36)*   The class of stock that represents residual ownership of the corporation.

corporation *(p. 27)*   A form of organization in which ownership is evidenced by shares of stock owned by stockholders; its features such as limited liability make this the principal form of organization for most business activity.

cost of goods sold *(p. 33)*   Cost of merchandise sold during the period; an expense deducted from net sales to arrive at gross profit.

current assets *(p. 32)*   Cash and those assets that are likely to be converted to cash or used to benefit the entity within one year of the balance sheet date.

current liabilities *(p. 32)*   Those liabilities due to be paid within one year of the balance sheet date.

depreciation *(p. 31)* The accounting process of recognizing that the cost of an asset is used up over its useful life to the entity.

depreciation expense *(p. 38)* The expense recognized in a fiscal period for the depreciation of an asset.

dividend *(p. 36)* A distribution of earnings to the owners of a corporation.

earnings from operations *(p. 34)* The difference between gross profit and operating expenses. Also referred to as *operating income*.

equity *(p. 30)* The ownership right associated with an asset. See *owner's equity*.

expenses *(p. 32)* Outflows or other using up of assets or incurring a liability during a period from delivering or producing goods, rendering services, or carrying out other activities that constitute the entity's major operations.

fiscal year *(p. 29)* The annual period used for reporting to owners.

gains *(p. 32)* Increases in net assets from incidental transactions that are not revenues or investments by owners.

going concern concept *(p. 44)* A presumption that the entity will continue in existence for the indefinite future.

gross profit *(p. 33)* The difference between net sales and cost of goods sold. Sometimes called *gross margin*.

income statement *(p. 32)* The financial statement that summarizes the entity's revenues, expenses, gains, and losses for a period of time, and reports the entity's results of operations for that period of time.

liabilities *(p. 30)* Probable future sacrifices of economic benefits arising from present obligations of a particular entity to transfer assets or provide services to other entities in the future as a result of past transactions or events.

losses *(p. 32)* Decreases in net assets from incidental transactions that are not expenses or distributions to owners.

matching concept *(p. 46)* Results in a fair presentation of the results of a firm's operations during a period by requiring the deduction of all expenses incurred in generating that period's revenues from the revenues earned in the period.

merchandise inventory *(p. 31)* Items held by an entity for sale to potential customers in the normal course of business.

net assets *(p. 30)* The difference between assets and liabilities; also referred to as *owners' equity*.

net income *(p. 33)* The difference between revenues and gains, and expenses and losses for the period.

net income per share of common stock outstanding *(p. 34)* Net income available to the common stockholders divided by the average number of shares of common stock outstanding during the period. Usually referred to as *earnings per share*.

net sales *(p. 33)* Gross sales, less sales discounts and sales returns and allowances.

net worth *(p. 30)*   Another term for *net assets* or *owners' equity,* but not as appropriate because the term *worth* may be misleading.

opportunity cost *(p. 49)*   An economic concept relating to income forgone because an opportunity to earn income was not pursued.

owners' equity *(p. 30)*   The equity of the entity's owners in the assets of the entity. Sometimes called *net assets;* the difference between assets and liabilities.

paid-in capital *(p. 35)*   The amount invested in the entity by the owners.

par value *(p. 35)*   An arbitrary value assigned to a share of stock when the corporation is organized. Sometimes used to refer to the stated value or face amount of a security.

partnership *(p. 27)*   A form of organization indicating ownership by two or more individuals or corporations without the limited liability and other features of a corporation.

profit *(p. 32)*   The excess of revenues and gains over expenses and losses for a fiscal period.

profit and loss statement *(p. 32)*   Another name for the income statement.

proprietorship *(p. 27)*   A form of organization indicating individual ownership without the limited liability and other features of a corporation.

retained earnings *(p. 35)*   Cumulative net income that has not been distributed to the owners of a corporation as dividends.

revenues *(p. 32)*   Inflows of cash or increases in other assets, or settlement of liabilities during a period from delivering or producing goods, rendering services, or performing other activities that constitute the entity's major operations.

statement of cash flows *(p. 37)*   The financial statement that explains why cash changed during a fiscal period. Cash flows from operating, investing, and financing activities are shown.

statement of changes in capital stock *(p. 35)*   The financial statement that summarizes changes during a fiscal period in capital stock and additional paid-in capital. This information may be included in the statement of changes in owners' equity.

statement of changes in owners' equity *(p. 35)*   The financial statement that summarizes the changes during a fiscal period in capital stock, additional paid-in capital, retained earnings, treasury stock, and other elements of owners' equity.

statement of changes in retained earnings *(p. 35)*   The financial statement that summarizes the changes during a fiscal period in retained earnings. This information may be included in the statement of changes in owners' equity.

statement of earnings *(p. 32)*   Another name for the income statement; it shows the revenues, expenses, gains, and losses for a period of time, and the entity's results of operations for that period of time.

statement of financial position *(p. 28)*   Another name for the *balance sheet;* a listing of the entity's assets, liabilities, and owners' equity at a point in time.

stock *(p. 27)*   The evidence of ownership of a corporation.

stockholders *(p. 27)*   The owners of a corporation's stock; sometimes called *share owners.*

subsidiary *(p. 45)*   A corporation whose stock is more than 50% owned by another corporation.

transactions *(p. 26)*   Economic interchanges between entities that are accounted for and reflected in financial statements.

EXERCISES AND PROBLEMS

2–1. Listed below are a number of financial statement captions. Indicate in the spaces to the right of each caption the category of each item, and the financial statement(s) on which the item can usually be found. Use the following abbreviations:

Category		*Financial Statement*	
Asset	A	Balance sheet	BS
Liability	L	Income statement	IS
Owners' equity	OE	Statement of changes	
Revenue	R	in owners' equity	SOE
Expense	E	Statement of cash flows	SCF
Gain	G		
Loss	LS		

Cash	A	BS
Accounts payable	L	BS
Common stock	OE	SOE, BS
Depreciation expense	E	IS, SCF
Net sales	R	IS
Income tax expense	E	IS
Short-term investments	A	BS
Gain on sale of land	G	IS
Retained earnings	OE	BS, SOE
Dividends payable	L	BS
Accounts receivable	A	BS
Short-term debt	L	BS

2–2. Listed below are a number of financial statement captions. Indicate in the spaces to the right of each caption the category of each item, and the financial statement(s) on which the item can usually be found. Use the following abbreviations:

Category		Financial Statement	
Asset	A	Balance sheet	BS
Liability	L	Income statement	IS
Owners' equity	OE	Statement of changes	
Revenue	R	in owners' equity	SOE
Expense	E	Statement of cash flows	SCF
Gain	G		
Loss	LS		

Accumulated depreciation _____ _____
Long-term debt _____ _____
Equipment _____ _____
Loss on sale of
   short-term investments _____ _____
Net income _____ _____
Merchandise inventory _____ _____
Other accrued liabilities _____ _____
Dividends paid _____ _____
Cost of goods sold _____ _____
Additional paid-in capital _____ _____
Interest income _____ _____
Selling expenses _____ _____

2–3. Select the appropriate data from that given below and calculate the Retained Earnings balance at December 31, 1993.

Retained earnings, December 31, 1992.	$318,000
Cost of building purchased in 1993	250,000
Net income for year ended December 31, 1993	97,000
Dividends declared and paid in 1993.	43,000
Decrease in cash balance from January 1, 1992, to	
December 31, 1993	21,000
Proceeds from sale of common stock in 1993	80,000

2–4. Select the appropriate data from that given below and calculate the Retained Earnings balance at December 31, 1993.

Retained earnings, December 31, 1994	$87,000
Increase in total assets during 1994.	22,000
Gain on sale of land during 1994	3,000
Net income for 1994	7,000
Increase in long-term debt during 1994	75,000
Dividends declared and paid during 1994	12,000

2–5. Tammy Triedhard is thinking about liquidating her business and retiring. The company has $8,000 of cash and $20,000 of total liabilities. Owners' equity is $5,000. Tammy estimates that if she sold all of the assets, except cash, she would get $12,500 from the sale.

Required:

Compute the balance of Tammy's owners' equity in the company if the assets were sold for the amount expected, and all of the liabilities were paid off. (*Hint: Set up the accounting equation before the sale of the assets, then do the arithmetic indicated by the sale of the noncash assets.*)

2–6. Goferbroke is planning to go out of business. The firm's most recent balance sheet shows cash of $2,200 and other assets totaling $21,800, and owners' equity of $8,300. It is estimated that the other assets can be sold for $14,200 cash in a quick going out of business sale.

Required:

Calculate the amount of cash that would be available for the owners if the other assets were sold and the liabilities paid off.

2–7. At the beginning of its current fiscal year, Radax Corp.'s balance sheet showed assets of $12 and liabilities of $7. During the year, liabilities decreased $1. Net income for the year was $3, and net assets at the end of the year were $6. There were no changes in paid-in capital during the year.

Required:

Calculate the dividends, if any, declared during the year. (*Hint: Set up an accounting equation for the beginning of the year, changes during the year, and at the end of the year. Enter known data and solve for the unknowns.*)

2–8. At the beginning of its current fiscal year, the balance sheet for Salco, Inc., showed owners' equity of $46. During the year liabilities decreased $3 to $17, paid-in capital increased $5 to $15, and assets decreased $8. Dividends declared and paid during the year were $4.

Required:

Calculate the net income or loss for the year.

(A)rmstrong

2–9. Review the Armstrong World Industries, Inc., 1991 annual report in Appendix A and answer the following questions about it:

   a. There is material presented in the report that could be classified as a financial statement but it isn't like one of the four financial statements described in this chapter. What is this material labeled, and what page of the report is it on?
   b. What was the independent CPA's opinion about the financial statements?
   c. Based on your review of the entire annual report, what would you say are the primary and secondary purposes of the report?
   d. What is your overall impression of the report?

2–10. Prepare a personal balance sheet for yourself as of today. Work at identifying your assets and liabilities; use rough estimates for the amounts associated with them.

2–11. A partially completed balance sheet for Blue Co., Inc., as of January 31, 1994, is presented. Where amounts are shown for various items, the amounts are correct.

$A = L + OE$

Assets		Liabilities		
Cash.	$ 700	Note payable. . . .	$_____	2200 ?
Accounts receivable .	3400	Accounts payable. .	3,400	
Land.	7000			
Automobile.	9000	Total liabilities . . .	$ 5606	
Less: Accumulated depreciation . .	(3000)	Owners' equity		
		Capital stock. . .	$ 8,000	
		Retained earnings	3500	
		Total owners' equity	$ 11,500	
		Total liabilities + owners' equity . .	$ 17,160 5600	
Total assets.	$ 17100			

Required:

Using the following data, complete the balance sheet.

Ac. Rec~ 4000
− 600
3400

a. Blue Co.'s records show that current and former customers owe the firm a total of $4,000; $600 of this amount has been due for over a year from two customers who are now bankrupt.   NOT EXPECTED −

b. The automobile, which is still being used in the business, cost $9,000 new; a used car dealer's blue book shows that it is now worth $5,000. Management estimates that the car has been used for one-third of its total potential use.

c. The land cost Blue Co. $7,000; it was recently assessed for real estate tax purposes at a value of $11,000.

d. Blue Co.'s president isn't sure of the amount of the note payable, but he does know that he signed a note. ?

e. Since the date Blue Co. was formed, net income has totaled $23,000, and dividends to stockholders have totaled $19,500.   23000 − 19500 3500 = RetaIned earning

Homework

• **2–12.** Presented below is a partially completed balance sheet for Epsico, Inc., at December 31, 1994, together with comparative data for the year ended December 31, 1993. From the statement of cash flows for the year ended December 31, 1994, you determine that:

Net income for the year ended December 31, 1994, was $26.

Dividends paid during the year ended December 31, 1994, were $8.

Cash increased $8 during the year ended December 31, 1994.

The cost of new equipment acquired during 1994 was $15; no equipment was disposed of.

There were no transactions affecting the land account during 1994, but it is estimated that the fair market value of the land at December 31, 1994, is $42.

Required: Complete the balance sheet at December 31, 1994.

EPSICO, INC.
Balance Sheets
December 31, 1994, and 1993

	1994	*1993*		*1994*	*1993*
Assets			**Liabilities**		
Current assets:			Current liabilities:		
Cash	$38	$ 30	Note payable . .	$ 49	$ 40
Accounts			Accounts		
receivable.	126	120	payable	123	110
Inventory	241	230			
Total current			Total current		
assets	$___	$ 380	liabilities . .	$172	$150
			Long-term debt . .	$___	$ 80
Land	$___	25	**Owners' equity**		
Equipment	$___	375	Capital stock. . . .	$200	$200
Less: Accumulated			Retained earnings .	$___	190
depreciation. . . .	(180)	(160)	Total owners'		
Total land &			equity.	$___	$390
equipment . . .	$___	$ 240	Total liabilities and		
Total assets	$___	$ 620	owners' equity . .	$___	$620

2–13. Presented below are comparative balance sheets for Millco, Inc., at January 31 and February 28, 1994.

MILLCO, INC.
Balance Sheets
January 31 and February 28, 1994

	February 28	*January 31*
Assets		
Cash.	$ 42,000	$ 37,000
Accounts receivable	64,000	53,000
Merchandise inventory	81,000	94,000
Total current assets	$187,000	$184,000
Plant and equipment:		
Production equipment	166,000	152,000
Less: Accumulated depreciation . .	(24,000)	(21,000)
Total assets	$329,000	$315,000

(continued)

	February 28	January 31
Liabilities		
Short-term debt	$ 44,000	$ 44,000
Accounts payable	37,000	41,000
Other accrued liabilities	21,000	24,000
Total current liabilities	$102,000	$109,000
Long-term debt	33,000	46,000
Total liabilities	$135,000	$155,000
Owners' Equity		
Common stock, no par value, 40,000 shares authorized, 30,000 and 28,000 shares issued, respectively	$104,000	$ 96,000
Retained earnings:		
Beginning balance	$ 64,000	$ 43,000
Net income for month	36,000	29,000
Dividends	(10,000)	(8,000)
Ending balance	$ 90,000	$ 64,000
Total owners' equity	$194,000	$160,000
Total liabilities and owners' equity . . .	$329,000	$315,000

Required:

Prepare a statement of cash flows that explains the change that occurred in cash during the month. Follow the format of Exhibit 2–4. You may assume that the change in each balance sheet amount is due to a single event (e.g., the change in the amount of production equipment is *not* the result of both a purchase and sale of equipment).

(Hints: What is the purpose of the statement of cash flows? How is this purpose accomplished?)

Use the space to the right of the January 31 data to enter the difference between the February 28 and January 31 amount of each balance sheet item; these are the amounts that will be in your solution.

2–14. Presented below is the statement of cash flows for Optico, Inc., for the year ended December 31, 1993, and the company's balance sheet at December 31, 1992.

OPTICO, INC.
Statement of Cash Flows
For the Year Ended December 31, 1993

Cash flows from operating activities:

Net income	$ 37,000
Add (deduct) items not affecting cash:	
Depreciation expense	15,000
Decrease in accounts receivable	12,000

(continued)

Increase in merchandise inventory.	(14,000)
Decrease in short-term debt.	(20,000)
Increase in accounts payable	7,000
Decrease in other accrued liabilities	(8,000)
Net cash provided by operating activities.	$ 29,000

Cash flows from investing activities:

Purchase of buildings.	$(40,000)

Cash flows from financing activities:

Increase in long-term debt	$ 18,000
Payment of cash dividend on common stock	(12,000)
Net cash provided by financing activities	$ 6,000
Net decrease in cash for the year	$ (5,000)

OPTICO, INC.
Balance Sheets
December 31, 1992

Assets		Liabilities and Owners' Equity	
Current assets:		Current liabilities:	
Cash.	$ 15,000	Short-term debt.	$ 20,000
Accounts receivable	22,000	Accounts payable.	13,000
Merchandise		Other accrued	
inventory.	31,000	liabilities.	17,000
Total current		Total current	
assets	$ 68,000	liabilities.	$ 50,000
		Long-term debt.	21,000
		Total liabilities	$ 71,000
Plant and equipment:			
Land.	8,000	Owners' equity:	
Building	82,000	Capital stock, no par . . .	$ 10,000
Less: Accumulated		Retained earnings.	41,000
depreciation . . .	(36,000)		
	$ 54,000	Total owners'	
		equity	$ 51,000
		Total liabilities and	
Total assets.	$122,000	owners' equity	$122,000

Required:

Using the information in the above financial statements, prepare the balance sheet for Optico, Inc., at December 31, 1993.

2–15. Using data from the 1991 annual report of Armstrong World Industries, Inc., reproduced in Appendix A, enter amounts in the summary financial statements presented on the following page. (*Note: changes in Armstrong World Industries, Inc., shareholders' equity are summarized on page 28 of the annual report in the Financial Review section of the report.*)

Ⓐrmstrong

Balance Sheet
December 31, 1990

Assets

Cash
All other assets

Total assets

Liabilities and Owners' Equity

Liabilities

Owners' equity:
Retained earnings

All other owners' equity

Total owners' equity

Total liabilities +
owners' equity

Income Statement
For the Year Ended Dec. 31, 1991

Revenues
Expenses
Net income

Statement of Cash Flows
For the Year Ended Dec. 31, 1991

Cash provided by
operating activities
Cash used for
investing activities
Cash used for
financing activities
Effect of exchange
rate changes
Cash at the beginning
of the year

Cash at the end
of the year

Statement of Changes
in Owners' Equity
For the Year Ended Dec. 31, 1991

Retained earnings:
Balance, Dec. 31,
1990
Net Income
Dividends

Balance, Dec. 31, 1991

All other owners'
equity:
Balance, Dec. 31,
1990
Changes

Balance, Dec. 31, 1991

Balance Sheet
December 31, 1991

Assets

Cash
All other assets

Total assets

**Liabilities and
Owners' Equity**

Liabilities

Owners' equity:
Retained earnings

All other owners'
equity

Total owners'
equity

Total liabilities +
owners' equity

Chapter 3

Fundamental Interpretations Made from Financial Statement Data

Now that you have some familiarity with the financial statements that result from the financial accounting process, it is appropriate to preview some of the interpretations made by financial statement users to support the decisions and informed judgments that they make. Current and potential stockholders are interested in making their own assessments about management's stewardship of the resources made available by the owners. For example, judgments about profitability will affect the investment decision. Creditors make judgments about the entity's ability to repay loans and pay for purchased products and services. These assessments about profitability and paying ability involve interpreting the relationships between amounts reported in the financial statements. Most of these relationships will be referred to in subsequent chapters. They are introduced now to illustrate how management's financial objectives for the firm are quantified, and to prepare you to better understand the impact of alternative accounting methods on these relationships when accounting alternatives are explained.

This chapter introduces some financial statement analysis concepts. Chapter 11, Financial Statement Analysis, is a comprehensive explanation of how to use financial statement data to analyze financial condition and results of operations. You will better understand topics in that chapter after you have studied the financial accounting material in Chapters 5 through 10.

LEARNING OBJECTIVES

After studying this chapter you should understand:

- Why financial statement ratios are important.
- How ratio trends can be used most effectively.
- The significance and calculation of return on investment.
- The DuPont model, an expansion of the basic return on investment calculation, and the terms *margin* and *turnover*.
- The significance and calculation of return on equity.
- The meaning of liquidity, and why it is important.
- The significance and calculation of three measures of liquidity: working capital, the current ratio, and the acid-test ratio.
- How a credit relationship is established.

FINANCIAL RATIOS AND TREND ANALYSIS

The large numbers on the financial statements of many companies, and the varying size of companies, make ratio analysis the only really sensible method of evaluating the various financial characteristics of a company. Students seem frequently to be awed by the number of ratio measurements that are suggested as appropriate to learn, and are sometimes put off by the mere thought of calculating a ratio. Be neither awed nor intimidated! A ratio is simply the relationship between two numbers, and the name of virtually every financial ratio describes the numbers to be related, and usually how the ratio is calculated. As you study this material, concentrate on understanding why the ratio is considered to be important, and work to understand the meaning of the ratio. If you do these things, you should avoid much of the stress sometimes associated with understanding financial ratios.

In most cases, a single ratio does not describe very much about the company whose statements are being studied. Much more meaningful analysis is accomplished when the *trend* of a particular ratio over several time periods is examined. Of course, consistency in financial reporting and in defining the ratio components is crucial if the trend is to be meaningful.

Most industry and trade associations publish industry average ratios based on aggregated data compiled by the association from reports submitted by association members. Comparison of an individual company's ratio with the comparable industry ratio is frequently made as a means of assessing a company's relative standing in its industry. Again, however, comparison of a single observation for the company with that of the industry may not be very meaningful because one company may use a financial accounting alternative that is different from that used by the rest of the industry. **Trend analysis** results in a much more meaningful comparison because even though the data used in the ratio may have been developed under different financial accounting alternatives, internal consistency within each of the trends will permit useful trend comparisons.

Trend analysis is described later in this chapter, but a brief example now will illustrate it. Suppose that a student's grade point average for last semester was 2.8 on a 4.0 scale. That GPA may be interesting, and it says a little about the student's work. But suppose you learn that this student's GPA was 1.9 four semesters ago, 2.3 three semesters ago, and 2.6 in the semester prior to last semester. The upward trend of grades suggests that the student is working "smarter and harder." This conclusion would be reinforced if you knew that the average GPA for all students in this person's class was 2.6 for each of the four semesters. You still don't know everything about the individual student's academic performance, but the comparative trend data do let you make a more informed judgment than was possible with just the grades from one semester.

Return on Investment

Imagine that you are presented with two investment alternatives. Each investment will be made for a period of one year, and each investment is equally risky. At the end of the year you will get your original investment back, plus from investment A income of $80, and from investment B income of $90. Which investment alternative would you choose? The answer seems so obvious that you believe that the question is loaded, so you hesitate to answer—a very sensible strategy. But why is this a trick question? A little thought should make you think of a question to which you need an answer before you can select between investment A and investment B. Your question? "How much money would I have to invest in either alternative?" If the amount to be invested is the same, for example, $1,000, then clearly you would select investment B because your income would be greater than for the same investment in investment A. If the amount to be invested in investment B is more than that required for investment A, you would have to calculate the **rate of return** on each investment in order to choose the one that would be more profitable for you.

Rate of return is calculated by dividing the amount of return (the income of $80 or $90 in the above example) by the amount of the investment. For example, using an investment of $1,000 for each alternative:

Investment A:

$$\text{Rate of return} = \frac{\text{Amount of return}}{\text{Amount invested}} = \frac{\$80}{\$1,000} = 8\%$$

Investment B:

$$\text{Rate of return} = \frac{\text{Amount of return}}{\text{Amount invested}} = \frac{\$90}{\$1,000} = 9\%$$

Your intuitive selection of investment B as the better investment is confirmed by the fact that its rate of return is higher than that of investment A.

It is important to remember that the example situation assumed that the investment would be made for one year. Unless otherwise specified, rate of return calculations assume that the time period of the investment and return is one year.

The rate of return calculation is derived from the interest calculation that you probably learned many years ago. Recall that:

$$\text{Interest} = \text{Principal} \times \text{Rate} \times \text{Time}$$

Interest is the income or expense from investing or borrowing money.

Principal is the amount invested or borrowed.

Rate is the **interest rate** per year expressed as a percent.

Time is the length of time the funds are invested or borrowed, expressed in years.

Note that when time is assumed to be one year, that term of the equation becomes 1/1 or 1, and so it disappears. Thus the rate of return calculation is simply a rearranged interest calculation that solves for the annual interest rate.

Return to the example situation and assume that the amounts required to be invested are $667 for investment A and $750 for investment B. Now which alternative would you select on the basis of rate of return? You should have made these calculations:

Investment A:

$$\text{Rate of return} = \frac{\text{Amount of return}}{\text{Amount invested}} = \frac{\$80}{\$667} = 12\%$$

Investment B:

$$\text{Rate of return} = \frac{\text{Amount of return}}{\text{Amount invested}} = \frac{\$90}{\$750} = 12\%$$

All other things being equal (and they seldom are except in textbook illustrations), you would be indifferent with respect to the alternatives available to you, because each has a rate of return of 12% (per year).

Rate of return and riskiness related to an investment go hand in hand. **Risk** relates to the range of possible outcomes from an activity. The wider the range of possible outcomes, the greater the risk. An investment in a bank savings account is less risky than investment in the stock of a corporation because the investor is virtually assured of receiving his/her principal and interest from the savings account, but the market value of stock may fluctuate widely over a short period of time. Thus the investor anticipates a higher rate of return from the stock investment than from the savings account, but the greater risk of the stock investment means that the actual rate of return earned could be considerably less (even negative), or much greater than the interest earned on the savings account. For now understand that the higher the rate of return of one investment relative to another, the greater the risk associated with the higher return investment.

Rate of return is a universally accepted measure of profitability. Because it is a ratio, profitability of unequal investments can be compared, and risk/reward relationships can be evaluated. Bank advertisements for certificates of deposit feature the interest rate, or rate of return, that will be earned by the depositor. All investors evaluate the profitability of an investment by making a rate of return calculation.

Return on investment (ROI) is the label usually assigned to the rate of return calculation made using data from financial statements. There are many ways of defining both the amount of return and the amount invested. For now, we shall use net income as the amount of return, and average total assets during the year as the amount invested. It is not appropriate to use total assets as reported on a single year-end balance sheet because that is the total at one point in time: the balance sheet date. Net income was earned over the entire fiscal year, so it should be related to the assets that were used for the whole year. Average assets used for the year are usually estimated by averaging the assets reported at the beginning of the year (the prior year-end balance sheet total) and assets reported at the end of the year. If seasonal fluctuations in total assets are significant (the materiality concept) and if quarter-end or month-end balance sheets are available, a more refined average asset calculation may be made.

The ROI of a firm is significant to most financial statement readers because it describes the rate of return management was able to earn on the assets that it had available to use during the year. Investors especially will make decisions and informed judgments about the quality of management and the relative profitability of a company based on ROI. This author believes that ROI is the most meaningful measure of a company's profitability. Knowing net income alone is not enough; *an informed judgment about the firm's profitability requires relating net income to the assets used to generate that net income.*

Calculation of ROI is illustrated below, using data from the condensed balance sheets and income statement of Cruisers, Inc., a hypothetical company, which are presented in Exhibit 3–1:

> From the firm's balance sheets:
> Total assets, September 30, 1992. . . . . . $364,720
> Total assets, September 30, 1993. . . . . . $402,654
> From the firm's income statement for
> the year ended September 30, 1993:
> Net income . . . . $ 32,936

EXHIBIT 3–1 **Condensed Balance Sheets and Income Statement of Cruisers, Inc., A Hypothetical Company**

Cruisers, Inc. Comparative Condensed Balance Sheets September 30, 1993 and 1992			Cruisers, Inc. Condensed Income Statement For the Year Ended September 30, 1993	
Current assets:				
Cash and marketable securities	$ 22,286	$ 16,996	Net sales	$611,873
			Cost of good sold	428,354
Accounts receivable	42,317	39,620	Gross margin	$183,519
Inventories	53,716	48,201	Operating expenses	122,183
Total current assets	$118,319	$104,817	Earnings before interest and taxes	$ 61,336
Other assets	284,335	259,903	Interest expense	6,400
Total assets	$402,654	$364,720	Earnings before taxes	$ 54,936
Current liabilities	$ 57,424	$ 51,400	Income taxes	22,000
Other liabilities	80,000	83,000	Net income	$ 32,936
Total liabilities	$137,424	$134,400	Earnings per share	$ 1.21
Owners' equity	265,230	230,320		
Total liabilities and owners' equity	$402,654	$364,720		

$$\text{Return on investment} = \frac{\text{Net income}}{\text{Average total assets}}$$

$$= \frac{\$32,936}{(\$364,720 + \$402,654)/2} = 8.6\%$$

Some financial analysts prefer to use operating income (or earnings before interest and income taxes) and average operating assets in the ROI calculation because they believe that excluding interest expense, income taxes, and assets not used in operations results in a better measure of the operating results of the firm. Other analysts will make other adjustments to arrive at the amounts used in the ROI calculation. Consistency in the definition of terms is more important than the definition itself because the trend of ROI will be more significant for decision making and informed judgments than the absolute result. However, it is appropriate to understand the definitions used in any ROI results that you see.

The DuPont Model, an Expansion of the ROI Calculation

Financial analysts at E.I. DuPont de Nemours & Co. are credited with developing the **DuPont model,** an expansion of the basic ROI calculation, in the late 1930s. They reasoned that profitability from sales and utilization of assets to generate sales revenue were both important factors to be considered when evaluating a company's overall profitability. One popular adaptation of their model introduces total sales revenue into the ROI calculation as follows:

$$\text{Return on investment} = \frac{\text{Net income}}{\text{Sales}} \times \frac{\text{Sales}}{\text{Average total assets}}$$

The first term, net income/sales, is **margin.** The second term, sales/average total assets, is **asset turnover,** or simply **turnover.** Of course, the sales quantities cancel out algebraically, but they are introduced to this version of the ROI model because of their significance. *Margin* emphasizes that from every dollar of sales revenue, some amount must work its way to the bottom line, net income, if the company is to be profitable. *Turnover* relates to the efficiency with which the firm's assets are used in the revenue-generating process.

Another quick quiz will illustrate the significance of turnover. Many of us look forward to a 40-hour per week job, generally thought of as five 8-hour days. Imagine a company's factory operating on such a schedule — one shift per day, five days a week. The question: What percentage of the available time is that factory operating? You may have answered 33 percent or one-third of the time, because eight hours is one-third of a day. But what about Saturday and Sunday? In fact, there are 21 shifts available in a week (7 days × 3 shifts per day), so a factory operating 5 shifts per week is only being used ⁵⁄21 of the time — less than 25 percent! The factory is idle more than 75 percent of the time! And as you can imagine, many of the occupancy costs (real estate taxes, utilities, insurance) are incurred whether or not the plant is in use. This explains why many firms operate their plant on a two-shift, three-shift, or even seven-day basis rather than build additional plants. Even when the higher costs of multiple shift operations (e.g., shift premiums for workers, and additional shipping costs relative to shipping from a second location closer to some customers) are reflected in lower margin, ROI is increased relative to having additional plants because turnover is increased proportionately more than margin is reduced.

Calculation of ROI using the DuPont model is illustrated below, using data from the financial statements of Cruisers, Inc., in Exhibit 3–1:

From the firm's balance sheets:
Total assets, September 30, 1992. . . . . . $364,720
Total assets, September 30, 1993. . . . . . $402,654
From the firm's income statement for
the year ended September 30, 1993:
Net sales $611,873
Net income . . . . $ 32,936

Return on investment = Margin × Turnover

$$= \frac{\text{Net income}}{\text{Sales}} \times \frac{\text{Sales}}{\text{Average total assets}}$$

$$= \frac{\$32,936}{\$611,873} \times \frac{\$611,873}{(\$364,720 + \$402,654)/2}$$

$$= 5.4\% \times 1.6$$

$$= 8.6\%$$

The significance of the DuPont model is that it has led many managements to consider utilization of assets, including keeping investment in assets as low as feasible, to be just as important to overall performance as generating profit from sales.

A rule of thumb useful for putting ROI in perspective is that average ROI, based on net income, for most American merchandising and manufacturing companies is between 5% and 8%. Average ROI based on operating income (earnings before interest and taxes) for the same set of firms is between 10% and 15%. Average margin, based on net income, ranges from about 5% to 8%. Using operating income, average margin ranges from 10% to 15%. Asset turnover is usually in the range of 1.0 to 1.5.

Return on Equity

Recall that the balance sheet equation is:

$$Assets = Liabilities + Owners' \ equity$$

The return on investment calculation relates net income (perhaps as adjusted for interest, income taxes, or other items) to assets. Assets (perhaps adjusted to exclude nonoperating assets or other items) represent the amount invested to generate earnings. The balance sheet equation indicates that the investment in assets can result from either amounts borrowed from creditors (liabilities) or amounts invested by the owners. Owners (and others) are interested in expressing the profits of the firm as a rate of return on the amount of owners' equity; this is called **return on equity** (ROE), and it is calculated as follows:

$$Return \ on \ equity = \frac{Net \ income}{Average \ owners' \ equity}$$

Return on equity is calculated using average owners' equity during the period for which the net income was earned for the same reason that average assets is used in the ROI calculation; net income is earned over a period of time, so it should be related to the owners' equity over that same period of time.

Calculation of ROE is illustrated below using data from the financial statements of Cruisers, Inc., in Exhibit 3–1:

From the firm's balance sheets:
Total owners' equity, September 30, 1992 . . . . $230,320
Total owners' equity, September 30, 1993 . . . . $265,230
From the firm's income statement for
the year ended September 30, 1993:
Net income . . . . $ 32,936

$$Return \ on \ equity = \frac{Net \ income}{Average \ owners' \ equity}$$

$$= \frac{\$32,936}{(\$230,320 + \$265,230)/2}$$

$$= \$32,936/\$247,775$$

$$= 13.3\%$$

A rule of thumb useful for putting ROE in perspective is that average ROE for most American merchandising and manufacturing companies is between 10% and 15%.

Adjustments to both net income and average owners' equity may be appropriate, and some of these will be explained later in the text. For now, you should understand that both return on investment and return on equity are fundamental measures of the profitability of a firm, and that the data for making these calculations come from the firm's financial statements.

Return on equity is a special case application of the rate of return concept. ROE is important to current and prospective owners because it relates earnings to the owners' investment, that is, the owners' equity in the assets of the entity.

Working Capital and Measures of Liquidity

Working capital is the excess of a firm's current assets over its current liabilities. **Liquidity** refers to a firm's ability to meet its current obligations, and is measured by relating its current assets and current liabilities as reported on the balance sheet. Current assets are cash and other assets that are likely to be converted to cash within a year (principally accounts receivable and merchandise inventories). Current liabilities are those obligations that are expected to be paid within a year, including loans, accounts payable, and other accrued liabilities. Most financially healthy firms have positive working capital. Even though a firm is not likely to have cash on hand at any point in time equal to its current liabilities, it will expect to collect its accounts receivable, or sell its merchandise inventories and then collect the resulting accounts receivable in time to pay the liabilities when they are scheduled for payment. Of course, in the process of converting inventories to cash, the firm will be purchasing additional merchandise for its inventory, and the suppliers will want to be assured of collecting the amounts due according to the previously agreed provisions for when payment is due.

There are three principal measures of liquidity:

1. Working capital = Current assets − Current liabilities

2. Current ratio = $\dfrac{\text{Current assets}}{\text{Current liabilities}}$

3. Acid-test ratio = $\dfrac{\text{Cash (including temporary cash investments)} + \text{Accounts receivable}}{\text{Current liabilities}}$

The dollar amount of a firm's working capital is not as significant as the ratio of is current assets to current liabilities because the amount can be misleading unless it is related to another quantity (e.g., how large is large?). Therefore, it is the *trend* of a company's **current ratio** that is most useful in judging its current bill-paying ability. The **acid-test ratio,** also known as the *quick ratio,* is a more short-term measure of liquidity because merchandise inventories are excluded from the computation. This ratio provides information about an almost worst-case situation — the firm's ability to meet its current obligations even if none of the inventory can be sold.

Liquidity measure calculations are illustrated below using September 30, 1993, data from the financial statements of Cruisers, Inc., in Exhibit 3–1:

$$\text{Working capital} = \text{Current assets} - \text{Current liabilities}$$

$$= \$118,319 - \$57,424$$

$$= \$60,895$$

$$\text{Current ratio} = \frac{\text{Current assets}}{\text{Current liabilities}} = \frac{\$118,319}{\$57,424} = 2.1$$

$$\text{Acid-test ratio} = \frac{\text{Cash (including temporary cash investments)} + \text{Accounts receivable}}{\text{Current liabilities}}$$

$$= \frac{\$22,286 + \$42,317}{\$57,424}$$

$$= 1.1$$

From these data it can be concluded that Cruisers, Inc., has a high degree of liquidity. It should not have any trouble meeting its current obligations. As a general rule, a current ratio of 2 and an acid-test ratio of 1 are considered indicative of good liquidity.

Remember, however, that judgments made from the results of any of these calculations using data from a single balance sheet are not as meaningful as the trend of the results over several periods. It is also important to note the composition of working capital, and to understand the impact on the ratios of equal changes in current assets and current liabilities. As the following illustration shows, if a short-term bank loan were repaid just before the balance sheet date, working capital would not change (because current assets and current liabilities would each decrease by the same amount), but the current ratio (and the acid-test ratio) would change.

	Before Loan Repayment	*After $20,000 Loan Repaid*
Current assets	$200,000	$180,000
Current liabilities	100,000	80,000
Working capital	$100,000	$100,000
Current ratio	2.0	2.25

If a new loan were taken out just after the balance sheet date, the level of the firm's liquidity at the balance sheet date would have been overstated.

Measures of liquidity are used primarily by potential creditors who are seeking to make a judgment about their prospects of being paid promptly if they enter into a creditor relationship with the firm whose liquidity is being analyzed (see Business Procedure Capsule 5 — Establishing a Credit Relationship).

The statement of cash flows is also useful in assessing the reasons for a firm's liquidity (or illiquidity). Recall that this financial statement identifies the reasons for the change in a firm's cash during the period (usually a year) by reporting the changes during the period in noncash items on the balance sheet.

Illustration of Trend Analysis

Trend analysis of return on investment, return on equity, and working capital and liquidity measures is illustrated in the following tables and exhibits. Data used in this illustration come primarily from the 1991 Annual Report of Armstrong World Industries, Inc., which is Appendix A. Data are presented first in tabular form, and then graphs are presented.

Most of the data in Table 3–1 come from the "six-year summary" of financial information on page 38 of Armstrong's 1991 Annual Report. Refer to Appendix A and find in it the data in Table 3–1.

The data in Table 3–1 are presented graphically in Exhibits 3–2 through 3–4. Note that the presentation of the years involved in the table is opposite from that of the years in the graph. Tabular data are frequently presented so the most recent year is closest to the captions of the table. Graphs of time series data usually flow from left to right. In any event, it is necessary to notice and understand the captions of both tables and graphs.

The graph in Exhibit 3–2 illustrates that ROI declined steadily from 1987 through 1990, and then dropped sharply in 1991. Al-

---

TABLE 3–1 Armstrong World Industries, Inc. (profitability and liquidity data, 1991–1987)

	1991	*1990*	*1989*	*1988*	*1987*
Earnings from continuing business as a percentage of:					
Sales (margin)	2.5%	5.8%	6.3%	6.8%	7.2%
Average monthly total assets (ROI)	2.9%	7.1%	8.3%	10.2%	11.6%
Net earnings as a percentage of average common stockholders' equity (ROE)	3.3%	13.0%	17.9%	17.0%	17.6%
Asset turnover*	1.2	1.2	1.3	1.5	1.6
Year-end position (in millions)					
Current assets†	$718.8	$726.6	$724.3	$839.1	$726.5
Current liabilities†	479.9	544.8	400.8	700.1	471.2
Working capital	$238.9	$181.8	$323.5	$139.0	$255.3
Current ratio‡	1.5	1.3	1.8	1.2	1.5

* Not included in the Six-Year Summary. Calculated using margin and ROI (ROI = Margin × Turnover; Turnover = ROI/Margin)
† Not included in the Six-Year Summary. These amounts are from the balance sheets of this and prior annual reports. (Amounts at year-end 1991 and 1990 can be found on page 19 of the annual report in Appendix A.)
‡ Not included in the Six-Year Summary; calculated using current assets and current liabilities (Current ratio = Current assets/Current liabilities).

Source: Armstrong World Industries, Inc., 1991 Annual Report, pp. 19, 38.

though ROE was relatively steady for the 1987–89 period, it dropped sharply in 1990 and 1991. These trends clearly illustrate the effect of the economic slowdown of the early 1990s on the profitability of Armstrong World Industries, Inc.

The graph in Exhibit 3–3 illustrates that it is the change in margin that has caused most of the change in ROI and ROE. Turnover declined sharply in 1989, but has been relatively steady since then.

Both working capital and the current ratio, plotted in Exhibit 3–4, have shown no trend in spite of the profit pressures reflected in declining ROI and ROE. Armstrong World Industries, Inc., has maintained its liquidity over this four-year period.

A potential investor in the common stock of Armstrong World Industries, Inc., would probably be interested in the company's profitability compared to the industry within which it operates.

• **BUSINESS PROCEDURE CAPSULE 5**
Establishing a Credit Relationship

Most transactions between businesses, and many transactions between individuals and businesses, are credit transactions. That is, the sale of the product or provision of the service is completed some time before payment is made by the purchaser. Usually, before delivering the product or service, the seller wants to have some assurance that the bill will be paid when due. This involves determining that the buyer is a good **credit risk.**

Individuals usually establish credit by submitting to the potential creditor a completed credit application, which includes information about employment, salary, bank accounts, liabilities, and other credit relationships (e.g., charge accounts) established. Most credit grantors are looking for a good record of having made timely payments on existing credit accounts. This is why an individual's first credit account is usually the most difficult to obtain. Potential credit grantors may also check an individual's credit record as maintained by the credit bureau in the city in which the applicant lives or has lived.

Businesses seeking credit may follow a procedure similar to that used by individuals. Alternatively, they may provide financial statements and names of firms with which a credit relationship has been established. A newly organized firm may have to pay for its purchases in advance, or on delivery (**COD**) until it has been in operation for several months. Then the seller may set a relatively low credit limit for sales on credit. Once a record is established of having paid bills when due, the credit limit will be raised. After a firm has been in operation for a year or more, its credit history may be reported by the Dun & Bradstreet credit reporting service—a type of national credit bureau to which many companies subscribe. Even after a credit relationship has been established, it is not unusual for a firm to continue providing financial statements to its principal creditors.

Table 3–2 summarizes data taken from the Value Line Investment Survey, an investment advisory service. Value Line classifies Armstrong World Industries, Inc., in the building materials industry. Note that the Value Line calculations are based on net worth, a synonym for total owners' equity, and that the amounts are different from the return on common stockholders' equity reported in the six-year summary of the Armstrong World Industries, Inc., annual report and in Table 3–1. This definitional distinction will be clarified in a later chapter; for now note that the trend of the Armstrong World Industries, Inc., data is essentially the same for both sets of data.

EXHIBIT 3–2   Armstrong World Industries, Inc., Return on Investment (ROI) and Return on Equity (ROE), 1987–1991

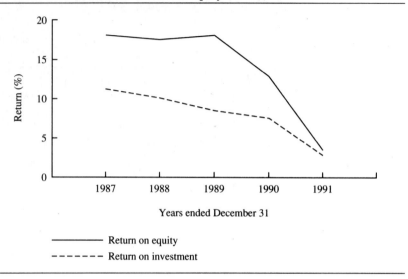

EXHIBIT 3–3   Armstrong World Industries, Inc. (margin and turnover, 1987–1991)

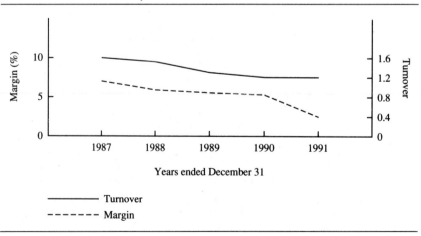

EXHIBIT 3–4 Armstrong World Industries, Inc. (working capital and current ratio, 1987–1991)

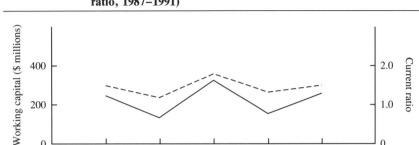

The downward trend in ROE of Armstrong World Industries, Inc., illustrated in Exhibit 3–2 does not seem quite so alarming when compared with industry performance as shown in Exhibit 3–5. It is clear that the reduced level of economic activity in the building materials industry from 1989 through 1991 has had an adverse effect on the profitability of firms in that industry.

Exhibit 3–5 illustrates a subtle point about graphical presentations. Note that the vertical axis scale of Exhibit 3–5 is compressed

TABLE 3–2 Value Line Investment Survey (percentage earned on net worth, 1987–1991)

Armstrong World Industries, Inc., and the Building Materials Industry

	For the Year				
	1991	*1990*	*1989*	*1988*	*1987*
Armstrong World Industries, Inc. .	6.8	12.9	15.7	15.9	16.5
Building materials industry	13.0	16.1	22.0	23.6	16.6

EXHIBIT 3–5 **Armstrong World Industries, Inc., and Building Materials Industry (percentage earned on net worth, 1987–1991)**

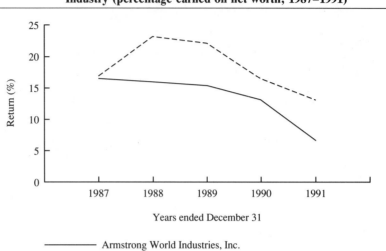

Years ended December 31

———————— Armstrong World Industries, Inc.

– – – – – – – Building materials industry

Copyright © 1992 by Value Line, Inc. Used by permission.

to about 80 per cent that of Exhibit 3–2. That is, the vertical distance equal to 25 percentage points in Exhibit 3–5 is about equal to the vertical distance of 20 percentage points in Exhibit 3–2. Thus, the lines in Exhibit 3–2 are steeper than if the graph had been constructed using the same scale as Exhibit 3–5. The visual message conveyed by a graph can be influenced by the scale selected. It is important to note the scale before jumping to a conclusion about the significance of the changes suggested by the slope of the lines on a graph.

All of the graphs presented in this chapter use an arithmetic vertical scale. This means that the distance between values shown on the vertical axis is the same, so if the data being plotted increase at a constant rate over the period of time shown on the horizontal scale, the plot will be a line that curves upward more and more steeply. Many analysts prefer to plot data that will change significantly over time (a company's sales, for example) on a graph that has a logarithmic vertical scale. This is called a **semilogarithmic graph** because the horizontal scale is still arithmetic. The intervals between years, for example, will be equal. The advantage of a semilogarithmic presentation is that a constant rate of growth results in a straight-line plot. Exercise 3–17 illustrates this point.

SUMMARY

Financial statement users express financial statement data in ratio format to facilitate making informed judgments and decisions. Users are especially interested in the trend of a company's ratios over time, and the comparison of the company's ratio trends with those of its industry as a whole.

The rate of return on investment is a universally accepted measure of profitability. Rate of return is calculated by dividing the amount of return, or profit, by the amount invested. Rate of return is expressed as an annual percentage rate.

Return on investment (ROI) is one of the most important measures of profitability because it relates the income earned during a period to the assets that were invested to generate those earnings. The DuPont model for calculating ROI expands the basic model by introducing sales to calculate margin (net income/sales) and asset turnover (sales/average assets); ROI is the product of margin × turnover. *Margin* describes the profit from each dollar of sales, and *turnover* expresses the sales generating capacity (efficiency) of the firm's assets.

Return on equity (ROE) relates net income earned for the year to the average owners' equity for the year. This rate of return measure is important to current and prospective owners because it relates earnings to the owners' investment.

Creditors are interested in an entity's liquidity, that is, its ability to pay its liabilities when due. The amount of working capital, and the current ratio and acid-test ratio are measures of liquidity. These calculations are made using the amounts of current assets and current liabilities reported on the balance sheet.

When ratio trend data are plotted graphically, it is easy to determine the significance of ratio changes, and to evaluate a firm's performance. However, it is necessary to pay attention to how graphs are constructed, because the visual image presented can be influenced by the scales used.

KEY TERMS AND CONCEPTS

acid-test ratio *(p. 74)*   The ratio of the sum of cash (including temporary cash investments) and accounts receivable to current liabilities. A primary measure of a firm's liquidity.

asset turnover *(p. 70)*   The quotient of sales divided by average assets for the year or other fiscal period.

COD *(p. 77)*   Cash on delivery, or collect on delivery.

credit risk *(p. 77)* The risk that an entity to which credit has been extended will not pay the amount due on the date set for payment.

current ratio *(p. 74)* The ratio of current assets to current liabilities. A primary measure of a firm's liquidity.

DuPont model *(p. 70)* An expansion of the return on investment calculation to margin × turnover.

interest *(p. 67)* The income or expense from investing or borrowing money.

interest rate *(p. 67)* The percentage amount used, together with principal and time, to calculate interest.

liquidity *(p. 73)* Refers to a firm's ability to meet its current financial obligations.

margin *(p. 70)* The percentage of net income to net sales. Sometimes margin is calculated using operating income, or other intermediate subtotals of the income statement. The term can also refer to the *amount* of gross profit, operating income, or net income.

principal *(p. 67)* The amount of money invested or borrowed.

rate of return *(p. 66)* A percentage calculated by dividing the amount of return on an investment for a period of time by the average amount invested for the period. A primary measure of profitability.

return on equity *(p. 72)* The percentage of net income divided by average owners' equity for the fiscal period in which the net income was earned; frequently referred to as ROE. A primary measure of a firm's profitability.

return on investment *(p. 68)* The rate of return on an investment; frequently referred to as ROI. A primary measure of a firm's profitability.

risk *(p. 68)* A concept that describes the range of possible outcomes from an action. The greater the range of possible outcomes, the greater the risk.

semilogarithmic graph *(p. 80)* A graph format in which the y-axis is a logarithmic scale.

trend analysis *(p. 66)* Evaluation of the trend of data over time.

turnover *(p. 70)* The quotient of sales divided by the average assets for the year, or some other fiscal period. A descriptor, such as total asset, inventory, or plant and equipment, usually precedes the turnover term. A measure of the efficiency with which assets are used to generate sales.

working capital *(p. 73)* The difference between current assets and current liabilities. A measure of a firm's liquidity.

EXERCISES AND PROBLEMS

3–1. Two acquaintances have approached you about investing in business activities in which each is involved. Julie is seeking $560 and Sam needs $620. One year from now, your original investment will be returned, along with

$50 income from Julie, or with $53 income from Sam. You can make only one investment.

Required:

a. Which investment would you prefer? Why?

b. What other factors should be considered before making either investment?

3–2. A friend has $600 that has been saved from her part-time job. She will need her money, plus any interest earned on it, in six months, and has asked for your help in deciding whether to put the money in a bank savings account at 5.5 percent interest, or to lend it to Judy. Judy has promised to repay $620 after six months.

Required:

a. Calculate the interest earned on the savings account for six months.

b. Calculate the rate of return if the money is loaned to Judy.

c. Which alternative would you recommend? Explain your answer.

3–3. You have two investment opportunities. One will have a 10% rate of return on an investment of $500; the other will have a 10.5 percent rate of return on principal of $550. You would like to take advantage of the higher yielding investment, but have only $500 available.

Required:

What is the maximum rate of interest that you would pay to borrow the $50 needed to take advantage of the higher yield?

3–4. You have accumulated $800 and are looking for the best rate of return that can be earned over the next year. A bank savings account will pay 6 percent. A one-year bank certificate of deposit will pay 8 percent, but the minimum investment is $1,000.

Required:

a. Calculate the amount of return you would earn if the $800 were invested for one year at 6 percent.

b. Calculate the net amount of return you would earn if $200 were borrowed at a cost of 15 percent, and then $1,000 were invested for one year at 8 percent.

c. Calculate the net rate of return on your investment of $800 if you accept the strategy of part (*b*).

3–5. *a.* Firm A has a margin of 12 percent, sales of $600,000, and ROI of 18 percent. Calculate the firm's average total assets.

b. Firm B has net income of $78,000, turnover of 1.3, and average total assets of $950,000. Calculate the firm's ROI.

c. Firm C has net income of $132,000, turnover of 2.1, and ROI of 7.37 percent. Calculate the firm's margin.

3–6. *a.* Firm D has net income of $27,900, sales of $930,000, and average total assets of $415,000. Calculate the firm's margin, turnover, and ROI.

b. Firm E has net income of $75,000, sales of $1,250,000, and ROI of 15 percent. Calculate the firm's turnover and average total assets.

c. Firm F has ROI of 12.6 percent, average total assets of $1,730,159, and turnover of 1.4. Calculate the firm's sales, margin, and net income.

3–7. At the beginning of the year, the net assets of Jansan Co. were $346,800. The only transactions affecting owners' equity during the year were net income of $42,300, and dividends of $12,000.

Required: Calculate Jansan Co.'s return on equity (ROE) for the year.

3–8. For the year ended December 31, 1993, Metro, Inc., earned an ROI of 12 percent. Sales for the year were $12 million, and average asset turnover was 2.4. Average owners' equity was $3 million.

Required:
a. Calculate Metro's margin and net income.
b. Calculate Metro's return on equity.

3–9. Frank's Furniture Store has been in business for several years. The firm's owners have described the store as a "high-price, high-service" operation that provides lots of assistance to its customers. Margin has averaged a relatively high 32 percent per year for several years, but turnover has been a relatively low 0.4 based on average total assets of $800,000. A discount furniture store is about to open in the area served by Frank's, and management is considering lowering prices in order to compete effectively.

Required:
a. Calculate current sales and ROI for Frank's Furniture Store.
b. Assuming that the new strategy would reduce margin to 15 percent, and assuming that average total assets would stay the same, calculate the sales that would be required to have the same ROI as that currently earned.

3–10. Manyops, Inc., is a manufacturing firm that has experienced strong competition in its traditional business. Management is considering joining the trend to the "service economy" by eliminating its manufacturing operations and concentrating on providing specialized maintenance services to other manufacturers. Management of Manyops, Inc., has had a target ROI of 15 percent on an asset base that has averaged $6 million. To achieve this ROI, average asset turnover of 2 was required. If the company shifts its operations from manufacturing to providing maintenance services, it is estimated that average assets will decrease to $1 million.

Required:
a. Calculate net income, margin, and sales required for Manyops, Inc., to achieve its target ROI as a manufacturing firm.
b. Calculate the company's net income if it can earn on ROI of 15 percent from providing maintenance services.
c. Assume that the average margin of maintenance service firms is 2.5 percent. Calculate the sales and asset turnover that Manyops, Inc., will have if the change to services is made, and the firm is able to earn an average margin and achieve a 15 percent ROI.

(A)rmstrong

3–11. Using data from the financial statements of Armstrong World Industries, Inc., in Appendix A, calculate:
a. ROI for 1991.
b. ROE for 1991.
c. Working capital at December 31, 1991, and December 31, 1990.
d. Current ratio at December 31, 1991, and December 31, 1990.
e. Acid-test ratio at December 31, 1991, and December 31, 1990.

3–12. Presented below are the comparative balance sheets of Millco, Inc., at December 31, 1993, and 1992. Sales for the year ended December 31, 1993, totaled $520,000.

MILLCO, INC.
Balance Sheets
December 31, 1993, and 1992

	1993	1992
Assets		
Cash	$ 42,000	$ 37,000
Accounts receivable	64,000	53,000
Merchandise inventory	81,000	94,000
Total current assets	$187,000	$184,000
Plant and equipment:		
Production equipment	166,000	152,000
Less: Accumulated depreciation	(24,000)	(21,000)
Total assets	$329,000	$315,000
Liabilities		
Short-term debt	$ 44,000	$ 44,000
Accounts payable	37,000	41,000
Other accrued liabilities	21,000	24,000
Total current liabilities	$102,000	$109,000
Long-term debt	33,000	46,000
Total liabilities	$135,000	$155,000
Owners' Equity		
Common stock, no par value, 40,000 shares authorized, 30,000 and 28,000 shares issued, respectively	$104,000	$ 96,000
Retained earnings:		
Beginning balance	$ 64,000	$ 43,000
Net income for year	36,000	29,000
Dividends for year	(10,000)	(8,000)
Ending balance	$ 90,000	$ 64,000
Total owners' equity	$194,000	$160,000
Total liabilities and owners' equity	$329,000	$315,000

Required:

a. Calculate ROI for 1993.
b. Calculate ROE for 1993.
c. Calculate working capital at December 31, 1993.
d. Calculate the current ratio at December 31, 1993.
e. Calculate the acid-test ratio at December 31, 1993.

3–13. The following presents the current asset and current liability sections of the balance sheets for Freedom, Inc., at January 31, 1993, and 1992 (in millions).

	January 31, 1993	*January 31, 1992*
Current assets		
Cash	$ 5	$ 2
Accounts receivable	3	6
Inventories	4	8
Other prepaids	2	2
Total current assets	$14	$18
Current liabilities		
Note payable	$ 3	$ 3
Accounts payable	4	1
Other accrued liabilities . . .	2	2
Total current liabilities	$ 9	$ 6

Required:

a. Calculate the current ratio and working capital at each balance sheet date.

b. Evaluate the firm's liquidity at each balance sheet date.

c. The firm operated at a loss during the year ended January 31, 1993. How could cash have increased during the year?

3–14. The following presents the current asset and current liability sections of the balance sheets for Calketch, Inc., at August 31, 1993, and 1992 (in millions).

	August 31, 1993	*August 31, 1992*
Current assets		
Cash	$ 3	$ 6
Marketable securities	7	10
Accounts receivable	13	8
Inventories	18	8
Total current assets	$41	$32
Current liabilities		
Note payable	$ 3	$ 8
Accounts payable	10	14
Other accrued liabilities	9	7
Total current liabilities	$22	$29

Required:

> *a.* Calculate the current ratio and working capital at each balance sheet date.
>
> *b.* Describe the change in the firm's liquidity from 1992 to 1993.

3–15. Management of Shady Co. anticipates that its year-end balance sheet will show current assets of $12,639 and current liabilities of $7,480, but is considering paying $3,850 of accounts payable before year-end, even though payment isn't due until later.

Required:

> *a.* Calculate the firm's working capital and current ratio under each situation. Would you recommend early payment of the accounts payable? Why?
>
> *b.* Assume that Shady Co. had negotiated a short-term bank loan of $5,000 that can be drawn down either before or after the end of the year. Calculate working capital and the current ratio at year-end under each situation, assuming that early payment of accounts payable is not made. When would you recommend that the loan be taken? Why?

3–16. Metro, Inc., had current liabilities at November 30 of $68,700. The firm's current ratio at that date was 1.8.

Required:

> *a.* Calculate the firm's current assets and working capital at November 30.
>
> *b.* Assume that management paid $15,300 of accounts payable on November 29. Calculate the current ratio and working capital at November 30 as if the November 29 payment had not been made.
>
> *c.* Explain the changes, if any, between working capital and the current ratio given the original data, and assuming that the November 29 payment was not made.

3–17. Time-series data are frequently plotted on graph paper having a semilogarithmic scale rather than on graph paper having an arithmetic scale. To understand the results of both methods, plot the following sales for a hypothetical firm on each kind of graph paper.

Year	Sales (in millions)
1987	$15.0
1988	19.5
1989	25.4
1990	32.9
1991	42.8
1992	55.6

> *a.* What is your conclusion about the rate of change in sales by looking at each graph?
>
> *b.* What is the actual rate of sales increase each year?
>
> *c.* What is the advantage of using the logarithmic scale for the data?

Chapter 4

The Bookkeeping Process and Transaction Analysis

In order to understand how different transactions affect the financial statements, and in turn understand how to make sense of the data on the financial statements, it is necessary to understand the mechanical operation of the bookkeeping process. The objectives of this chapter are to have you understand this mechanical process, and to introduce a method of analyzing the effects of a transaction on the financial statements.

LEARNING OBJECTIVES

After studying this chapter you should understand:

- How the income statement is linked to the balance sheet through owners' equity.
- The expansion of the basic accounting equation to include revenues and expenses.
- How the expanded accounting equation stays in balance after every transaction.
- That the bookkeeping system is a mechanical adaptation of the expanded accounting equation.
- The meaning of the bookkeeping terms *journal, ledger, T-account, account balance, debit, credit,* and *closing the books.*
- The five questions of transaction analysis.
- How to analyze a transaction, prepare a journal entry, and determine the effect of a transaction on working capital.

THE BOOKKEEPING/ACCOUNTING PROCESS

The bookkeeping/accounting process starts with **transactions** (economic interchanges between entities that are accounted for and reflected in financial statements) and culminates in the financial statements. This flow was illustrated in Chapter 2 as follows:

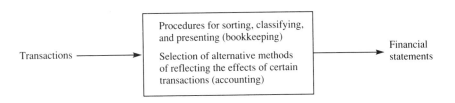

This chapter presents an overview of bookkeeping procedures. Your objective is not to become a bookkeeper but to learn part of the mechanical process of bookkeeping so you will be able to determine the effects on the financial statements of any transaction. This is crucial to being able to make informed judgments and decisions from the financial statements. Bookkeepers (and accountants) use some special terms to describe the bookkeeping process, and you will have to learn these terms. The bookkeeping process itself is a mechanical process, however, and once you understand it in the language of bookkeeping, you will see that it is quite straightforward.

The Balance Sheet Equation — A Mechanical Key

You now know that the **balance sheet equation** expresses the equality between an entity's assets and the claims to those assets. This is expressed:

$$\text{Assets} = \text{Liabilities} + \text{Owners' equity}$$

For present illustration purposes, let us consider a firm without liabilities. What do you suppose happens to the amounts in the equation if the entity operates at a profit? Well, assets (perhaps cash) increase, and, if the equation is to balance (and it must), then clearly owners' equity must also increase. Yes, profits increase owners' equity, and to keep the equation in balance, assets will increase and/or liabilities will decrease. Every financial transaction that is accounted for will cause a change somewhere in the balance sheet equation, and the equation will remain in balance after every transaction.

You have already seen that a firm's net income (profit) or loss is the difference between the revenues and expenses reported on its income statement (Exhibit 2–2), and you saw that in the statement of changes in owners' equity (Exhibit 2–3), net income from the income statement is reported as one of the factors causing a change in the retained earnings part of owners' equity from the beginning of the reporting period to the end of the reporting period. The other principal element of owners' equity is the amount of capital invested by the owners, that is, the paid-in capital of Exhibit 2–3. Given these components of owners' equity, it is possible to modify the basic balance sheet equation as follows:

$$\text{Assets} = \text{Liabilities} + \text{Owners' equity}$$

$$\text{Assets} = \text{Liabilities} + \text{Paid-in capital} + \text{Retained earnings}$$

$$\text{Assets} = \text{Liabilities} + \text{Paid-in capital} + \begin{array}{c}\text{Retained}\\\text{earnings}\\\text{(beginning}\\\text{of period)}\end{array} + \text{Revenues} - \text{Expenses}$$

To illustrate the operation of this equation and the effect of several transactions, study how the following transactions are reflected in Exhibit 4–1. Note that in the exhibit some specific assets and liabilities have been identified within those general categories, and columns have been established for each.

EXHIBIT 4–1   Transaction Summary

		Assets			=	Liabilities	+		Owners' equity		
Trans-action	Cash +	Account Receiv-able +	Merchan-dise Inventory +	Equip-ment =		Notes Pay-able +	Accounts Pay-able +	Paid-In Capital +	Retained Earnings +	Reve-nue −	Expenses
1.	+30							+30			
2.	−25			+25							
3.	+15					+15					
4.	−10		+20				+10				
5.	+ 2	+ 5		− 7							
6.	+ 5	− 5									
Total	17 +	0 +	20 +	18 =		15 +	10 +	30			
7. Revenues	+20									+20	
7. Expenses			−12								−12
8.							+ 3				− 3
Total	17 +	20 +	8 +	18 =		15 +	13 +	30	+ 5 ◄──────┘	+20	−15

Transactions

1. Investors organized the firm and invested $30. (In this example the category title *Paid-In Capital* is used rather than *Common Stock* and, possibly, *Additional Paid-In Capital*. There isn't any beginning balance in Retained Earnings because the firm is just getting started.)
2. Equipment costing $25 was purchased for cash.
3. The firm borrowed $15 from a bank.
4. Merchandise costing $20 was purchased for inventory; $10 cash was paid and $10 of the cost was charged on account.
5. Equipment that cost $7 was sold for $7; $2 was received in cash, and $5 will be received later.
6. The $5 account receivable from the sale of equipment was collected.

Each column of the exhibit has been totaled after transaction *(6)*. Does the total of all the asset columns equal the total of the liability and owners' equity columns? (They had better equal!)

The firm hasn't had any revenue or expense transactions yet, and it's hard to make a profit without them, so the transactions continue:

7. Sold merchandise inventory that had cost $12 for a selling price of $20; the sale was made **on account** (that is, on credit), and the customer will pay later. Notice that in Exhibit 4–1 this transaction is shown on two lines; one reflects the revenue of $20 and the other reflects the expense, or cost of the merchandise sold, of $12.
8. Wages of $3 earned by the firm's employees are accrued. This means that the expense is recorded even though it has not yet been paid. The wages have been earned by employees (the expense has been incurred), and are owed but have not yet been paid; they will be paid in the next accounting period. The accrual is made in this period so that revenues and expenses of the current period will be matched (the matching concept), and net income will reflect the economic results of this period's activities.

Again, each column of the exhibit has been totaled, and the total of all the asset columns equals the total of all the liability and owners' equity columns. If the accounting period were to end after transaction *(8)*, the income statement would report net income of $5, and the balance sheet would show total owners' equity of $35. A simplified balance sheet and an income statement after transaction *(8)* are presented in Exhibit 4–2.

Notice especially in Exhibit 4–2 how net income on the income statement gets into the balance sheet via the Retained Earnings section of owners' equity. In the equation of Exhibit 4–1, revenues and expenses were treated as a part of owners' equity to keep the

EXHIBIT 4–2   Balance Sheet and Income Statement after Transaction (8)

	Exhibit 4–1 Data *Balance Sheet after Transaction (8)*		*Exhibit 4–1 Data* *Income Statement for* *Transactions (1)* *through (8)*	
Assets		**Liabilities & Owners' Equity**		
Cash	$17	Note payable	$15	Revenues $20
Accounts receivable . .	20	Accounts payable	13	Expenses 15
Merchandise inventory .	8	Current liabilities . . .	$28	Net income . . . . $ 5
Current assets	$45			
Equipment	18	Owners' equity:		*Exhibit 4–1 Data*
		Paid-in capital	$30	*Statement of Change in*
		Retained earnings . . .	5	*Retained Earnings*
		Total owners' equity .	$35	Beginning balance . $ 0
		Total liabilities +		Net income 5
Total assets	$63	owners' equity	$63	Ending balance . . $ 5

equation in balance. For financial reporting purposes, however, revenues and expenses are shown in the income statement. In order to have the balance sheet balance, it is necessary that net income be reflected in the balance sheet, and this is done in retained earnings. If any retained earnings are distributed to the owners as a dividend, the dividend does not show on the income statement, but is a deduction from retained earnings, shown in the statement of changes in retained earnings. This is because a dividend is not an expense (it is not incurred in the process of generating revenue). A dividend is a distribution of earnings to the owners of the firm.

What you have just learned is the essence of the bookkeeping process. Transactions are analyzed to determine which asset, liability, or owners' equity category is affected and how each is affected. The amount of the effect is recorded, the amounts are totaled, and financial statements are prepared.

Bookkeeping Jargon and Procedures

Because of the complexity of most business operations, and the frequent need to refer to past transactions, a bookkeeping system has evolved to facilitate record-keeping. The system may be manual or computerized, but the general features are virtually the same.

Transactions are initially recorded in a **journal.** A journal (derived from the French word *jour*, meaning *day*) is a day-by-day, or chronological, record of transactions. Transactions are then recorded in — **posted** to — a **ledger.** The ledger serves the function of Exhibit 4–1, but rather than having a large sheet with a column for each asset, liability, and owners' equity category, there is an **account** for each category. In a manual bookkeeping system, each account is a separate page in a book much like a loose-leaf binder. Accounts are arranged in a sequence to facilitate the posting process. Usually the sequence is assets, liabilities, owners' equity, revenues, and expenses. A **chart of accounts** serves as an index to the ledger, and each account is numbered to facilitate the frequent written references that are made to it.

A key part of the bookkeeping system that has evolved is the account. The account format that has been used for several hundred years looks like a "T." (In the following illustration notice the T under the captions for Assets, Liabilities, and Owners' Equity.) On one side of the T, additions to the account are recorded, and on the other side of the T, subtractions are recorded. The **account balance** at any point in time is the arithmetic difference between the prior balance and the additions and subtractions, just as in Exhibit 4–1 the account balance shown after transactions *(6)* and *(8)* is the sum of the prior balance, plus the additions, minus the subtractions.

To facilitate making reference to account entries and **balances** (and to confuse neophytes), the left-hand side of a **T-account** is called the *debit* side, and the right-hand side of a T-account is called the *credit* side. In bookkeeping and accounting, **debit** and **credit** mean left and right, respectively, and nothing more (see Business Procedure Capsule 6 — Bookkeeping Language in Everyday English). A record of a transaction involving a posting to the left-hand side of an account is called a *debit entry*. An account that has a balance on its right-hand side is said to have a *credit balance*.

The beauty of the bookkeeping system is that debit and credit entries to accounts, and account balances, are set up so that if debits equal credits, the balance sheet equation will be in balance. The key to this is that asset accounts will normally have a debit balance: increases to assets are recorded as debit entries to these accounts, and decreases in assets are recorded as credit entries to these accounts. For liabilities and owners' equity accounts, the opposite will be true. To illustrate:

Assets		=	Liabilities		+	Owners' Equity	
Debit	Credit		Debit	Credit		Debit	Credit
–	–		–	–		–	–
Increases	Decreases		Decreases	Increases		Decreases	Increases
–	–		–	–		–	–
Normal balance				Normal balance			Normal balance

It is no coincidence that the debit and credit system of normal balances coincides with the balance sheet presentation illustrated earlier. In fact, the balance sheets illustrated so far have been presented in what is known as the *account format*. An alternative approach is to use the *report format*, in which assets are shown above liabilities and owners' equity.

Entries to revenue and expense accounts follow a pattern that is consistent with entries to other owners' equity accounts. Revenues are increases in owners' equity, so revenue accounts will normally have a credit balance, and will increase with credit entries. Expenses are decreases in owners' equity, so expense accounts will normally have a debit balance, and will increase with debit entries. Gains and losses are recorded like revenues and expenses, respectively.

The debit or credit behavior of accounts for assets, liabilities, owners' equity, revenues, and expenses is summarized in the following illustration:

Account Name	*Account number*
Debit side	Credit side
Normal balance for:	Normal balance for:
Assets	Liabilities
Expenses	Owners' equity accounts
	Revenues
Debit entries increase:	Credit entries increase:
Assets	Liabilities
Expenses	Owners' equity accounts
	Revenues
Debit entries decrease:	Credit entries decrease:
Liabilities	Assets
Owners' equity accounts	Expenses
Revenues	

Referring to the transactions that were illustrated in Exhibit 4–1, a bookkeeper would say that in transaction *(1)*, which was the investment of $30 in the firm by the owners, that Cash had been debited—it had been increased—and that Paid-In Capital had

---

• **BUSINESS PROCEDURE CAPSULE 6**
Bookkeeping Language in Everyday English

Many bookkeeping and accounting terms have found their way into the language, especially in the business context. Debit and credit are no exceptions to this, and some brief examples may stress the left-right definition. The terms *debit* and *credit* are used by banks to describe additions to or subtractions from an individual's checking account. For example, your account is credited for interest earned, and is debited for a service charge or for the cost of checks that are furnished to you. From the bank's perspective your account is a liability; that is, the bank owes you the balance in your account. Interest earned by your account increases that liability of the bank; hence the interest is credited. Service charges reduce your claim on the bank—its liability to you—so those are debits. Perhaps because of these effects on a checking or savings account balance, many people think that debit is a synonym for bad, and that credit means good. In certain contexts these synonyms may be appropriate, but they do not apply in accounting.

A synonym for debit that is used in accounting is *charge*. To **charge** an account is to make a debit entry to the account. This usage carries over to the terminology used when merchandise or services are purchased on credit; that is, they are received now and will be paid for later. This arrangement is frequently called a *charge account* because from the seller's perspective, an asset (accounts receivable) is increasing as a result of the transaction, and assets increase with a debit entry. The fact that a credit card is used and that this is called a *credit transaction* may refer to the increase in the purchaser's liability.

An alternative to the credit card that merchants and banks are developing is the "debit card." This term is used from the bank's perspective because when a debit card is used at an electronic point-of-sale terminal, the purchaser's bank account balance will be immediately reduced by the amount of the purchase, and the seller's bank account balance will be increased. As you can imagine, consumers have been reluctant to switch from credit cards to debit cards because they would rather pay later than sooner for several reasons, not the least of which is that they may not have the cash until later.

---

been credited, each for $30. Transaction *(2)*, the purchase of equipment for $25 cash, would be described as a $25 debit to Equipment and a $25 credit to Cash. Pretend that you are a bookkeeper, and describe the remaining transactions of that illustration.

The bookkeeper would say, after transaction *(8)* has been recorded, that the Cash account had a debit balance of $17, the Note Payable account had a credit balance of $15, and that the Expense account had a debit balance of $15. (There was only one expense account in the example; usually there will be a separate account for each category of expense and each category of revenue.) What kind of balance did the other accounts have after transaction *(8)*?

The journal was identified earlier as the chronological record of the firm's transactions. The journal is also the place where transactions are first recorded, and it is sometimes referred to as the *book of original entry*. The **journal entry** format is a useful and convenient way of describing the effect of a transaction on the accounts involved, and will be used in subsequent chapters of this text, so it is introduced now and is worth learning now.

The general format of the journal entry is:

Date   Dr. Account Name . . .   Amount
            Cr. Account Name .   Amount

Notice these characteristics of the journal entry:

The date is recorded to provide a cross-reference to the transaction. In many of our examples a transaction reference number will be used instead of a date; the point is that a cross-reference is provided.

The name of the account to be debited and the debit amount are to the left (remember, debit means *left*) of the name of the account to be credited and the credit amount.

The abbreviations *Dr.* and *Cr.* are used for *debit* and *credit*, respectively. These identifiers are frequently omitted from the journal entry to reduce writing time and because the indenting practice is universally followed and understood.

It is possible for a journal entry to have more than one debit account and amount, and/or more than one credit account and amount. The only requirement of a journal entry is that the total of the debit amounts equals the total of the credit amounts. Frequently there will be a brief explanation of the transaction beneath the journal entry, especially if the **entry** is not self-explanatory.

The journal entry for transaction *(1)* of Exhibit 4–1 would appear as follows:

(1) Dr. Cash. 30
        Cr. Paid-in Capital   30
     To record investment in the firm by the owners.

Technically, the journal entry procedure illustrated here is a *general journal entry*. Most bookkeeping systems also use specialized journals, but they are still books of original entry, recording transactions chronologically, involving various accounts, and resulting in entries in which debits equal credits. If you understand the basic general journal entry illustrated above, you will be able to understand a specialized journal if you ever see one.

Transactions generate **source documents,** such as an invoice from a supplier, a copy of a credit purchase made by a customer, a check stub or check copy, or a tape printout of the totals from a cash register's activity for a period, to name a few. These source documents are the raw materials used in the bookkeeping process, and support the journal entry.

The following flowchart illustrates the bookkeeping process that we have explored:

Transactions ——recorded in——→ Journal ————posted to————→ Ledger

Supported by	Dr.	Account Name	. . .	$xx		**Account**
source documents		Cr.	Account Name. .		$xx	**Name**

debit | credit

Understanding the Effects of Transactions on the Financial Statements

T-accounts and journal entries are models used by accountants to explain and understand the effects of transactions on the financial statements. These models are frequently difficult for a nonaccountant to use because one must know what kind of account (asset, liability, owners' equity, revenue, or expense) is involved, where in the financial statements (balance sheet or income statement) the account is found, and how the account is affected by the debit or credit characteristic of the transaction.

An alternative to the T-account and journal entry models that should be useful to you is the following horizontal financial statement relationship model first introduced in Chapter 2. The **horizontal model** is as follows:

Balance sheet	Income statement
Assets = Liabilities + Owners' equity	← Net income = Revenues − Expenses

The key to using this model is to keep the balance sheet in balance. The arrow from net income in the income statement to owners' equity in the balance sheet indicates that net income affects retained earnings, which is a component of owners' equity. For a transaction affecting both the balance sheet and income statement, the balance sheet will balance when the income statement effect on owners' equity is considered. In this model the account name is entered under the appropriate financial statement category, and the dollar effect of the transaction on that account is entered with a plus or minus sign below the account name. For example, the journal entry shown above, which records the investment of $30 in the firm by the owners, would be shown in this horizontal model as follows:

Balance sheet	Income statement
Assets = Liabilities + Owners' equity	← Net income = Revenues − Expenses

Cash   Paid-In Capital
+ 30   + 30

To further illustrate the model's use, assume a transaction in which the firm paid $12 for advertising, and that this represents an expense of the current period. The effect on the financial statements is:

Balance sheet	Income statement
Assets = Liabilities + Owners' equity	← Net income = Revenues − Expenses

Cash   Advertising
− 12   Expense
          − 12

Notice that the amount of advertising expense is shown with a minus sign. This is because the expense reduces net income, which reduces owners' equity. A plus or minus sign is used in the context of each financial statement equation. Thus a minus sign for expenses means that net income is reduced (expenses are greater), not that expenses are lower.

It is possible that a transaction can affect two accounts in a single balance sheet or income statement category. For example, assume a transaction in which a firm receives $40 that was owed to it by a customer for services performed in a prior period. The effect of this transaction is shown as follows:

Balance sheet	Income statement
Assets = Liabilities + Owners' equity	← Net income = Revenues − Expenses

Cash
+ 40

Accounts Receivable
− 40

It is also possible for a transaction to affect more than two accounts. For example, assume a transaction in which a firm provided services to a client for a price of $60, $45 of which was collected when the services were provided and $15 of which will be collected later. The following is the effect on the financial statements:

Balance sheet	Income statement
Assets = Liabilities + Owners' equity	← Net income = Revenues − Expenses

Cash	Fee Revenues
+ 45	+ 60

Accounts Receivable
+15

The horizontal model and its financial statement equations can be combined into the single equation:

$$\text{Assets} = \text{Liabilities} + \text{Owners' equity} + \text{Revenues} - \text{Expenses}$$

The operational equal sign in the horizontal model is the one between assets and liabilities. You can check that a transaction recorded in the horizontal model at least keeps the balance sheet in balance by mentally (or actually) putting an equal sign between assets and liabilities on the amount line of the model.

Spend some time now becoming familiar with the horizontal model (by working problem 4–1, for example) so it will be easier for you to understand the effects on the financial statements of transactions that you will encounter later in this book, and in practice. As a financial statement user (as opposed to a financial statement preparer), you will find that the horizontal model is an easily used tool. With practice you will also become proficient at understanding how an amount on either the balance sheet or income statement probably affected other parts of the financial statements.

Adjustments/Adjusting Entries

After the end of the accounting period the bookkeeper will probably have to record some **adjusting journal entries.** These entries are made to reflect accrual accounting in the financial statements. As discussed in Chapters 1 and 2, **accrual** accounting recognizes revenues and expenses as they occur, even though the cash receipt from the revenue or the cash disbursement related to the expense may occur before or after the event that causes revenue or expense recognition. Although prepared after the end of the accounting period, adjustments are dated and recorded as of the end of the period.

Adjustments result in revenues and expenses being reported in the appropriate fiscal period. For example, revenue may be earned in fiscal 1993 from selling a product or providing a service, and the customer/client may not pay until fiscal 1994. (Most firms pay for products purchased or services received within a week to a month after receiving the product or service.) It is also likely that some expenses *incurred* in fiscal 1993 will not be paid for until fiscal 1994. (Utility costs and employee wages are examples.) Alternatively, it is possible that a customer/client will pay the entity for a product or service in fiscal 1992, and the product will not be sold or the service provided until fiscal 1993. (Subscription fees and insurance premiums are usually paid in advance.) Likewise, the entity may pay for an item in fiscal 1992, but the expense applies to fiscal 1993. (Insurance premiums and rent are usually paid in advance.) These alternative activities are illustrated on the following time line:

Fiscal 1992	12/31/92	Fiscal 1993	12/31/93	Fiscal 1994
Cash received		Product sold or service provided and revenue earned		Cash received
Cash paid		Expense incurred		Cash paid

There are two categories of adjusting entries:

1. **Accruals** — Transactions for which cash has not yet been received or paid, but the effect of which must be recorded in the accounts in order to accomplish a matching of revenues and expenses, and accurate financial statements.
2. **Reclassifications** — The initial recording of a transaction, although a true reflection of the transaction at the time, does not result in assigning revenues to the period in which they were earned or expenses to the period in which they were incurred, so an amount must be reclassified from one account to another.

The first type of adjustment is illustrated by the accrual of wages expense and wages payable. For example, work performed by employees during March, for which they will be paid in April, results in wages expense to be included in the March income statement and a wages payable liability to be included in the March 31 balance sheet. To illustrate this accrual, assume that employees earned $60 in March that will be paid to them in April. Using the horizontal model, the **accrued** wages adjustment has the following effect on the financial statements:

Balance sheet		Income statement	
Assets = Liabilities + Owners' equity	←	Net income = Revenues − Expenses	
	Wages Payable		Wages
	+ 60		Expense
			− 60

Thus the March 31 balance sheet will reflect the wages payable liability, and the income statement for March will include all of the wages expense incurred in March. Again, note that the recognition of the expense of $60 is shown with a minus sign because as expenses increase, net income and owners' equity (retained earnings) decrease. The balance sheet remains in balance after this adjustment because the $60 increase in liabilities is offset by the $60 decrease in owners' equity. When the wages are paid in April, both the Cash and Wages Payable accounts will be decreased; Wages Expense is not affected.

Similar adjustments are made to accrue revenues (e.g., for services performed but not yet billed, or for interest earned but not yet received) and other expenses including various operating expenses, interest expense, and income tax expense.

The effect on the financial statements, using the horizontal model, of accruing $50 of interest income that has been earned but not yet received is shown as follows:

Balance sheet		Income statement	
Assets = Liabilities + Owners' equity	←	Net income = Revenues − Expenses	
Interest			Interest
Receivable			Income
+ 50			+ 50

An example of the second kind of adjustment is the reclassification for supplies. If the purchase of supplies at a cost of $100 during February was initially recorded as an increase in the Supplies (asset) account (and a decrease in Cash), the cost of supplies used during February must be removed from the asset and recorded as Supplies Expense for February. Assuming that supplies costing $35 were used during February, the reclassification adjustment would be reflected in the horizontal model as follows:

Balance sheet		Income statement	
Assets = Liabilities + Owners' equity	←	Net income = Revenues − Expenses	
Supplies			Supplies
− 35			Expense
			− 35

Conversely, if the purchase of supplies during February at a cost of $100 was originally recorded as an increase in Supplies Expense for February, the cost of supplies still on hand at the end of February ($65, if supplies costing $35 were used during February) must be removed from the Supplies Expense account for February and recorded as an asset at the end of February. The reclassification adjustment for the $65 of supplies still on hand at the end of February would be reflected in the horizontal model as follows:

Balance sheet	Income statement
Assets = Liabilities + Owners' equity ←	Net income = Revenues − Expenses
Supplies	Supplies
+ 65	Expense
	+ 65

What's going on here? Supplies costing $100 were originally recorded as an expense (a minus 100 in the expense column offset by a minus 100 of cash in the asset column). The expense should be only $35 because $65 of the supplies are still on hand at the end of February, so Supplies Expense is reduced to $35 by showing a plus 65 in the expense column. The model is kept in balance by increasing Supplies in the asset column by 65.

Adjustments for prepaid insurance (insurance premiums paid in a fiscal period before the insurance expense has been incurred) and revenues received in advance (cash received from customers before the service has been performed or the product has been sold; advance payments for example) are also reclassification adjustments.

Generally speaking, every adjusting entry affects both the balance sheet and the income statement. That is, if one part of the entry—either the debit or the credit—affects the balance sheet, the other part affects the income statement. The result of adjusting entries is to make both the balance sheet at the end of the accounting period and the income statement for the accounting period more accurate. That is, asset and liability account balances are appropriately stated, all revenues earned during the period have been reported, and all expenses incurred in generating those revenues are subtracted to arrive at net income. The matching concept has been applied. The results of ROI, ROE, and liquidity calculations will be valid measures of results of operations and financial position.

After the adjustments have been posted to the ledger accounts, account balances are determined. The financial statements are prepared using the account balance amounts, which are usually summarized to a certain extent. For example, if the company has only one ledger account for cash, the balance in that account is shown on the balance sheet as Cash. If the company has several separate selling expense accounts (e.g., Advertising Expense, Salesforce Travel Expense, and Salesforce Commissions), the selling expense ledger account balances are added together to get the selling expense amount shown on the income statement.

This entire procedure is called **closing the books,** and usually takes at least several working days to complete. At the end of the fiscal year for a large, publicly owned company, a period from 4 to 10 weeks may be required for this process because of the complexities involved, including the annual audit by the firm's public accountants.

It should be clear that the bookkeeping process itself is procedural, and that the same kinds and sequence of activities are repeated each fiscal period. These procedures and the sequence are system characteristics that make mechanization and computerization feasible. Mechanical bookkeeping system aids were developed many years ago. Today there are a large number of computer programs that use transaction data as input, and with minimum operator intervention complete the bookkeeping procedures and prepare financial statements. Accounting knowledge and judgment are as necessary as ever, however, to ensure that transactions are initially recorded in an appropriate manner, that required adjustments are made, and that the output of the computer processing is sensible.

Transaction Analysis Methodology

The key to being able to understand the effect of any transaction on the financial statements is having the ability to analyze the transaction. **Transaction analysis methodology** involves answering five questions:

1. What's going on?
2. What accounts are affected?
3. How are they affected?
4. Does the balance sheet balance? (Do the debits equal the credits?)
5. Does my analysis make sense?

What's going on? To analyze any transaction it is necessary to understand the transaction, that is, to understand the activity that is taking place between the entity for which the accounting is being done and the other entity involved in the transaction. This is why most elementary accounting texts, including this one, explain many business procedures. It is impossible to understand the effect of a transaction on the financial statements if the basic activity being accounted for is not understood. One of your principal objectives is to learn about business activities.

What accounts are affected? This question is frequently answered by the answer to "What's going on?" because the specific account name is often included in that explanation. This question may also be answered by a process of elimination. First, think about whether one of the accounts is an asset, liability, owners' equity, revenue, or expense. From the broad category it is usually possible to identify a specific account.

How are they affected? Answer this question with the word *increasing* or *decreasing,* and then, if you are using the journal entry or T-account model, translate to *debit* or *credit.* Accountants learn to think directly in debit and credit terms after much more practice than you will probably have. Note that when using the horizontal model, the debit/credit issue is avoided.

Does the balance sheet balance? If the horizontal model is being used, it is possible to determine easily that the balance sheet equation is in balance by observing the arithmetic sign and amounts of the transaction. Alternatively, the journal entry for the transaction can be written, or T-accounts can be sketched, and the equality of the debits and credits can be verified. You know by now that if the balance sheet equation is not in balance, or if the debits do not equal the credits, your analysis of the transaction is wrong!

Does my analysis make sense? This is the most important question, and it involves standing back from the trees to look at the forest, that is, determining whether the journal entry that results from your analysis causes changes in account balances and the financial statements that are consistent with your understanding of what's going on. If the analysis doesn't make sense to you, then go back to question number 1 and start again.

Application of this five-question transaction analysis routine is illustrated in Exhibit 4–3, which also illustrates the determination of the effect of a transaction on a firm's working capital. You are learning transaction analysis to help you better understand how the amounts reported on financial statements got there, which in turn will improve your ability to make decisions and informed judgments from those statements.

As described in the earlier discussion of "reclassification" adjusting entries, some transactions can quite legitimately be recorded in at least two ways, with neither entry being "wrong." Regardless of how the transaction was originally recorded, an adjusting entry prepared at the end of the accounting period will

---

EXHIBIT 4–3   Transaction Analysis

Situation:
On September 1 Cruisers, Inc., borrowed $2,500 from its bank; a note was signed that provided that the loan, plus interest, was to be repaid in 10 months.

Required:
a. Analyze the transaction and prepare a journal entry for it.
b. Describe the effect of this transaction on the working capital and current ratio of Cruisers, Inc.

a. Analysis of transaction:

What's going on? The firm signed a note at the bank and is receiving cash from the bank.

What accounts are affected? Note Payable (a liability) and Cash (an asset).

How are they affected? Note Payable is increasing and Cash is increasing.

Does the balance sheet balance? Using the horizontal model, the effect of this transaction on the financial statements is:

Balance sheet	Income statement
Assets = Liabilities + Owners' equity ←	Net income = Revenues − Expenses

Cash   Note Payable
+ 2,500   + 2,500

Yes, the balance sheet does balance; assets and liabilities each increased by $2,500. The journal entry for this transaction, in which debits equal credits, follows:

Sept. 1   Dr. Cash   2,500
                   Cr.   Note Payable . . .   2,500
             Bank loan received.

Does this make sense? Yes, because a balance sheet prepared immediately after this transaction will show an increased amount of cash, and the liability to the bank. The interest associated with the loan is not reflected in this entry because at this point Cruisers, Inc., has not incurred any interest expense, nor does the firm owe any interest; if the loan were to be immediately repaid, there would not be any interest due to the bank. Interest expense, and the liability for the interest payable, will be recorded as adjustments over the life of the loan. Let's get a preview of things to come by looking at how the interest would be accrued each month (the expense and liability have been incurred, but the liability has not yet been paid), and by looking at the ultimate repayment of the loan and accrued interest. Assume that the interest rate on the note is 12 percent (remember, an interest rate is an annual rate unless otherwise specified). Interest expense for one month would be calculated as follows:

Annual interest = Principal × Annual rate × Time (in years)

(*continued*)

EXHIBIT 4–3   *(continued)*

$$\text{Monthly interest} = \text{Principal} \times \text{Annual rate} \times \text{Time}/12$$

$$= \$2,500 \times .12 \times 1/12$$

$$= \$25$$

It is appropriate that the financial statements of Cruisers's, Inc., that are prepared each month reflect accurately the firm's interest expense for the month and its interest payable liability at the end of the month. To achieve this accuracy, the following adjusting entry would be made at the end of every month of the 10-month life of the note:

Each	Dr.	Interest Expense	25	
month-end		Cr. Interest Payable		25
		To accrue monthly interest on		
		bank loan.		

Using the horizontal model, the effect of this adjustment on the financial statements is:

Balance sheet	Income statement
Assets = Liabilities + Owners' equity ←	Net income = Revenues − Expenses
Interest	Interest
Payable	Expense
+ 25	− 25
	(A reduction in net income,
	an increase in expenses.)

Remember, a minus sign for expenses means that net income is reduced, not that expenses are reduced. As explained earlier, if the two financial statement equations are combined into

$$\text{Assets} = \text{Liabilities} + \text{Owners' equity} + \text{Revenues} - \text{Expenses}$$

the equation's balance will be preserved after each transaction or adjustment.

At the end of the 10th month, when the loan and accrued interest are paid, the following entry would be made:

June 30	Dr.	Note Payable	2,500	
	Dr.	Interest Payable	250	
		Cr. Cash		2,750
		Payment of bank loan and		
		accrued interest.		

Using the horizontal model, the effect of this transaction on the financial statements is:

EXHIBIT 4–3 *(concluded)*

Balance sheet	Income statement
Assets = Liabilities + Owners' equity ←	Net income = Revenues − Expenses

Cash　Note Payable
− 2,750　− 2,500

　　　　Interest Payable
　　　　− 250

Apply the five questions of transaction analysis to both the monthly interest expense–interest payable accrual, and to the payment. Also think about the effect of each of these entries on the financial statements. What is happening to net income each month? What has happened to net income for the 10 months? What has happened to working capital each month? What happened to working capital when the loan and accrued interest were paid?

b. Effect on working capital:
Remember from the discussion of working capital in Chapter 3 that working capital is the arithmetic difference between current assets and current liabilities. Cash is a current asset. The note payable is a current liability because it is to be paid within a year. Because both current assets and current liabilities are increasing by the same amount, working capital will not be affected. The current ratio is the ratio of current assets to current liabilities. Assuming that prior to this transaction the firm had positive working capital, its current ratio would have been greater than 1. Because both current assets and current liabilities have increased by the same amount, the proportionate increase in current assets is less than the proportionate increase in current liabilities. Therefore the current ratio has decreased. This can be shown by calculating the current ratio using assumed amounts for current assets and current liabilities.

$$\text{Before: Current ratio} = \frac{\text{Current assets}}{\text{Current liabilities}} = \frac{\$10,000}{\$5,000} = 2.0$$

$$\text{After: Current ratio} = \frac{\text{Current assets}}{\text{Current liabilities}} = \frac{\$12,500}{\$7,500} = 1.7$$

You can test this conclusion using other assumed amounts for current assets and current liabilities before the transaction, and then increasing each by the borrowed $2,500. If working capital had been negative prior to the transaction (an unusual situation because it reflects very low liquidity), the transaction would have increased the current ratio, but still not have affected the amount of working capital.

---

result in the appropriate recognition of balance sheet and income statement amounts.

For example, assume that the balance in the Supplies (asset) account on November 1 was $2,200, that on November 18 an additional $3,500 of supplies were purchased on account, and that $2,500 of supplies were on hand November 30. (The amount of supplies on hand at the end of the accounting period can be determined by counting them, and calculating their total cost. Alternatively, supplies expense can be determined by keeping track of the cost of supplies used.) Thus for the month of November, the Supplies Expense account balance should be $3,200 (beginning asset balance of $2,200 + purchases of $3,500 − ending asset balance of $2,500). The purchase of supplies can be recorded either as an increase (debit) in the Supplies (asset) account or as an increase (debit) in the Supplies Expense account. In either case a reclassification adjusting entry will result in correct account balances at November 30. The entries and T-account pictures are:

I. Purchase recorded as an increase in the supplies asset:
    Purchase transaction entry:
        Dr.   Supplies (asset)   3,500
            Cr.   Accounts Payable   3,500
    Adjusting entry:
        Dr.   Supplies Expense   3,200
            Cr.   Supplies (asset)   3,200

The T-accounts will show:

Supplies (asset)		Supplies Expense	
Balance			
Nov. 1 2,200	Adjust-	Adjust-	
Purchase 3,500	ment 3,200	ment 3,200	
Balance		Balance	
Nov. 30 2,500		Nov. 30 3,200	

The effect of this transaction and adjustment on the financial statements using the horizontal model is shown below. Note that the balance in the Supplies (asset) account before and after the transaction and adjustment has been entered in the model. The model does not seem to be "in balance" on these lines because only the balances for this one asset account are shown. It would be possible to show the beginning and ending balance of each asset, liability, owners' equity, revenue, and expense account, but that would make the presentation unnecessarily complicated.

Balance sheet		Income statement
Assets = Liabilities + Owners' equity	←	Net income = Revenues − Expenses

Balance, Nov. 1
Supplies
+ 2,200

Transaction:

	Accounts	
Supplies	Payable	
+ 3,500	+ 3,500	

Adjustment:

		Supplies
Supplies		Expense
− 3,200		− 3,200
		(A reduction in net income, an increase in expenses.)

Balance, Nov. 30

	Accounts		Supplies
Supplies	Payable		Expense
+ 2,500	+ 3,500		− 3,200

Note that the net result is a $300 increase in the supplies asset, a $3,500 increase in liabilities, and $3,200 of Supplies Expense (a decrease in retained earnings if this is the only revenue or expense item).

II. Purchase recorded as an increase in supplies expense:
    Purchase transaction entry:
          Dr. Supplies Expense   3,500
                 Cr. Accounts Payable   3,500

    Adjusting entry:
          Dr. Supplies (asset)   300
                 Cr. Supplies Expense   300

The T-accounts will show:

Supplies (asset)			Supplies Expense		
Balance					
Nov. 1	2,200		Purchase	3,500	
Adjustment	300				Adjustment 300
Balance			Balance		
Nov. 30	2,500		Nov. 30	3,200	

The effect of this transaction and adjustment on the financial statements using the horizontal model is shown below. Again, note that the beginning and ending balances have been entered in the model, and that the model does not seem to be "in balance" on these lines because only the balances for these accounts are shown.

Balance sheet	Income statement
Assets = Liabilities + Owners' equity	← Net income = Revenues − Expenses

Balance, Nov. 1
Supplies
+ 2,200

Transaction:

Accounts Payable + 3,500	Supplies Expense − 3,500 (A reduction in net income, an increase in expenses.)

Adjustment:

Supplies + 300	Supplies Expense + 300

Balance, Nov. 30

	Accounts		Supplies
Supplies	Payable		Expense
+ 2,500	+ 3,500		− 3,200

Note that the net result of this adjustment and transaction is the same as that illustrated earlier. In both cases the November 30 balance of the Supplies (asset) account and the November 30 balance of the Supplies Expense account are the same. In one sense if you know what the financial statements should show — November Supplies Expense of $3,200 and November 30 Supplies (asset) of $2,500 — an appropriate adjusting entry will result in these amounts regardless of how the transaction during the month was originally recorded. The point of this discussion is not to show you how to do bookkeeping. The point is that the last question of the transaction analysis methodology ("Does it make sense?") and the knowledge of how accounts operate can be extended to permit you to understand how financial statement amounts reflect accurately the financial position and results of operations of an entity.

Transaction analysis methodology and knowledge about the arithmetic operation of a T-account can also be used to understand the activity that is recorded in an account. For example, assume that the Interest Receivable account shows the following activity for a month:

Interest Receivable

Beginning balance	2,400		
		Transactions	1,700
Month-end adjustment	1,300		
Ending balance	2,000		

What transactions caused the credit to this account? Since the credit to this asset account represents a reduction in the account balance, the question can be rephrased to: "What transaction would cause interest receivable to decrease?" The answer: receipt of cash from entities that owed this firm interest. The journal entry summarizing these transactions is:

```
Dr.  Cash . . . . . . . . . . . . . .   1,700
     Cr.  Interest Receivable . . . . . . .        1,700
```

What is the month-end adjustment that caused the debit to the account? The rephrased question is: "What causes interest receivable to increase?" The answer: accrual of interest income that was earned this month. The adjusting journal entry to record this accrual is:

```
Dr.  Interest Receivable . . . . .   1,300
     Cr.  Interest Income . . . . .        1,300
```

By using the horizontal model, the effect of this transaction and of the adjustment on the financial statements is:

Balance sheet	Income statement
Assets = Liabilities + Owners' equity ←	Net income = Revenues − Expenses

Transaction:
Cash
+ 1,700

Interest
Receivable
− 1,700

Adjustment:	
Interest	Interest
Receivable	Income
+ 1,300	+ 1,300

The T-account format is a useful way of visualizing the effect of transactions and adjustments on the account balance. In addition, because of the arithmetic operation of the T-account (beginning balance +/− transactions and adjustments = ending balance), if all of the amounts except one are known, the unknown can be calculated.

Transaction analysis is a skill that is learned with practice. For our purposes showing the effects of a transaction in the horizontal model, writing out a journal entry, and/or recording a transaction directly in T-accounts that have been sketched on a piece of paper are ways of understanding the effects of a transaction on the financial statements.

You should learn to use transaction analysis procedures, and understand the horizontal model, journal entries, and T-accounts, because these are tools used in subsequent chapters to describe the impact of transactions on the financial statements. Although these models are part of the bookkeeper's "tool kit," you are not learning them to become a bookkeeper—you are learning them to become an informed user of financial statements.

SUMMARY

Financial statements result from the bookkeeping (procedures for sorting, classifying, and presenting the effects of a transaction) and accounting (the selection of alternative methods of reflecting the effects of certain transactions) processes. Bookkeeping procedures for recording transactions are built on the framework of the accounting equation (Assets = Liabilities + Owners' equity) that must be kept in balance.

The income statement is linked to the balance sheet through the retained earnings component of owners' equity. Revenues and expenses of the income statement are really subparts of retained earnings that are reported separately as net income (or net loss). Net income or net loss for a fiscal period is added to (or subtracted from) retained earnings at the beginning of the fiscal period in the process of determining retained earnings at the end of the fiscal period.

Bookkeeping procedures involve establishing an account for each asset, liability, owners' equity element, revenue, and expense. Accounts can be represented by a "T"; the left side is the debit side and the right side is the credit side. Transactions are recorded in journal entry format, which is:

```
Dr.  Account Name . . . . . . . .   Amount
     Cr.  Account Name . . . . . .              Amount
```

The journal entry is the source of amounts recorded in an account. The ending balance in an account is the positive difference between the debit and credit amounts recorded in the account, including the beginning balance. Asset and expense accounts normally have a debit balance; liability, owners' equity, and revenue accounts normally have a credit balance.

The horizontal model is an easy and meaningful way of understanding the effect of a transaction on the balance sheet and/or income statement. The representation of the horizontal model is:

Balance sheet	Income statement
Assets = Liabilities + Owners' equity ←	Net income = Revenues − Expenses

The key to using this model is to keep the balance sheet in balance. The arrow from net income in the income statement to owners' equity in the balance sheet indicates that net income affects retained earnings, which is a component of owners' equity. For a transaction affecting both the balance sheet and income statement, the balance sheet will balance when the income statement effect on owners' equity is considered. In this model the account name is entered under the appropriate financial statement category, and the dollar effect of the transaction on that account is entered with a plus or minus sign below the account name. It is possible to show in the model the account balance for any account at the beginning of the period, before any transactions or adjustments or at the end of the period. If the beginning and/or end of the period balance for every account is shown, the model should be "in balance." The horizontal model can be shortened to the single equation:

Assets = Liabilities + Owners' equity + Revenues − Expenses

Adjusting journal entries describe accruals or reclassifications rather than transactions. Adjustments usually affect both a balance sheet account and an income statement account. Adjustments are part of accrual accounting, and they are required to achieve a matching of revenue and expense, that is, to have the financial statements reflect accurately the financial position and results of operations of the entity.

Transaction analysis is the process of determining how a transaction affects the financial statements. Transaction analysis involves asking and answering five questions:

1. What's going on?
2. What accounts are affected?
3. How are they affected?
4. Does the balance sheet balance? (Do the debits equal the credits?)
5. Does my analysis make sense?

Transactions can be initially recorded in virtually any way that makes sense at the time. Prior to the preparation of period-end financial statements, a reclassification adjustment can be made to reflect the appropriate asset/liability and revenue/expense recognition with respect to the accounts affected by the transaction (e.g., purchase of supplies) and subsequent activities (e.g., use of supplies).

KEY TERMS AND CONCEPTS

account *(p. 93)*   A record in which transactions affecting individual assets, liabilities, owners' equities, revenues, and expenses are recorded.

account balance *(p. 93)* The arithmetic sum of the additions and subtractions to an account through a given date.

accrual *(p. 99)* The process of recognizing revenue that has been earned but not collected, or an expense that has been incurred but not paid.

accrued *(p. 100)* Describes revenue that has been earned and a related asset that will be collected, or an expense that has been incurred and a related liability that will be paid.

adjusting journal entry *(p. 99)* A journal entry usually made during the process of "closing the books" that results in more accurate financial statements. Adjusting journal entries involve accruals and reclassifications.

balance *(p. 93)* See *account balance.*

balance sheet equation *(p. 89)* Assets = Liabilities + Owners' equity (A = L + OE) expresses the fundamental structure of the balance sheet and is the basis of bookkeeping procedures. Also called *the accounting equation.*

charge *(p. 95)* In bookkeeping, a synonym for *debit.*

chart of accounts *(p. 93)* An index of the accounts contained in a ledger.

closing the books *(p. 103)* The process of posting transactions and adjustments to the ledger and preparing the financial statements.

credit *(p. 93)* The right side of an account. A decrease in asset and expense accounts; an increase in liability, owners' equity, and revenue accounts.

debit *(p. 93)* The left side of an account. An increase in asset and expense accounts; a decrease in liability, owners' equity, and revenue accounts.

entry *(p. 96)* A journal entry or a posting to an account.

horizontal model *(p. 97)* A representation of the balance sheet and income statement relationship that is useful for understanding the effect of transactions and adjustments on the financial statements. The model follows:

Balance sheet	Income statement
Assets = Liabilities + Owners' equity ←	Net income = Revenues − Expenses

journal *(p. 93)* A chronological record of transactions.

journal entry *(p. 96)* A description of a transaction in a format that shows the debit account(s) and amount(s) and credit account(s) and amount(s).

ledger *(p. 93)* A book or file of accounts.

on account *(p. 91)* Used to describe a purchase or sale transaction for which cash will be paid or received at a later date. A "credit" transaction.

post *(p. 93)* The process of recording a transaction in the ledger using a journal as the source of the information recorded.

source document *(p. 97)* Evidence of a transaction that supports the journal entry recording the transaction.

T-account *(p. 93)* An account format with a debit (left) side and a credit (right) side.

transactions *(p. 89)* Economic interchanges between entities that are accounted for and reflected in financial statements.

transaction analysis methodology *(p. 103)* The process of answering five questions to ensure that a transaction is understood. The questions are:

1. What's going on?
2. What accounts are affected?
3. How are they affected?
4. Does the balance sheet balance? (Do the debits equal the credits?)
5. Does my analysis make sense?

EXERCISES AND PROBLEMS

4–1. The transactions relating to the formation of Blue Co. Stores, Inc., and its first month of operations are shown below. Prepare an answer sheet with the columns shown. Record each transaction in the appropriate columns of your answer sheet. Show the amounts involved, and indicate how each account is affected (+ or −). After all transactions have been recorded, calculate the total of assets, liabilities, and owners' equity at the end of the month, and calculate the amount of net income for the month.

a. The firm was organized and the owners invested cash of $180.
b. The firm borrowed $100 from the bank; a short-term note was signed.
c. Display cases and other store equipment costing $75 were purchased for cash. The original list price of the equipment was $90, but a discount was received because the seller was having a sale.
d. A store location was rented, and $40 was paid for the first month's rent.
e. Inventory of $150 was purchased; $90 cash was paid to the suppliers, and the balance will be paid in 30 days.
f. During the first week of operations, merchandise that had cost $40 was sold for cash of $65.
g. A newspaper ad costing $20 was arranged for; it ran during the second week of the stores's operations. The ad will be paid for in the next month.
h. Additional inventory costing $400 was purchased; cash of $120 was paid, and the balance is due in 30 days.
i. In the last three weeks of the first month, sales totaled $450, of which $320 was sold on account. The cost of the goods sold totaled $300.
j. Employee wages for the month totaled $35; these will be paid during the first week of the next month.

Assets = Liabilities + Owners' equity

Trans-action	Cash +	Accounts Receivable +	Merchandise Inventory +	Equip-ment =	Notes Payable +	Accounts Payable +	Paid-In Capital +	Retained Earnings +	Revenues −	Expenses

4–2. The following are the transactions relating to the formation of Cardinal Mowing Services, Inc., and its first month of operations. Prepare an answer sheet with the columns shown. Record each transaction in the appropriate columns of your answer sheet. Show the amounts involved, and indicate how each account is affected (+ or −). After all transactions have been recorded, calculate the total of assets, liabilities, and owners' equity at the end of the month, and calculate the amount of net income for the month.

Transactions:
a. The firm was organized and the owners invested cash of $600.
b. The company borrowed $450 from a relative of the owners; a short-term note was signed.
c. Two lawn mowers costing $280 each, a trimmer costing $65, and a gas can costing $9 were purchased for cash. The original list price of each mower was $340, but a discount was received because the seller was having a sale.
d. Gasoline, oil, and several packages of trash bags were purchased for cash of $52.
e. Advertising flyers announcing the formation of the business and a newspaper ad were purchased. The cost of these items, $75, will be paid in 30 days.
f. During the first two weeks of operations, 19 lawns were mowed. The total revenue for this work was $210; $90 was collected in cash and the balance will be received within 30 days.
g. Employees were paid $150 for their work during the first two weeks.
h. Additional gasoline, oil, and trash bags costing $67 were purchased for cash.
i. In the last two weeks of the first month revenues totaled $260, of which $90 was collected.
j. Employee wages for the last two weeks totaled $190; these will be paid during the first week of the next month.
k. Trash bags that had cost $10 were sold to a customer for $15 cash.
l. It was determined that at the end of the month the cost of the gasoline, oil, and trash bags still on hand was $8.
m. A customer paid $40 due from mowing services provided during the first two weeks. The revenue for these services was recognized in transaction (f).

Assets = Liabilities + Owners' equity

Trans-action	Cash +	Accounts Receivable +	Supplies +	Equip-ment =	Notes Payable +	Accounts Payable +	Paid-In Capital +	Retained Earnings +	Revenues −	Expenses

4–3. Write the journal entry(ies) for each of the transactions of Problem 4–1.

4–4. Write the journal entry(ies) for each of the transactions of Problem 4–2.

4–5. On February 1, 1993, the balance of the retained earnings account of Blue Power Corporation was $630,000. Revenues for February totaled $123,000, of which $115,000 was collected in cash. Expenses for February totaled $131,000, of which $108,000 was paid in cash. Dividends declared and paid during February were $12,000.

Required: Calculate the retained earnings balance at February 28, 1993.

4–6. During the month of April, Macon Co. had cash receipts from customers of $79,000. Expenses totaled $52,000, and accrual basis net income was $14,000. There were no gains or losses during the month.

Required:
a. Calculate the revenues for Macon Co. for April.
b. Explain why cash receipts from customers can be different from revenues.

4–7. On April 1, 1993, Tabor Co. received a $6,000 note from a customer in settlement of a $6,000 account receivable from that customer. The note bore interest at the rate of 15 percent per annum, and the note plus interest was payable March 31, 1994.

Required:
a. Write the journal entry to record receipt of the note on April 1, 1993.
b. Write the journal (adjusting) entry to accrue interest at December 31, 1993.
c. Write the journal entry to record collection of the note and interest on March 31, 1994.
(*Note: As an alternative to writing journal entries, use the horizontal model to show the transactions and adjustments.*)

4–8. Proco had an account payable of $4,200 due to Shirmoo, Inc., one of its suppliers. The amount was due to be paid on January 31. Proco did not have enough cash on hand then to pay the amount due, so Proco's treasurer called Shirmoo's treasurer and agreed to send a note payable for the amount due. The note was dated February 1, had an interest rate of 9 percent per annum, and was payable with interest on May 31.

Required: Write the journal entry that would be appropriate for Proco to record on:
a. February 1, to show that the account payable had been changed to a note payable.
b. March 31, to accrue interest expense for February and March.
c. May 31, to record payment of the note and all of the interest due to Shirmoo.
(*Note: As an alternative to writing journal entries, use the horizontal model to show the transactions and adjustments.*)

4–9. On January 10, 1993, the first day of the spring semester, the cafeteria of Hardnox College purchased for cash enough paper napkins to last the entire 16-week semester. The total cost was $4,800.

Required:
a. Write the journal entry to record the purchase of the paper napkins, assuming that the purchase was recorded as an expense.
b. At January 31 it was estimated that the cost of the paper napkins used during the first three weeks of the semester totaled $950. Write the adjusting journal entry that should be made as of January 31 so that the appropriate amount of expense will show in the income statement for the month of January.
c. Write the journal entry to show the alternative way of recording the initial purchase of napkins.

d. Write the adjusting journal entry that would be appropriate at January 31 if the initial purchase had been recorded as in (c).

e. What is the effect of the difference between the two sets of entries (a) and (b) versus (c) and (d) on the:
1. Income statement for the month of January?
2. Balance sheet at January 31?

(*Note: As an alternative to writing journal entries, use the horizontal model to show the transactions and adjustments.*)

4–10. Calco, Inc., rents its store location. Rent is $220 per month, payable quarterly in advance. On July 1 a check for $660 was issued to the landlord for the July-September quarter.

Required:

a. Write the journal entry to record the payment, assuming that all $660 is recorded as Rent Expense.

b. Write the adjusting journal entry that would be appropriate at July 31 if your entry in (a) had been made.

c. Write the journal entry to record the initial payment as Prepaid Rent.

d. Write the adjusting journal entry that would be appropriate at July 31 if your entry in (c) had been made.

e. Write the adjusting journal entry that would be appropriate at August 31 and September 30, regardless of how the initial payment had been recorded.

f. If you were supervising the bookkeeper, how would you suggest that the July 1 payment be recorded? Explain your answer.

(*Note: As an alternative to writing journal entries use the horizontal model to show the transactions and adjustments.*)

4–11. Big Blue Rental Corp. provides rental agent services to apartment building owners. As shown on Big Blue Corp.'s income statement for August, 1993, and its August 31, 1993, balance sheet, consideration was not given to the following facts:

a. Rental commissions of $200 had been earned in August, but had not yet been received from or billed to building owners.

b. When supplies are purchased, their cost is recorded as an asset. As supplies are used, a record of those used is kept. The record sheet shows that $180 of supplies were used in August.

c. Interest on the note payable is to be paid on May 31 and November 30. Interest for August has not been accrued, that is, it has not yet been recorded. (The Interest Payable of $40 on the balance sheet is the amount of the accrued liability at July 31.) The interest rate on this note is 10 percent.

d. Wages of $130 for the last week of August have not been recorded.

e. The Rent Expense of $510 represents rent for August, September, and October, which was paid early in August.

f. Interest of $140 has been earned on notes receivable, but has not yet been received.

g. Late in August the board of directors met and declared a cash dividend of $1,400, payable September 10. Once declared, the dividend is a liability of the corporation until it is paid.

Required:

Using the columns provided on the income statement and balance sheet for Big Blue Rental Corp., make the appropriate adjustments/corrections to the statements, and enter the correct amount in the Final

		Adjustments/Corrections		
Big Blue Rental Corp. **Income Statement — August**	*Prelimi-* *nary*	*Debit*	*Credit*	*Final*
Commission revenue . . .	$ 4,500	$	$	$
Interest revenue	850			
Total revenue.	$ 5,350	$	$	$
Rent expense	$ 510	$	$	$
Wages expense	1,190			
Supplies expense	—			
Interest expense	—			
Total expenses	$ 1,700	$	$	$
Net income.	$ 3,650	$	$	$
Big Blue Rental Corp. **Balance Sheet —** **August 31, 1993**				
Cash.	$ 400	$	$	$
Notes receivable	13,000			
Commissions receivable . .	—			
Interest receivable	—			
Prepaid rent	—			
Supplies	650			
Total assets	$14,050	$	$	$
Accounts payable	$ 120	$	$	$
Notes payable	2,400			
Interest payable.	40			
Wages payable	—			
Dividend payable	—			
Total liabilities	$ 2,560	$	$	$
Paid-in capital	$ 2,400	$	$	$
Retained Earnings:				
Balance, August 1. . . .	$ 5,440	$	$	$
Net income.	3,650			
Dividends	—			
Balance, August 31 . .	$ 9,090	$	$	$
Total owners' equity	$11,490	$	$	$
Total liabilities and owners' equity	$14,050	$	$	$

column. Key your adjustments/corrections with the letter of the item in the above list. Captions/account names that you will have to use are on the statements. (*Hints: Use the five questions of transaction analysis. What is the relationship between net income from the income statement and the balance sheet?*)

4–12. A bookkeeper prepared the year-end financial statements of Giftwrap, Inc. The income statement showed net income of $16,400, and the balance sheet showed ending retained earnings of $83,000. The firm's accountant reviewed the bookkeeper's work and determined that adjusting entries should be made that would increase revenues by $3,000, and increase expenses by $5,700.

Required: Calculate the amounts of net income and retained earnings after the above adjustments are recorded.

4–13. This exercise provides practice in understanding the operation of T-accounts and transaction analysis. For each situation, solve for the required item. Use a T-account for the balance sheet account, prepare journal entries for the other data and the requirement, and show the effect of each entry in the account. In each case there is only one debit entry and one credit entry in the account during the month.

Balance Sheet				
Account	*Balance February 1*	*Balance February 28*	*Other Data*	*Required*
Example:				
Accounts payable	3,000	2,700	Payments to suppliers were $8,000	Purchases on account

Solution:

Accounts Payable

	Beginning balance	3,000	Dr. Accounts Dr. Inventory 7,700
Payment 8,000	Purchase	?=7,700	Payable 8,000 Cr. Accounts
	Ending balance	2,700	Cr. Cash 8,000 Payable 7,700

a.

Accounts receivable	1,200	900	February sales revenue from credit sales totaled $12,000.	Cash collected from customers in February.

b.

Supplies on hand	540	730	Cost of supplies used in February totaled $2,340.	Cost of supplies purchased in February.

	Balance Sheet			
Account	Balance February 1	Balance February 28	Other Data	Required
c. Wages payable	410	?	Wages paid in February totaled $3,800. Wages expenses accrued in February totaled $4,100.	Wages payable at February 28.

4–14. Answer these questions that are related to the following account:

   a. What is the amount of the February 28 adjustment?

   b. What account would most likely have been credited for the amount of the February transactions?

   c. What account would most likely have been debited for the amount of the February 28 adjustment?

   d. Why would this adjusting entry have been made?

Interest Payable

February transactions	1,500	February 1 balance	1,200
		February 28 adjustment	?
		February 28 balance	2,100

4–15. Enter the following column headings across the top of a sheet of paper.

Transaction/ Situation	Assets	Liabilities	Owners' Equity	Net Income

Enter the transaction/situation number in the first column and show the effect, if any, of the transaction entry or adjusting entry on the appropriate balance sheet category or on the income statement by entering the amount and indicating whether it is an addition (+) or a subtraction (−). Column headings reflect the expanded balance sheet equation; items that affect net income should not be shown as affecting owners' equity. In some cases only one column may be affected because all of the specific accounts affected by the transaction are included in that category. The first transaction has been done as an illustration.

   a. Provided services to a client on account; revenues totaled $550.

   1. Paid an insurance premium of $360 for the coming year. An asset, Prepaid Insurance, was debited.

2. Recognized insurance expense for one month from the above premium via a reclassification adjusting entry.
3. Paid $800 of wages accrued at the end of the prior month.
4. Paid $2,600 of wages for the current month.
5. Accrued $600 of wages at the end of the current month.
6. Received cash of $1,500 on accounts receivable accrued at the end of the prior month.

Transaction/ Situation	Assets	Liabilities	Owners' Equity	Net Income
a.	+550			+550

4–16. Enter the following column headings across the top of a sheet of paper.

Transaction/ Situation	Assets	Liabilities	Owners' Equity	Net Income

Enter the transaction/situation number in the first column and show the effect, if any, of the transaction entry or adjusting entry on the appropriate balance sheet category or on the income statement by entering the amount and indicating whether it is an addition (+) or a subtraction (−). Column headings reflect the expanded balance sheet equation; items that affect net income should not be shown as affecting owners' equity. In some cases only one column may be affected because all of the specific accounts affected by the transaction are included in that category. Transaction *a.* has been done as an illustration.

a. During the month Supplies Expense was debited for $1,800 of supplies purchases. The cost of supplies actually used during the month was $1,400.
1. During the month Supplies (asset) was debited $1,800 for supplies purchased. The total cost of supplies actually used during the month was $1,400.
2. Received $800 of cash from clients for services provided during the current month.
3. Paid $500 of accounts payable.
4. Received $300 of cash from clients for revenues accrued at the end of the prior month.
5. Received $900 of interest income accrued at the end of the prior month.
6. Received $1,200 of interest income for the current month.
7. Accrued $700 of interest income earned in the current month.
8. Accrued $600 of interest expense at the end of the month.
9. Paid $1,900 of interest expense for the month.
10. Accrued $2,500 of commissions payable to sales staff for the current month.

Transaction/ Situation	Assets	Liabilities	Owners' Equity	Net Income
a.	+400			+400

Armstrong

4–17. Set up a horizontal model in the following format:

Balance sheet			Income statement		
Assets = Liabilities + Owners' equity			← Net income = Revenues − Expenses		
Cash		Retained Earnings			

Beg. balance

Net earnings

Dividends

Ending Balance

Required:

a. Enter the beginning (December 31, 1990) and ending (December 31, 1991) account balance for Retained Earnings. Find these amounts in the Shareholders' Equity summary on page 28 in the annual report for Armstrong World Industries, Inc., in Appendix A. Find Net Earnings for the year ended December 31, 1991, and enter that amount in the model.

b. Record in the model all of the dividends for the year ended December 31, 1991, as a single transaction, assuming that all dividends were paid in cash.

c. Explain how the amount of dividends recorded in requirement *(b)* can be proved correct.

4–18. Set up a horizontal model in the following format:

	Assets			*Liabilities*	*Revenues*	*Expenses*	
	Cash	*Accounts Receivable*	*Inventories*	*Accounts Payable & Accrued Expenses*	*Sales*	*Cost of Goods Sold*	*Selling & Administrative Expense*

Armstrong

Beginning balance

Net sales

Cost of goods sold

Selling & administrative expenses

Purchases on Account

Collections of accounts receivable

Payment of accounts payable & accrued liabilities

Ending balance

Required:

a. Enter the beginning (December 31, 1990) and ending (December 31, 1991) account balances for Accounts Receivable, Inventories, and Accounts Payable and Accrued Expenses (Payable). Find these amounts on the balance sheet for Armstrong World Industries, Inc., in Appendix A.

b. From the income statement (Statement of Earnings) for Armstrong World Industries, Inc., for the year ended December 31, 1991, in Appendix A, record the following transactions in the model:

Net sales, assuming all sales were made on account.

Cost of goods sold, assuming all costs were transferred from inventories.

Selling and administrative expenses, assuming that all of these expenses were accrued in the Accounts Payable and Accrued Expenses liability account as they were incurred.

c. Assuming that the only other transactions affecting the balance sheet were those described below, calculate the amount of each transaction:

Purchases of inventories on account.

Collection of accounts receivable.

Payment of accounts payable and accrued expenses.

4–19. a. Give an example of a reclassification adjusting journal entry, and explain why such an adjusting entry may be required.

b. Give an example of an accrual adjusting entry, and explain why such an adjusting entry may be required.

4–20. Assume that Cater Co.'s accountant neglected to record the payroll expense accrual adjusting entry at the end of October.

Required:

a. Explain the effect of this omission on net income reported for October.

b. Explain the effect of this omission on net income reported for the month of November.

c. Explain the effect of this omission on total net income for the two months of October and November taken together.

d. Explain why the accrual adjusting entry should have been recorded as of October 31.

Chapter 5

Accounting for and Presentation of Current Assets

Current assets include cash and those assets that are expected to be converted to cash or used up in the operating activities of the entity within one year. Current asset captions usually seen in a balance sheet are:

Cash.

Marketable (or Short-Term) Securities.

Accounts and Notes Receivable.

Inventories.

Prepaid Expenses or Other Current Assets.

Refer to the Armstrong World Industries, Inc., Consolidated Balance Sheets on page 19 of Appendix A. Note that Armstrong's current assets at December 31, 1991, total $718.8 million, and account for about 33% of the company's total assets. Look at the components of current assets. Cash equivalents are short-term investments. Why does Armstrong invest in short-term securities rather than hold very large cash balances? Notice that the largest components of current assets are Accounts and Notes Receivable, and Inventories. Now refer to the balance sheets in other annual reports that you may have, and examine the composition of current assets. Do they differ significantly from Armstrong's balance sheet? The objective of this chapter is to permit you to make sense of the current asset presentation of any balance sheet.

LEARNING OBJECTIVES

After studying this chapter you should understand:

• What is included in the cash amount reported on the balance sheet.

• The bank reconciliation procedure.

- How and why a petty cash fund is used.
- How short-term marketable securities are reported on the balance sheet.
- The accrual of interest income and interest receivable.
- How accounts receivable are reported on the balance sheet, including the valuation allowances for estimated uncollectible accounts and estimated cash discounts.
- The features of a system of internal control, and why internal controls are important.
- How notes receivable and related accrued interest are reported on the balance sheet.
- How inventories are reported on the balance sheet.
- The alternative inventory cost-flow assumptions, and their respective effects on the income statement and balance sheet when price levels are changing.
- What prepaid expenses are, and how they are reported on the balance sheet.

CASH

The amount of cash reported on the balance sheet represents the cash that is available to the entity as of the close of business on the balance sheet date. This includes cash on hand in change funds, **petty cash** funds (see Business Procedure Capsule 7 — Petty Cash), undeposited cash receipts, and the amount of cash available to the firm in its various bank accounts.

The Bank Reconciliation

To determine the amount of cash available in the bank, it is appropriate that the Cash account balance as shown in the general ledger be reconciled with the balance reported by the bank. The **bank reconciliation** process, which you do (or should do) for your own checking account, involves bringing into agreement the account balance reported by the bank on the bank statement with the account balance in the ledger. The balances might differ for two reasons: timing differences, and errors.

Timing differences arise because the firm knows about some transactions affecting the cash balance about which the bank is not yet aware, or the bank has recorded some transactions about which

---

• **BUSINESS PROCEDURE CAPSULE 7**
Petty Cash Funds

Although most of the cash disbursements of a firm should be and are made by check for security and record-keeping purposes, many firms have one or more petty cash funds for small payments for which writing a check is inconvenient. For example, postage-due or **collect on delivery (COD)** delivery charges, or the cost of an office supply item that is needed immediately and is not in the storeroom, could be paid from the petty cash fund.

The petty cash fund is an **imprest account;** that term means that the sum of the cash on hand in the petty cash box and the receipts (called *petty cash vouchers*) in support of disbursements should equal the amount initially put in the petty cash fund.

Periodically (usually at the end of the accounting period), the petty cash fund is reimbursed; that is, the cash in the fund is brought back to the original amount. It is at this time that the expenses paid through the fund are recognized in the accounts.

The amount of the petty cash fund is included in the cash amount reported on the firm's balance sheet.

---

the firm is not yet aware. The most common timing differences involve:

Deposits in transit, which have been recorded in the firm's Cash account, but which have not yet been added to the firm's balance on the bank's records. From the entity's point of view, the deposit in transit represents cash on hand because it has been received.

Outstanding checks, which have been recorded as credits (reductions) to the firm's cash balance, but which have not yet been presented to the bank for payment. From the firm's point of view, outstanding checks should not be included in its cash balance because its intent was to disburse cash when it issued the checks.

Charges by the bank for its services, and interest added to the account balance by the bank because of the balance maintained over the period. The **bank service charge** and interest income should be recognized by the entity in the period incurred or earned. They will affect the cash balance at the end of the period.

NSF (not sufficient funds) checks, which are checks that have "bounced" from the maker's bank because the account did not have enough funds to cover the check. Because the firm that received the check recorded it as a cash receipt and added the check amount to the balance of its cash account, it is necessary to establish an account receivable for the amount due from the maker of the NSF check.

Errors, which can be made by either the firm or the bank, are detected in what may be a trial-and-error process if the book balance and bank balance do not reconcile after timing differences have been recognized. Finding errors is a tedious process involving verification of the timing difference amounts (e.g., double-checking the makeup and total of the list of outstanding checks), verifying the debits and credits to the firm's ledger account, and verifying the arithmetic and amounts included on the bank statement. If the error is in the recording of cash transactions on the firm's books, then an appropriate journal entry must be made to correct the error. If the bank has made the error, the bank is notified but no change is made to the cash account balance.

There are a number of ways of mechanically setting up the bank reconciliation. The reverse side of the bank statement usually has a reconciliation format printed on it. A simple and clear technique for setting up the reconciliation is illustrated in Exhibit 5–1.

EXHIBIT 5–1   A Bank Reconciliation

Assumptions:

The balance in the Cash account of Cruisers, Inc., at September 30 was $4,614.58.

The bank statement showed a balance of $5,233.21 as of September 30.

Included with the bank statement were notices that the bank had deducted a service charge of $42.76, and had credited the account with interest of $28.91 earned on the average daily balance.

An NSF check for $35.00 from a customer was returned with the bank statement.

A comparison of deposits recorded in the cash account with those shown on the bank statement showed that the September 30 deposit of $859.10 was not on the bank statement. This is not surprising because the September 30 deposit was put in the bank's night depository on the evening of September 30.

A comparison of the record of checks issued with the checks returned in the bank statement showed that the amount of outstanding checks was $1,526.58.

Reconciliation as of September 30:

(continued)

EXHIBIT 5–1 *(concluded)*

From Bank Records		*From Company Books*	
Indicated balance . . .	5,233.21	Indicated balance . . .	4,614.58
Add: Deposit in transit .	859.10	Add: Interest earned . .	28.91
Less: Outstanding		Less: Service charge . .	(42.76)
checks	(1,526.58)	NSF check . . .	(35.00)
Reconciled balance . .	4,565.73	Reconciled balance . .	4,565.73

The following adjusting journal entry would be made to adjust the balance in the company's general ledger account before reconciliation (the "Indicated balance") to the reconciled balance.

Dr.	Service Charge Expense	42.76	
Dr.	Accounts Receivable.	35.00	
	Cr. Interest Income		28.91
	Cr. Cash		48.85

Using the horizontal model, the effect of this adjustment on the financial statements is:

Balance sheet			Income statement	
Assets = Liabilities + Owners' equity			← Net income = Revenues − Expenses	
Accounts			Interest	Service
Receivable			Income	Charge
+ 35.00			+ 28.91	Expense
Cash				− 42.76
− 48.85				

Alternatively, a separate adjusting journal entry could be made for each reconciling item. The amount from this particular bank account to be included in the cash amount shown on the balance sheet for September 30 is $4,565.73. There would not be an adjusting journal entry for the reconciling items that affect the bank balance because those items have already been recorded on the company's books.

SHORT-TERM MARKETABLE SECURITIES

Do you remember the cash equivalents (short-term securities) that are part of Armstrong World Industries, Inc.'s, current assets? In order to increase profits and return on investment, most firms have a cash management program that involves investing cash balances over and above those required for day-to-day operations in **short-term marketable securities.** An integral part of the cash management program is the firm's forecast of cash receipts and disbursements (forecasting, or budgeting, is discussed in Chapter 14). The broad objective of the cash management program is to maximize earnings by having as much cash as feasible invested for the longest possible time. Cash managers are usually interested in minimizing investment risks, and this is accomplished by investing in U.S. Treasury securities, securities of agencies of the federal government, bank certificates of deposit, and/or commercial paper. (**Commercial paper** is like an IOU issued by a very creditworthy corporation.) Securities selected for investment will usually have a maturity date that is within a year of the investment date, and that corresponds to the time when the cash manager thinks the cash will be needed.

Balance Sheet Valuation

Short-term marketable securities are reported in the balance sheet at their cost to the entity, unless the current market value of the securities, in the aggregate, is less than cost. The market value is not likely to be less than cost because of the high quality and short time until the maturity date of the securities, but if it is, the matching concept and conservatism principle require that the loss in value be reflected in the period in which it occurs.

Interest Accrual

Of course, it is appropriate that interest income on short-term marketable securities be accrued as earned so that both the balance sheet and income statement reflect more accurately the financial position at the end of the period and results of operations for the period. The asset involved is called *Interest Receivable,* and *Interest Income* is the income statement account. The accrual is made with the following adjusting entry:

Dr.   Interest Receivable   xx
    Cr.   Interest Income   xx

The effect of the interest accrual on the financial statements is:

Balance sheet	Income statement
Assets = Liabilities + Owners' equity	← Net income = Revenues − Expenses

+ Interest
  Receivable
	+ Interest
	  Income

The amount in the Interest Receivable account is combined with other receivables in the current asset section of the balance sheet.

ACCOUNTS RECEIVABLE

Recall from the Armstrong World Industries, Inc., balance sheet that Accounts Receivable is one of the largest current assets. Accounts receivable from customers for merchandise and services delivered are reported at realizable value—the amount that is expected to be received from customers in settlement of their obligations. Two factors will cause this amount to be different from the amount of the receivable originally recorded: bad debts and cash discounts.

Bad Debts/Uncollectible Accounts

Whenever a firm permits its customers to purchase merchandise or services on credit, it knows that some of the customers will not pay. Even a thorough check of the potential customer's credit rating and history of payments to other suppliers will not assure that the customer will pay in the future. Based on experience tempered by the current state of economic affairs of the industry in which a firm is operating, credit managers can estimate with a high degree of accuracy the probable **bad debts expense (or uncollectible accounts expense)** of the firm.

When the amount of accounts receivable estimated to be uncollectible has been determined, a **valuation adjustment** can be recorded to reduce the carrying value of the asset and recognize the bad debt expense. The adjusting entry is:

Dr. Bad Debts Expense (or Uncollectible Accounts Expense) xx
      Cr. Allowance for Bad Debts (or Allowance for Uncollectible Accounts) xx

The effect of this adjustment on the financial statements is:

Balance sheet	Income statement
Assets = Liabilities + Owners' equity	← Net income = Revenues − Expenses
− Allowance for Bad Debts	− Bad Debts Expense

In bookkeeping language the **Allowance for Uncollectible Accounts** or **Allowance for Bad Debts** account is considered a **contra**

asset because it is reported as a subtraction from an asset in the balance sheet. The presentation of the Allowance for Bad Debts in the current asset section of the balance sheet (using assumed amounts) is:

Accounts receivable	$10,000
Less: Allowance for bad debts.	(500)
Net accounts receivable	$ 9,500

or:

Accounts receivable, less allowance for bad debts of $500	$ 9,500

The debit and credit mechanics of a contra asset account are the opposite of those of an asset account; that is, a contra asset increases with credit entries and decreases with debit entries, and it normally has a credit balance.

During the year as accounts are determined to be uncollectible, they are *written off* against the allowance account with the following entry:

Dr.	Allowance for Bad Debts	xx
	Cr. Accounts Receivable	xx

The effect of this entry on the financial statements is:

Balance sheet	Income statement
Assets = Liabilities + Owners' equity ←	Net income = Revenues − Expenses

− Accounts
  Receivable
+ Allowance
  for Bad Debts	

Note that the **write off** of an account receivable has no effect on the income statement, nor should it. The expense was recognized in the year in which the revenue from the transaction with this customer was recognized. The write-off entry removes from Accounts Receivable an amount that is never expected to be collected. Also note that the write-off of an account will not have any effect on the net accounts receivable reported on the balance sheet because both the asset (Accounts Receivable) and the contra asset (Allowance for Bad Debts) are affected the same way (each is reduced) by the same amount.

Although some bad debt losses are inevitable when a firm makes credit sales, policies and procedures will exist in most firms to keep losses at a minimum, and to ensure that every reasonable effort is

---

• BUSINESS PROCEDURE CAPSULE 8
The Internal Control System

An organization's **internal control system** is made up of those policies and procedures that are designed to:

1. Assure the accuracy of its bookkeeping records and financial statements.
2. Protect its assets.
3. Encourage adherence to the policies established by management.
4. Provide for efficient operations of the organization.

   Items 1 and 2 above are known as financial controls, and items 3 and 4 are administrative controls. Although the system of internal control is frequently discussed in the context of the firm's accounting system, it is equally applicable to every activity of the firm, and it is appropriate for everyone to understand the need for and significance of internal controls.
   Financial controls include the series of checks and balances that remove from one person the sole involvement in a transaction from beginning to end. For example, most organizations require that checks be signed by someone other than the person who prepares them. The check signer is expected to review the documents supporting the disbursement, and to raise questions about unusual items. Another internal control requires the credit manager who authorizes the write-off of an account receivable to have that write-off approved by another officer of the firm. Likewise, a bank teller or cashier who has made a mistake in initially recording a transaction must have a supervisor approve the correction.
   Administrative controls are frequently included in policy and procedure manuals, and are reflected in management reviews of reports of operations and activities. For example, a firm's credit policy might specify that no customer is to have an account receivable balance in excess of $10,000 until the customer has had a clean payment record for at least a year. The firm's internal auditors might periodically review the accounts receivable detail to determine whether or not this policy is being followed.
   The system of internal control does not exist because top management thinks that the employees are dishonest. Internal controls provide a framework within which employees can operate, knowing that their work is being performed in a way that is consistent with the desires of top management. To the extent that temptation is removed from a situation that might otherwise lead to an employee's dishonest act, the system of internal control provides an even more significant benefit.

---

made to collect all amounts that are due to the firm (see Business Procedure Capsule 8 — The Internal Control System). Some companies, however, willingly accept high credit risk customers and know that they will experience high bad debt losses. These firms maximize their ROI by having a very high margin and requiring a down payment that equals or approaches the cost of the item being sold. Sales volume is higher than it would be if credit standards were tougher, and thus even though bad debts are relatively high, all or most of the product cost is recovered, and bad debt losses are more than offset by the profits from greater sales volume.

Providing for bad debt expense in the same year in which the related sales revenue is recognized is an application of the matching concept. The Allowance for Bad Debts (or Allowance for Doubtful Accounts) account is a **valuation account** and its credit balance is subtracted from the debit balance of Accounts Receivable to arrive at the amount of net receivables reported in the Current Asset section of the balance sheet. This procedure results in stating Accounts Receivable at the amount expected to be collected. If an appropriate allowance for bad debts is not provided, then Accounts Receivable and net income will be overstated, and the ROI, ROE, and liquidity measures will be distorted. The amount of the allowance is usually reported parenthetically in the Accounts Receivable caption so financial statement users can make a judgment about the credit and collection practices of the firm.

Cash Discounts

To encourage prompt payment by their customers, many firms permit their customers to deduct up to 2 percent of the amount owed if the bill is paid within a stated period — usually 10 days — of the date of the sale, usually referred to as the *invoice date*. Most firms' **credit terms** provide that if the invoice is not paid within the discount period, it must be paid in full within 30 days of the invoice date. This term is abbreviated as 2/10, n30. The 2/10 refers to the discount terms and the n30 means that the net amount of the invoice is due within 30 days. To illustrate, assume that Cruisers, Inc., has credit sales terms of 2/10, n30. On April 8, Cruisers, Inc., made a $5,000 sale to Mount Marina. Mount Marina has the option of paying $4,900 (5,000 − [2% × $5,000]) by April 18, or paying $5,000 on May 8.

Most firms will take advantage of the **cash discount** because it represents a high rate of return (see Business Procedure Capsule 9 — Cash Discounts). The discount is clearly a cost to the seller because the selling firm will not receive the full amount of the account receivable resulting from the sale.

Cash discounts on sales are usually subtracted from Sales in the income statement to arrive at the net sales amount that is reported, because the discount is in effect a reduction of the selling price.

• **BUSINESS PROCEDURE CAPSULE 9**
Cash Discounts

Cash discounts for prompt payment represent a significant cost to the seller and a benefit to the purchaser. Not only do they encourage prompt payment, but they also represent an element of the pricing decision, and will be considered when evaluating the selling prices of competitors.

Converting the discount to an annual return on investment will illustrate its significance. Assume that an item sells for $100, with credit terms of 2/10, n30. If the invoice is paid by the 10th day, a $2 discount is taken, and the payor gives up the use of the $98 paid for 20 days because the alternative is to keep the money for another 20 days and then pay $100. The return on investment for 20 days is $2/$98, or slightly more than 2 percent; however, there are 18 available 20-day periods in a year (360 days/20 days), and so the annual return on investment is over 36%! Very few firms are able to earn this high an ROI on their principal activities. Most firms have a rigidly followed internal control policy of taking all cash discounts possible.

One of the facts that credit rating agencies and credit grantors want to know about a firm when evaluating its liquidity and creditworthiness is whether or not the firm takes cash discounts. If it does not, that is a signal that either the management doesn't understand their significance, or that the firm can't afford to borrow money at a lower interest rate to earn the higher rate from the cash discount. Either of these reasons indicates a potentially poor credit risk.

Since the purchaser's benefit is the seller's burden, why do sellers allow cash discounts if they represent such a high cost? The principal reasons are to encourage prompt payment and to be competitive. Obviously, however, cash discounts represent a cost that must be covered for the firm to be profitable.

On the balance sheet date, Accounts Receivable includes the full amount of sales made in the discount period preceding the balance sheet date. In order to report Accounts Receivable at the amount expected to be realized as cash, it is appropriate to reduce Accounts Receivable by the estimated cash discounts that will be taken by customers when they pay within the discount period following the balance sheet date. These estimated cash discounts are recognized as cash discounts on sales in the fiscal period in which the sale was made. The basis for the estimate is past experience with cash discounts taken. The valuation adjustment entry is:

Dr. Cash Discounts on Sales.   xx
    Cr. Allowance for Cash Discounts   xx

The Allowance for Cash Discounts account is another contra asset, and the balance in this account is subtracted from Accounts Receivable to determine the amount reported for Accounts Receivable in the balance sheet. The balance sheet presentation of the Allowance for Cash Discounts is the same as previously illustrated for the Allowance for Bad Debts. Many firms combine the amount of the allowance for cash discounts and the allowance for bad debts and report this total parenthetically in the Accounts Receivable caption. Note that in Appendix A Armstrong World Industries, Inc., has done this in its balance sheet.

NOTES RECEIVABLE

If a firm has an account receivable from a customer that has developed difficulties paying its accounts when due, the firm may convert that account receivable to a **note receivable.** The entry to reflect this transaction is:

Dr.   Note Receivable   xx
      Cr.   Accounts Receivable   xx

The effect of this entry on the financial statements is:

Balance sheet	Income statement
Assets = Liabilities + Owners' equity ← Net income = Revenues − Expenses	
− Accounts Receivable	
+ Note Receivable	

One asset has been exchanged for another. Does the entry make sense?

A note receivable differs from an account receivable in several ways. A note is a formal document that includes specific provisions with respect to its maturity date (when it is to be paid), agreements or *covenants* made by the borrower (e.g., to supply financial statements to the lender or refrain from paying dividends until the note is repaid), identification of security or **collateral** pledged by the borrower to support the loan, penalties to be assessed if it is not paid on the maturity date, and, most importantly, the interest rate associated with the loan. Although some firms assess an interest charge or service charge on invoice amounts that are not paid when due, this practice is unusual for transactions between firms. Thus if an account receivable is not going to be paid promptly, the seller will ask the customer to sign a note so interest is earned on the overdue account.

Under other circumstances a firm may lend money to another entity and take a note from that entity; for example, a manufacturer may lend money to a distributor that is also a customer or potential customer in order to help the distributor build its business. This transaction is another rearrangement of assets; Cash is decreased and Note Receivable is increased.

Interest Accrual

If interest is to be paid at the maturity of the note (a common practice), it is appropriate that the holder of the note accrue interest income, usually on a monthly basis. This is appropriate because interest revenue has been earned and accruing the revenue and increasing interest receivable result in more accurate monthly financial statements. The entry to do this is the same as that for interest accrued on short-term cash investments:

```
Dr.  Interest Receivable . . . . . . . . . . . . . . . . .   xx
      Cr.  Interest Income . . . . . . . . . . . . . . . .        xx
```

The effect of this entry on the financial statements is:

Balance sheet	Income statement
Assets = Liabilities + Owners' equity ←	Net income = Revenues − Expenses

+ Interest
  Receivable
	+ Interest
	  Income

This accrual entry reflects interest income that has been earned in the period, and increases current assets by the amount earned but not yet received.

Interest Receivable is frequently combined with the Note Receivable in the balance sheet for reporting purposes. Amounts to be received within a year of the balance sheet date are classified as current assets. If the note has a maturity date beyond a year, it will be classified as a noncurrent asset.

It is appropriate to recognize any probable loss from uncollectable notes and interest receivable just as is done for accounts receivable, and the bookkeeping process is the same. Cash discounts do not apply to notes, so there is no discount valuation allowance.

INVENTORIES

Inventories represent the most significant current asset for many merchandising and manufacturing firms. For Armstrong World Industries, Inc., inventories account for almost 47 percent of current assets, and are greater than the amount of accounts and notes receivable. Accounting for inventories is one of the areas in which alternative generally accepted practices can result in major differences between the assets and expenses reported by companies that might otherwise be alike in all respects.

Just as warehouse bins and store shelves hold inventory until the product is sold to the customer, the inventory accounts of a firm hold the *cost* of a product until that cost is released to the income statement to be subtracted from (matched with) the revenue from the sale. The cost of a purchased or manufactured product is recorded as an asset, and carried in the asset account until the product is sold (or becomes worthless, or is lost or stolen), at which point the cost becomes an expense to be reported in the income statement. The cost of an item purchased for inventory includes not only the price paid to the supplier, but also other costs associated with the purchase of the item such as freight and material handling charges. Cost is reduced by the amount of any cash discount allowed on the purchase. The income statement caption used to report this expense is Cost of Goods Sold (see Exhibit 2–2). The effects of purchase and sale transactions on specific accounts are:

Dr. Inventory	xx	
Cr. Accounts Payable (or Cash)		xx
Purchase (or manufacture) of inventory.		
Dr. Cost of Goods Sold	xx	
Cr. Inventory		xx
To transfer cost of item sold to income statement.		

These transactions are illustrated in the horizontal model as follows:

Balance sheet	Income statement
Assets = Liabilities + Owners' equity ←	Net income = Revenues − Expenses

Purchase of inventory:
+ Inven-   + Accounts
   tory   Payable

Recognize cost of goods sold:
− Inven-   − Cost of
   tory   Goods
                                                                     Sold

Recognizing cost of goods sold is a process of accounting for the *flow of costs* from the Inventory (asset) account of the balance sheet to the Cost of Goods Sold (expense) account of the income statement. T-accounts can also be used to illustrate this flow of

---

EXHIBIT 5–2   Flow of Costs from Inventory to Cost of Goods Sold

---

Balance Sheet / Income Statement

Inventory (asset)		Cost of Goods Sold (expense)
Purchases of merchandise for resale increase inventory (credit to accounts payable or cash)	When merchandise is sold, the cost flows from the inventory asset account to ——→	the cost of goods sold expense account

---

costs as shown in Exhibit 5–2. Of course, the sale of merchandise also generates revenue, but *recognizing revenue is a separate transaction* involving Accounts Receivable (or Cash) and the Sales Revenue accounts. This discussion focuses only on the accounting for the cost of the inventory sold.

Inventory Cost-Flow Assumptions

The accounting alternatives permitted relate to the assumption about how costs flow from the Inventory account to the Cost of Goods Sold account. There are four principal alternative **cost-flow assumptions:**

1. Specific identification.
2. Weighted average.
3. First-in, first-out (FIFO) (pronounced FIE-FOE).
4. Last-in, first-out (LIFO) (pronounced LIE-FOE).

It is important to recognize that these are *cost-flow assumptions,* and that FIFO and LIFO do not refer to the physical flow of product. Thus it is possible for a firm to have a FIFO physical flow (a grocery store usually tries to accomplish this) and to use the LIFO cost-flow assumption.

The **specific identification** alternative links cost and physical flow. When an item is sold, the cost of that specific item is determined from the firm's records, and that amount is transferred from the inventory account to cost of goods sold. The amount of the ending inventory is the cost of the items that are in inventory at the end of the year. This alternative is appropriate for a firm dealing with specifically identifiable products, such as automobiles, that have an identifying serial number and are purchased and sold by specific unit. This assumption is not practical for a firm having a large number of inventory items that are not easily identified individually.

The **weighted-average** alternative is applied to individual items of inventory, and involves calculating the average cost of the items in the beginning inventory plus purchases made during the year, and using this average to determine the cost of goods sold and the carrying value of the ending inventory. This method is illustrated in Exhibit 5–3. Notice that the average cost is not a simple average of the unit costs, but is instead an average weighted by the number of units in beginning inventory and each purchase.

First-in, first-out, or FIFO, means more than first-in, first-out; it means that the first costs *in to inventory* are the first costs *out to cost of goods sold.* The first cost in is the cost of the beginning inventory. The effect of this inventory cost-flow assumption is to transfer to the Cost of Goods Sold account the oldest costs incurred for the quantity of merchandise sold, and to leave in the Inventory asset account the most recent costs of merchandise purchased or manufactured for the quantity of merchandise in inventory. This cost-flow assumption is also illustrated in Exhibit 5–3.

Last-in, first-out, or LIFO, is an alternative cost-flow assumption opposite to FIFO. Remember, we are thinking about cost flow, not physical flow, and it is possible for a firm to have a FIFO physical flow (like the grocery store) and still use the LIFO cost-flow assumption. Under LIFO, the most recent costs incurred for merchandise purchased or manufactured are transferred to the income statement when items are sold, and the inventory on hand at the balance sheet date is costed at the oldest costs, including those used to value the beginning inventory. This cost-flow assumption is also illustrated in Exhibit 5–3.

The way the cost-flow assumption is specifically applied depends on the inventory accounting system in use. The two systems — *periodic* and *perpetual* — are described later in this chapter. The examples in Exhibit 5–3 use the periodic system.

To recap the results of the three alternatives presented in Exhibit 5–3:

Cost-Flow Assumption	Cost of Ending Inventory	Cost of Goods Sold
Weighted average	$13,152	$60,828
FIFO	13,680	60,300
LIFO	12,300	61,680

EXHIBIT 5–3   Inventory Cost-Flow Alternatives Illustrated

Situation:

On September 1, 1992, the inventory of Cruisers, Inc., consisted of five Model OB3 boats. Each boat had cost $1,500. During the year ended August 31, 1993, 40 boats were purchased on the dates and at the costs that follow. During the year, 37 boats were sold.

Required:

Determine the August 31, 1993, inventory amount, and the cost of goods sold, using the weighted-average, FIFO, and LIFO cost-flow assumptions.

Solution:

Date of Purchase	Number of Boats	Cost per Boat	Total Cost
9/1/92 (Beginning inventory).	5	$1,500	$ 7,500
11/7/92	8	1,600	12,800
3/12/93	12	1,650	19,800
5/22/93	10	1,680	16,800
7/28/93	6	1,700	10,200
8/30/93	4	1,720	6,880
Total of boats available to sell	45		$73,980
Number of boats sold	37		
Number of boats in 8/31/93 inventory	8		

a. Weighted-average cost-flow assumption:

$$\text{Weighted-average cost} = \frac{\text{Total cost of boats available to sell}}{\text{Number of boats available to sell}}$$

$$= \frac{\$73,980}{45}$$

$$= \$1,644 \text{ per boat}$$

Cost of ending inventory = $1,644 × 8 = $13,152
Cost of goods sold = $1,644 × 37 − $60,828

b. FIFO cost-flow assumption:

   The cost of ending inventory is the cost of the eight most recent purchases:

4 boats purchased 8/30/93 @ $1,720 ea =	$ 6,880
4 boats purchased 7/28/93 @ $1,700 ea =	6,800
Cost of 8 boats in ending inventory	$13,680

(continued)

EXHIBIT 5–3   *(concluded)*

The cost of 37 boats sold is the sum of the costs for the first 37 boats purchased:

Beginning inventory . . .	5 boats @ $1,500 =	$ 7,500
11/7/92 purchase	8 boats @ 1,600 =	12,800
3/12/93 purchase	12 boats @ 1,650 =	19,800
5/22/93 purchase	10 boats @ 1,680 =	16,800
7/28/93 purchase*	2 boats @ 1,700 =	3,400
Cost of goods sold. . . .		$60,300

* Applying the FIFO cost-flow assumption, the cost of two of the six boats purchased this date is transferred from Inventory to Cost of Goods Sold.

Note that the cost of goods sold could also have been calculated by subtracting the ending inventory amount from the total cost of the boats available for sale.

Total cost of boats available for sale	$73,980
Less cost of boats in ending inventory	(13,680)
Cost of goods sold	$60,300

c. **LIFO cost-flow assumption:**

The cost of ending inventory is the cost of the eight oldest purchases:

5 boats in beginning inventory @ $1,500 ea =	$ 7,500
3 boats of 11/7/92 purchase @ $1,600 ea =	4,800
Cost of 8 boats in ending inventory	$12,300

The cost of the 37 boats sold is the sum of costs for the last 37 boats purchased:

8/30/93 purchase	4 boats @ $1,720 =	$ 6,880
7/28/93 purchase	6 boats @ 1,700 =	10,200
5/22/93 purchase	10 boats @ 1,680 =	16,800
3/12/93 purchase	12 boats @ 1,650 =	19,800
11/7/92 purchase*	5 boats @ 1,600 =	8,000
Cost of goods sold		$61,680

* Applying the LIFO cost-flow assumption, the cost of five of the eight boats purchased this date is transferred from Inventory to Cost of Goods Sold.

Note that the cost of goods sold could also have been calculated by subtracting the ending inventory amount from the total cost of the boats available for sale.

Total cost of boats available for sale	$73,980
Less cost of boats in ending inventory	(12,300)
Cost of goods sold	$61,680

Although the differences between amounts seem small in this Illustration, under real-world circumstances with huge amounts of inventory the differences become large and are material (the materiality concept). Why do the differences occur? Because, as you have probably noticed, the cost of the boats purchased changed over time. If the cost had not changed, there would not have been any difference in the ending inventory and cost of goods sold among the three alternatives. But in practice, costs do change. Notice that the amounts resulting from the weighted-average cost-flow assumption are between those for FIFO and LIFO; this is to be expected. Weighted-average results will never be outside the range of amounts resulting from FIFO and LIFO.

The crucial point to understand about the inventory cost-flow assumption issue is the impact on cost of goods sold, operating income, and net income of the alternative assumptions. On page 24 of the 1991 Armstrong World Industries, Inc., Annual Report in Appendix A, this paragraph appears: "Approximately 47 percent in 1991 and 45 percent in 1990 of the company's total inventory is valued on a LIFO (last-in, first-out) basis. Such inventory values were lower than would have been reported on a total FIFO (first-in, first-out) basis by $104.3 million at the end of 1991 and $101.6 million at year-end 1990." LIFO inventory values $104.3 million lower than FIFO means that cost of goods sold over the years has

TABLE 5–1   Inventory Cost-Flow Assumptions Used by 600 Publicly Owned Industrial and Merchandising Corporations–1990

	Number of Companies
Methods:	
Last-in, first-out (LIFO)	366
First-in, first-out (FIFO)	411
Average cost	195
Other	44
Use of LIFO:	
All inventories	20
50% or more of inventories	186
Less than 50% of inventories	92
Not determinable	68
Companies using LIFO	366

Source: AICPA, *Accounting Trends and Techniques*, Table 2–8 (New York, 1991).

been $104.3 million higher and operating income has been $104.3 million lower than would have been the case under FIFO! To put this number in perspective, Armstrong World Industries, Inc.'s inventories at December 31, 1991, totaled $336.4 million, and retained earnings at that date totaled $1,208.7 million. The impact of LIFO on Armstrong World Industries Inc.'s financial position and results of operations has been significant, and this company is not unique (see Table 5–1). Clearly, Armstrong World Industries, Inc.'s ROI, ROE, and measures of liquidity have been impacted by the choice of inventory cost-flow assumption. Because of the impact of the inventory cost-flow assumption on a firm's measures of profitability and liquidity, the impact of this assumption must be understood if these measures are to be used effectively in making judgments and informed decisions, especially if comparisons are made between entities.

The Impact of Changing Prices (Inflation/Deflation)

It is important to understand how the inventory cost-flow assumption used by a firm interacts with the direction of cost changes to affect both inventory and cost of goods sold. In times of rising costs LIFO results in lower inventory cost and higher cost of goods sold than FIFO. These changes occur because the LIFO assumption results in most recent, and higher, costs being transferred to cost of goods sold. When purchase costs are falling, the opposite is true. These relationships are illustrated graphically in Exhibit 5–4.

The graphs in Exhibit 5–4 are helpful in understanding the relative impact on cost of goods sold and inventory when costs move in one direction. Of course, in the real world, costs rise and fall over time, and the impact of a strategy chosen during a period of rising costs will reverse when costs decline. Thus in the mid-1980s some firms that had switched to LIFO during a prior inflationary period began to experience falling costs. These firms then reported higher profits under LIFO than they would have under FIFO.

The Impact of Inventory Quantity Changes

Changes in the quantities of inventory will have an impact on profits that is dependent on the cost-flow assumption used and the extent of cost changes during the year.

Under FIFO, whether inventory quantities rise or fall, the cost of the beginning inventory is transferred to Cost of Goods Sold because the quantity of goods sold usually exceeds the quantity of beginning inventory. As previously explained, when costs are ris-

EXHIBIT 5–4 **Effect of Changing Costs on Inventory and Cost of Goods Sold under FIFO and LIFO**

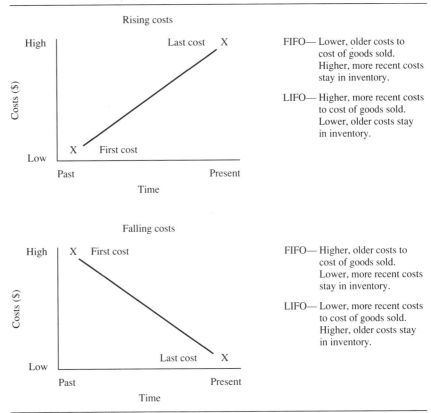

Rising costs

FIFO— Lower, older costs to cost of goods sold. Higher, more recent costs stay in inventory.

LIFO— Higher, more recent costs to cost of goods sold. Lower, older costs stay in inventory.

Falling costs

FIFO— Higher, older costs to cost of goods sold. Lower, more recent costs stay in inventory.

LIFO— Lower, more recent costs to cost of goods sold. Higher, older costs stay in inventory.

ing, costs of goods sold will be lower and profits will be higher than under LIFO. The opposite is true if costs fall during the year.

When inventory quantities rise during the year and LIFO is used, a "layer" of inventory value is added to the book value of inventories at the beginning of the year. If costs have risen during the year, LIFO results in higher cost of goods sold and lower profits than FIFO. The opposite is true if costs fall during the year.

When inventory quantities decline during the year and LIFO is used, the inventory value layers built up when inventory quantities were rising are transferred to cost of goods sold, with costs of the most recently added layer transferred first. The effect on cost of goods sold, and profits, of LIFO versus FIFO depends on the costs in each value layer relative to current costs of inventory if FIFO is used. Generally, costs have increased over time, so inventory reductions of LIFO layers result in lower cost of goods sold and higher profits than with FIFO.

In recent years many firms have sought to increase their ROI by reducing assets while maintaining or increasing sales and margin. Thus turnover (sales/average assets) is increasing, with a resulting increase in ROI. When lower assets are achieved by reducing inventories in a LIFO environment, older and lower costs are released from inventory to cost of goods sold. Since revenues reflect current selling prices, which are independent of the cost-flow assumption used, profit is higher than it would be under the FIFO cost-flow assumption when inventory quantity reductions cause older, lower LIFO costs to be included in cost of goods sold.

Selecting an Inventory Cost-Flow Assumption

What factors influence the selection of a cost-flow assumption? When rates of inflation were relatively low and the conventional wisdom was that they would always be low, most financial managers selected the FIFO cost-flow assumption because that resulted in slightly lower cost of goods sold, and hence higher net income. Financial managers have a strong motivation to report higher, rather than lower, net income to the share owners. However, when double-digit inflation was experienced, the higher net income from the FIFO assumption resulted in higher income taxes. (Federal income tax law requires that if the LIFO cost-flow assumption is used for tax purposes, it must also be used for reporting to stockholders. This tax requirement is a constraint that does not exist in other areas where alternative accounting methods exist.) Rapidly rising costs result in **inventory profits,** or **phantom profits,** when the FIFO assumption is used because the release of older, lower costs to the income statement results in higher profits than if current costs were recognized. Since taxes must be paid on these profits, and the cost of replacing the merchandise sold is considerably higher than the old cost, users of the financial statements can be misled about the firm's real economic profitability. To avoid inventory profits, many firms changed from FIFO to LIFO during the years of high inflation for at least part of their inventories. (Generally accepted accounting principles do not require that the same cost-flow assumption be used for all inventories.) This change to LIFO resulted in higher cost of goods sold than FIFO costs, and lower profits, lower taxes, and (in the opinion of some analysts) more realistic financial reporting of net income. Note, however, that even though net income may better reflect a matching of revenues (which also usually rise on a per unit basis during periods of inflation) and costs of merchandise sold, the inventory amount on the balance sheet will be reported at older, lower costs. The balance sheet will not reflect current costs for items in inventory. This is consistent with the original cost concept, and underscores the fact that balance sheet amounts do not reflect current values of most assets.

But what about consistency, the concept that requires whatever accounting alternative selected for one year be used for subsequent financial reporting? With respect to the inventory cost-flow assumption, the Internal Revenue Service permits a one-time, one-way change from FIFO to LIFO. Since tax reporting and financial reporting must be consistent in this area, firms are able to change from FIFO to LIFO for financial reporting also. However, if they do change, it is required that the effect of the change on both the balance sheet inventory amount and cost of goods sold be disclosed, so financial statement users can evaluate the impact of the change on the firm's financial position and results of operations.

Table 5–1 summarizes the methods used to determine inventory cost by 600 industrial and merchandising corporations whose annual reports are reviewed and summarized by the AICPA. It is significant that many companies use at least two methods, and that only 20 companies use LIFO for all inventories. A footnote on page 24 of the 1991 Armstrong World Industries, Inc., Annual Report in Appendix A discloses that approximately 47 percent of the company's total inventory is valued on a LIFO basis. The mix of inventory cost-flow assumptions used in practice emphasizes the complex ramifications of selecting a cost-flow assumption.

Inventory Accounting System Alternatives

The system to account for inventory cost flow is very complex in practice because most firms have hundreds or thousands of inventory items. There are two principal **inventory accounting systems:** perpetual and periodic. In a **perpetual inventory system,** a record is made of every purchase and every sale, and a continuous record of the quantity and cost of each item of inventory is maintained. Computers have made using a perpetual inventory system feasible in many organizations. In a **periodic inventory system,** a count of the inventory on hand (taking **a physical inventory**) is made periodically—frequently at the end of the fiscal year—and the cost of the inventory on hand, based on the cost-flow assumption being used, is determined and subtracted from the sum of the beginning inventory and purchases to determine the cost of goods sold. This calculation is illustrated using the following **cost of goods sold**

model using data from the FIFO cost-flow assumption of Exhibit 5–3.

Beginning inventory	$ 7,500
Purchases.	66,480
Cost of goods available for sale . . .	$73,980
Less: Ending inventory	(13,680)
Cost of goods sold.	$60,300

The examples in Exhibit 5–3 use the periodic inventory system. Although less detailed record-keeping is needed for the periodic system than for the perpetual system, the efforts involved in counting and costing the inventory on hand are still significant.

Even when a perpetual inventory system is used, it is appropriate periodically to verify that the quantity of an item shown by the perpetual inventory record to be on hand is the quantity actually on hand because errors and theft or mysterious disappearance will cause differences between these amounts. When differences are found, it is appropriate to reflect these as inventory losses, or corrections to the inventory account, as appropriate. If the losses are significant, management would probably authorize an investigation to determine the cause of the loss and develop recommendations for strengthening the system of internal control over inventories.

This discussion of accounting for inventories has focused on the products available for sale to the entity's customers. A retail firm would use the term **merchandise inventory** to describe this inventory category; a manufacturing firm would use the term **finished goods inventory.** Besides finished goods inventory, a manufacturing firm will have two other broad inventory categories: raw materials and work in process. In a manufacturing firm the **Raw Materials Inventory** account is used to hold the costs of raw materials until the materials are released to the factory floor, at which time the costs are transferred to the **Work in Process Inventory** account. Direct labor costs (wages of production workers) and factory overhead costs (e.g., factory utilities, maintenance costs for production equipment, and factory building and equipment depreciation expense) are also recorded in the Work in Process Inventory account. These costs, *incurred in making the product* as opposed to costs of selling or administering the company generally, are appropriately related to the product and become part of the product cost to be accounted for as an asset (inventory) until the product is sold, and as an expense (cost of goods sold) when the product has been sold. Accounting for production costs is a large part of cost accounting, a topic that will be explored in more detail in Chapter 12.

Inventory Errors

Errors in the amount of ending inventory have a direct dollar-for-dollar effect on cost of goods sold and net income. This direct link between inventory amounts and reported profit or loss causes independent auditors, income tax auditors, and financial analysts to look closely at reported inventory amounts. The following T-account diagram illustrates this link:

Balance Sheet / Income Statement

Inventory		**Cost of Goods Sold**	
Beginning balance			
Cost of goods purchased or manufactured	Cost of goods sold	→ Cost of goods sold	
Ending balance			

If the beginning balance of inventory, and the cost of goods purchased or manufactured are accurate, an error in the ending inventory affects cost of goods sold. For example, if the periodic inventory system is used, and ending inventory is understated, then the cost of goods sold amount (which is calculated by adding the beginning balance and the cost of goods purchased or manufactured, and subtracting the ending balance) will be overstated. Overstated cost of goods sold results in understated gross profit and net income.

The error will also affect cost of goods sold and net income of the subsequent accounting period, but in the opposite direction because one period's ending inventory is the next period's beginning inventory. Therefore, when the periodic inventory system is used, a great deal of effort is made to have the inventory count and valuation be as accurate as possible.

Balance Sheet Valuation at Lower of Cost or Market

Inventory carrying values on the balance sheet are reported at the **lower of cost or market.** This reporting is an application of accounting conservatism, and is similar to the treatment of short-term marketable securities. The "market" of lower of cost or market is generally the replacement cost of the inventory on the balance sheet date. If market value is lower than cost, then a loss is reported in the accounting period in which the inventory was acquired. The loss is recognized because the decision to buy or make the item was costly, to the extent that the item could have been bought or manufactured at the end of the accounting period for less than its original cost.

The lower-of-cost-or-market determination can be made with respect to individual items of inventory, broad categories of inventory, or to the inventory as a whole. A valuation adjustment will be made to reduce the carrying value of inventory items that have become obsolete or that have deteriorated and will not be salable at normal prices.

PREPAID EXPENSES AND OTHER CURRENT ASSETS

Other current assets are principally **prepaid expenses,** that is, expenses that have been paid in the current fiscal period but that will not be subtracted from revenue until a subsequent fiscal period. This is the opposite of an accrual, and is referred to in accounting and bookkeeping jargon as a *deferral* or *deferred charge* (or *deferred debit,* since *charge* is a bookkeeping synonym for *debit*). An example of a **deferred charge** transaction is a premium payment to an insurance company. It is standard business practice to pay an insurance premium at the beginning of the period of insurance coverage. Assume that a one-year casualty insurance premium of $1,800 is paid on November 1, 1993. At December 31, 1993, insurance coverage for two months has been received, and it is appropriate to recognize the cost of that coverage as an expense. However, the cost of coverage for the next 10 months should be deferred, that is, not shown as an expense but reported as **prepaid insurance,** an asset. Usual bookkeeping practice is to record the premium payment transaction as an increase in the Prepaid Insurance asset account, and then to transfer the expense to the Insurance Expense account as the expense is incurred. The journal entries are:

```
Nov. 1   Dr.  Prepaid Insurance . . . . . . . . . . .   1,800
              Cr.  Cash . . . . . . . . . . . . . . .          1,800
              Payment of one-year premium.
Dec. 31  Dr.  Insurance Expense . . . . . . . . . .     300
              Cr.  Prepaid Insurance . . . . . . . . .          300
              Insurance expense for two months incurred.
```

With the horizontal model, this transaction and the adjustment affect the financial statements as follows:

Balance sheet	Income statement
Assets = Liabilities + Owners' equity ←	Net income = Revenues − Expenses

Payment of premium for the year:

Cash − 1,800	
Prepaid Insurance + 1,800	

Recognition of expense for two months:

Prepaid Insurance − 300	Insurance Expense − 300

The balance in the Prepaid Insurance asset account at December 31 would be $1,500, which represents the premium for the next 10 months' coverage that has already been paid, and that will be transferred to Insurance Expense over the next 10 months.

Other expenses that could be prepaid and included in this category of current assets include rent, travel expense advances to salespeople and other employees, postage, and office supplies. The key to deferring these expenses is that they can be objectively associated with a benefit to be received in a future period. Advertising expenditures are not properly deferred because it is not possible to determine objectively how much of the benefit of advertising occurred in the current period and how much of the benefit will be received in future periods. The accountant's principal concerns are that the prepaid item be a properly deferred expense, and that it will be used up, that is, become an expense, within the one-year time frame for classification as a current asset.

SUMMARY

This chapter has discussed the accounting for and the presentation of the following balance sheet current assets and related income statement accounts:

Balance sheet	Income statement
Assets = Liabilities + Owners' equity ←	Net income = Revenues − Expenses
Cash Marketable Securities	

Balance sheet		Income statement
Assets = Liabilities + Owners' equity	←	Net income = Revenues − Expenses

Interest	Interest
Receivable	. Income
Accounts	Sales
Receivable	. Revenue
(Allowance for	Bad Debts
Bad Debts)	Expense
(Allowance for	(Cash
Cash Discounts).	Discounts)
Inventory.	Cost of
	Goods Sold
Prepaid.	Operating
Expenses	Expenses

    The amount of cash reported on the balance sheet represents the cash available to the entity as of the close of business on the balance sheet date. Cash available in bank accounts is determined by reconciling the bank statement balance with the entity's book balance. Reconciling items are caused by timing differences (such as deposits in transit, or outstanding checks) and errors.

    Petty cash funds are used as a convenience for making small disbursements of cash.

    Entities temporarily invest excess cash in short-term marketable securities in order to earn interest income. Cash managers invest in short-term, low-risk securities that are not likely to have a widely fluctuating market value. Marketable securities are reported in the balance sheet at cost unless their market value on the balance sheet date is less than cost.

    Accounts receivable are valued in the balance sheet at the amount expected to be collected. This valuation principle, as well as the matching concept, requires that the estimated losses from uncollectible accounts be recognized in the fiscal period in which the receivable arose. A valuation adjustment recognizing bad debt expense and using the Allowance for Uncollectible Accounts account is used to accomplish this. When an account receivable is determined to be uncollectible, it is written off against the allowance account.

    Firms encourage customers to pay their bills promptly by allowing a cash discount if the bill is paid within a specified period such as 10 days. Cash discounts are classified in the income statement as a deduction from sales revenue. It is appropriate to reduce accounts receivable with an allowance for cash discounts, which accomplishes the same objectives associated with the allowance for uncollectible accounts.

Organizations have a system of internal control to ensure the accuracy of the bookkeeping records and financial statements, to protect assets, to encourage adherence to management policies, and to provide for efficient operations.

Notes receivable usually have a longer term than accounts receivable, and they bear interest. The accounting for notes receivable is similar to that for accounts receivable.

Accounting for inventories involves using a cost-flow assumption, that is, assuming how costs flow from the Inventory asset account to the Cost of Goods Sold income statement account. The alternative cost-flow assumptions are specific identification; weighted average; first-in, first-out; and last-in, first-out. The cost flow will probably differ from the physical flow of the product. When price levels change, different cost-flow assumptions result in different cost of goods sold amounts in the income statement, and different inventory account balance amounts in the balance sheet. The cost-flow assumption used also influences the effect of inventory quantity changes on the balance in both cost of goods sold and the inventory accounts. Because of the significance of inventories in most balance sheets, and the direct relationship between inventory and cost of goods sold, accurate accounting for inventories must be achieved if the financial statements are to be meaningful.

Prepaid expenses (or deferred charges) arise in the accrual accounting process. To achieve an appropriate matching of revenue and expense, the expense recognition for amounts paid in a fiscal period prior to the period in which the expense should be recognized is deferred in this asset category.

Refer to the Armstrong World Industries, Inc. balance sheet in Appendix A, and to other balance sheets you may have, and observe how current assets are presented.

KEY TERMS AND CONCEPTS

administrative controls *(p. 133)* Features of the internal control system that emphasize adherence to management's policies and operating efficiency.

allowance for uncollectible accounts (or allowance for bad debts) *(p. 131)* The valuation allowance that results in accounts receivable being reduced by the amount not expected to be collected.

bad debts expense (or uncollectible accounts expense) *(p. 131)* An estimated expense, recognized in the fiscal period of the sale, representing accounts receivable that are not expected to be collected.

bank reconciliation *(p. 126)* The process of bringing into agreement the balance in the cash account in the entity's ledger and the balance reported on the bank statement.

bank service charge *(p. 127)* The fee charged by a bank for maintaining the entity's checking account.

cash discount *(p. 134)* A discount offered for prompt payment.

cash on delivery (COD) *(p. 127)* A requirement that an item be paid for when it is delivered. Sometimes COD is defined as *Collect on Delivery*.

collateral *(p. 136)* The security provided by a borrower that can be used to satisfy the obligation if payment is not made when due.

commercial paper *(p. 130)* A short-term security usually issued by a large, creditworthy corporation.

contra asset *(p. 131)* An account that normally has a credit balance and that is subtracted from a related asset on the balance sheet.

cost-flow assumption *(p. 139)* An assumption made for accounting purposes that identifies how costs flow from the inventory account to cost of goods sold. Alternatives include specific identification; weighted average; first-in, first-out; and last-in, first-out.

cost of goods sold model *(p. 147)* The way to calculate cost of goods sold when the periodic inventory system is used. The model follows:

Beginning inventory
Purchases
———————————
Cost of goods available for sale

Less: Ending inventory
———————————
Cost of goods sold

credit terms *(p. 134)* A seller's policy with respect to when payment of an invoice is due, and what cash discount (if any) is allowed.

deferred charge *(p. 150)* An expenditure made in one fiscal period that will be recognized as an expense in a future fiscal period. Another term for a *prepaid expense*.

deposit in transit *(p. 127)* A bank deposit that has been recorded in the entity's cash account but that does not appear on the bank statement because the bank received the deposit after the date of the statement.

financial controls *(p. 133)* Features of the internal control system that emphasize accuracy of bookkeeping and financial statements, and protection of assets.

finished goods inventory *(p. 148)* The term used primarily by manufacturing firms to describe inventory ready for sale to customers.

first-in, first-out (FIFO) *(p. 140)* The inventory cost-flow assumption that the first costs in to inventory are the first costs out to cost of goods sold.

imprest account *(p. 127)* An asset account that has a constant balance in the ledger that is physically composed of cash and receipts or vouchers that total the account balance. Used especially for petty cash funds.

internal control system *(p. 133)* Policies and procedures designed to:
1. Ensure the accuracy of the bookkeeping records and financial statements.
2. Protect the assets.

3. Encourage adherence to policies established by management.

4. Provide for efficient operations of the organization.

inventory accounting system *(p. 147)*   The method used to account for the movement of items in to inventory and out to cost of goods sold. The alternatives are the periodic system and the perpetual system.

inventory profits *(p. 146)*   Profits that result from using the FIFO cost-flow assumption rather than LIFO during periods of inflation. Sometimes called *phantom profits.*

last-in, first-out (LIFO) *(p. 140)*   The inventory cost-flow assumption that the last costs in to inventory are the first costs out to cost of goods sold.

lower of cost or market *(p. 149)*   A valuation process that may result in an asset being reported at an amount less than cost.

merchandise inventory *(p. 148)*   The term used primarily by retail firms to describe inventory ready for sale to customers.

note receivable *(p. 136)*   A formal document that supports the claim of one entity against another.

NSF (not sufficient funds) check *(p. 127)*   A check returned by the maker's bank because there were not enough funds in the account to cover the check.

outstanding check *(p. 127)*   A check that has been recorded as a cash disbursement by the entity, but that has not yet been processed by the bank.

periodic inventory system *(p. 147)*   A system of accounting for the movement of items in to inventory and out to cost of goods sold that involves periodically making a physical count of the inventory on hand.

perpetual inventory system *(p. 147)*   A system of accounting for the movement of items in to inventory and out to cost of goods sold that involves keeping a continuous record of items received, items sold, and inventory on hand.

petty cash *(p. 126)*   A fund used for small payments for which writing a check is inconvenient.

phantom profits *(p. 146)*   See *inventory profits.*

physical inventory *(p. 147)*   The process of counting the inventory on hand, and determining its cost based on the inventory cost-flow assumption being used.

prepaid expenses *(p. 150)*   Expenses that have been paid in the current fiscal period but that will not be subtracted from revenue until a subsequent fiscal period. Usually a current asset. Another term for *deferred charge.*

prepaid insurance *(p. 150)*   An asset account that represents an expenditure made in one fiscal period for insurance that will be recognized as an expense in the subsequent fiscal period to which the coverage applies.

raw materials inventory *(p. 148)*   Inventory of materials ready for the production process.

short-term marketable securities *(p. 129)*   Investments made with cash not needed for current operations.

specific identification *(p. 139)*   The inventory cost-flow assumption that matches cost flow with physical flow.

valuation account *(p. 134)*   An account that reduces the carrying value of an asset to a realizable value that is less than cost.

valuation adjustment *(p. 131)*   An adjustment that results in an asset being reported at a realizable value that is less than cost.

weighted average *(p. 140)*   The inventory cost-flow assumption that is based on an average of the cost of beginning inventory and the cost of purchases during the year, weighted by the quantity of items at each cost.

Work in Process Inventory *(p. 148)*   Inventory account for the costs (raw materials, direct labor, and manufacturing overhead) of items that are in the process of being manufactured.

write off *(p. 132)*   The process of removing an account receivable that is not expected to be collected from the Accounts Receivable account. Also used generically to describe the reduction of an asset and the related recognition of an expense.

EXERCISES AND PROBLEMS

5–1. Prepare a bank reconciliation as of October 31 from the following information:

   a. The October 31 cash balance in the general ledger is $844.
   b. The October 31 balance shown on the bank statement is $373.
   c. Checks issued but not returned with the bank statement were No. 462 for $13, and No. 483 for $50.
   d. A deposit made late on October 31 for $450 is included in the general ledger balance but not in the bank statement balance.
   e. Returned with the bank statement was a notice that a customer's check for $75 that had been deposited on October 25 had been returned because the customer's account was overdrawn.
   f. During a review of the checks that were returned with the bank statement, it was noted that the amount of Check No. 471 was $65, but that in the company's records supporting the general ledger balance, the check had been erroneously recorded in the amount of $56.

5–2. Prepare a bank reconciliation as of January 31 from the following information:

   a. The January 31 balance shown on the bank statement is $1,860.
   b. There is a deposit in transit of $210 at January 31.
   c. Outstanding checks at January 31 totaled $315.
   d. Interest credited to the account during January, but not recorded on the company's books, amounted to $18.
   e. A bank charge of $6 for checks was made to the account during January. Although the company was expecting a charge, its amount was not known until the bank statement arrived.
   f. In the process of reviewing the canceled checks, it was determined that

a check issued to a supplier in payment of accounts payable of $316 had been recorded as a disbursement of $361.

g. The January 31 balance in the general ledger Cash account, before reconciliation, is $1,698.

5–3. *a.* Write the adjusting journal entry (or entries) that should be prepared to reflect the reconciling items of Problem 5–1 or show the reconciling items in a horizontal model.

b. What is the amount of cash to be included in the October 31 balance sheet for the bank account reconciled in Problem 5–1?

5–4. *a.* Write the adjusting journal entry (or entries) that should be prepared to reflect the reconciling items of Problem 5–2 or show the reconciling items in a horizontal model.

b. What is the amount of cash to be included in the January 31 balance sheet for the bank account reconciled in Problem 5–2?

5–5. Marco Sales Co. has its home office in Chicago, and operates a sales branch in Denver. The firm's fiscal year ends January 31. On January 30, the Denver branch issued a check payable to the home office for $4,390 to transfer cash to the home office. On January 31, the branch reported its year-end cash balance to the home office as $1,500—its reconciled bank account balance. The home office did not receive the $4,390 from the branch until February 3, when it was deposited in the bank. The home office bank reconciliation as of January 31, on which the transfer from the branch did not appear as a reconciling item, showed a reconciled balance of $12,535.

Required: What cash balance should be reported on the January 31 balance sheet of Marco Sales Co?

5–6. Holly Corp. operates eight sales offices scattered throughout the country. Customer payments are made to the nearest sales office, and the sales office deposits receipts in a local bank account. Local account balances in excess of $1,000 are automatically transferred from the local bank accounts to the corporate account in Chicago every evening. On the evening of December 31, amounts in transit to the corporate account totaled $47,892. The reconciled balance of the corporate account as of December 31, including the amounts in transit from the regional offices, was $126,459.

Required: *a.* What is the amount of cash to be reported on Holly Corp.'s December 31 balance sheet with respect to the sales office accounts and the corporate account?

b. Why does Holly Corp. make daily transfers from the sales office accounts to the corporate account?

5–7. Find the description of the valuation of short-term investments on page 24 of the Armstrong World Industries, Inc., Annual Report in Appendix A. Under what circumstance would the short-term investments be carried (valued on the balance sheet) at less than cost? Why is the statement about market value made?

Armstrong

5–8. If you have the annual report of a company other than Armstrong World Industries, Inc., write the caption(s) used for cash and short-term securities (or cash equivalents) that is/are on the balance sheet. Search the footnotes or financial review for a reference to the short-term securities. Summarize the differences between the balance sheet presentation and footnote discussion of this annual report and Armstrong's report.

5–9. On January 1, 1993, the balance in Tabor Co.'s Allowance for Bad Debts account was $13,400. During the first 11 months of the year, bad debt expense of $21,462 was recognized. The balance in the Allowance for Bad Debts account at November 30, 1993, was $9,763.

Required:

a. What was the total of accounts written off during the first 11 months? (*Hint: Make a T-account for the Allowance for Bad Debts account.*)

b. As the result of a comprehensive analysis, it is determined that the December 31, 1993, balance of the Allowance for Bad Debts account should be $9,500. Show, in general journal format, the adjusting entry required or show the adjustment in the horizontal model.

c. During a conversation with the credit manager, one of Tabor's sales representatives learns that a $1,230 receivable from a bankrupt customer has not been written off, but it was considered in the determination of the appropriate year-end balance of the Allowance for Bad Debts account balance. Write a brief explanation to the sales representative explaining the effect that the write-off of this account receivable would have had on 1993 net income.

5–10. The following is a portion of the current asset section of the balance sheets of HiROE Co. at December 31, 1993, and 1992:

	December 31, 1993	*December 31,1992*
Accounts receivable, less allowance for uncollectable accounts of $9,000 and $3,000, respectively	151,000	117,000

Required:

a. Describe how the allowance amount at December 31, 1993, was most likely determined.

b. If bad debt expense for 1993 totaled $8,000, what was the amount of accounts receivable written off during the year? (*Hint: Use the T-account model of the allowance account, plug in the three amounts that you know, and solve for the unknown.*)

c. The December 31, 1993, Allowance account balance includes $3,500 for a past due account that is not likely to be collected. This account has *not* been written off. *If it had been written off,* what would have been the effect of the write off on:

1. Working capital at December 31, 1993?

2. Net income and ROI for the year ended December 31, 1993?

d. What do you suppose was the level of HiROE's sales in 1993, compared to 1992? Explain your answer.

e. Calculate the ratio of the Allowance for Uncollectible Accounts balance to the Accounts Receivable balance at the end of each year. What factors might have caused the change in this ratio?

5–11. Find and read "Management's Statement of Responsibility" on page 31 of the Armstrong World Industries, Inc. Annual Report in Appendix A. How do "selection and training of personnel" relate to the elements of a system of internal control identified in Business Procedure Capsule 8?

(A)rmstrong

5–12. "Management's Statement of Responsibility" on page 31 of the Armstrong World Industries, Inc. Annual Report in Appendix A refers to the Internal Audit Department and states that "a review of controls and practices to assure compliance with corporate ethical policy is performed as a part of each audit."

(A)rmstrong

Required:

a. To which of the four elements of a system of internal control identified in Business Procedure Capsule 8 does this statement relate?
b. Identify three items that might be included in Armstrong World Industries, Inc.'s corporate ethical policy.

5–13. Annual credit sales of Nadak Co. total $340 million. The firm gives a 2 percent cash discount for payment within 10 days of the invoice date; 90 percent of Nadak's accounts receivable are paid within the discount period.

Required:

a. What is the total amount of cash discounts allowed in a year?
b. If Nadak's sales are made evenly throughout the year, calculate the appropriate year-end Allowance for Cash Discounts balance. (*Hint: What is the amount of sales for the last 10 days of the year?*)
c. Calculate the approximate annual rate of return on investment that Nadak Co.'s cash discount terms represent to customers who take the discount.

5–14. *a.* Calculate the approximate annual rate of return on investment of the following cash discount terms:

1. 1/15, net 30
2. 2/10, net 60
3. 1/10, net 90

b. Which of the above terms, if any, is not likely to be a significant incentive to the customer to pay promptly? Explain your answer.

5–15. Agrico, Inc., took a 10-month, 13.8 percent (annual rate), $4,500 note from one of its customers on June 15; interest is payable with the principal at maturity.

Required:

a. Write the entry, in general journal format, to record the interest earned by Agrico during its fiscal year ended October 31.
b. Write the entry, in general journal format, to record collection of the note and interest at maturity.
(*Note: As an alternative to writing journal entries, use the horizontal model to show the interest accrual and collection.*)

5–16. Decdos Co.'s assets include notes receivable from customers. During fiscal 1993, the amount of notes receivable averaged $46,800, and the interest rate of the notes averaged 9.2 percent.

Required:

a. Calculate the amount of interest income earned by Decdos Co. during fiscal 1993, and write a journal entry that accrues the income interest earned from the notes.

b. If the balance in the Interest Receivable account increased by $1,100 from the beginning to the end of the fiscal year, how much interest receivable was collected during the fiscal year? Write the journal entry to show the collection of this amount.

(*Note: As an alternative to writing journal entries, use the horizontal model to show the interest accrual and collection.*)

5–17. Mower-Blower Sales Co. started business on January 20, 1993. Products sold were snow blowers and lawn mowers. Each product sold for $350. Purchases during 1993 were:

	Blowers	Mowers
January 21	20 @ $200	
February 3	40 @ 195	
February 28	30 @ 190	
March 13.	20 @ 190	
April 6.		20 @ $210
May 22		40 @ 215
June 3		40 @ 220
June 20		60 @ 230
August 15		20 @ 215
September 20.		20 @ 210
November 7	20 @ 200	

In inventory at December 31, 1993, were 10 blowers and 25 mowers.

Required:

a. What will be the *difference* between ending inventory valuation at December 31, 1993, and cost of goods sold for 1990, under the FIFO and LIFO cost-flow assumptions?

b. If the cost of mowers had increased to $240 each by December 1, and if management had purchased 30 mowers at that time, which cost-flow assumption is probably being used by the firm? Explain your answer.

5–18. The following data are available for Sellco for the month of January:

Sales	800 units
Beginning inventory	250 units @ $4.00
Purchases, in chronological order . .	300 units @ $5.00
	400 units @ $6.00
	200 units @ $8.00

Required:

    a. Calculate cost of goods sold and ending inventory under the following cost-flow assumptions:
      1. FIFO.
      2. LIFO.
      3. Weighted average.
    b. Assume that net income using the weighted average cost-flow assumption is $14,500. Calculate net income under FIFO and LIFO.

5–19. Many firms are adopting inventory management practices that result in reduced levels of inventory. If a firm adopted LIFO in the early 1970s or earlier, and selling prices and costs of products sold have generally risen since then, what is the income statement impact of reducing inventories? How does this income statement impact differ from that of a firm that has used FIFO since the 1970s, but that is still lowering inventory levels?

5–20. Proponents of the LIFO inventory cost-flow assumption argue that this costing method is superior to the alternatives because it results in better matching of revenue and expense.

Required:

    a. Explain why "better matching" occurs with LIFO.
    b. What is the impact on the carrying value of inventory in the balance sheet when LIFO rather than FIFO is used during periods of inflation?

5–21. Natco, Inc., uses the FIFO inventory cost-flow assumption. In a year of rising costs and prices, the firm reported net income of $120 and average assets of $600. If Natco had used the LIFO cost-flow assumption in the same year, its cost of goods sold would have been $20 more than under FIFO, and its average assets would have $20 less than under FIFO.

Required:

    a. Calculate the firm's ROI under each cost-flow assumption.
    b. Suppose that two years later costs and prices were falling. Under FIFO, net income and average assets were $130 and $650, respectively. If LIFO had been used through the years, inventory values would have been $30 less than under FIFO, and current year cost of goods sold would have been $10 less than under FIFO. Calculate the firm's ROI under each cost-flow assumption.

5–22. *a.* If the beginning balance of the Inventory account, and the cost of items purchased or made during the period are correct, but an error resulted in overstating the firm's ending inventory balance by $5,000, how would the firm's cost of goods sold be affected? Explain your answer by drawing T-accounts for Inventory and Cost of Goods Sold, and entering amounts that illustrate the difference between correctly stating and overstating the ending inventory balance.
    b. If management wanted to understate profits, would ending inventory be understated or overstated? Explain your answer.

5–23. Why are prepaid expenses reflected as an asset instead of being recorded as an expense in the accounting period in which the item is paid?

5–24. *a.* Write the journal entry to record the payment of a one-year insurance premium of $3,000 on March 1.

b. Write the adjusting entry that will be made at the end of every month to show the amount of insurance premium "used" that month.

c. Calculate the amount of prepaid insurance that should be reported on the August 31 balance sheet with respect to this policy.

d. If the premium had been $6,000 for a two-year period, theoretically, how should the prepaid amount at August 31 of the first year be reported on the balance sheet?

(*Note: As an alternative to writing journal entries, use the horizontal model to show the premium payment and monthly adjustment.*)

5–25. Prepare an answer sheet with the column headings shown below. For each of the following transactions or adjustments you are to indicate the effect of the transaction or adjustment on the appropriate balance sheet category and on net income by entering for each account affected the account name and amount, and indicating whether it is an addition (+) or a subtraction (−). Transaction *a* has been done as an illustration. Net income is *not* affected by every transaction. In some cases, only one column may be affected because all of the specific accounts affected by the transaction are included in that category.

	Current Assets	Current Liabilities	Owners' Equity	Net Income
a. Accrued interest income of $15 on a note receivable	Int. Receivable + 15			Int. Income + 15

1. Determined that the Allowance for Doubtful Accounts Balance should be increased by $2,200.
2. Recognized bank service charges of $30 for the month.
3. Received $25 cash for interest accrued in a prior month.
4. Purchased 5 units of a new item of inventory on account at a cost of $35 each.
5. Purchased 10 more units of the above item at a cost of $38 each.
6. Sold 8 of the items purchased in 4 and 5, and recognized the cost of goods sold using the FIFO cost flow assumption.

5–26. Prepare an answer sheet with the column headings shown below. For each of the following transactions or adjustments you are to indicate the effect of the transaction or adjustment on the appropriate balance sheet category and on net income by entering for each account affected the account name and amount, and indicating whether it is an addition (+) or a subtraction (−). Transaction *a* has been done as an illustration. Net income is *not* affected by every transaction. In some cases, only one column may be affected because all of the specific accounts affected by the transaction are included in that

	Current Assets	Current Liabilities	Owners' Equity	Net Income
a. Accrued interest income of $15 on a note receivable.				
	Int. Receivable + 15			Int. Income + 15

1. Determined that the Allowance for Doubtful Accounts Balance should be decreased by $1,600 because expense during the year had been overestimated.
2. Wrote off an account receivable of $720.
3. Received cash from a customer in full payment of an account receivable of $250 that was paid within the 2% discount period.
4. Purchased 8 units of a new item of inventory on account at a cost of $20 each.
5. Purchased 17 more units of the above item at a cost of $19 each.
6. Sold 20 of the items purchased in 4 and 5, and recognized the cost of goods sold using the LIFO cost flow assumption.
7. Paid an insurance premium of $240 that applied to the next fiscal year.
8. Recognized insurance expense related to the above policy during the first month of the fiscal year to which it applied.

Accounting for and Presentation of Property, Plant and Equipment, and Other Noncurrent Assets

The presentation of property, plant and equipment, and other noncurrent assets on the Consolidated Balance Sheets of Armstrong World Industries, Inc., on page 19 of Appendix A, appears straightforward. However, there are several business and accounting matters involved in understanding this presentation, and the objective of this chapter is to learn about those matters.

There are four issues related to the accounting for property, plant, and equipment. These are:

1. Accounting for the acquisition of the asset.
2. Reflecting depreciation expense.
3. Accounting for maintenance and repairs.
4. Accounting for the disposition of the asset.

Other noncurrent assets are primarily intangible, and include assets such as leaseholds, patents, trademarks, and goodwill.

LEARNING OBJECTIVES

After studying this chapter you should understand:

- How the cost of land, buildings, and equipment is reported on the balance sheet.
- The use of the terms *capitalize* and *expense,* with respect to expenditures related to property, plant and equipment.

- How depreciation is reflected in the balance sheet and in the income statement.
- Alternative methods of calculating depreciation for financial accounting purposes, and the relative effect of each on depreciation expense.
- Why depreciation for income tax purposes is an important concern of taxpayers, and how tax depreciation differs from financial accounting depreciation.
- The accounting for maintenance and repair expenditures.
- The effect on the financial statements of disposing of an asset either by abandonment, sale, or trade-in.
- The difference between an operating lease and a capital lease.
- That the financial statement effect of using a capital lease to acquire an asset is essentially the same as buying the asset, and how this occurs.
- The concept of present value.
- What intangible assets are, and how their cost is reflected in the income statement.
- The accounting for various intangible assets.
- What goodwill is when this term appears as an asset in a balance sheet.

LAND

Land owned and used in the operation of the firm is shown on the balance sheet at its original cost. Original cost is not usually difficult to determine, but if the land is acquired in a single transaction with some other assets such as a building, and both are to be used in the business, then an allocation of the purchase price of the package, based on relative appraised values, will have to be made. If land with a building on it is purchased, and the building is razed so that a new building can be built to the firm's specifications, then the cost of the land, old building, and razing (less any salvage proceeds) all become the cost of the land and are *capitalized* (see Business Procedure Capsule 10—Capitalizing versus Expensing) because all of the costs were incurred to acquire the land to be used by the firm.

Land acquired for investment purposes, or for some potential future but undefined use, is classified as a separate noncurrent and nonoperating asset. This asset is reported at its original cost. A land development company would treat land under development as inventory, and all development costs would be included in the asset carrying value. As lots are sold, the costs are transferred from inventory to cost of goods sold.

Because land is not used up, no accounting depreciation is associated with land.

When land is sold, the difference between the selling price and cost will be a gain or loss to be reported in the income statement of the period in which the sale occurred. For example, if a parcel of land on which the firm had had a plant is sold this year for a price of $140,000, and the land had cost $6,000 when it was acquired 35 years earlier, the entry would be:

```
Dr.  Cash . . . . . . . . . . . . . . . . . . . . . .   140,000
      Cr.  Land . . . . . . . . . . . . . . . . . . . .              6,000
      Cr.  Gain on Sale of Land. . . . . . . . . .            134,000
```

The effect of this transaction on the financial statements is:

Balance sheet	Income statement
Assets = Liabilities + Owners' equity ←	Net income = Revenues − Expenses
Cash	Gain on
+ 140,000	Sale of
Land	Land
− 6,000	+ 134,000

The financial statements for each of the years between purchase and sale would *not* have reflected the increasing value of the land. All of the gain is reported in the income statement of the year in which the land is sold. The gain would not be included with operating income; it would be highlighted in the income statement as a nonrecurring, nonoperating item so that financial statement users would not be led to expect a similar gain in future years.

BUILDINGS AND EQUIPMENT

Cost of Assets Acquired

Buildings and equipment are recorded at their original cost, which is the purchase price plus all the ordinary and usual costs incurred to get the building or equipment ready to use in the operations of the firm. Interest costs associated with loans used to finance the construction of a building are included in the building cost until the building is put into operation. Installation and shakedown costs (costs associated with adjusting and preparing the equipment to be used in production) incurred for a new piece of equipment should

• BUSINESS PROCEDURE CAPSULE 10
Capitalizing versus Expensing

Capitalize is the term applied to recording an expenditure as an asset. If an expenditure is recorded as an expense, it is said to have been **expensed.** Although this jargon applies to any expenditure, it is most prevalent in discussions about property, plant and equipment.

Expenditures should be capitalized if the item acquired will have an economic benefit to the entity that extends beyond the end of the current fiscal year. However, expenditures for preventative maintenance and normal repairs, even though they are needed to maintain the usefulness of the asset over a number of years, are expensed as incurred. The capitalize versus expense issue is resolved by applying the matching concept, under which costs incurred in generating revenues are subtracted from revenues in the period in which the revenues are earned.

When an expenditure is capitalized, or treated as a capital expenditure, plant assets increase, and, if the asset is depreciable—and all plant assets except land are depreciable—depreciation expense is recognized over the estimated useful life of the asset. If the expenditure is expensed, then the full cost is reflected in the current period's income statement. There is a broad gray area between expenditures that are clearly capital, and those that are obviously expenses. This gray area leads to differences of opinion that have a direct impact on the net income reported for a fiscal period.

The materiality concept (see Chapter 2) is often applied to the issue of accounting for capital expenditures.

Other factors that can influence the capitalize or expense decision are the potential income tax reduction in the current year that results from treating an expenditure as an expense, and the administrative effort involved in capitalizing and depreciating the cost of an asset. Although depreciation would be claimed, and income taxes reduced, over the life of a capitalized expenditure, many managers prefer the immediate income tax reduction that results from expensing. Many computer software programs have been developed to ease the administrative burden of depreciation calculations, so that burden is not a valid reason for failing to capitalize.

Generally speaking, most accountants will expense items that are not material. Thus the cost of a $5 wastebasket may be expensed, rather than capitalized and depreciated, even though the wastebasket clearly has a useful life of many years and should theoretically be accounted for as a capital asset. This capitalize versus expense issue is another area in which accountants' judgments can have a significant effect on an entity's financial position and results of operations. Explanations in this text will reflect sound accounting theory; recognize that in practice there may be some deviation from theory.

be capitalized. If a piece of equipment is made by a firm's own employees, all of the material, labor, and overhead costs that would be recorded as inventory costs if the machine were being made for an outside customer should be capitalized. The reason for capitalizing these costs is that they are directly related to assets that will be used by the firm over several accounting periods, and are not related just to earning revenue in the current period.

Depreciation for Financial Accounting Purposes

In financial accounting, depreciation is an application of the matching concept. To the extent that the cost of an asset is used up in the operations of the entity, that cost should be subtracted from the revenue that has been generated through the use of the asset. Depreciation is *not* an attempt to recognize a loss in market value or any difference between the original cost and replacement cost of an asset. Depreciation expense is recorded in each fiscal period with this adjusting entry:

Dr.   Depreciation Expense   xx
    Cr.   Accumulated Depreciation   xx

The effect of this adjusting entry on the financial statements is:

Balance sheet	Income statement
Assets = Liabilities + Owners' equity ←	Net income = Revenues − Expenses

− Accumulated
  Depreciation
	− Depreciation
	  Expense

Accumulated depreciation is another contra asset, and the balance in this account is the sum of all the depreciation expense that has been recorded over the life of the asset up to the balance sheet date. It is classified with the related asset on the balance sheet, as a subtraction from the cost of the asset. The difference between the cost of an asset and the accumulated depreciation on that asset is the **net book value** of the asset. The presentation of a building asset and the related accumulated depreciation in the balance sheet (using assumed amounts) is:

Building $100,000
    Less: Accumulated depreciation . . . .   (15,000)
Net book value of building . . . . $ 85,000

or:

> Building, less accumulated
> depreciation of $15,000 . . . . $ 85,000

With either presentation, the user can determine how much of the cost has been recognized as expense since the asset was acquired.

Note that cash is not involved in the depreciation expense entry. The entity's Cash account was affected when the asset was purchased, or as it is being paid for if a liability was incurred when the asset was acquired. The fact that depreciation expense does not affect cash is important in understanding the statement of cash flows, which identifies the sources and uses of a firm's cash during a fiscal period.

There are several alternative methods of calculating depreciation expense for financial accounting purposes. Each involves spreading the amount to be depreciated, which is the asset's cost minus its expected salvage value, over the asset's useful life to the entity. The depreciation method selected will not affect the total depreciation expense to be recognized over the life of the asset; however, the different methods will result in different patterns of depreciation expense by fiscal period. There are two broad categories of depreciation calculation methods: the straight-line methods and accelerated methods. Depreciation expense patterns resulting from these alternatives are illustrated in Exhibit 6–1.

The **accelerated depreciation method** results in greater depreciation expense and lower net income than straight-line depreciation during the early years of the asset's life. During the later years of

EXHIBIT 6–1   Depreciation Expense Patterns

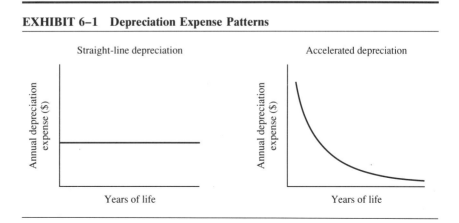

the asset's life, annual depreciation expense using accelerated methods is less than it would be using straight-line depreciation, and net income is higher.

Which method is used, and why? For purposes of reporting to stockholders most firms use the **straight-line depreciation method** because it results in lower depreciation expense, and hence higher reported net income in the early years of an asset's life, than accelerated depreciation. In later years, when accelerated depreciation is less than straight-line depreciation, total depreciation expense using the straight-line method will still be less than under an accelerated method if the amount invested in new assets has grown each year. Such a regular increase in depreciable assets is not unusual if the firm is growing, and if the prices of new and replacement equipment are rising.

The specific depreciation calculation methods are:

Straight line:
    Straight-line.
    Units of production.
Acclerated:
    Sum-of-the-years' digits.
    Declining-balance.

Each of these depreciation calculation methods is illustrated in Exhibit 6–2.

Depreciation calculations using the straight-line, units of production, and sum-of-the-years' digits methods involve determining the amount to be depreciated by subtracting the estimated salvage value from the cost of the asset. Salvage is considered in the declining-balance method only near the end of the asset's life when salvage value becomes the target for net book value.

The declining-balance calculation illustrated in Exhibit 6–2 is known as *double-declining-balance* because the depreciation rate used was double the straight-line rate. In some instances, the rate used is 1.5 times the straight-line rate; this is referred to as *150 percent declining-balance* depreciation. Whatever rate is used, it is applied to the declining balance of the net book value.

Although many firms will use a single depreciation method for all of their depreciable assets, the consistency concept is applied to the depreciation method used for a particular asset acquired in a particular year. Thus it is possible for a firm to use an accelerated depreciation method for some of its assets, and the straight-line method for other assets. Differences can even occur between similar assets purchased in the same or different years. In order to make sense of the income statement and balance sheet, it is neces-

EXHIBIT 6–2   Depreciation Calculation Methods

Assumptions:

Cruisers, Inc., purchased a molding machine at the beginning of 1992 at a cost of $22,000.

The machine is estimated to have a useful life to Cruisers, Inc., of five years, and has an estimated salvage value of $2,000.

It is estimated that the machine will produce 200 boat hulls before it is worn out.

a. Straight-line depreciation:

$$\text{Annual depreciation expense} = \frac{\text{Cost} - \text{Estimated salvage value}}{\text{Estimated useful life}}$$

$$= \frac{\$22,000 - \$2,000}{5 \text{ years}}$$

$$= \$4,000$$

Alternatively, a straight-line depreciation rate could be determined and multiplied by the amount to be depreciated.

$$\text{The straight-line depreciation rate} = \frac{1}{\text{Life}} = \frac{1}{5} = 20\%$$

Then, $20\% \times \$20,000 = \$4,000$ annual depreciation expense.

b. Units of production depreciation:

$$\text{Depreciation expense per unit produced} = \frac{\text{Cost} - \text{Estimated salvage value}}{\text{Estimated total units to be made}}$$

$$= \frac{\$22,000 - \$2,000}{200 \text{ hulls}}$$

$$= \$100$$

Each year's depreciation expense would be $100 multiplied by the number of hulls produced.

c. Sum-of-the-years'-digits depreciation:

$$\text{Annual depreciation expense} = (\text{Cost} - \text{Estimated salvage value}) \times \frac{\text{Remaining life}}{\text{Sum of digits of years of life}}$$

$$\text{1992 depreciation expense} = (\$22,000 - \$2,000) \times \frac{5 \text{ years}}{1 + 2 + 3 + 4 + 5}$$

$$= \$20,000 \times \frac{5}{15}$$

$$= \$6,667$$

(continued)

EXHIBIT 6–2 (*continued*)

Subsequent years' depreciation expense:

$$1993 \ldots \$20,000 \times \frac{4}{15} = \$5,333$$

$$1994 \ldots \$20,000 \times \frac{3}{15} = 4,000$$

$$1995 \ldots \$20,000 \times \frac{2}{15} = 2,667$$

$$1996 \ldots \$20,000 \times \frac{1}{15} = 1,333$$

Total depreciation expense over 5 years = \$20,000

d. **Declining-balance depreciation:**

Annual depreciation expense = Double the straight-line depreciation rate ×
Asset's net book value at beginning of year

$$\text{The straight-line depreciation rate} = \frac{1}{\text{life in years}}$$

$$= \frac{1}{5}$$

$$= 20\%$$

Double the straight-line depreciation rate is 40 percent.

Year	Net Book Value at Beginning of Year		Factor	Depreciation Expense for the Year	Accumulated Depreciation	Net Book Value at End of Year
1992		$22,000	× 0.4 =	$8,800	$ 8,800	$13,200
1993		13,200	× 0.4 =	5,280	14,080	7,920
1994		7,920	× 0.4 =	3,168	17,248	4,752
1995		4,752	× 0.4 =	1,901	19,149	2,851
1996		2,851	× 0.4 =	851*	20,000	2,000

* Depreciation expense at the end of the asset's life is equal to an amount that will cause the net book value to equal the asset's estimated salvage value.

Recap of depreciation expense by year by method:

Year	Straight-Line	Sum-of-the-Years' Digits	Declining Balance
1992	$ 4,000	$ 6,667	$ 8,800
1993	4,000	5,333	5,280
1994	4,000	4,000	3,168
1995	4,000	2,667	1,901
1996	4,000	1,333	851
Total	$20,000	$20,000	$20,000

EXHIBIT 6–2 *(concluded)*

Note that the total depreciation expense for the five years is the same for each method; it is the pattern of the expense that differs. Since depreciation is an expense, the effect on operating income of the alternative methods will be opposite; that is, 1992 operating income will be highest if the straight-line method is used, and lowest if the declining-balance method is used.

sary to find out from the footnotes to the financial statements just how depreciation has been calculated.

The estimates made of useful life and salvage value are educated guesses to be sure, but accountants, frequently working with engineers, are able to estimate these factors with great accuracy. A firm's experience and equipment replacement practices are considered in the estimating process.

There are a number of technical accounting challenges to be considered when calculating depreciation in practice. These include part-year depreciation for assets acquired during a year, changes in estimated salvage value and/or useful life after the asset has been depreciated for some time, and asset grouping to facilitate the depreciation calculation. These are beyond the scope of this text; your task is to understand the basic calculation procedures and the different effect of each on both depreciation expense in the income statement and accumulated depreciation (and net book value) on the balance sheet.

Depreciation for Income Tax Purposes

Depreciation is a deductible expense for income tax purposes. Although depreciation expense does not directly affect cash, it does reduce taxable income. Therefore, most firms would like to have deductible depreciation expense as large an amount as possible because this would mean lower taxable income and lower taxes payable. The Internal Revenue Code has permitted taxpayers to use an accelerated depreciation calculation method for many years. Estimated useful life is generally the most significant factor (other than calculation method) affecting the amount of depreciation expense, and for many years this was a contentious issue between taxpayers and the Internal Revenue Service.

In 1981 the Internal Revenue Code was amended to permit use of the **Accelerated Cost Recovery System (ACRS),** frequently pronounced "acres," for depreciable assets put in service after 1980. The effects of ACRS were to simplify useful life determination and achieve a rapid write-off having a pattern similar to that for accelerated depreciation, so most firms started using ACRS for tax purposes. Unlike the LIFO inventory cost-flow assumption (which, if selected, must be used for both financial reporting and income tax determination purposes), there is no requirement that "book" (i.e., financial statement) and tax depreciation calculation methods be the same. Most firms continued to use straight-line depreciation for book purposes.

ACRS used relatively short, and arbitrary, useful lives, and ignored salvage value. The intent was more to permit relatively quick "cost recovery" and thus encourage investment, than it was to recognize traditional depreciation expense. For example, ACRS permitted the write-off of most machinery and equipment over three to five years.

However, in the Tax Reform Act of 1986, Congress changed the original ACRS provisions. The system is now referred to as the **Modified Accelerated Cost Recovery System (MACRS).** Recovery periods were lengthened, additional categories for classifying assets were created, and the method of calculating the depreciation deduction was specified. Cost recovery periods are specified based on the type of asset and its class life defined by the Internal Revenue Service. Most machinery and equipment is depreciated using the double-declining-balance method, but the 150% declining-balance method is required for some longer lived assets, and the straight-line method is specified for buildings.

The use of ACRS for book depreciation was discouraged because of the arbitrarily short lives involved. MACRS lives are closer to actual useful lives, but basing depreciation expense for financial accounting purposes on tax law provisions, which are subject to frequent change, is not appropriate.

Maintenance and Repair Expenditures

Preventative maintenance expenditures and routine repair costs are clearly expenses of the period in which they are incurred. There is a gray area with respect to some maintenance expenditures, however, and accountants' judgments may differ. If a maintenance expenditure will extend the useful life or salvage value of an asset beyond those used in the depreciation calculation, it is appropriate that the expenditure be capitalized, and that the new net book value of the asset be depreciated over the asset's remaining useful life.

In practice, most accountants will decide in favor of expensing rather than capitalizing for several reasons. To revise the depreciation calculation data is frequently time-consuming, with little perceived benefit. Because depreciation involves estimates of useful life and salvage value to begin with, revising those estimates without overwhelming evidence that they are significantly in error is an exercise of questionable value. For income tax purposes, most taxpayers would rather have a deductible expense now (expensing) rather than later (capitalizing and depreciating).

Because of the possibility that net income could be affected either favorably or unfavorably by inconsistent judgments about the accounting for repair and maintenance expenditures, auditors (internal and external) and the Internal Revenue Service usually look closely at these expenditures when they are reviewing the firm's reported results.

Disposal of Depreciable Assets

When a depreciable asset is sold or scrapped, both the asset and accumulated depreciation accounts must be reduced by the appropriate amounts. For example, throwing out a fully depreciated piece of equipment, for which no salvage value had been estimated, would result in the following entry:

```
Dr.  Accumulated Depreciation . . . . . . . . . . . . .    xx
      Cr.  Equipment . . . . . . . . . . . . . . . . . .          xx
```

Note that this entry does not affect *total* assets, or any other parts of the financial statements.

Balance sheet	Income statement
Assets = Liabilities + Owners' equity ← Net income = Revenues − Expenses
− Equipment
+ Accumulated
Depreciation

When the asset being disposed of has a positive net book value, either because a salvage value was estimated, or because it has not reached the end of its estimated useful life to the firm, a gain or loss on the disposal will result unless the asset is sold for a price that is equal to the net book value. For example, if equipment that cost $6,000 new has a net book value equal to its estimated salvage value of $900, and is sold for $1,200, the following entry will result:

```
Dr.  Cash. . . . . . . . . . . . . . . . . . . . .    1,200
Dr.  Accumulated Depreciation . . . . . . . . . .    5,100*
     Cr.  Equipment . . . . . . . . . . . . . . .              6,000
     Cr.  Gain on Sale of Equipment. . . . . . . .              300
     Sold equipment.
```

        * Net book value = Cost − Accumulated depreciation
                      900 = 6,000 − Accumulated depreciation
        Accumulated depreciation = 5,100

The effect of this entry on the financial statements is:

Balance sheet	Income statement
Assets = Liabilities + Owners' equity ←	Net income = Revenues − Expenses
Cash	Gain on
+1,200	Sale
Accumulated	+ 300
Depreciation	
+ 5,100	
Equipment	
− 6,000	

Alternatively, assume that the above equipment had to be scrapped without any salvage value. The entry would be:

```
Dr.  Accumulated Depreciation  . . . . . . . . . . .    5,100
Dr.  Loss on Disposal of Equipment . . . . . . . .       900
     Cr.  Equipment  . . . . . . . . . . . . . . . .              6,000
     Scrapped equipment.
```

The effect of this entry on the financial statements is:

Balance sheet	Income statement
Assets = Liabilities + Owners' equity ←	Net income = Revenues − Expenses
Accumulated	Loss on
Depreciation	Disposal
+ 5,100	− 900
Equipment	
− 6,000	

The gain or loss on the disposal of a depreciable asset is in effect a correction of the depreciation expense that has been recorded over the life of the asset. If salvage value and useful life estimates had been correct, the net book value of the asset would be equal to the proceeds (if any) received from its sale or disposal. Depreciation expense is never adjusted retroactively, so the significance of these gains or losses gives the financial statement user a basis for judging the accuracy of the accountant's estimates of salvage value and useful life. Gains or losses on the disposal of depreciable assets are not part of the operating income of the entity. If significant, they will be reported separately as elements of other income or expense. If not material, they will be reported with miscellaneous other income.

Frequently an old asset is traded in on a similar new asset. In this kind of transaction a trade-in allowance is determined by the seller of the new equipment. The trade-in allowance is then subtracted from the list price of the new asset to determine the amount of cash to be paid for it. Assume that you have an old car to trade in on a new one. Which is more important to you —the trade-in allowance on the old car or the amount you have to pay to get the new car? Clearly, it is the amount you have to pay. If you focused on the trade-in allowance, an unscrupulous dealer could offer a trade-in allowance much greater than the market value of your old car, and then work from a list price that had been inflated by an even larger amount. Because of the lack of objectivity that frequently applies to a trade-in allowance, using the trade-in allowance as if it were the same thing as the proceeds from a sale of the asset could lead to a fictitious gain or loss. For income tax purposes a trade-in transaction results in neither a gain nor a loss to the entity trading in an old asset and acquiring a new asset. Generally accepted accounting principles provide for recognizing a loss, but not a gain, on a trade-in transaction (accounting conservatism). When no gain or loss is recognized, the cost of the new asset becomes the net book value of the old asset, plus the cash (or "boot," as in "I got the new car for my old car and $3,000 to boot.") paid or liability assumed in the transaction. The new asset cost, less estimated salvage value, will be depreciated over the estimated useful life to the entity of the new asset. Accounting for a trade-in transaction is illustrated in Exhibit 6–3.

If the trade-in transaction involves dissimilar assets, both generally accepted accounting principles and the Internal Revenue Code consider two transactions to have occurred: the "sale" of the old asset and the purchase of a new asset. Thus a gain or loss is recognized on the sale of the old asset, with the trade-in allowance being considered the proceeds from the sale. The cost of the new asset is the fair market value of the old asset plus the cash paid and/ or liability incurred.

EXHIBIT 6–3   Trade-in Transaction Accounting

Assumptions:

The cost of the old car was $9,300.

Accumulated depreciation on the old car is $8,100.

The new car list price is $12,800; a $2,600 trade-in allowance is given.

The buyer is going to pay $1,500 cash and sign a note for the balance due to the new car dealer.

The entry to record this trade-in transaction is:

Dr.	Accumulated Depreciation (on old car)	8,100	
Dr.	Automobiles (cost of new car)	11,400	
	Cr. Automobiles (cost of old car)		9,300
	Cr. Cash		1,500
	Cr. Note payable		8,700

Trade of old car for new car.

The effect of this transaction on the financial statements is shown below. Notice that the income statement is not affected.

Balance sheet	Income statement

Assets = Liabilities + Owners' equity ←	Net income = Revenues − Expenses

Accumulated   Note
Depreciation   Payable
(on old car)   + 8,700
+ 8,100

New Car cost
+ 11,400

Old Car cost
− 9,300

Cash
− 1,500

Recap of amounts:

New car list price	$12,800
Old car trade-in allowance	2,600
Amount required by buyer	$10,200
Amount paid in cash	1,500
Amount of note payable	$ 8,700
Net book value of old car ($9,300–$8,100)	$ 1,200
Amount required from buyer to get new car (boot)	10,200
Cost of new car	$11,400

ASSETS ACQUIRED BY CAPITAL LEASE

Many firms will lease, or rent, assets rather than purchase them. There are two broad categories of leases: operating leases and capital leases.

Operating leases are ordinary, frequently short-term, leases that do not involve any attributes of ownership. Assets rented under an operating lease are not reflected on the lessee's (renter's) balance sheet, and the rent expense involved is reported in the income statement as an operating expense.

A **capital lease** results in the lessee (renter) assuming virtually all of the benefits and risks of ownership of the leased asset. A lease is a capital lease if it has any of the following characteristics:

1. It transfers ownership of the asset to the lessee.
2. It permits the lessee to purchase the asset for a nominal sum at the end of the lease period.
3. The lease term is at least 75 percent of the economic life of the asset.
4. The **present value** (see Business Procedure Capsule 11) of the lease payments is at least 90 percent of the fair value of the asset.

The economic impact of a capital lease isn't really any different from buying the asset outright and signing a note payable that will be paid off, with interest, over the life of the asset. Therefore it is appropriate that the asset and related liability be reflected in the lessee's balance sheet. In the lessee's income statement the cost of the leased asset will be reflected as depreciation expense, rather than rent expense, and the financing cost will be shown as interest expense.

Prior to an FASB standard issued in 1976, many companies did not record assets acquired under a capital lease, because they did not want to reflect the related lease liability in their balance sheet. This practice was known as *off-balance-sheet financing,* and was deemed inappropriate because the full disclosure concept was violated.

Assets acquired by capital lease are included with purchased assets on the balance sheet. The amount recorded as the cost of the asset involved in a capital lease, and as the related lease liability, is the present value of the lease payments to be made, based on the interest rate used by the lessor to determine the periodic lease payments. The effects of a capital lease on the financial statements are:

Balance sheet	Income statement
Assets = Liabilities + Owners' equity ←	Net income = Revenues − Expenses

1. Date of Acquisition
+ Equipment   + Capital
            Lease Liability

2. Annual Depreciation Expense:
− Accumulated   − Depreciation
   Depreciation   Expense

3. Annual Lease Payment:
− Cash   − Capital   − Interest
              Lease Liability   Expense

The first effect shows the asset acquisition and the related financial obligation that has been incurred. The second effect shows depreciation expense in the same way it is recorded for purchased assets. The third effect shows the lease payment effect on cash, reflects the interest expense for the year on the amount that has been borrowed, in effect, from the lessor, and reduces the lease liability by what is really a payment on the principal of the loan from the lessor.

To illustrate the equivalence of capital lease payments and a loan, assume that a firm purchased a computer system at a cost of $217,765, and borrowed the money by giving a note payable that had an annual interest rate of 10 percent and that required payments of $50,000 per year for six years. The purchase would be recorded using the following entry:

```
Dr.  Computer Equipment. . . . . . . . . . .   217,765
     Cr.  Note Payable . . . . . . . . . . . .           217,765
```

Using the horizontal model, the following is the effect on the financial statements:

Balance sheet	Income statement
Assets = Liabilities + Owners' equity ←	Net income = Revenues − Expenses

Computer   Note
Equipment   Payable
+ 217,765   + 217,765

• BUSINESS PROCEDURE CAPSULE 11
Present Value

Organizations and individuals are frequently confronted with the choice of paying for a purchase today, or at a later date. Intuition suggests that all other things being equal, it would be better to pay later, because in the meantime the cash could be invested to earn interest. This reflects the fact that money has value over time. Of course, other things aren't always equal, and sometimes the choice is between paying one amount—say $100—today, and a larger amount—say $110—a year later. Or in the opposite case, the choice may be between receiving $100 today or $110 a year from now. Present value analysis is used to determine which date alternative is financially preferable.

The present value concept is an application of compound interest—the process of earning interest on interest. If $1,000 is invested in a savings account earning interest at the rate of 10 percent compounded annually, and if the account is left alone for four years, the results shown in the following table will occur:

Year	Principal at Beginning of Year	Interest Earned at 10 Percent	Principal at End of Year
1	$1,000	$100	$1,100
2	1,100	110	1,210
3	1,210	121	1,331
4	1,331	133	1,464

This is an example of future value, and most of us think of a future amount when we think about compound interest. That is, we understand that the future value of $1,000 invested for four years at 10 percent interest compounded annually is $1,464. This relationship can be illustrated on a time line as follows:

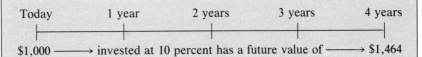

Today   1 year   2 years   3 years   4 years

$1,000 ———→ invested at 10 percent has a future value of ———→ $1,464

(There is a formula for calculating future value, and there are tables of future value factors. Many computer program packages include a future value function.)

Present value involves looking at the same compound interest concept from a different perspective. Using data in the above table, you can say that the present value of $1,464 to be received four years from now, assuming an interest rate of 10 percent compounded annually, is $1,000. On a time-line

(continued)

representation, the direction of the arrow representing the time perspective is reversed.

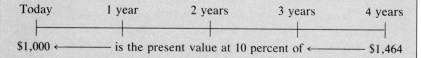

| Today | 1 year | 2 years | 3 years | 4 years |

$1,000 ⟵——— is the present value at 10 percent of ⟵——— $1,464

That is, if someone owed you $1,464 to be paid four years from now, and if you and that person agreed that 10 percent was a fair interest rate for that period of time, both you and your debtor would be satisfied to settle the debt for $1,000 today. Or, alternatively, if you owed $1,464 payable four years from now, both you and your creditor would be satisfied to settle the debt for $1,000 today (still assuming agreement on the 10 percent interest rate). That is because $1,000 invested at 10 percent interest compounded annually will be $1,464 in four years. Stated differently, the future value of $1,000 at 10 percent interest in four years is $1,464, and the present value of $1,464 in four years at 10 percent is $1,000.

Present value analysis involves determining the present amount that is equivalent to an amount to be paid or received in the future. Present value analysis recognizes that money does have value over time, and that that value is represented by the interest that can be earned on money. In present value analysis **discount rate** is a term frequently used for *interest rate*. Thus in the above example, the present value of $1,464, discounted at 10 percent for four years, is $1,000.

Present value analysis does not recognize inflation, although inflationary expectations will influence the discount rate used in the present value calculation. Generally, the higher the inflationary expectations, the higher the discount rate used in present value analysis.

The above example deals with the present value of a single amount to be received or paid in the future. Some transactions involve receiving or paying the same amount each period for a number of periods. This sort of receipt or payment pattern is an **annuity.** The present value of an annuity is simply the sum of the present value of each of the annuity payment amounts.

There are formulas and computer program functions for calculating the present value of a single amount and the present value of an annuity. In all cases the amount to be received or paid in the future, the discount rate, and the number of years (or other time periods) are used in the present value calculation. Table 6–1 presents factors for calculating the present value of $1, and Table 6–2 gives the factors for the present value of an annuity of $1 for several discount rates and for a number of periods. To find the present value of any amount, the appropriate factor from the table is multiplied by the amount to be received or paid in the future. Using the data from the initial example described above, we can calculate the present value of

(*continued*)

$1,464 to be received four years from now, based on a discount rate of 10 percent, as:

$1,464 × 0.6830 (from the 10 percent column, four-period row of
Table 6–1) = $1,000 (rounded)

What is the present value of a lottery prize of $3,200,000, payable in 20 annual installments of $160,000 each, assuming a discount (interest) rate of 12 percent? The time-line representation of this situation is:

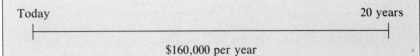

The present value of this annuity is calculated by multiplying the annuity amount ($160,000) by the annuity factor from Table 6–2. The solution:

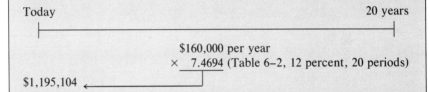

The answer of $1,195,104 shouldn't make the winner feel less wealthy; but it does mean that the lottery authority needs to deposit today in an account earning 12 percent interest only the amount of $1,195,104 in order to be able to pay the winner $160,000 a year for 20 years beginning a year from now because interest will be earned each year on the balance of the deposit.

Let's look at another example calculation. Assume that you have accepted a job from a company willing to pay you a signing bonus. You must choose the bonus plan you want. The plan A bonus is $3,000 payable today. The plan B bonus is $4,000 payable three years from today. The plan C bonus is three annual payments of $1,225 each (an annuity) with the first payment to be made one year from today. Assuming a discount rate of 8 percent, which bonus should you accept? The solution requires calculation of the present value of each bonus. Using the time-line approach:

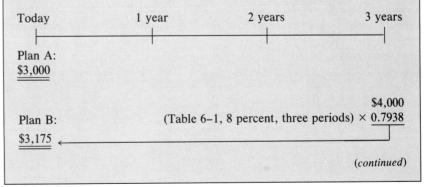

(continued)

TABLE 6-1 **Factors for Calculating the Present Value of $1**

No. of Periods	4%	6%	8%	10%	12%	14%	16%	18%	20%	22%
1	0.9615	0.9434	0.9259	0.9091	0.8929	0.8772	0.8621	0.8475	0.8333	0.8197
2	0.9246	0.8900	0.8573	0.8264	0.7972	0.7695	0.7432	0.7182	0.6944	0.6719
3	0.8890	0.8396	0.7938	0.7513	0.7118	0.6750	0.6407	0.6086	0.5787	0.5507
4	0.8548	0.7921	0.7350	0.6830	0.6355	0.5921	0.5523	0.5158	0.4823	0.4514
5	0.8219	0.7473	0.6806	0.6209	0.5674	0.5194	0.4761	0.4371	0.4019	0.3700
6	0.7903	0.7050	0.6302	0.5645	0.5066	0.4556	0.4104	0.3704	0.3349	0.3033
7	0.7599	0.6651	0.5835	0.5132	0.4523	0.3996	0.3538	0.3139	0.2791	0.2486
8	0.7307	0.6274	0.5403	0.4665	0.4039	0.3506	0.3050	0.2660	0.2326	0.2038
9	0.7026	0.5919	0.5002	0.4241	0.3606	0.3075	0.2630	0.2255	0.1938	0.1670
10	0.6756	0.5584	0.4632	0.3855	0.3220	0.2697	0.2267	0.1911	0.1615	0.1369
11	0.6496	0.5268	0.4289	0.3505	0.2875	0.2366	0.1954	0.1619	0.1346	0.1122
12	0.6246	0.4970	0.3971	0.3186	0.2567	0.2076	0.1685	0.1372	0.1122	0.0920
13	0.6006	0.4688	0.3677	0.2897	0.2292	0.1821	0.1452	0.1163	0.0935	0.0754
14	0.5775	0.4423	0.3405	0.2633	0.2046	0.1597	0.1252	0.0985	0.0779	0.0618
15	0.5553	0.4173	0.3152	0.2394	0.1827	0.1401	0.1079	0.0835	0.0649	0.0507
16	0.5339	0.3936	0.2919	0.2176	0.1631	0.1229	0.0930	0.0708	0.0541	0.0415
17	0.5134	0.3714	0.2703	0.1978	0.1456	0.1078	0.0802	0.0600	0.0451	0.0340
18	0.4936	0.3503	0.2502	0.1799	0.1300	0.0946	0.0691	0.0508	0.0376	0.0279
19	0.4746	0.3305	0.2317	0.1635	0.1161	0.0829	0.0596	0.0431	0.0313	0.0229
20	0.4564	0.3118	0.2145	0.1486	0.1037	0.0728	0.0514	0.0365	0.0261	0.0187
21	0.4388	0.2942	0.1987	0.1351	0.0926	0.0638	0.0443	0.0309	0.0217	0.0154
22	0.4220	0.2775	0.1839	0.1228	0.0826	0.0560	0.0382	0.0262	0.0181	0.0126
23	0.4057	0.2618	0.1703	0.1117	0.0738	0.0491	0.0329	0.0222	0.0151	0.0103
24	0.3901	0.2470	0.1577	0.1015	0.0659	0.0431	0.0284	0.0188	0.0126	0.0085
25	0.3751	0.2330	0.1460	0.0923	0.0588	0.0378	0.0245	0.0160	0.0105	0.0069
30	0.3083	0.1741	0.0994	0.0573	0.0334	0.0196	0.0116	0.0070	0.0042	0.0026
35	0.2534	0.1301	0.0676	0.0356	0.0189	0.0102	0.0055	0.0030	0.0017	0.0009
40	0.2083	0.0972	0.0460	0.0221	0.0107	0.0053	0.0026	0.0013	0.0007	0.0004
45	0.1712	0.0727	0.0313	0.0137	0.0061	0.0027	0.0013	0.0006	0.0003	0.0001
50	0.1407	0.0543	0.0213	0.0085	0.0035	0.0014	0.0006	0.0003	0.0001	0.0000

TABLE 6–2   Factors for Calculating the Present Value of an Annuity of $1

No. of Periods	4%	6%	8%	10%	12%	14%	16%	18%	20%	22%
1	0.9615	0.9434	0.9259	0.9091	0.8929	0.8772	0.8621	0.8475	0.8333	0.8197
2	1.8861	1.8334	1.7833	1.7355	1.6901	1.6467	1.6052	1.5656	1.5278	1.4915
3	2.7751	2.6730	2.5771	2.4869	2.4018	2.3216	2.2459	2.1743	2.1065	2.0422
4	3.6299	3.4651	3.3121	3.1699	3.0373	2.9137	2.7982	2.6901	2.5887	2.4936
5	4.4518	4.2124	3.9927	3.7908	3.6048	3.4331	3.2743	3.1272	2.9906	2.8636
6	5.2421	4.9173	4.6229	4.3553	4.1114	3.8887	3.6847	3.4976	3.3255	3.1669
7	6.0021	5.5824	5.2064	4.8684	4.5638	4.2883	4.0386	3.8115	3.6046	3.4155
8	6.7327	6.2098	5.7466	5.3349	4.9676	4.6389	4.3436	4.0776	3.8372	3.6193
9	7.4353	6.8017	6.2469	5.7590	5.3282	4.9464	4.6065	4.3030	4.0310	3.7863
10	8.1109	7.3601	6.7101	6.1446	5.6502	5.2161	4.8332	4.4941	4.1925	3.9232
11	8.7605	7.8869	7.1390	6.4951	5.9377	5.4527	5.0286	4.6560	4.3271	4.0354
12	9.3851	8.3838	7.5361	6.8137	6.1944	5.6603	5.1971	4.7932	4.4392	4.1274
13	9.9856	8.8527	7.9038	7.1034	6.4235	5.8424	5.3423	4.9095	4.5327	4.2028
14	10.5631	9.2950	8.2442	7.3667	6.6282	6.0021	5.4675	5.0081	4.6106	4.2646
15	11.1184	9.7122	8.5595	7.6061	6.8109	6.1422	5.5755	5.0916	4.6755	4.3152
16	11.6523	10.1059	8.8514	7.8237	6.9740	6.2651	5.6685	5.1624	4.7296	4.3567
17	12.1657	10.4773	9.1216	8.0216	7.1196	6.3729	5.7487	5.2223	4.7746	4.3908
18	12.6593	10.8276	9.3719	8.2014	7.2497	6.4674	5.8178	5.2732	4.8122	4.4187
19	13.1339	11.1581	9.6036	8.3649	7.3658	6.5504	5.8775	5.3162	4.8435	4.4415
20	13.5903	11.4699	9.8181	8.5136	7.4694	6.6231	5.9288	5.3527	4.8696	4.4603
21	14.0292	11.7641	10.0168	8.6487	7.5620	6.6870	5.9731	5.3837	4.8913	4.4756
22	14.4511	12.0416	10.2007	8.7715	7.6446	6.7429	6.0113	5.4099	4.9094	4.4882
23	14.8568	12.3034	10.3711	8.8832	7.7184	6.7921	6.0442	5.4321	4.9245	4.4985
24	15.2470	12.5504	10.5288	8.9847	7.7843	6.8351	6.0726	5.4509	4.9371	4.5070
25	15.6221	12.7834	10.6748	9.0770	7.8431	6.8729	6.0971	5.4669	4.9476	4.5139
30	17.2920	13.7648	11.2578	9.4269	8.0552	7.0027	6.1772	5.5168	4.9789	4.5338
35	18.6646	14.4982	11.6546	9.6442	8.1755	7.0700	6.2153	5.5386	4.9915	4.5411
40	19.7928	15.0463	11.9246	9.7791	8.2438	7.1050	6.2335	5.5482	4.9966	4.5439
45	20.7200	15.4558	12.1084	9.8628	8.2825	7.1232	6.2421	5.5523	4.9986	4.5449
50	21.4822	15.7619	12.2335	9.9148	8.3045	7.1327	6.2463	5.5541	4.9995	4.5452

Plan C: $1,225 per year for three years
                   ×2.5771 (Table 6–2, 8 percent, three periods)
$3,157 ←

Bonus plan B has the highest present value, and for that reason would be the plan selected based on present value analysis.

The frequency with which interest is compounded affects both future value and present value. You would prefer to have the interest on your savings account compounded monthly, weekly, or even daily, rather than annually, because you will earn more interest the more frequently compounding occurs. This is recognized in present value calculations by converting the annual discount rate to a discount rate per compounding period by dividing the annual rate by the number of periods per year. Likewise, the number of periods is adjusted by multiplying the number of years involved by the number of compounding periods per year. For example, the present value of $1,000 to be received or paid six years from now, at a discount rate of 18 percent compounded annually, is $370.40 (the factor 0.3704 from the 18 percent column, six-period row, multiplied by $1,000). If interest were compounded every four months, or three times per year, the present value calculation uses the factor from the 6 percent (18 percent per year/three periods per year) column, 18-period (six years × three periods per year) row, which is 0.3503. The present value of $1,000 to be received or paid in six years, but with compounding every four months, is $350.03. Using the time-line approach:

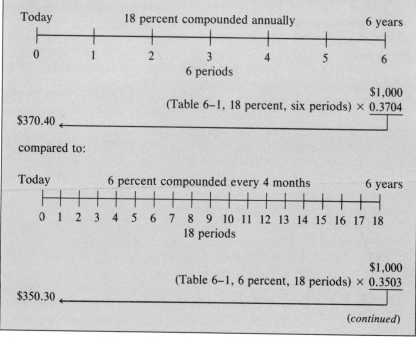

compared to:

(continued)

You can make sense of the fact that the present value of a single amount is lower the more frequent the compounding by visualizing what you could do with either $370.40 or $350.03 if you were to receive the amount today rather than $1,000 in six years. Each amount could be invested at 18 percent, but interest would compound on the $370.40 only once a year, and you would have $1,000 after six years. However, interest on the $350.03 would compound every four months, so even though you start with a lower amount, you'll still have $1,000 after six years. Test your comprehension of this calculation process by verifying that the present value of an annual annuity of $100 for 10 years, discounted at an annual rate of 16 percent is $483.32, and that the present value of $50 paid every six months for 10 years, discounted at the same annual rate (which is an 8 pecent semiannual rate) is $490.91. (The present value of an annuity is greater the more frequent the compounding because the annuity amount is paid sooner than when the compounding period is longer.)

There are several applications of present value to business transactions, and some of these will be illustrated in subsequent chapters. An investment of time now in understanding this concept will be rewarded with quicker understanding later.

Each year the firm will accrue and pay interest expense on the note, and make principal payments, as shown in the following table:

Year	Principal Balance at Beginning of Year	Interest at 10 percent	Payment Applied to Principal ($50,000—Interest)	Principal Balance at End of Year
1 . .	$217,765	$21,776	$28,224	$189,541
2 . .	189,541	18,954	31,046	158,495
3 . .	158,495	15,849	34,151	124,344
4 . .	124,344	12,434	37,566	86,778
5 . .	86,778	8,677	41,323	45,455
6 . .	45,455	4,545	45,455	–0–

After six years, the note will have been fully paid.

If the firm were to lease the computer system and agree to make annual lease payments of $50,000 for six years, instead of borrowing the money and buying the computer system outright, the financial statements should reflect the transaction in essentially the same way. This will happen because the present value of all of the lease payments (which include principal and interest) is $217,765.

(From Table 6–2, in the 10 percent column and six-period row, the factor is 4.3553. This factor multiplied by the $50,000 annual lease payment is $217,765.) The entry at the beginning of the lease will be:

Dr. Computer Equipment.   217,765
    Cr. Capital Lease Liability   217,765

Using the horizontal model, the following is the effect on the financial statements:

Balance sheet		Income statement

Assets = Liabilities + Owners' equity ← Net income = Revenues − Expenses

Computer	Capital
Equipment	Lease
+ 217,765	Liability
	+ 217,765

Each year the principal portion of the lease payment will reduce the capital lease liability, and the interest portion will be recognized as an expense. In addition, the computer equipment will be depreciated each year. Thus liabilities on the balance sheet and expenses in the income statement will be the same as under the borrow and purchase alternative.

Again, the significance of capital lease accounting is that the economic impact of capital leasing isn't really any different from buying the asset outright; the impact on the financial statements shouldn't differ either.

INTANGIBLE ASSETS

Intangible assets are long-lived assets that differ from property, plant and equipment that has been purchased outright or acquired under a capital lease, either because the asset is represented by a contractual right, or because the asset results from a purchase transaction but is not physically identifiable. Examples of the first type of intangible asset are leaseholds, patents, and trademarks; the second type of intangible asset is known as *goodwill*.

Just as the cost of plant and equipment is transferred to expense over time through accounting depreciation, the cost of most intangibles also becomes expense over time. **Amortization,** which means spreading an amount over time, is the term used to describe the spreading of the cost of an intangible asset to the income statement. The cost of tangible assets is depreciated; the cost of intangible assets is amortized. The terms are different but the process is the same. Most intangibles are amortized on a straight-line basis based on useful life to the entity. Although an Accumulated Amortization account is sometimes used, amortization expense is usually recorded as a reduction in the carrying value of the related intangible asset. Thus, periodic amortization would be recorded as follows:

Dr. Amortization Expense.   xx
    Cr. Intangible Asset.   xx

The effect of this entry on the financial statements is:

Balance sheet	Income statement
Assets = Liabilities + Owners' equity	← Net income = Revenues − Expenses
− Intangible	− Amortization
Asset	Expense

Amortization expense is usually included with depreciation expense in the income statement. Note that neither depreciation expense nor amortization expense involves a cash disbursement; cash is disbursed when the asset is acquired, or, if a loan were used to finance the acquisition, when the loan payments are made.

Leasehold Improvements

When the tenant of an office building makes modifications to the office space, such as having private offices constructed, the cost of these modifications is a capital expenditure to be amortized over their useful life to the tenant, or over the life of the lease, whichever is shorter. The concept is the same as that applying to buildings or equipment, but the terminology is different. Entities that use rented facilities extensively, such as smaller shops or retail store chains that operate in shopping malls, may have a significant amount of **leasehold improvements.**

Patents, Trademarks, and Copyrights

A **patent** is a monopoly license granted by the government for a period of 17 years. A **trademark** (or trade name), when registered with the Federal Trade Commission, can be used only by the entity that owns it, or by another entity that has secured permission from the owner. A trademark has an unlimited life, but it can be terminated by lack of use. A **copyright** is a protection granted to writers and artists that is designed to prevent unauthorized copying of printed or recorded material. A copyright is granted for a period of time equal to the life of the writer or artist, plus 50 years.

To the extent that an entity has incurred some cost in obtaining a patent, trademark, or copyright, that cost should be capitalized and amortized over its estimated remaining useful life to the entity, or its statutory life if that is shorter. The cost of developing a patent, trademark, or copyright is not usually significant. Most intangible assets in this category arise when one firm purchases a patent, trademark, or copyright from another entity. An intangible that becomes very valuable because of the success of a product (e.g., "Coke"), cannot be assigned a value and recorded as an asset. In some cases, a firm will include a caption for trademarks, or another intangible asset, in its balance sheet and report a nominal cost of $1, just to communicate to financial statement users that it does have this type of asset.

License fees or royalties earned from an intangible asset owned by a firm are reported as operating revenues in the income statement. Likewise, license fees or royalty expenses incurred by a firm using an intangible asset owned by another entity are operating expenses.

Goodwill

Goodwill results from the purchase of one firm by another for a price that is greater than the fair value of the net assets acquired. Why would one firm be willing to pay more for a business than the fair market value of the inventory, plant and equipment, and other assets being acquired? Because the purchasing firm does not see the transaction as the purchase of assets, but instead evaluates the transaction as the purchase of *profits*. The purchaser will be willing to pay such an amount because the profits expected to be earned from the investment will generate an adequate return on the investment. If the firm being purchased has been able to earn a greater than average rate of return on its invested assets, then the owners of that firm will be able to command a price for the firm that is greater than the fair market value of its assets. This greater than average return may result from excellent management, a great location, unusual customer loyalty, a unique product or service, or some other factor.

When one firm purchases another, the purchase price is first assigned to the physical assets acquired. The cost recorded for these assets is their fair market value, usually determined by appraisal. This cost then becomes the basis for depreciating plant and equipment, or determining cost of goods sold if inventory is involved. To the extent that the total price exceeds the fair market value of the physical assets acquired, the excess is recorded as goodwill. Goodwill is an intangible asset, and it will be amortized over its expected economic life, which is the period that the expected higher than average rate of return will continue, or over 40 years, whichever is less. Accounting conservatism would suggest a period of much less than 40 years, but because it is difficult to determine objectively the economic life of goodwill, 40 years is a frequently used amortization period. The effect of goodwill amortization is:

Balance sheet	Income statement
Assets = Liabilities + Owners' equity ← Net income = Revenues − Expenses − Goodwill	− Amortization Expense

Goodwill amortization expense is not an allowable expense for federal income tax purposes. Therefore, many accountants will choose the 40-year amortization period to keep the expense reported in the income statement at a minimum.

Goodwill cannot be recorded by a firm because its management believes that goodwill exists, or even if the firm receives an offer to purchase it for more than the carrying value of its assets. Goodwill can be recorded by a purchasing firm only under the circumstances summarized above.

Another way of describing goodwill is to say that it is the present value of the greater than average earnings of the acquired firm, discounted for the period they are expected to last, at the acquiring firm's desired return on investment. That is, goodwill is the amount a firm is willing to pay now for expected future earnings that are greater than the earnings expected on the fair market value of the assets acquired. In fact, when analysts at the acquiring firm are calculating the price to offer for the firm to be acquired, they use a good deal of present value analysis.

Some critics suggest that goodwill is a fictitious asset that should be written off against the firm's retained earnings. Others point out that it is at best a "different" asset that must be carefully evaluated when it is encountered. However, if goodwill is included in the assets used in the return-on-investment calculation, the ROI measure will reflect management's ability to earn a return on this asset.

NATURAL RESOURCES

Accounting for natural resource assets, such as coal deposits, crude oil reserves, timber, and mineral deposits, parallels that for depreciable assets. **Depletion,** rather than depreciation, is the term for the using up of natural resources, but the concepts are exactly the same, even though depletion usually involves considerably more complex estimates.

For example, when a firm pays for the right to drill for oil or mine for coal, the cost of that right, and the costs of developing the well or mine, are capitalized. The cost is then reflected in the income statement as Depletion Expense, which is matched with the revenue resulting from the sale of the natural resource. Depletion is usually recognized on a straight-line basis, based on geological and engineering estimates of the quantity of the natural resource to be recovered. Thus if $1 million was the cost of a mine that held an estimated 20 million tons of coal, the depletion cost would be $.05 per ton. In most cases the cost of the asset is credited, or reduced directly, in the Depletion Expense entry, instead of using an Accumulated Depletion account.

In practice, estimating depletion expense is very complex. Depletion expense allowed for federal income tax purposes frequently differs from that recognized for financial accounting purposes because the tax laws have, from time to time, been used to provide special incentives to develop natural resources.

OTHER NONCURRENT ASSETS

Long-term investments, notes receivable that mature more than a year after the balance sheet date, and other noncurrent assets are included in this category. At such time as they become current, they will be reclassified to the current asset section of the balance sheet. The explanatory footnotes, or financial review, accompanying the financial statements will include appropriate explanations about these assets if they are significant.

SUMMARY

This chapter has discussed the accounting for and presentation of the following balance sheet long-lived asset and related income statement accounts.

Balance sheet	Income statement
Assets = Liabilities + Owners' equity ← Net income = Revenues − Expenses	
Land . . . . .Gain on or Loss on	
	Sale* Sale*
Purchased . . . . .Repairs and	
Buildings/Equipment	Maintenance Expense
Leased . . . . . .Capital . . . . .Interest	
Buildings/ Lease	Expense
Equipment Liability	
(Accumulated. .Depreciation	
Depreciation)	Expense
Natural . . . . .Depletion	
Resources	Expense
Intangible . . . . .Amortization	
Assets	Expense

* For any asset

Property, plant and equipment owned by the entity are reported on the balance sheet at their original cost, less (for depreciable assets) accumulated depreciation.

Expenditures representing the cost of acquiring an asset that will benefit the entity for more than the current fiscal period are capitalized. Routine repair and maintenance costs are expensed in the fiscal period in which they are incurred.

Accounting depreciation is the process of recognizing in a fiscal period the part of the cost of an asset that has been used up during that period. Depreciation does not affect cash, nor is it an attempt to recognize a loss in the market value of an asset.

Depreciation expense can be calculated several ways. The calculations result in a depreciation expense pattern that is straight line or accelerated. Straight-line methods are usually used for book purposes, and accelerated methods (based on the Modified Accelerated Cost Recovery System specified in the Internal Revenue Code) are usually used for income tax purposes.

When a depreciable asset is disposed of, both the asset and its related accumulated depreciation are removed from the accounts. A gain or loss results, depending on the relationship of any cash received in the transaction to the net book value of the asset disposed of.

When an asset is traded in on a similar asset, no gain or loss results. The cost of the new asset is the net book value of the old asset plus the cash paid and/or debt incurred to acquire the new asset.

When the use of an asset is acquired in a capital lease transaction, the asset and related lease liability are reported in the balance sheet. The cost of the asset is the present value of the lease payments, calculated using the interest rate used by the lessor to determine the periodic lease payments. The asset is depreciated, and interest expense related to the lease is recorded.

The present value concept recognizes that money does have value over time. The present value of an amount to be paid or received in the future is calculated by multiplying the future amount by a present value factor based on the discount (interest) rate and the number of periods involved. An annuity is a fixed amount to be paid or received each period for some number of periods. In the calculation of the present value of an annuity, the fixed periodic amount is multiplied by the appropriate factor. The present value concept is widely used in business and finance.

Intangible assets are represented by a contractual right, or are not physically identifiable. The cost of intangible assets is spread over the useful life to the entity of the intangible asset, and is called *amortization expense*. Intangible assets include leasehold improvements, patents, trademarks, copyrights, and goodwill.

The cost of natural resources is recognized as *depletion expense,* which is allocated to the natural resources recovered and used or sold.

Refer to the Armstrong World Industries, Inc., balance sheet and financial review in Appendix A, and to other financial statements you may have, and observe how information about property, plant and equipment, and other noncurrent assets is presented.

KEY TERMS AND CONCEPTS

Accelerated Cost Recovery System (ACRS) *(p. 173)* The method prescribed in the Internal Revenue Code for calculating the depreciation deduction; applicable to the years 1981–1986.

accelerated depreciation method *(p. 169)* A depreciation calculation method that results in greater depreciation expense in the early periods of an asset's life than in the later periods of its life.

amortization *(p. 188)* The process of spreading the cost of an intangible asset over its useful life.

annuity *(p. 182)* The receipt or payment of a constant amount over some period of time.

capital lease *(p. 179)* A lease that has the effect of financing the acquisition of an asset. Sometimes called a *financing lease*.

capitalize *(p. 167)* To record an expenditure as an asset as opposed to recording it as an expense.

copyright *(p. 190)* An intangible asset represented by the legally granted protection against unauthorized copying of a creative work.

declining-balance depreciation method *(p. 172)* An accelerated depreciation method in which the declining net book value of the asset is multiplied by a constant rate.

depletion *(p. 192)* The accounting process recognizing that the cost of a natural resource asset is used up as the natural resource is consumed.

discount rate *(p. 182)* The interest rate used in a present value calculation.

expensed *(p. 167)* An expenditure recorded as an expense, as opposed to capitalizing the expenditure.

goodwill *(p. 190)* An intangible asset arising from the purchase of a business for more than the fair market value of the net assets acquired. Goodwill is the present value of the earnings of the business in excess of the earnings that would represent an average return on the investment, discounted at the investor's required rate of return for the expected duration of the excess earnings.

intangible asset *(p. 188)* A long-lived asset represented by a contractual right, or one that is not physically identifiable.

leasehold improvement *(p. 189)* A depreciable asset represented by the cost of improvements made to a leasehold by the lessee.

Modified Accelerated Cost Recovery System (MACRS) *(p. 174)* The method prescribed in the Internal Revenue Code for calculating the depreciation deduction; applicable to years after 1986.

net book value *(p. 168)* The difference between the cost of an asset and the accumulated depreciation related to the asset.

operating lease *(p. 179)* A lease (usually short term) that does not involve any attribute of ownership.

patent *(p. 189)* An intangible asset represented by a government-sanctioned monopoly over the use of a product or process.

present value *(p. 179)* The value now of an amount to be received or paid at some future date, recognizing an interest (or discount) rate for the period from the present to the future date.

straight-line depreciation method *(p. 170)*   Calculation of periodic depreciation expense by dividing the amount to be depreciated by the number of periods over which the asset is to be depreciated.

sum-of-the-years' digits depreciation *(p. 171)*   An accelerated depreciation method in which the amount to be depreciated is multiplied by a rate that declines each year.

trademark *(p. 189)*   An intangible asset represented by a right to the exclusive use of an identifying mark.

units-of-production depreciation method *(p. 171)*   A depreciation method based on periodic use and life expressed in terms of asset utilization.

EXERCISES AND PROBLEMS

6–1. A parcel of land with a building on it was purchased for a total cost of $90,000. The appraised value of the land is $80,000, and the appraised value of the building is $20,000.

Required:

a. Assuming that the building is to be used in the purchaser's business activities, what cost should be recorded for the land?

b. Assuming that the building is razed at a cost of $10,000 so the land can be used for employee parking, what cost should be recorded for the land?

6–2. Crow Co. purchased some of the machinery of Hare, Inc., a bankrupt competitor, at a liquidation sale for a total cost of $8,400. Crow's cost of moving and installing the machinery totaled $800. The following data are available:

Item	Hare's Net Book Value on the Date of Sale	List Price of Same Item if New	Appraiser's Estimate of Fair Value
Punch press	$5,040	$9,000	$6,000
Lathe	4,032	4,500	3,000
Welder	1,008	1,500	1,000

Required:

a. Calculate the amount that should be recorded by Crow Co. as the cost of each piece of equipment.

b. Which of the following alternatives should be used as the depreciable life for Crow Co.'s depreciation calculation? Explain your answer.

The remaining useful life to Hare, Inc.

The life of a new machine.

The useful life of the asset to Crow Co.

6–3. Should the cost of repairing damage resulting from the careless unloading of a new machine be capitalized as part of the cost of the new machine? Explain your answer.

6–4. Tater Co. has expanded its operations by purchasing the assets of Oak Co. for $250,000. Included in the assets of Oak Co. are land, buildings, equipment, and inventories.

Required:

a. Explain why, for income tax purposes, Tater Co.'s management would want as little of the purchase price as possible allocated to the land.

b. Would Oak Co.'s original cost of the assets or the market value at the date of Tater's purchase be used as the basis of allocating the $250,000 cost to the assets acquired by Tater? Explain your answer.

6–5. During the first month of its current fiscal year, Green Co. incurred repair costs of $20,000 on a machine that had five years of remaining depreciable life. The repair cost was inappropriately capitalized. Green Co. reported operating income of $160,000 for the current year.

Required:

a. Assuming that Green Co. took a full year's straight-line depreciation expense in the current year, calculate the operating income that should have been reported for the current year.

b. Assume that Green Co.'s total assets at the end of the prior year and at the end of the current year were $940,000 and $1,020,000, respectively. Calculate ROI (based on operating income) for the current year using the originally reported data and for the current year using corrected data.

c. Explain the effect on ROI of subsequent years if the error is not corrected.

6–6. Early in January 1993, Tellco, Inc., acquired a new machine and incurred $10,000 of interest, installation, and overhead costs that should have been capitalized but were expensed. The company earned net income of $100,000 on average total assets of $800,000 for 1993. Assume that the total cost of the new machine will be depreciated over 10 years using the straight-line method.

Required:

a. Calculate the ROI for Tellco Inc., for 1993.

b. Calculate the ROI for Tellco Inc., for 1993, assuming that the $10,000 had been capitalized and depreciated over 10 years using the straight-line method. *(Hint: There is an effect on net income and average assets.)*

c. Given your answers to *(a)* and *(b),* why would the company want to account for this expenditure as an expense?

d. Assuming that the $10,000 is capitalized, what will be the effect on ROI for 1994 and subsequent years, compared to expensing the interest, installation, and overhead costs in 1993? Explain your answer.

6–7. Millco, Inc., acquired a machine that cost $80,000 early in 1993. The machine is expected to last for eight years, and its estimated salvage value at the end of its life is $8,000.

Required:

a. Using straight-line depreciation, calculate the depreciation expense to be recognized in the first year of the machine's life, and calculate the accumulated depreciation after the fifth year of the machine's life.

b. Using declining-balance depreciation at twice the straight-line rate, calculate the depreciation expense for the third year of the machine's life.

c. Using sum-of-the-years' digits depreciation, calculate the amount of accumulated depreciation after the fifth year of the machine's life. Compare this amount to the accumulated depreciation calculated in *(a)*.

d. What will be the net book value of the machine at the end of its eighth year of use before it is disposed of, under each depreciation method?

6–8. Kleener Co. acquired a new delivery truck at the beginning of its current fiscal year. The truck cost $26,000 and has an estimated useful life of four years and an estimated salvage value of $4,000.

Required:

a. Calculate depreciation expense for each year of the truck's life using:

1. Straight-line depreciation.
2. Sum-of-the-years' digits depreciation.
3. Double-declining balance depreciation.

b. Calculate the truck's net book value at the end of its third year of use under each depreciation method.

c. Assume that Kleener Co. had no more use for the truck after the end of the third year, and that at the beginning of the fourth year, it had an offer from a buyer who was willing to pay $6,200 for the truck. How should the depreciation method used affect the decision to sell the truck? *(Hint: How will the cost of having used the truck for three years differ?)*

6–9. With respect to new assets, Misty Co. has adopted a depreciation policy of starting depreciation at the beginning of the month following the month in which the asset is acquired. On March 3, 1993, it acquired a machine costing $9,600. The machine has an estimated life of seven years and estimated salvage value of $1,200.

Required:

Calculate depreciation expense for calendar 1993 and 1994 using:

1. Straight-line depreciation.
2. Sum-of-the-years' digits depreciation.

6–10. Freedom Co. purchased a new machine on July 2, 1993, at a total installed cost of $44,000. The machine has an estimated life of five years, and an estimated salvage value of $6,000.

Required:

a. Calculate the depreciation expense for each year of the asset's life using:
1. Straight-line depreciation.
2. Sum-of-the-years' digits depreciation.
3. Double-declining balance depreciation.

b. How much depreciation expense should be recorded by Freedom Co. for its fiscal year ended December 31, 1993, under each of the three methods? *(Note: The machine will have been used for one-half of its first year of life.)*

c. Calculate the accumulated depreciation and net book value of the machine at December 31, 1994, under each of the three methods.

Armstrong

6-11. Find the discussion of depreciation methods used by Armstrong World Industries, Inc., on page 21 of the Annual Report in Appendix A. Explain why the particular method is used for the purpose described.

6-12. Answer the following questions using data from the Armstrong World Industries, Inc., Annual Report in Appendix A.

Required:

Armstrong

   a. Calculate the ratio of the depreciation and amortization (expense) for 1991 reported on page 21 in the Financial Review to the cost (*not* net book value) of property, plant, and equipment reported in the December 31, 1991, balance sheet.
   b. Based on the ratio calculated in part *(a),* and the depreciation method being used by Armstrong World Industries, Inc., what is the average useful life being used for its depreciation calculation?
   c. If the use of an accelerated depreciation method had resulted in twice as much accumulated depreciation at December 31, 1991, and all of that difference had affected retained earnings, what would be the percentage reduction from the retained earnings amount reported at December 31, 1991?

6-13. Alpha, Inc., and Beta Co. are sheet metal processors that supply component parts for consumer product manufacturers. Alpha, Inc., has been in business since 1960, and is operating in its original plant facilities. Much of its equipment was acquired in the 1960s. Beta Co. was started two years ago and acquired its building and equipment then. Each firm has about the same sales revenue, and material and labor costs are about the same for each firm. What would you expect Alpha's ROI to be, relative to the ROI of Beta Co.? Explain your answer. What are the implications of this ROI difference for a firm seeking to enter an established industry?

6-14. Assume that a company chooses an accelerated method of calculating depreciation expense for financial statement reporting purposes for an asset with a 10-year life.

Required:

State the effect (higher, lower, no effect) of accelerated depreciation relative to straight-line depreciation on:

   a. Depreciation expense in the first year.
   b. The asset's net book value after two years.
   c. Cash flows from operations (excluding income taxes).

6-15. Nalco, Inc., acquired its computer several years ago at a cost of $85,000. The net book value of the computer is now $21,000. Nalco is going to acquire a new HAL computer that has a list price of $110,000, and the company will be given a trade-in allowance of $12,000 on its old computer and will pay cash for the balance.

Required:

   a. Calculate the cost at which Nalco will record the new computer.
   b. Use the horizontal model (or write the journal entry) to show the effect of the trade-in transaction.

6–16. The balance sheets of HIROE, Inc., showed the following at December 31, 1993, and 1992:

	December 31, 1993	December 31, 1992
Equipment, less accumulated depreciation of $31,500 at December 31, 1993, and $22,500 at December 31, 1992	40,500	49,500

Required:

a. If there have not been any purchases or sales, or other transactions affecting this equipment account since the equipment was first acquired, what is the amount of the depreciation expense for 1993?

b. Assume the same facts as in *(a),* and assume that the estimated useful life of the equipment to HIROE, Inc., is eight years and that there is no estimated salvage value.
Determine:

  1. What depreciation method is apparently being used.
  Explain your answer.
  2. When the equipment was acquired.

c. Assume that this equipment account represents the cost of 10 identical machines. Calculate the gain or loss on the sale of one of the machines on January 2, 1993, for $4,500.

d. Assume that one of the machines was traded in on a new machine on January 2, 1992. The list price of the new machine was $12,000, and a $3,000 trade-in allowance was given on the old machine. Use the horizontal model (or write the journal entry) to show the effect of the trade-in transaction.

6–17. When an asset now owned is traded in on a new asset, the trade-in allowance offered on the old asset is frequently emphasized by the seller of the new asset. If this approach is used, what other amount (besides cash to be paid) must be considered by the purchaser of the new asset? Explain your answer.

6–18. The company car owned by Charlie's Chili Co. is near the end of its life. The car cost $9,800 and has a net book value of $2,000. Charlie has approached two dealers who have made the following offers for the same new car model. Dealer A will allow a $2,900 trade-in allowance on the old car and sell Charlie a new car at its list price of $14,800. Dealer B isn't interested in taking the old car in trade; B's selling price for the new car is $13,000. If Charlie buys the new car from Dealer B, he'll be able to sell the old car outright for $900.

Required:

a. Which offer do you suggest Charlie accept? Explain your answer.
b. What caused the difference between the net book value of the old car and its trade-in allowance and cash value?

6–19. If capital leases were not capitalized, but were ignored from the balance sheet point of view (which used to be the case), what would be the impact of leasing rather than borrowing and buying plant assets on ROI and on the ratio of long-term liabilities to total owners' equity?

6–20. Included in the Debt summary on page 24 of the Armstrong World Industries, Inc., Annual Report in Appendix A is an amount for capitalized leases. What does this item represent?

6–21. Using a present value table, or a computer program present value function, calculate the present value of:

a. A car down payment of $3,000 that will be required in two years, assuming an interest rate of 10 percent.
b. A lottery prize of $6 million to be paid at the rate of $300,000 a year for 20 years, assuming an interest rate of 10 percent.
c. The same annual amount as in *(b),* but assuming an interest rate of 14 percent.
d. A capital lease obligation that calls for the payment of $8,000 per year for 10 years, assuming a discount rate of 8 percent.

6–22. Renter Co. acquired the use of a machine by agreeing to pay the manufacturer of the machine $900 per year for 10 years. At the time the lease was signed, the interest rate for a 10-year loan was 12 percent.

Required:

a. Use the appropriate factor from Table 6–2 to calculate the amount that Renter Co. could have paid at the beginning of the lease to buy the machine outright.
b. What causes the difference between the amount you calculated in *(a)* and the total of $9,000 ($900 per year for 10 years) that Renter Co. will pay under the terms of the lease?
c. What is the appropriate amount of cost to be reported in Renter Co.'s balance sheet with respect to this asset?

6–23. Assume that fast-food restaurants generally provide an ROI of 15 percent, but that such a restaurant near a college campus has an ROI of 18 percent because its relatively large volume of business generates an above average turnover (sales/assets). The replacement value of the restaurant's plant and equipment is $200,000. If you were to invest that amount in a restaurant elsewhere in town, you could expect a 15 percent ROI.

Required:

a. Would you be willing to pay more than $200,000 for the restaurant near the campus? Why?
b. If you purchased the restaurant near the campus for $240,000, and the fair value of the assets you acquired was $200,000, what balance sheet accounts would be used to record the cost of the restaurant?

6–24. Goodwill arises when one firm acquires the assets of another firm and pays more for those assets than their current fair market value. Suppose that Target Co. had operating income of $60,000 and assets with a fair market value of $200,000. Takeover Co. pays $300,000 for Target Co.'s assets and business activities.

Required:

a. How much goodwill will result from this transaction?

b. Calculate the ROI for Target Co. based on its present operating income and the fair market value of its assets.

c. Calculate the ROI that Takeover Co. will earn if the operating income of the acquired assets continues to be $60,000. (Ignore goodwill amortization.)

d. What reasons can you think of to explain why Takeover Co. is willing to pay $100,000 more than fair market value for the assets acquired from Target Co.?

Chapter 7

Accounting for and Presentation of Liabilities

Liabilities are obligations of the entity. Most liabilities arise because credit has been obtained in the form of a loan or in the normal course of business, as when a supplier ships merchandise before payment is made, or when an employee works one week not expecting to be paid until the next week. As has been illustrated in previous chapters, many liabilities are recorded in the accrual process that matches revenues and expenses. Sometimes the liability that results from accruing an expense is called an *accrued expense*; one way to resolve the confusion that this mixing of terms may cause is to understand that any amount reported in the liability section of the balance sheet is a liability because expenses and revenues are reported only in the income statement. Current liabilities are those that must be paid, or that are related to an obligation that must be satisfied, within a year of the balance sheet date; noncurrent liabilities are those that will be paid or satisfied more than a year after the balance sheet date.

Review the liabilities section of the Armstrong World Industries, Inc., Consolidated Balance Sheets on page 19 of the Annual Report in Appendix A. Note that of the eight captions, three have to do with debt and two relate to income taxes. The business and accounting practices relating to these items make up a major part of this chapter.

Some of the most significant and controversial issues that the FASB has addressed in recent years, including accounting for income taxes, accounting for pensions, and consolidation of subsidiaries, relate to this section of the balance sheet. A principal reason for the interest generated by these topics is that the recognition of a liability usually involves recognizing an expense as well. Expenses reduce net income, and lower net income means lower ROI. Keep these relationships in mind as you study this chapter.

LEARNING OBJECTIVES

After studying this chapter you should understand:

- Why short-term debt is incurred.
- The difference between interest calculated on a straight basis and on a discount basis.
- How short-term debt is presented in the balance sheet.
- The financial statement presentation of current maturities of long-term debt.
- Two methods of accounting for cash discounts on purchases.
- What unearned revenues are, and how they are accounted for.
- That certain liabilities must be estimated, and how these are presented in the balance sheet.
- What leverage is, and how it is provided by long-term debt.
- Different characteristics of a bond, which is the formal document representing most long-term debt.
- Why bond discount or premium arises, and how it is accounted for.
- The financial statement effects of retiring a bond before its maturity.
- What deferred income taxes are, and why they arise.
- What minority interest is, why it arises, and what it means in the balance sheet.

CURRENT LIABILITIES

Short-Term Debt

Most firms experience seasonal fluctuations during the year in the demand for their products or services. For instance, a firm like Cruisers, Inc., a manufacturer of small boats, is likely to have a greater demand for its product during the spring and early summer than in the winter. In order to utilize its production facilities most efficiently, Cruisers, Inc., will plan to produce boats on a level basis during the year. This means that during the fall and winter seasons, its inventory of boats will be increased in order to have enough product on hand to meet spring and summer demand. In order to finance this inventory increase, and be able to keep its payments to suppliers and employees current, Cruisers, Inc., will obtain a **working capital loan** from its bank. This type of short-term loan is made with the expectation that it will be repaid from the collections of accounts receivable that will be generated by the sale of inventory. The short-term loan usually has a **maturity date** specifying when the loan is to be repaid. Sometimes a firm will negotiate a **revolving line of credit** with its bank. There will be a predetermined maximum loan amount, but the firm has flexibility in the timing and amount borrowed. There may be a specified repayment schedule, or an agreement that all amounts borrowed will be repaid by a particular date. Whatever the specific loan arrangement may be, the borrowing is recorded by the following entry:

```
Dr.  Cash. . . . . . . . . . . . . . . . . . . . . . .    xx
        Cr.  Short-Term Debt . . . . . . . . . . . . . . .        xx
     Borrowed money from bank.
```

The effect of this transaction on the financial statements is:

Balance sheet	Income statement
Assets = Liabilities + Owners' equity ← Net income = Revenues − Expenses	
+ Cash + Short-Term	
Debt	

The short-term debt resulting from this type of transaction is sometimes called a **note payable.** The note is a formal promise to pay a stated amount at a stated date, usually with interest at a stated rate, and sometimes secured by collateral.

Interest expense is associated with almost any borrowing, and it is appropriate that the interest expense for a fiscal period be recorded in each period during which the money is borrowed. The alternative methods of calculating interest are explained in Business Procedure Capsule 12—Interest Calculation Methods.

Prime rate is the term frequently used to express the interest rate on short-term loans. The prime rate is established by the lender, presumably for its most creditworthy borrowers, but is in reality just a benchmark rate. The prime rate is raised or lowered by the lender in response to credit market forces. The borrower's rate may be expressed as "prime plus 1," for example, which means that the interest rate for the borrower will be the prime rate plus 1 percent. It is quite possible for the interest rate to change during the term of the loan, in which case a separate calculation of interest is made for each period having a different rate.

For a loan on which interest is calculated on a straight basis, interest is accrued each period with the following entry:

```
Dr.  Interest Expense . . . . . . . . . . . . . . . . . . . .    xx
     Cr.  Interest Payable. . . . . . . . . . . . . . . . . .         xx
     Accrued interest for period.
```

The effect of this entry on the financial statements is:

Balance sheet	Income statement
Assets = Liabilities + Owners' equity ←	Net income = Revenues − Expenses
+ Interest	− Interest
Payable	Expense

Interest Payable is a current liability because it will be paid within a year of the balance sheet date. It may be disclosed in a separate caption, or included with other accrued liabilities in the current liability section of the balance sheet.

Using the data in the discount example in Business Procedure Capsule 12, the effect on the borrower's financial statements when discount is subtracted from the principal (maturity value) amount to determine the loan proceeds is:

Balance sheet	Income statement
Assets = Liabilities + Owners' equity ←	Net income = Revenues − Expenses
Cash Short-Term	
+ 880 Debt	
+ 1,000	
Discount on	
Short-Term Debt	
− 120	

The Discount on Short-Term Debt account is a **contra liability,** classified with the Short-Term Debt on the balance sheet.

In this situation interest expense is recognized by amortizing the Discount on Short-Term Debt to Interest Expense as the expense is incurred, as follows:

Balance sheet	Income statement
Assets = Liabilities + Owners' equity ←	Net income = Revenues − Expenses
+ Discount on	− Interest
Short-Term Debt	Expense

The amortization of the discount to interest expense affects neither cash nor interest payable.

• BUSINESS PROCEDURE CAPSULE 12
Interest Calculation Methods

Lenders calculate interest on either a straight (or simple interest) basis, or on a discount basis. The straight calculation involves charging interest on the money actually available to the borrower for the length of time it was borrowed. Interest on a **discount loan** is based on the principal amount of the loan, but the interest is subtracted from the principal and only the difference is made available to the borrower. In effect the borrower pays the interest in advance. Assume the borrowing of $1,000 for one year at an interest rate of 12 percent.

Straight Interest

The **interest calculation—straight basis** is made as follows:

$$\text{Interest} = \text{Principal} \times \text{Rate} \times \text{Time (in years)}$$

$$= \$1,000 \times 0.12 \times 1$$

$$= \$120$$

At the maturity date of the note, the borrower will repay the principal of $1,000 plus the interest owed of $120. The borrower's effective interest rate—the **annual percentage rate (APR)** is 12 percent:

$$\text{APR} = \text{Interest paid/Money available to use} \times \text{Time (in years)}$$

$$= \$120/\$1,000 \times 1$$

$$= 12\%$$

You should understand that this is another application of the present value concept described in Chapter 6. The amount of the liability on the date the money is borrowed is the present value of the amount to be repaid in the future, calculated at the effective interest rate, which is the rate of return desired by the lender. To illustrate, the amount to be repaid in one year is $1,120, the sum of the $1,000 principal plus the $120 of interest. From Table 6–1, the factor in the 12 percent column and one-period row is 0.8929; $1,120 × 0.8929 = $1,000 (rounded). These relationships are illustrated on the following time line:

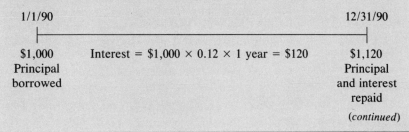

1/1/90   12/31/90

$1,000   Interest = $1,000 × 0.12 × 1 year = $120 $1,120
Principal   Principal
borrowed   and interest
                                                                   repaid

(continued)

• **BUSINESS PROCEDURE CAPSULE 12** *(concluded)*

Discount

The interest calculation—discount basis is made as illustrated above, but the interest amount is subtracted from the loan principal, and the borrower receives the difference. In this case, the loan **proceeds** would be $880 ($1,000 − $120). At the maturity of the note, the borrower will repay just the principal of $1,000 because the interest of $120 has already been paid—it was subtracted from the principal amount when the loan was obtained. Illustrated on a time-line, the discount situation is:

1/1/90   12/31/90

$880   Interest = $1,000 × 0.12 × 1 year = $120 $1,000
Proceeds   Principal
                                                                      repaid

But, because the full principal amount was not available to the borrower, the effective interest rate is much higher than the rate used to calculate the interest:

$$\text{APR} = \text{Interest paid/Money available to use} \times \text{Time (in years)}$$

$$= \$120/\$880 \times 1$$

$$= 13.6\%$$

Applying present value analysis, the amount of the liability on the date the money is borrowed is the amount to be repaid, $1,000, multiplied by the present value factor for 13.6 percent for one year. The factor is 0.8803, and although it is not explicitly shown in Table 6–1, it can be derived approximately by interpolating between the factors for 12 percent and 14 percent.

If the loan is to be repaid on an installment basis over the year, and the discount method is used to calculate interest, the effective interest rate is about twice that of the discount method with a lump-sum repayment of principal at the maturity date. This results from the fact that for the term of the loan, only about half of the proceeds are available to use for the entire term because the principal is being repaid ratably over the loan's life.

In the final analysis, it isn't important whether interest is calculated using the straight method or the discount method; what is important is the APR, or effective interest rate. The borrower's objective is to keep that rate at a minimum.

Current Maturities of Long-Term Debt

When funds are borrowed on a long-term basis (a topic to be discussed later in this chapter), it is not unusual for principal repayments to be required on an installment basis. That is, every year a portion of the debt matures and is to be repaid by the borrower. Because a liability is classified as current if it is to be paid within a year of the balance sheet date, any portion of a long-term borrowing that is to be repaid within a year of the balance sheet date is reclassified from the noncurrent liability section of the balance sheet to the current liability section. The current liability account used is **Current Maturities of Long-Term Debt.** These amounts are reported separately from short-term debt because the liability arose from a long-term borrowing transaction. Interest payable on long-term debt is classified with other interest payable, and may be combined with other accrued liabilities for reporting purposes.

Accounts Payable

Amounts owed to suppliers for goods and services that have been provided to the entity on credit are the principal components of **accounts payable.** Unlike accounts receivable, which are reported net of estimated cash discounts expected to be taken, the liability to suppliers that permit a cash discount for prompt payment is not usually reduced by the amount of the cash discount expected to be taken. This treatment is supported by the materiality concept, because the amount involved is not likely to have a significant effect on the financial position or results of the operations of the firm. However, accounts payable for firms that record purchases net of anticipated cash discounts (see Business Procedure Capsule 13— Methods of Recording Purchases) will be reported at the amount expected to be paid.

Unearned Revenue or Deferred Credits

There are several situations in which customers pay for services or even products before the service or product is delivered. These situations result in **unearned revenue,** or a **deferred credit,** which is included with current liabilities. The accounting for revenue received in advance was discussed with adjusting entries in Chapter 4. To recap, the effect on the financial statements of a magazine publisher that requires a subscriber to pay in advance for a subscription is:

Balance sheet	Income statement

Assets = Liabilities + Owners' equity ← Net income = Revenues − Expenses

Cash received with subscription:

+ Cash   + Unearned
        Subscription
        Revenue

Adjustment in fiscal period in which revenue is earned (magazines delivered):

    − Unearned   + Subscription
       Subscription   Revenue
       Revenue

As you think about this situation, you should understand that it is the opposite of the prepaid expense/deferred charge transaction described in Chapter 5. In that kind of transaction, cash was *paid* in the current period, and *expense* was recognized in subsequent periods. Deferred credit transactions involve the *receipt* of cash in the current period, and the recognition of *revenue* in subsequent periods.

Deposits received from customers are also accounted for as deferred credits. If the deposit is an advance payment for a product or service, the deposit is transferred from a liability account to a revenue account when the product or service is delivered. Or, for example, if the deposit is security for a returnable container, when the container is returned, the refund of the deposit reduces (is a credit to) cash and eliminates (is a debit to) the liability.

An interesting issue is the accounting for deposits that will never be claimed. For example, a soft drink bottler receives more container deposits from customers than it will repay, because some of the containers will be broken and others will be permanently lost. What accounting makes sense in this situation? Based on experience and estimates, an adjusting entry is made to transfer some of the deposit liability to income. This adjustment offsets some of the cost of the lost containers. Although the deposit amount is usually less than the cost of the container, the bottler has in effect "sold" the container for the deposit amount.

Unearned revenues/deferred credits are usually classified with other accrued liabilities in the current liability section of the balance sheet.

Other Accrued Liabilities

Included in this caption are liabilities for accrued payroll, accrued payroll taxes (which include the employer's share of social security taxes, and federal and state unemployment taxes), accrued prop-

• BUSINESS PROCEDURE CAPSULE 13
Methods of Recording Purchases

Purchase transactions for which a cash discount is allowed are recorded using either the gross or net method. The difference between the two is the timing of the recognition of the cash discount. The gross method results in recognizing the cash discount when the invoice is paid. The net method recognizes the cash discount when the purchase is recorded.

Because cash discounts represent such a high return on investment (see Business Procedure Capsule 9 in Chapter 5), and to strengthen the system of internal control with respect to taking all cash discounts offered, some firms use the net method, which assumes that cash discounts will be taken. Then, if the discount is missed because the invoice is paid after the cash discount date, an expense is recognized. This expense highlights in the financial statements the fact that a discount was missed, and management can then take the appropriate action to eliminate or minimize future missed discounts.

To illustrate and contrast the net and gross methods of recording purchases, assume that a $1,000 purchase is made with terms 2/10, n30. The financial statement effects of each method are:

Balance sheet	Income statement

Assets = Liabilities
        + Owners' equity
	← Net income = Revenues
	        − Expenses

A. Gross method
   1. Record purchase:

Inventory   Accounts
+ 1,000   Payable
          + 1,000

   2. Pay within the discount period:

Cash   Accounts   Purchase
− 980   Payable   Discounts*
          − 1,000   + 20
                      *(A reduction of cost of goods sold)

   3. Pay after the discount period:

Cash   Accounts
− 1,000   Payable
          − 1,000

B. Net method
   1. Record purchase:

Inventory   Accounts
+ 980   Payable
          + 980

(continued)

• **BUSINESS PROCEDURE CAPSULE 13**   (*concluded*)

Balance sheet	Income statement

2. Pay within the discount period:

Cash   Accounts
− 980   Payable
          − 980

3. Pay after the discount period:

Cash   Accounts   Purchase
− 1,000   Payable   Discounts
          − 980   Lost
                                                   − 20

The gross method treats cash discounts as a reduction of cost of goods sold in the income statement, but the income statement doesn't show that every cash discount offered was taken. Under the net method, however, if a discount is missed, the expense Purchase Discounts Lost is recorded, and any amount in this account means that discounts were missed. Thus the net method has the advantage of strengthening the firm's system of internal control because any breakdown in the policy of taking every possible cash discount is highlighted.

---

erty taxes, accrued interest (if not reported separately), and other accrued expenses. These items have in common the fact that the expense has been incurred but not yet paid. The expense is recognized and the liability is shown so that the financial statements present a more complete summary of the results of operations (income statement) and financial position (balance sheet) than would be presented without the accrual. The term *accrued expenses* is used on some balance sheets, but this is shorthand for the *liability resulting from the accrual of expenses.*

A firm's estimated liability under product warranty or performance guarantees is another example of an accrued liability. It is appropriate to recognize the estimated warranty expense that will be incurred on a product in the same period in which the revenue from the sale is recorded. Although the expense and liability must be estimated, past experience and statistical analysis can be used to develop very accurate estimates. The effect of warranty accounting on the financial statements is:

Balance sheet	Income statement

Assets = Liabilities + Owners' equity ← Net income = Revenues − Expenses

Fiscal period in which product is sold:

        + Estimated   − Warranty

           Liability   Expense

           under Warranty

Fiscal period in which warranty is honored:

− Cash   − Estimated

  and/or   Liability

  Repair   under

  Parts   Warranty

  Inventory

One accrued liability that is usually shown separately, because of its significance, is the accrual for income taxes. The accrual of the current liability for income taxes is related to the long-term liability for deferred taxes. Both are discussed later in this chapter.

LONG-TERM LIABILITIES

Long-Term Debt

For many nonfinancial firms, **long-term debt** accounts for up to half of a corporation's capital structure; that is the mix of debt and owners' equity that is used to finance the firm's assets. One of the advantages of using debt is that interest expense is deductible in calculating taxable income, whereas dividends (distributions of earnings to stockholders) are not deductible. Thus debt usually has a lower economic cost to the firm than owners' equity. Another reason for using debt is to obtain favorable **financial leverage.** Financial leverage refers to the difference between the rate of return earned on assets (ROI) and the rate of return earned on owners' equity (ROE). This difference results from the fact that the interest cost of debt is usually fixed; that is, it is not a function of the return on assets. Thus, if the firm can borrow money at an interest cost of 10 percent and use that money to buy assets on which it earns a return greater than 10 percent, then the owners will have a greater return on their investment (ROE) than if they had provided all of the funds. This is illustrated in Exhibit 7–1.

This simplified illustration in Exhibit 7–1 shows positive financial leverage. If a firm earns a lower return on investment than the interest rate on the borrowed funds, financial leverage will be nega-

---

EXHIBIT 7–1   Financial Leverage

Two firms have the same assets and operating income. Current liabilities and income taxes are ignored for simplification. The firm without financial leverage has, by definition, no long-term debt. The firm with financial leverage has a capital structure that is 40 percent long-term debt with an interest rate of 10 percent and 60 percent owners' equity. Return on investment and return on equity are shown below.

Note that the return on investment calculation has been modified from the model introduced in Chapter 3. ROI is based on income from operations and total assets, rather than net income and total assets. Income from operations (which is net income before interest expense) is used because the interest expense reflects a financing decision, not an operating result. Thus ROI becomes an evaluation of the operating activities of the firm.

Firm without Leverage		*Firm with Leverage*	
Balance sheet:		Balance sheet:	
Assets	$10,000	Assets	$10,000
Liabilities	$ 0	Liabilities (10%) . . .	$ 4,000
Owners' equity	10,000	Owners' equity	6,000
Total liabilities +		Total liabilities +	
owner's equity . . .	$10,000	owners' equity . . .	$10,000
Income from		Income from	
operations	$ 1,200	operations	$ 1,200
Interest expense . . .	0	Interest expense . . .	400
Net income.	$ 1,200	Net income.	$ 800

Return on investment (ROI = Income from operations/Assets)

$$\text{ROI} = \$1,200/\$10,000 \qquad\qquad \text{ROI} = \$1,200/\$10,000$$

$$= 12\% \qquad\qquad\qquad\qquad = 12\%$$

Return on equity (ROE = Net income/Owners' equity)

$$\text{ROE} = \$1,200/\$10,000 \qquad\qquad \text{ROE} = \$800/\$6,000$$

$$= 12\% \qquad\qquad\qquad\qquad = 13.3\%$$

The firm with financial leverage has a higher return on owner's equity because it was able to borrow money at a cost of 10 percent and to use the money to buy assets on which it earned 12 percent.

---

tive, and ROE will be less than ROI. Financial leverage adds risk to the firm, because if the firm does not earn enough to pay the interest on the debt, the debt holders can force the firm into bankruptcy.

Financial leverage is discussed in greater detail in Chapter 11. For now you should understand that financial leverage, the use of long-term debt with a fixed interest cost, usually results in ROE being different from ROI. Whether financial leverage is good or bad for the shareowners depends on the relationship between ROI and the interest rate of the long-term debt.

Long-term debt is usually issued in the form of bonds. A **bond** or **bond payable** is a formal document, usually issued in denominations of $1,000. Bond prices, both when issued and later when they are bought and sold in the market, are expressed as a percentage of the bond's **face amount,** the principal amount printed on the face of the bond. A $1,000 face amount bond that has a market value of $1,000 is priced at 100. (This means 100 percent; usually the term *percent* is neither written nor stated.) A $1,000 bond trading at 102.5 can be purchased for $1,025; such a bond priced at 96 has a market value of $960. When a bond has a market value greater than its face amount, it is trading at a premium; the amount of the **bond premium** is the excess of its market value over its face amount. A **bond discount** is the excess of the face amount over market value. The reason for a premium or discount is explained in Exhibit 7–2.

Accounting and financial reporting considerations for bonds can be classified into three categories: the original issuance of the bonds, interest expense recognition, and accounting for bond retirement or conversion.

If a bond is issued at its face amount, the effect on the financial statements is straightforward:

Balance sheet	Income statement
Assets = Liabilities + Owner's equity ←	Net income = Revenues − Expenses
+ Cash + Bonds	
for payable	
Face for Face	
Amount Amount	

As was the case with short-term notes payable, the amount of the liability is the present value of the amounts to be paid in the future with respect to the bonds, discounted at the return on investment desired by the lender. For example, assume that a 10 percent bond with a 10-year maturity is issued to investors who desire a 10 percent return on their investment. There are two components to

EXHIBIT 7–2 Bond Discount and Premium

The interest paid by a borrower to its bond holders each period is fixed; that is, the same amount of interest (equal to the stated or coupon rate multiplied by the face amount of the bond) will be paid on each bond each period regardless of what happens to market interest rates. When an investor buys a bond, he or she wants, and is entitled to, an interest rate that reflects market conditions at the time the investment is made. Because the amount of interest the investor is to receive is fixed, the only way the investor can earn an interest rate different from the stated rate is to buy the bond for more or less than its face amount (i.e., buy the bond at a premium or discount). As already illustrated, the amount the investor is willing to pay for the bond is the present value of the cash flows to be received from the investment, discounted at the investor's desired rate of return.

Assumptions   Cruiser's, Inc., issues a 10 percent, $1,000 bond when market interest rates are 12 percent. The bond will mature in eight years. Interest is paid semiannually.

Required   Calculate the proceeds from the bond issue, and the premium or discount to be recognized.

The solution involves calculating the present value of the cash flows to be received by the investor, discounted at the investor's desired rate of return, which is the market interest rate. There are two components to the cash flows: the semiannual interest payment, and the payment of principal at maturity. Note that the interest is an annuity because the same amount is paid each period. Because the interest is paid semiannually, it is appropriate to recognize semiannual compounding in the present value calculation. This is accomplished by using the number of semiannual periods in the life of the bonds. Since the bonds mature in eight years, there are 16 semiannual periods. However, the interest rate per semiannual period is half of the annual interest rate. To be consistent, the same approach is used to calculate the present value of the principal. Thus, the solution calculations use factors from the 6 percent (one-half the investors' desired ROI) column and the 16-period (twice the term of the bonds) row of the present value tables. (If interest were paid quarterly, the annual ROI would be divided by 4, and the term of the bonds in years would be multiplied by 4.) Using present value factors from Tables 6–1 and 6–2, the present values are:

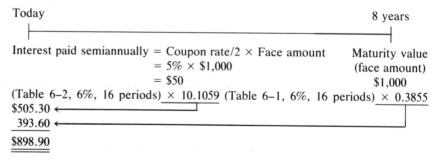

Today   8 years

Interest paid semiannually = Coupon rate/2 × Face amount   Maturity value
                     = 5% × $1,000   (face amount)
                     = $50 $1,000
(Table 6–2, 6%, 16 periods) × 10.1059 (Table 6–1, 6%, 16 periods) × 0.3855
$505.30 ←
  393.60 ←
$898.90

The proceeds received by Cruisers, Inc., as well as the amount invested by the buyer of the bond, are the sum of the present value of the interest payments and the present value of the principal. This sum is $898.90 ($505.30 + $393.60). Thus the bond is priced at a discount; the discount is $101.10.

EXHIBIT 7–2   *(concluded)*

Two important points about the calculation process to learn from the above illustration are:

1. The *stated interest rate* of the bond is the rate to use to calculate the amount of interest paid; the payment amount per payment period is the amount of the annuity used in the calculation of the present value of the interest.
2. The *market rate of interest,* or the investors' desired ROI, adjusted for the compounding frequency, is the discount rate used in the present value calculation.

In this illustration, because the market interest rate is higher than the bond's stated interest rate, the investor must pay less than the face amount of the bond if the $50 to be received each six months and the $1,000 to be received at maturity are to provide a market rate of return.

The issuance of the $1,000 bond by Cruisers, Inc., will be recorded with the following entry:

Dr. Cash	898.90	
Dr. Discount on Bond Payable	101.10	
Cr. Bond Payable		1,000.00
Issued bond at a discount.		

The effect of this entry on the financial statements is:

Balance sheet	Income statement

Assets = Liabilities + Owners' equity ← Net income = Revenues − Expenses

Cash   Bonds Payable
+ 898.90 + 1,000

            Discount on
            Bonds Payable
            − 101.10

If market rates are less than the stated interest rate on the bond, the opposite will be true (i.e., the investor will be willing to pay a premium over the face amount of the bond). Use the above model to prove to yourself that if the market interest rate is 12 percent, then a 13 percent, $1,000 face amount, 10-year bond on which interest is paid semiannually would be issued for $1,057.34 (i.e., the bond is issued at a premium of $57.34).

This exhibit illustrates the fundamental reason for bonds being issued for a price (or having a market value) that is different from the face amount. The actual premium or discount is a function of the magnitude of the difference between the stated interest rate of the bond and the market interest rate, and the number of years to maturity because present value factors reflect the time value of money. For any given difference between the bond's stated interest rate and the market interest rate, the closer a bond is to maturity, the smaller the premium or discount will be.

the cash flows from the issuer of the bonds to the investors in the bonds: the annual interest payments, and the payment of principal at maturity. Note that the interest is an annuity because the same amount is paid each period. Using present value factors from Tables 6–1 and 6–2, the present values are:

Today   10 years

```
Interest paid annually = Coupon rate × Face amount        Maturity value
                       = 10% × $1,000                      (face amount)
                       = $100                                   $1,000
(Table 6–2, 10%, 10 periods) × 6.1446   (Table 6–1, 10%, 10 periods) × 0.3855
$614.46  ←
 385.50  ←
$999.96
```

The present value of the liability is the sum of the present value of the interest payments and the present value of the principal. This sum is $999.96, which, except for a rounding difference in the present value factors, is the same as the face amount of the bonds.

Because of the mechanics involved in a bond issue, there is usually a time lag between the establishment of the interest rate that is printed on the face of the bond and the actual issue date. During this time lag, market interest rates will fluctuate, and the market rate on the issue date will probably differ from the **stated rate** (or **coupon rate**) used to calculate interest payments to bond holders. This difference in interest rates causes the proceeds (cash received) from the sale of the bonds to be more or less than the face amount; the bonds are issued at a premium or discount, respectively. The reason for this is illustrated in Exhibit 7–2.

Because bond premium or discount arises from a difference between the bond's stated interest rate and the market interest rate, it should follow that the premium or discount will affect the issuing firm's interest expense. Bond discount really represents additional interest expense because the interest that will be paid (based on the stated rate) is less than the interest would be if it were based on the market rate at the date the bonds were issued. Bond discount is a deferred charge that is amortized to interest expense over the life of the bond. The amortization increases interest expense over the amount actually paid to bondholders. Bond discount is classified in the balance sheet as a contra account to the Bonds Payable liability. Bond premium is a deferred credit that is amortized to interest expense, and its effect is to reduce interest expense below the amount actually paid to bond holders. Bond premium is classified in the balance sheet with the Bonds Payable liability. The effects of interest accrual, interest payment, and discount or premium amortization are:

Balance sheet	Income statement

Assets = Liabilities + Owners' equity ← Net income = Revenues − Expenses

Interest accrual (each fiscal period, for example, monthly):

| + Interest Payable | − Interest Expense |

Interest payment (periodically, perhaps semiannually):

− Cash − Interest Payable

Amortization (each time interest is accrued):

Discount:

| +Discount on Bonds | − Interest Expense (An increase in interest expense) |

Premium:

| − Premium on Bonds | + Interest Expense (A reduction in interest expense) |

Discount or premium is sometimes amortized on a straight-line basis over the life of the bonds. However, it is more appropriate to use a compound interest method that results in amortization related to the **carrying value** (face amount plus unamortized premium or minus unamortized discount) of the bonds; using this method, amortization is largest in the first year of the bonds' life, and it decreases in subsequent years. The compound interest method of premium or discount amortization results in interest expense for a fiscal period being equal to the product of the market interest rate at the date the bonds were issued times the carrying value of the bonds at the beginning of that fiscal period.

Bonds payable are reported on the balance sheet at their carrying value. Sometimes this amount is referred to as the **book value** of the bonds.

When bonds are paid off, or retired, at maturity, all of the premium or discount will have been amortized to interest expense over the life of the bonds, and the effect of the transaction is:

Balance sheet	Income statement

Assets = Liabilities + Owners' equity ← Net income = Revenues − Expenses
− Cash   − Bonds
         Payable

If the bonds are called, or redeemed prior to maturity, it is appropriate to write off the unamortized balance of premium or discount as part of the transaction. Since a call premium is usually involved in an early retirement of bonds, a loss on the retirement will usually be recognized, although a gain on the retirement is possible. The effect of an early retirement of bonds having a book value of $95,000 by redeeming them for a total payment of $102,000 is:

Balance sheet	Income statement

Assets = Liabilities + Owners' equity ← Net income = Revenues − Expenses

Cash	Bonds Payable		Loss on
− 102,000	− 100,000		Retirement
			of Bonds
	Discount on		− 7,000
	Bonds Payable		
	+ 5,000		

The loss or gain on the retirement of the bonds is reported as an extraordinary item (explained in more detail in Chapter 9) in the income statement. The loss or gain is not considered part of operating income or interest expense. The firm is willing to retire the bonds and recognize the loss because it will save, in future interest expense, more than the loss incurred.

A discussion of bonds involves quite a bit of specialized terminology, and although it all doesn't have to be mastered to understand the financial statement impact of bond transactions, it is relevant to understanding bonds.

The contract between the issuer of the bonds and the bond holders is the **bond indenture,** and it is frequently administered by a third party, the **trustee of bonds**—often a bank trust department. Bonds are issued in one of two forms: **registered bonds** and **coupon bonds.**

The name and address of the owner of a registered bond is known to the issuer, and interest payments are mailed to the bond holder on a quarterly or semiannual basis, as called for in the indenture. The owner of a coupon bond is not known to the issuer; the bond holder receives interest by clipping a coupon on the interest payment date and depositing it in her/his bank account. The coupon is then sent to the trustee, and is honored as if it were a check. Coupon bonds are no longer issued because federal income tax regulations have been changed to require interest payers to report the name and social security number of payees, but coupon bonds issued prior to that regulation are still outstanding.

Bonds are also classified according to the security, or collateral, that is pledged by the issuer. **Debenture bonds** (or **debentures**) are bonds that are secured only by the general credit of the issuer. **Mortgage bonds** are secured by a lien against real estate owned by the issuer. **Collateral trust bonds** are secured by the pledge of securities or other intangible property.

Another classification of bonds relates to when the bonds mature. **Serial bonds** are repaid in installments. The installments may or may not be equal in amount; the first installment is usually scheduled for a date several years after the issuance of the bonds. Most bonds are **callable bonds;** this means that the issuer may pay off the bonds before the scheduled maturity date. Bonds will be called if market interest rates have dropped below the rate being paid on the bonds and the firm can save interest costs by issuing new bonds at a lower rate, or, if the firm has enough cash that will not be needed for operations in the immediate future, it can redeem the bonds to save more interest expense than the interest income that could be earned by investing the excess cash. There is usually a **call premium** paid to the bond holder if the bond is called; that is, the bond holder receives more than the face amount of the bond because she/he must reinvest the proceeds, usually at a lower interest rate than was being earned on the called bonds. **Convertible** bonds may be converted into stock of the issuer corporation. The number of shares of stock into which a bond is convertible is established when the bond is issued. If the stock price has risen substantially while the bonds have been outstanding, the bond holder may elect to receive shares of stock that will be worth more than the face amount of the bonds when the bonds mature or are called.

The specific characteristics, the interest rate, and the maturity date are usually included in a bond's description. For example, you may hear or read about long-term debt described as Cruiser, Inc.'s, 12 percent convertible debentures due in 1998, or its 12.5 percent First Mortgage Serial Bonds with maturities from 1995 to 2005.

Deferred Income Taxes

This long-term liability reflects income taxes that are expected to be paid more than a year after the balance sheet date. The firm does not have a present obligation to pay the amount of **deferred**

income taxes to the Internal Revenue Service or state and local governments; this liability arises from the accounting process of matching revenues and expenses, and the appropriateness of recognizing a liability for the tax consequences of events that have taken place up to the balance sheet date. Some of these events cause temporary differences between factors recognized in the determination of book income and those recognized in the determination of taxable income.

The most significant temporary difference item for most firms relates to depreciation expense. As previously explained, a firm may use straight-line depreciation for financial reporting purposes, and the Modified Accelerated Cost Recovery System (prescribed in the Internal Revenue Code) for calculating depreciation expense for income tax determination purposes. To calculate the amount of the current liability to be recorded as Income Taxes Payable, the company's actual tax liability is determined. A deferred tax liability is calculated at the end of the fiscal period by multiplying temporary differences that will result in taxable income in future years by tax rates provided in the current tax law. Income tax expense on the income statement is the sum of the current taxes payable plus the increase (or less the decrease) in the deferred tax liability from the beginning to the end of the fiscal period.

If income tax rates do not decrease, the deferred income tax liability of most firms will increase over time, because as firms grow, they acquire more and more depreciable assets, and price-level increases cause costs for replacement assets to be higher than the cost of assets being replaced. Thus the temporary difference between book and tax depreciation expense grows each year because the excess of book depreciation expense over income tax depreciation for older assets is more than offset by the excess of tax depreciation over book depreciation for newer assets. The effect of recognizing income tax liabilities and expense for firms with a growing deferred tax liability is:

Balance sheet	Income statement
Assets = Liabilities + Owners' equity ←	Net income = Revenues − Expenses
+ Current Tax Liability	− Income Tax Expense
+ Deferred Tax Liability	

Some accountants have questioned the appropriateness of showing deferred taxes as a liability, since in the aggregate the balance of this account has grown larger and larger for many firms and therefore never seems to actually become payable. Note from the Consolidated Balance Sheets on page 19 of Appendix A that Armstrong World Industries, Inc.'s deferred income taxes at December 31, 1991, amounted to about 18 percent of the company's owners' equity. The amount of Armstrong's deferred income taxes has grown steadily over the years.

Most deferred income taxes result from the temporary difference between book and tax depreciation expense, but there are other temporary differences as well. For example, when the temporary difference involves an expense that is recognized for financial accounting purposes before it is deductible for tax purposes, a deferred tax asset can arise. This is an extremely complex issue that has caused a great deal of debate within the accounting profession.

The accounting described here is based on a standard about accounting for income taxes issued by the FASB in 1987. This standard, referred to as *FAS 96,* was the result of an extensive review of past pronouncements and suggestions for change. FAS 96 reaffirmed the comprehensive recognition of deferred taxes, but, as explained above, did provide that the amount of the deferred income tax liability be a function of the tax consequences of temporary differences based on provisions in the current tax law, including tax rates specified for future years. This is a significant change from prior accounting for deferred income taxes that will probably cause the deferred income tax liability of many companies to fall because of a 1986 reduction in federal corporate income tax rates. The provisions of this standard were to become effective for fiscal years beginning after December 15, 1988. However, in late 1988 the FASB deferred the effective date to years beginning after December 15, 1989, to give companies more time to deal with implementation issues. During 1989 the FASB received heavy pressure from companies about the impact of FAS 96, and the costs of implementing it. In December 1989, the implementation date was moved forward to years beginning after December 15, 1991. During 1992 the FASB proposed revisions in the standard to reduce its complexity and to address concerns about the criteria for recognizing and measuring deferred tax assets. Because of these revisions, which would take effect for years beginning after December 15, 1992, the implementation date of FAS 96 was deferred to years beginning after December 15, 1992. In spite of these developments and postponements, some companies (including Armstrong World Industries, Inc.) have already adopted the new standard. The history of accounting for deferred taxes is an example of the way accounting standards evolve over time.

Other Long-Term Liabilities

Frequently included in this balance sheet category are obligations to pension plans and other employee benefit plans, including deferred compensation and bonus plans. Expenses of these plans are accrued and reflected in the income statement of the fiscal period in which the benefit is earned by the employee. Because benefits are frequently conditional upon continued employment, future salary levels, and other factors, and because the cost to the employing company will depend upon income earned on funds in the pension or other benefit plan trust accounts that have been or will be invested over a period of time, actuaries and other experts are involved in estimating the expense to be reported in a given fiscal period. Because of the large number of significant factors that must be estimated in the expense and liability calculations, accounting for pension plans is a complex topic that has been controversial over the years. In 1985 the FASB issued an accounting standard to increase the uniformity of accounting for pensions. One of the significant provisions of the standard requires the recognition of a minimum liability on the balance sheet if the fair market value of the pension plan assets is less than the accumulated benefit obligation to pension plan participants.

An issue related to pensions is accounting for postretirement benefit plans other than pensions. These plans provide medical, hospitalization, life insurance, and other benefits to retired employees. The cost of these plans was generally reported as an expense in the fiscal period in which payments were made to the plans that provide the benefits, and an entity's liabilities under these plans were not reflected in the balance sheet. Late in 1990, after several years of study and quite a bit of controversy, the FASB issued a standard that requires, beginning no later than in 1993 financial statements, recognition of the accumulated liability and accrual of costs during the employees' working years when the benefits are earned. Thus, the concept of matching revenues and expenses is to be applied on the same basis as for pension plans. One major difference between pension plans and other postretirement benefit plans is that very few firms had funded their other postretirement benefit plans. This means that the liabilities to be recognized are very large—in some cases more than half of a firm's owners' equity. The FASB standard gives firms the choice of recognizing the expense and accumulated liability all at once, or deferring the expense and recognizing it over 20 years (or the remaining service life of the covered employees, if longer). As you read about the reported profits of firms for 1992 and 1993, be alert for discussion about the financial statement impact of this FASB standard.

Another item included with other long-term liabilities of some firms is estimated liability under lawsuits in progress, product warranty programs, and other expenses. The liability is reflected at its estimated amount, and the related expense is reported in the income statement of the period in which the expense was incurred or the liability was identified. Sometimes the term *reserve* is used to describe these items, as in "reserve for product warranty claims." However, the term *reserve* is misleading because this amount refers to an estimated liability, not an amount of money that has been set aside to meet the liability.

The last caption in the long-term liability section of many balance sheets is **minority interest in subsidiaries.** A subsidiary is a corporation that is more than 50 percent owned by the firm for which the financial statements have been prepared. (See Business Procedure Capsule 4 in Chapter 2 for more discussion about a subsidiary.) The financial statements of the parent company and its subsidiaries are combined through a process known as *consolidation*. The resulting financial statements are referred to as the **consolidated financial statements** of the parent and its subsidiary(ies). In consolidation, most of the assets and liabilities of the parent and subsidiary are added together. Reciprocal amounts (e.g., a parent's account receivable from a subsidiary and the subsidiary's account payable to the parent) are eliminated, or offset. The parent's investment in the subsidiary (an asset) is offset against the owners' equity of the subsidiary. Minority interest arises if the subsidiary is not 100 percent owned by the parent company because the parent's investment will be less than the owners' equity of the subsidiary. Minority interest is the equity of the other, or the minority, stockholders in the owners' equity of the subsidiary. This amount does not represent what the parent company would have to pay to acquire the rest of the stock of the subsidiary, nor is it a liability in the true sense of the term. The minority interest reported on a consolidated balance sheet is included because the subsidiary's assets and liabilities (except those eliminated to avoid double counting) have been added to the parent company's assets and liabilities, and the parent's share of owners' equity of the subsidiary is included in consolidated owners' equity, so to keep the balance sheet in balance, the equity of the minority stockholders in the owners' equity of the subsidiary must be shown.

Although usually included with noncurrent liabilities, some accountants believe that minority interest should be shown as a separate item between liabilities and owners' equity because this amount is not really a liability of the consolidated entity.

SUMMARY

This chapter has discussed the accounting for and presentation of the following liabilities and related income statement accounts. Contra liabilities and reductions of expense accounts are in parentheses.

Balance sheet	Income statement
Assets = Liabilities + Owners' equity ← Net income = Revenues − Expenses	
Current Liabilities:	
Short-Term Debt	Interest Expense
(Discount on Short- . . . . Term Debt)	Interest Expense
Current Maturities of Long-Term Debt	
Accounts Payable	(Purchase Discounts)
	or:
	Purchase Discounts Lost
Unearned Revenue	Revenue
Other Accrued . . . . Liabilities	Various Expenses
Long-Term Liabilities:	
Bonds Payable	Interest Expense
(Discount on . . . . Bonds Payable)	Interest Expense
Premium on . . . . Bonds Payable	(Interest Expense)
Deferred Income . . . . Taxes	Income Tax Expense

Liabilities are obligations of the entity. Most liabilities arise because funds have been borrowed or an obligation is recognized as a result of the accrual accounting process. Current liabilities are those that are expected to be paid within a year of the balance sheet date. Noncurrent, or long-term, liabilities are expected to be paid more than a year after the balance sheet date.

Short-term debt, such as a bank loan, is obtained to provide cash for seasonal buildup of inventory. The loan is expected to be repaid when the inventory is sold and the accounts receivable from the sale are collected. The interest cost of short-term debt is sometimes calculated on a discount basis. Discount results in a higher annual percentage rate than straight interest because the discount is based on the maturity value of the loan, and the proceeds available to the borrower are calculated as the maturity value minus the discount. Discount is recorded as a contra liability, and is amortized to interest expense. The amount of discounted short-term debt shown as a liability on the balance sheet is the maturity value minus the unamortized discount.

Long-term debt principal payments that will be made within a year of the balance sheet date are classified as a current liability.

Accounts payable represents amounts owed to suppliers of inventories and other resources. Some accounts payable are subject to a cash discount if paid within a time frame specified by the supplier. The internal control system of most entities will attempt to encourage adherence to the policy of taking all cash discounts offered.

Unearned revenue and other deferred credits, and other accrued liabilities, arise primarily because of accrual accounting procedures that result in the recognition of expenses in the fiscal period in which they are incurred. Many of these liabilities are estimated because the actual liability isn't known when the financial statements are prepared.

Long-term debt is a significant part of the capital structure of many firms. Funds are borrowed, rather than invested by the owners, because the firm expects to take advantage of the financial leverage associated with debt. If borrowed money can be invested to earn a higher return (ROI) than the interest cost, the return on the owners' investment (ROE) will be greater than ROI. However, the opposite is also true. Leverage adds to the risk associated with an investment in an entity.

Long-term debt is frequently in the form of bonds payable. Bonds have a stated interest rate that is almost always a fixed percentage, a face amount or principal, and a maturity date when they must be paid. Because the interest rate on a bond is fixed, changes in the market rate of interest result in fluctuations in the market value of the bond. As market interest rates rise, bond prices fall, and vice versa. The market value of a bond is the present value of the interest payments and maturity value, discounted at the market interest rate. When bonds are issued and the market rate at the date of issue is different from the stated rate of the bond, a premium or discount results. Both bond premium and discount are amortized to interest expense over the life of the bond. Premium amortization reduces interest expense below the amount of interest paid. Discount amortization increases interest expense over the amount of interest paid. A bond is sometimes retired before its maturity date because market interest rates have dropped significantly below the stated interest rate of the bond. Early retirement of bonds can result in a gain or loss.

Deferred income taxes result from temporary differences between book and taxable income. The most significant temporary difference is caused by the different depreciation expense calculation methods used for each purpose. The amount of deferred income tax liability is the amount of income tax expected to be paid in future years, based on tax rates provided in the current law applied to the total amount of temporary differences.

Other long-term liabilities may relate to pension obligations, other postretirement benefit plan obligations, warranty obligations, or estimated liabilities under lawsuits in process. Also included in this caption in the balance sheet of some companies is the equity of minority stockholders in the net assets of less than wholly owned subsidiaries, all of whose assets and liabilities are included in the entity's consolidated balance sheet.

Refer to the Armstrong World Industries, Inc., balance sheet and financial review in Appendix A, and to other financial statements you may have, and observe how information about liabilities is presented.

KEY TERMS AND CONCEPTS

account payable *(p. 209)*   A liability representing an amount payable to another entity, usually because of the purchase of merchandise or a service on credit.

annual percentage rate (APR) *(p. 207)*   The effective (true) annual interest rate on a loan.

bond discount *(p. 215)*   The excess of the face amount of a bond or bonds issued over the market value of a bond or the proceeds of the issue.

bond indenture *(p. 220)*   The formal agreement between the borrower and investor(s) in bonds.

bond premium *(p. 215)*   The excess of the market value of a bond or the proceeds of a bond issue over the face amount of a bond or the bonds issued.

bond or **bond payable** *(p. 215)*   A long-term liability with a stated interest rate and maturity date, usually issued in denominations of $1,000.

book value *(p. 219)*   The balance of the ledger account (including related contra accounts, if any), for an asset, liability, or owners' equity account. Sometimes referred to as *carrying value*.

callable bonds *(p. 221)* Bonds that can be redeemed by the issuer, at its option, prior to the maturity date.

call premium *(p. 221)* An amount paid in excess of the face amount of a bond when the bond is repaid prior to its established maturity date.

carrying value *(p. 219)* The balance of the ledger account (including related contra accounts, if any) for an asset, liability, or owners' equity account. Sometimes referred to as *book value*.

collateral trust bond *(p. 221)* A bond secured by the pledge of securities or other intangible property.

consolidated financial statements *(p. 225)* Financial statements resulting from the combination of parent and subsidiary company financial statements.

contra liability *(p. 206)* An account that normally has a debit balance and that is subtracted from a related liability on the balance sheet.

convertible bonds *(p. 221)* Bonds that can be converted to preferred or common stock of the issuer, at the bond holder's option.

coupon bond *(p. 220)* A bond for which the owner's name and address are not known by the issuer and/or trustee. Interest is received by clipping interest coupons that are attached to the bond and submitting them to the issuer.

coupon rate *(p. 216)* The rate used to calculate the interest payments on a bond. Sometimes called the *stated rate*.

current maturity of long-term debt *(p. 209)* Principal payments on long-term debt that are scheduled to be paid within one year of the balance sheet date.

debentures *(p. 221)* Bonds secured by the general credit of the issuer.

deferred credit *(p. 209)* An account with a credit balance that will be recognized as a revenue or as an expense reduction in a future period.

deferred income taxes *(p. 221)* A long-term liability that arises because of temporary differences between when an item (principally depreciation expense) is recognized for book purposes and tax purposes.

discount loan *(p. 207)* A loan on which interest is paid at the beginning of the loan period.

face amount *(p. 215)* The principal amount of a bond.

financial leverage *(p. 213)* The use of debt (with a fixed interest rate) that causes a difference between return on investment and return on equity.

interest calculation—discount basis *(p. 208)* Interest calculations in which the principal is the amount of money to be repaid by the borrower. The interest (called *discount*) is subtracted from the principal to determine the amount of money (the proceeds) made available to the borrower.

interest calculation—straight basis *(p. 207)* Interest calculation in which the principal is the amount of money made available to the borrower.

long-term debt *(p. 213)* A liability that will be paid more than one year from the balance sheet date.

maturity date *(p. 205)* The date when a loan is scheduled to be repaid.

minority interest in subsidiaries *(p. 225)*   An account that arises in the preparation of consolidated financial statements when some subsidiaries are less than 100 percent owned by the parent company.

mortgage bond *(p. 221)*   A bond secured by a mortgage on real estate.

note payable *(p. 205)*   Usually a short-term liability that arises from issuing a note; a formal promise to pay a stated amount at a stated date, usually with interest at a stated rate, and sometimes secured by collateral.

prime rate *(p. 205)*   The interest rate charged by banks on loans to large and most creditworthy customers; a benchmark interest rate.

proceeds *(p. 208)*   The amount of cash received in a transaction.

registered bond *(p. 220)*   A bond for which the owner's name and address are recorded by the issuer and/or trustee.

revolving line of credit *(p. 205)*   A loan on which regular payments are to be made, but which can be increased to a predetermined limit as additional funds must be borrowed.

serial bond *(p. 221)*   A bond that is to be repaid in installments.

stated rate *(p. 218)*   The rate used to calculate the amount of interest payable on a bond. Sometimes called the *coupon rate*.

trustee of bonds *(p. 220)*   The agent who coordinates activities between the bond issuer and the investor in bonds.

unearned revenue *(p. 209)*   A liability arising from receipt of cash before the related revenue has been earned. See *deferred credit*.

working capital loan *(p. 205)*   A short-term loan that is expected to be repaid from collections of accounts receivable.

EXERCISES AND PROBLEMS

7–1. On April 15, 1993, Arbyco, Inc., obtained a six-month working capital loan from its bank. The face amount of the note signed by the treasurer was $300,000. The interest rate charged by the bank was 9 percent. The bank made the loan on a discount basis.

Required:
  a. Calculate the loan proceeds made available to Arbyco.
  b. Calculate the amount of interest expense applicable to this loan during the six months ended June 30, 1993.
  c. What is the amount of the current liability related to this loan to be shown in the June 30, 1993, balance sheet?

7–2. On August 1, 1993, Colombo Co.'s treasurer signed a note promising to pay $240,000 on December 31, 1993. The proceeds of the note were $232,000.

Required:
  a. Calculate the discount rate used by the lender.
  b. Calculate the effective interest rate on the loan.
  c. Use the horizontal model (or write the journal entry) to show the effect of recording interest expense for the month of September.

7–3. At March 31, 1993, the end of the first year of operations at Grencon, Inc., the firm's accountant neglected to accrue payroll taxes of $4,800 that were applicable to payrolls for the year then ended.

Required:

a. Use the horizontal model (or write the journal entry) to show the effect of the accrual that should have been made as of March 31, 1993.

b. Explain the impact on Grencon's income statement for the year ended March 31, 1993, and on the balance sheet at March 31, 1993, of the failure to make the payroll tax accrual.

c. Assume that when the payroll taxes were paid in April 1993, the payroll tax expense account was charged. Assume that at March 31, 1994, the accountant again neglected to accrue the payroll tax liability, which was $5,000 at that date. Explain the impact on Grencon's income statement for the year ended March 31, 1994, and on the balance sheet at March 31, 1994, of the failure to have made the payroll tax accruals.

7–4. Spartan Co. operates in a city in which real estate tax bills for one year are issued in May of the subsequent year. Thus tax bills for 1993 are issued in May 1994. Taxes are payable in two installments: half on June 1 and half on September 1.

Required:

a. Explain how the amount of tax expense for calendar 1993, and the amount of taxes payable (if any) at December 31, 1993, can be determined.

b. Use the horizontal model (or write the journal entry) to show the effect of accruing 1993 taxes of $7,200 at December 31, 1993.

c. Spartan Co.'s real estate taxes have been increasing at the rate of 5 percent annually. Determine the income statement and balance sheet effects of not accruing 1993 taxes at December 31, 1993 (assuming that taxes in *(b)* are not accrued).

7–5. Assume that Blueco Button Co. offered its customers, which are primarily retail fabric stores, an advertising allowance equal to 5 percent of the amount of purchases from Blueco during December, if the retail store would spend the money for advertising in January. Blueco's sales in December totaled $2,700,000, and it was expected that 60 percent of those sales were made to retailers who would take advantage of the advertising allowance offer.

Required:

Use the horizontal model (or write the journal entry) to show the effect of the accrual (if any) that should be made as of December 31 with respect to the advertising allowance offer.

7–6. Prist Co. has not provided a warranty on its products, but competitive pressures forced management to add this feature at the beginning of 1993. Based on an analysis of customer complaints made over the past two years, the cost of a warranty program was estimated at 0.2 percent of sales. During 1993 sales totaled $4,600,000. Actual costs of servicing products under warranty totaled $12,700.

Required:

a. Use the horizontal model (or a T-account of the Estimated Liability under Warranty) to show the effect of having the warranty program during 1993.

        b. What type of accrual adjustment should be made at the end of 1993?

        c. Describe how the amount of the accrual adjustment could be determined.

7–7. Coolfroth Brewing Company distributes its products in an aluminum keg. Customers are charged a deposit of $15 per keg; deposits are recorded in the Keg Deposits account.

Required:

        a. Where on the balance sheet will the Keg Deposits account be found? Explain your answer.

        b. Use the horizontal model (or write the journal entry) to show the effect of a refund.

        c. A keg use analyst who works for Coolfroth estimates that 200 kegs for which deposits were received during the year will never be returned. What accounting, if any, would be appropriate for the deposits associated with these kegs?

        d. Describe the accounting that would be appropriate for the cost of the kegs.

7–8. Kirkland Theater sells season tickets for six events at a price of $42. For the 1993 season 1,200 season tickets were sold.

Required:

        a. Use the horizontal model (or write the journal entry) to show the effect of the sale of the season tickets.

        b. Use the horizontal model (or write the journal entry) to show the effect of presenting an event.

        c. Where on the balance sheet would the account balance representing funds received for performances not yet presented be classified?

7–9. Gramm Co. issued $1 million face amount of 11 percent 20-year bonds on April 1, 1993.

Required:

        a. Assume that market interest rates were slightly higher than 11 percent when the bonds were sold. Would the proceeds from the bond issue have been more than, less than, or equal to the face amount? Explain.

        b. Assume that the proceeds were $1,080,000. Use the horizontal model (or write the journal entry) to show the effect of issuing the bonds.

        c. Calculate the interest expense that Gramm Co. will show with respect to these bonds in its income statement for the year ended September 30, 1993, assuming that the premium of $80,000 is amortized on a straight-line basis.

7–10. On March 1, 1988, Joe Investor purchased $7,000 of White Co.'s 8 percent 20-year bonds at face amount. White Co. has paid the interest due on the bonds regularly. On March 1, 1993, market interest rates had risen to 12 percent, and Joe is considering selling the bonds.

Required:

Using the present value tables in Chapter 6, calculate the market value of Joe's bonds on March 1, 1993.

7–11. Riley Co. has outstanding $4 million face amount of 15 percent bonds that were issued several years ago, and that mature in the year 2008. The bonds are callable at 102 (i.e., they can be paid off now by paying the bond holders 102 percent of the face amount).

Required:

a. Under what circumstances would Riley Co. managers consider calling the bonds?

b. If the bonds were called, how would this transaction be reported on the statement of cash flows?

7–12. Howard Stone Co. issued $25 million face amount of 9 percent bonds when market interest rates were 8.92 percent for bonds of similar risk and other characteristics.

Required:

a. How much interest will be paid annually on these bonds?

b. Were the bonds issued at a premium or discount? Explain your answer.

c. Will the annual interest expense on these bonds be more than, equal to, or less than the amount of interest paid each year? Explain your answer.

7–13. Describe the risks associated with financial leverage.

7–14. A firm that issues long-term debt that has a cost of 10 percent and that can be invested at an ROI of 12 percent is using financial leverage. What effect will this leverage have on the firm's ROE relative to having the same amount of funds invested by the owners?

7–15. Refer to the Armstrong World Industries, Inc., Annual Report in Appendix A.

Required:

Ⓐrmstrong

a. Using data from the December 31, 1991, balance sheet, calculate the percentage of the deferred income tax liability to total owners' equity. Is the deferred income tax amount material?

b. Find the amount of deferred income tax expense included in total income tax expense, as reported in the detail of taxes table on page 23. Find the amount of deferred tax expense arising from the difference between book and tax depreciation for the years 1989, 1990, and 1991. What factors have caused this pattern?

c. Some financial analysts maintain that the deferred tax liability should be considered as part of owners' equity, rather than as a liability, for purposes of evaluating the relationship between debt and equity, and calculating return on equity. Why might analysts do this?

7–16. The difference between the amounts of book and tax depreciation expense, as well as the desire to report income tax expense that is related to book income before taxes, causes a long-term liability to be created and reported on the balance sheet.

Required:

a. What is the name of this long-term liability?

b. The amount of this liability reported on the balance sheets of many firms has been increasing over the years, thus creating the impression that the liability is never paid. Why has the amount of this liability risen steadily for many firms?

7–17. Enter the following column headings across the top of a sheet of paper.

Transaction/ Adjustment	Current Assets	Current Liabilities	Long-Term Debt	Net Income

Enter the transaction/adjustment letter in the first column, and show the effect, if any, of each of the transactions/adjustments on the appropriate balance sheet category or on the income statement by entering the amount and indicating whether it is an addition (+) or a subtraction (−).

a. Wages of $867 for the last three days of the fiscal period have not been accrued.
b. Interest of $170 on a bank loan has not been accrued.
c. Interest on bonds payable has not been accrued for the current month. The company has outstanding $240,000 of 8.5 percent bonds.
d. During the fiscal period advance payments from customers totaling $1,500 were received and recorded as sales revenues. The items will not be delivered to the customers until the next fiscal period.

7–18. Enter the following column headings across the top of a sheet of paper.

Transaction/ Adjustment	Current Assets	Current Liabilities	Long-Term Debt	Net Income

Enter the transaction/adjustment letter in the first column, and show the effect, if any, of each of the transactions/adjustments on the appropriate balance sheet category or on the income statement by entering the amount and indicating whether it is an addition (+) or a subtraction (−).

a. Wages of $768 accrued at the end of the prior fiscal period were paid this fiscal period.
b. Real estate taxes of $2,400 applicable to the current period have not been accrued.
c. Interest on bonds payable has not been accrued for the current month. The company has outstanding $360,000 of 7.5 percent bonds.
d. The premium related to the above bonds has not been amortized for the current month. The current month amortization is $823.
e. Based on past experience with its warranty program, it is estimated that warranty expense for the current period should be 0.2 percent of sales of $918,000.
f. Analysis of the company's income taxes indicates that taxes currently payable are $76,000, and that the deferred tax liability should be increased $21,000.

7–19. Enter the following column headings across the top of a sheet of paper.

Transaction/ Adjustment	Current Assets	Long-Lived Assets	Current Liabilities	Long-Term Liabilities	Owners' Equity	Net Income

Enter the transaction/adjustment letter in the first column, and show the effect, if any, of each transaction or adjustment on the appropriate balance sheet category or on net income by entering for each category affected the account name and amount, and indicating whether it is an addition (+) or a subtraction (−). Items that affect net income should not also be shown as affecting owners' equity.

a. Income tax expense of $700 for the current period is accrued. Of the accrual, $200 represents deferred income taxes.

b. Bonds payable with a face amount of $5,000 are issued at a price of 99.

c. Of the proceeds from the above bonds, $3,000 is used to purchase land for future expansion.

d. Because of warranty claims, finished goods inventory costing $64 is sent to customers to replace defective products.

7–20. Enter the following column headings across the top of a sheet of paper.

Transaction/ Adjustment	Current Assets	Long-Lived Assets	Current Liabilities	Long-Term Liabilities	Owners' Equity	Net Income

Enter the transaction/adjustment letter in the first column, and show the effect, if any, of each transaction or adjustment on the appropriate balance sheet category or on net income by entering for each category affected the account name and amount, and indicating whether it is an addition (+) or a subtraction (−). Items that affect net income should not also be shown as affecting owners' equity.

a. Recorded the financing lease of a truck. The present value of the lease payments is $32,000; the total of the lease payments to be made is $58,000.

b. Paid, within the discount period, an account payable of $1,500 on which terms were 1/15,n30. The purchase had been recorded at the gross amount.

c. Issued $7,000 of bonds payable at a price of 102.

d. Adjusted the estimated liability under a warranty program by reducing previously accrued warranty expense by $3,000.

e. Retired bonds payable with a carrying value of $3,000 by calling them at a redemption value of 101.

f. Accrued estimated health care costs for retirees; $43 is expected to be paid within a year and $628 is expected to be paid in more than a year.

Chapter 8

Accounting for and Presentation of Owners' Equity

Owners' equity is the claim of the entity's owners to the assets shown in the balance sheet. Another term for owners' equity is *net assets,* which is assets minus liabilities. Neither the liabilities nor the elements of owners' equity are specifically identifiable with particular assets, although certain assets may be pledged as collateral for some liabilities, as was explained in Chapter 7.

The specific terminology used to identify owners' equity will depend on the form of the entity's legal organization. For an individual proprietorship the term **proprietor's capital,** or *capital,* perhaps combined with the owner's name, is frequently used. For example, in the balance sheet of a single proprietorship owned by Mary Powers, owner's equity would be labeled Mary Powers, Capital. For a partnership **partners' capital** is the term used, and sometimes the capital account balance of each partner is shown on the balance sheet. In both proprietorships and partnerships no distinction is made between invested, or paid-in, capital and retained earnings.

Because the corporate form of organization is used for firms that account for most of the business activity in our economy, this text focuses on corporation owners' equity. As previously explained, there are two principal components of corporation owners' equity: paid-in capital and retained earnings. The financial statements of many small businesses that use the corporate form of organization are likely to show in owners' equity only capital stock (which is paid-in capital) and retained earnings. However, as shown by the shareholders' equity section of the Consolidated Balance Sheets of Armstrong World Industries, Inc., on page 19 of Appendix A, the owners' equity section can become quite complex. The owners'

EXHIBIT 8–1   Owners' Equity Section of Racers, Inc., Balance Sheets at August 31, 1993 and 1992

	August 31	
	1993	*1992*
Owners' equity:		
Paid-in capital:		
Preferred stock, 6%, $100 par value, cumulative, callable at $102, 5,000 shares authorized, issued, and outstanding	$ 500,000	$ 500,000
Common stock, $2 par value, 1,000,000 shares authorized, 240,000 shares issued at August 31, 1993, and 200,000 shares issued at August 31, 1992	480,000	400,000
Additional paid-in capital	3,260,000	2,820,000
Total paid-in capital	$4,240,000	$3,720,000
Retained earnings	2,900,000	2,600,000
Less: Common stock in treasury, at cost; 1,000 shares at August 31, 1993	(12,000)	—
Total owners' equity	$7,128,000	$6,320,000

equity section of the balance sheets in other annual reports that you have may appear equally complex. The learning objectives of this chapter relate to explaining those complexities, and in that process having you understand many characteristics of owners' equity that are relevant to the personal investment decisions you are likely to be making in the future.

For the purposes of our discussion, the owners' equity section of the balance sheets of Racers, Inc., in Exhibit 8–1 will be explained.

LEARNING OBJECTIVES

After studying this chapter you should understand:

- The characteristics of common stock, and how common stock is presented in the balance sheet.
- Two methods that common stockholders have to exercise their right/ obligation to elect members of the board of directors.
- What preferred stock is, and what its advantages and disadvantages to the corporation are.

- How preferred stock is presented in the balance sheet.
- The accounting for a cash dividend, and the dates involved in the dividend transaction.
- What stock dividends and stock splits are, and why each is used.
- What treasury stock is, why it is acquired, and how treasury stock transactions affect owners' equity.
- What the cumulative foreign currency translation adjustment is, and why it appears in owners' equity.
- How owners' equity transactions for the year are reported in the financial statements.

PAID-IN CAPITAL

Common Stock

As already explained, **common stock** (called **capital stock** at times, especially when there are no other classes of stock authorized) represents residual ownership (i.e., the common stockholders are the ultimate owners of the corporation). Common stockholders have claim to all assets that remain in the entity after all liabilities and preferred stock claims (described in the next section) have been satisfied. In the case of bankruptcy or forced liquidation, this residual claim may not have any value because the liabilities and preferred stock claims may exceed the amount realized from the assets in liquidation. In this severe case the liability of the common stockholders is limited to the amount they have invested in the stock; common stockholders cannot be forced by creditors and/or preferred stockholders to invest additional amounts to make up their losses. In the more positive, and usual, case the common stockholders prosper because the profits of the firm exceed the fixed claims of the creditors (interest) and preferred stockholders (preferred dividends). All of these profits accrue to the common stockholders—there is no upper limit to the value of their ownership interest. Of course, it is the market value of the common stock that reflects the profitability (or lack thereof) and ultimate dividend-paying capability of the corporation.

An important right/obligation of the common stockholders is that of electing the members of the board of directors of the corporation. The election process can take one of two forms; these are described in Business Procedure Capsule 14—Electing Directors. The board of directors hires the officers of the corporation, and the officers execute the strategies for achieving corporate objectives.

• **BUSINESS PROCEDURE CAPSULE 14**
Electing Directors

Directors are elected by a **cumulative voting** procedure, or on a slate basis. Under cumulative voting each stockholder is entitled to cast a number of votes equal to the number of shares owned multiplied by the number of directors to be elected. Thus if five directors are to be elected, the owner of 100 shares of common stock is entitled to 500 votes that can all be cast for one candidate, that can be cast as 100 votes for each of five candidates, or that can be cast in any combination between these two extremes. In **slate voting** the common stockholder is entitled to one vote for each share owned, but each vote is for an entire slate of candidates.

In most cases the voting method doesn't affect the outcome. A committee of the board of directors nominates director candidates (equal to the number of directors to be elected), a proxy committee made up of members of the board seeks proxies from the stockholders, and the required number of nominees are duly elected. Occasionally, however, an outside group challenges the existing board; under these circumstances the election can be exciting. Each group nominates director candidates and solicits stockholder votes. Under slate voting the successful group will be the one that gets a majority of the vote; that group's entire slate will be elected. Of course, controlling 50.1 percent of the voting shares will ensure success. Under cumulative voting, however, it is possible for a minority group of share owners to concentrate their votes on one or two of their own candidates, thus making it easier to secure representation on the board of directors. For example, if five directors are to be elected, the votes of approximately 17 percent of the outstanding common stock are required to elect one director.

Many people, especially proponents of corporate democracy, favor cumulative voting. Some states require corporations organized under their laws to have cumulative voting for directors. Some corporations prefer to maintain a slate voting practice because this method makes getting a seat on the board more difficult for corporate raiders and others. Another tactic designed to reduce outsiders' chances of securing a director position is to provide for rolling terms for directors. That is, for a nine-member board three directors will be elected each year for a three-year term. Thus, even with cumulative voting, the votes of many more shares are required to elect one director than would be required if all nine directors are elected each year.

Some officers may also be directors **(inside directors),** but current practice is to have most boards made up primarily of **outside directors,** individuals who are not employed by the firm and who can bring an outside viewpoint to the considerations and deliberations of the board.

Common stockholders must also approve changes to the corporate charter (for example, when the number of shares of stock authorized is changed so that additional shares can be sold to raise more capital), and may have to approve transactions such as mergers or divestitures.

Common stock can have **par value,** or can be of a no-par-value variety. When it is used, par value is usually a nominal amount assigned to each share when the corporation is organized. In today's business world par value has virtually no financial reporting or economic significance with respect to common stock. In most states the par value of the issued shares represents the **legal capital** of the corporation. Most state corporation laws provide that stock with par value cannot be issued for a price less than par value, and they provide that total owners' equity cannot be reduced to less than legal capital by dividends or the purchase from shareowners of previously issued shares of stock. If the stock has par value, the amount reported in the balance sheet will be the par value multiplied by the number of shares issued. Any difference between par value and the amount realized from the sale of the stock is recorded as additional paid-in capital. Some firms assign a **stated value** to the common stock, which is essentially par value by another name. If a firm issues true no-par-value stock, then the total amount received from the sale of the shares is recorded as common stock.

The sale of common stock is illustrated for Racers, Inc., in Exhibit 8–1 and in the following horizontal model. During the year ended August 31, 1993, Racers sold 40,000 additional shares of its $2 par value common stock at a price of $13 per share. The effect of this stock issue on the financial statements of Racers, Inc., was:

Balance sheet		Income statement
Assets = Liabilities + Owners' equity	←	Net income = Revenues − Expenses
Cash	Common Stock	
+520,000	+ 80,000	
(40,000 shares × $13)	(40,000 shares × $2)	
	Additional Paid-In Capital	
	+ 440,000	
	(40,000 shares × $11)	

Refer to Exhibit 8–1 and notice the increase in common stock and additional paid-in capital.

A survey of the annual reports for 1990 of 600 publicly owned merchandising and manufacturing companies indicated that only

EXHIBIT 8–2 Balance Sheet Disclosure for Shares of Stock

Terminology	*Number of Shares Disclosed*	*Dollar Amount Disclosed*
Shares authorized	Number specified in the corporate charter	None
Shares issued	Number of shares that have been issued to shareowners	Number of shares × par or stated value or If no par or stated value, amount received from sale of shares
Shares outstanding	Number of shares still held by shareowners	None
Treasury stock	Number of issued shares purchased by corporation from shareowners and not formally retired	Cost of treasury stock owned by corporation

66 companies had no-par-value common stock. Of those 66 companies, 17 had an assigned or stated value per share.[1]

On the balance sheet the number of shares *authorized, issued,* and *outstanding* will be disclosed. The number of **authorized shares** is stated in the corporate charter that is filed with the state according to its laws regarding corporate organization. The number of **issued shares** is the number of shares of stock that have actually been transferred from the corporation to shareholders. The number of **outstanding shares** will differ from the number of issued shares if the firm has **treasury stock.** As explained in more detail later in this chapter, treasury stock is a firm's own stock that has been acquired by the firm. The relationship between these terms and the balance sheet disclosure required for each is summarized in Exhibit 8–2. The difference between the number of shares authorized and the number of shares issued represents the potential for additional shares to be issued. The common stock of many firms has a **preemptive right,** which gives present shareholders the right to purchase shares from any additional share issues in proportion to their

---

[1] *Accounting Trends and Techniques* (New York, AICPA, 1991), Table 2–33.

present percentage of ownership. The preemptive right is usually most significant in smaller, closely held corporations (i.e., those with only a few stockholders) in which existing stockholders want to prevent their existing ownership interest from being diluted. Even though they are not bound by a preemptive right provision, many large corporations offer existing stockholders the right to purchase additional shares when more capital is needed. This maintains stockholder loyalty, and can be a relatively inexpensive way to raise capital.

Preferred Stock

Preferred stock is a class of paid-in capital that is different from common stock, the principal type of paid-in capital, in that preferred stock has several debt-like features and a limited claim on assets in the event of liquidation. Also, in most cases, preferred stock does not have a voting privilege. (Common stock represents residual equity; that is, it has claim to all assets remaining after the liabilities and preferred stock claims have been met in the liquidation of the corporation.) Historically, preferred stock has been viewed as having less risk than common stock, and in the early years of the industrial revolution, when firms sought to raise the large amounts of capital that were required to finance factories and railroads, investors were more willing to acquire preferred stock in a firm than take the risks associated with common stock ownership. As firms have prospered and many investors have experienced the rewards of common stock ownership, preferred stock has become a less significant factor in the capital structure of many manufacturing, merchandising, and service-providing firms. However, utilities and financial corporations continue to issue preferred stock.

The preferences of preferred stock, relative to common stock, relate to dividends and claim on assets in the event of liquidation of the corporation, or redemption of the preferred stock. A **dividend** is a distribution of the earnings of the corporation to its owners. The dividend requirement of preferred stock must be satisfied before a dividend can be paid to the common stockholders. Most preferred stocks call for a quarterly or semiannual dividend, which must be kept current if there is to be a dividend on the common stock. The amount of the dividend is expressed in dollars and cents, or as a percentage of the par value of the preferred stock. As shown in Exhibit 8–1, the preferred stock of Racers, Inc., is referred to as "6%, $100 par value," This means that each share of preferred stock is entitled to an annual dividend of $6 (6% × $100). The same dividend result could have been accomplished by creating a $6 cumulative preferred stock. The terms of the stock issue will specify whether the dividend is to be paid at the rate of $1.50 per quarter, $3 semiannually, or $6 annually. Preferred stock issues, including that of Racers, Inc., usually provide a **cumulative dividend,** which means that if a dividend payment is not made, missed dividends must be paid subsequently before any dividend can be paid to the common stockholders. Occasionally, preferred stock issues have **participating dividends,** which means that after the common stockholders have received a specified dividend, any further dividends are shared by the preferred and common stockholders in a specified ratio. Calculation of a preferred stock dividend amount is illustrated in Exhibit 8–3. A preferred stock issue's claim on the assets in the event of liquidation **(liquidating value)** or redemption **(redemption value)** is an amount specified at the time the preferred stock is issued. If the preferred stock has a par value, the liquidating value or redemption value is usually equal to the par value, or the par value plus a slight premium. If the preferred stock has no par value, then the liquidating value or redemption value is a stated amount. In either case the claim in liquidation must be fulfilled before the common stockholders receive anything. However, once the liquidating claim is met, the preferred stockholders will not receive any additional amounts.

Callable preferred stock is redeemable (usually at a slight premium over par or liquidating value) at the option of the corporation. **Convertible preferred stock** may be exchanged for common stock of the corporation at the option of the stockholder at a conversion rate (e.g., six shares of common stock for each share of preferred stock) established when the preferred stock is issued. Note in Exhibit 8–1 that the preferred stock of Racer's, Inc., is callable at a price of $102.

You have probably noticed that preferred stock seems to have some of the characteristics of bonds payable, and you are right. Exhibit 8–4 summarizes the principal similarities and differences of the two. The tax deductibility of interest expense causes many financial mangers to prefer debt to preferred stock. After all, they reason, if a fixed amount is going to have to be paid out regularly, it might as well be in the form of deductible interest rather than nondeductible preferred dividends. Of 600 publicly owned industrial and merchandising companies whose annual reports for 1990 were reviewed by the AICPA, 447 had no preferred stock outstanding.[2]

---

[2] Ibid., Table 2–32.

EXHIBIT 8–3   Illustration of Preferred Stock Dividend Calculation

Case 1

6%, $100 par value cumulative preferred stock, 50,000 shares authorized, issued, and outstanding. Dividend payable semiannually, no dividends in arrears.

Semiannual dividend amount:

$$6\% \times \$100 \times 50{,}000 \text{ shares outstanding} \times \tfrac{1}{2} \text{ year} = \$150{,}000$$

Case 2

$4.50, $75 par value cumulative preferred stock, 50,000 shares authorized and issued, 40,000 shares outstanding. (There are 10,000 shares of treasury stock.) Dividend payable quarterly, no dividends in arrears.

Quarterly dividend amount:

$$\$4.50 \times 40{,}000 \text{ shares outstanding} \times \tfrac{1}{4} \text{ year} = \$45{,}000$$

Case 3

$4, $50 par value cumulative preferred stock, 100,000 shares authorized, 60,000 shares issued, 54,000 shares outstanding (there are 6,000 shares of treasury stock). Dividend payable annually. Dividends were not paid in prior two years.

Dividend required in current year to pay prior years' and current year's dividend:

$$\$4 \times 54{,}000 \text{ shares outstanding} \times 3 \text{ years} = \$648{,}000$$

Case 4

$2, $25 par value cumulative participating preferred stock, 30,000 shares authorized, 28,000 shares issued and outstanding. Dividend payable annually, no dividends in arrears. After a $2 per share dividend has been paid on the common stock, the preferred stock and common stock are to share equally on a per share basis in any additional dividends. The company has 100,000 shares of common stock outstanding, and dividends for the year total $300,000.

Allocation of $300,000 total dividend payments:
  Preferred stock base dividend:

$$\$2 \times 28{,}000 \text{ shares outstanding} = \$56{,}000$$

  Common stock base dividend:

$$\$2 \times 100{,}000 \text{ shares outstanding} = \$200{,}000$$

Additional dividends to be shared = $44,000

$$\text{Dividend per share} = \$44{,}000 \ / \ 128{,}000 \text{ shares} = \$.34375/\text{share}$$

Recap:
  Preferred stock: $2.34375/share × 28,000 shares = $ 65,625
  Common stock: $2.34375/share × 100,000 shares =   234,375
Total dividends $300,000

EXHIBIT 8–4 Comparison of Preferred Stock and Bonds Payable

Preferred Stock	*Bonds Payable*
	Similarities
Dividend is (usually) a fixed claim to income.	Interest is a fixed claim to income.
Redemption value is a fixed claim to assets.	Maturity value is a fixed claim to assets.
Is usually callable and may be convertible.	Is usually callable and may be convertible.
	Differences
Dividend may be skipped, even though it usually must be caught up if dividends are to be paid on the common stock.	Interest must be paid or firm faces bankruptcy.
No maturity date.	Principal must be paid at maturity.
Dividends are not an expense and are not deductible for income tax purposes.	Interest is a deductible expense for income tax purposes.

The reasons for having preferred stock include the facts that it is owners' equity and, from the creditors' point of view, it reduces the risk associated with financial leverage (introduced in Chapter 7). Financial firms (such as banks, insurance companies, and finance companies) and utilities frequently have a significant portion of their owners' equity represented by preferred stock. This is because a significant proportion of the capital requirements of these firms is provided by investors who prefer the relative security of preferred stock rather than debt and/or common stock.

In the balance sheet the par value and dividend rate (or the amount of the annual dividend requirement), the liquidating or redemption value, the number of shares authorized by the corporate charter, the number of shares issued, and the number of shares outstanding will be reported. Any difference between the number of shares issued and the number of shares outstanding is caused by shares held in the firm's treasury, or treasury stock, a topic to be explained in detail later. In addition, the amount of any dividends that have been missed (that are in *arrears*) will be disclosed.

Additional Paid-In Capital

As has already been illustrated, **additional paid-in capital** is an owners' equity category that reflects the excess of the amount received from the sale of preferred or common stock over par value. In addition, this account is used for other relatively uncommon capital transactions that cannot be reflected in the common or preferred stock accounts, or that should not be reflected in retained earnings. (Remember that the amount in the common or preferred stock account is equal to par value multiplied by the number of shares issued, or the amount received from the sale of no-par-value stock.)

Capital in excess of par value (or stated value) is a term that is sometimes used for additional paid-in capital. Capital in excess of par value is descriptive of how the amount arises, but is a wordy term, and as stated in the preceding paragraph, it does not necessarily describe how all of the additional paid-in capital amount arose. Some firms still use **capital surplus** for this caption. This term was widely used many years ago before the term *surplus* fell into disfavor because of its connotation as something "extra," and because uninformed financial statement readers might think that this amount was somehow available for dividends.

To summarize and emphasize, the paid-in capital of a corporation represents the amount invested by the owners, and if par value stock is involved, paid-in capital includes par value and additional paid-in capital. If no-par-value stock is issued, paid-in capital represents the owners' investment.

RETAINED EARNINGS

The **retained earnings** account is what the caption describes; it refers to the earnings of the corporation that have been retained for use in the business rather than having been disbursed to the stockholders as dividends. *Retained earnings is not cash!* Retained earnings is increased by the firm's net income, and the accrual basis of accounting results in a net income amount that is different from the cash increase during a fiscal period. To the extent that operating results increase cash, that cash may be used for operating, investing, or financing activities.

Virtually the only factors affecting retained earnings are net income or loss reported on the income statement, and dividends. Under certain very restricted circumstances generally accepted accounting principles permit direct adjustment of retained earnings for correction of errors (referred to as *prior period adjustments*), but these cases are rare. For example, new information about an estimate made in a prior year (e.g., for depreciation or bad debts) does not warrant a direct entry to retained earnings. Accounting principles emphasize that the income statement is to reflect all transactions affecting owners' equity, except for the following:

1. Dividends to stockholders (which are a reduction in retained earnings).
2. Transactions involving the corporation's own stock (which are reflected in the paid-in capital section of the balance sheet).
3. A cumulative foreign currency translation adjustment, to be explained later in this chapter.

Cash Dividends

In order for a corporation to pay a cash dividend, it must meet several requirements. The firm must have retained earnings, the board of directors must declare the dividend, and the firm must have enough cash to pay the dividend. If the firm has agreed in a bond indenture or other contract to maintain certain minimum standards of financial health (e.g., a current ratio of at least 2.2:1), the dividend must not cause any of these measures to fall below their agreed-upon level. From both the corporation's and the stockholders' perspectives there are several key dates related to the dividend (see Business Procedure Capsule 15—Dividend Dates). Once the board of directors has declared the dividend, it becomes a liability of the corporation. A dividend declaration and its subsequent payment affect the financial statements this way:

Balance sheet	Income statement
Assets = Liabilities + Owners' equity ← Net income = Revenues − Expenses

Dividend declaration:
　　　　+ Dividends　− Retained
　　　　　Payable　　 Earnings

Dividend payment:
− Cash　− Dividends
　　　　　Payable

If a balance sheet is issued between the date the dividend is declared and the date it is paid, the liability will be included in the current liability section of the balance sheet.

If the retained earnings account has a negative balance because cumulative losses and dividends have exceeded cumulative net income, this account is referred to as **deficit.**

Stock Dividends and Stock Splits

In addition to a cash dividend, or sometimes instead of a cash dividend, a corporation may issue a **stock dividend.** A stock dividend is the issuance of additional shares of common stock to the existing stockholders in proportion to the number of shares each currently owns. It is expressed as a percentage; for example, a 5 percent stock dividend would result in the issuance of 5 percent of the currently outstanding shares. A stockholder who owns 100 shares would receive 5 additional shares of stock. (Fractional shares are not issued; an owner of 90 shares would receive 4 shares and cash equal to the market value of half of a share in a 5 percent stock dividend transaction.)

The motivation for a stock dividend is usually to maintain the loyalty of the stockholders when the firm does not have enough cash to pay or increase the cash dividend. Although many stockholders like to receive a stock dividend, such a distribution is not income to the stockholders. To understand why there is no income to the stockholder, the impact of the stock dividend on the company must be understood. From the issuing corporation's point of view, a stock dividend does not cause any change in either assets or liabilities; therefore it cannot affect the total of owners' equity. However, since additional shares of stock are issued, and because the common stock account must reflect the product of the number of shares issued multiplied by par value, there is a change within the owners' equity section of the balance sheet. Because the issuance of shares is called a *dividend,* it is appropriate for retained earnings to be reduced. The amount of the reduction in retained earnings is the number of the dividend shares issued multiplied by the market price per share. Any difference between market price and par value is recorded in the Additional Paid-In Capital account. If the shares are without par value, then the Common Stock account is increased by the market value of the dividend shares issued. The effect on the financial statements of a 6 percent stock dividend for a firm having 50,000 shares of $7 par value stock

---

• **BUSINESS PROCEDURE CAPSULE 15**
Dividend Dates

Three dates applicable to every dividend are the declaration date, the record date, and the payment date. In addition, there will be an ex-dividend date applicable to companies whose stock is publicly traded. There is no reason that the declaration, record, and payment dates for a closely held company couldn't be the same date.

The **declaration date** is the date on which the board of directors declares the dividend. The **record date** is used to determine who receives the dividend; the owner of the shares is considered to be the person listed on the stockholder records of the corporation on the record date. The owner of record is the person to whom the check is made payable and mailed to on the **payment date.** If shares have been sold but the ownership change has not yet been noted on the corporation's records, the prior owner (the one in the records) receives the dividend (and may have to settle with the new owner, depending upon their agreement with respect to the dividend). The **ex-dividend date** relates to this issue of who receives the dividend. When the stock of a publicly traded company is bought or sold, the seller has a settlement period of five business days in which to deliver the stock certificate. The buyer also has five business days to pay for the purchase. Since there will be no chance to change the ownership records of the corporation during the settlement period because the certificate will not have been delivered to the buyer, the stock trades "ex-dividend" five business days (usually a calendar week) before the record date. On the ex-dividend date, the stock trades without the dividend (i.e., the seller retains the right to receive the dividend if the stock is sold on or after the ex-dividend date). If the stock is sold before the ex-dividend date, then the buyer is entitled to receive the dividend. As you can imagine, all other things being equal, the price of the stock in the market falls by the amount of the dividend on the ex-dividend date.

There is no specific requirement dealing with the number of days that should elapse between the declaration, record, and payment dates for publicly traded stocks. It is not unusual for two to four weeks to elapse between each date.

---

outstanding ($6\% \times 50,000 = 3,000$ dividend shares) and having a market value of $22 per share is:

Balance sheet	Income statement

Assets = Liabilities + Owners' equity ← Net income = Revenues − Expenses

Retained Earnings
(3,000 shares × $22)
− 66,000

Common Stock
(3,000 shares × $7)
+ 21,000

Additional Paid-In
Capital
(3,000 shares × $15)
+ 45,000

Note that the stock dividend affects *only* the owners' equity of the firm.

If the stock dividend percentage is more than 20 to 25 percent, only the par value or stated value of the additional common shares issued is transferred from retained earnings to common stock.

Capitalizing retained earnings is the term sometimes used to refer to the effect of a stock dividend transaction because the dividend results in the permanent transfer of some retained earnings to paid-in capital.

What happens to the market value of a share of stock when a firm issues a stock dividend? Is the share owner any wealthier? As already explained, nothing happens to the firm's assets, liabilities, or earning power as a result of the stock dividend; therefore the *total* market value of the firm should not change. Since more shares of stock are now outstanding and the total market value of all the shares remains the same, the market value of each share will drop. This is why the stock dividend does not represent income to the stockholder. However, under some circumstances the market value per share of the common stock will not settle at its theoretically lower value. This will be true especially if the cash dividend per share is not adjusted to reflect the stock dividend. Thus if the firm had been paying a per share cash dividend of $1.00 before the stock dividend, and the same cash dividend rate is continued, there has been an effective increase in the dividend rate, and the stock price will probably rise to reflect this.

Sometimes the managers of a firm want to lower the market price of the firm's common stock by a significant amount because they believe that a stock trading in a price range of $20 to $50 per share is a more popular investment than a stock priced at more than $50 per share. A **stock split** will accomplish this objective. A stock split involves issuing additional shares to existing stockholders and, if the stock has a par value, reducing the par value proportionately. For example, if a firm had 60,000 shares of $10 par value stock outstanding, with stock trading in the market at a price of $80 per share, a 4-for-1 stock split would involve issuing 3 additional shares to each stockholder for each share owned. Then the share-owner who had owned 200 shares would receive an additional 600 shares, bringing the total shares owned to 800. As in the case of a stock dividend, nothing has happened to the assets or liabilities of the firm, so nothing can happen to owners' equity. The total market value of the company would not change, but the market price of each share would fall from $80 to $20. There is no accounting entry required for a stock split. The common stock caption of owners' equity indicates the drop in par value per share and the proportionate increase in the number of shares authorized, issued, and outstanding. If the corporation has used no-par-value stock, only the number of shares changes.

Sometimes a stock split is accomplished in the form of a very large (e.g., 100 percent) stock dividend. As explained earlier, when this happens only the par or stated value of the additional shares issued is transferred from retained earnings to the common stock account. There is no adjustment to the par value of the stock.

TREASURY STOCK

Many corporations will, from time to time, purchase shares of their own stock. Any class of stock that is outstanding can be acquired as treasury stock. Rather than retire this stock, it is held for future use for employee stock purchase plans, acquisitions of other companies, or even to be resold for cash if additional capital is needed. Sometimes treasury stock is acquired as a defensive move to thwart a takeover by another company, and frequently a firm buys treasury stock with excess cash because the market price is low and the company's own stock is thought to be a good investment. Whatever the motivation, the purchase of treasury stock is in effect a partial liquidation of the firm, because the firm's assets are used to reduce the number of shares of stock outstanding. For this reason, treasury stock is not reflected in the balance sheet as an asset; it is reported as a contra owners' equity account (i.e., treasury stock is deducted from the sum of paid-in capital and retained earnings).

   Because treasury stock transactions are capital transactions, the income statement is never affected by the purchase or sale of treasury stock. When treasury stock is acquired, it is recorded at cost. When treasury stock is sold or issued, any difference between its cost and the consideration received is recorded in the Additional Paid-In Capital account. As can be seen in Exhibit 8–1, Racers, Inc., purchased 1,000 shares of its own common stock at a total cost of $12,000 during the year ended August 31, 1993. The journal entry to record this purchase is:

```
Dr.  Treasury Stock . . . . . . . . . . . . . . .    12,000
     Cr.  Cash . . . . . . . . . . . . . . . . . .             12,000
     Purchase 1,000 shares of treasury stock at a cost of
     $12 per share.
```

The effect of this transaction on the financial statements is:

Balance sheet		Income statement
Assets = Liabilities + Owners' equity	←	Net income = Revenues − Expenses
Cash	Treasury Stock	
− 12,000	(A contra owners' equity account)	
	− 12,000	

   If 500 shares of this treasury stock were sold at a price of $15 per share in fiscal 1994, the journal entry to record the sale would be:

```
Dr.  Cash . . . . . . . . . . . . . . . . . . . . .    7,500
     Cr.  Treasury Stock . . . . . . . . . . . . .             6,000
     Cr.  Additional Paid-In Capital. . . . . . . . .           1,500
     Sale of 500 shares of treasury stock at a price of $15
     per share.
```

The effect of this transaction on the financial statements is:

Balance sheet		Income statement
Assets = Liabilities + Owners' equity	←	Net income = Revenues − Expenses
Cash	Treasury Stock	
+ 7,500	+ 6,000	
	Additional Paid-In Capital	
	+ 1,500	

Cash dividends are not paid on treasury stock. However, stock dividends are issued on treasury stock, and stock splits affect treasury stock.

CUMULATIVE FOREIGN CURRENCY
TRANSLATION ADJUSTMENT

When the financial statements of a foreign subsidiary are consolidated with those of its U.S. parent company, the financial statements of the subsidiary, originally expressed in the currency of the country in which it operates, must be converted to U.S. dollars. The conversion process is referred to as *foreign currency translation*. Because of the mechanics used in the translation process, and because exchange rates fluctuate over time, a debit or credit difference between the translated value of the subsidiary's assets and liabilities and the translated value of the subsidiary's owners' equity arises in the translation and consolidation process. Prior to 1983 this debit or credit difference was reported as a loss or gain in the consolidated income statement. Because of large gyrations in exchange rates, a firm might report a large translation gain in one year and an equally large translation loss in the next year. The translation gain or loss had a material effect on reported results, but did not have a significant economic impact because the gain or loss was never actually realized. Therefore, the Financial Accounting Standards Board issued an accounting standard that provided that the translation gain or loss be reported separately in owners' equity rather than as a gain or loss in the income statement. The effect of this accounting standard is to make reported net income more meaningful, and to highlight as a separate item in owners' equity the cumulative translation adjustment. To the extent that exchange rates of the U.S. dollar rise and fall relative to the foreign currencies involved, the amount of this **cumulative foreign currency translation adjustment** will fluctuate over time. This treatment of the translation adjustment is consistent with the going concern concept because as long as the entity continues to operate with foreign subsidiaries, the translation adjustment will not be realized.

REPORTING CHANGES IN OWNERS' EQUITY ACCOUNTS

It is appropriate that the reasons for changes to any owners' equity account during a fiscal period be presented in the balance sheet, in a separate statement of changes in owners' equity, or in the footnotes or financial review accompanying the financial statements. One possible format for a statement of changes in owners' equity is presented for Racers, Inc., in Exhibit 8–5. (Amounts for net income and dividends on common stock are assumed. You should prove to yourself the amount of the cash dividends on the preferred

EXHIBIT 8–5 Statement of Changes in Owners' Equity

RACERS, INC.
Statement of Changes in Owners' Equity
For the Year Ended August 31, 1993

	Preferred Stock		Common Stock		Additional Paid-In Capital	Retained Earnings	Common Treasury Stock	
	No. of Shares	$	No. of Shares	$	$	$	No. of Shares	$
Balance, August 31, 1992	5,000	500,000	200,000	400,000	2,820,000	2,600,000	—	—
Sale of common stock			40,000	80,000	440,000			
Purchase of common treasury stock							1,000	12,000
Net income						390,000		
Cash dividends:								
Preferred stock						(30,000)		
Common stock						(60,000)		
Stock dividend:								
2% on 240,000 shares when market value was $15 per share			4,800	9,600	62,400	(72,000)		
Balance, August 31, 1993	5,000	$500,000	244,800	$489,600	$3,321,400	$2,828,000	1,000	$12,000

EXHIBIT 8–6 Statement of Changes in Retained Earnings

RACERS, INC.
Statement of Changes in Retained Earnings
For the Year Ended August 31, 1993

Retained earnings balance, beginning of year	$2,600,000
Add: Net income	390,000
Less: Cash dividends:	
Preferred stock	(30,000)
Common stock	(60,000)
2% stock dividend on common stock	(72,000)
Retained earnings balance, end of year	$2,828,000

---

stock and the share and dollar amounts for the stock dividend.) Alternative formats may be used.

Even if there are no changes to the paid-in capital accounts, and there is no treasury stock or foreign subsidiary, an analysis of retained earnings is presented. This can be done in a separate statement, as illustrated for Racers, Inc., in Exhibit 8–6, or by appending the beginning balance, dividend, and ending balance to the bottom of the income statement, which then becomes a combined statement of income and retained earnings.

Note that in the Armstrong World Industries, Inc., Annual Report in Appendix A, changes in shareholders' equity are presented in a footnote located on page 28 of the report. What approach is used in the other annual reports that you have?

SUMMARY

This chapter has described the accounting for and presentation of the following owners' equity accounts. Treasury stock is shown in parentheses because it is a contra account. Note that, except for the fact that net income is added to retained earnings, transactions affecting owners' equity do not affect the income statement.

Balance sheet	Income statement

Assets = Liabilities + Owners' equity ← Net income = Revenues − Expenses

Paid-In Capital:
Preferred Stock
Common Stock
Additional Paid-In
Capital

Balance sheet	Income statement
Assets = Liabilities + Owners' equity ←	Net income = Revenues − Expenses
Retained Earn- ←	Net income
ings	
Cumulative Foreign	
Currency Translation	
Adjustment	
(Treasury Stock)	

Owners' equity is also referred to as *net assets*. For single proprietorships and partnerships the term *capital* is frequently used instead of owners' equity. For a corporation, the components of owners' equity are paid-in capital, retained earnings, treasury stock, and the cumulative foreign currency translation adjustment.

Paid-in capital is made up of common stock, and may include preferred stock and additional paid-in capital. Common stock represents the basic ownership of the corporation. Common stock may have a par value, or may be no par value. If there is a par value, the difference between the par value of the common stock issued and the total amount paid in to the corporation when the stock was issued is additional paid-in capital. If no-par-value stock has a stated value, the stated value operates as a par value. If no-par-value common stock has no stated value, the total amount paid in to the corporation when the stock was issued is reported as the dollar amount of common stock. The principal right and obligation of the common stock is to elect the board of directors of the corporation. Voting for directors can be on either a cumulative basis or a slate basis.

Preferred stock is different from common stock in that preferred has a prior claim to dividends and a prior claim on assets when the corporation is liquidated. In most cases, preferred stock does not have a voting privilege. Preferred stock is in some respects similar to bonds payable. The most significant difference between the two is that interest on bonds is a tax-deductible expense, and dividends on preferred stock are a nondeductible distribution of the corporation's earnings.

Additional paid-in capital is sometimes given the more descriptive caption "capital in excess of par (or stated) value."

Retained earnings represents earnings reinvested in the business. If earnings are not reinvested, they are distributed to stockholders as dividends. Retained earnings is not cash. The Retained Earnings account is increased by net income, and decreased by dividends (and a net loss).

Dividends are declared by the board of directors, and paid to owners of the stock on the record date. Dividends can be paid with any frequency; quarterly or semiannual dividend payments are most usual. Cash dividends are paid in cash. Stock dividends represent the issuance of additional shares of stock to stockholders in proportion to the number of shares owned on the record date. Stock dividends do not affect the assets, liabilities, or total owners' equity of the firm. They do result in the transfer of an amount of retained earnings to paid-in capital. Stock dividends are expressed as a percentage of the predividend shares to be issued as the dividend; that percentage is usually relatively small (i.e., less than 20 percent).

Stock splits also involve issuing additional shares of stock to stockholders in proportion to the number of shares owned on the record date but usually result in at least doubling the number of shares held by each stockholder. Stock splits are expressed as a ratio of the number of shares held after the split to the number held before the split (e.g., 2 for 1). The reason for and effect of a stock split is to reduce the market value per share of the stock.

Treasury stock is the corporation's own stock that has been purchased from stockholders and is being held in the treasury for future reissue. Treasury stock is reported as a contra owners' equity account. When treasury stock is reissued at a price different from its cost, no gain or loss is recognized. The difference between its cost and reissue price affects paid-in capital.

The cumulative foreign currency translation adjustment is an amount reported in owners' equity of corporations having foreign subsidiaries. The adjustment arises in the process of translating the financial statements of subsidiaries, expressed in foreign currency units, to the U.S. dollar. Because exchange rates can fluctuate widely, net income could be distorted if this adjustment were reported in the income statement. To avoid this distortion, the adjustment is reported in owners' equity.

The relationship between the elements of owners' equity is illustrated in the following listing. It is possible that a firm might have only capital stock and retained earnings (or deficit) as components of owners' equity.

Owners equity:
  Paid-in capital
    Capital stock (Legal capital)
      Common stock
      Preferred stock (optional)
    Additional paid-in capital
  Retained earnings (Deficit if negative)
  Cumulative foreign currency translation adjustment
  Less: Treasury stock

Changes in owners' equity may be reported in a comprehensive statement that summarizes the changes of each element of owners' equity. If there have not been significant changes in paid-in capital accounts, only a statement of change in retained earnings may be presented. Sometimes the statement of change in retained earnings is combined with the income statement.

Refer to the Armstrong World Industries, Inc., balance sheet, and shareholders' equity analysis in the financial review in Appendix A, and to other financial statements you may have, and observe how information about owners' equity is presented.

KEY TERMS AND CONCEPTS

additional paid-in capital *(p. 246)*   The excess of the amount received from the sale of par value stock over the par value of the shares sold.

authorized shares *(p. 241)*   The number of shares of stock of a class authorized by the corporation's charter.

callable preferred stock *(p. 243)*   Preferred stock that can be redeemed by the corporation at its option.

capital in excess of par value *(p. 246)*   Another term for *additional paid-in capital*.

capital stock *(p. 238)*   The generic term for stock issued by a corporation.

capital surplus *(p. 246)*   A less generally accepted term for *additional paid-in capital*.

capitalizing retained earnings *(p. 250)*   The transfer of retained earnings to paid-in capital that occurs when a stock dividend is declared.

common stock *(p. 238)*   The class of stock that represents residual ownership of the corporation.

convertible preferred stock *(p. 243)*   Preferred stock that can be converted to common stock of the corporation at the option of the stockholder.

cumulative dividend *(p. 243)*   A feature of preferred stock that requires that any missed dividends be paid before dividends can be paid on common stock.

cumulative foreign currency translation adjustment *(p. 253)*   A component of owners' equity arising from the translation of foreign subsidiary financial statements included in the consolidated financial statements.

cumulative voting *(p. 239)*   A system of voting for the directors of a firm in which the number of votes that can be cast for one or more candidates is equal to the number of shares of stock owned multiplied by the number of directors to be elected.

declaration date *(p. 249)*   The date a dividend is declared by the board of directors.

deficit *(p. 248)*   Retained earnings with a negative (debit) balance.

dividend *(p. 242)*   A distribution of earnings to the owners of a corporation.

ex-dividend date *(p. 249)*   The date on and after which the buyer of a publicly traded stock will not receive a dividend that has been declared but not yet paid.

inside director *(p. 239)*   A member of the firm's board of directors who is also an officer or employee of the firm.

issued shares *(p. 241)*   The number of shares of a class of stock that has been issued to stockholders.

legal capital *(p. 240)*   The amount associated with the capital stock that has been issued by a corporation. Legal capital is generally the par value or stated value of the shares issued.

liquidating value *(p. 243)*   The stated claim of preferred stock in the event the corporation is liquidated. Sometimes called *redemption value*.

outside director *(p. 239)*   A member of the firm's board of directors who is not also an officer or employee of the firm.

outstanding shares *(p. 241)*   The number of shares of a class of stock held by stockholders.

par value *(p. 240)*   An arbitrary value assigned to a share of stock when the corporation is organized. Sometimes used to refer to the stated value or face amount of a security.

participating dividend *(p. 243)*   A feature of preferred stock that provides that the preferred stock shares in additional dividends at a specified ratio after a base amount of dividends has been paid on the common stock.

partners' capital *(p. 236)*   The owners' equity in a partnership.

payment date *(p. 249)*   The date a dividend is paid.

preemptive right *(p. 241)*   The right of a stockholder to purchase shares from any additional share issues in proportion to the stockholder's present percentage of ownership.

preferred stock *(p. 242)*   The class of stock that represents ownership of a corporation that has certain preferences, usually including a priority claim to dividends, relative to the common stock.

proprietor's capital *(p. 236)*   The owners' equity of an individual proprietorship.

record date *(p. 249)*   The date used to determine the stockholders who will receive a dividend.

redemption value *(p. 243)*   The stated claim of preferred stock in the event the corporation is liquidated. Sometimes called *liquidating value*.

retained earnings *(p. 246)*   Cumulative net income that has not been distributed to the owners of a corporation as dividends.

slate voting *(p. 239)*   A system of voting for the directors of a firm in which votes equal to the number of shares owned are cast for a single slate of candidates.

stated value *(p. 240)*   An arbitrary value assigned to shares of no-par-value stock.

stock dividend *(p. 248)*   A distribution of additional shares to existing stockholders in proportion to their existing holdings. The additional shares issued usually amount to less than 20 percent of the previously issued shares.

stock split *(p. 251)*   A distribution of additional shares to existing stockholders in proportion to their existing holdings. The additional shares issued usually amount to 100 percent or more of the previously issued shares.

treasury stock *(p. 241)*   Shares of a firm's stock that have been reacquired by the firm.

EXERCISES AND PROBLEMS

8–1. The balance sheet caption for common stock is:

Common stock, $5 par value, 2,000,000 shares authorized, 1,400,000 shares issued, 1,250,000 shares outstanding

Required:
a. Calculate the dollar amount that will be presented opposite this caption.
b. Calculate the total amount of a cash dividend of $.15 per share.
c. What accounts for the difference between issued shares and outstanding shares?

8–2. The balance sheet caption for common stock is:

Common stock without par value, 4,000,000 shares
   authorized, 800,000 shares issued and
   outstanding $2,600,000

Required:
a. Calculate the average price at which the shares were issued.
b. If these shares had been assigned a stated value of $1 each, show how the above caption would be different.
c. If a cash dividend of $.18 per share were declared, calculate the total amount of cash that would be paid to stockholders.

8–3. Calculate the annual cash dividends required to be paid for each of the following preferred stock issues:

a. $3.75 cumulative preferred, no par value; 161,821 shares authorized, 161,522 shares issued. (The treasury stock caption of the stockholders' equity section of the balance sheet indicates that there are 43,373 shares of this preferred stock issue owned by the company.)
b. 6 percent, $40 par value preferred, 73,621 shares authorized, issued, and outstanding.
c. 11.4 percent cumulative preferred, $100 stated value, $104 liquidating value; 50,000 shares authorized, 43,200 shares issued, 37,600 shares outstanding.

8–4. Calculate the cash dividends required to be paid for each of the following preferred stock issues:

a. Semiannual dividend on 9 percent cumulative preferred, $60 par value; 10,000 shares authorized, issued, and outstanding.

b. The annual dividend on $2.40 cumulative preferred, 100,000 shares authorized, 60,000 shares issued, 53,200 shares outstanding. Prior years' dividends have been paid.

c. The quarterly dividend on 13.2 percent cumulative preferred, $100 stated value, $103 liquidating value, 60,000 shares authorized, 52,000 shares issued and outstanding. No dividends are in arrears.

8–5. Anderco, Inc., did not pay dividends on its $6.50, $50 par value, cumulative preferred stock during 1991 or 1992. Since 1986 22,000 shares of this stock have been outstanding. Anderco, Inc., has been profitable in 1993 and is considering a cash dividend on its common stock that would be payable in December 1993.

Required: Calculate the amount of dividends that would have to be paid on the preferred stock before a cash dividend could be paid to the common stockholders.

8–6. Poorco, Inc., did not pay dividends in 1993 or 1994, even though 45,000 shares of its 8.5 percent, $70 par value cumulative preferred stock were outstanding during those years. The company has 263,000 shares of $2.50 par value common stock outstanding.

Required:
a. Calculate the annual dividend per share obligation on the preferred stock.

b. Calculate the amount that would be received by an investor who has owned 200 shares of preferred stock and 450 shares of common stock since 1992 if a $.25 per share dividend on the common stock is paid at the end of 1995.

8–7. Blanker, Inc., has paid a regular quarterly cash dividend of $.50 per share for several years. The common stock is publicly traded. On February 21 of the current year, Blanker's board of directors declared the regular first quarter dividend of $.50 per share payable on March 30 to stockholders of record on March 15.

Required: As a result of this dividend action, state what would you expect to happen to the market price of the common stock of Blanker, Inc., on each of the following dates. Explain your answers.

a. February 21.
b. March 8.
c. March 15.
d. March 30.

8–8. Find and review the Dividend News section of an issue of *The Wall Street Journal* that is at least one week old. Find the list of stocks that will trade ex-dividend a few days later. From the stock listings in *The Wall Street Journal* on the ex-dividend date, determine what happened to the market price of the stock on the ex-dividend date. Does this price action make sense? Explain your answer.

8–9. Knight, Inc., is expecting to incur a loss for the current year. The chairman of the board of directors wants to have a cash dividend so that the company's record of having paid a dividend during every year of its existence will continue. What factors will determine whether or not the board can declare a dividend?

Armstrong

8–10. Refer to the Armstrong World Industries, Inc., 1991 Annual Report in Appendix A. From the table of quarterly financial information on page 32 and the Six-Year Summary on page 38, find the information relating to cash dividends on common stock.

Required:

a. How frequently are cash dividends paid?

b. What has been the pattern of the cash dividend amount per share relative to the pattern of earnings per share? How can this be possible?

c. Calculate the rate of change in the annual dividend per share for each of the four years from 1988 through 1991.

8–11. Under what circumstances would you prefer to have a company in which you have an ownership interest pay cash dividends rather than issue stock dividends? Under what circumstances would you prefer stock dividends to cash dividends?

8–12. Assume that you own 200 shares of Blueco, Inc., common stock and that you currently receive cash dividends of $.84 per share per year.

Required:

a. If Blueco, Inc., declared a 5 percent stock dividend, how many shares of common stock would you receive as a dividend?

b. Calculate the cash dividend per share amount that would result in the same total dividend after the stock dividend as before it.

c. If the cash dividend remained at $.84 per share after the stock dividend, what per share cash dividend amount without a stock dividend would have accomplished the same total cash dividend?

d. Why would a company have a dividend policy of paying a $.10 per share cash dividend and issuing a 5 percent stock dividend every year?

8–13. Assume that you own 100 shares of common stock of a company and the company has a 2-for-1 stock split.

Required:

a. How many shares of common stock will you own after the stock split?

b. What will probably have happened to the market price per share of the stock?

8–14. Assume that you own 75 shares of common stock of a company, that you have been receiving cash dividends of $3 per share per year, and that the company has a 4-for-3 stock split.

Required:

a. How many shares of common stock will you own after the stock split?

b. What stock dividend percentage could have accomplished the same end result as the 4-for-3 stock split?

c. What new cash dividend per share will result in the same total dividend income as you received before the stock split?

8–15. On May 4, 1993, Docker, Inc., purchased 800 shares of its own common stock in the market at a price of $18.25 per share. On September 11, 1993, 600 of these shares were sold in the open market at a price of $19.50 per share. There were 36,200 shares of Docker common stock outstanding prior to the May 4 purchase of treasury stock. A $.35 per share cash dividend on the common stock was declared and paid in June.

Required:

a. Use the horizontal model (or write the journal entry) to show the effect on Docker's financial statements of:
  1. The purchase of the treasury stock on May 4.
  2. The sale of the treasury stock on September 11.
b. Calculate the total amount of the cash dividend paid in June.

8–16. At the beginning of its fiscal year, Metco, Inc., had outstanding 287,300 shares of $2 par value common stock. At the end of the first fiscal quarter, Metco, Inc., purchased for its treasury 2,200 shares of its common stock at a price of $37.50 per share. During the third fiscal quarter, 700 of these treasury shares were sold for $42 per share. Metco's directors declared cash dividends of $.60 per share during the second quarter, and again during the fourth quarter, payable at the end of each quarter. A 2 percent stock dividend was issued at the end of the year. There were no other transactions affecting common stock during the year.

Required:

a. Use the horizontal model (or write the journal entry) to show the effect of the treasury stock purchase at the end of the first quarter, and the treasury stock sale during the third quarter.
b. Calculate the total amount of the cash dividends paid in the second quarter, and for the entire year.
c. Calculate the number of shares of stock issued in the stock dividend.

8–17. Enter the following column headings across the top of a sheet of paper:

Trans-action	Cash	Other Assets	Liabil-ities	Paid-In Capital	Retained Earnings	Treasury Stock	Net Income

Enter the transaction letter in the first column, and show the effect (if any) of each of the following transactions on each financial statement category by entering a plus (+) or minus (−) sign in the appropriate column. Do not show items that affect net income in the retained earnings column.

a. Sold $50 par value preferred stock at par.
b. Declared the annual dividend on the preferred stock.
c. Purchased 50 shares of preferred stock for the treasury.
d. Declared and issued a 4 percent stock dividend on the common stock.
e. Issued 2,000 shares of common stock in exchange for land.

8–18. Enter the following column headings across the top of a sheet of paper:

Trans-action	Cash	Other Assets	Liabil-ities	Paid-In Capital	Retained Earnings	Treasury Stock	Net Income

Enter the transaction letter in the first column, and show the effect (if any) of each of the following transactions on each financial statement category by entering a plus (+) or minus (−) sign and the amount in the appropriate column. Do not show items that affect net income in the retained earnings column. You should assume that the transactions occurred in this chronological sequence.

a. Sold 5,000 previously unissued shares of $1 par value common stock for $18 per share.

b. Issued 1,000 shares of previously unissued 8 percent cumulative preferred stock, $40 par value, in exchange for land and a building appraised at $40,000.

c. Declared and issued the annual cash dividend on the preferred stock issued in transaction b.

d. Purchased 250 shares of common stock for the treasury at a total cost of $4,750.

e. Declared a cash dividend of $.15 per share on the 45,000 shares of common stock outstanding.

f. Sold 130 shares of the treasury stock purchased in transaction d at a price of $20 per share.

g. Declared and issued a 3 percent stock dividend on the common stock when the market value per share of common stock was $21. There were 45,000 shares of common stock issued before transaction f took place.

h. Split the common stock 3 for 1.

8–19. Allyn, Inc., has the following owners' equity section in its November 30, 1993, balance sheet:

Paid-in capital:
    12% Preferred stock, $60 par value, 1,500 shares
        authorized, issued, and outstanding . . . . $?
    Common stock, $8 par value, 100,000 shares authorized,
        ____?____ shares issued   240,000
    Additional paid-in capital on common stock   540,000
    Additional paid-in capital from treasury stock   13,000
Retained earnings   97,000
Less: Treasury stock, at cost (2,000 shares of common) . .   (18,000)
        Total stockholders' equity . . . . $?

Required:

a. Calculate the amount of the total annual dividend requirement on the preferred stock.

b. Calculate the amount that should be shown on the balance sheet for preferred stock.

c. Calculate the number of shares of common stock that are issued, and the number of shares of common stock that are outstanding.

d. On January 1, 1993, the firm's balance sheet showed common stock of $210,000 and additional paid-in capital on common stock of $468,750. The only transaction affecting these accounts during 1993 was the sale of some common stock. Calculate the number of shares that were sold and the selling price per share.

e. Describe the transaction that resulted in the additional paid-in capital from treasury stock.

f. The retained earnings balance on January 1, 1993, was $90,300. Net income for the past 11 months has been $24,000. Preferred stock dividends for all of 1993 have been declared and paid. Calculate the amount of dividends on common stock during the first 11 months of 1993.

8–20. Bacon, Inc., has the following owners' equity section in its May 31, 1994, comparative balance sheets (in thousands):

	May 31, 1994	April 30, 1994
Paid-in capital:		
Preferred stock, $120 par value, 8%, cumulative, 50,000 shares authorized, 40,000 shares issued and outstanding	$4,800	$ 4,800
Common stock, $6 par value, 300,000 shares authorized, 200,000 and 190,000 shares issued, respectively.	?	1,140
Additional paid-in capital.	8,400	8,240
Retained earnings	6,950	6,812
Less: Treasury common stock, at cost; 9,000 shares and 8,500 shares, respectively.	(830)	(816)
Total stockholders' equity . . .	$?	$20,176

Required:

a. Calculate the amount that should be shown on the balance sheet for common stock at May 31, 1994.

b. The only transaction affecting additional paid-in capital during the month of May was the sale of additional common stock. At what price per share were the additional shares sold?

c. What was the average cost per share of the common stock purchased for the treasury during the month?

d. During May dividends on preferred stock equal to one-half of the 1994 dividend requirement were declared and paid. There were no common dividends declared or paid in May. Calculate net income for May.

e. Assume that on June 1 the board of directors declares a cash dividend of $.42 per share on the outstanding shares of common stock. The dividend will be payable on July 15 to stockholders of record on June 15.
1. Calculate the total amount of the dividend.
2. Explain the impact this action will have on the June 30 balance sheet, and on the income statement for June.

f. Assume that on June 1 the market value of the common stock is $36 per share and that the board of directors declares a 3 percent stock dividend on the issued shares of common stock. Use the horizontal model (or write the journal entry) to show the issuance of the stock dividend.

g. Assume that instead of the stock dividend described in *f* above, the board of directors authorizes a 3-for-1 stock split on June 1 when the market price of the common stock is $36 per share.

1. What will be the par value, and how many shares of common stock will be authorized after the split?
2. What will be the market price per share of the common stock after the split?
3. How many shares of common stock will be in the treasury after the spilt?

h. By how much will total stockholders' equity change as a result of:
1. The stock dividend?
2. The stock split?

Chapter 9

The Income Statement and the Statement of Cash Flows

The income statement answers some of the most important questions that users of the financial statements have: What were the financial results of the entity's operations for the fiscal period? How much profit (or loss) did the firm have? Many income statement accounts were introduced when transactions also affecting asset and liability accounts were explained. However, because of the significance of the net income figure to managers, share owners, potential investors, and others, it is appropriate to focus on the form and content of this financial statement.

The income statement of Armstrong World Industries, Inc., is on page 18 of the Annual Report in Appendix A. This page of the annual report has been reproduced as Exhibit 9–1. Note that comparative statements for the years ended December 31, 1991, 1990, and 1989 are presented. This permits the reader of the statement to assess quickly the recent trend of these important data.

Armstrong's income statement includes several subtotals between "net sales" (revenues), and what in popular jargon is referred to as the *bottom line,* which on this statement is labeled "net earnings," which precedes the earnings per share data that require considerable disclosure in the bottom part of the statement. The significance of earnings per share will be explained in detail in Chapter 11. The principal focus of the first part of this chapter is on understanding the components of the income statement.

The second part of this chapter explores the statement of cash flows in detail. Remember that as presented in Chapter 2, this statement explains the change in the entity's cash from the beginning to the end of the fiscal period by summarizing the cash effects

EXHIBIT 9–1

ARMSTRONG WORLD INDUSTRIES, INC. AND SUBSIDIARIES
Consolidated Statements of Earnings
(millions except for per-share data)

Years ended December 31	1991	1990	1989
Current earnings			
Net sales	$2,439.3	$2,518.8	$2,488.7
Cost of goods sold	1,801.1	1,816.6	1,764.0
Gross profit	638.2	702.2	724.7
Selling and administrative expense. . .	468.3	462.6	436.6
Earnings from continuing businesses before other income (expense) and income taxes	169.9	239.6	288.1
Other income (expense):			
Interest expense	(45.8)	(37.5)	(40.5)
Gain on sale of woodlands	—	60.4	9.5
Miscellaneous income (expense). . .	(23.8)	(39.4)	(13.5)
	(69.6)	(16.5)	(44.5)
Earnings from continuing businesses before income taxes	100.3	223.1	243.6
Income taxes	39.7	76.7	85.9
Earnings from continuing businesses. .	60.6	146.4	157.7
Discontinued businesses:			
Earnings (losses) net of income tax benefit of $1.9 in 1991, and $2.2 in 1990 and tax expense of $6.1 in 1989	(3.8)	(4.3)	8.2
Provision for (loss) gain on disposition of discontinued businesses, net of income tax benefit of $4.6 in 1991, and $3.8 in 1990 and tax expense of $8.0 in 1989	(8.6)	(9.1)	21.7
Cumulative effect of change in accounting for income taxes . . .	—	8.0	—
Net earnings	$ 48.2	$ 141.0	$ 187.6
Per share of common stock:			
Primary:			
Earnings from continuing businesses	$ 1.11	$ 3.26	$ 3.26
Earnings (losses) from discontinued businesses	(.11)	(.11)	.18
Provision for (loss) gain on disposition of discontinued businesses	(.23)	(.23)	.48
Cumulative effect of change in accounting for income taxes . .	—	.20	—
Net earnings	$ .77	$ 3.12	$ 3.92

EXHIBIT 9–1 *(concluded)*

Fully diluted:

Earnings from continuing businesses	$ 1.11	$ 2.99	$ 3.11
Earnings (losses) from discontinued businesses	(.11)	(.11)	.16
Provision for (loss) gain on disposition of discontinued businesses	(.23)	(.20)	.45
Cumulative effect of change in accounting for income taxes	—	.18	—
Net earnings	$ .77	$ 2.86	$ 3.72

of the firm's operating, investing, and financing activities during the period.

Armstrong's statements of cash flows are presented on page 20 of Appendix A. Comparative statements for each of the past three years are again shown. Pay more attention to the captions of the subtotals in the statements than to the captions of the detailed amounts. Notice that the subtotal captions describe the activities—operating, investing, and financing—that caused cash to be provided and used.

The income statement and statement of cash flows have in common the fact that they report what has happened for the fiscal period (usually, but not necessarily, for the year ended on the balance sheet date). The balance sheet, as you should understand, is focused on a single point in time—usually the end of the fiscal year, but one can be prepared as of any date.

LEARNING OBJECTIVES

After studying this chapter you should understand:

- What revenue is, and what the two criteria are that permit revenue recognition.
- The reasons for the difference between gross sales and net sales.
- How shipping terms are described, and their significance in determining who owns merchandise that is in transit between seller and buyer.

- The percentage-of-completion method of recognizing revenue, and why it is sometimes used.
- How cost of goods sold is determined under both perpetual and periodic inventory accounting systems.
- The significance of gross profit (or gross margin), and how the gross profit (or gross margin) ratio is calculated and used.
- How other operating expenses are reported on the income statement.
- What income from operations includes, and why this income statement subtotal is significant to managers and financial analysts.
- The nature of the items that make up other income and expenses.
- The components of the earnings per share calculation, and the reasons for some of the refinements made in that calculation.
- The unusual items that may appear on the income statement, including:
  Discontinued operations.
  Extraordinary items.
  Minority interest in earnings of subsidiaries.
- The alternative income statement presentation models.
- The presentation of unusual items in the income statement.
- The purpose and general format of the statement of cash flows.
- Why the statement of cash flows is significant to financial analysts and investors who rely on the financial statements for much of their evaluative data.

INCOME STATEMENT

Revenues

The FASB defines **revenues** as "inflows or other enhancements of assets of an entity or settlements of its liabilities (or a combination of both) from delivering or producing goods, rendering services, or other activities that constitute the entity's ongoing major or central operations."[1] In its simplest and most straightforward application, this definition means that when a firm sells a product or provides services to a client or customer, and receives cash, creates an account receivable, or satisifies an obligation created when cash

---

[1] FASB, *Statement of Financial Accounting Concepts No. 6,* "Elements of Financial Statements" (Stamford, Conn., 1985), para. 78. Copyright © by the Financial Accounting Standards Board, High Ridge Park, Stamford, Connecticut 06905, U.S.A. Quoted with permission. Copies of the complete document are available from the FASB.

was received prior to delivering the product or service, the firm has revenue. Most revenue transactions fit this simple and straightforward situation. Revenues are generally measured by the amount of cash received or expected to be received from the transaction. If the cash is not expected to be received within a year, then the revenue is usually the present value of the amount expected to be received.

In *Concepts Statement No. 5* the FASB expands upon the above definition of revenues to provide guidance in applying the fundamental criteria involved in recognizing revenue. To be recognized, revenues must be realized or realizable, and earned. Sometimes one of these criteria is more important than the other.

Realization means that the product or service has been exchanged for cash, claims to cash, or an asset that is readily convertible to a known amount of cash or claims to cash. Thus the expectation that the product or service provided by the firm will result in a cash receipt has been fulfilled.

Earned means that the entity has completed, or substantially completed, the activities it must perform to be entitled to the revenue benefits (i.e., the increase in cash or some other asset, or the satisfaction of its liability).

The realization and earned criteria for recognizing revenue are usually satisfied when the product or merchandise being sold is delivered to the customer, or when the service is provided. Thus revenue from selling and servicing activities is commonly recognized when the sale is made, which means when the product is delivered, or when the service is provided to the customer.

An example of a situation in which the earned criterion is more significant than the realization criterion is the magazine publishing company that receives cash at the beginning of a subscription period. In this case, revenue is recognized as earned by delivery of the magazine. On the other hand, if a product is delivered or a service is provided without any expectation of receiving cash or satisfying a liability, for example when a donation is made, there is no revenue to be recognized.

When the revenue is related to the use of assets over a period of time, such as the renting of property or the lending of money, revenues are recognized as earned as time passes based on the contractual prices that had been established in advance.

Some agricultural products, precious metals, and marketable securities have readily determinable prices and can be sold without significant effort. Where this is the case, revenues (and some gains or losses) may be recognized when production is completed or when prices of the assets change.

In spite of these (and prior) guidelines for recognizing revenues, a number of revenue recognition problems have arisen over the years because of the increasing complexity of some business activities, and other newly developed transactions. The FASB and its predecessors within the American Institute of Certified Public Accountants have issued numerous pronouncements about the topic of revenue recognition for various industries and transactions. Revenue recognition is straightforward an overwhelming proportion of the time. But because they are the key to the entire income statement, revenues that are misstated (usually on the high side) lead to significantly misleading financial statements.

Sales is the term used to describe the revenues of firms that sell products that have been manufactured or purchased. In the normal course of business some sales transactions will be subsequently voided because the purchaser returns the merchandise for credit, or for a refund. In some cases, rather than have a shipment returned (especially if it is only slightly damaged or defective, and so is still usable by the customer), the seller will make an allowance on the amount billed, and credit the account receivable from the customer for the allowance amount. If the customer has already paid, a refund is made. These **sales returns and allowances** are accounted for separately for internal control and analysis purposes, but are subtracted from the gross sales amount to arrive at **net sales.** In addition, if the firm allows a cash discount for prompt payment, the cash discounts are also subtracted from gross sales for reporting purposes. A fully detailed income statement prepared for use within the company might have the following revenue section captions:

Sales	$
Less: Sales returns and allowances	( )
Less: Cash discounts	( )
Net sales	$

The first caption usually seen in the annual report income statement of a merchandising or manufacturing company is Net sales, as illustrated in Exhibit 9–1.

Firms that generate significant amounts of revenue from providing services in addition to, or instead of, selling a product will label the revenue source appropriately in the income statement. Thus a leasing company might report Rental and service revenues as the lead item on its income statement, or a consulting service firm might show simply Fees, or Fee revenues. If a firm has several types of revenue, the amount of each could be shown if each amount is significant and is judged by the accountant to increase the usefulness of the income statement.

From a legal perspective, the sale of a product involves the passing of title, or rights of ownership, to the product from the seller to the purchaser. The point at which title passes is usually specified by the shipment terms (see Business Procedure Capsule 16 — Shipping Terms). This issue becomes especially significant in two situations. The first involves shipments made near the end of a fiscal period. The shipping terms will determine whether revenue is recognized in the period in which the shipment was made, or in the subsequent period if that is when the shipment was received by the customer. Achieving an accurate "sales cutoff" may be important to the accuracy of the financial statements if the period-end shipments are material in amount. The second situation relates to the loss or damage of the merchandise while it is in transit from the seller to the buyer since the legal owner of the merchandise is the one who suffers the loss (or who seeks to recover the amount of the loss from the party responsible for the damage).

Most of the time revenue recognition based on transfer of ownership or provision of service is quite straightforward. However, when a firm takes more than a year to construct the item being sold (for example, a shipbuilder or a manufacturer of complex custom machinery), delaying revenue recognition until the product has been delivered may result in a misleading income statement. Because these items are being manufactured under a contract with the buyer that specifies a price, it is possible to recognize revenue (and costs and profits) under what is known as the **percentage-of-completion method.** If, based on engineers' analyses and other factors, 40 percent of a job has been completed in the current year, 40 percent of the expected revenue (and 40 percent of the expected costs) will be recognized in the current year.

Companies should disclose any unusual revenue recognition methods, such as the percentage-of-completion method, in the notes or financial review accompanying the financial statements. Because profits will be directly affected by revenue, the user of the financial statements must be alert to, and understand the effect of, any revenue recognition method that differs from the usual and generally accepted practice of recognizing revenue when the product or service has been delivered to the customer.

Gains, which are increases in an entity's net assets resulting from incidental transactions or nonoperating activities, are usually not included with revenues at the beginning of the income statement. Gains are reported as other income after the firm's operating expenses have been shown, and operating income has been reported. Interest income is an example of an "other income" item. The reporting of gains will be explained in more detail later in this chapter.

Expenses

The FASB defines **expenses** as "outflows or other using up of assets or incurrences of liabilities (or a combination of both) from delivering or producing goods, rendering services, or carrying out other activities that constitute the entity's ongoing major or central operations."[2] Some expenses (cost of goods sold is an example) are recognized concurrently with the revenues that are related to them. This is the **matching principle,** which has been previously described and emphasized. Some expenses (administrative salaries, for example) are recognized in the period in which they are incurred because the benefit of the expense is used up simultaneously or soon after incurrence. Other expenses (depreciation) result from an allocation of the cost of an asset to the periods that are expected to benefit from its use. Each of these categories of expense relates to the matching principle because these expenses support the revenue-generating process. The amount of an expense is measured by the cash or other asset used up to obtain the economic benefit it represents. When the outflow of cash related to the expense will not occur within a year, it is appropriate to recognize the present value of the future cash flow as the amount of the expense.

Most of the time the identification of expenses to be recognized in the current period's income statement is straightforward. Cost of goods sold, compensation of employees, uncollectible accounts receivable, utilities consumed, and depreciation of long-lived assets are all examples. In other cases (advertising, for example), the impact on the revenues of future periods is not readily determinable. For expenditures like this the concepts of objectivity and conservatism are used to justify recording all of the expense in the period in which it was incurred because there is no sound method of matching the expenditure with the revenues that may be earned over several periods.

Other types of expense involve complex recognition and measurement issues. Income tax expense and pension expense are just two examples of this kind of item. Recall the discussion of these topics in Chapter 7, when the liabilities related to these expenses were discussed.

Losses, which are decreases in an entity's net assets resulting from incidental transactions or nonoperating activities, are not included with expenses. Losses are included with other income and expenses reported after income from operations, as discussed later in this chapter.

---

[2] Ibid., para. 80.

> **• BUSINESS PROCEDURE CAPSULE 16**
> **Shipping Terms**
>
> Many products are shipped from the seller to buyer instead of being picked up by the buyer at the time of sale. **Shipping terms** define the owner of the product while it is in transit. **FOB destination** and **FOB shipping point** are the terms used. (FOB means *free on board,* and is jargon that has carried over from the days when much merchandise was shipped by boat.) When an item is shipped FOB destination, the seller owns the product until it is accepted by the buyer at the buyer's designated location. FOB shipping point means that the buyer accepts ownership of the product at the seller's shipping location. Thus title to merchandise shipped FOB destination passes from seller to buyer when the merchandise is received by the buyer.
>
> Shipping terms also describe which party to the transaction is to *incur* the shipping cost. The *seller* incurs the freight cost for shipments made FOB destination; the *buyer* incurs the cost for shipments made FOB shipping point. *Payment* of the freight cost is another issue, however. The freight cost for products shipped **freight prepaid** is paid by the shipper; when a shipment arrives **freight collect,** the buyer pays the freight cost. Ordinarily, items shipped FOB destination will have freight prepaid, and items shipped FOB shipping point will be shipped freight collect. However, depending on freight company policies or other factors, an item having shipping terms of FOB destination may be shipped freight collect, or vice versa. If this happens the firm paying the freight subsequently collects the amount paid to the freight company from the other firm, which *incurred* the freight cost under the shipping terms.

This discussion of expenses will follow the sequence in which expenses are presented in most income statements.

Cost of Goods Sold

Cost of goods sold is the most significant expense for many manufacturing and merchandising companies. The term means what it says, and you should recall from your study of the accounting for inventories in Chapter 5 that the **inventory cost-flow assumption** (FIFO, LIFO, weighted average) being used by the firm affects this expense. **Inventory shrinkage,** the term that describes inventory losses from obsolescence, errors, and theft, is usually included in cost of goods sold unless the amount involved is material. In that case the inventory loss would be reported separately as a loss after operating income has been reported.

Determination of the cost of goods sold amount is a function of the inventory cost-flow assumption and the system used to account for inventories. The two systems, described in Chapter 5, are the perpetual system and the periodic system.

Under the perpetual system, a detailed record of quantities received and sold, and costs, is maintained. When an item is sold, its cost (as determined according to the cost-flow assumption) is transferred from the inventory asset to the cost of goods sold expense with the following entry:

```
Dr.  Cost of Goods Sold . . . . . . . . . . . . . . . . .      xx
      Cr.  Inventory . . . . . . . . . . . . . . . . . . . . .          xx
```

The effect of this entry on the financial statements is:

Balance sheet	Income statement
Assets = Liabilities + Owners' equity	← Net income = Revenues − Expenses
− Inventory	− Cost of Goods Sold

The key point about a perpetual inventory system is that cost is determined when the item is sold. As you can imagine, a perpetual inventory system requires much data processing, but can give management a great deal of information about which inventory items are selling well and which are not. The computer has enabled many firms to adopt a perpetual inventory system. Regular counts of specific inventory items will be made on a cycle basis during the year, and actual quantities on hand will be compared to the computer record of the quantity on hand. This is an internal control procedure designed to determine whether the perpetual system is operating accurately, or to trigger investigation of significant differences.

In a periodic inventory system the cost of goods sold is determined periodically by counting the inventory on hand at the end of a period, and then multiplying the quantity of each item by its cost (determined according to the cost-flow assumption) to get the total cost of the merchandise on hand. This cost is then subtracted from the sum of the cost of the beginning inventory (i.e., the ending inventory of the prior period) and the cost of the merchandise purchased during the current period. (For a manufacturing firm the cost of goods manufactured—discussed in Chapter 12—rather than purchases is used.) This **cost of goods sold model** is illustrated below using 1991 data from the Armstrong World Industries, Inc., financial statements in Appendix A. Can you find the inventory amounts in Appendix A? The amounts for net purchases and goods available for sale have been forced in the model. All amounts are in millions of dollars.

Cost of beginning inventory	$ 349.2
+ Net purchases.	1,788.3
= Cost of goods available for sale	$2,137.5
− Cost of ending inventory	(366.4)
= Cost of goods sold	$1,801.1

The cost of goods sold, of inventory, and of purchases includes not only the price paid to the supplier, but also other costs associated with the purchase of the item such as freight and material handling charges. Cost is reduced by the amount of any cash discount allowed on the purchase. When the periodic inventory system is used, freight charges, purchases discounts, and **purchases returns and allowances** (the purchaser's side of the sales return and allowance transaction) are usually recorded in a separate account for each item, and each account balance is classified with purchases. Thus the net purchases amount is made up of the following:

Purchases
Add: Freight charges
Less: Purchases discounts
       Purchase returns and allowances
Net purchases

Note that selling expenses (discussed later in the Other Operating Expense section of this chapter) are **not** included as part of cost of goods sold!

Although the periodic system may require a less complicated record-keeping system than the perpetual system, the need to take a complete physical inventory to determine accurately the cost of goods sold is a disadvantage. Also, although it can be estimated or developed from special analysis, inventory shrinkage (losses from theft, errors, etc.) is not really known when the periodic system is used because these losses are included in the total cost of goods sold.

Cost of goods sold, ending inventory, and gross profit for periods in which a physical inventory has not been taken can be estimated. This process uses the gross profit ratio (see below) and is illustrated in Exhibit 9–2. This is the procedure used to estimate the amount of inventory lost in a fire, flood, or other circumstance in which a physical inventory cannot be taken. Note that the key to the calculation is the estimated gross profit ratio.

EXHIBIT 9–2   Using the Gross Profit Ratio to Estimate Ending Inventory and Cost of Goods Sold

---

Assume that a firm expects to have a gross profit ratio of 30% for the current fiscal year. Beginning inventory is known because it is the amount of the physical inventory taken at the end of the prior fiscal year. Net sales and net purchases are known from the accounting records of the current fiscal period.

The model (with assumed known data entered):

Net sales	$100,000	100%
Cost of goods sold:		
Beginning inventory	$ 19,000	
Net purchases	63,000	
Cost of goods available for sale	$ 82,000	
Less: Ending inventory	?	
Cost of goods sold	$?	
Gross profit	$?	30%

Solution:

$$\text{Gross profit} = 30\% \times \$100,000 = \$30,000$$

$$\text{Cost of goods sold} = \$100,000 - \$30,000 = \$70,000$$

$$\text{Ending inventory} = \$82,000 - \$70,000 = \$12,000$$

Gross Profit or Gross Margin

The difference between sales revenue and cost of goods sold is **gross profit,** or **gross margin.** Using data from Exhibit 9–1, the income statement for Armstrong World Industries, Inc., to this point is:

ARMSTRONG WORLD INDUSTRIES, INC., AND SUBSIDIARIES
Consolidated Statements of Earnings
(millions except for per-share data)

Years ended December 31	1991	1990	1989
Current earnings			
Net sales	$2,439.3	$2,518.8	$2,488.7
Cost of goods sold	1,801.1	1,816.6	1,764.0
Gross profit	638.2	702.2	724.7

When the amount of gross profit is expressed as a percentage of the sales amount, the resulting **gross profit ratio** (or **gross margin**

ratio) is an especially important statistic for managers of merchandising firms. The calculation of the gross profit ratio for Armstrong World Industries, Inc., for 1991 is illustrated in Exhibit 9–3.

Because the gross profit ratio is a measure of the amount of each sales dollar that is available to cover operating expenses and profit, one of its principal uses by the manager is to estimate whether or not the firm is operating at a level of sales that will lead to profitability in the current period. The manager knows from past experience that if the firm is to be profitable, a certain gross profit ratio and level of sales must be achieved. Sales can be determined on a daily basis from cash register tapes or sales invoice records, and then that amount can be multiplied by the estimated gross profit ratio to determine the estimated gross profit amount. This amount can be related to estimated operating expenses, which are made up of an amount that seldom changes much from month to month and of an amount that does change and that can be anticipated, to estimate the firm's operating results. In many cases just knowing the amount of sales is enough to be able to estimate whether or not the firm has reached profitability. This is especially true for firms that have virtually the same gross profit ratio for every item sold. However, if the gross profit ratio differs by class of merchandise, and it usually does, then the proportion of the sales of each class to total sales (the **sales mix**) must be considered when estimating total gross profit. For example, if Armstrong World Industries, Inc., has a 20 percent gross profit ratio on floor coverings, and a 30 percent gross profit ratio on furniture, and the proportion of floor coverings and furniture sold each month changes, then the sales of both product categories must be considered to estimate total gross profit anticipated for any given month.

EXHIBIT 9–3

ARMSTRONG WORLD INDUSTRIES, INC.
Gross Profit Ratio—1991
(dollars in millions)

Net sales	$2,493.3
Cost of goods sold	1,801.1
Gross profit (or gross margin)	$ 638.2

Gross profit ratio = Gross profit/Net sales

= $638.2/$2,439.3

= 26.2%

Another important use of the gross profit ratio is to set selling prices. If the manager knows the gross profit ratio required to achieve profitability at a given level of sales, the cost of the item can be divided by the complement of the gross profit ratio (or the cost of goods sold ratio) to determine the selling price. This is illustrated in Exhibit 9–4.

Of course, competitive pressures, the manufacturer's recommended selling price, and other factors will also influence the price finally established, but the desired gross profit ratio and the item's cost are frequently the starting points in the pricing decision.

The gross profit ratio required to achieve profitability will vary among firms as a result of their operating strategies. For example, a discount store seeks a high sales volume and a low level of operating expenses, so a relatively low gross profit ratio is accepted. A boutique, on the other hand, has a relatively low sales volume and higher operating expenses, and so needs a relatively high gross profit ratio.

Even though gross profit and the gross profit ratio are widely used internally by the managers of the firm, many companies do not present gross profit as a separate item in their published income statements. Even though gross profit is not reported separately, however, cost of goods sold is usually shown as a separate item. Thus, the user of the income statement can make the calculation for comparative and other evaluation purposes.

EXHIBIT 9–4   Using Desired Gross Profit Ratio to Set Selling Price

---

Assume that a retail store's cost for a particular carpet is $8 per square yard. What selling price per square yard should be established for this product if a 20 percent gross profit ratio is desired?

$$\text{Selling price} = \text{Cost of product}/(1 - \text{Desired gross profit ratio})$$

$$= \$8/(1 - 0.2)$$

$$= \$10$$

Proof:

Calculated selling price	$10 per square yard
Cost of product.	8 per square yard
Gross profit	$ 2

$$\text{Gross profit ratio} = \text{Gross profit/Selling price}$$

$$= \$2/\$10$$

$$= 20\%$$

Other Operating Expenses

The principal categories of other **operating expenses** frequently reported on the income statement are:

Selling expenses.

General and administrative expenses.

Research and development expenses.

Sometimes these three categories are combined into one or two categories. Armstrong World Industries, Inc., uses the single category "Selling and administrative expense."

Sometimes other operating expenses that management believes should be highlighted (e.g., repairs and maintenance, or taxes other than income taxes) are reported separately. The financial statement footnotes, or financial review, will sometimes include disclosure of certain expense items that are combined with others in the income statement. Total depreciation and amortization expense is frequently reported this way because, as already explained, these expenses do not result in the disbursement of cash. The total of depreciation and amortization expense also appears in the statement of cash flows, as will be illustrated later in this chapter.

Income from Operations

The difference between gross profit and operating expenses represents **income from operations,** or **operating income.** Armstrong World Industries, Inc., has given this subtotal a different but more descriptive caption, as shown in the following partial income statement from Exhibit 9–1:

Armstrong World Industries, Inc., and Subsidiaries
Consolidated Statements of Earnings (millions except for per-share data)

Years ended December 31	1991	1990	1989
Current earnings			
Net sales	$2,439.3	$2,518.8	$2,488.7
Cost of goods sold	1,801.1	1,816.6	1,764.0
Gross profit	638.2	702.2	724.7
Selling and administrative expense. . . .	468.3	462.6	436.6
Earnings from continuing businesses before other income (expense) and income taxes	169.9	239.6	288.1

Although only an intermediate subtotal on the income statement, income from operations is frequently interpreted as the most appropriate measure of management's ability to utilize the firm's operating assets because the other income and expense items, and income taxes, reflect the effect of nonoperating transactions. As discussed in Chapter 3, income from operations is frequently used in the return on investment calculation, which relates operating income to average operating assets.

Managers of those firms that do not report income from operations as a separate item believe that other income and expense items (i.e., gains and losses) should receive as much attention in the evaluation process as revenues and expenses from the firm's principal operations because they do exist and do affect overall profitability. There is no single best presentation for all firms; this is another area in which the accountant's judgment is used to select among equally acceptable alternatives.

Other Income and Expenses

Other income and expenses are reported after income from operations. These nonoperating items include interest expense, interest income, gains, and losses.

Interest expense is the item of other income and expenses most frequently identified separately. It is shown separately because most financial statement users want to know the amount of this expense because it is a contractural obligation.

Interest income earned from excess cash that has been temporarily invested is not subtracted from interest expense. Interest income is reported as a separate item if it is material in amount relative to other nonoperating items. The full disclosure principle is applied to determine the extent of the details reported in this section of the income statement. Significant items that would facilitate the reader's understanding of net income or loss are separately identified, either in the statement itself or in the footnotes or financial review. For example, in the Armstrong World Industries, Inc., income statement in Exhibit 9–1, a gain on the sale of woodlands is reported in 1990 and 1989. Items that are not significant are combined in an "other" or "miscellaneous" category. Examples of nonoperating gains or losses are those resulting from litigation, the sale or disposal of depreciable assets (including plant closings), and inventory obsolescence losses.

Income before Income Taxes and Income Tax Expense

Because income taxes are assessed on operating income and gains and losses, the income statement usually has a subtotal labeled **"Income before income taxes,"** followed by the caption "Income taxes" or "Provision for income taxes" and the amount of this expense. Some income statements do not use the "Income before income taxes" caption; income taxes are listed as another expense in these statements. There will almost always be a footnote or financial review disclosure of the details of the income tax expense calculation.

Net Income and Earnings per Share

Net income (or net loss), sometimes called *the bottom line,* is the arithmetic sum of the revenues and gains minus the expenses and losses. Because retained earnings, which results from having net income, is a necessary prerequisite to dividends, share owners and potential investors are especially interested in net income. Reinforce your understanding of information presented in the income statement by referring again to Exhibit 9–1, and studying the income statements in other annual reports you may have.

To facilitate interpretation of net income (or loss), it is also reported on a per share of common stock basis. In its simplest form, **earnings per share** is calculated by dividing net income by the average number of shares of common stock outstanding during the year. There are two principal complications in the calculation that should be understood. First, a weighted-average number of shares of common stock is used. This is sensible because if shares are issued early in the year, the proceeds from their sale have been used longer in the income-generating process than the proceeds from shares issued later in the year. The weighting basis usually used is the number of months each number of shares has been outstanding. The weighted average calculation is illustrated in Exhibit 9–5.

The other complication exists in the calculation of earnings per share of common stock in those situations in which a firm has preferred stock outstanding. Remember that preferred stock is entitled to its dividend before dividends can be paid on common stock. Because of this prior claim to earnings, the amount of the preferred stock dividend requirement is subtracted from net in-

---

EXHIBIT 9–5   Weighted-Average Shares Outstanding Calculation

Assumptions:

On September 1, 1992, the beginning of its fiscal year, Cruisers, Inc., had 200,000 shares of common stock outstanding.

On January 3, 1993, 40,000 additional shares were issued for cash.

On June 25, 1993, 15,000 shares of common stock were acquired as treasury stock (and so are no longer outstanding).

Weighted-average calculation:

Period	Number of Months	Number of Shares Outstanding	Months × Shares
9/1–1/3.	4	200,000	800,000
1/3–6/25	6	240,000	1,440,000
6/25–8/31. . . .	2	225,000	450,000
Totals	12		2,690,000

Weighted-average number of shares outstanding = 2,690,000/12

= 224,167

---

come to arrive at the numerator in the calculation of earnings per share of common stock outstanding. The preferred stock dividend requirement is not shown as a deduction in the income statement, however. Thus if Cruisers, Inc., had earned net income of $1,527,000 for the year ended August 31, 1991, and had 80,000 shares of a 7 percent $50 par value preferred stock outstanding during the year, using the weighted average number of shares of common stock outstanding from Exhibit 9–5 would result in earnings per share of common stock of $5.56, calculated as follows:

Net income	$1,527,000
Less preferred stock dividend requirement (7% × $50 par value × 80,000 shares outstanding)	280,000
Net income available for common stock	$1,247,000

Earnings per share of common stock outstanding =

$$\frac{\text{Net income available for common stock}}{\text{Weighted average number of shares of common stock, outstanding}}$$

= $1,247,000/224,167

= $5.56

In addition to the two principal complications just discussed, several other issues (not discussed here) can add to the complexity of the calculation. The result of the calculation illustrated above is called primary earnings per share. Because of its significance, primary earnings per share of common stock outstanding is reported on the income statement just below the amount of net income. Note the presentation in Exhibit 9–1.

In addition to primary earnings per share, a firm may be required to report fully diluted earnings per share. If the firm has issued long-term debt or preferred stock that is convertible into common stock, it is possible that the conversion of the debt or preferred stock could result in a lower earnings per share of common stock outstanding. This can happen because the increase in net income available to the common stock (if interest expense is reduced, or preferred dividends are not required) is proportionately less than the number of additional common shares issued in the conversion. The reduction in earnings per share of the common stock is referred to as **dilution.** If significant, the effect of the potential dilution is reported on the income statement by showing the fully diluted earnings per share of common stock as well as the primary earnings per share. Fully diluted earnings per share are calculated under the assumption that the convertible debt and/or preferred stock had been converted at the beginning of the year.

The income statement presentation of net income and earnings per share when potential dilution exists is shown below. (Data are from the previous Cruisers, Inc., illustrations, with an assumed fully diluted earnings per share amount.)

Net income	$1,527,000
Earnings per share of common stock:	
Assuming no dilution	$ 5.56
Assuming full dilution	$ 4.98

As illustrated in the Armstrong World Industries, Inc., income statement in Exhibit 9–1, if there are any unusual items on the income statement (see below), the per share amount of each item is disclosed, and earnings per share is the sum of earnings per share before the unusual items and the per share amounts of the unusual items. This is done for both primary and fully diluted earnings per share data.

Unusual Items Sometimes Seen on an Income Statement

One of the ways that investors and potential investors use the income statement is to predict probable results of future operations from the results of current operations. Transactions that have an effect on the predictive process are highlighted and reported separately from the results of recurring transactions. Two of the more frequently encountered of these uncommon items relate to discontinued operations and extraordinary items. Other captions sometimes seen on an income statement relate to the cumulative effect of a change in the application of an accounting principle, or to the earnings of subsidiaries. When any of these items affect income tax expense, the amount disclosed in the income statement is the amount of the item net of the income tax effect. Each of these unusual items is discussed in the following paragraphs.

Discontinued Operations.   When a segment, or major portion of a business, is disposed of, it is appropriate to disclose separately the impact that the discontinued operation has had on the operations of the firm. This separate disclosure is made to help users of the financial statements understand how future income statements may differ because of the discontinued operation. This is accomplished by reporting the income or loss, after income taxes, of the discontinued operation separately after a subtotal amount labeled **income from continuing operations.** Income from continuing operations is the income after income taxes of continuing operations. The effect of this reporting is to exclude all of the effects of the discontinued operation from the revenues, expenses, gains, and losses of continuing operations. This presentation is illustrated in Part III of Exhibit 9–6.

Extraordinary Items.   A transaction that has a significant income statement effect after income taxes, that is unusual in nature, and that occurs infrequently qualifies for reporting as an **extraordinary item.** The reason for such separate reporting is to emphasize that the item is extraordinary, and that the income statements for subsequent years are not likely to include this kind of item. Examples of extraordinary items are gains or losses from early repayment of long-term debt, pension plan terminations, some litigation settlements, and utilization of tax loss carryforwards (see Business Procedure Capsule 17—Tax Loss Carryovers).

• BUSINESS PROCEDURE CAPSULE 17
Tax Loss Carryovers

The Internal Revenue Code provides that a business that experiences an operating loss in any year can offset that loss against profits that have been earned in the past or that may be earned in the future, and can recover the income taxes that were paid in the past, or escape taxation on the future profits. Generally speaking, losses can be carried back 3 years, and carried forward for 15 years. To illustrate, assume the following pattern of profits and losses for a firm that began business in 1988:

	1988	1989	1990	1991	1992
Profit/(Loss)	$50,000	$30,000	$(100,000)	$(40,000)	$70,000

The corporation would have paid taxes in 1988 and 1989 based on its income in those years. In 1990, no taxes would be payable because the firm operated at a loss. Under the **tax loss carryover** rules, $50,000 of the 1990 loss would be carried back to 1988, and $30,000 of the 1990 loss would be carried back to 1989, and the taxes previously paid in each of those years would be refunded to the corporation. The remaining $20,000 of "unused" loss from 1990 would be carried forward, to be offset against profits of the next 15 years. No taxes would be payable in 1991 because of the loss in that year, but there would be no carryback of that loss because the 1990 carryback absorbed the 1988 and 1989 profits; the 1991 loss would be carried forward. In 1992, the $70,000 of profits would be reduced by the $20,000 loss carryforward from 1990 and the $40,000 loss carryforward from 1991, so only $10,000 of 1992 profits would be subject to tax.

In the income statement it is desirable to relate income tax expense, or recovery of income taxes previously paid, to results from operations. Thus for the firm in the example, income tax expense for 1988 and 1989 would be reported in the usual way, as illustrated below. In the 1990 income statement, the income tax refund from 1988 and 1989 would be shown as an income tax recovery, or negative tax expense. The potential income tax reduction in the future from the carryforward is not reflected in the financial statements because it will not be realized unless profits are earned in the future. The 1991 income statement will not show either expense or potential future reduction of income taxes. The 1992 income statement will reflect income tax expense based on pre-tax income of $70,000; then, the tax reduction because of the $60,000 of loss carryover would be reported as an extraordinary item in 1992.

(continued)

- **BUSINESS PROCEDURE CAPSULE 17**   *(concluded)*

The income tax expense (recovery) for each year would be reported as follows, assuming an income tax rate of 40 percent:

	1988	1989	1990	1991	1992
Income (loss) before taxes . . .	$50,000	$30,000	$(100,000)	$(40,000)	$70,000
Income tax expense/(recovery)	20,000	12,000	(32,000)	—	28,000
Net income (loss) . .	$30,000	$18,000	$ (68,000)	$(40,000)	$42,000
For 1992 only: Extraordinary item: Utilization of tax loss carryforward					24,000
Net income and extraordinary item					$66,000

When an extraordinary item is reported, earnings per share of common stock outstanding is reported for income before the extraordinary item, for the extraordinary item, and for net income (after the extrordinary item). This presentation is also illustrated in Part III of Exhibit 9–6.

Minority Interest in Earnings of Subsidiaries.   As explained in Chapter 7, the financial statements of a subsidiary are consolidated with those of the parent even though the parent owns less than 100 percent of the stock of the subsidiary. The consolidated income statement includes all of the revenues, expenses, gains, and losses of the subsidiary. However, only the parent company's equity in the subsidiary's earnings is included in consolidated net income. The minority shareowners' equity in the subsidiary's earnings is reported in the consolidated income statement as a deduction from income after income taxes when this minority interest is significant. When the **minority interest in the earnings of the subsidiary** is not significant, this deduction is included with other income and expense.

Cumulative Effect of a Change in Accounting Principle.   A change from one generally accepted principle or method to another (from

EXHIBIT 9–6   Income Statement Format Alternatives

I. Single-step format

CRUISERS, INC. AND SUBSIDIARIES
Consolidated Income Statement
For the Years Ended August 31, 1993, and 1992
(000 omitted)

	1993	*1992*
Net sales	$77,543	$62,531
Cost of goods sold	48,077	39,870
Selling expenses	13,957	10,590
General and administrative expenses	9,307	7,835
Interest expense	3,378	2,679
Other income (net)	385	193
Minority interest	432	356
Income before taxes	$ 2,777	$ 1,394
Provision for income taxes	1,250	630
Net income	$ 1,527	$ 764
Earnings per share of common stock outstanding .	$ 5.56	$ 2.42

II. Multiple-step format

CRUISERS, INC. AND SUBSIDIARIES
Consolidated Income Statement
For the Years Ended August 31, 1993, and 1992
(000 omitted)

	1993	*1992*
Net sales	$77,543	$62,531
Cost of goods sold	48,077	39,870
Gross profit	$29,466	$22,661
Selling, general, and administrative expenses . . .	23,264	18,425
Income from operations	$ 6,202	$ 4,236
Other income (expense):		
Interest expense	(3,378)	(2,679)
Other income (net)	385	193
Minority interest	(432)	(356)
Income before taxes	$ 2,777	$ 1,394
Provision for income taxes	1,250	630
Net income	$ 1,527	$ 764
Earnings per share of common stock outstanding	$ 5.56	$ 2.42

The principal difference between these two formats is that the multiple-step
format provides subtotals for gross profit and income from operations. As
previously discussed, each of these amounts is useful in evaluating the
performance of the firm, and proponents of the multiple-step format believe
that it is appropriate to highlight these amounts.

(continued)

EXHIBIT 9–6 *(concluded)*

III. Under either format, discontinued operations and an extraordinary item would be disclosed in captions following income taxes, and the rest of the income statement would appear as follows:

	1993	1992
. . . .		
Income from continuing operations before income taxes	$2,777	$1,394
Provision for income taxes	1,250	630
Income from continuing operations	$1,527	$ 764
Discontinued operations, net of income taxes:		
Loss from operations.	(162)	—
Loss on disposal.	(79)	—
Loss from discontinued operations.	$ (241)	—
Earnings before extraordinary item	$1,286	$ 764
Extraordinary item:		
Gain on termination of pension plan net of income taxes	357	—
Net income	$1,643	$ 764
Earnings per share of common stock outstanding:		
Continuing operations	$ 5.56	$ 2.42
Discontinued operations:		
Loss from operations.	(.72)	—
Loss on disposal.	(.35)	—
Extraordinary item.	1.59	—
Net income	$ 6.08	$ 2.42

---

straight-line to accelerated depreciation, for example) is permitted only if there has been a change promulgated by a standard-setting body (such as the FASB), or if the change can be justified by the entity because of a change in its economic circumstances. The cumulative effect of the change on the reported net income of prior years, net of any income tax effect, is reported in the income statement for the year of the change, after income from continuing operations. Income statements of prior years that are presented for comparative purposes are not revised to reflect the change; however, the effect that the change would have had on those years is disclosed in the explanatory notes to the financial statements (see

Chapter 10). An exception to this procedure occurs for some changes mandated by the FASB, for which restatement of prior years' financial statements is required. In these cases the cumulative effect of the change is reflected in the beginning retained earnings balance of the earliest year presented in the comparative financial statements. Note in Exhibit 9–1 that Armstrong World Industries, Inc., reported the cumulative effect of a change in accounting for income taxes that occurred in 1990. The change reflected the requirements of a new financial accounting standard issued by the FASB that Armstrong World Industries, Inc., elected to implement in 1990 even though the FASB permitted later implementation. (The new financial accounting standard is discussed in Chapter 7, in the section on deferred income taxes.)

Summary of Income Statement Presentation Alternatives

There are two principal alternative presentations of income statement data: the **single-step format** and the **multiple-step format.** These are illustrated in Exhibit 9–6, using hypothetical data for Cruisers, Inc., for fiscal years 1992 and 1993. Examples of the unusual income statement captions are also presented in that exhibit.

You may notice an inconsistency in the use of parentheses in the single-step and multiple-step formats in Exhibit 9–6. No parentheses are used in the single-step format; the user is expected to know by reading the captions which items to add and which to subtract in the calculation of net income. In the multiple-step format the caption for "Other income (expense)" indicates that *in this section of the statement*, items without parentheses are added and items in parentheses are subtracted. In other parts of the statement the caption indicates the arithmetic operation. With either format, the statement reader must be alert to make sense of the information presented in the statement.

Note especially that in Part III of Exhibit 9–6 the earnings per share information is presented separately for income from continuing operations and the elements of discontinued operations and the extraordinary item. This is done to alert the reader to the fact that future years' earnings per share will not include the impact of these nonrecurring items.

Table 9–1 summarizes the income statement format used by 600 publicly owned industrial and merchandising corporations whose annual reports are summarized by the AICPA. Note the trend to the use of the multiple-step format over the four years.

STATEMENT OF CASH FLOWS

Content and Format of the Statement

The **statement of cash flows** (and its predecessor, the statement of changes in financial position) is a relatively new financial statement that illustrates the way accounting evolves to meet the requirements of users of financial statements. The importance of understanding the cash flows of an entity has been increasingly emphasized over the years. The accrual basis income statement is not designed to present cash flows from operations, and, except for related revenues and expenses, it shows no information about cash flows from investing and financing activities.

In the early 1960s some companies began presenting information about changes in balance sheet items. In 1963 the Accounting Principles Board of the AICPA recommended that this statement be called the *statement of source and application of funds*. The term *funds* usually meant working capital, and this statement explained the change in working capital that had occurred between the dates of the balance sheets presented in the annual report. In 1971 the Accounting Principles Board made the statement mandatory and gave it the title "Statement of Changes in Financial Position." In late 1987 the Financial Accounting Standards Board issued a standard requiring the presentation of a statement of cash flows. This statement replaces the "Statement of Changes in Financial Position," and is required for financial statements issued for years ending after July 15, 1988.

TABLE 9–1 Income Statement Format

	1990	1989	1988	1987
Single-step format:				
Federal income tax shown as a separate last item	206	229	233	251
Federal income tax listed among operating items	9	3	7	8
Multiple-step format:				
Costs and expenses deducted from sales to show operating income.	229	220	225	220
Costs deducted from sales to show gross margin	156	148	135	121
Total companies	600	600	600	600

Source: AICPA, *Accounting Trends and Techniques* (New York, 1991), Table 3–2.

The primary purpose of the statement of cash flows is to provide relevant information about the cash receipts and cash payments of an enterprise during a period.[3] The statement shows why cash (including short-term investments that are essentially equivalent to cash) changed during the period by reporting net cash provided or used by operating activities, investing activities, and financing activities.

There are two approaches to achieving the statement objective—the direct-method presentation and the indirect-method presentation. The direct method involves listing each major class of cash receipts transactions and cash disbursements transactions for each of the three activity areas. The operating activity transactions include cash received from customers, cash paid to merchandise or raw material suppliers, cash paid to employees for salaries and wages, cash paid for other operating expenses, cash payments of interest, and cash payments for taxes. A direct-method statement of cash flows is illustrated in Exhibit 9–7. The FASB standard encourages enterprises to use the direct method.

The indirect method explains the change in cash by explaining the change in each of the noncash accounts in the balance sheet. A statement of cash flows prepared this way shows net income as the first source of operating cash. However, net income is an accrual concept amount, and must be adjusted for revenues and expenses that did not affect cash. The most significant of these are usually expenses for depreciation and amortization. These expenses do not involve payment of cash; remember that their effect on the financial statements is:

Balance sheet	Income statement
Assets = Liabilities + Owners' equity ←	Net income = Revenues − Expenses
− Accumulated Depreciation	− Depreciation Expense
or	
− Intangible Asset	− Amortization Expense
or	
+ Discount on Bonds Payable	− Interest Expense

---

[3] FASB, *Statement of Financial Accounting Standards No. 95*, "Statement of Cash Flows" (Stamford, Conn., 1987), para. 4. Copyright © by the Financial Accounting Standards Board, High Ridge Park, Stamford, Connecticut 06905, U.S.A. Quoted with permission. Copies of the complete document are available from the FASB.

EXHIBIT 9–7   Statement of Cash Flows

I. Direct Method

CRUISERS, INC., AND SUBSIDIARIES
Consolidated Statements of Cash Flows
For the Years Ended August 31, 1993, and 1992
(000 omitted)

	1993	1992
Cash flows from operating activities:		
Cash received from customers	$14,929	$13,021
Cash paid to suppliers	6,784	8,218
Payments for compensation of employees . . .	2,137	1,267
Other operating expenses paid	1,873	1,002
Interest paid	675	703
Taxes paid	1,037	532
Net cash provided by operating activities. . . .	$ 2,423	$ 1,299
Cash flows from investing activities:		
Proceeds from sale of land	$ —	$ 200
Investment in plant and equipment	(1,622)	(1,437)
Net cash used for investing activities	$(1,622)	$(1,237)
Cash flows from financing activities:		
Additional long-term borrowing	$ 350	$ 180
Payment of long-term debt	(268)	(53)
Purchase of treasury stock	(37)	(26)
Payment of dividends on capital stock	(363)	(310)
Net cash used for financing activities	$ (318)	$ (209)
Increase (Decrease) in cash.	$ 483	$ (147)
Cash balance, August 31, 1992, and 1991.	276	423
Cash balance, August 31, 1993, and 1992.	$ 759	$ 276
Reconciliation of net income and		
net cash provided by operating activities:		
Net income	$ 1,390	$ 666
Add (Deduct) items not affecting cash:		
Depreciation expense	631	526
Minority interest.	432	356
Gain on sale of land	—	(110)
Increase in accounts receivable	(30)	(44)
Increase in inventories	(21)	(168)
Increase in current liabilities	16	66
Other (net)	5	7
Net cash provided by operating activities. . . .	$ 2,423	$ 1,299

(continued)

EXHIBIT 9–7   *(concluded)*

II. Indirect method

CRUISERS, INC., AND SUBSIDIARIES
Consolidated Statements of Cash Flows
For the Years Ended August 31, 1993, and 1992
(000 omitted)

	1993	*1992*
Cash flows from operating activities:		
Net income	$ 1,390	$ 666
Add (Deduct) items not affecting cash:		
Depreciation expense	631	526
Minority interest.	432	356
Gain on sale of land	—	(110)
Increase in accounts receivable	(30)	(44)
Increase in inventories	(21)	(168)
Increase in current liabilities	16	66
Other (net)	5	7
Net cash provided by operating activities. . . .	$ 2,423	$ 1,299
Cash flows from investing activities:		
Proceeds from sale of land	$ —	$ 200
Investment in plant and equipment	(1,622)	(1,437)
Net cash used for investing activities	$ (1,622)	$ (1,237)
Cash flows from financing activities:		
Additional long-term borrowing	$ 350	$ 180
Payment of long-term debt	(268)	(53)
Purchase of treasury stock	(37)	(26)
Payment of dividends on capital stock	(363)	(310)
Net cash used for financing activities	$ (318)	$ (209)
Increase (Decrease) in cash.	$ 483	$ (147)
Cash balance, August 31, 1992, and 1991	276	423
Cash balance, August 31, 1993, and 1992	$ 759	$ 276

Therefore depreciation and amortization expense that have been deducted to arrive at net income are added back to the net income amount to determine more accurately the amount of cash generated from operations. Other income statement items that need to be considered in a similar way are:

Income tax expense not currently payable (i.e., deferred income taxes resulting from temporary differences in the recognition of revenue and expenses for book and tax purposes).

Gains or losses on the sale or abandonment of assets. The *proceeds* from the sale, not the gain or loss, affect cash. Losses are added back to net income, and gains are subtracted from net income. The sale proceeds are reported as an investing activity, described below.

Changes in the noncash accounts must also be shown. Thus increases in current assets such as accounts receivable and inventories, and decreases in current liabilities such as accounts payable are reported as uses of cash because one way to look at these changes is to see that cash would have increased had the change not occurred. Conversely, decreases in current assets and increases in current liabilities are reported as sources of cash. An indirect-method statement of cash flows is also illustrated in Exhibit 9–7.

Investing activities include transactions involving plant and equipment, as well as investment in debt or equity securities of other entities.

Financing activities include transactions involving the entity's own debt or capital stock, including dividends paid.

Exhibit 9–7 illustrates hypothetical statements of cash flow using the alternative methods. Most statements of changes in financial position prepared prior to 1988 used the indirect method. What method was used in the statement of cash flows in the annual report that you obtained?

Note that the difference between the two methods is in the presentation of cash flows from operating activities. When the direct-method format is used, a separate schedule reconciling net income reported on the income statement with net cash provided by operating activities is required. This reconciliation is in the form of the indirect method presentation of net cash provided by operating activities. A survey of the 1990 annual reports of 600 publicly owned merchandising and manufacturing companies indicated that 585 firms used the indirect-method presentation, and 15 companies used the direct-method presentation.[4]

Interpreting the Statement of Cash Flows

The statement of cash flows focuses on cash receipts and cash payments during the period, so the first question to be answered is: "Did the company's cash balance increase or decrease during the year?" The answer is usually found near the bottom of the statement. In the annual report of a publicly owned corporation, com-

---

[4] AICPA, *Accounting Trends and Techniques* (New York, 1991), Table 5–3.

parative statements for the most recent and prior two years will be presented, and the change in each of the three years can be noted. If the change in the cash balance during a year has been significant (more than 10% of the beginning cash balance), the financial statement user will try to understand the reason for the change by focusing on the relative totals of each of the three categories of cash flows—operating activities, investing activities, and financing activities. Even if the change in the cash balance during a year is not significant, the relationship between the three activity categories will be observed.

A firm should have a positive cash flow provided by operating activities. If operating activities did not generate cash, the firm would have to seek outside funding to finance its day-to-day activities, as well as its investment requirements, unless a large cash balance was brought forward from the prior year. Although negative cash flow from operating activities might apply to a firm just starting up, it would be a sign of possible financial weakness for a mature company.

Virtually all financially healthy firms have growth in revenues as a financial objective. This growth usually requires increasing capacity to manufacture or sell products, or provide services. Thus a principal investing activity is the acquisition of plant and equipment. The total cash used for investing activities is compared to the total cash provided by operating activities. If cash provided by operating activities exceeds cash used for investing activities, the indication is that the firm is generating the cash it needs to finance its growth, and that is probably positive. If the cash used for investing activities exceeds the cash provided by operating activities, the difference will have to be provided by financing activity, or come from the cash balance carried forward from the prior year. This is not necessarily negative, because investment requirements in any one year may be unusually high. If, however, cash used for investing activities exceeds cash provided from operating activities year after year, and the difference is provided from financing activities, a question about the firm's ability to continue raising funds from financing activities must be raised.

Financing activities include the issue and repayment of debt, the sale of stock and purchase of treasury stock, and the payment of dividends on stock (although some companies report cash dividends separately in the reconciliation of beginning and ending cash). For most companies, it would be desirable to have the cash dividend covered by the excess of cash provided from operating activities over cash used for investing activities.

After the big picture of the entity's cash flows has been obtained, it may be necessary to look at the details of each category of cash flows for clues that will explain the overall change. For example, if cash flows from operating activities are less than cash used for investing activities, or if they are decreasing even though profits are increasing, it may be that accounts receivable and/or inventories are increasing at a higher rate than sales. This is a signal that the firm may have liquidity problems that would not necessarily be reflected by the change in working capital, the current ratio, or the acid-test ratio, because those measures of liquidity include other items besides cash.

The details of an entity's investing activities frequently describe its growth strategy. Besides investing in more plant and equipment, some firms acquire capacity by purchasing other companies. Other firms will invest in the securities of other companies. Occasionally a firm will sell some of its plant and equipment, in which case cash is provided. The reasons for and consequences of such a sale of assets are of interest to the financial statement user.

To illustrate these interpretation techniques, refer to the Armstrong World Industries, Inc., Consolidated Statements of Cash Flows on page 20 of the annual report in Appendix A. There was a significant decrease in cash in 1989, followed by an increase in 1990 and a decrease in 1991. In all three years, cash provided by operating activities exceeded cash used for investing activities, a relationship generally considered desirable. The pace of the company's purchases of property, plant and equipment has been slowing over the past three years. The company has sold some facilities and discontinued some businesses, and the financial statement footnotes (see Chapter 10) will be reviewed to learn more about this. In all three years financing activities resulted in a net use of cash, with the purchase of treasury stock being a significant use in 1989 and 1990. In 1989, cash was raised by the sale of convertible preferred stock, but a considerable amount of short-term debt was repaid. In 1990 short-term debt was increased. In 1991 the issuance of long-term debt was a significant source of cash, and about 60 percent of the cash so raised was used to retire short-term debt. Cash dividends were paid all three years. The overall picture for Armstrong World Industries, Inc., is good; cash provided from operating activities is covering investment requirements and, except in 1991, was also covering the cash dividends. The firm's debt/equity structure was modified during 1989 and 1990, and further financial statement analysis (see Chapter 11) will evaluate this change.

The statement of cash flows provides useful information for owners, managers, employees, suppliers, potential investors, and others interested in the economic activities of the entity. This statement provides information that is difficult, if not impossible, to obtain from the other three financial statements alone.

SUMMARY

This chapter has described the income statement and the statement of cash flows. The income statement summarizes the results of the firm's profit-generating or loss-generating activities for a fiscal period. The statement of cash flows explains the change in the firm's cash from the beginning to the end of the fiscal period by summarizing the cash effects of the firm's operating, investing, and financing activities during the period.

Revenues are reported at the beginning of the income statement. Revenues result from the sale of a product or the provision of a service, not necessarily from the receipt of cash. The revenues of most manufacturing and merchandising firms are called *sales*. Net sales, which is gross sales minus sales returns and allowances and cash discounts, is usually the first caption of the income statement. Service entities will describe the source of their revenues (e.g., rental fees or consulting fees).

Expenses are subtracted from revenues in the income statement. A significant expense for many firms is cost of goods sold. The actual calculation of cost of goods sold is determined by the system used to account for inventories. With a perpetual inventory system, cost can be determined and recognized when a product is sold. With a periodic inventory system, cost of goods sold is calculated at the end of the fiscal period using beginning and ending inventory amounts, and the purchases (or cost of goods manufactured) amount. Sometimes cost of goods sold is reported separately and subtracted from net sales to arrive at gross profit or gross margin in what is called a *multiple-step income statement presentation*. Other firms will include cost of goods sold with operating expenses in a single-step income statement presentation.

Gross profit (or gross margin) is frequently expressed as a ratio. The gross profit ratio can be used to monitor profitability and set selling prices.

Selling, general, and administrative expenses are the costs of operating the firm. They are deducted from gross profit to arrive at operating income, an important measure of management performance.

Interest expense is usually shown as a separate item in the other income and expense category of the income statement. Other significant gains or losses will be identified.

Income before income taxes is frequently reported as a subtotal before income tax expense is shown because this expense is a function of all income statement items reported to this point in the statement.

Net income, or net earnings, is reported in total and on a per share of outstanding common stock basis. If there is a significant potential dilution from convertible debt or preferred stock, earnings per share on a fully diluted basis will also be reported.

To facilitate users' comparisons of net income with that of prior years, and to provide a basis for future expectations, income or loss from discontinued operations and extraordinary items are reported separately in the income statement.

The income statement reflects accrual accounting. Financial statement users are interested in the cash flows of an entity. The statement of cash flows provides information about the cash flows from operating activities, investing activities, and financing activities.

The determination of cash flows from operating activities is essentially a conversion of the accrual accounting income statement to a cash basis income statement. The principal reasons net income doesn't affect cash directly are that not all accounts receivable from sales are collected in the fiscal period of the sale, and not all of the expenses reported in the income statement are disbursements of cash in the fiscal period in which the expense was incurred.

Investing activities include purchases of plant and equipment, investments in other companies, and other long-term investments.

Financing activities include issuance and redemption of bonds and stock, including treasury stock transactions, and cash dividends on stock.

The statement of cash flows shows the change in cash during the year, and reports cash provided from or used by operating activities, investing activities, and financing activities.

There are two presentation formats for the statement of cash flows. The difference between the two is primarily in the presentation of cash flows from operating activities. Most entities will use the indirect-method presentation alternative.

Interpretation of the statement of cash flows involves observing the relationship between the three broad categories of cash flows (operating activities, investing activities, and financing activities) and the change in the cash balance for the year. It is desirable to have cash provided from operating activities that is equal to or greater than cash used for investing activities, although large investment requirements in any one year may result in cash being raised from financing activities or in a reduction in the beginning of the year cash balance. The details of each activity category will be reviewed and their effect on the overall cash position of the firm evaluated. The statement of cash flows provides important information that is not easily obtained from the other financial statements.

Refer to the income statement and statement of cash flows for Armstrong World Industries, Inc., in Appendix A, and to these statements in other annual reports you may have, to observe content and presentation alternatives.

KEY TERMS AND CONCEPTS

cost of goods sold *(p. 275)*   Cost of merchandise sold during the period; an expense deducted from net sales to arrive at gross profit.

cost of goods sold model *(p. 276)*   The formula for calculating cost of goods sold by adding beginning inventory and purchases and subtracting ending inventory.

dilution *(p. 285)*   The reduction in "earnings per share of common stock" that may occur if convertible securities are actually converted to common stock.

earned *(p. 271)*   A revenue recognition criterion that relates to completion of the revenue-generating activity.

earnings per share *(p. 283)*   Net income available to the common stockholders divided by the average number of shares of common stock outstanding during the period.

expenses *(p. 274)*   Outflows or other using up of assets or incurring a liability during a period from delivering or producing goods, rendering services, or carrying out other activities that constitute the entity's major operations.

extraordinary item *(p. 286)*   A gain or loss from a transaction that is both unusual in nature and occurs infrequently; it is reported separately in the income statement.

FOB destination *(p. 275)*   The shipping term that means that title passes from seller to buyer when the merchandise arrives at its destination.

FOB shipping point *(p. 275)*   The shipping term that means that title passes from seller to buyer when the merchandise leaves the seller's premises.

freight prepaid *(p. 275)*   A freight payment alternative meaning that freight is paid by the shipper.

freight collect *(p. 275)*   A freight payment alternative meaning that freight is payable when the merchandise arrives at its destination.

gains *(p. 273)*   Increases in net assets from incidental transactions and other events affecting an entity during a period except those that result from revenues or investments by owners.

gross margin *(p. 278)*   Another term for *gross profit*.

gross margin ratio *(p. 278)*   Another term for *gross profit ratio*.

gross profit *(p. 278)*   The difference between net sales and cost of goods sold. Sometimes called *gross margin*.

gross profit ratio *(p. 278)*   The ratio of gross profit to net sales. Sometimes called *gross margin ratio*.

income before income taxes *(p. 283)*   An income statement subtotal on which income tax expense is based.

income from continuing operations *(p. 286)*   An income statement subtotal that is presented before income or loss from discontinued operations; excluded from operating income to facilitate judgments about and comparisons with operating income of future periods.

income from operations *(p. 281)*   The difference between gross profit and operating expenses. Also called *operating income*.

inventory cost-flow assumption *(p. 275)*   The application of FIFO, LIFO, weighted-average, or specific identification procedures to determine the cost of goods sold.

inventory shrinkage *(p. 275)*   Inventory losses resulting from theft, deterioration, and record-keeping errors.

losses *(p. 274)*   Decreases in net assets from incidental transactions and other events affecting an entity during a period except those that result from expenses or distributions to owners.

matching principle *(p. 274)*   Results in a fair presentation of the results of a firm's operations during a period by requiring the deduction of all expenses incurred in generating that period's revenues from the revenues earned in the period.

minority interest in earnings of subsidiary *(p. 288)*   An income statement item representing the minority stockholders' share of the earnings of a subsidiary that have been included in the consolidated income statement.

multiple-step format *(p. 291)*   An income statement format that includes subtotals for gross profit, operating income, and income before taxes.

net income *(p. 283)*   The difference between revenues and gains, and expenses and losses for the period.

net sales *(p. 272)*   Gross sales, less sales discounts and sales returns and allowances.

operating expenses *(p. 281)*   Expenses, other than cost of goods sold, incurred in the day-to-day activities of the entity.

operating income *(p. 281)*   The difference between gross profit and operating expenses. Also referred to as *earnings from operations*.

other income and expenses *(p. 282)*   An income statement category that includes interest expense, interest income, and gain or loss items not related to the principal operating activities of the entity.

percentage-of-completion method *(p. 273)*   A method of recognizing revenue based on the completion percentage of a long-term construction project.

purchases returns and allowances *(p. 277)*   Reductions in purchases from products returned to the supplier, or adjustments in the purchase cost.

realization *(p. 271)*   A revenue recognition criterion that relates to the receipt of cash or a claim to cash in exchange for the product or service.

revenues *(p. 270)*   Inflows of cash or increases in other assets, or settlement of liabilities, during a period from delivering or producing goods, rendering services, or performing other activities that constitute the entity's major operations.

sales *(p. 272)*   Revenues resulting from the sale of product.

sales mix *(p. 279)*   The proportion of total sales represented by various products or categories of products.

sales returns and allowances *(p. 272)*   Reductions in sales from product returns or adjustments in selling price.

shipping terms *(p. 275)*   The description of the point at which title passes from seller to buyer.

single-step format *(p. 291)*   An income statement format that excludes subtotals such as gross profit and operating income.

statement of cash flows *(p. 292)*   The financial statement that explains why cash changed during a fiscal period. Cash flows from operating, investing, and financing activities are shown in the statement.

tax loss carryover *(p. 287)*   A loss for tax purposes for the current year that can be carried back or forward to offset taxable income of other years.

EXERCISES AND PROBLEMS

9–1. Big Blue University has a fiscal year that ends on June 30. The 1993 Summer Session of the university runs from June 9 through July 28. The total tuition paid by students for the summer session amounted to $112,000.

Required:

a. How much revenue should be reflected in the fiscal year ended June 30, 1993? Explain your answer.

b. Would your answer to (*a*) be any different if the university had a tuition refund policy that stated that no tuition would be refunded after the end of the third week of summer session classes? Explain your answer.

9–2. Kirkland Theater sells season tickets for six events at a price of $42. In pricing the tickets, the planners assigned the leadoff event a value of $10 because the program was an expensive symphony orchestra. The last five events were priced equally; 1,200 season tickets were sold for the 1993 season.

Required:

a. Calculate the theater's earned revenue after the first three events have been presented.

b. About 95 percent of the season ticket holders attended the first event. Subsequent events were attended by about 80 percent of the season ticket holders. To what extent, if any, should the attendance data impact revenue recognition? Explain your answer.

(A)rmstrong

9–3. Refer to the description of the amounts reported as net sales on page 21 of the Armstrong Annual Report in Appendix A. What might cause the difference between "sales billed" and shipments of a product that involve transfer of title? What internal controls would exist to ensure that a sale is billed after title has passed?

(A)rmstrong

9–4. Refer to the discussion of discontinued businesses under the Operating Statement Items section in the Financial Review on page 21 of the Armstrong World Industries, Inc., Annual Report in Appendix A.

Required:

a. Calculate the amount that would have been reported as net sales for each of the years ended December 31, 1991, 1990, and 1989, if the net sales of the discontinued businesses had not been reclassified.

b. Explain why amounts applicable to discontinued businesses are reclassified to the Discontinued Businesses section of the income statement.

9–5. If the ending inventory of a firm is overstated by $50,000, by how much and in what direction (overstated or understated) will the firm's operating income be misstated? (*Hint: Use the cost of goods sold model, enter hypothetically "correct" data, and then reflect the ending inventory error and determine the effect on cost of goods sold.*)

9–6. Assume that the ending inventory of a merchandising firm is overstated by $40,000.

Required:

a. By how much and in what direction (overstated or understated) will the firm's cost of goods sold be misstated?

b. If this error is not corrected, what effect will it have on the subsequent period's operating income?

c. If this error is not corrected, what effect will it have on the total operating income of the two periods (i.e., the period in which there is an error and the subsequent period) combined?

(A)rmstrong

9–7. *a.* Refer to the consolidated statements of earnings on page 18 of the Armstrong Annual Report in Appendix A. Calculate the gross profit ratio for each of the past three years.

b. Assume that Armstrong's net sales for the first four months of 1992 totaled $845 million. Calculate an estimated cost of goods sold and gross profit for the four months.

9–8. MBI, Inc., had sales of $37.9 million for fiscal 1993. The company's gross profit ratio for that year was 22.6 percent.

Required:

a. Calculate the gross profit and cost of goods sold for MBI, Inc., for fiscal 1993.

b. Assume that a new product is developed, and that it will cost $485 to manufacture. Calculate the selling price that must be set for this new product if its gross profit ratio is to be the same as the average achieved for all products for fiscal 1993.

9–9. If you were interested in evaluating the profitability of a company and could have only limited historical data, would you perfer to know operating income or net income for the past five years? Explain your answer.

9–10. Refer to the Six-Year Summary on page 38 of the Armstrong World Industries, Inc., Annual Report in Appendix A.

Required:

/

a. Calculate operating income (earnings from continuing businesses before other income and expense and income taxes) for each of the five years from 1987 through 1991.

b. Compare the trend of the above data with the trend of net earnings over the same period. Which series of data is more meaningful? Explain your answer.

9–11. Use the appropriate amounts from the following list to calculate operating income for the year ended October 31, 1993. (Amounts are in thousands.)

Net sales	$784
Advertising expense	62
Extraordinary gain from sale of land,	
net of income taxes of $37	53
Gross profit	305
General and administrative expenses	98
Income tax expense	39
Other selling expenses	51

9–12. Use the appropriate amounts from the following list to calculate operating income for this company for its fiscal year ended March 31, 1993. (Amounts are in thousands.)

Provision for income taxes	$ 36
Selling, general, and administrative expenses	210
Net sales	987
Interest expense	112
Cost of goods sold	534
Extraordinary gain from patent	
infringement suit settlement	140
Research and development expenses	96
Loss from discontinued operations	76

9–13. Kiwi Mfg. Co. has experienced gross profit ratios for 1992, 1991, and 1990 of 33 percent, 30 percent, and 31 percent, respectively. On April 3, 1993, the firm's plant and all of its inventory were destroyed by a tornado. Accounting records for 1993, which were available because they were stored in a protected vault, showed the following:

Sales from January 1 thru April 2	$142,680
January 1 inventory amount	63,590
Purchases of inventory from	
January 1 thru April 2	118,652

Required:

Calculate the amount of the insurance claim to be filed for the inventory destroyed in the tornado. (*Hint: Use the cost of goods sold model and a gross profit ratio that will result in the largest claim.*)

9–14. On April 8, 1993, a flood destroyed the warehouse of Stuco Distributing Co. From the waterlogged records of the company, management was able to determine that the firm's gross profit ratio had averaged 29 percent for the past several years and that the inventory at the beginning of the year was $17,350. It was also determined that during the year until the date of the flood, sales had totaled $32,700 and purchases totaled $21,860.

Required: Calculate the amount of inventory loss from the flood.

9–15. Ringemup, Inc., had net income of $473,700 for its fiscal year ended October 31, 1993. During the year the company had outstanding 38,000 shares of $4.50, $50 par value preferred stock, and 105,200 shares of common stock.

Required: Calculate the earnings per share of common stock for fiscal 1993.

9–16. Thrifty Co. reported net income of $745,600 for its fiscal year ended January 31, 1994. At the beginning of that fiscal year, 240,000 shares of common stock were outstanding. On October 31, 1993, an additional 40,000 shares were issued. No other changes in common shares outstanding occurred during the year. During the year the company paid the annual dividend on the 30,000 shares of 5 percent, $40 par value preferred stock that were also outstanding the entire year.

Required:
a. Calculate primary earnings per share of common stock for the year ended December 31, 1994.
b. If Thrifty Co.'s preferred stock was convertible into common stock, what additional calculation would be required?

9–17. Refer to the consolidated statements of earnings on page 18 of the Armstrong Annual Report in Appendix A. Does Armstrong use the single-step format on the multiple-step format? Which format do you prefer? Explain your answer.

9–18. Refer to the earnings per share of common stock data on page 17 and the earnings per common share comments under the Operating Statement Items section on page 21 of the Armstrong World Industries, Inc., Annual Report in Appendix A.

Required: Explain why all of this disclosure is appropriate.

9–19. Refer to the consolidated statements of cash flows on page 20 of the Armstrong World Industries, Inc., Annual Report in Appendix A.

Required:
a. Identify the two most significant sources of cash from operating activities during 1990. How much of a cash source amount do these items represent?
b. What were the firm's investing activities during 1990, and how much cash did they use or generate?
c. Identify the two most significant financing activities, other than dividends, during 1990. What was the net effect on cash of these items?
d. What was the amount of dividends paid during 1990?
e. Prepare a simplified statement of cash flows for 1990, using amounts rounded to the nearest million, based on your answers to (*a*) through (*d*), and using the following additional data:

All other operating activities (net) . . . .   (70.9)

All other financing activities (including exchange
rate change effect—net) 44.4

9–20. Refer to the consolidated statements of cash flows on page 20 of the Armstrong World Industries, Inc., Annual Report in Appendix A.

   a. Identify the two most significant sources of cash from operating activities during 1991. How much of a cash source amount do these items represent?

   b. What were the firm's investing activities during 1991, and how much cash did they use or generate?

   c. Identify the two most significant financing activities, other than dividends, during 1991. What was the net effect on cash of these items?

   d. What was the amount of dividends paid during 1991?

   e. Prepare a simplified statement of cash flows for 1991, using amounts rounded to the nearest million, based on your answers to (*a*) through (*d*), and using the following additional data:

   All other operating activities (net). . . . . $(33.5)

   All other financing activites (including
   exchange rate change effect) (net). . . . .   (8.4)

   f. What information does the statement of cash flows disclose that is not readily available from the income statement, statement of change in shareholders' equity, or the balance sheets?

9–21. Evaluate the cash flows of Armstrong World Industries, Inc., for the year ended December 31, 1990.

9–22. Evaluate the cash flows of Armstrong World Industries, Inc., for the year ended December 31, 1991.

9–23. Refer to the statement of cash flows in the annual report you have obtained either as a result of completing Exercise 1–1, or otherwise.

Required:

   a. Which method, direct or indirect, is used in the statement?

   b. List the principal sources and uses of cash for this firm.

   c. Evaluate the change in cash. Has the firm generated most of its cash requirements from operations, or has it had to borrow extensively? Have its uses of cash been balanced between investment and dividends?

   d. Has the cash balance been increasing or decreasing? What seem to be the implications of this pattern for dividends?

Chapter 10

Explanatory Notes and Other Financial Information

Because of the complexities related to financial reporting, and because of the number of alternative generally accepted accounting principles that can be used, **explanatory notes to the financial statements** are included as an integral part of the financial statements. These notes, or **financial review,** are referred to on each individual financial statement and are presented immediately following the financial statements. In Appendix A, the 1991 Annual Report of Armstrong World Industries, Inc., the financial review is on pages 21 through 30.

At first glance the notes to the financial statements can appear quite intimidating because they frequently require more pages than the financial statements themselves, contain a great deal of detailed information, and include much financial management terminology. However, the reader cannot fully understand the financial statements without referring to the notes.

Financial statements of companies whose securities are publicly traded must be audited by independent auditors, and the annual report of such a company must include disclosures required by the Securities and Exchange Commission. An understanding of the auditors' report, and a review of the other disclosures lead to a more complete picture of a company's financial condition, results of operations, and cash flows.

The objective of this chapter is to explain the meaning of the explanatory notes and other financial information found in most corporate annual reports.

LEARNING OBJECTIVES

After studying this chapter you should understand:

- That the explanatory notes are an integral part of the financial statements, and that they must be referred to if more than a cursory, and perhaps misleading, impression of a firm's financial position and its results of operations is to be achieved.
- The kinds of significant accounting policies that are explained in the notes.
- The nature of, and the overall content of, disclosures relating to:

    Accounting changes.
    Business combinations.
    Contingencies and commitments.
    Events subsequent to the balance sheet date.
    Impact of inflation.
    Segment information.

- The role of the Securities and Exchange Commission, and some of its reporting requirements.
- Why a statement of management's responsibility is included with the notes.
- The significance of management's discussion and analysis of the firm's financial condition and results of operations.
- What is included in the five-year (or longer) summary of financial information.
- The meaning and content of the independent auditors' report.

GENERAL ORGANIZATION

The explanatory notes that refer to specific financial statement items are generally presented in the same sequence as the financial statements, and in the same sequence that items appear in the financial statements. The financial statement sequence is usually:

1. Income statement.
2. Balance sheet.
3. Statement of cash flows.

Placement of the statement of changes in owners' equity usually depends on the complexity of that statement. If paid-in capital has not changed during the year, only a statement of changes in retained earnings may be presented. This statement frequently is on the same page as the income statement and may even be combined with it because net income is the principal item affecting retained earnings. If there have been several capital stock transactions during the year, a full statement of changes in owners' equity, which includes changes in retained earnings, would be presented separately following the balance sheet. Some companies, including Armstrong World Industries, Inc., present the statement of changes in owners' equity as part of the notes or financial review (see page 28 of the Armstrong World Industries, Inc., report in Appendix A).

In addition to the notes or financial review, many firms include in the annual report a narrative section called **management's discussion and analysis.** This is a description of the firm's activities for the year, including comments about its financial condition and results of operations. Also included in most annual reports is a comparative summary of key financial data for several years. Both of these components can be quite helpful to users of the annual report.

Significant Accounting Policies

Because of the alternative accounting practices that are generally acceptable, disclosure of the specific practices being followed by the firm is necessary for the reader to make sense of the financial statements. **Significant accounting policies** disclosed include those relating to:

Depreciation method—The method (straight-line, units of production, sum-of-the-years' digits, or declining-balance) being used for financial reporting purposes and the range of useful lives assumed for broad categories of asset types are usually disclosed. The amount of depreciation expense may also be disclosed in the notes, although it is also reported in the statement of cash flows as an add back to net income.

Inventory valuation method—The method (weighted average, FIFO, or LIFO) being used is disclosed. If different methods are being used for different categories of inventory, the method used for each category is disclosed. When LIFO is used, a comparison of the cumulative difference in the balance sheet inventory valuation under LIFO, with what it would have been under FIFO, is usually disclosed.

Basis of consolidation—A brief statement confirms the fact that the consolidated financial statements include the financial data of all subsidiaries or if not, why not.

Income taxes—A reconciliation of the statutory income tax rate (presently about 34 percent) with the effective tax rate indicated by the firm's income tax expense as a percentage of pre-tax income is provided. Reasons for this difference include tax credits (e.g., for investment in new plant and equipment) and other special treatment given certain items for income tax purposes. An explanation is also made of the deferred taxes resulting from temporary differences between the fiscal year in which an expense (or revenue) is reported for book purposes and the fiscal year in which it is reported for tax purposes. As already discussed, the principal factor in deferred taxes is the use of straight-line depreciation for book purposes and accelerated depreciation for tax purposes.

Employee benefits—The cost of employee benefit plans that has been included as an expense in the income statement will be disclosed. The significant actuarial assumptions made with respect to funding pension plans may be discussed, and certain estimated future pension liabilities may be disclosed. The two elements of pension expense are current service cost and past service cost. Current service cost is the actuarily determined cost to provide future pension benefits based on employees' earnings and service in the current year. Past service cost is the actuarily determined cost of providing future pension benefits based on employees' earnings and service in prior years. Past service cost arises when a pension plan is started or modified and the future pension benefit will be affected by the employees' earnings and service in prior years. This past service cost is recognized in future income statements over a period of years. This past service amortization process is most significant in understanding the firm's current and probable future pension expense. Many firms have a significant unfunded past service liability that is not reflected on the balance sheet but is disclosed in the explanatory notes.

Amortization of intangible assets—If the balance sheet includes the intangible asset goodwill, the method of amortizing this intangible asset and the amount of amortization expense recorded in the current year will be disclosed. The maximum amortization period allowed by generally accepted accounting principles is 40 years, but many firms use a shorter period. As discussed in Chapter 6, accounting for goodwill is a very sticky problem for accountants.

Earnings per share of common stock—An explanation of the calculation, perhaps including the details of the calculation of the weighted average number of shares outstanding, and the adjustments to net income for preferred stock dividends will be provided. The potential dilution of the earnings per share figure resulting from convertible bonds or convertible preferred stock if conversions had taken place during the year will also be explained.

Stock option and stock purchase plans—Many firms have a **stock option plan** under which officers and key employees are given an option to buy a certain number of shares of stock at some time in the future, but at a price equal to the market value of the stock when the option is granted. The stock option presumably provides an incentive to increase the profitability of the firm so that the stock price will rise. Then, when the option is exercised, the owner has an immediate profit that is in effect additional compensation for a job well done. Under a stock purchase plan the employees can purchase shares of the company's common stock at a slight discount from market value. The objective is to permit the employees to become part owners of the firm, and thus to have more of an owner's attitude about their jobs and the company. From the employees' point of view both of these plans are usually good fringe benefits. From the investors' point of view the shares that are issuable under these plans represent potential dilution of the equity of the investor. Thus the nature of these plans is described, and the potential dilution from them is disclosed.

Details of Other Financial Statement Amounts

Many firms will include in the explanatory notes the details of amounts that are reported as a single amount in the financial statements. For example, the amount of research and development expenses included in a broader income statement operating expense category, the details of the "other income" category of the income statement, or details of the cost and accumulated depreciation of plant and equipment that are reported in total on the balance sheet may be provided. Long-term debt, frequently reported as a single amount on the balance sheet, is usually made up of several obligations. A descriptive listing of the obligations, including a schedule of the principal payments required for each of the next five years, is usually reported. The extent of such detail to be reported is decided by the financial officers of the firm and is generally based on their judgment of the benefit of such detail to the broad user audience that will receive the financial statements. In some cases disclosure requirements of the Securities and Exchange Commission and the desire to conform the stockholders' report with the report required to be filed with the SEC (see Business Procedure Capsule 18) result in these details.

Other Disclosures

Accounting Change.   An **accounting change** is a change in an accounting principle that has been adopted and that has a material effect on the comparability of the current period financial state-

• BUSINESS PROCEDURE CAPSULE 18
Reporting to the Securities and Exchange Commission

The Securities and Exchange Commission (SEC) was created by the Securities and Exchange Act of 1934 to administer the provisions of that act and the Securities Act of 1933. Subsequently Congress assigned to the SEC the authority and responsibility for administering other securities laws. Securities issued by corporations (principally stocks and bonds) that are offered for sale to more than a very few investors must be registered with the SEC. The basic objective of this registration is to provide to potential investors a full and fair disclosure of the securities being issued, the issuer's business activities and financial position, and an explanation of the use to be made of the proceeds of the security issue. Registration does not result in a "seal of approval" or a guarantee against loss. It is up to the investor to decide whether or not the investor's objectives are likely to be achieved. Registration is required for additional issues of previously unregistered securities (for example, if the corporation wants to raise capital by selling additional shares of stock) and for issues of newly created securities (for example, bonds that will be offered to the public). A **prospectus** summarizing the complete registration statement must be provided to investors prior to or concurrently with purchase of the security. A prospectus is provided by the company or the broker through whom the securities are being sold.

Registered securities can be traded publicly on a stock exchange or in the over-the-counter market. Firms that issue these securities are required to file an annual report with the SEC. This report is referred to as *Form 10-K*. The requirements of Form 10-K have had a significant impact on the scope of material included in the annual report to stockholders. Most companies include in their annual report to stockholders all of the financial statement information required in the Form 10-K.

Form 10-K requires some information not usually found in the financial statements, including data about executive compensation and ownership of voting stock by directors and officers. This information is also included in the proxy statement sent to stockholders along with the notice of the annual meeting and a description of the items expected to be acted upon by the stockholders at that meeting. Stockholders who do not expect to attend the annual meeting are invited to return a **proxy.** Although the proxy gives another person (usually a director of the corporation) the right to vote the stockholder's shares, the owner can indicate her/his preference for how the shares are to be voted on the indicated issues.

The registration statement, prospectus, Form 10-K, and proxy statement are public documents, and copies can be obtained from the corporation, or from the SEC.

ments with those of prior periods. The effect of an accounting change must be disclosed. For example, if a firm changes its inventory cost-flow assumption from FIFO to LIFO, this fact and the dollar effect of the change on both the income statement and balance sheet must be disclosed. Likewise, a change in depreciation methods, a change in the method of accounting for pension costs, or any other change having a significant effect on the financial statements must be disclosed.

Sometimes the accounting change is the result of a Financial Accounting Standards Board pronouncement. In 1982 the FASB changed the generally accepted accounting for the translation of foreign subsidiaries' financial statements to U.S. dollars. This change was adopted by all affected corporations, and the nature and effect of this change were disclosed in their explanatory notes.

Business Combinations. If the firm has been involved in a **business combination** (i.e., a merger, acquisition, or disposition), the transaction(s) involved will be described and the effect on the financial statements will be explained. Recall that in the case of the disposition of part of the business, the income statement will segregate the impact on the current year's results of discontinued operations.

Most mergers and acquisitions are accounted for using **purchase accounting.** Under purchase accounting the assets acquired are recorded by the acquiring company at their fair market value at the date of acquisition. Any amount paid for the acquired assets (or company) in excess of the fair market value of the assets is recorded as goodwill—that intangible asset that is then amortized to expense over a period of time. An alternative accounting method, **pooling of interests accounting,** can be used in certain circumstances. Under pooling the assets acquired are recorded by the acquiring company at the book value at which they are carried by the acquired company, and the stock issued in the merger is recorded at the book value of the acquired company, not the market value of the shares issued. This accounting alternative eliminates any necessity for goodwill but usually results in the acquired assets being recorded by the acquiring company at less than fair market value. The notes will explain the accounting method used in the merger or acquisition.

Contingencies and Commitments. It is not unusual for a firm to be involved in litigation, the results of which are not known when the financial statements are prepared. If the firm is denying liability in a lawsuit in which it is a defendant, it is appropriate to disclose the fact of the lawsuit to readers of the financial statements. Of course, the concept of matching revenue and expense requires that any anticipated cost of verdicts that the company expects to have to pay be recognized as an expense or a loss and as a related liability in the period affected. Even if the lawsuit is one that the company and its legal counsel believe will not result in any liability to the company, the fact of the potential loss and liability should be disclosed. The nature of the legal action, the potential damages, and a statement to the effect that the claims against the company are not likely to be sustained are included in the notes.

In some cases a firm or one of its subsidiaries may act as a guarantor of the indebtedness of another entity. In such cases it is appropriate for the amount of the potential liability and a brief description of the circumstances to be disclosed in the notes.

If the firm has made commitments to purchase a significant amount of plant and equipment, or has committed to pay significant amounts of rent on leased property for several years into the future, these commitments will be disclosed. This is because the commitment is like a liability, but is not recorded on the balance sheet.

A firm may have quite a few other kinds of **contingencies** and **commitments.** Most will have a negative impact on the financial position of the firm, or its results of operations, if they materialize. The purpose of disclosing them is to provide full disclosure to the user of the financial statements.

Events Subsequent to the Balance Sheet Date. If, subsequent to the balance sheet date, a significant event occurs that has a material impact on the balance sheet or income statement, it is appropriate that the subsequent event and its probable impact on future financial statements be explained. Examples of such significant events include the issuance of a large amount of long-term debt, the restructuring of long-term debt, a business combination, the issuance of a large amount of capital stock, and the sale of a significant part of the company's assets.

Impact of Inflation. It has been emphasized that the financial statements do not reflect the impact of inflation. The original cost concept and the objectivity principle result in assets being recorded at original cost and transactions being recorded at amounts based on current dollars involved. In 1979, because of the significant inflation that the United States had experienced in the prior decade, the Financial Accounting Standards Board required large companies to report, as supplementary data in the explanatory notes to the financial statements, certain inflation-adjusted data. This was done on a trial basis for a period of five years. In effect the income statement, earnings per share of common stock, and total net assets were adjusted based on two methods of reflecting the impact of changing prices: a price index method and a current replacement cost method. The effect of each of these methods was usually to reduce reported earnings, because of higher expenses in two areas. Depreciation expense was greater than recorded because asset values had increased and, for firms that used the FIFO cost-flow assumption, cost of goods sold increased because inventory replacement costs were higher than the historical cost used in traditional accounting. Firms that used LIFO did not experience as much of a cost of goods sold increase because LIFO releases more current costs to the income statement. Net assets were generally increased significantly under each method of reflecting inflation. In 1986 the FASB rescinded the requirement, and now firms are merely encouraged to report the effects of inflation.

Reporting the effects of inflation is a controversial and complex area of accounting. If the economy experiences high rates of inflation in the future, efforts to reflect the impact of inflation directly in the financial statements will likely be renewed.

Segment Information. Most large corporations operate in several lines of business and in several international geographic areas. In addition, some firms have major customers (frequently the U.S. government) that account for a significant part of the total business. A **business segment** is a group of the firm's business activities that have a common denominator. The components of each business segment are identified and defined by management. Segments may reflect the company's organizational structure, manufacturing processes, product-line groups, or industries served, for example. The required disclosure of segment, geographic, and major customer information is designed to permit the financial statement user to make judgments about the impact on the firm of factors that might influence specific lines of business, geographic areas, or specific major customers.

Data shown for each segment include sales to unaffiliated customers, operating profit, capital expenditures, depreciation and amortization expense, and identifiable assets. Note that from these data it is possible to make a DuPont model return-on-investment calculation, and to prepare for each segment a simple statement of cash flows showing cash flows from operating activities (net income plus depreciation expense), minus cash used for investing activities (capital expenditures). This simple statement of cash flows omits financing activities (such as long-term debt and dividend transactions) but it does highlight the principal cash flows related to each segment. Although these segment measures cannot be combined to equal the total company's ROI or cash flows (because of assets and expenses applicable to the corporation as a whole that have not been arbitrarily allocated to segments), segment trends over time can be determined.

Sales to unaffiliated customers, operating profits, and identifiable assets are also reported by geographic areas in which the firm operates. For example, the areas in the geographic breakdown used by many firms with international operations are the United States, Europe, Africa, Pan America, and the Pacific.

If a firm has a major customer that accounts for more than 10 percent of its total sales, it is appropriate that this fact be disclosed to the financial statement user so that a judgment about the influence of that customer on the firm's continued profitability can be made.

Management's Statement of Responsibility

Many firms include in the explanatory notes **management's statement of responsibility,** which explains that the responsibility for the financial statements lies with the management of the firm, not the external auditors/certified public accountants who express an opinion about the fairness with which the financial statements present the financial condition and results of operations of the company. The statement of responsibility usually refers to the firm's system of internal controls, the internal audit function, the audit committee of the board of directors, and other policies and procedures designed to ensure that the company operates at a high level of ethical conduct.

MANAGEMENT'S DISCUSSION AND ANALYSIS

For many years, the Securities and Exchange Commission has required companies that must file a Form 10-K annual report with the Commission to include in the report a discussion by management of the firm's activities during the year, and its financial condition and results of operations. This discussion is being included in more and more annual reports to stockholders. Management's discussion and analysis should enhance disclosure to the public of information about the corporation. It is a part of the annual report that should be read by current and potential investors. In the Armstrong World Industries, Inc., report in Appendix A, management's discussion and analysis of financial condition and results of operations is on pages 33 through 37.

FIVE-YEAR (OR LONGER) SUMMARY OF FINANCIAL DATA

Most corporate annual reports will present a summary of financial data for at least the five most recent years. Many firms report these data for longer periods, and at least one firm reports for every year since it was organized. Included in the summary are key income statement data, or even the entire income statement in condensed form. In addition to amounts, significant ratios such as earnings as a percentage of sales, average assets, and average owners' equity are also included. Earnings and dividends per share, the average number of shares outstanding each year, and other operating statistics may be reported. Year-end data from the balance sheet such as working capital; property, plant and equipment (net of accumulated depreciation); long-term debt; and owners' equity are usually reported. Book value per share of common stock and the year-end market price of the common stock are frequently reported. When stock dividends or stock splits have occurred, the per share data of prior years are adjusted retroactively so that the per share data are comparable.

As an illustration of the adjustment of per share data for stock dividends or stock splits, assume that Cruisers, Inc., reported earnings per share and cash dividends per share of $4.50 and $2.00, respectively, for fiscal 1991. Assume also that in 1992 the firm had a 2-for-1 stock split. In the annual report for 1992 earnings and dividends for 1991 should reflect the fact that because of the split there are now twice as many shares of common stock outstanding as there were when 1991 amounts were first reported. Therefore, in the 1992 annual report 1991 earnings per share and dividends per share will be reported at $2.25 and $1.00, respectively. Assume further that in 1993 Cruisers had a 10 percent stock dividend that results in 110 shares outstanding for every 100 shares that were outstanding before the stock dividend. The 1993 annual report will report 1991 earnings per share and dividends per share as $2.05 ($2.25/1.10) and $.91 ($1.00/1.10), respectively.

The **five-year summary** is not included in the scope of the outside auditors' work, nor does their opinion relate to the summary. Therefore, the summary appears in the annual report after the outside auditors' opinion. Likewise, the summary is not a part of the explanatory notes to the financial statements; it is a supplementary disclosure.

INDEPENDENT AUDITORS' REPORT

The independent auditors' report is a brief (usually three paragraphs), often easily overlooked, report that relates to the financial statements and the accompanying explanatory notes. The SEC requires an audit of the financial statements of a publicly owned company. Many privately owned firms will have an audit of their financial statements to support their bank loan negotiations.

The independent auditors' report for Armstrong World Industries, Inc., which is on page 31 of the annual report in Appendix A, is reproduced in Exhibit 10–1. The report format has been standardized by the Auditing Standards Board of the AICPA, and the format illustrated in Exhibit 10–1 is almost universal.

The report is usually addressed to the board of directors and stockholders of the corporation. The first, or introductory paragraph, identifies the financial statements that were audited and

---

EXHIBIT 10-1   Independent Auditors' Report

The Board of Directors and Shareholders,
Armstrong World Industries, Inc.:

We have audited the consolidated balance sheets of Armstrong World Industries, Inc., and subsidiaries as of December 31, 1991 and 1990, and the related statements of earnings and cash flows for each of the years in the three-year period ended December 31, 1991. These consolidated financial statements are the responsibility of the company's management. Our responsibility is to express an opinion on these consolidated financial statements based on our audits.

We conducted our audits in accordance with generally accepted auditing standards. Those standards require that we plan and perform the audit to obtain reasonable assurance about whether the financial statements are free of material misstatements. An audit includes examining, on a test basis, evidence supporting the amounts and disclosures in the financial statements. An audit also includes assessing the accounting principles used and significant estimates made by management, as well as evaluating the overall financial statement presentation. We believe that our audits provide a reasonable basis for our opinion.

In our opinion, the consolidated financial statements referred to above present fairly, in all material respects, the financial position of Armstrong World Industries, Inc., and subsidiaries, at December 31, 1991 and 1990, and the results of their operations and their cash flows for each of the years in the three-year period ended December 31, 1991, in conformity with generally accepted accounting principles.

KPMG PEAT MARWICK

Philadelphia, Pa.
February 17, 1992

---

briefly describes the responsibilities of both management and the auditors with respect to the financial statements. It is important to note here that management is responsible for the financial statements; the auditors' task is to express an opinion about them.

The second paragraph describes the scope of the auditors' work. Note that their concern is with obtaining reasonable assurance about whether the financial statements are free of material misstatements, and that their work involves tests. Auditors give no guarantee that the financial statements are free from error, or that there have not been any fraudulent transactions reflected in the statements. However, generally accepted auditing standards do require extensive audit procedures as a means of obtaining reasonable assurance.

The third paragraph is the opinion paragraph, and in that sense it is the most important. The benchmark for fair presentation is generally accepted accounting principles. Again, note the reference to materiality. If, during the course of the audit, the auditor determines that the financial statements taken as a whole do not "present fairly," the auditor will require a change in the presentation or withdraw from the audit. The latter action is very rare.

The name of the auditing firm, sometimes presented as a facsimile signature, and the date of the report are shown. The date of the report is the date the audit work was completed, and a required audit procedure is to review transactions subsequent to the balance sheet date up to the date of the report. Unusual transactions that occur during this period must be disclosed in the financial statements or in the explanatory notes.

Occasionally the auditors' report will include an explanatory paragraph that describes a situation that does not affect fair presentation but that should be disclosed to keep the financial statements from being misleading. Items that require additional explanation include the following:

1. Basing the opinion in part on the work of another auditor.
2. Uncertainties about the outcome of certain events that would have affected the presentation if the outcome could be estimated.
3. Substantial doubt about the entity's ability to continue as a going concern.
4. A material change between periods in an accounting principle or its method of application.

The auditor can issue a qualified opinion if the scope of the audit was restricted and essential audit work could not be performed, or if there is a material departure from generally accepted accounting principles that affects only part of the financial statements. The reason for the qualification is explained in the report, and the opinion about fair presentation is restricted to the unaffected parts of the financial statements. Qualified opinions are very rare.

It is appropriate for the financial statement reader to review the independent auditors' report and determine the effect of any departure from the standard report.

SUMMARY

Explanatory notes to the financial statements are an integral part of the statements. These notes, sometimes called *the financial review,* result from the application of the full disclosure concept discussed in Chapter 2. The notes disclose details of amounts summarized for financial statement presentation, explain which permissible alternative accounting practices have been used by the entity, and provide detailed disclosure of information needed to have a full understanding of the financial statements.

Accounting policies disclosed include the depreciation method, inventory cost-flow assumption, and basis of consolidation. Accounting for the entity's income taxes, employee benefits, and amortization of intangible assets is described. Details of the calculation of earnings per share of common stock are sometimes provided. There is a discussion of employee stock option and stock purchase plans. The materiality concept is applied to the extent of each of these disclosures.

If there have been changes in the accounting for a material item, the consistency concept requires disclosure of the effect of the change on the financial statements. Sometimes accounting or reporting changes are required by new FASB standards.

There is a full discussion of any business combinations in which the entity has been involved.

Significant contingencies and commitments, such as litigation or loan guarantees, as well as significant events that have occurred since the balance sheet date, are described. This is a specific application of the full disclosure concept.

The impact of inflation on the historical cost amounts used in the financial statements may be reported, although this information is not currently required to be shown.

Segment information summarizes some financial information for the principal activity areas of the firm. The intent of this disclosure is to permit judgment about the significance to the entity's overall results of its activities in certain business segments and geographic areas.

The financial statements are the responsibility of management, not the auditors, and management's statement of responsibility acknowledges this. This acknowledgment usually refers to the system of internal control.

Management's discussion and analysis of the firm's financial condition and results of operations provide an important and useful summary of the firm's activities.

Although not usually a part of the explanatory notes to the financial statements, most annual reports do include a summary of key financial data for a period of several years. This summary permits financial statement users to make trend evaluations easily.

The independent auditors' report includes their opinion about the fair presentation, in accordance with generally accepted accounting principles, of the financial statements, and calls attention to special situations. Auditors do not guarantee that the company will be profitable, nor do they give assurance that the financial statements are absolutely accurate.

The Securities and Exchange Commission is responsible for administering federal securities laws. One of its principal concerns is that investors have full disclosure about securities and the companies that issue them. The reporting requirements of the SEC have led to many of the disclosures contained in corporate annual reports.

Refer to the financial review in the Armstrong World Industries, Inc., Annual Report in Appendix A, and to the comparable part of other annual reports that you may have. Observe the organization of this part of the financial statements and the comprehensive explanation of the material discussed. Read management's discussion and analysis of the firm's financial condition and results of operations. Find the summary of key financial data for several years, and evaluate the trends disclosed for sales, profits, total owners' equity, and other items reported in the summary. The next chapter will describe and illustrate some of the ways of analyzing the financial statement data to support the informed judgments and decisions made by users of financial statements.

KEY TERMS AND CONCEPTS

accounting change *(p. 312)*   A change in the application of an accounting principle.

business combination *(p. 314)*   A merger between two or more firms, or the purchase of one firm by another.

business segment *(p. 316)*   A group of the firm's similar business activities; most large firms have several segments.

commitment *(p. 315)*   A transaction that has been contractually agreed to but that has not yet occurred and is not reflected in the financial statements.

contingency *(p. 315)* An event that has an uncertain but potentially significant effect on the financial statements.

explanatory notes to financial statements *(p. 308)* An integral part of the financial statements that contains explanations of accounting policies and descriptions of financial statement details.

financial review *(p. 308)* Another name for the footnotes to the financial statements.

five-year summary *(p. 318)* A summary of key financial data included in an organization's annual report; it is not a financial statement included in the scope of the independent auditor's report.

management's discussion and analysis *(p. 310)* A narrative description of the firm's activities for the year, including comments about its financial condition and results of operations.

management's statement of responsibility *(p. 317)* A discussion included in the explanatory notes to the financial statements describing management's responsibility for the financial statements.

pooling of interests accounting *(p. 314)* A method of accounting for the acquisition of another company that results in the book values of the acquired company's assets and liabilities being recorded by the acquiring company.

prospectus *(p. 313)* A summary of the characteristics of a security being offered for sale, including a description of the business and financial position of the firm selling the security.

proxy *(p. 313)* An authorization given by a stockholder to another person to vote the shares owned by the stockholder.

purchase accounting *(p. 314)* A method of accounting for the purchase of another company that records as the cost of the investment the value of the cash and/or securities paid, less the liabilities assumed in the transaction.

significant accounting policies *(p. 310)* A brief summary or description of the specific accounting practices followed by the entity.

stock option plan *(p. 311)* A plan for compensating key employees by providing an option to purchase a company's stock at a future date at the market price of the stock when the option is issued.

EXERCISES AND PROBLEMS

Armstrong

10–1. Refer to the Armstrong World Industries, Inc., Annual Report for 1991 in Appendix A. Find and scan the Financial Review. Read management's statement of responsibility, the independent auditors' report, and management's discussion and analysis of financial condition and results of operations.

10–2. Find and read management's statement of responsibility in the annual report that you obtained as a result of completing Exercise 1–1. Identify the principal topics covered in that statement. Are there other topics that you believe would be appropriate to have included in the statement? Explain your answer.

(A)rmstrong

10–3. Refer to the industry segment data on page 27 of the Armstrong World Industries, Inc., Annual Report in Appendix A.

Required:

Calculate the ROI for the floor coverings and industry products segments for each of the past three years. Use the DuPont model format with net trade sales, operating profit, and identifiable assets.

(A)rmstrong

10–4. Solve the requirements of Problem 10–3 for the building products and furniture segments.

10–5. *a.* For the year ended December 31, 1992, Finco, Inc., reported earnings per share of $3.12. During 1993 the company had a 3-for-1 stock split. Calculate the 1992 earnings per share that will be reported in Finco's 1993 annual report for comparative purposes.
b. During 1994 Finco had a 2-for-1 stock split. Calculate the 1992 earnings per share that will be reported in Finco's 1994 annual report for comparative purposes.
c. If Finco had issued a 10 percent stock dividend in 1993 and did not have a stock split, calculate the 1992 earnings per share that will be reported in Finco's 1993 annual report for comparative purposes.

10–6. During the year ended December 31, 1993, Gluco, Inc., split its stock on a 3-for-1 basis. In its annual report for 1992, the firm reported net income of $874,290 for 1992, with an average 284,700 shares of common stock outstanding for that year. There was no preferred stock.

Required:

a. What amount of net income for 1992 will be reported in Gluco's 1993 annual report?
b. Calculate Gluco's earnings per share for 1992 that would have been reported in the 1992 annual report.
c. Calculate Gluco's earnings per share for 1992 that will be reported in the 1993 annual report.

10–7. During the fiscal year ended September 30, 1993, Rentco, Inc., had a 2-for-1 stock split and a 5 percent stock dividend. In its annual report for 1993, the company reported earnings per share for the year ended September 30, 1992, on a restated basis, of $.60.

Required:

Calculate the originally reported earnings per share for the year ended September 30, 1992.

10–8. For several years Dorcel, Inc., has followed a policy of paying a cash dividend of $.20 per share and having a 10 percent stock dividend. In the 1993 annual report, Dorcel reported restated earnings per share for 1991 of $.72.

Required:

a. Calculate the originally reported earnings per share for 1991.
b. Calculate the restated cash dividend per share for 1991 reported in the 1993 annual report.

10–9. It is impossible for an auditor to "guarantee" that a company's financial statements are free of all error because the cost to the company to achieve absolute accuracy even if that were possible, and the cost of the auditor's verification would be prohibitively expensive. How does the auditor's opinion recognize this absence of absolute accuracy?

10–10. To what extent is the auditor's opinion an indicator of a company's future financial success and future cash dividends to stockholders?

Chapter 11

Financial Statement Analysis

Chapters 5 through 10 have explained the accounting for almost all of the transactions that an entity may experience. The reporting of the effects of these transactions on the financial statements has been described and explained. Understanding that material will permit you to make sense of an entity's financial statements so that you will be able to make decisions and informed judgments about the financial conditions and the results of the operations of that entity. The process of interpreting an entity's financial statements can be facilitated by certain ratio computations, and if one entity's financial condition and results of operations are to be compared to those of another entity, ratio analysis of the financial statements is mandatory. This chapter focuses on such ratio analysis.

In Chapter 3 you learned about some of the fundamental interpretations made from financial statement data. The importance of financial statement ratios and the significance of *trends* in the ratio results were explained. The calculation of return on investment (ROI) and the use of the DuPont model, which recognizes margin and turnover in the ROI calculation, were described. In addition, the calculation and significance of return on equity (ROE) and the liquidity measures of working capital, current ratio, and acid-test ratio were explained. It would be appropriate for you to review Chapter 3 if you don't thoroughly understand these analytical tools.

LEARNING OBJECTIVES

After studying this chapter you should understand:

- How liquidity measures can be influenced by the inventory cost-flow assumption used.

- How individual suppliers and creditors use a customer's payment practices to judge liquidity.
- The calculation and significance of various turnover factors, and the influence of alternative inventory cost-flow assumptions and depreciation methods on the turnover ratio.
- How the number of days' sales in accounts receivable and inventory are calculated, and how these measures are used to evaluate the effectiveness of the management of receivables and inventory.
- The significance of the price/earnings ratio in the evaluation of the market price of a company's common stock.
- How dividend yield and the dividend payout ratio are used by investors to evaluate a company's common stock.
- What financial leverage is, and why it is significant to management, creditors, and owners.
- What a leveraged buyout transaction is, and why some analysts are concerned about the significant increase in the number of these transactions that occurred in the mid- and late-1980s.
- What book value per share of common stock is, how it is calculated, and why it is not a very meaningful amount for most companies.
- How operating statistics using physical, or nonfinancial, data can be used to help management evaluate the results of the firm's activities.

FINANCIAL STATEMENT ANALYSIS RATIOS

The ratios used to facilitate the interpretation of an entity's financial position and results of operations can be grouped into four categories that have to do with:

1. Liquidity.
2. Activity.
3. Profitability.
4. Debt situation, called *financial leverage*.

Liquidity Measures

The liquidity measures of working capital, current ratio, and acid-test ratio were discussed in Chapter 3. One point that deserves reemphasis is the **effect of the inventory cost-flow assumption on working capital.** The balance sheet carrying value of inventories will depend on whether the weighted-average, FIFO, or LIFO assumption is used. In periods of rising prices, a firm using the FIFO cost-flow assumption will report a relatively higher asset value for inventories than a similar firm using the LIFO cost-flow assumption. Thus, even though the firms may be similar in all other respects, they will report different amounts of working capital, and they will have a different current ratio. Therefore a direct comparison of the liquidity of the two firms by using these measures is not possible. Of greater significance would be the relative *trend* of each measure for each company.

Of course, even more significant to suppliers or potential suppliers/creditors of the firm than the aggregate working capital or liquidity ratios is the firm's current and recent payment experience. Suppliers/creditors want to know whether or not the firm is paying its bills promptly. One indication of this is whether or not all cash discounts for prompt payment (e.g., for payment terms of 2/10, net 30) are being taken. Information about current and recent payment practices can be obtained by contacting other suppliers or credit bureaus and reviewing Dun & Bradstreet reports.

Activity Measures

The impact of efficient utilization of assets on the firm's return on investment was explained in Chapter 3, in the discussion of the asset turnover component of the DuPont model (ROI = Margin × Turnover). Activity measures focus primarily on the relationship between asset levels and sales (i.e., turnover).

Recall that the general model for calculating turnover is:

$$Turnover = Sales/Average\ assets$$

Because sales are generated over a period of time, it is appropriate that the average asset investment over the same period be used rather than the amount of assets at a single point in time (e.g., the balance sheet amount reported at the end of the period). Usually the average assets amount is determined by using the balance sheet amounts reported at the beginning and end of the period; however, if appropriate and available, monthly or quarterly balance sheet data can be used in the calculation of the average. Turnover is frequently calculated for:

Accounts receivable.

Inventories.

Plant and equipment.

Total operating assets.

Total assets.

• **BUSINESS PROCEDURE CAPSULE 19**
  Credit Rating and Financial Analysis Services

To help potential creditors and investors evaluate the financial condition and investment prospects of companies, a credit rating and financial analysis industry has developed. Firms in this industry gather and report data about individual companies, industries, segments of the economy, and the economy as a whole.

Credit rating firms such as Dun & Bradstreet and credit bureaus collect data from companies (and individuals) and their creditors, and sell credit history data to potential suppliers and others. These firms usually have a rating system and assign a credit risk value based on that system. These services apply primarily to smaller firms and individuals. A company or individual can request to see the data in the file so that erroneous data can be eliminated or corrected.

The financial statements of larger firms whose stock or bonds have been issued to the public are analyzed and reported on by firms such as Standard & Poor's Corporation or Moody's Investors Services, Inc. A rating is assigned to bonds to reflect the rating firm's assessment of the risk associated with the security. The ratings range from triple A to C, or no rating at all for a speculative bond. Summary financial statements, ratio calculation results, and bond ratings are published in manuals that are available in many libraries. In addition to rating bonds, these firms and many others (such as Value Line, Inc., and stock brokerage firms) evaluate the common and preferred stock issues of publicly owned companies, and report summary financial data and ratios and their opinions about the investment prospects for the stocks. A potential investor will likely use reports from one or more of these sources as well as the company's annual report to support the investment decision.

Alternative inventory cost-flow assumptions and alternative depreciation calculation methods will affect the comparability of turnover between companies. Of more significance than intercompany or company-industry comparisons as of a given date is the trend of turnover for the company relative to the trend of turnover for other companies or the industry.

When calculating inventory turnover, some analysts substitute the cost of goods sold amount for the sales amount in the calculation because inventories are reported at cost, and because making the calculation this way eliminates distortions that could be caused by sales mix changes between product categories with different gross profit ratios or mark-up percentages. This is certainly an appropriate modification to make in the calculation, but even if it is not made and sales is used in the numerator consistently, the inventory turnover trend will not be significantly affected unless there are major relative mark-up differences and major sales mix changes.

Some analysts use the cost of plant and equipment rather than the net book value (cost minus accumulated depreciation) when calculating plant and equipment turnover. This removes the impact of different depreciation calculation methods and may make intercompany and industry turnover data more comparable. This may be an illusory improvement, however, because the assets of each firm are reported at original cost, not current value or replacement cost. If they were acquired over different periods of time, the cost data are not likely to be comparable.

Exhibit 11–1 illustrates some turnover calculations for Armstrong World Industries, Inc., with data from the company's 1991 annual report, which is Appendix A of this text. Calculation results are usually not carried beyond one decimal place because aggregate financial statement data are being used, and the accuracy implied by additional decimal places is not warranted.

Two other activity measures that permit assessment of the efficiency of asset management are the **number of days' sales in accounts receivable** and the **number of days' sales in inventory.** The sooner that accounts receivable can be collected, the sooner cash is available to use in the business or to permit temporary investment, and the less cash needs to be borrowed for prompt payment of liabilities. Likewise, the lower that inventories can be maintained relative to sales, the less inventory needs to be financed with debt or owners' equity, and the greater the return on investment. However, the risk of having minimum inventories is that an unanticipated increase in demand or a delay in receiving raw materials or finished product can result in an out-of-stock situation that may result in lost sales. Inventory management is a very important activity for many firms, and many quantitative and operational techniques have been developed to assist in this activity. The "just-in-time" system pioneered by some Japanese firms and adopted by many firms in this country has as its objective keeping the investment in inventories at a minimum by forecasting needs and having suppliers deliver components as they are needed in the production process.

Each of the number of days' sales calculations involves calculating an average day's sales (or cost of sales) and dividing that average into the year-end balance sheet amount. A 365-day year is usually assumed for the average day's sales (or cost of sales) calculation. As in the calculation of inventory turnover, it is more appropriate to use cost of sales data in the days' sales in inventory

---

EXHIBIT 11–1   **Armstrong World Industries, Inc., Asset Turnover Calculations Illustrated**

Accounts receivable turnover for 1991 ($ millions)

Sales for 1991	$2,439.3
Accounts receivable, 12/31/91	305.3
Accounts receivable, 12/31/90	302.7

$$\text{Accounts receivable turnover} = \frac{\text{Sales}}{\text{Average accounts receivable}}$$

$$= \frac{\$2,439.3}{(\$305.3 + \$302.7)/2}$$

$$= 8.0 \text{ times}$$

Inventory turnover for 1991 ($ millions)

Cost of goods sold for 1991	$1,801.1
Inventories, 12/31/91	336.4
Inventories, 12/31/90	349.2

$$\text{Inventory turnover} = \frac{\text{Cost of goods sold}}{\text{Average inventories}}$$

$$= \frac{\$1,801.1}{(\$336.4 + \$349.2)/2}$$

$$= 5.3 \text{ times}$$

Plant and equipment turnover for 1991 ($ millions)

Sales for 1991	$2,439.3
Plant and equipment (net), 12/31/91	1,152.9
Plant and equipment (net), 12/31/90	1,147.4

$$\text{Plant and equipment turnover} = \frac{\text{Sales}}{\text{Average plant and equipment}}$$

$$= \frac{\$2,439.3}{(\$1,152.9 + \$1,147.4)/2}$$

$$= 2.1 \text{ times}$$

---

calculation. Year-end balance sheet amounts are used instead of the average of the beginning and ending balance sheet amounts used in the turnover calculation because the focus here is on the number of days' sales (or cost of sales) in the year-end balance sheet amount. The results of these calculations can also be referred to, for receivables, as the average collection period for accounts receivable, or the number of days' sales outstanding; and for inventories, as the average sales period for inventories. It must be stressed again that the inventory cost-flow assumption will influence the result of the inventory activity calculations. Exhibit 11–2 illustrates these calculations for Armstrong World Industries, Inc., for 1991.

EXHIBIT 11–2   Armstrong World Industries, Inc., Number of Days' Sales Calculations

---

Number of days' sales in accounts receivable ($ millions)

Sales for 1991	$2,439.3
Accounts receivable at 12/31/91	305.3

$$\text{Average day's sales} = \frac{\text{Annual sales}}{365}$$

$$= \$2,439.3/365$$

$$= \$6.683$$

$$\text{Days' sales in accounts receivable} = \frac{\text{Accounts receivable}}{\text{Average days' sales}}$$

$$= \$305.3/\$6.683$$

$$= 45.7 \text{ days}$$

The result of this calculation can also be expressed as the average age of accounts receivable, the number of days' sales outstanding, or the average collection period for accounts receivable.

Number of days' sales in inventory ($ millions)

Cost of goods sold for 1991	$1,801.1
Inventories at 12/31/91	336.4

$$\text{Average day's cost of goods sold} = \frac{\text{Annual cost of goods sold}}{365}$$

$$= \$1,801.1/365$$

$$= \$4.934$$

$$\text{Days' sales in inventory} = \frac{\text{Inventory}}{\text{Average day's cost of goods sold}}$$

$$= \$336.4/\$4.934$$

$$= 68.2 \text{ days}$$

The result of this calculation can also be expressed as the average age of the inventory or the average sales period for inventory.

Again, in evaluating the firm's operating efficiency it is the trend of these calculation results that is important. A single year's days' sales in receivables or inventory is not very useful. Armstrong World Industries, Inc., having 45.7 days' of sales in accounts receivable when its payment terms are probably a combination of 2/10, net 30, and net 30 (without a discount), doesn't make much sense, or indicates that its credit managers do not do a very good job collecting the accounts receivable promptly. If the calculation were based on 260 business days in the year (52 weeks of five days each), the average age of the accounts receivable works out to 32.5 days, which is more reasonable. In fact, if the credit manager wanted to know how many days' sales were in receivables at any time, the most accurate result could be determined by following this procedure:

1. Obtain the daily sales amounts for the period ending with the date of the total accounts receivable.
2. Add the daily sales amounts, beginning with the date of the total accounts receivable and working backward by day, until the sum of the daily sales amounts equals the total accounts receivable.
3. Count the number of days' sales that had to be included to equal the total accounts receivable.

Because of the different operating characteristics of various industries, rules of thumb for activity measures are difficult to develop. In general, the higher the turnover or the fewer the number of days' sales in accounts receivable and inventory, the greater the efficiency. Again, it should be emphasized that the answer from any financial statement analysis calculation is not important by itself; the *trend* of the result over time is most meaningful. An increase in the age of accounts receivable, an increase in inventory relative to sales, or a reduction in plant and equipment turnover are all early warning signs that the liquidity and profitability of a firm may be weakening.

Profitability Measures

Two of the most significant measures of profitability, return on investment and return on equity, were explained and illustrated in Chapter 3. Each of these measures relates net income, or an income statement subtotal (e.g., operating income), to an element of the balance sheet. Operating income, which excludes Other income and expense (principally interest expense) and income taxes, is frequently used in the ROI calculation because it is a more direct measure of the results of management's activities than is net income. Interest expense is a function of the board of directors' decisions about capital structure (the relationship between debt and owners' equity); income taxes are a function of the tax laws. Thus ROI based on operating income becomes an evaluation of the operating activities of the firm. The balance sheet element in this calculation is average total assets (or average operating assets) for ROI, and average common stockholders' equity for ROE. You know enough about accounting principles and how financial statement data are developed to have some healthy skepticism about the relationship of these rates of return to what a "true" rate of return based on real economic profit related to fair market values would be. Of course, the problem is that there is no agreement among managers, accountants, or financial analysts about what constitutes real economic profit, or how to determine objectively fair market values of the balance sheet data. In addition, the unique characteristics of individual companies and industries make the development of benchmark or target profitability ratios difficult if not impossible. Although many valid exceptions exist, a very broad rule of thumb useful for putting ROI in perspective is that average ROI, based on net income, for most American merchandising and manufacturing companies, is between 5% and 8%. Average ROI based on operating income (earnings before interest and taxes) for the same set of firms is between 10% and 15%. Average margin, based on net income, ranges from about 5% to 8%. Using operating income, average margin ranges from 10% to 15%. Asset turnover is usually in the range of 1.0 to 1.5. A rule of thumb useful for putting ROE in perspective is that average ROE, for most American merchandising and manufacturing companies, is between 8% and 13%. Do not draw firm conclusions based on these rules of thumb. Profitability evaluations are likely to be more valid when they are based on the *trend* of one company's ROI and ROE relative to the *trend* of industry and competitors' rates of return.

Earnings per share, originally discussed in detail in Chapter 9, is a profitability measure that is the denominator of a ratio that is used extensively by investors to evaluate the market price of a company's common stock relative to that of other companies and relative to the market as a whole. This ratio is the **price/earnings ratio,** or simply the P/E ratio. It is calculated by dividing the market price of a share of common stock by the earnings per share of common stock. **Earnings multiple** is another term for the price/earnings ratio. This term merely reflects the fact that the market price of stock is equal to the earnings per share multiplied by the P/E ratio. The following calculation illustrates this concept using data for Armstrong World Industries, Inc., as of December 31, 1991:

$$\begin{aligned} \text{Price earnings ratio} \\ \text{(or earnings multiple)} \end{aligned} = \frac{\text{Market price of common stock}}{\text{Earnings per share of common stock}}$$

$$= \frac{\$29.25^*}{\$0.77^\dagger}$$

$$= 38.0$$

To understand the significance of the P/E ratio, think about the reason an individual invests in the common stock of a company. The obvious objective is to "make money" (i.e., to achieve the desired return on the investment that is made). It is anticipated that return on investment will be realized in two ways: (1) the firm will pay cash dividends and (2) the market price of the stock will increase. The change in market value is usually called a *capital gain* or *loss*. A number of factors can cause the market price to change; one of the most significant of these is the prospect for future cash dividends. Both present and future cash dividends are a function of earnings. So in a very real sense the market price of a company's common stock reflects investors' expectations about the firm's future earnings. The greater the probability of increased earnings, the more investors are willing to pay for a claim to those earnings. Relating market price and earnings per share in a ratio is a way to express investors' expectations without confusing the issue by focusing on just market price per share. To illustrate, assume the following market price per share of common stock for each of two companies:

	Company A	Company B
Market price per share	$48.00	$75.00

Based on market price alone, the tempting conclusion is that the stock of Company B is more expensive than the stock of Company A. However, when earnings per share are considered, the table looks like this:

	Company A	Company B
Market price per share	$48.00	$75.00
Earnings per share	$ 4.00	$ 7.50

---

* Bottom row of five-year summary on page 38 of 1991 Annual Report in Appendix A.

† Bottom of consolidated statement of current earnings on page 18 of 1991 Annual Report in Appendix A.

It is now possible and appropriate to calculate the price/earnings ratio by dividing market price per share by the earnings per share. The results of this calculation are:

	Company A	*Company B*
Market price per share Earnings per share	$\dfrac{\$48.00}{\$4.00} = 12$	$\dfrac{\$75.00}{\$7.50} = 10$

Company A's stock is the more expensive because investors are willing to pay 12 times earnings for it, but they will pay only 10 times earnings for Company B. In essence, investors are showing that they expect greater future earnings growth and dividend payments from Company A than from Company B; therefore they are willing to pay relatively more for a given amount of earnings.

The price/earnings ratio, or earnings multiple, is one of the most important measures used by investors to evaluate the market price of a firm's common stock. This is one reason that earnings per share is reported prominently on the face of the income statement and that, as explained in Chapter 9, the effect of extraordinary items and potential dilution from any convertible long-term debt and/or convertible preferred stock is disclosed separately. The P/E ratio is disclosed in the stock listing tables of *The Wall Street Journal* and other periodicals because of its significance. Although the above illustration of the P/E ratio calculation was based on earnings for the past year, sometimes analysts use expected future earnings per share and current market price in the calculation in order to evaluate the prospects for changes in the stock's market price. Another approach to forecast market price is to use expected future earnings per share and the current (or expected future) earnings multiple.

A rule of thumb useful for putting the price/earnings ratio in perspective is that for the common stocks of most merchandising and manufacturing companies, an average P/E ratio will be in the range of 13 to 16 most of the time. A higher P/E ratio indicates that the common stock price is high relative to current earnings, probably because investors anticipate relatively favorable future developments, such as increased earnings per share or higher dividends per share. The relatively high P/E ratio for Armstrong World Industries, Inc., probably reflects investors' recognition that 1991 earnings were temporarily and unusually low due to the 1991 recession, and an expectation that earnings will recover when the economy recovers. Low P/E ratios usually indicate relatively poor expectations.

Another ratio used by both common stock investors and preferred stock investors (to whom the P/E ratio is not significant because the dividend on preferred stock will not fluctuate as earnings change) is the **dividend yield.** This is calculated by dividing the annual dividend by the current market price of the stock. This calculation is illustrated here, again using Armstrong World Industries, Inc., per share data for the year ended December 31, 1991:

$$\text{Dividend yield} = \frac{\text{Annual dividend per share}}{\text{Market price per share of stock}}$$

Dividend yield on:

$$\text{Common stock} = \frac{\$1.19^*}{\$29.75\dagger} = 4.0\%$$

$$\text{Preferred stock} = \frac{\$3.462^*}{\$35.00\ddagger} = 9.9\%$$

The dividend yield would be compared to the yield available on alternative investments to help the investor evaluate the extent to which the investment objectives were being met. In many cases investors will accept a low current dividend yield from a common stock if they believe that the firm is reinvesting the earnings retained for use in the business at a relatively high ROI because investors anticipate that future earnings will permit higher future dividends. In the case of preferred stock, investors will compare the yield to that available on other fixed income investments with comparable risk to determine whether or not to continue holding the preferred stock as an investment.

The average dividend yield on common stocks is usually in the range of 3% to 6%. For preferred stocks, the yield is usually somewhat greater, in a range of 5% to 8%.

Another ratio involving the dividend on common stock is the **dividend payout ratio.** This ratio, computed by dividing the dividend per share of common stock by the earnings per share of common stock, reflects the dividend policy of the company. Most firms have a policy of paying dividends that are a relatively constant proportion of earnings (e.g., 40 to 50 percent, or 10 to 15 percent). Knowing the dividend payout ratio permits the investor to project dividends from an assessment of the firm's earnings

---

* Retained earnings summary, page 28 of 1991 Annual Report in Appendix A.

† Bottom row of five-year summary on page 36 of 1991 Annual Report in Appendix A.

‡ Arbitrarily selected for illustrative purposes.

prospects. Armstrong World Industries, Inc.'s dividend payout ratio for 1991 was 155 percent, calculated as follows:

$$\text{Dividend payout ratio} = \frac{\text{Annual dividend per share}}{\text{Annual earnings per share}}$$

$$= \$1.19^*/0.77^\dagger$$

$$= 155\%$$

Most firms try to avoid having significant fluctuations in the amount of the cash dividend per share because investors prefer to be relatively assured of the dividend amount; therefore very few firms use the payout ratio as the sole, or even the principal, determinant of the dividend amount. To help communicate its dividend policy to the shareowners, a firm refers to its dividends in two ways: **regular dividends** are the stable, or gradually changing, periodic (quarterly, semiannual, or annual) dividends; **extra dividends** are larger dividends that may be declared and paid after an especially profitable year. The significance of the extra dividend is that it indicates to share owners that they should not expect to receive the larger amount every year.

As a rule of thumb, the dividend payout ratio for most merchandising and manufacturing companies is usually in the range of 30% to 50%.

From the preferred stockholders' point of view the ratio of net income to the total preferred stock dividend requirement indicates the margin of safety of the preferred dividend. If net income is less than three or four times the preferred dividend requirement and has been falling over time, the preferred stockholders would become concerned about the firm's ability to generate enough earnings and cash to be able to pay the preferred dividend. This **preferred dividend coverage ratio** for Armstrong World Industries, Inc., for 1991 was an adequate 2.5, calculated as follows:

$$\frac{\text{Preferred dividend}}{\text{coverage ratio}} = \frac{\text{Net income}}{\text{Preferred dividend requirement}}$$

$$= \frac{\$48.2 \text{ million}^\ddagger}{\$19.4 \text{ million}^\S}$$

$$= 2.5 \text{ times}$$

---

* Retained earnings summary, page 28 of 1991 Annual Report in Appendix A.

† Bottom of consolidated statement of current earnings on page 18 of 1991 Annual Report in Appendix A.

‡ Consolidated statement of earnings, page 18 of 1991 Annual Report in Appendix A.

§ Retained earnings, summary, page 28 of 1991 Annual Report in Appendix A.

Financial Leverage Ratios

Financial leverage (frequently called just *leverage*) refers to the use of debt (and, in the broadest context of the term, of preferred stock) to finance the assets of the entity. Leverage, the use of debt, adds risk to the operation of the firm because if the firm does not earn enough operating and other income to pay the interest on its debt, the creditors may force the firm into bankruptcy. However, because the interest on debt is fixed (i.e., is the same amount for any given amount of debt regardless of the amount of earnings), leverage also magnifies the return to the owners (ROE) relative to the return on assets (ROI). This magnification is illustrated in Exhibit 11–3.

EXHIBIT 11–3 Financial Leverage

I. No financial leverage
   Assume the following balance sheet and income statement:

Balance Sheet		*Income Statement*	
Assets	$10,000	Earnings before interest	
		and taxes	$2,000
		Interest	0
Liabilities	$none	Earnings before taxes .	$2,000
Owners' Equity	10,000	Income taxes (40%) . .	$ 800
Total L + OE	$10,000	Net income	$1,200

$$\text{Return on investment (assets)} = \text{Earnings before interest}$$
$$\text{before interest and taxes} \qquad \text{and taxes/Total assets}$$

$$= \$2,000/\$10,000$$

$$= 20\%$$

$$\text{Return on equity, after taxes} = \text{Net income/Owners' equity}$$

$$= \$1,200/\$10,000$$

$$= 12\%$$

Return on investment measures the efficiency with which management has used the operating assets to generate operating income. Note that the return on investment calculation is based on earnings before interest and taxes (operating income) and total assets, rather than net income and total assets. Earnings before interest and taxes (operating income) is used because the interest expense reflects a financing decision, not an operating result, and income taxes are beyond the control of operating management. Thus, ROI becomes an evaluation of the operating activities of the firm.

(continued)

EXHIBIT 11–3   *(concluded)*

Return on equity measures the rate of return that net income provides to the owners.

ROI and ROE differ only because income taxes have been excluded from ROI but have been included in ROE.

II. With financial leverage
Assume the following balance sheet and income statement:

Balance Sheet		*Income Statement*	
Assets	$10,000	Earnings before interest	
		and taxes	$2,000
		Interest	360
Liabilities (9% interest) .	$ 4,000	Earnings before taxes .	$1,640
Owners' Equity	6,000	Income taxes (40%) . .	656
Total L + OE	$10,000	Net income	$ 984

$$\text{Return on investment (assets)} = \text{Earnings before interest}$$
$$\text{before interest and taxes} \qquad \text{and taxes/Total assets}$$

$$= \$2,000/\$10,000$$

$$= 20\%$$

$$\text{Return on equity, after taxes} = \text{Net income/Owners' equity}$$

$$= \$984/\$6,000$$

$$= 16.4\%$$

The use of financial leverage has not affected ROI; financial leverage refers to how the assets are financed, not how efficiently the assets are used to generate operating income.

The use of financial leverage has caused the ROE to increase from 12 percent to 16.4 percent because ROI exceeds the cost of the debt used to finance a portion of the assets.

As illustrated in Exhibit 11–3, borrowing money at an interest rate cost that is less than the rate of return that can be earned on that money increases (or magnifies) the return on owners' equity. This is common financial sense; who wouldn't borrow money at a 6 percent interest cost if the money could be invested to earn more than 6 percent? Of course, if the return on investment were less than the cost of the borrowing, the result is a reduction of owners' equity (a loss) at best, bankruptcy at worst. This is the risk of leverage—the magnification works both ways! Highly leveraged firms or individuals (i.e., those with lots of debt relative to owners' equity) are exposed to the risk of losses or bankruptcy if the return on investment falls below the cost of borrowing. This does happen in economic recessions and industry business cycles, and this is why most nonfinancial firms try to limit the debt in their capital structure to no more than 50 percent of total capital (debt plus owners' equity).

The characteristic of debt and preferred stock that provides leverage is the fact that the interest cost (or dividend rate) is fixed. When debt is issued, the interest rate is set and remains unchanged for the life of the debt issue. If the interest rate were to fluctuate as a function of the entity's ROI, or as a result of inflation or deflation in the economy, the magnification of ROE would be diminished or eliminated.

Another feature of debt illustrated in Exhibit 11–3 is the deductibility of interest as an expense in determining income subject to income taxes. The after-tax cost of debt is its interest rate multiplied by the complement of the firm's tax rate. In this example the assumed tax rate is 40 percent, so the after-tax cost of the debt is 9 percent $\times$ (1 − 0.40) = 5.4 percent. Since preferred stock dividends are not deductible as an expense, financial managers prefer to use debt, rather than preferred stock, as the source of fixed cost capital.

Two **financial leverage ratios** are used to indicate the extent to which a firm is using financial leverage. They are the debt ratio, and the debt/equity ratio. Each of the ratios expresses the relationship between debt and equity, but each does it differently.

The **debt ratio** is the ratio of total liabilities to the total of liabilities and owners' equity. The **debt/equity ratio** is the ratio of total liabilities to total owners' equity. Thus a debt ratio of 50 percent would be the same as a debt/equity ratio of 1 (or 1 : 1). To illustrate these ratios, assume the following capital structure (i.e., right-hand side of the balance sheet) for a firm:

Liabilities	$ 40,000
Owners' equity	60,000
Total L + OE	$100,000

$$\text{Debt ratio} = \frac{\text{Total liabilities}}{\text{Total liabilities and owners' equity}}$$

$$= \frac{\$40,000}{\$100,000}$$

$$= 40\%$$

$$\text{Debt/Equity ratio} = \frac{\text{Total liabilities}}{\text{Total owners' equity}}$$
$$= \frac{\$40,000}{\$60,000}$$
$$= 66.7\%$$

As already indicated, most nonfinancial firms will usually have a debt ratio below 50 percent — a debt/equity ratio of less than 1 — because of the risk associated with having a greater proportion of debt in the capital structure.

Holders of a company's long-term debt will frequently want to know the **times interest earned ratio** for the firm. This measure is similar to the preferred dividend coverage ratio previously explained; it shows the relationship of earnings before interest and taxes to interest expense. The greater the ratio, the more confident the debt holders can be about the firm's prospects for continuing to have enough earnings to cover the interest expense, even if the firm experiences a decline in the demand for its products or services. Using data from the Armstrong World Industries, Inc., annual report for 1991, the calculation of times interest earned is:

Earnings before income taxes	$100.3* million
Add back interest expense	45.8* million
Earnings before interest and taxes	$146.1 million

* Consolidated statement of earnings, page 18 of 1991 Annual Report in Appendix A.

$$\text{Times interest earned} = \frac{\text{Earnings before interest and taxes}}{\text{Interest expense}}$$
$$= \$146.1/\$45.8$$
$$= 3.2 \text{ times}$$

The debt holders of Armstrong would not be too concerned about Armstrong's ability to continue to earn enough to cover its interest expense unless sales and operating income continued to fall.

As a general rule of thumb, a times interest earned ratio of 5 or higher is considered by creditors to indicate a relatively low risk that a firm will not be able to pay interest in the future.

OTHER ANALYTICAL TECHNIQUES

Book Value per Share of Common Stock

The **book value per share of comon stock** is calculated by dividing the total common stockholders' equity by the number of shares of common stock outstanding. **Net asset value per share of common stock** is another name for this measure.

If there is preferred stock in the capital structure of the firm, the liquidating value of the preferred stock is subtracted from total owners' equity to get the common stockholders' equity.

The following illustration using data as of December 31, 1991, for Armstrong World Industries, Inc., illustrates the calculation (in millions of dollars):

Total stockholders equity	$885.5*
Less: Preferred stock	($267.7)*
Add: Reduction for ESOP loan guarantee	256.0*
Common stockholders' equity	$873.8

$$\text{Book value per share of common stock} = \frac{\text{Common stockholders' equity}}{\text{Number of shares of common stock outstanding}}$$

$$= \frac{\$873.8 \text{ million}}{37.1 \text{ million}†}$$

$$= \$23.55$$

* From stockholders' equity section of consolidated balance sheets, page 19 of 1991 Annual Report in Appendix A.

† Common shares issued, from balance sheet	51,878,910
Less: Common shares in treasury, from balance sheet	14,776,338
Common shares outstanding	37,102,572

Because total common stockholders' equity reflects the application of generally accepted accounting principles, and the specific accounting policies that have been selected, book value per share is not a number that can be meaningfully compared to the market value per share of stock for most companies, especially if the market value is greater than the book value. If market value is less than book value, then careful analysis may indicate that the total market value of the company is less than the fair value of its assets. *The book value per share of a manufacturing or merchandising company is not a very useful measure most of the time.*

Common Size Financial Statements

When comparing and evaluating the operating results of a company over a number of years, many analysts like to express the balance sheet and income statement in a percentage format. This type of presentation is a **common size statement**. To prepare a common size balance sheet, each asset is expressed as a percentage of total assets, and each liability and owners' equity amount is expressed as a percentage of that total. For the income statement sales is set at 100 percent, and each item on the income statement is expressed as a percentage of sales. This type of percentage analysis makes spotting trends in the composition of balance sheet and income statement items much easier than looking at dollar amounts. Thus inventories that represent an increasing percentage of total assets may indicate a weakness in inventory control procedures. An increase in the ratio of cost of goods sold to sales (which would be a decrease in the gross profit ratio — the complement of the cost of goods sold ratio) would indicate that management is either not able or not willing to increase selling prices in response to cost increases, thus causing downward pressure on operating income. Of course, a well-designed graphical display of key balance sheet and income statement percentage data can also greatly help a reader interpret the data.

Exhibit 11–4 presents common size income statements for Armstrong World Industries, Inc., for each of the years 1987 through 1991. It is quite easy to see the impact of various items on Armstrong's profitability over this period. The decline in net earnings is due to a falling gross profit ratio, proportionately higher selling and administrative expenses, and discontinued businesses. Proportionately lower income taxes only partly offset these other changes.

Other Operating Statistics

Physical measures of activity, rather than the financial measures included in the financial statements, are frequently useful. For example, reporting sales in units provides a perspective that may be hidden by price changes when only sales dollars are reported. Or reporting the total number of employees (or employees by division or department) may be more useful for some purposes than reporting payroll costs.

EXHIBIT 11–4   Common Size Income Statements

ARMSTRONG WORLD INDUSTRIES, INC.
Common Size Income Statements
For the Years Ended December 31, 1987–1991

	1991	1990	1989	1988	1987
Sales	100.0%	100.0%	100.0%	100.0%	100.0%
Cost of goods sold	73.8	72.1	70.9	71.2	70.2
Gross profit	26.2%	27.9%	29.1%	28.8%	29.8%
Selling and administrative expense	19.2	18.4	17.5	17.3	17.2
Earnings from continuing businesses before other income (expense) and income taxes	7.0%	9.5%	11.6%	11.5%	12.6%
Other income (expense)	−2.9	−0.7	−1.8	−0.6	−0.5
Earnings from continuing businesses before income taxes	4.1%	8.8%	9.8%	10.9%	12.1%
Income taxes	1.6	3.0	3.5	4.1	4.9
Earnings from continuing businesses	2.5%	5.8%	6.3%	6.8%	7.2%
Discontinued businesses	−0.5	−0.5	1.2	0.4	0.5
Cumulative effect of change in accounting for income taxes	—	0.3	—	—	—
Net earnings	2.0%	5.6%	7.5%	7.2%	7.6%

Many analysts combine physical and financial measures to develop useful statistics to show trends or make comparisons of firms. For example, sales dollars per employee and operating income per employee each indicates a type of productivity measure. Plant operating expenses per square foot of plant space or gross profit per square foot of selling space might also be useful indicators of efficiency. There is no "cookbook" of quantitative measures for management to follow; the challenge is to understand the

---

• BUSINESS PROCEDURE CAPSULE 20
The Leveraged Buyout

The mid- and late-1980s was a period of relatively high corporate ownership rearrangement activity featuring friendly and unfriendly mergers and acquisitions, as well as leveraged buyouts. In a merger or acquisition one firm acquires another, either by issuing stock of the surviving company to the share owners of the firm being acquired (usually a merger) or by buying the stock of the company being acquired by paying cash (and sometimes other securities) to the share owners of the other firm. This is a *takeover*. Changes in top management and operations of the acquired company frequently result. A leveraged buyout is a transaction in which the present top management of a publicly held firm buys the stock of the nonmanagement share-owners, and the firm becomes "privately owned" (i.e., its shares are no longer traded in the public market). Neither management nor the operations of the firm change significantly. Some firms that have been takeover targets have "gone private" through a leveraged buyout in order to avoid being acquired by another firm.

The leveraged buyout transaction gets its label from the fact that the company goes heavily into debt in order to get the funds needed to buy the shares of the public stockholders. In many cases the debt ratio will be substantially higher than is usually considered prudent, but investors are willing to invest in the debt because of their confidence in management's ability, which has been proven in the past, to operate the firm profitably.

The debt issued in a leveraged buyout is usually considered speculative or high risk (the term *junk bond* has been applied to much of it), because of concern about the impact of a major economic recession on the ability of these firms to meet the interest and principal payment requirements of this debt. In the early 1990s many firms were forced into bankruptcy, sales of assets, or merger with other firms for this reason. Other financially healthier firms took advantage of rising stock market values to realign their capital structure by selling stock (going public again) and using the proceeds to reduce high-cost long-term debt.

---

firm's objectives and procedures, and then to develop measurement and reporting techniques to help people accomplish their goals.

SUMMARY

Financial statement analysis using ratio measurements and trend analysis assists the user of financial statements to make informed judgments and decisions about the entity's financial condition and results of operations.

Rate of return calculations in general, and the return on investment (ROI) and return on equity (ROE) measures in particular, are essential in evaluating profitability. These measures were discussed in detail in Chapter 3.

The trend of a ratio over time contains much more information than a single ratio at one point in time. Trend comparisons between the entity and broad industry averages are also useful.

Creditors especially are interested in the entity's liquidity. Working capital and the calculation of the current ratio and acid-test ratio were also discussed in Chapter 3.

Because financial statement analysis uses the data shown in the financial statements, and because alternative accounting methods affect the financial statement data differently, it is important that readers know which alternatives (e.g., FIFO and LIFO for inventory) have been used in the financial statements being analyzed.

Activity measures reflect the efficiency with which assets have been utilized to generate sales revenue. Most activity ratios focus on turnover. Activity can also be expressed in terms of the number of days of activity (e.g., sales) in the year-end balance (e.g., accounts receivable).

In addition to ROI and ROE based on total data, certain per share ratios are also important. The price/earnings ratio, dividend yield, dividend payout ratio, and preferred dividend coverage ratios are examples.

Leverage ratios focus on the financial leverage of the firm. Financial leverage will magnify return on equity relative to return on assets, and it adds risk to the securities issued by the firm.

Book value per share of common stock is frequently reported, but because it is based on the financial statement value of the firm's assets instead of their market value, book value is not very useful in most circumstances.

An effective way to compare the financial condition and results of operations of different sized firms is to express balance sheet data as a percentage of total assets, and income statement data as a percentage of sales. This process results in common size financial statements.

Investors, managers, employees, and others are frequently interested in other operating statistics that use data not contained in the financial statements. More than financial data are needed to develop a complete picture about a company.

Financial statement analysis ratios are summarized below by category of ratio.

I. Profitability measures
  A. Return on investment (ROI)
    1. General model

$$ROI = \frac{Return}{Investment}$$

Return is frequently net income, and investment is frequently average total assets.

This ratio gives the rate of return that has been earned on the assets invested, and is the key measure of profitability.

    2. DuPont model

$$ROI = Margin \times Turnover$$

$$= \frac{Net\ income}{Sales} \times \frac{Sales}{Average\ total\ assets}$$

Margin expresses the net income resulting from each dollar of sales. Turnover shows the efficiency with which assets are used to generate sales.

    3. Variations of the general model use operating income, income before taxes, or some other intermediate income statement amount in the numerator and average operating assets in the denominator to focus on the rate of return from operations before taxes.

  B. Return on equity (ROE)
    1. General model

$$ROE = \frac{Net\ income}{Average\ total\ owners'\ equity}$$

This ratio gives the rate of return on that portion of the assets provided by the owners of the entity.

    2. A variation of the general model occurs when there is preferred stock. Net income is reduced by the amount of the preferred stock dividend requirement, and only common stockholders' equity is used in the denominator. This distinction is made because the ownership rights of the preferred and common stockholders differ.

  C. Price/Earnings ratio (P/E Ratio)

$$\frac{Price\ earnings\ ratio}{(or\ earnings\ multiple)} = \frac{Market\ price\ of\ common\ stock}{Earnings\ per\ share\ of\ common\ stock}$$

This ratio expresses the relative expensiveness of a share of a firm's common stock because it shows how much investors are willing to pay for the stock relative to earnings. Generally speaking, the greater a firm's ROI and rate of earnings growth, the higher the P/E ratio of its common stock will be.

D. Dividend yield

$$\text{Dividend yield} = \frac{\text{Annual dividend per share}}{\text{Market price per share of stock}}$$

The dividend yield expresses part of the stockholder's ROI: the rate of return represented by the annual dividend. The other part of the stockholder's total rate of return from the investment comes from the change in the market value of the stock during the year; this is usually called the *capital gain or loss*.

E. Dividend payout ratio

$$\text{Dividend payout ratio} = \frac{\text{Annual dividend per share}}{\text{Annual earnings per share}}$$

The dividend payout ratio expresses the proportion of earnings paid as dividends. It can be used to estimate dividends of future years if earnings can be estimated.

F. Preferred dividend coverage ratio

$$\frac{\text{Preferred dividend}}{\text{coverage ratio}} = \frac{\text{Net income}}{\text{Preferred dividend requirement}}$$

The preferred dividend coverage ratio expresses the ability of the firm to meet its preferred stock dividend requirement. The higher this coverage ratio, the lower the probability that dividends on common stock will be discontinued because of low earnings and failure to pay dividends on preferred stock.

II. Liquidity measures

A. Working capital

$$\text{Working capital} = \text{Current assets} - \text{Current liabilities}$$

The arithmetic relationship between current assets and current liabilities is a measure of the firm's ability to meet its obligations as they come due.

B. Current ratio

$$\text{Current ratio} = \frac{\text{Current assets}}{\text{Current liabilities}}$$

This ratio measurement permits evaluation of liquidity that is more comparable over time and between firms than the amount of working capital.

C. Acid-test ratio

$$\text{Acid-test ratio} = \frac{\text{Cash (including temporary cash investments)} + \text{Accounts receivable}}{\text{Current liabilities}}$$

By excluding inventories and other nonliquid current assets, this ratio gives a conservative assessment of the firm's bill-paying ability.

III. Activity measures
   A. Total asset turnover

$$\text{Total asset turnover} = \frac{\text{Sales}}{\text{Average total assets}}$$

Turnover shows the efficiency with which assets are used to generate sales. Refer also to the DuPont model under Profitability measures.

   B. Inventory turnover

$$\text{Inventory turnover} = \frac{\text{Cost of goods sold}}{\text{Average inventories}}$$

Inventory turnover is an efficiency measure that focuses on inventories. Cost of goods sold is used in the numerator because inventories are carried at cost, not selling price. Even so, in practice the numerator is frequently sales. This does not usually distort significantly the trend of this measure.

   C. Number of days' sales in
      1. Accounts receivable

$$\frac{\text{Number of days' sales in}}{\text{Accounts receivable}} = \frac{\text{Accounts receivable}}{\text{Average day's sales}}$$

$$\text{Average day's sales} = \frac{\text{Annual sales}}{365}$$

This measure shows the average age of the accounts receivable, and reflects the efficiency of the firm's collection policies relative to its credit terms.

      2. Inventory

$$\frac{\text{Number of days' sales}}{\text{in Inventory}} = \frac{\text{Inventory}}{\text{Average day's cost of goods sold}}$$

$$\frac{\text{Average day's cost}}{\text{of good sold}} = \frac{\text{Annual cost of goods sold}}{365}$$

This shows the number of days' of sales that could be made from the inventory on hand. The trend of this measure reflects management's ability to control inventories relative to sales.

IV. Leverage measures
   A. Debt ratio

$$\text{Debt ratio} = \frac{\text{Total liabilities}}{\text{Total liabilities and owners' equity}}$$

B. Debt/Equity ratio

$$\text{Debt/Equity ratio} = \frac{\text{Total liabilities}}{\text{Total owners' equity}}$$

Each of these measures shows the proportion of debt in the capital structure. Note that a debt ratio of 50 percent is the same as a debt/equity ratio of 100 percent. These ratios reflect the risk caused by the interest and principal requirements of debt. Variations of these models involve the definition of total liabilities. Current liabilities are not included by some analysts because they are being paid currently from current assets. Some analysts exclude the liability for deferred taxes from total liabilities because for many firms this liability has never been reduced, causing the impression that deferred taxes will never be paid.

C. Times interest earned

$$\text{Times interest earned} = \frac{\text{Earnings before interest and taxes}}{\text{Interest expense}}$$

This is a measure of the firm's ability to earn enough to cover its annual interest requirement.

V. Book value per share of common stock

$$\text{Book value per share of common stock} = \frac{\text{Common stockholders' equity}}{\text{Number of shares of common stock outstanding}}$$

An easily calculated but generally meaningless measure.

KEY TERMS AND CONCEPTS

book value per share of common stock *(p. 343)* The quotient of total common stockholders' equity divided by the number of shares of common stock outstanding. Sometimes called *net asset value per share of common stock*. Not a very useful measure most of the time.

common size statement *(p. 344)* A financial statement in which amounts are expressed in percentage terms. In a common size balance sheet, total assets are 100 percent, and all other amounts are expressed as a percentage of total assets. In a common size income statement net sales or revenues are 100 percent, and all other amounts are expressed as a percentage of that amount.

debt ratio *(p. 341)* The ratio of total liabilities to the sum of total liabilities and total owners' equity. Sometimes long-term debt is the only liability used in the calculation.

debt/equity ratio *(p. 341)* The ratio of total liabilities to total owners' equity. Sometimes only long-term debt is used for the numerator of the ratio.

dividend payout ratio *(p. 337)*   On common stock the ratio of the dividend per share to the earnings per share.

dividend yield *(p. 337)*   The ratio of the annual dividend per share to the market price per share of the stock.

earnings multiple *(p. 334)*   Another term for the *price/earnings ratio;* an indicator of the relative expensiveness of a firm's common stock.

effect of inventory cost-flow assumption on working capital *(p. 327)*   When the cost of items being purchased for inventory is changing, the amount of the balance in the inventory account and total current assets are influenced by the inventory cost-flow assumption used (e.g., FIFO or LIFO).

extra dividend *(p. 338)*   A dividend that is not likely to be incorporated as part of the regular dividend in the future.

financial leverage ratios *(p. 341)*   The "debt ratio" and "debt/equity ratio," that indicate the extent to which financial leverage is being used.

net asset value per share of common stock *(p. 343)*   The quotient of total common stockholders' equity divided by the number of shares of common stock outstanding. Sometimes called *book value per share of common stock.*

number of days' sales in accounts receivable *(p. 330)*   An indicator of the efficiency with which accounts receivable are collected.

number of days' sales in inventory *(p. 330)*   An indicator of the efficiency with which inventories are managed.

preferred dividend coverage ratio *(p. 338)*   The ratio of net income to the annual preferred stock dividend requirement.

price/earnings ratio *(p. 334)*   An indicator of the relative expensiveness of a firm's common stock.

regular dividend *(p. 338)*   A dividend that is likely to be declared on a repetitive, periodic (quarterly, semiannual) basis.

times interest earned ratio *(p. 342)*   The ratio of earnings before interest and taxes to interest expense. An indicator of the risk associated with financial leverage.

EXERCISES AND PROBLEMS

11–1. Review the accompanying financial statements (Statements 1, 2, 3, and 4) for Sample Co. Note especially the format of the balance sheet, which is Statement 3, the Consolidated Financial Position at December 31. Study the financial statements and see how they are interrelated.

Required: *a.* Calculate the following ratios for the year ended December 31, 1991:

Return on investment, using the DuPont model, based on operating income.

Return on equity, based on net income.

b. Calculate the following activity measures for the year ended December 31, 1991:

Number of days' sales in accounts receivable based on a 365-day year.

Inventory turnover.

Turnover of buildings, machinery and equipment, and land.

c. Calculate the following leverage measures:

Debt (long-term debt due after one year) to owners' equity at December 31, 1991.

Debt (long-term debt due after one year) to debt (as above) plus owners' equity at December 31, 1991.

Times interest earned for the year ended December 31, 1991.

d. The market price of Sample Co.'s common stock was $42 per share at the end of 1991. Calculate the following ratios at that date:

Price/earnings ratio.

Dividend payout ratio.

Dividend yield.

STATEMENT 1

SAMPLE CO.
Consolidated Results of Operations
For the Years Ended December 31
(millions of dollars except per share data)

	1992	*1991*	*1990*
Sales	**$10,359**	$8,251	$7,362
Operating costs:			
Cost of goods sold	**8,011**	6,523	6,064
Selling, general, and administrative expenses	**1,242**	1,071	980
Research and development expenses	**182**	159	178
	9,435	7,753	7,222
Operating profit . . *No mem* .	**924**	498	140
Interest expense	**264**	209	197
	660	289	(57)
Other income	**182**	170	160
	842	459	103
Provision for income taxes	**262**	118	21
Profit of consolidated companies .	**580**	341	82

(continued)

STATEMENT 1 (*concluded*)

	1992	1991	1990
Equity in profit (loss) of affiliated companies	36	(22)	(6)
Profit — before extraordinary tax benefit	616	319	76
Extraordinary tax benefit from foreign tax credit carryforwards .	—	31	—
Profit	$ 616	$ 350	$ 76
Profit per share of common stock before extraordinary tax benefit .	$ 6.07	$ 3.20	$ .77
Profit per share of common stock after extraordinary tax benefit . .	$ 6.07	$ 3.51	$ .77
Dividends paid per share of common stock	$ .75	$ .50	$ .50

STATEMENT 2

SAMPLE CO.
Changes in Consolidated Ownership
For the Years Ended December 31
(dollars in millions)

	1992	1991	1990
Common stock:			
Balance at beginning of year . . .	$ 827	$ 714	$ 696
Common shares issued, including treasury shares resissued: 1992 — 1,317,485; 1991 — 2,601,332; 1990 — 452,959 . . .	83	113	18
Treasury shares purchased: 1992 — 1,326,058	(86)	—	—
Balance at year-end	824	827	714
Profit employed in the business:			
Balance at beginning of year . . .	2,656	2,363	2,349
Add: Profit	616	350	76
Deduct: Dividends paid and payable	88	57	62
Balance at year-end	3,184	2,656	2,363
Foreign currency translation adjustment:			
Balance at beginning of year . . .	82	72	23
Aggregate adjustment for year . .	23	10	49
Balance at year-end	105	82	72
Ownership at year-end	$4,113	$3,565	$3,149

STATEMENT 3

SAMPLE CO.
Consolidated Financial Position
At December 31
(dollars in millions except per share data)

	1992	1991	1990
Current assets:			
Cash and short-term investments	$ 74	$ 155	$ 166
Receivables	2,669	2,174	1,808
Refundable income taxes	114	130	92
Deferred income taxes and prepaid expenses allocable to the following year	474	224	208
Inventories	1,986	1,323	1,211
	5,317	4,006	3,485
Current liabilities:			
Short-term borrowings	1,072	623	696
Payable to material suppliers and others	1,495	1,351	1,182
Wages, salaries, and contributions for employee benefits	485	431	450
Dividends payable	30	19	12
Income taxes	118	48	10
Long-term debt due within one year	235	286	122
	3,435	2,758	2,472
Net current assets	1,882	1,248	1,013
Buildings, machinery, and equipment—net	2,802	2,467	2,431
Land—at original cost	107	96	97
Patents, trademarks, and other intangibles	71	47	60
Investments in and advances to affiliated companies	288	227	185
Long-term receivables	902	665	413
Other assets	199	123	90
Total assets less current liabilities	6,251	4,873	4,289
Long-term debt due after one year	1,953	1,287	1,134
Deferred income taxes	185	21	6
Net assets	$4,113	$3,565	$3,149

(continued)

STATEMENT 3 (*concluded*)

	1992	1991	1990
Ownership (Statement 2):			
Common stock of $1.00 par value:			
Authorized shares: 200,000,000			
Outstanding shares (1992—			
101,414,138 and 1991—			
101,422,711 [after deducting			
23,470 and 2,961 treasury			
shares, respectively]; 1990—			
98,832,079) at paid-in amount .	$ 824	$ 827	$ 714
Profit employed in the business . .	3,184	2,656	2,363
Foreign currency translation ad-			
justment	105	82	72
	$4,113	$3,565	$3,149

STATEMENT 4

SAMPLE CO.
Consolidated Statement of Cash Flows
For the Years Ended December 31
(millions of dollars)

	1992	1991	1990
Cash flows from operating activities:			
Profit	$ 616	$ 350	$ 76
Adjustments for noncash items:			
Depreciation and amortization .	434	425	453
Other	(74)	144	86
Changes in assets and liabilities:			
Receivables	(777)	(699)	(765)
Refundable income taxes . . .	15	(34)	1
Inventories	(598)	(124)	(68)
Payable to material suppliers			
and others.	348	252	(14)
Other—net	(39)	(80)	(4)
Net cash provided by operating			
activities	(75)	234	(235)

(*continued*)

STATEMENT 4 (*concluded*)

	1992	1991	1990
Cash flows from investing activities:			
Expenditures for land, buildings, machinery, and equipment . .	**(793)**	(493)	(331)
Proceeds from disposals of land, buildings, machinery, and equipment.	**30**	32	16
Investments in and advances to affiliated companies	**(24)**	(65)	(52)
Other—net	**(50)**	(25)	41
Net cash used for investing activities	**(1,259)**	(931)	(637)
Cash flows from financing activities:			
Dividends paid.	**(77)**	(50)	(49)
Common shares issued, including treasury shares reissued . . .	**4**	6	3
Treasury shares purchased . . .	**(86)**	—	—
Proceeds from long-term debt issued.	**371**	503	156
Payments on long-term debt. . .	**(298)**	(102)	(307)
Short-term borrowings—net . .	**965**	(91)	578
Net cash provided by financing activities	**879**	266	381
Effect of exchange rate changes on cash	**(48)**	40	41
Decrease in cash and short-term investments	**$ (81)**	$ (11)	$ (139)

11–2. Solve the requirements of Problem 11–1 for the year ended December 31, 1992. The market price of Sample Co.'s common stock was $65 at December 31, 1992.

11–3. Look forward to the day when you will have accumulated $2,000, and assume that you have decided to invest that hard-earned money in the common stock of a publicly owned corporation. What data about that company will you be most interested in, and how will you arrange those data so they are most meaningful to you? What information about the company will you want on a weekly basis, on a quarterly basis, and on an annual basis? How will you decide whether to sell, hold, or buy some more of the firm's stock?

11–4. Presented below are summarized data from the balance sheets and income statements of Wiper, Inc.:

WIPER, INC.
Condensed Balance Sheets
March 31, 1993, 1992, 1991
(in millions)

	1993	1992	1991
Current assets	$ 677	$ 891	$ 736
Other assets	2,413	1,920	1,719
	$3,090	$2,811	$2,455
Current liabilities	$ 562	$ 803	$ 710
Long-term liabilities.	1,521	982	827
Owners' equity	1,007	1,026	918
	$3,090	$2,811	$2,455

WIPER, INC.
Selected Income Statement and Other Data
For the years ended March 31, 1993 and 1992
(in millions)

	1993	1992
Income statement Data:		
Sales	$3,050	$2,913
Operating income.	296	310
Interest expense	84	65
Net income	192	187
Other data:		
Average number of common shares outstanding .	41.3	46.7
Total dividends paid	$ 50.0	$ 52.3

Required:

a. Calculate return on investment, based on net income and average total assets, for 1993 and 1992. Show both margin and turnover in your calculation.

b. Calculate return on equity for 1993 and 1992.

c. Calculate working capital and the current ratio for each of the past three years.

d. Calculate earnings per share for 1993 and 1992.

e. If Wiper's stock had a price/earnings ratio of 13 at the end of 1993, what was the market price of the stock?

f. Calculate the cash dividend per share for 1993, and the dividend yield based on the market price calculated in (*e*).

g. Calculate the dividend payout ratio for 1993.

h. Assume that accounts receivable at December 31, 1993, totaled $309 million. Calculate the number of days' sales in receivables at that date.

i. Calculate Wiper's debt ratio and debt/equity ratio at December 31, 1993, and 1992.

j. Calculate the times interest earned factor for 1993 and 1992.

k. Review the results of these calculations, evaluate the profitability and liquidity of this company, and state your opinion about its suitability as an investment for a young, single professional person with funds to invest in common stock.

ⒶArmstrong

11–5. Refer to the consolidated balance sheets on page 19 of the Armstrong World Industries, Inc., Annual Report in Appendix A.

Required:

Prepare a common size balance sheet at December 31, 1990, using the following captions:

> Total current assets
> Property, plant, and equipment (net)
> Other noncurrent assets
>   Total assets
> Total current liabilities
> Total noncurrent liabilities
> Total shareholders' equity
>   Total liabilities and shareholders' equity

ⒶArmstrong

11–6. Solve the requirements of Problem 11–5 for the year ended December 31, 1991.

11–7. If your library has a common stock investment advisory service such as *Moody's Handbook of Common Stocks*, Standard and Poor's *Corporation Stock Market Encyclopedia*, or Value Line Reports, find in one of these sources the report about a company you have heard about or in which you have an interest. Alternatively, visit a brokerage firm office and ask for a report from one of the above sources, or a report prepared by the brokerage firm's research division. Review the report and notice the analytical data that it contains. What other data besides those in the report would you like to obtain? Why do you want this other data? How would you get them?

ⒶArmstrong

11–8. Refer to the Six-Year Summary section on page 38 of the Armstrong World Industries, Inc., Annual Report in Appendix A.

Required:

a. Identify five ratios that are not given in the six-year summary that would be useful for your evaluation of the suitability of an investment in Armstrong World Industries, Inc., common stock for a young, single professional person with funds to invest in common stock.

b. Calculate the ratios identified above for each of the five years.

c. Make a graph plot of each of the above ratios, plus five amounts or ratios that are reported in the six-year summary.

d. Write a conclusion about the appropriateness of an investment in the common stock of Armstrong World Industries, Inc., for that young, single professional person with funds to invest in common stock.

PART II

Managerial Accounting

Chapter 12

Managerial/Cost Accounting and Cost Classifications

Managerial accounting, sometimes called *management accounting,* involves using economic and financial information to plan and control many of the activities of the entity, and to support the management decision-making process. **Cost accounting** is a subset of managerial accounting that relates primarily to the determination and accumulation of product, process, or service costs. Managerial accounting and cost accounting have primarily an internal orientation, as opposed to the primarily external orientation of financial accounting. Much of the same data used in or generated by the financial accounting process is used in managerial and cost accounting, but the latter are more likely to have a future orientation, such as in the preparation of budgets.

As with financial accounting, managerial accounting and cost accounting have special terminology or, as many would say, *jargon.* Most of these terms relate to different types of costs. An important lesson about managerial and cost accounting to be learned early is that *there are different costs for different purposes.* When a marketing or production manager asks a management accountant what a certain item or activity costs, the accountant is not being sassy or disrespectful when asking: "Why do you want to know?" Costs used for valuing inventory are different from the costs that should be considered when analyzing a product modification or potential new product.

In this chapter we shall look briefly at the management process, identify several of the contributions that the managerial accountant makes to that process, and then focus on cost classifications and descriptions. Subsequent chapters will describe how costs are used in the planning and controlling processes.

LEARNING OBJECTIVES

After studying this chapter you should understand:

- The overall activities involved in the management process, and how managerial accounting supports those activities.
- The major differences between financial accounting and managerial accounting.
- That there are different costs for different purposes.
- The broad cost classification structure that relates different ways of identifying costs to the uses made of those costs.
- The difference between product costs and period costs, and the three components of product cost.
- The general operation of a product costing system, and how costs flow through the inventory accounts to cost of goods sold.
- The difference between direct and indirect costs.
- The difference between variable and fixed cost behavior patterns, and the simplifying assumptions made in this classification method.
- How the behavior of a cost can be expressed in a cost formula.
- Why expressing fixed costs on a per unit of activity basis is misleading and may result in faulty decisions.
- That all costs are controllable by someone at some time, but that in the short run some costs may be classified as uncontrollable.
- The difference between committed costs and discretionary costs.
- What a differential cost is, and how identifying and using differential costs may simplify the decision-making process.
- What an allocated cost is, and why cost allocation may result in misleading data for decision makers.
- What a sunk cost is, and why it doesn't affect the evaluation of alternative future actions.
- What an opportunity cost is, and why it should be considered in the decision-making process, even though it is never recognized in the accounting records.

MANAGERIAL ACCOUNTING CONTRASTED TO FINANCIAL ACCOUNTING

Management accounting supports the internal planning (future-oriented) decisions made by management. Financial accounting has more of a score-keeping, historical orientation, although data produced by the financial accounting process form some of the foundation on which plans are based. Planning is a key part of the **management process,** and although there are many descriptions of that process, a generally acceptable definition would include reference to the process of planning, organizing, and controlling an entity's activities so that the organization can accomplish its purpose. A schematic model of the process looks like this:

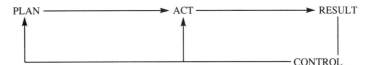

The diagram suggests that controls provide feedback. Actual results are compared to planned results, and if a variance exists between the two, then either the plan or the actions, or perhaps both, are changed.

Not all of a firm's objectives are stated in financial terms by any means. For example, market share, employee morale, absence of layoffs, and responsible corporate citizenship are all appropriate objectives that are expressed in nonfinancial terms. However, many of the firm's goals will be financial in nature (e.g., ROI, ROE, growth in sales, earnings, and dividends, to name just a few) and the accountant plays a major role in identifying these goals, in helping to achieve them, and in measuring the degree to which they have been accomplished.

Emphasis on the future is a principal characteristic that makes managerial accounting different from financial accounting. Anticipating what revenues will be and forecasting the expenses that will be incurred to achieve those revenues are principal activities of the budgeting process. Another difference between managerial accounting and financial accounting that is emphasized in planning is breadth of focus. Financial accounting deals primarily with the financial statements for the organization as a whole; managerial accounting is more concerned with units within the organization. Thus, even though an overall company ROI objective is established, effective planning requires that the planned impact of the activities and results of each unit (division, product line, plant, sales territory, and so on) of the organization be considered.

Measuring results involves using the historical data of financial accounting, and because of the time required to perform financial accounting procedures, there is usually a time lag of weeks or months between the end of an accounting period and the issuance of financial statements. However, for performance feedback to be most effective, it should be provided as quickly as possible after action has been completed. Management accounting is not constrained by generally accepted accounting principles, and so approximate results can be quickly generated for use in the control process. In other words, relevant data, even though not absolutely accurate in a financial accounting sense, are useful for evaluating performance soon after an activity has been completed.

Exhibit 12–1 summarizes the principal differences between managerial accounting and financial accounting.

If time and effort have been devoted to develop a plan, it is appropriate to attempt to control the activities of the organization so that the goals of the plan are accomplished. Many of the activities of the managerial accountant are related to cost control; this control emphasis will be seen in most of the managerial accounting ideas that are explained in these chapters.

Another management concept relevant to the control process is that if an individual is to be held accountable, or responsible, for the results of an activity, that individual must also have the authority to influence those results. If a manager is to be held responsible for costs incurred by a unit of the organization, the financial results reported for that unit should not include costs incurred by other units that have been arbitrarily assigned to the unit being evaluated, nor should the results reflect costs that the manager being held responsible cannot control.

Management accountants work extensively with people in other

EXHIBIT 12–1 Managerial Accounting Compared to Financial Accounting

Characteristic	Managerial Accounting	Financial Accounting
Service perspective	Internal to managers	External to stockholders
Time frame	Present and future for planning and control	Past—financial statements are historical
Breadth of concern	Micro—individual units of the organization plan and act	Macro—financial statements are for the organization as a whole
Reporting frequency and promptness	Control reports issued frequently (e.g., daily) and promptly (e.g., one day after period-end)	Most financial statements issued monthly, a week or more after month-end
Degree of precision of data used	Reasonable accuracy desired, but "close counts"	High accuracy desired, with time usually available to achieve it
Reporting standards	None imposed because of internal and pragmatic orientation	Imposed by generally accepted accounting principles and FASB

functional areas of the organization. For example, industrial engineers and management accountants work together to develop **production standards,** which are the expected or allowed times and costs to make a product or perform an activity. Management accountants help production people interpret performance reports, which compare actual and planned production and costs. Sales personnel, the marketing staff, and management accountants are involved in estimating a future period's sales. Personnel professionals and management accountants work together to determine the cost effect of compensation changes. These few examples illustrate the need for management accountants to have a breadth of knowledge and interest about the organization in particular and its operating environment in general. The examples also suggest that it is appropriate for persons in other functional areas to have a general understanding of managerial accounting. Helping you to achieve that general understanding is the objective of this and the next four chapters of this book. The topics to be discussed are:

Cost classifications and cost accounting systems.

Cost-profit-volume analysis.

Budgeting and performance reporting.

Standard costs and variance analysis.

Capital budgeting.

COST CLASSIFICATIONS

The term *cost* means different things to different people, and in the management planning and decision-making process, it is important that costs appropriate to the situation be used, and that everyone involved in any given situation understand the costs being used. The cost classifications most frequently encountered are:

For cost accounting purposes:
  Product cost
  Period cost

Relationship to product or activity:
  Direct cost
  Indirect cost

Relationship between total cost and volume of activity:
  Variable cost
  Fixed cost

Time-frame perspective:
  Controllable cost
  Noncontrollable cost

For other analytical purposes:
Differential cost
Allocated cost
Sunk cost
Opportunity cost

These classifications are not mutually exclusive. Thus a cost might be identified as a "controllable, variable, direct, product cost."

Costs for Cost Accounting Purposes

Cost accounting relates to the determination of product, process, or service costs. In addition to being useful for management planning and control, **product costs** are used by manufacturers and merchandisers to determine inventory values and, when the product is sold, the amount of cost of goods sold. This is, of course, a financial accounting use of product cost. Even though service firms do not usually produce items for inventory, their costs of providing services will also be identified and analyzed for management planning and control purposes.

The product costing emphasis in the financial accounting chapters of this book focused on the cost-flow assumption (FIFO, LIFO, weighted average) used by merchandising firms. We now focus on the components of product cost of a manufacturing firm, although the cost-flow assumption issues apply to the inventories of manufacturing firms too.

Product costing for a manufacturer is more complex than for a merchandiser because making a product is more complex than buying an already finished product. However, the accounting concepts involved are the same. The cost of the product is recorded and reported as an asset (inventory) until the product is sold, when the cost is transferred to the income statement (cost of goods sold) as an expense to be matched with the revenue that resulted from the sale. The difference between a manufacturer and a merchandiser is illustrated schematically in the following diagram.

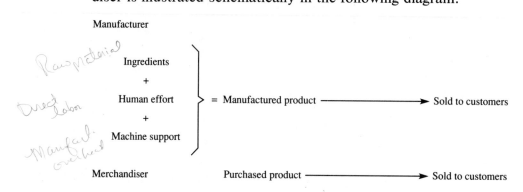

The cost associated with each of the inputs of a manufactured product is classified as raw materials, direct labor, or manufacturing overhead.

Raw materials are the ingredients of the product—the materials that are put into the production process and from which the finished product is made. The cost of raw materials includes the same items as the product cost of a merchandiser. The finished product of one process or company may be the raw material of another process or company. For example, corn is the raw material of a corn processor, and one of the processor's finished products may be corn syrup. The candy manufacturer uses the corn syrup as a raw material of its products.

Direct labor is the effort provided by workers who are directly involved with the manufacture of the product. For example, workers who perform machine operations on raw materials, workers who operate or control raw material conversion equipment (melters, mixers, heat treaters, coolers, and evaporators), workers who assemble or package the product, and supervisors of these workers are directly involved in manufacturing. Their compensation costs would be considered direct labor costs.

Manufacturing overhead, or **overhead,** includes all manufacturing costs except those for raw materials and direct labor. Overhead is an indirect cost because it is not feasible to specifically relate overhead items to individual products. Examples of overhead

EXHIBIT 12–2   Accounting for Product and Period Costs

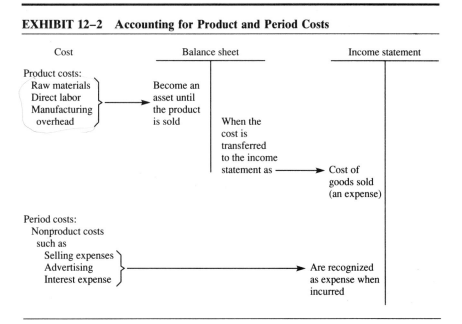

costs include factory utilities, maintenance and housekeeping costs (both materials and labor), depreciation expense for the factory building and production equipment, and compensation of production managers and supervisors.

As the manufacturing process becomes more complex and more technologically oriented, overhead costs generally become more significant. The development of robotic production methods, for example, has resulted in increased overhead costs. Planning and controlling overhead has become an increasingly important activity in many firms.

Costs not included in inventory as product costs are reported in the income statement as incurred. These are the selling, general, and administrative costs or operating expenses of the firm, and are called **period costs** because they are recorded as expense in the accounting period in which they were incurred. Accounting for product and period costs is illustrated in Exhibit 12–2.

Cost Accounting Systems — General

Every manufacturing firm has a cost accounting system that is used to accumulate the cost of the products made. Very few firms manufacture a single unit of a unique product; most firms produce a quantity of product in a production run. Cost accounting systems are frequently very complex and are designed for the specific needs of individual companies, but virtually all systems have the general characteristics described below.

A manufacturing cost accounting system involves three inventory accounts: *Raw Materials, Work in Process,* and *Finished Goods.* The **Raw Materials Inventory** account holds the cost of materials (e.g., for a sailboat manufacturer — glass fiber cloth, epoxy resin, wood, sailcloth, deck fittings, and rope), parts, and assemblies that will be used in the manufacturing process. The **Work in Process Inventory** account is used to accumulate all of the manufacturing costs, including raw materials, direct labor, and manufacturing overhead. When the manufacturing process is complete, the cost of the items made is transferred to the **Finished Goods Inventory** account. At the end of the accounting period each of these inventory accounts may have a balance. For Raw Materials and Finished Goods the balance represents the cost of the items on hand at the end of the month. For Work in Process, the balance represents the sum of the costs incurred to that date for products that have been started in production but that have not been completed at the end of the period. The Work in Process Inventory account balance will be relatively small (or zero) for production processes that are of short duration or that are cleared out at the end of the period (e.g., candy manufacturing or food processing). Work in Process Inventory is likely to exist for firms that have relatively long-duration manufacturing processes, but the account balance will usually be low relative to Raw Materials and Finished Goods. When a manufactured item is sold, its cost is transferred from the balance sheet Finished Goods Inventory account to cost of goods sold in the income statement. Exhibit 12–3 illustrates and compares the flow of product costs for a manufacturing firm and a merchandising firm.

Determining the cost of a single unit of a manufactured product is done by averaging the total material, labor, and overhead costs incurred in the manufacture of some quantity of the product. Determining the raw material and labor costs is usually fairly easy; raw material inventory usage records and time records for direct labor workers provide these data. It is the assignment of overhead costs that presents the challenge. Most cost systems apply overhead to production by using a single, or at most a very few, surrogate measures of overhead behavior. One of the most popular bases is direct labor hours. Other bases include direct labor cost, machine hours, raw material usage, and number of units made. The simplifying assumption is that overhead is incurred because product is being made, and the number of direct labor hours (or other base) used on a particular production run is a fair indicator of the overhead incurred for that production run. Given this relationship, at the beginning of the year an estimate is made of both the total overhead expected to be incurred during the year and the total direct labor hours (or other base) expected to be used. Estimated total overhead cost is divided by the estimated total direct labor hours (or other base) to get a **predetermined overhead application rate** per direct labor hour (or other base). To illustrate product costing and other cost and managerial accounting concepts, the hypothetical firm Cruisers, Inc., a manufacturer of fiber-glass sailboats, will be used. Exhibit 12–4 illustrates how the cost of a boat made during the month of April can be determined. Note that the first step is the determination of the predetermined overhead application rate. This is shown in Section I of Exhibit 12–4. Then overhead is assigned to specific production runs based on this predetermined overhead application rate. This is illustrated in Section II of Exhibit 12–4. If multiple overhead application bases (e.g., direct labor hours and quantity of a certain raw material used) are used, the estimated overhead cost associated with each base is divided by the estimated usage of each base to develop the separate **overhead application rates.** Study Exhibit 12–4 to see how cost components are accumulated and then averaged to get the cost of a single unit.

EXHIBIT 12–3   Flow of Cost Comparison — Manufacturer and Merchandiser

I. Manufacturer

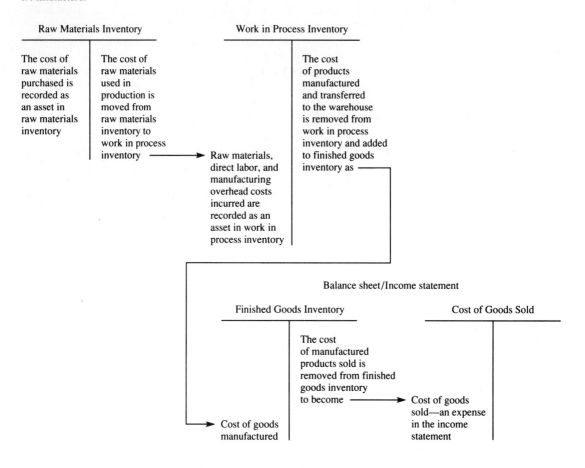

II. Merchandiser

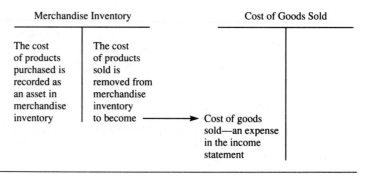

EXHIBIT 12–4 Product Costing Illustration

I. Determination of overhead application rate

Assumptions:

Overhead costs are incurred in proportion to the number of direct labor hours worked; therefore the overhead application rate is based on direct labor hours.

Estimated total overhead cost to be incurred for the year: $840,000.

Estimated total direct labor hours to be worked in the year: 60,000.

$$\text{Overhead application rate} = \frac{\text{Estimated total overhead cost}}{\text{Estimated total direct labor hours}}$$

$$= \$840,000/60,000 \text{ hours}$$

$$= \$14/\text{direct labor hour}$$

II. Determination of product cost

Assumptions:

During April, 86 Model 21 sailboats were made. Costs incurred and time involved were:

Raw materials cost	$368,510
Direct labor cost	$330,240
Direct labor hours	20,640 hours

The cost of each boat is determined by dividing the total cost of making the boats by the number of boats made:

Raw materials	$368,510
Direct labor	330,240
Overhead (20,640 direct labor hours × the overhead application rate of $14/hour)	288,960
Total cost	$987,710
Cost per boat ($987,710/86 boats)	$ 11,485

In recent years overhead costs have become an increasingly significant part of product cost, and managers have needed higher quality cost information to permit greater control and better responses to increased competition. The application of overhead on the basis of a single or a few broad rates based on direct labor hours and or machine hours has been replaced in many firms by an **activity based costing** (ABC) system. An ABC system involves accumulating overhead cost by activity, such as machine setup, quality inspection, production order preparation, materials handling activity, and so on, and then applying overhead to production based on the activity required for each job or product. This refinement in the identification of the activity base used for manufacturing overhead application has led to more accurate costing and has supported more effective management of the production process. The development of an ABC system is a complex process involving considerable analysis and a significant investment, but for most firms the planning, controlling, and decision-making benefits of the system have exceeded the development costs.

Although the costing process involves estimates and provides an overall average, many firms do an excellent job of estimating both total overhead costs and total activity, resulting in quite accurate overhead application and product costing. Because the predetermined overhead application rate calculation is based on estimates, at the end of the year there will be a difference between the total overhead costs actually incurred and the costs applied to production during the year. This difference is called **overapplied overhead** or **underapplied overhead.** At the end of the year, if the overapplied or underapplied overhead is small relative to total overhead costs incurred, it is transferred to cost of goods sold. If it is material, it is allocated between inventories and cost of goods sold in proportion to the total overhead included in each. On a monthly basis the overapplied or underapplied overhead is carried forward in the Manufacturing Overhead account. The reason for this is that estimates for the whole year were used to calculate the predetermined overhead application rate, and variations in cost and activity that occur one month may be offset in a subsequent month. Thus, a better matching of revenue and expense usually occurs if the overapplied or underapplied overhead adjustment is made only at the end of the year.

Exhibit 12–5 illustrates the flow of these costs through the accounts of Cruisers, Inc., for April. Note the use of the Manufacturing Overhead account. This is an account that functions as an asset-type clearing account. Actual manufacturing overhead costs incurred are recorded as increases (debits) in this account, and the manufacturing overhead applied to Work in Process is a reduction (credit) to the account. The Manufacturing Overhead account will not have any balance at the beginning or end of the year because, as already stated, the balance represents overapplied or underapplied overhead that is transferred to Cost of Goods Sold or allocated between inventories and Cost of Goods Sold. However, at month-ends during the year the account is likely to have a relatively small overapplied or underapplied balance. This is the case in the Exhibit 12–5 illustration.

EXHIBIT 12–5   Cruisers, Inc., Flow of Costs for April

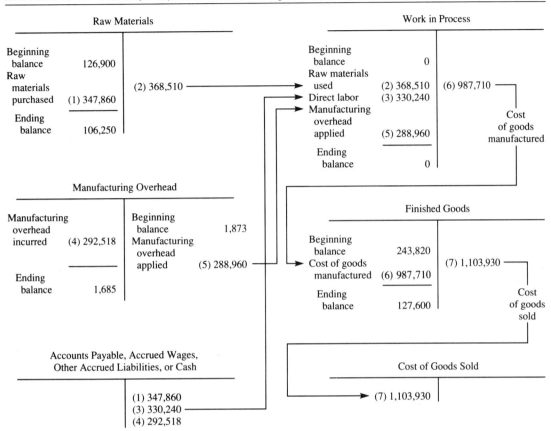

Explanation of transactions:
(1) Purchase of raw materials on account.
(2) Cost of raw materials used transferred to Work in Process.
(3) Direct labor costs for the month increase Work in Process and increase Accrued Wages or decrease Cash.
(4) Actual manufacturing overhead costs incurred for the month increase Manufacturing Overhead and increase Accounts Payable, Accrued Wages, or Other Accrued Liabilities, or decrease Cash.
(5) Manufacturing Overhead applied to Work in Process using the predetermined overhead application rate and the actual activity base (direct labor hours, for example).
(6) Cost of goods manufactured transferred from Work in Process to Finished Goods inventory.
(7) Cost of good sold transferred from Finished Goods inventory to Cost of Good Sold.

Manufacturing costs can be summarized and reported in a **statement of cost of goods manufactured.** Such a statement using amounts for Cruisers, Inc., for April is illustrated in Exhibit 12–6. Although it was assumed that there were no beginning or ending inventories for work in process, Exhibit 12–6 illustrates how work in process balances would be reported in this statement.

EXHIBIT 12–6

CRUISERS, INC.
Statement of Cost of Goods Manufactured
For the Month of April

Raw Materials:

Inventory, March 31	$126,900	
Purchases during April	347,860	
Raw materials available for use	$474,760	
Less: Inventory, April 30	(106,250)	
Cost of raw materials used		$368,510
Direct labor cost incurred during April		330,240
Manufacturing overhead applied during April		288,960
Total manufacturing costs incurred in April		$987,710
Add: Work in process inventory, March 31		–0–
Less: Work in process inventory, April 30		–0–
Cost of goods manufactured during April		$987,710

To calculate cost of goods sold for April the cost of goods manufactured is added to the beginning inventory of finished goods to get the cost of goods available for sale. The ending inventory of finished goods is subtracted from goods available for sale to arrive at cost of goods sold.

The determination of cost of goods sold for April will depend on the type of inventory system in use. If the periodic system is used, the cost of the ending inventory will be determined and the cost of goods sold model will be used:

Beginning inventory	$ 243,820
Cost of goods manufactured	987,710
Cost of goods available for sale	$1,231,530
Less: Ending inventory	(127,600)
Cost of goods sold	$1,103,930

If the perpetual system is used, the cost of each unit of product will be calculated, and cost of goods sold is the number of units sold multiplied by the cost of each.

To summarize, product costs attach themselves to the product being manufactured and are treated as an expense when the product is sold (or is lost, becomes worthless from obsolescence, or is otherwise no longer an asset to the firm). Period costs—selling, general, and administrative expenses — are reported in the income statement of the period in which those costs were incurred. Another way to distinguish between product and period costs is to think of product costs as manufacturing costs, and period costs as nonmanufacturing costs.

Cost Accounting Systems — Job Order Costing, Process Costing, and Hybrid Costing

The general cost accounting system illustrated in the prior section must be adapted to fit the manufacturing environment of the entity. A **job order costing system** is used when discrete products, such as a sailboat, are manufactured. Each production run is treated as a separate "job." Costs are accumulated for each job, as illustrated in Exhibit 12–4 for Cruisers' production of 86 Model 21 sailboats, and the cost per unit is determined by dividing the total costs incurred by the number of units made. During any accounting period a number of "jobs," or production runs of different products, may be worked on. For any "job" or production run, costs are accumulated, and cost per unit of product made is calculated as illustrated for the Model 21 sailboat.

When the manufacturing environment involves essentially homogeneous products that are made in a more or less continuous process, frequently involving several departments, it is not feasible to accumulate product cost by job so a **process costing system** is used. The processing of corn into meal, starch, and syrup is an example of an activity for which process costing would be applicable. The objectives of process costing and job order costing are the same: to assign raw material, direct labor, and manufacturing overhead costs to products and to provide a means to compute the unit cost of each item made. In process costing, costs are accumulated by department (rather than by job) and are assigned to the products processed through the department.

The accumulation of costs by department is relatively straightforward, but the existence of work in process inventories that are partially complete adds a complexity to the determination of the number of units of product over which the departmental costs are to be spread. For example, assume that during the month 100,000 units were transferred from the first department in the manufacturing sequence to the next department, and at the end of the month 15,000 units in inventory were 50 percent completed. Production during the month is stated in **equivalent units of production,** the number of units that would have been produced if all production efforts during the month had resulted in completed products. In this example the costs incurred by the first department during the period (including costs in the beginning inventory) would be spread over 107,500 units — the 100,000 units completed plus 50 percent × 15,000 ending inventory units — to get the cost per unit for work of this department. This is the cost per unit for items transferred to the next department, and the cost used to value the first department's ending inventory. Costs of subsequent departments include costs of prior departments. Ultimately, all production costs are transferred to Finished Goods Inventory.

As manufacturing firms have sought to increase efficiency and to lower costs in recent years, production processes have been developed that mix elements of job order and continuous process manufacturing environments. Whether labeled flexible manufacturing, batch manufacturing, just-in-time manufacturing, or something else, most of these processes involve streamlined work flow, tighter inventory controls, and extensive use of automated equipment. Hybrid costing systems have evolved for these processes. Hybrid cost accounting systems mix elements of job order and process costing systems to accomplish the objective of assigning manufacturing costs to units produced. It is important to recognize that cost accounting systems will change in response to changes in the production process; the opposite should not be true.

Cost Accounting Systems — Absorption Costing and Direct Costing

The cost accounting systems described above are **absorption costing** systems because all of the manufacturing costs incurred are absorbed in to the product cost. An alternative system, called **direct costing** or **variable costing,** assigns only variable costs to products; fixed manufacturing costs are treated as operating expenses of the period in which they are incurred. (Variable and fixed costs are described in the following section.) Absorption costing must be used for financial and income tax reporting purposes because fixed manufacturing overhead is part of the cost of a product. However, some managers are willing to incur the additional expense of using a direct (or variable) costing system for internal planning and control purposes, because it results in product and inventory values that reflect the relationship between total cost and volume of activity (see below).

The distinction between absorption costing and direct costing focuses on *manufacturing overhead* costs only. Raw material and direct labor are always product costs, and selling, general, and administrative expenses are always treated as operating expenses of the period in which they are incurred. Under absorption costing *both* variable and fixed manufacturing overhead are considered product cost and are applied to work in process. Under direct costing only variable manufacturing overhead is a product cost applied to work in process; fixed manufacturing overhead is treated as a period cost and recorded as an operating expense when incurred. Exhibit 12–7 is a schematic diagram illustrating these alternative systems.

The significance of the distinction between absorption costing and direct costing is a function of the change in ending inventory. If inventories have increased, under absorption costing the fixed manufacturing overhead related to the inventory increase is in the balance sheet, but under direct costing it is an expense in the income statement. Thus when inventories increase, under absorption costing expenses are lower and profits are higher than under direct costing. The opposite is true when inventories decrease. Direct costing advocates point out that absorption costing gives an erroneous profit signal to managers. These advocates maintain that greater profits should result in periods when the firm's sales result in inventory decreases than in periods when production has exceeded sales and inventories increase.

EXHIBIT 12–7   Cost Flows — Absorption Costing and Direct (Variable) Costing

Balance sheet / Income statement

I. Absorption costing

Manufacturing Overhead		Work in Process	Operating Expenses
Variable and fixed overhead incurred	Variable and fixed overhead applied to work in process ⟶		

II. Direct (variable) costing

Manufacturing Overhead		Work in Process	Operating Expenses
Variable overhead incurred	Variable overhead applied to work in process ⟶		Fixed overhead incurred

For financial reporting and income tax purposes, firms that use direct costing must make a year-end adjustment to reclassify from the income statement Operating Expense account to the Finished Goods and Work in Process Inventory account balances that part of the fixed manufacturing overhead incurred during the year that relates to the ending inventory. The amount of fixed manufacturing overhead to be reclassified can be calculated fairly easily based on the proportion of the variable cost of ending inventory to the total variable manufacturing costs incurred during the year.

Do not confuse the product costing procedure with what you may have experienced in a repair shop where the price you pay is based on material cost and labor hours multiplied by a rate that includes the labor cost, overhead cost, and an amount to cover administrative costs and profit. This is a technique for arriving at the price a customer is to be charged and, although similar in concept to product costing, the result is selling price, not product cost.

Relationship of Cost to Product or Activity

Direct cost and **indirect cost** are terms used to relate a cost to a product or activity.

Whether a cost is direct or indirect depends on the context within which the term is being used. When describing product cost, raw materials and direct labor are direct costs, and overhead is an indirect cost. However, when evaluating the profitability of a product line, the total product cost would be a direct cost, as would be the specific advertising and marketing costs associated with the product. The costs of a training program designed to make the sales force more effective with all of the firm's product lines would be an indirect cost. One way of distinguishing between a direct and an indirect cost is to think of a direct cost as a cost that would *not* be incurred if the product or activity were discontinued. An indirect cost is one that would continue to be incurred if the product or activity were discontinued.

The classification of a cost as direct or indirect is significant only in the context of the cost's relationship to a product or activity.

Relationship of Total Cost to Volume of Activity

The relationship of total cost to volume of activity describes the **cost behavior pattern,** one of the most important cost classification methods to understand. The two cost behavior patterns are variable and fixed. A **variable cost** is one that changes *in total* as the volume of activity changes. A cost that does not change *in total* as the volume of activity changes is a **fixed cost.** For example, raw material costs have a variable cost behavior pattern because the greater the number of units produced, the higher the total raw material costs incurred. On the other hand, factory building depreciation expense is a fixed cost because total depreciation expense will not change regardless of the level of production (unless, of course, a units-of-production method to calculate depreciation is used — in which case this cost would be variable). The distinction between fixed and variable cost behavior patterns is illustrated graphically in Exhibit 12–8.

The fixed or variable label refers to the behavior of *total* cost relative to a change in activity. When referring to the behavior of unit costs, however, the labels may be confusing because variable costs are constant per unit, but fixed costs per unit will change based on the change in the units of activity. Thus it is necessary to understand the behavior pattern on both a total cost basis and a per unit basis. Variable costs change in total as activity changes but are constant per unit. Fixed costs do not change in total as activity changes but will vary if expressed on a per unit of activity basis.

Knowledge of cost behavior pattern is important to the planning process, and several simplifying assumptions are usually made to facilitate the use of this cost characteristic. The most significant assumption has to do with the range of activity over which the identified or assumed cost behavior pattern exists. This is the **relevant range** assumption, and it is most applicable to fixed costs.

EXHIBIT 12–8   Cost Behavior Patterns

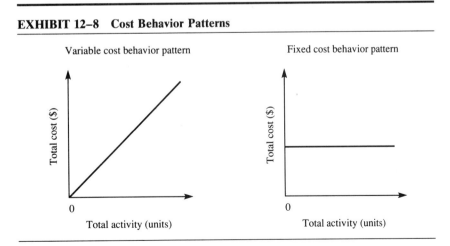

Returning to the depreciation expense example, it is clear that at some point an increase in the volume of production would require more plant capacity, and depreciation expense would increase. On the other hand, if substantially lower production volumes were anticipated in the future, some of the factory would be closed down or converted to other use, and depreciation expense would decrease. To say that depreciation expense is fixed is to say that over some relevant range of production the total cost will not change. Different fixed expenses will have different relevant ranges over which they have a fixed cost behavior pattern. When a cost is identified as fixed and cost projections are made based on that cost behavior pattern classification, the limits of the relevant range assumption must be considered. The other major simplifying assumption is that the cost behavior pattern is linear, not curvilinear. This assumption relates primarily to variable costs. Because of economies of scale, quantity discounts, and other factors, variable costs will change slightly when expressed on a per unit basis. These changes are usually not significant, but if they are, appropriate adjustment in unit costs should be made in analyses based on cost behavior patterns. These assumptions are illustrated and described in more detail in the next chapter.

It is clear that not all costs can be classified as either variable or fixed. Some costs are partly fixed and partly variable. Sometimes costs with this mixed behavior pattern are called **semivariable costs.** Utilities for the factory, for example, have a mixed behavior pattern because when the plant isn't operating, some lights must be kept on for safety and security, but as production increases more electricity is required. Analytical techniques can break this type of cost into its fixed and variable components, and a **cost formula** can be developed, expressed as:

Total cost = Fixed cost + Variable cost

= Fixed amount + (Variable rate per unit × Activity)

This cost formula can then be used to forecast the total cost expected to be incurred at various levels of activity. For example, assume that it has been determined that the fixed cost for utilities is $850 per month, and that the variable rate for utilities is 3 cents per direct labor hour. Total utilities cost for a month in which 6,000 direct labor hours were planned would be estimated to be:

Total cost = $850 + ($.03 × 6,000 direct labor hours)

= $1,030

Great care must be taken with the use of fixed cost per unit data because any change in the volume of activity will change the per

---

EXHIBIT 12–9   The Error of Unitizing Fixed Costs

Assume the following university business office costs per month associated with providing a student check cashing privilege.

Salary	$ 900
Allocated Space Cost	
(depreciation, utilities, etc.) . . .	300
Total.	$1,200 per month

If 2,000 checks are cashed in a month, the "cost" per check is
($1,200/2,000 checks) . . . . . . $ .60
If 6,000 checks are cashed in a month, the "cost" per check is
($1,200/6,000 checks) . . . . . . $ .20

How much does it "cost" to cash a check?

What action would students take if they learned that a check-cashing fee was being considered based on the "cost" of cashing a check during the coming month?

---

unit cost. As a general rule, *do not unitize fixed expenses because they do not behave on a per unit basis!* For example, most of the costs of a college business office — salaries, depreciation, and utilities — are fixed; to calculate the "cost" of cashing student checks by dividing a portion of business office costs by the number of checks cashed in a period of time gives a misleading result because if more or fewer checks were cashed, the total cost would probably not change. Sometimes fixed costs must be unitized, as in the development of a predetermined overhead application rate described earlier. Sometimes it is important to recognize that the relevant range is quite wide, and significant increases in activity can be achieved without increasing fixed costs (i.e., there are economies of scale to be achieved that result in efficiencies and a reduction of fixed cost per unit). However, whenever fixed costs are unitized, be very careful about the conclusions that you draw from the data. Exhibit 12–9 focuses on the error of unitizing fixed costs.

Cost Classification According to a Time-Frame Perspective

Frequently, reference is made to a "noncontrollable" cost, which implies that there is really nothing the manager can do to influence the amount of the cost. This may be true in the short run (e.g., for the coming quarter or year), but in the long run every cost incurred by the organization is controllable by someone. For example, real estate taxes on a firm's plant and office facilities cannot usually be influenced by management in the short run because the assessed valuation and tax rates are established by the taxing authorities. However, when the decision was made to build or buy the facilities, the relative level of property taxes was established. Land in a prime location and a fancy building with plenty of space for possible expansion could be expected to result in higher property taxes over the years than more modest facilities. The point is not whether appropriate facilities were obtained; the point is that the decision makers (top management or board of directors) had control over the general level of property taxes when the decision was being made. It is not appropriate to think of any cost as being noncontrollable over all time frames.

To eliminate the potential for fuzzy thinking that the controllable/noncontrollable classification may encourage, many firms use the terms *committed cost* and *discretionary cost*. A **committed cost** is one that is going to be incurred because of long-range policy decisions that have been made. A **discretionary cost** is one that can be adjusted in the short-run. Examples are presented here.

Committed Costs	*Discretionary Costs*
Real estate taxes	Support of company softball
Advertising (especially for	team
a consumer products	Contributions
company)	Junior executive attendance
Quality control	at conventions
Depreciation	

The control issue with respect to committed costs is not that they are incurred but that control efforts should instead be focused on whether the cost is appropriate for the value received from its incurrence.

There are significant nonfinancial considerations to be made when beginning or curtailing discretionary costs, but managers do have short-term discretion about the level of cost to be incurred.

Cost Classifications for Other Analytical Purposes

Differential costs are brought into focus when possible future activities are analyzed. A differential cost is one that will differ according to the alternative activity that is selected. For example, if a modification of an existing product is being considered, only the changes in cost resulting from the modification need to be considered relative to the additional revenues expected to result from the modification. Those costs that will continue to be incurred whether or not the modification is made are not relevant to the modification decision.

Allocated costs are those that have been assigned to a product or activity (a "cost center") using some sort of arithmetic process. For example, overhead costs are allocated to production runs using the overhead application rate, the derivation of which was described earlier. The topic of cost allocation will be covered in more detail in Chapter 14, but at this point a warning about cost allocations is appropriate. Many cost allocation methods are very arbitrary and do not result in assigning costs in a way that reflects the reasons the costs were incurred. Therefore, managers must be very careful about the conclusions made from an analysis that includes allocated costs. A general rule, similar to that proscribing the unitization of fixed costs, is appropriate to learn: *Do not arbitrarily allocate costs to a cost center because the allocated costs may not behave the way assumed in the allocation method.*

A **sunk cost** is a cost that has been incurred and cannot be unincurred, or reversed, by some future action. For example, if a firm has acquired a special purpose asset that would not be useful to any other organization, the cost of the asset represents a sunk cost. If the asset is put in use, its cost will be shown as depreciation expense over its life; if scrapped, its net book value will be recorded as a loss. Either way, the cost of the asset will be reflected in the income statement. When a new car is driven out of the dealer's lot, a sunk cost equal to the loss in value that occurs because the car is now "used" has been incurred. Sunk costs are never relevant to the analysis of alternative future actions (i.e., they are never differential costs) because they have been incurred and will not change.

Opportunity cost is an economic concept that is too frequently overlooked in accounting analyses. Opportunity cost is the income that has not been earned because an asset was not invested at a rate of return that could have been earned. For example, if you keep a $200 minimum balance in a noninterest earning checking account for which no service charge would be assessed regardless of balance, instead of investing the $200 in a 6 percent savings account, the opportunity cost of that decision is $12 per year (6% × $200). Because opportunity cost relates to a transaction that did not occur, no record of it is made in the accounting records; thus it is often overlooked. Awareness of opportunity cost raises the question: What other alternatives are there for earning a return on a particular asset?

SUMMARY

Management is the process of planning, organizing, and controlling an organization's activities to accomplish its goals. Managerial accounting (sometimes called *management accounting*) supports the management process.

Managerial accounting differs from financial accounting in several ways. The most significant differences are in the areas of who is served and of the time dimension. Managerial accounting is internally oriented and has a future perspective.

There are different costs for different purposes. Cost terminology is important to understand if cost data are to be used appropriately.

Cost accounting systems distinguish between product costs and period costs. Product costs for a merchandising firm are the costs associated with the product that is for sale. Product costs for a manufacturing firm include raw materials, direct labor, and manufacturing overhead. Period costs, such as selling, general, and administrative expenses, are reported as expenses in the fiscal period in which they are incurred.

Cost accounting systems account for the flow of product costs into work in process inventory, the transfer of cost of goods manufactured out of work in process inventory into finished goods inventory, and finally to cost of goods sold when the product is sold. One of the challenging objectives of the cost accounting system is assigning manufacturing overhead to products made. Whatever the cost accounting system, ultimately the cost of a single unit of product is the sum of the costs incurred to make a quantity of units divided by the number of units made.

The difference between absorption costing and direct (or variable) costing is in the accounting for fixed manufacturing overhead. In absorption costing, fixed manufacturing overhead is a product cost. In direct (or variable) costing, fixed manufacturing overhead is a period cost.

Costs can be classified as direct or indirect, relative to a particular product or activity.

The cost behavior pattern of a cost relates to the change in total cost for a change in activity. Variable costs change, in total, as activity changes. Fixed costs remain constant in total as activity changes. Assumptions about linearity and relevant range are implicit when a cost is described as variable or fixed. Many costs have a mixed behavior pattern (i.e., they are partly variable and partly fixed).

A cost formula expresses the total amount of a cost for a given level of activity by combining the fixed and variable elements of the total cost.

It is inappropriate, and may be misleading, to express a fixed cost on a per unit basis because by definition a fixed cost is constant over a range of activity.

Costs that are controllable in the short run are usually called *discretionary costs*. Costs that are controllable only in the long run are called *committed costs*. However, all costs are controllable by someone over some time frame.

When an analysis of costs involved in alternative plans is made, differential costs are those that differ between alternatives. Sometimes cost allocations are made for analytical purposes. If the allocation is made on an arbitrary basis rather than by recognizing causal factors, users of the data must be very careful about the conclusions they reach because cost behavior has not been accurately reflected. Sunk costs have been incurred and cannot be reversed. Opportunity cost is not reflected in the accounting records but should be recognized when making an economic analysis.

KEY TERMS AND CONCEPTS

absorption costing *(p. 378)*   A product costing process in which both variable and fixed manufacturing costs are included in product costs.

activity based costing *(p. 373)*   The process of accumulating manufacturing overhead cost by production support activity (e.g., machine setup) and then applying manufacturing overhead to production based on the activity required for each job or product.

allocated cost *(p. 385)*   A cost that has been assigned to a product or activity using some sort of arithmetic process.

committed cost *(p. 384)*   A cost that is incurred because of a long-range policy decision.

cost accounting *(p. 363)*   A subset of managerial accounting that relates to the determination and accumulation of product, process, or service costs.

cost behavior pattern *(p. 380)*   Identification of whether a cost is fixed or variable.

cost formula *(p. 382)*   An arithmetic expression that reflects the fixed and variable elements of a cost.

differential cost *(p. 384)*   A cost that will differ based on the selection of an alternative activity.

direct cost *(p. 380)*   A cost directly related to the product or activity under consideration; the cost would not be incurred if the product or activity were discontinued.

direct costing *(p. 378)*   A product costing process in which only variable manufacturing costs are included in product cost. Sometimes called *variable costing*.

direct labor *(p. 369)*   Effort provided by workers who are directly involved in the manufacture of a product.

discretionary cost *(p. 384)* A cost that can be raised or lowered in the short run.

equivalent units of production *(p. 377)* In a process costing system the number of units that would have been produced if all production efforts during the period had resulted in completed products.

finished goods inventory *(p. 370)* Inventory ready for sale to customers.

fixed cost *(p. 381)* A cost that does not change in total as the level of activity changes within a relevant range.

indirect cost *(p. 380)* A cost that is indirectly related to the product or activity under consideration; the cost would continue to be incurred if the product or activity were discontinued.

job order costing system *(p. 377)* A product costing system used when discrete products, or "jobs," are manufactured.

management process *(p. 365)* Planning, organizing, and controlling the activities of an organization so it can accomplish its purpose.

managerial accounting *(p. 363)* Accounting that uses economic and financial information to plan and control many of the activities of an entity, and to support the management decision-making process. Sometimes called *management accounting.*

manufacturing overhead, or overhead *(p. 369)* All manufacturing costs except those classified as raw materials or direct labor.

opportunity cost *(p. 385)* An economic concept relating to income forgone because an opportunity to earn income was not pursued.

overapplied overhead *(p. 374)* A credit balance in the manufacturing overhead account that results from applied overhead in excess of actual overhead costs.

overhead application rate *(p. 371)* The rate used to allocate overhead to specific production runs. See *predetermined overhead application rate.*

period costs *(p. 370)* Noninventoriable costs, *including selling, general, and administrative expenses,* that relate to an accounting period.

predetermined overhead application rate *(p. 371)* The rate per unit of activity (e.g., direct labor hour) used to apply manufacturing overhead to work in process.

process costing system *(p. 377)* A costing system used to accumulate costs for a production process that is more or less continuous, frequently involving several departments.

product costs *(p. 368)* Inventoriable costs including raw materials, direct labor, and manufacturing overhead.

production standard *(p. 367)* Expected or allowed times and costs to make a product or to perform an activity.

raw materials *(p. 369)* The ingredients of a product.

raw materials inventory *(p. 370)* Inventory of materials ready for the production process.

relevant range *(p. 381)* The range of activity over which the fixed or variable cost behavior pattern exists.

semivariable cost *(p. 382)* A cost that has both fixed and variable elements.

statement of cost of goods manufactured *(p. 375)* A supplementary financial statement that supports cost of goods sold, which is an element of the income statement. This statement summarizes raw materials, direct labor, and manufacturing overhead costs incurred during the period.

sunk cost *(p. 385)* A cost that has been incurred and that cannot be unincurred or reversed by some future action.

underapplied overhead *(p. 374)* A debit balance in the Manufacturing Overhead account that results from actual overhead costs in excess of applied overhead.

variable cost *(p. 381)* A cost that changes in total as the volume of activity changes.

variable costing *(p. 378)* A product costing process in which only variable manufacturing costs are included in product cost. Sometimes called *direct costing*.

work in process inventory *(p. 370)* Inventory account for the costs (raw materials, direct labor, and manufacturing overhead) of items that are in the process of being manufactured.

EXERCISES AND PROBLEMS

12–1. For each of the following costs, check the columns that most likely apply.

	Product				
	Direct	Indirect	Period	Variable	Fixed
Raw materials	____	____	____	____	____
Staples used to secure packed boxes of product	____	____	____	____	____
Plant janitors' wages	____	____	____	____	____
Order processing clerks' wages	____	____	____	____	____
Advertising expenses	____	____	____	____	____
Production workers' wages	____	____	____	____	____
Supervisors' salaries	____	____	____	____	____
Sales force commissions	____	____	____	____	____
Maintenance supplies used	____	____	____	____	____
President's salary	____	____	____	____	____
Electricity cost	____	____	____	____	____

	Product				
Real estate taxes for:	*Direct*	*Indirect*	*Period*	*Variable*	*Fixed*
Factory	———	———	———	———	———
Office building	———	———	———	———	———

12–2. Campus Carriers manufactures backpacks that are sold to students for use as book bags.

Required: Identify a specific item in this company's manufacturing, selling, or administrative processes for which the cost would be classified as:
a. Raw material.
b. Direct labor.
c. Variable manufacturing overhead.
d. Fixed manufacturing overhead.
e. Fixed administrative expense.
f. Indirect selling expense.
g. Variable, direct selling expense.

12–3. Assume that you have decided to drive your car to Florida for the spring break. A classmate learns about your plans and asks about riding with you. Explain how you would apply each of the following cost concepts to the task of determining how much, if any, cost you would take into consideration for the purposes of setting a price to be charged for taking the classmate with you.
a. Differential cost.
b. Allocated cost.
c. Sunk cost.
d. Opportunity cost.

12–4. Attending college involves incurring many costs. Give an example of a college cost that could be assigned to each of the following classifications. Explain your reason for assigning each cost to the classification.
a. Sunk cost.
b. Discretionary cost.
c. Committed cost.
d. Opportunity cost.

12–5. Halle Manufacturing Company makes wood products, including bowls, trays, and boxes. Manufacturing overhead is assigned to production using an application rate based on direct labor hours.

Required:
a. For 1993 the company's cost accountant estimated that total overhead costs incurred would be $118,000, and that a total of 36,875 direct labor hours would be worked. Calculate the amount of overhead to be applied to each production run for each direct labor hour worked on that production run.
b. A production run of 800 bowls required raw materials that cost $1,440, and 140 direct labor hours at a cost of $9.20 per direct labor hour. Calculate the cost of each bowl manufactured.
c. At the end of May 1993, 550 of the bowls made in the above production

run had been sold; the rest were still in inventory. Calculate the cost of the bowls sold that would have been reported in the income statement, and the cost to be included in the May 31, 1993, finished goods inventory.

12–6. Throwpot Co. makes ceramic vases. Manufacturing overhead is assigned to production on a machine-hour basis. For 1993 it was estimated that manufacturing overhead would total $45,000 and that 6,000 machine hours would be used.

Required:

a. Calculate the predetermined overhead application rate that will be used for absorption costing purposes during 1993.

b. During February 800 model CVG2 vases were made. Raw materials costing $960 were used, and direct labor costs totaled $4,400. Actual manufacturing overhead costs incurred during February totaled $4,000. Calculate the cost per vase made during February.

c. At the end of February, 670 of the vases were in finished goods inventory. Calculate the cost of the ending inventory and the cost of the vases sold during February.

12–7. Apple Polishing Co. processes slabs of raw granite into pieces for building walls and floors. Overhead is applied to finished product on the basis of machine hours required for cutting and polishing. A predetermined overhead application rate of $9.70 per machine hour was established for 1993.

Required:

a. If 8,400 machine hours were expected to be used during 1993, how much overhead was expected to be incurred?

b. Actual overhead incurred during 1993 totaled $81,480, and 8,200 actual machine hours were used during 1993. Calculate the amount of over- or underapplied overhead for the year.

c. Explain the accounting necessary for the over- or underapplied overhead for the year.

12–8. Waite Co. makes desk accessories. Manufacturing overhead is applied to production on a direct labor hours basis. During the first month of the company's fiscal year, $32,680 of manufacturing overhead was applied to Work in Process Inventory using the predetermined overhead application rate of $4 per direct labor hour.

Required:

a. Calculate the number of hours of direct labor used during March.

b. Actual manufacturing overhead costs incurred during March totaled $30,520. Calculate the amount of over- or underapplied overhead for March.

c. Identify two possible explanations for the over- or underapplied overhead.

d. Explain the accounting appropriate for the over- or underapplied overhead at the end of March.

12–9. The Regimental Tie Co. manufactures neckties and scarves. Two overhead application bases are used; some overhead is applied on the basis of raw material cost at a rate of 215 percent of material cost, and the balance of the overhead is applied at the rate of $3.10 per direct labor hour.

Required:

Calculate the cost per unit of a production run of 250 neckties that required:

a. Raw materials costing $820.

b. 32 direct labor hours at a total cost of $208.

12–10. Continental Mfg. Co. makes hand tools. Two manufacturing overhead application bases are used; some overhead is applied on the basis of machine hours at a rate of $6.30 per machine hour, and the balance of the overhead is applied at the rate of 280 percent of direct labor cost.

Required:

a. Calculate the cost per unit of a production run of 3,500 eight-inch screwdrivers that required:

1. Raw materials costing $380.
2. 16 direct labor hours costing $224.
3. 28 machine hours.

b. At the end of April, 2,800 of the above screwdrivers had been sold. Calculate the ending inventory value of the screwdrivers still in inventory at April 30.

12–11. The following table shows the amount of cost incurred in March for the cost items indicated. During March 3,000 units of the firm's single product were manufactured.

Raw materials.	$12,000
Factory depreciation expense.	9,000
Direct labor.	21,000
Factory manager's salary.	5,000
Computer rental expense.	4,800
Equipment repair expense	2,100

Required:

How much cost would you expect to be incurred for each of the above items during April when 4,500 units of the product are planned for production?

12–12. Sam estimated that the costs of insurance, license, depreciation, and so forth to operate his car totaled $240 per month, and that the gas, oil, and maintenance costs were 6 cents per mile. Sam also estimates that on average, he drives his car 1,200 miles per month.

Required:

a. How much cost would Sam expect to incur during April if he drove the car 1,146 miles?

b. Would it be meaningful for Sam to calculate an estimated average cost per mile for the car for a typical 1,200-mile month? Explain your answer.

12–13. Endeavor Co. manufactures kitchen utensils. During 1993 total costs associated with manufacturing 20,000 5-inch spatulas (a new product first introduced in 1993) were as follows:

Raw materials.	$25,720
Direct labor.	18,930

Manufacturing overhead:
Variable overhead	14,570
Fixed overhead	10,320

Required:

a. Calculate the cost per spatula under both direct (or variable) costing and absorption costing.

b. If 3,800 of these spatulas were in finished goods inventory at the end of 1993, by how much and in what direction (higher or lower) would 1993 gross profit be different under direct (or variable) costing than under absorption costing?

c. Express this spatula product cost in a cost formula. What does this cost formula suggest would be the total cost of making 100 more spatulas?

12–14. Hardshell Co. makes storage cases for 3.5-inch computer diskettes. Costs incurred making 15,000 cases in a typical recent month included $35,700 of fixed manufacturing overhead. The total absorption cost of a storage case is $5.62.

Required:

a. Calculate the direct (or variable) cost per storage case.

b. The ending inventory of 3.5-inch storage cases was 3,200 cases lower at the end of the month than at the beginning of the month. By how much and in what direction (higher or lower) would cost of goods sold for the month be different under direct (or variable) costing than under absorption costing?

c. Express the monthly costs of a 3.5-inch storage case in a cost formula.

d. If Hardshell Co. had an opportunity to sell 2,000 storage cases to an exporter at a price of $4.50 each and this incremental business would not affect the company's regular business, should the sale be considered? Explain your answer.

12–15. Curpay, Inc., incurred the following costs during March:

Raw materials	$36,800
Direct labor	79,300
Manufacturing overhead	47,200
Selling expenses	24,700
Administrative expenses	17,300
Interest expense	8,100

During the month 3,800 units of product were manufactured, and 3,500 units of the product were sold. There were no beginning inventories.

Required:

a. Calculate the total cost of goods manufactured during March and the average cost of a single unit of product.

b. Calculate the cost of goods sold during March.

c. Where in the financial statements will the difference between total cost of goods manufactured and total cost of goods sold be classified?

12–16. Sanderco, which manufactures a single product, incurred the following costs during January:

Raw materials	$25,300
Direct labor (1,600 hours)	20,800
Manufacturing overhead	37,000
Advertising expense	8,000
Administrative expenses	13,200

Manufacturing overhead is applied to work in process at the predetermined overhead application rate of $22 per direct labor hour. During the month 2,100 units of product were made, and 1,900 units were sold. There were no beginning inventories.

Required:

a. Calculate the average cost of a unit produced during the month.

b. Calculate the cost of the January 31 inventory of finished goods.

c. Comment about the usefulness of this product cost information for management planning and control purposes.

12–17. The following table summarizes the beginning and ending inventories of Demetro Co. for the month of September:

	August 31	September 30
Raw materials	$45,790	$53,430
Work in process	18,930	15,340
Finished goods	63,650	68,280

Raw materials purchases during September totaled $217,580. Direct labor costs incurred and manufacturing overhead costs applied during the month totaled $392,100 and $169,300, respectively.

Required:

a. Calculate the cost of goods manufactured during September.

b. Calculate the cost of goods sold during September.

12–18. Marble Co. uses an absorption cost system for accumulating product cost. The following data are available for the past year:

Raw materials purchases totaled $370,000.

Direct labor costs incurred for the year totaled $420,000.

Overhead is applied on the basis of machine hours used. When plans for the year were being made, it was estimated that total overhead costs would be $286,000, and that 22,000 machine hours would be used during the year.

Actual machine hours used during the year totaled 21,000 hours.

Actual general and administrative expenses for the year totaled $320,000.

Inventory balances at the beginning and end of the year were as follows:

	Beginning of Year	End of Year
Raw materials	21,000	16,000
Work in process	–0–	–0–
Finished goods	82,000	97,000

Required:

Calculate the following and show your work in a "model":

a. Predetermined overhead application rate.

b. Cost of raw materials used.

c. Overhead applied to Work in Process.

d. Cost of goods manufactured.

e. Cost of goods sold.

Chapter 13

Cost-Volume-Profit Analysis

Cost-volume-profit (CVP) analysis involves the use of knowledge about cost behavior patterns to interpret and forecast the changes in operating income that result from changes in revenues, changes in costs, or changes in the volume of activity. One especially important application of CVP analysis is determination of the break-even point for a company, or one of its units or products. Because CVP analysis emphasizes the cost behavior pattern of various costs and the impact on costs and profits of changes in the volume of activity, or products sold, it is very useful for planning and for evaluating actual results achieved.

LEARNING OBJECTIVES

After studying this chapter you should understand:

- What kinds of costs are likely to have a variable cost behavior pattern, and what kinds of costs are likely to have a fixed cost behavior pattern.
- How to use the high-low method to determine the cost formula for a cost that has a mixed—partly variable and partly fixed—behavior pattern.
- The difference between the traditional income statement format and the contribution margin income statement format.
- The importance of using the contribution margin format to analyze the impact of sales volume changes on operating income.
- The concept of operating leverage.
- How an expanded version of the contribution margin format, or model, can be used to analyze the impact of cost and volume changes on operating income.

- How contribution margin ratio is calculated, and how it can be used in cost-volume-profit analysis.
- How changes in sales mix can affect projections made with the contribution margin model.
- The meaning and significance of break-even point, and how the break-even point is calculated.

APPLICATIONS OF CVP ANALYSIS

Cost Behavior Pattern: The Key

Recall the cost behavior patterns described in Chapter 12. Variable costs change *in total* as activity changes, but are constant when expressed on a per unit basis. Fixed costs *do not change in total* as activity changes; if expressed on a per unit of activity basis (which is dangerous to do because the cost doesn't behave that way, and erroneous decisions or judgments could result), fixed costs change as activity changes.

Two simplifying assumptions are made in connection with cost behavior pattern determination. First, the behavior pattern is true only within a relevant range; if activity moves beyond the relevant range, the cost will change. Second, the cost behavior pattern identified is assumed to be linear within the relevant range, not curvilinear. These concepts were first mentioned in Chapter 12.

The relevant range idea relates to the level of activity over which a particular cost behavior pattern exists. For example, if the production capacity of the plant of Cruisers, Inc., is 90 Model 21 sailboats per month, additional equipment would be required if production of 120 boats per month was desired. The investment in additional equipment would result in an increase in depreciation expense. On the other hand, if long-term demand for the boat could be satisfied with a capacity of only 50 boats per month, it is likely that management would "mothball," or dispose of, some of the present capacity, and depreciation expense would fall. The graph on the following page illustrates a possible relationship between depreciation expense and capacity. The relevant range for depreciation expense of $12,000 per month is production capacity of 61 to 90 boats. As long as capacity remains in this range, the total fixed expense for depreciation will not change, but if capacity changes to another relevant range, then the amount of this fixed expense will also change.

The linearity assumption means that the cost behavior pattern will plot as a straight line within the relevant range. Although appli-

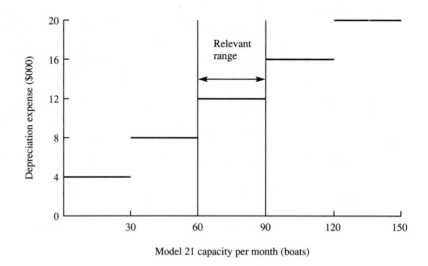

Model 21 capacity per month (boats)

cable to both fixed and variable costs, the significance of this assumption is best illustrated with a variable cost like raw materials such as glass fiber cloth. Because of quantity discounts and shipping efficiencies, the cost per unit of this raw material will decrease as the quantity purchased increases. This is illustrated in the left graph below. For analytical purposes, however, it may be assumed that the cost is linear within a relevant range, as shown in the right graph. Even though the cost per yard does vary slightly, for purposes of using cost-volume-profit analytical techniques it will be assumed constant per yard (variable in total) when purchases total between 8,000 and 16,000 yards per month.

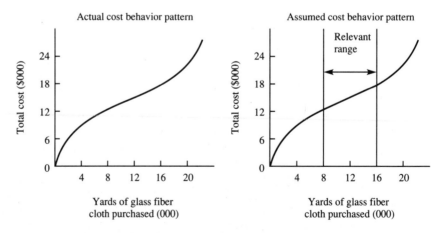

It is clear that if these assumptions are overlooked, or if costs are incorrectly classified or described, the results of the analytical process illustrated later in this chapter will be inaccurate. Cost-volume-profit analysis is a valuable and appropriate tool to use in many situations, but the cost behavior assumptions made are crucial to the validity and applicability of its results, and must be kept in mind when evaluating these results.

Generally speaking, raw materials and direct labor costs are variable costs. In addition, some manufacturing overhead costs will have a variable behavior pattern. For example, maintenance and housekeeping materials used, as well as the variable portion of factory utilities, will be a function of the quantity of product made. Other manufacturing overhead costs are fixed, including depreciation expense, supervisory salaries, and the fixed portion of utility costs.

Selling, general, administrative, and other operating expenses also fit both patterns. Sales commissions, for example, vary in proportion to sales revenue or the quantity of product sold. The wages associated with those employees who process orders from customers, or who handle payments from customers, may be variable if those functions are organized so that the number of workers can be expanded or contracted rapidly in response to changes in sales volume. On the other hand, advertising costs are usually fixed in the short run; once approved, the money is spent, and it is difficult to relate sales volume changes directly to advertising expenditures.

A particular cost's estimated behavior pattern is determined by analyzing cost and activity over a period of time. One of the analytical techniques involves using a scattergram to identify high and low cost-volume data, and then simple arithmetic to compute the variable rate and cost formula. This "high-low" method is illustrated in Exhibit 13–1. More complex techniques, including simple and multiple regression analysis, can also be used, but at some point the perceived increase in accuracy is offset by the simplifying assumptions involved in using the cost formula for planning and control purposes.

A Modified Income Statement Format

The traditional income statement format classifies costs according to the reason they were incurred: cost of goods sold, selling expenses, administrative expenses, research and development expenses, and so on. The income statement format used in CVP analysis, frequently referred to as the **contribution margin format,** classifies costs according to their behavior pattern—variable or fixed. The alternative formats are:

EXHIBIT 13–1   High-Low Method of Estimating a Cost Behavior Pattern

---

Assumption: During the months of January through June the following utility costs were incurred at various production volumes:

Month	Total Utility Cost	Total Production Volume
January	$2,500	8,000 units
February . . .	3,500	13,000 units
March	4,000	16,000 units
April	5,500	12,000 units
May	2,000	6,000 units
June	5,000	18,000 units

I. The scattergram

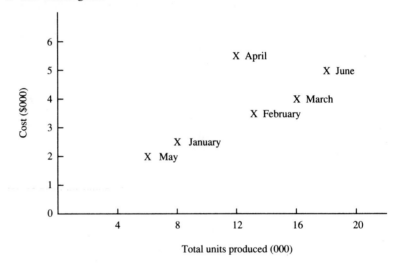

It can be observed in the scattergram that a cost-volume relationship does exist because of the approximate straight-line pattern of most of the observations. However, the April data do not fit the pattern. This may be due to an error, or some unusual condition. This observation is an "outlier" and will be ignored in the calculation of the cost formula because of its variation from the cost-volume relationship that exits between other data.

II. Calculation of the variable cost behavior pattern

The high-low method of calculating the variable cost behavior pattern, or variable cost rate, relates the change in cost to the change in activity, using the highest and lowest relevant observations.

$$\text{Variable rate} = \frac{\text{High cost} - \text{Low cost}}{\text{High activity} - \text{Low activity}}$$

$$= \frac{\$5,000 - \$2,000}{18,000 \text{ units} - 6,000 \text{ units}}$$

(continued)

EXHIBIT 13–1 (*concluded*)

$$= \$3,000/12,000 \text{ units}$$
$$= \$.25 \text{ per unit}$$

III. The cost formula

Knowing the variable rate, the fixed cost element can be calculated at either the high or low set of data, and the cost formula can be developed because total cost is equal to variable cost plus fixed cost.

At 18,000 units of activity, the total variable cost is 18,000 units × $.25 per unit = $4,500.

Fixed cost calculation:

$$\text{Total cost at 18,000 units} = \$5,000$$
$$\text{Variable cost at 18,000 units} = \underline{\quad 4,500}$$
$$\text{Fixed cost} = \underline{\underline{\$ \quad 500}}$$

The cost formula for utilities is:

$$\text{Total cost} = \text{Fixed cost} + \text{Variable rate}$$
$$= \$500 + \$.25 \text{ per unit made}$$

At 6,000 units made, total cost would be:

$$\$500 + (\$.25 \times 6,000) = \$2,000$$

Likewise, the cost formula could be used to estimate total utility costs at any level of activity (within the relevant range). Note that it is coincidence if the cost formula explains total cost accurately at points not used in the high-low calculation because the calculation assumes a linear relationship between the observations used, and in practice exact linearity will not exist.

Traditional Format		*Contribution Margin Format*	
Revenues	$	Revenues	$
Cost of goods sold	———	Variable expenses	———
Gross profit	$	Contribution margin	$
Operating expenses	———	Fixed expenses	———
Operating income	$____	Operating income	$____

Revenues and operating income (income before interest and taxes) are the same under either alternative. The difference is in the classification of expenses: functional in the traditional format, and according to cost behavior pattern in the contribution margin format. Although the behavior pattern classification could be carried beyond operating income to other income and expense, and income taxes, it usually isn't because the greatest benefits of the contribution margin approach are realized in the planning and control/ evaluation processes applied to a firm's operations.

The contribution margin format derives its name from the difference between revenues and variable expenses. **Contribution margin** means that this amount is the contribution to fixed expenses and operating income from the sale of product or provision of service. The significance of this concept lies in understanding cost behavior patterns. As revenue increases as a result of selling more products or providing more services, variable expenses will increase proportionately, and so will contribution margin. However, *fixed expenses will not increase* because they are not a function of the level of revenue-generating activity.

Use of the traditional income statement model can result in misleading and erroneous conclusions when changes in activity levels are being considered because it is assumed that all expenses change in proportion to changes in activity. This error is made because cost behavior patterns are not disclosed. The error is avoided when the contribution margin model is used correctly. For example, assume that a firm currently has revenues of $100,000, and operating income of $10,000. If revenues were to drop by 20 percent to $80,000, a quick conclusion would be that operating income would also decline by 20 percent, to $8,000. However, analysis using the contribution margin format results in a much more accurate, and disturbing, result:

	Current Results	Results Assuming a 20% Decline in Volume
Revenues	$100,000	$80,000
Variable expenses (60%)	60,000	48,000
Contribution margin (40%).	$ 40,000	$32,000
Fixed expenses.	30,000	30,000
Operating income.	$ 10,000	$ 2,000

Because fixed expenses did not change (the firm did not move into a different relevant range), the $8,000 reduction in contribution margin resulting from the reduction in revenues carried right through to reduce operating income by the same amount. This is an example of why it is misleading to think of fixed costs on a per unit basis. Fixed costs, and especially the relevant range assumption, cannot be overlooked by the manager, but it must be recognized that they behave differently from variable costs.

The **contribution margin ratio** is the ratio of contribution margin to revenues. This ratio can be used to calculate directly the change in contribution margin for a change in revenues. Continuing with the same data used above, a $12,000 increase in revenue would result in a $4,800 (40 percent × $12,000) increase in contribution margin, and a $4,800 increase in operating income.

Operating Leverage

When an entity's revenues change because the volume of activity changes, variable expenses and contribution margin will change proportionately. But the presence of fixed expenses, which do not change as the volume of activity changes, means that operating income will change proportionately more than the change in revenues. This magnification of the effect on operating income of a change in revenues is called **operating leverage.** This is illustrated in the above example of a 20 percent decline in volume, where revenues, variable expenses, and contribution margin all declined 20 percent, but operating income declined 80 percent (from $10,000 to $2,000). Note the similarity of operating leverage to financial leverage, explained in Chapter 11, in which fixed interest expense causes a proportionately greater change in ROE than the percentage change in ROI resulting from any given change in operating income.

Just as high financial leverage increases the risk that a firm may not be able to meet its required interest payments, high operating leverage increases the risk that a small percentage decline in revenues will cause a very large percentage decline in operating income. The higher a firm's contribution margin ratio, the greater its operating leverage. Management can influence the operating leverage of a firm by its decisions about incurring variable versus fixed costs. For example, if a firm substitutes automated production equipment for employees, it has changed a variable cost (assuming the employees could be laid off if demand for the firm's products declined) to a fixed cost (the machine will depreciate, be insured, and be included in the property tax base whether or not it is being used), and has increased its contribution margin ratio and operating leverage. If the management of a firm anticipates a decline in demand for the firm's products or services, it may be reluctant to change its cost structure by shifting variable costs to fixed costs, even though productivity increases could be attained, because the equipment has to be operating in order to realize the benefits of

EXHIBIT 13–2 Operating Leverage

I. Assume that two companies make similar products, but that the companies have adopted different cost structures. Company A's product is made in a labor-intensive operation with relatively high variable costs but relatively low fixed costs, and Company B's product is made in an equipment-intensive operation with relatively low variable costs but relatively high fixed costs. Each firm presently sells 6,000 units of product. A contribution margin model for each firm is presented below.

	Company A — *Lower Operating Leverage*				*Company B —* *Higher Operating Leverage*			
	Per Unit	*× Volume*	*= Total*	*%*	*Per Unit*	*× Volume*	*= Total*	*%*
Revenue	$ 50				$ 50			
Variable expenses .	35				20			
Contribution margin.	$ 15	× 6,000	= $90,000	30%	$ 30	× 6,000	= $180,000	60%
Fixed expenses . .			60,000				150,000	
Operating income .			$30,000				$ 30,000	

II. Effect on operating income of an increase in volume to 7,000 units:

Contribution margin.	$ 15	× 7,000	= $105,000	30%	$ 30	× 7,000	= $210,000	60%
Fixed expenses . .			60,000				150,000	
Operating income .			$ 45,000				$ 60,000	
Percentage change in volume		+17%				+17%		
Percentage change in operating income		+50%				+100%		

Note that Company B's operating income increased at a much greater rate, and to a considerably higher amount, than Company A's operating income. Operating leverage resulted in the operating income of each firm increasing proportionately more than the change in volume of activity. Company B's higher operating leverage results from a greater contribution margin per unit and contribution margin ratio of its product relative to Company A's product.

III. Effect on operating income of a decrease in volume to 5,000 units:

Contribution margin.	$ 15	× 5,000	= $75,000	30%	$ 30	× 5,000	= $150,000	60%
Fixed expenses . .			60,000				150,000	
Operating income .			$15,000				$ 0	
Percentage change in volume		−17%				−17%		

(continued)

EXHIBIT 13–2 *(concluded)*

| Percentage change in operating income | −50% | −100% |

Note that Company B's operating income decreased at a much greater rate, and to a considerably lower amount, than Company A's operating income. Operating leverage resulted in the operating income of each firm decreasing proportionately more than the change in volume of activity. With a decrease in volume, the greater contribution margin per unit and contribution margin ratio of Company B's product resulted in a greater reduction of its operating income than of that of Company A.

---

productivity gains. The effect of different cost structures on operating leverage is illustrated in Exhibit 13–2.

An Expanded Contribution Margin Model

The benefits of using the contribution margin model for planning can be best understood, and illustrated, by applying the model to a single product. For analytical purposes, an expanded version of the model, using the captions already illustrated, but adding some columns, is helpful. The expanded model is:

	Per Unit × *Volume* = *Total*	%
Revenue.	$	
Variable expenses	_____	
Contribution margin	$_____ ×_____ = $_____	_____%
Fixed expenses	_____	
Operating Income	$_____	

Notice that this model is used in Exhibit 13–2. The preferred route through the model is to express revenue, variable expense, and contribution margin on a per unit basis, multiply contribution margin per unit by volume to get total contribution margin, then subtract fixed expenses from total contribution margin to get operating income. Note that *fixed expenses are not unitized!* The contribution margin ratio is calculated (contribution margin per unit divided by revenue per unit) because it can frequently be used to answer quickly the "what if" questions that may be asked in the planning process.

To illustrate the use of the model, assume that mangement wants to know the operating income from a product that has the following revenue, cost, and volume characteristics:

Selling price per case	$ 15
Variable cost per case	8
Fixed expenses associated with the product	$ 40,000
Sales volume in cases	8,000 cases

Using these data in the model results in the following analysis:

	Per Unit	×	Volume	=	Total	%
Revenue.	$ 15					
Variable expenses	8					
Contribution margin.	$ 7	×	8,000	=	$56,000	46.7%
Fixed expenses.					40,000	
Operating income.					$16,000	

Now suppose that management wants to know what would happen to operating income if a $3 per unit price cut would result in a volume increase of 5,000 units, to a total of 13,000 units. The solution:

	Per Unit	×	Volume	=	Total	%
Revenue.	$ 12					
Variable expenses	8					
Contribution margin.	$ 4	×	13,000	=	$52,000	33.3%
Fixed expenses.					40,000	
Operating income.					$12,000	

Based on the quantitative analysis, the price reduction would not be made.

Next suppose that management proposes a $3 per unit price cut and a $5,000 increase in advertising, with the expectation that volume would increase to 18,000 units. The analysis of the effect on operating income is:

	Per Unit	×	Volume	=	Total	%
Revenue.	$ 12					
Variable expenses	8					
Contribution margin.	$ 4	×	18,000	=	$72,000	33.3%

	Per Unit × Volume =	Total	%
Fixed expenses.		45,000	
Operating income.		$27,000	

Note that the advertising expense increase is reflected in fixed expenses. The analysis suggests that if the volume increase can be achieved with the price cut and increased advertising combination, operating income will increase from its present level. But watch out for the relevant range assumption; the impact on fixed expenses of such a large increase in sales volume must be questioned.

The expanded contribution margin model can also be used to calculate the volume of activity required to achieve a target level of operating income. For example, using the original data for selling price, variable cost, and fixed expenses, suppose management wanted to know the sales volume required to have operating income of $23,000. The solution involves entering the known data in the model, and working to the middle to obtain the required volume:

	Per Unit × Volume =		Total	%
Revenue.	$ 15			
Variable expenses	8			
Contribution margin.	$ 7 × ?	=	$63,000	46.7%
Fixed expenses.			40,000	
Operating income.			$23,000	

The required sales volume is $63,000/$7 = 9,000 units.

The contribution margin ratio is used to calculate directly the effect on contribution margin and operating income when the change in operations is expressed in terms of total revenues. For example, if the contribution margin ratio is 33.3 percent, and total revenues are expected to increase by $12,000, a $4,000 increase in contribution margin and operating income would result, assuming that fixed expenses didn't change.

Another use of the contribution margin ratio is to determine the increase in revenues and sales volume that would be necessary to cover an increase in fixed expenses. For example, if fixed expenses were to increase by $5,000, contribution margin would have to increase by the same amount if operating income isn't going to change. If the contribution margin ratio is 33.3 percent, revenues would have to increase by $15,000 ($5,000/33.3 percent) to generate a $5,000 increase in contribution margin. The sales volume increase needed to generate the additional revenue is determined by dividing $15,000 by the selling price per unit. (Of course, the volume increase could also be calculated by dividing the increased contribution margin required, $5,000, by the contribution margin per unit.)

The contribution margin ratio is also used to determine revenue and contribution margin changes when per unit data are not available, or not applicable. For example, the contribution margin model is frequently used to analyze the impact on the operating income of an entire product line (e.g., a candy bar brand) that is sold in a variety of package or size configurations, and for which each configuration has the same, or very nearly the same, contribution margin ratio. Thus if a product line had a contribution margin ratio of 40 percent, would an advertising program costing $20,000 be cost effective if it generated an additional $60,000 of revenue? The increase in contribution margin would be $24,000 (40 percent × $60,000), which is $4,000 more than the cost of the additional advertising; yes, the program would be cost effective. Alternatively, the increased fixed expenses divided by the contribution margin ratio ($20,000/40 percent) shows that an additional $50,000 of revenue would be needed to cover the increased fixed expense; because the revenue increase is estimated to be $60,000, which is $10,000 more than required, an operating income increase of $4,000 (40 percent × $10,000) can be expected.

Although all of the examples used so far have expressed volume as units of product, the contribution margin model is also applicable to and useful for organizations that provide services rather than sell products. For example, a day care center could identify variable costs by type of activity, and then set charges to achieve a target contribution margin ratio that would be expected to generate enough total contribution margin to cover fixed expenses and operating income. Using the expanded contribution margin model, expected variable expenses of $18 per week per child, and a target contribution margin ratio of 40 percent, we calculate the revenue needed to be charged per week per child as follows:

	Per *Child* × *Volume* = *Total*			%
Revenue	$?			100%
Variable expenses	18			?
Contribution margin	$? × ? = $	?	40%

If the contribution margin ratio is 40 percent, the variable expense ratio is 60 percent (revenues = 100%); 60 percent of revenue per

EXHIBIT 13–3 Multiple Products and Sales Mix

I. Assume that a company has two products. Per unit revenue and variable expenses, and product volumes for present operations are shown below:

	Product A				Product B				Total Company	
	Per Unit	× Volume =	Total	%	Per Unit	× Volume =	Total	%	Total	%
Revenue	$ 40 ×	2,000 =	$80,000		$ 30 ×	2,000 =	$60,000		$140,000	100%
Variable expenses . . .	30				18					
Contribution margin . .	$ 10 ×	2,000 =	$20,000	25%	$ 12 ×	2,000 =	$24,000	40%	$ 44,000	31.4%
Fixed expenses									30,000	
Operating income . . .									$ 14,000	

Note that fixed expenses are shown in the total company column only because they apply to the company as a whole, not to individual products.

II. Now assume that the sale mix changes and that instead of sales volume of 2,000 units of each product, sales volume becomes 2,500 units of Product A and 1,500 units of Product B. The company's contribution margin format income statement becomes:

	Product A				Product B				Total Company	
	Per Unit	× Volume =	Total	%	Per Unit	× Volume =	Total	%	Total	%
Revenue	$ 40 ×	2,500 =	$100,000		$ 30 ×	1,500 =	$45,000		$145,000	100%
Variable expenses . . .	30				18					
Contribution margin . .	$ 10 ×	2,500 =	$ 25,000	25%	$ 12 ×	1,500 =	$18,000	40%	$ 43,000	29.7%
Fixed expenses									30,000	
Operating income . . .									$ 13,000	

Note that even though total sales volume was the same, total revenues increased, but total contribution margin and operating income decreased. This is due to the fact that proportionately more units of Product A, with its relatively low contribution margin ratio, were sold than of Product B, which has a relatively high contribution margin ratio.

child = \$18; revenue per child = \$18/0.60 = \$30. This process is virtually the same as that described in Chapter 9 to calculate a required selling price when the cost of the item and the desired gross profit ratio are known.

When the contribution margin model is applied using data for more than one product, the **sales mix** issue must be considered. Sales mix refers to the relative proportion of total sales accounted for by different products. Because different products are likely to have different contribution margin ratios, the average contribution margin ratio for a mix of products will change if the sales mix of the products changes.

The effect of a sales mix change is illustrated in Exhibit 13–3. Sales mix is an important concept to understand, because almost all firms have multiple products or services. When there is a range of quality to a firm's products (e.g. good, better, best), the higher-quality products generally have higher contribution margin ratios, so marketing efforts are frequently focused on those products. A strategy that some firms try to follow is to have all of their products have a contribution margin ratio that is about the same. A company that is able to achieve this approximate parity in contribution margin ratios among its products doesn't have to be concerned, from a product profitability standpoint, about sales mix changes, so marketing efforts can be more broadly based than if sales mix were a consideration.

Break-Even Point Analysis

The **break-even point** is usually expressed as the amount of revenue that must be realized in order for the firm (or product or activity or group of products or activities) to have neither profit nor loss (i.e., operating income equal to zero). The break-even point is useful to managers because it expresses a minimum revenue target, and frequently managers find it easier to think in terms of revenues rather than variable and fixed expenses. In addition, the amount of sales (or revenues) generated by the firm is easily determined on a daily basis from the accounting system.

The contribution margin model is used to determine the break-even point by setting operating income to zero and solving the model for the revenue or physical sales volume that will cause that result. The calculation of break-even point in terms of total revenues and units is illustrated below:

Selling price per unit	\$ 12
Variable expenses per unit	8
Total fixed expenses	\$45,000

	Per Unit	×	Volume	=	Total	%
Revenue.	$ 12					
Variable expenses	8					
Contribution margin.	$ 4	×	?	= $	?	33.3%
Fixed expenses.					45,000	
Operating Income.					$ 0	

According to the model, contribution margin clearly must be equal to fixed expenses of $45,000.

$$\text{Total revenues at break even} = \frac{\text{Contribution margin}}{\text{Contribution margin ratio}}$$

$$= \$45,000/33.3\%$$

$$= \$135,000$$

$$\text{Volume in units at break even} = \frac{\text{Contribution margin}}{\text{Contribution margin per unit}}$$

$$= \$45,000/\$4$$

$$= 11,250 \text{ units}$$

or

$$\text{Volume in units at break even} = \frac{\text{Total revenues required}}{\text{Revenue per unit}}$$

$$= \$135,000/\$12$$

$$= 11,250 \text{ units}$$

Break-even analysis is frequently illustrated in graph format, as illustrated in Exhibits 13–4 and 13–5 with data from the above example. Note that in these graphs, the x axis is sales volume in units, and the y axis is total dollars. In Exhibit 13–4 the horizontal line represents fixed expenses, and variable expenses are added to fixed expenses to produce the total expense line. Revenues start at the origin and rise in proportion to the sales volume in units. The intersection of the total expense line and the total revenue line is the break-even point. The sales volume in units required to break even is on the x axis directly below this point, and total revenues required to break even can be read on the y axis opposite the intersection. The amount of operating income or loss can be read as the dollar amount of the vertical distance between the total revenue line and total expense line for the sales volume actually achieved. Sometimes the area between the two lines is marked as "profit area" or "loss area."

EXHIBIT 13–4   Break-Even Graph

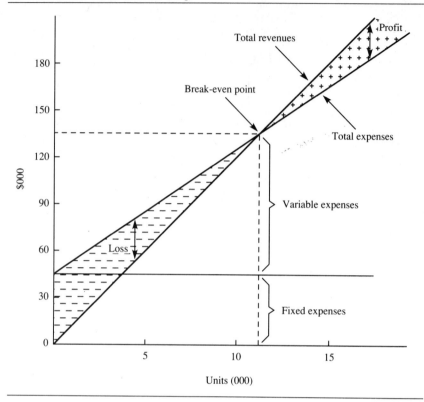

Exhibit 13–5 is another version of the break-even graph. The variable expense line begins at the origin, with fixed expenses added to total variable expenses. Although expenses are rearranged compared to Exhibit 13–4, the total expense line stays the same, and the break-even point and the profit and loss areas are the same. This version permits identification of contribution margin and shows how contribution margin grows as volume increases.

The key to the break-even point calculation (and graphic presentation) is that fixed expenses remain fixed in total regardless of the level of activity, subject to the relevant range assumption. In addition to that assumption, the linearity and constant sales mix assumptions must also be considered. In spite of these simplifications, the contribution margin model and cost behavior pattern concepts are among the most important ideas to understand, and to be able to apply. The manager encounters many situations in which cost-volume-profit analysis supports decisions that contribute to

---

EXHIBIT 13–5   Break-Even Graph Featuring Contribution Margin

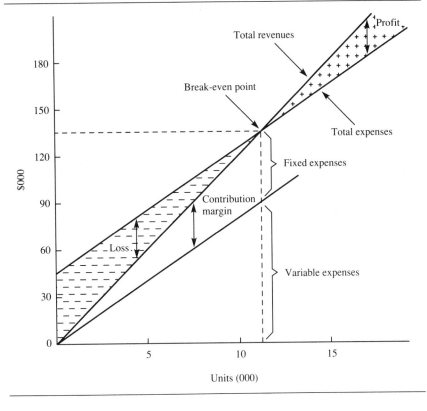

the achievement of the organization's objectives. One of these applications is described in Business Procedure Capsule 21.

SUMMARY

Cost-volume-profit (CVP) analysis uses knowledge about cost behavior patterns to interpret and forecast changes in operating income resulting from changes in revenue, or in the volume of activity.

Variable costs change in total as the volume of activity changes. Fixed costs remain constant in total as the volume of activity changes. The simplifying assumptions of linearity and relevant range must be kept in mind when cost behavior pattern data are used.

When a particular cost is partly fixed and partly variable, the high-low method can be used to develop a cost formula that recognizes both the variable and fixed elements of the cost.

The contribution margin format income statement reclassifies the functional cost categories of the traditional income statement to cost behavior pattern categories. Contribution margin is the difference between revenues and variable expenses. Unless there are changes in the composition of variable expenses, contribution margin changes in proportion to the change in revenues.

Operating leverage describes the percentage change in operating income for a given percentage change in revenues. Since fixed expenses don't change when revenues change, operating income changes by a greater percentage amount than revenues. The higher a firm's fixed expenses relative to its variable expenses, the greater the operating leverage and the greater the risk that a change in the level of activity will cause a much larger change in operating income. Operating leverage can influence management's decisions about whether to incur variable costs or fixed costs.

The expanded contribution margin format model provides a framework for analyzing the effect of revenue, cost, and volume changes on operating income. A key to using this model is that fixed costs are only recognized in total; they are not unitized.

The contribution margin ratio can sometimes be used to determine the effect of a volume change on operating income more quickly and more easily than using unit revenue and variable expense, and volume.

Sales mix describes the relative proportion of total sales accounted for by specific products. When different products or product lines have significantly different contribution margin ratios, changes in the sales mix will cause the percentage change in total contribution margin to be different from the percentage change in revenues.

The break-even point is the total sales volume (in units or dollars) at which operating income is zero. The sales volume required to break even can be calculated using the contribution margin model by calculating the sales volume required to have contribution margin equal fixed expenses. Break-even analysis can be illustrated graphically.

KEY TERMS AND CONCEPTS

break-even point *(p. 410)*   The amount of revenue required to have neither operating income nor operating loss.

contribution margin *(p. 402)*   The difference between revenues and variable costs.

• BUSINESS PROCEDURE CAPSULE 21
The 1-Cent Scale

An understanding of cost-volume-profit relationships is shown by the manager of a fast-food and soft ice cream business operating in a midwestern city when a 1-cent sale is held in February. Ice cream sundaes are featured —two for the price of one, plus 1 cent. None of the other menu items are on sale.

Those sundaes usually sell for a price of 55 cents to $1, but even with generous estimates, it is hard to come up with variable costs (ice cream, topping, cup, and spoon) much greater than 30 percent of the usual selling price. So even when the price is effectively cut in half, there is still a positive contribution margin. And what happens to the store's fixed costs during the sale? They are probably not affected at all. The fixed costs (including workers' wages) will be incurred whether or not extra customers come in for the sundae special. And of course, many of those customers will probably buy other items at the regular price.

The net result of the special promotion is that the store builds traffic and business at a time of otherwise low activity (assuming that normal demand for sundaes is low in February). All of the business has a positive contribution margin, fixed expenses are the same as they would be without the promotion, and operating income is increased over what it would otherwise have been.

contribution margin format *(p. 399)* An income statement format in which variable costs are subtracted from revenues to show contribution margin, from which fixed costs are subtracted to determine operating income.

contribution margin ratio *(p. 403)* The ratio of contribution margin to revenues.

cost-volume-profit analysis *(p. 396)* Analysis of the impact on profit of volume and cost changes using knowledge about the behavior patterns of the costs involved.

operating leverage *(p. 403)* The concept that operating income changes proportionately more than revenues for any given change in revenues as a result of a change in the level of activity.

sales mix *(p. 410)* The proportion of total sales represented by various products or categories of products.

EXERCISES AND PROBLEMS

13–1. A department of Gamma Co. incurred the following costs for the month of February. Variable costs, and the variable portion of the mixed costs, are a function of the number of units of activity.

Activity level in units	5,000
Variable costs.	$10,000
Fixed costs	30,000
Mixed costs.	20,000
Total costs	$60,000

During April the activity level was 7,000 units, and the total costs incurred were $68,000.

Required:

a. Calculate the variable costs, fixed costs, and mixed costs incurred during April.

b. Use the high-low method to calculate the cost formula for the mixed cost.

13–2. The following data have been extracted from the records of Puzzle Co.:

	March	October
Production level, in units	6,000	15,000
Variable costs	$18,000	$?
Fixed costs	?	25,000
Mixed costs	17,000	?
Total costs	$60,000	$105,000

Required:

a. Calculate the missing costs.

b. Calculate the cost formula for the mixed cost using the high-low method.

c. Calculate the total cost that would be incurred for the production of 20,000 units.

d. Identify the two key cost behavior assumptions made in the calculation of your answer to *(c)*.

13–3. Shown below is an income statement in the traditional format for a firm with a sales volume of 8,000 units. Cost formulas are shown.

Revenues.	$32,000
Cost of goods sold	
($6,000 + $2.10/unit).	22,800
Gross profit.	$ 9,200
Operating expenses:	
Selling ($1,200 + $.10/unit)	2,000
Administration ($4,000 + $.20/unit)	5,600
Operating income	$ 1,600

Required:

a. Prepare an income statement in the contribution margin format.

b. Calculate the contribution margin per unit and the contribution margin ratio.

c. Calculate the firm's net income (or loss) if the volume changed to:
   1. 12,000 units.
   2. 4,000 units.
d. Calculate the firm's net income (or loss) if unit selling price and variable expenses do not change, and total revenues:
   1. Increased $12,000.
   2. Decreased $7,000.

13–4. Presented below is the income statement for Docmag Co. for March:

Sales	$80,000
Cost of goods sold	37,000
Gross profit	$43,000
Operating expenses	38,000
Operating income.	$ 5,000

Based on an analysis of cost behavior patterns, it has been determined that the company's contribution margin ratio is 40 percent.

Required:

a. Rearrange the above income statement to the contribution margin format.
b. If sales increase by 8 percent, what will be the firm's operating income? *(Note: Do not construct an income statement to get your answer.)*
c. Calculate the amount of revenue required for Docmag to break even.

13–5. Penta Co. makes and sells a single product. The current selling price is $15 per unit. Variable costs are $9 per unit, and fixed expenses total $27,000 per month.

Required:

(Unless otherwise stated, consider each requirement separately.)

a. Calculate the monthly operating income (or loss) at a sales volume of 5,400 units per month.
b. Calculate monthly operating income (or loss) if a $2 per unit reduction in selling price results in a volume increase to 8,400 units per month.
c. What questions would have to be answered about the cost-volume-profit analysis simplifying assumptions before adopting the price-cut strategy of *(b)?*
d. Calculate monthly operating income (or loss) that would result from a $1 per unit price increase and a $6,000 per month increase in advertising expenses, both relative to the original data, and assuming a sales volume of 5,400 units per month.
e. Management is considering a change in the salesforce compensation plan. Currently, each of the firm's two salespersons is paid a salary of $2,500 per month. Calculate the monthly operating income (or loss) that would result from changing the compensation plan to a salary of $400 per month, plus a commission of $.80 per unit, assuming a sales volume of:

1. 5,400 units per month.
2. 6,000 units per month.

f. Assuming that the sales volume increase of 600 units per month achieved in *(e)* could also be achieved by increasing advertising by $1,000 per month instead of changing the salesforce compensation plan, which strategy would you recommend? Explain your answer.

g. Calculate the break-even point expressed in terms of total sales dollars, and sales volume.

13–6. Kiwi Manufacturing Co. makes a single product that sells for $23 per unit. Variable costs are $12 per unit, and fixed costs total $28,050 per month.

Required:

a. Calculate the number of units that must be sold each month for the firm to break even.

b. Calculate operating income if 3,000 units are sold in a month.

c. Calculate operating income if the selling price is raised to $24 per unit, advertising expenditures are increased by $3,000 per month, and monthly unit sales volume becomes 3,200 units per month.

d. Assume that the firm adds another product to its product line and that the new product sells for $20 per unit, has variable costs of $14 per unit, and causes fixed expenses in total to increase to $38,000 per month. Calculate the firm's operating income if 3,000 units of the original product and 2,000 units of the new product are sold each month. For the original product, use the selling price and variable cost data given in the problem statement.

e. Using the selling price and variable cost data from *(d)*, calculate the firm's operating income if 2,000 units of the original product and 3,000 units of the new product are sold each month.

f. Explain why operating income is different in *(d)* and *(e)*, even though sales totaled 5,000 units in each case.

13–7. Campus Canvas Co. currently makes and sells two models of a backpack/book sack. Data applicable to the current operation are summarized in the columns below labeled Current Operation. Management is considering an expansion—adding a Value model to its current Luxury and Economy models. Expected data if the new model is added are shown in the columns below labeled Proposed Expansion.

	Current Operation		*Proposed Expansion*		
	Luxury	*Economy*	*Luxury*	*Economy*	*Value*
Selling price per unit	$20	$12	$20	$12	$15
Variable costs per unit	9	7	9	7	8
Annual sales volume—units	10,000	20,000	6,000	17,000	8,000
Fixed expenses for year	Total of $70,000		Total of $84,000		

Required:

a. Calculate the company's current total contribution margin and the current overall contribution margin ratio.

b. Calculate the company's current break-even point in dollar sales.

c. Why might the company incur a loss, even if break-even sales dollars were achieved and selling prices and costs didn't change?

d. Calculate the company's total operating income under the proposed expansion.

e. Based on the proposed expansion data, would you recommend adding the Value model? Why or why not?

f. Would your answer to (e) change if the Value model sales volume were to increase to 10,000 units annually, and all other data stay the same? Why or why not?

13–8. Arithmetico makes three models of calculators. Data applicable to the current operation are summarized below in the columns labeled Current Operation. Management is considering eliminating the Math model. Expected data if this occurs are shown below in the columns labeled Proposed.

	Current Operation			Proposed	
	Business	Math	Student	Business	Student
Selling price per unit	$42	$54	$12	$40	$15
Contribution margin per unit	14	18	3	12	6
Monthly sales volume—units	3,000	800	2,500	3,500	3,000
Fixed expenses per month	Total of $52,000			Total of $47,000	

Required:

a. Calculate the contribution margin ratio of each product under the current and proposed operation.

b. Calculate the overall contribution margin ratio under the current and proposed operation.

c. Calculate the company's break-even point in dollar sales under the current and proposed operation.

d. Calculate the company's operating income under both the current and proposed operation.

e. If the increased sales volume of the Business model comes from what would otherwise have been Math model sales, should the Math model be discontinued? Explain your answer.

f. Assume that the Math model is discontinued. Explain what really accounts for the change in the company's operating income.

g. Assume that the Math model is discontinued. On which of the remaining models should the company concentrate its marketing efforts as it seeks to maximize operating income as a result of a sales mix change? Explain your answer.

13–9. Sevprod, Inc., makes and sells a large number of consumer products. The firm's average contribution margin ratio is 35 percent. Management is considering adding a new product that will require an additional $15,000 per month of fixed expenses and will have variable costs of $7.80 per unit.

Required:

a. Calculate the selling price that will be required for the new product if it is to have a contribution margin ratio equal to 35 percent.

b. Calculate the number of units of the new product that would have to be sold if the new product is to increase the firm's monthly operating income by $6,000.

13–10. Clampet Co. has annual revenues of $890,000, an average contribution margin ratio of 32 percent, and fixed expenses of $216,200.

Required:

a. Management is considering adding a new product to the company's product line. The new item will have a variable cost of $5.78 per unit. Calculate the selling price that will be required if this product is not to affect the average contribution margin ratio.

b. If the new product adds an additional $14,500 to Clampet's fixed expenses, how many units of the new product will have to be sold to break even on the new product?

c. If 20,000 units of the new product could be sold at a price of $10 per unit, and the company's other business did not change, calculate Clampet's total operating income and average contribution margin ratio.

d. Describe how the analysis of adding the new product would be complicated if it were to "steal" some volume from existing products.

13–11. Barb and Jan's ice cream shop charges $1.25 for a cone. Variable costs are $.35 per cone, and fixed costs total $1,800 per month. A "sweetheart" promotion is being planned for the second week of February. During this week, a person buying a cone at the regular price could receive a free cone for a friend. It is estimated that 400 additional cones would be sold and that 600 cones would be given away. Advertising costs for the promotion would be $120.

Required:

a. Calculate the effect of the promotion on operating income for the second week of February.

b. Do you think the promotion should occur? Explain your answer.

13–12. The management of Primo's Prime Pizzeria is considering a special promotion for the last two weeks of May, which is normally a relatively low demand period. The special promotion would involve selling two medium pizzas for the price of one, plus 1 cent. The medium pizza normally sells for $7.50 and has variable expenses of $2.20. Expected sales volume without the special promotion is 460 medium pizzas per week.

Required:

a. Calculate the total contribution margin generated by the normal volume of medium pizzas in a week.

b. Calculate the total number of medium pizzas that will have to be sold during the 1-cent sale to generate the same amount of contribution margin that results from the normal volume.

c. What other factors should management consider in evaluating the pros and cons of the special promotion?

13–13. Green Co. makes and sells a single product. The current selling price is $32 per unit. Variable costs are $20 per unit, and fixed expenses total $43,200 per month. Sales volume for January totaled 4,100 units.

Required:

a. Calculate operating income for January using the expanded contribution margin model.

b. Calculate the break-even point in terms of units sold and total revenues.

c. Management is considering installing automated equipment to reduce direct labor cost. If this were done, variable costs would drop to $14 per unit, but fixed expenses would increase to $67,800 per month.
   1. Calculate operating income at a volume of 4,100 units per month.
   2. Calculate the break-even point with the new cost structure.
   3. Why would you suggest that management seriously consider investing in the automated equipment and accepting the new cost structure?
   4. Why might management not accept your recommendation but decide instead to maintain the old cost structure?

13–14. Ace Binding Co. provides a magazine binding service to libraries, which send loose copies of periodicals for binding into a hardcover book for permanent use. The business is seasonal, with much binding to be done early in the calendar year, but less work to be done late in the year. The binding has been done manually. Ace uses temporary workers during its busy period and cuts back to a smaller permanent staff during the rest of the year. The firm's income statement for a recent year showed the following:

Revenues	$120,000
Variable expenses	80,000
Contribution margin	$ 40,000
Fixed expenses	25,000
Operating income	$ 15,000

An automated binding machine has been developed and could be purchased by Ace Binding. If the machine is acquired, fixed expenses will increase $30,000 a year. The firm's binding capacity will increase, and it is estimated that increased binding activity would result in a 25 percent increase in revenues. It is also estimated that the variable expense ratio would be half what it is now.

Required:

a. Calculate the firm's current contribution margin ratio and break-even point in terms of revenues.

b. Calculate the firm's contribution margin ratio and break-even point in terms of revenues if the new machine is acquired and the variable expense ratio change occurs.

c. Calculate the firm's operating income assuming that the machine is purchased and the other estimated changes occur.

d. Do you believe that management of Ace Binding should acquire the new machine? Explain your answer.

13–15. Integrated Circuits, Inc. (ICI), is presently operating at 50 percent of capacity and manufacturing 50,000 units of a patented electronic component. The cost structure of the component is as follows:

Raw materials	$ 1.50 per unit
Direct labor	1.50 per unit
Variable overhead	2.00 per unit
Fixed overhead	$100,000 per year

A Japanese firm has offered to purchase 30,000 of the components at a price of $6 per unit, FOB ICI's plant. The normal selling price is $8 per component. This special order will not affect any of ICI's "normal" business. Management figures that the cost per component is $7, so it is reluctant to accept this special order.

Required:

a. Show how management comes up with a cost of $7 per unit for this component.

b. Evaluate this cost calculation. Explain why it is or is not appropriate.

c. Should the offer from the Japanese firm be accepted? Why or why not?

13–16. Foreway Manufacturing Co. makes and sells several models of locks. The cost records for Model B–603 show that manufacturing costs total $13.26 per lock. An analysis of this amount indicates that $7.60 of the total cost has a variable cost behavior pattern, and the remainder is an allocation of fixed manufacturing overhead. The normal selling price of this model is $21 per lock. A chain store has offered to buy 8,000 B–603 locks from Foreway at a price of $12 each to sell in a market that would not compete with Foreway's regular business. Foreway has manufacturing capacity available and could make these locks without incurring additional fixed manufacturing overhead.

Required:

a. Calculate the effect on Foreway's operating income of accepting the order from the chain store.

b. If Foreway's costs had not been classified by cost behavior pattern, is it likely that a correct special order analysis would have been made? Explain your answer.

c. Identify the key qualitative factors that Foreway managers should consider with respect to this special order decision.

13–17. Assume that you are a sales representative for Saturn Candy Company. One of your customers is interested in buying some candy that will be given to the members of a high school Substance Abuse Awareness Club. The club members will be marching in a community parade and will give the candy to children who are watching the parade. Your customer has asked that you discount the normal selling price of the candy to be given to the club by 35 percent. You know that the contribution margin ratio of the candy, based on the regular selling price, is 40 percent.

Required:

Identify the pros and cons of complying with the customer's request, and state the recommendation you would make to your sales manager.

13–18. Bill Sparks is in charge of arranging the "attitude adjustment" period and dinner for the monthly meetings of the local chapter of the Young Executives Association. Bill is negotiating with a new restaurant that would like to have the group's business, and Bill wants to apply some of the cost-volume-profit analysis material he has learned. The restaurant is proposing its regular menu prices of $1.50 for a before-dinner drink, and $16.50 for dinner. Bill has determined that on average, the persons attending the meeting have 1.5 drinks before dinner. He also believes that the contribution margin ratios for the drinks and dinner are 60 percent and 45 percent, respectively.

Required:

Prepare a memo to Bill outlining the possible offers he might make to the restaurant owner and recommend an offer that he should make.

Chapter 14

Budgeting and Performance Reporting

Planning is an essential part of the management process. A **budget** is a financial plan. *Budgeting* is the process of planning, in financial terms, the organization's activities and the results of those activities. Budgeting involves the use of financial accounting concepts because ultimately the results of the organization's activities will be reported in financial terms in the financial statements. Budgeting also involves using managerial accounting techniques, especially knowledge about cost behavior patterns, because the aggregate financial plan of an organization is the sum of plans for individual products and units.

Budgets are useful because:

The preparation of a budget forces management to plan.

The budget provides a benchmark against which to compare performance.

The budget preparation process requires the different functional areas of the firm—finance, production, marketing, personnel, and so on— to communicate and coordinate activities if goals are to be achieved.

Although it may seem that these benefits should be achieved even without a budget, they are often not realized without a budgeting process because each functional area gets so wrapped up in its own activities that the impact on other functions is overlooked or given secondary significance.

Performance reporting involves the comparison of actual results with planned results, with the objective of highlighting those activities for which actual and planned results differed, either favorably or unfavorably, so that appropriate action can be taken. Appropriate actions may include changing the way activities are carried out or changing plans.

LEARNING OBJECTIVES

After studying this chapter you should understand:

- Why budgets are useful.
- How management philosophy can influence the budgeting process.
- The difference between the starting point for most budgeting and zero-based budgeting.
- How alternative budget time frames can be used.
- The steps involved in the budgeting process, and the various budgets that are frequently prepared as part of the overall operating budget.
- The significance of the sales or revenue forecast to the overall budget.
- How the purchases, or production, budget is developed.
- Why budget managers are concerned about budget slack, or "padding."
- That cost behavior pattern knowledge is essential to the budgeting of operating expenses.
- Why a budgeted income statement and budgeted balance sheet are prepared.
- The general format, and objective, of a performance report.
- How the performance report facilitates using the management-by-exception process.
- How the operating results of segments of an organization can be reported most meaningfully by avoiding the pitfalls of arbitrarily allocated costs.
- What a flexible budget is, and how it is used.

BUDGETING

The Budgeting Process in General

Many organizations commit substantial time and resources to the budgeting process. A useful budget is not prepared in a few hours or a few days; usually several months and the efforts of many people are devoted to the process. Once developed, a budget is not put on the shelf; it should become a useful tool to help managers accomplish the goals that were established.

How the budget is used in an organization will depend on the management philosophy of the top managers. In a highly structured, autocratically managed firm the budget may be seen as being "carved in stone," and managers may develop dysfunctional practices to avoid being criticized for failing to meet budgeted results. For example, in such an environment, the salesforce may defer entering customer orders in a month in which the sales target has already been achieved, sacrificing customer service levels and sales in order to get a head start on the next period's quota. Or a manager may commit funds for supplies that aren't really needed in order to use the full budget allowance, on the premise that doing so will facilitate justifying a budget allowance of at least that much for the next period. These and other budget "games" waste valuable time and resources.

The budget should be seen as a guide that reflects management's best thinking when it is prepared. However, the plan may have to change, or large differences between budgeted amounts and actual amounts may have to be anticipated and accepted if circumstances change from those envisioned when the budget was prepared. The objective of the organization should not be to have actual results equal budgeted results; the objective should be to operate profitably, as expressed and measured by rate of return, growth in profits, market share, levels of service, and other measures that reflect the purpose of the organization.

Management philosophy is reflected in whether the budget is prepared using **top-down budgeting** (a dictated approach), or an interactive, participative approach in which lower-level managers provide significant input to the budgeting process. One approach is not better than the other in all situations. The **participative budgeting** approach should result in lower-level managers identifying more closely with the budget objectives, but there may be times, as when a firm is under heavy pressure to survive, that dictated objectives are appropriate.

The beginning point for most budgets is the actual performance for the current period. The manager first determines what the revenues and/or costs have been recently, and then adjusts these amounts for changes that are expected to occur in the next period. The disadvantage of this approach is that inefficiencies in the present way of doing things tend to be carried into the future. **Zero-based budgeting** is a technique that became popular in the 1970s. Zero-based budgeting involves identifying and prioritizing the activities carried out by a department, determining the costs associated with each, and then authorizing for the future only those activities that satisfy certain priority constraints. Some firms and organizations—especially governmental and social service agencies—embarked on a zero-based budgeting program but discontinued it because of the heavy administrative and paperwork burdens it required. An alternative zero-based approach used by some organizations involves determining budget estimates by showing the details of all amounts to be expended, rather than just showing increments from the current period's budget or actual results.

The Budget Time Frame

Budgets can be prepared for a single period or for several periods. A **single-period budget** for a fiscal year would be prepared in the months preceding the beginning of the year, and used for the year. The disadvantage of this approach is that some budget estimates must be made for months more than a year in the future. For example, a firm operating on a calendar year will prepare its 1993 budget during the last few months of 1992. November and December 1993 activities are being planned before actual results for those months in 1992 are known.

A multiperiod, or **rolling budget,** involves planning for segments of a year on a repetitive basis. For example, in a three-month/one-year rolling budget, late in 1992 a budget for each quarter of 1993 will be prepared. During the first quarter of 1993 a budget for the next four quarters will be prepared. This will be the second budget for each of the last three quarters of 1993, and first budget for the first quarter of 1994. During the second quarter of 1993 the budgets for the third and fourth quarters of 1993 and the first quarter of 1994 will be revised as necessary, and the first budget for the second quarter of 1994 will be prepared. Budget time frames are illustrated in Exhibit 14–1.

The advantage of such a **continuous budget** is that the final budget for any quarter should be much more accurate because it has been prepared more recently. The obvious disadvantage to this process is the time, effort, and money required. However, in a rapidly changing environment, the benefit of a budget that requires frequent assessment of the organization's plans may be worth the cost. The periods of the multiperiod budget can be any that make sense for the organization, and for the activity being budgeted. Thus full financial statements may be budgeted on a six-month/one-year cycle, but cash receipt and disbursement details may be budgeted on a one-week/four-week cycle, or even a daily/one-week/four-week cycle (i.e., every day a budget by day for the next

EXHIBIT 14–1   Budget Time Frames

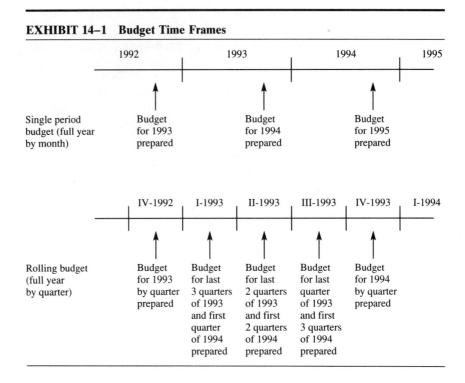

several days is prepared, and every week a budget by week for the next four weeks is prepared).

The Budgeting Process

The first step in the budgeting process is to develop and communicate a set of broad assumptions about the economy, the industry, and the organization's strategy for the budget period. This is frequently done by planners and economists, and is approved by top management. These assumptions represent the foundation on which the action plans for the budget period are built.

The **operating budget,** which is the operating plan expressed in financial terms, is made up of a number of detailed budgets. These include:

The sales/revenue budget (or forecast).

The purchases/production budget.

The operating expense budget(s).

The income statement budget.

The cash budget.

The balance sheet budget.

The key to every budget is the forecast of activity that is expected during the budget period. This is usually a sales or revenue forecast developed using an estimate of the physical quantity of goods or services to be sold multiplied by the expected selling price per unit. Merchandising firms may develop a **sales forecast** using expected revenues from groups of products. Commodity processing firms may forecast expected activity (e.g., bushels of corn to be processed) because revenues are based on the commodity price plus a "spread" or markup, and the commodity price can fluctuate widely. Service organizations forecast expected activity based on expected number of clients to be served and the quantity of service likely to be required by each client. Based on these activity measures and an anticipated revenue per service, total revenues can be estimated.

Once the sales forecast has been developed, the other budgets can be prepared because the items being budgeted are a function of sales or other measure of activity. For example, the quantity of product to make or buy depends on planned sales and desired inventory levels. Selling expenses will be a function of sales, and other operating expenses depend on quantities sold and purchased or made. After revenues and expenses have been forecast, an income statement can be completed. Next the cash budget (or projected statement of cash flows) can be prepared, given operating results and plans for investing and financing activities. Finally, by considering all of these expectations, a balance sheet as of the end of the budget period can be prepared. This hierarchy of budgets and key assumptions, as well as the way each budget is related to the balance sheet and income statement, is illustrated in Exhibit 14–2.

The sales or other activity forecast is the most challenging part of the budget to develop accurately because of the numerous factors over which the organization has little or no control that influence revenue-producing activities. These include the state of the economy and competitors' actions. Numerous quantitative models, many of which involve computer processing, have been developed to assist in forecasting revenues. The past experience of managers provides valuable input to the forecast. Information provided by the salesforce is important. But, in the final analysis, the sales or other activity forecast is only an educated guess resulting from a great deal of effort and, although the rest of the budgeting

---

EXHIBIT 14–2   Hierarchy of Budgets, Key Assumptions, and Financial Statement Relationships

	Key	Balance sheet	Income statement
Budget	*Assumption*	Assets = Liabilities + Owners' Equity ←	Net Income = Revenues − Expenses
Sales forecast	Sales	+ Accounts Receivable	+ Revenues
Purchases/ production	Sales and inventory levels	+ Inventories + Accounts Payable − Inventories	− Cost of Goods Sold
Operating expenses	Sales and production	+ Other Accrued Liabilities − Accumulated Depreciation	− Operating Expenses − Depreciation Expense
Income statement can be prepared		+ Net income ←	Net income
Cash	Operating	+ Cash − Accounts Payable − Accounts − Other Accrued Receivable Liabilities	
	investing,	− Cash + Long-term + Plant and Debt Equipment	
	and financing plans	+/− Cash +/− Long-term + Capital Debt Stock − Dividends − Treasury Stock	
Balance sheet can be prepared		Assets = Liabilities + Owners' Equity	

process flows from it, managers must remember that variations from the forecast will occur, and good managers will be prepared to respond quickly to those variations.

The Purchases/Production Budget

Recall that when a periodic inventory system was used to determine cost of goods sold, the following model was used:

Beginning inventory	$
Add: Purchases	____
Goods available for sale	$

Less: Ending inventory. . . . . .   (   )

Cost of goods sold . . . . $ \underline{\hspace{2cm}}

By changing dollars to physical quantities, the same model can be used to determine the quantity of merchandise to be purchased or manufactured. The captions change slightly, and the model would be as follows:

Beginning inventory		units
Add: Purchases (or production) . .	_____	units
Goods available for sale		units
Less: Ending inventory.	(_____)	units
Quantity of goods sold	_____	units

To use the model, inventory quantities based on the firm's inventory management policies and quantity of goods sold from the sales forecast are entered. The amount of goods available for sale is calculated by working from the bottom up (the quantity of goods sold is added to ending inventory), and then beginning inventory is subtracted from goods available for sale to get the purchase or production quantity. Of course, the model could be rearranged to permit calculation of the purchase or production quantity in a traditional equation format (Purchases or production = Quantity sold − Beginning inventory + Ending inventory), but that format requires learning another model.

A firm's inventory management policies recognize the lead time to receive or make finished goods and/or raw materials, and these policies provide an allowance for forecast errors. For example, a finished goods inventory policy might be to have on hand at the end of a month (or other period) a quantity of inventory equal to 1.4 times the quantity expected to be sold in the subsequent month (or period). And remember that one period's ending inventory is the next period's beginning inventory. The beginning inventory for the first budget period could be estimated using the inventory policy, or could be the estimated inventory for the end of the current period, which could be different from the policy quantity because the current period's actual sales or usage differs from the forecast for the current period.

The results of the production and purchases budget model will frequently be adjusted to reflect production efficiencies or appropriate order quantities. For example, if the production budget calculation calls for significantly different quantities of production each month for several months, management may elect to plan level production and ignore the ending inventory policy because the benefits of production efficiencies are greater than the costs of carrying inventory. Likewise, if the purchases budget calculation indicates that 38,400 units of raw material should be purchased but standard shipping containers contain 2,000 units each, the actual quantity ordered will be either 38,000 or 40,000 units. Inventories will absorb the difference between the budget calculation and the practical order quantity. Remember that in most cases, the budget calculations result in a guide to action; they do not produce absolute amounts to be followed at all costs.

To complete a budgeted income statement, physical quantities developed in the model must be converted to dollars. This is done by multiplying the cost of a unit by the budgeted quantity of each unit in each element of the model. (Standard costs, discussed in Chapter 15, and the use of computer software facilitate this task.)

A manufacturing firm would use the same approach to budget the number of units of product to be made by substituting production for purchases. Then when the number of units to be produced is known, the quantity of each raw material to be purchased would be forecast using the same model, with the quantity of each raw material required for that quantity of production being substituted for the quantity of goods sold. Exhibit 14–3 illustrates the development of a manufacturing firm's production budget and a raw materials purchases budget to support the budgeted level of production. A merchandising firm's purchases budget would be similar to a manufacturer's production budget. The computations involved are not complex, but they are numerous, and computer programs are widely used in the process.

If quantity forecast data are not required or desired because the cost of using the above approach is greater than its benefit, and/or because the inventory control system results in ordering raw materials and/or finished goods as they are needed, the approach can be easily modified to provide a dollar amount forecast for purchases or production. This is accomplished by using the complement of the budgeted gross profit ratio to calculate budgeted cost of goods sold. Beginning and ending inventories can be expressed as a function of budgeted cost of goods sold, and so the dollar amount of budgeted purchases can be determined. This process is illustrated in Exhibit 14–4.

The cost of goods manufactured budget for a manufacturing firm will include budgeted amounts for direct labor and manufacturing overhead. Determining these budget amounts frequently involves the use of a standard cost system (discussed in Chapter 15), which permits determination of budgeted direct labor and manufacturing overhead based on an analysis of the labor and overhead inputs that should be required to make a unit or batch of the product.

EXHIBIT 14–3   Development of a Production Budget and the Related Raw Materials Purchases Budget

I. Assumptions:
   A. Sales forecast in units per month:
      January   10,000 units
      February 12,000 units
      March   15,000 units
      April   11,000 units
   B. Inventory policy:
      Finished goods ending inventory should equal 1.4 times the subsequent month's forecasted sales.
      Raw materials ending inventory should equal 50 percent of the subsequent month's budgeted raw material usage.
   C. Three units of raw materials are required for each unit of finished product.

II. Production budget:
   A. Ending inventory of finished goods required:

	December	January	February	March
Ending inventory units required (1.4 × sales forecast for subsequent month)	14,000	16,800	21,000	15,400

   B. Production budget using the cost of goods sold model (assuming that December 31 inventory is equal to that required by the finished goods inventory policy).

	January	February	March
Beginning inventory (units)	14,000	16,800	21,000
Add: Production (units)	?	?	?
Goods available for sale (units)	?	?	?
Less: Ending inventory (units)	(16,800)	(21,000)	(15,400)
Quantity of goods sold (units)	10,000	12,000	15,000
By working from the bottom up, the quantity of goods available for sale is calculated first, and then beginning inventory is subtracted from goods available for sale to get production in units of	12,800	16,200	9,400

(*continued*)

EXHIBIT 14–3   *(concluded)*

III. Raw materials purchased budget:

	January	*February*	*March*
A. Quantity of raw material used each month to produce the number of units called for by the production budget (3 units of raw materials per unit of finished product)	38,400	48,600	28,200
B. Ending inventory required (equal to 50% of next month's usage)	24,300	14,000	*

C. Purchases budget using cost of goods sold model with known data (assuming that December 31 inventory is equal to that required by the raw materials inventory policy).

	January	*February*
Beginning inventory (units)	19,200	24,300
Add: Purchases	?	?
Goods available for use (units)	?	?
Less: Ending inventory (units)	(24,300)	(14,100)
Quantity of goods used (units)	38,400	48,600
By working from the bottom up, the quantity of goods available for use is calculated first, and then beginning inventory is subtracted from goods available for use to get purchases in units of	43,500	38,400

Note that the purchases budget for March cannot be established until the sales budget for May is available because the inventory of finished goods at the end of April is a function of May sales, and the inventory of raw materials at the end of March is a function of April production requirements.

* Won't be known until the April production budget is established.

Many manufacturing firms increase the accuracy of their cost of production and cost of goods sold forecasts by using the contribution margin model for manufacturing costs. (Note that in a merchandising firm the cost of goods sold is a variable expense.) Variable costs of manufacturing (raw materials, direct labor, and variable overhead) are determined, and the variable cost ratio (variable manufacturing costs as a percentage of selling price) is

---

EXHIBIT 14–4   Budgeted Purchases Using the Gross Profit Ratio

---

I. Assumptions:
Sales forecast as shown below.
Gross profit ratio budgeted at 30%.
Ending inventory planned to be 80% of next month's cost of goods sold.
Required: Budgeted purchases for April, May, June.

II. Budget calculations:

	March	April	May	June	July
Sales forecast. . . .	$85,000	$ 90,000	$ 75,000	$ 82,000	$92,000
Cost of goods sold (Sales × (1 − 0.3))	59,500	63,000	52,500	57,400	64,400
Ending inventory . .	50,400	42,000	45,920	51,520	
Beginning inventory.		$ 50,400	$ 42,000	$ 45,920	
Add: Purchases . . .		?	?	?	
Goods available for sale		$?	$?	$?	
Less: Ending inventory.		(42,000)	(45,920)	(51,520)	
Cost of goods sold .		$ 63,000	$ 52,500	$ 57,400	
By working from the bottom up, the amount of goods available for sale is calculated first, and then beginning inventory is subtracted from goods available for sale to get purchases of . . .		$ 54,600	$ 56,420	$ 63,000	

---

calculated. This ratio is then used instead of the cost of goods sold ratio as illustrated in Exhibit 14–4. Fixed manufacturing expenses are budgeted separately because they are not a function of the quantity produced or sold.

The Operating Expense Budget

The cost behavior patterns of selling, general, administrative, and other operating expenses are determined, and these expenses are budgeted accordingly. For example, sales commissions will be a function of the forecast of either sales dollars or units. The historical pattern of some expenses will be affected by changes in strategy that management may plan for the budget period. In a participative budgeting system the manager of each department or cost responsibility center will submit the anticipated cost of the department's planned activities, along with descriptions of the activities and explanations of significant differences from past experience. After review by higher levels of management, and perhaps negotiation, a final budget is established.

There is a natural tendency for managers to submit budget estimates that are slightly higher than what the costs are really expected to be. This practice gives the manager some **budget slack** for contingencies or cost increases that may not have been planned. Adding budget slack or ''padding the budget'' can result in a significantly misleading budget for the organization as a whole. In spite of budget managers' pleas and/or threats that padding be eliminated, the practice probably continues in virtually all organizations. Some budget managers deal with the problem by judgmentally reducing the grand total of all departmental expense budgets when the company budget is prepared.

The Budgeted Income Statement

The sales forecast, cost of goods sold budget, and operating expense budget data are used by management accountants to prepare a budgeted income statement. This is a complex process but a necessary one if the anticipated overall results of the budget period are to be evaluated.

In many cases, if the budgeted income statement that has been prepared shows unacceptable results, top management will request that operating departments review their budget proposals and make adjustments to them so that profitability goals can be achieved.

The Cash Budget

The cash budget is very much like a budgeted statement of cash flows, but with a relatively short time frame. The financial manager must be able to anticipate short-term borrowing requirements because arrangements for borrowing must be made in advance of the date the cash is needed. When considering a loan, the lending officer at the bank wants to know how much will be needed when, and will also want to know when the borrower expects to repay the loan. A potential borrower who cannot answer these questions because a cash budget has not been prepared may not receive a loan. The financial manager must also know when temporarily excess cash is available for investment, and when it will be needed, so that cash can be invested to earn interest income.

A number of assumptions about the timing of cash receipts and disbursements must be made when the cash budget is prepared. For example, how long after the sale will an account receivable be collected? The days' sales in receivables statistic will help answer this question. Again, the sales forecast comes into play. For example, assume that, based on past experience, the entity expects that 25 percent of a month's sales will be collected in the month of sale, 60 percent will be collected in the month following the month of sale, and 12 percent will be collected in the second month following the month of sale. (The last 3 percent will be collected over a several-month period and is ignored in the budgeting process because of its relatively small amount and uncertain collection pattern, or is written off as uncollectible.) A cash receipts analysis for March and April might look like this:

	January	*February*	*March*	*April*
Sales forecast	$40,000	$50,000	$30,000	$40,000
Collections:				
25% of current				
month's sales			$ 7,500	$10,000
60% of prior				
month's sales			30,000	18,000
12% of second prior				
month's sales			4,800	6,000
Total collections			$42,300	$34,000

If this cash receipts forecast were being made in late December for the next four months, collections of sales made prior to January would probably be based on an estimate of when the accounts receivable at the end of December would be collected, rather than on the estimated collection percentages of monthly sales because the resulting forecast will be more accurate. This approach, and an alternative format for the cash receipts forecast analysis, would look like this:

	January	*February*	*March*	*April*
Sales forecast	$40,000	$50,000	$30,000	$40,000
Collections:				
From December 31				
accounts receivable				
of $68,423	$38,000	$25,000	$ 3,000	$ 1,000

(*continued*)

	January	February	March	April
From January sales	10,000	24,000	4,800	—
From February sales		12,500	30,000	$ 6,000
From March sales			7,500	18,000
From April sales			—	10,000
Total collections	$48,000	$61,500	$45,300	$35,000

Note that the difference between the budgeted cash receipts for March and April in the two formats is the estimated collections in those months of December 31 accounts receivable. Even though the estimated collections from sales occur over three months, the estimated collections of December 31 accounts receivable are more realistically spread over a longer period, and it has been recognized that not all of the receivables are likely to be collected.

It should be clear that the keys to an accurate cash receipts forecast are the accuracy of the sales forecast and the accuracy of the collection percentage estimates. The actual calculation is clearly an ideal computer spreadsheet application.

On the cash disbursement side, the payment pattern for purchases must be determined. If suppliers' terms are 2/10, net 30, the financial manager will assume that two-thirds of a month's purchases will be paid for in the same month as the purchase, and one-third will be paid for in the subsequent month. The format of the analysis of payments on accounts payable will be similar to that illustrated above for cash receipts. As was the case for the cash receipts forecast, the accuracy of the cash payments forecast is a function of the accuracy of the sales forecast (on which the finished goods purchases or production and raw materials purchases budgets are based) and the accuracy of the payment pattern estimates.

The frequency with which the company pays its employees will be related to projected payroll expense to determine this significant disbursement. Capital expenditure plans and anticipated dividend payments will have to be considered. Of course, projected depreciation expense and other amortization expenses are ignored in cash budgeting because these are not expenses requiring a cash disbursement.

Once the assumptions about the timing of cash receipts and disbursements have been made, the preparation of the cash budget is a straightforward mechanical process easily accomplished on a computer spreadsheet program. Budgeted cash receipts are added to the beginning cash balance, budgeted disbursements are subtracted, and a preliminary ending balance is determined. The organization will have an established minimum cash balance to be maintained. This "inventory" of cash serves the same purpose as an inventory of product; it is a cushion that can absorb forecast errors. If the cash forecast indicates a preliminary balance that is less than the desired minimum, temporary investments must be liquidated or a loan must be planned to bring the forecast balance up to the desired level. If the preliminary balance is greater than the minimum desired working balance, the excess is available for repayment of loans or investment. The cash budget will be prepared for monthly periods at least; many organizations forecast cash flows on a daily basis for a week or two, and then weekly for a week or two, so optimum cash management results can be achieved. Exhibit 14–5 illustrates a cash budget format and shows sources of the budget amounts.

EXHIBIT 14–5 Cash Budget Illustration and Assumptions

CRUISERS, INC.
Cash Budget
For the Months of March and April

Date budget prepared: February 25

Activity	March	April	Source/Comments
Beginning cash balance	$ 5,000	$20,000	March: Forecast balance for March 1. April: Indicated cash balance at end of March.
Cash receipts:			
From sales made in prior periods	60,000	50,000	Analysis of accounts receivable detail when budget prepared, and sales forecast for subsequent periods with collection estimates based on past experience.
From sales made in current period	10,000	8,000	Sales forecast and estimates based on past experience.
From investing activities	1,000	—	Plans for sale of assets.
From financing activities	5,000	—	Plans for new borrowings or sale of stock.
Total cash available	$81,000	$78,000	
Cash disbursements:			
To suppliers for inventory purchases	30,000	36,000	Analysis of accounts payable detail for purchases that have been made, and purchases budget for subsequent periods with estimates based on supplier terms and past payment practices.

(continued)

EXHIBIT 14–5 (concluded)

CRUISERS, INC.
Cash Budget
For the Months of March and April

Activity	March	April	Source/Comments
To other creditors and employees for operating expenses and wages	20,000	24,000	Analysis of accrued liability detail for transactions that have occurred and production budget and operating expense budget for subsequent periods, and knowledge of past payment practices.
For investing activities	8,000	17,000	Plans for purchase of plant and equipment, and other investments.
For financing activities	3,000	—	Plans for dividend payments, debt repayments, or purchases of treasury stock.
Total disbursements	$61,000	$77,000	
Indicated cash balance	$20,000	1,000	
Desired cash balance	5,000	5,000	Based on financial operating needs and amount of "cushion" for error that is desired.
Excess/Deficiency)	$15,000	$(4,000)	Excess available for temporary investment or repayment of loans. Deficiency indicates a need to liquidate temporary investments or arrange financing.

The Budgeted Balance Sheet

The impact of all of the other budgets on the balance sheet is determined, and a budgeted balance sheet is prepared. This hierarchy is illustrated in Exhibit 14–2. For example, the production and purchases budgets include inventory budget estimates. The operating expense budget is the source of the depreciation and amortization impact on the balance sheet. The budgeted income statement indicates the effect of net income or loss on retained earnings. The cash budget, with its assumptions about collections of accounts receivable and payments of accounts payable and other liabilities, purchases of equipment, payment of dividends, and financing activities is the source of budgeted balance sheet amounts for current assets (except inventories), plant assets, liabilities, paid-in capital, treasury stock, and the dividend impact on retained earnings. In effect, the financial accounting process is applied using planned transaction amounts to generate an anticipated balance sheet. This balance sheet will be analyzed to determine that all of the appropriate ratios are within the limits established by top management. The reason for any discrepancies will be determined, and appropriate changes in plans will be considered. This process can very well require modifications to some of the other budgets, and if so, the entire budgeting process may have to be repeated. Although this may seem like a tedious and frustrating thing to have to do, it is better done in the planning process than after the company has already acted, with the result that its financial condition has been adversely affected. Recovery at that stage may be very difficult to accomplish.

The most challenging parts of the budgeting process are developing the sales forecast, coming up with the assumptions related to the timing of receipts and disbursements, and establishing policies for ending inventory quantities, the minimum desired cash balance, and other targets. The budget calculations, frequently a challenge for students learning about budgeting, are easily made for most organizations using computer spreadsheet models. These models make it feasible for planners to change various assumptions and quickly and easily see the effect of changes on budgeted results.

PERFORMANCE REPORTING

Characteristics of the Performance Report

The **performance report** compares actual results to budgeted amounts. The performance report is an integral part of the control process, because those activities that are performing differently from expectations are highlighted, and the managers responsible for achieving goals are provided with information about activities that need attention.

The general format of a performance report is:

Activity	Budget Amount	Actual Amount	Variance	Explanation

The **variance** is usually described as *favorable* or *unfavorable*, depending on the nature of the activity and the relationship between the budget and actual amounts. For revenues a **favorable variance** is the excess of actual revenues over the budget amount. An actual expense that is greater than a budgeted expense causes an **unfavorable variance.** Sometimes the favorable or unfavorable nature of the variance must be determined based on the relationship of one variance to another. For example, if a favorable variance in advertising expense resulted from not placing as many ads as planned, and this caused lower sales than were forecast, the variance is not really favorable to the company.

The Explanation column of the performance report is used to communicate to upper-level managers concise explanations of causes of significant variances. Because top management probably doesn't want to be inundated with details, a system of **responsibility reporting** is used by many organizations. Responsibility reporting involves successive degrees of summarization, such that each layer of management receives detailed performance reports for the activities immediately below that layer but summaries of the results of activities of lower layers in the chain of command.

The paramount concern of a manager should be with the action that is going to be taken to eliminate unfavorable variances and to capture favorable variances. Performance reports should not be used to find fault or place blame; such uses are likely to result in dysfunctional behavior in creating the budget amount and/or reporting actual results.

The concept of **management by exception** that is frequently used in connection with performance reporting permits managers to concentrate their attention on only those activities that are not performing according to plan. The presumption of this concept is that management time is a scarce resource, and that if a thorough job of planning is done, a manager's attention need be devoted only to those areas not performing according to plan. To facilitate the use of management by exception, the variance is frequently expressed as a percentage of the budget, and only those variances in excess of a predetermined percentage (e.g., 10 percent) are investigated.

Performance reports must be issued soon after the period in which the activity takes place if they are to be useful for influencing future activity because results must be linked to the actions that caused those results. If there is too long a time lag, the actions are forgotten, or confused with later activities. All performance reports need not be issued with the same frequency. Thus production supervisors might receive weekly reports, a supervisor responsible for the use of a very high-cost raw material might receive a daily report, and the advertising manager might receive a monthly report.

An issue that arises in the design of a performance report is the extent of the cost-generating activities to be listed for a particular responsibility area relative to the degree of short-term control that the manager has over those activities. For example, should the performance report for a production line show the depreciation expense, property taxes, insurance cost, and other "noncontrollable" expenses associated with that production line, or should the performance report be limited to those expenses over which the supervisor has real short-term control? Advocates of the all-inclusive report format suggest that it is appropriate for the supervisor to be aware of all costs, even though she/he may not be able to influence them in the short run. Advocates of the limited format believe that the report should focus on those costs that the supervisor can control and that including others causes confusion, and/or may focus attention on the wrong costs (i.e., those that can't be controlled in the short run). There is no "right" answer to this issue. One middle ground solution is periodically to provide the supervisor with all cost data, but to focus the performance report on those costs that can be controlled in the short run. Notice that at the heart of the issue is the allocation of fixed costs, and recall the previously discussed warning not to allocate fixed costs arbitrarily because "they don't behave that way."

A performance report for the April production of Model 21 sailboats made by Cruisers, Inc., is presented in Exhibit 14–6. (Actual costs in this exhibit have been brought forward from Exhibit 12–4.) Note that the manufacturing overhead has been classified accord-

---

EXHIBIT 14–6 Performance Report Illustration

CRUISERS, INC.
Performance Report—Model 21 Sailboat
April

Activity	Budget	Actual	Variance*	Explanation
Raw materials	$370,300	$368,510	$ 1,790 F	Variance not significant in total.
Direct labor	302,680	330,240	27,560 U	New workers not as efficient as planned.
Manufacturing overhead:				
Variable	89,400	103,160	13,760 U	Related to additional hours caused by labor inefficiency.
Fixed	193,200	185,800	7,400 F	Plant fire insurance premium credit received.
Totals	$955,580	$987,710	$32,130 U	

*F is favorable, U is unfavorable.

ing to cost behavior pattern. This is appropriate because the efforts made to control these costs will be a function of their cost behavior pattern. The performance report in Exhibit 14–6, although interesting and perhaps helpful to top management's determination of why budgeted results were not achieved, is not very useful for operating managers and supervisors. Some of the questions raised by this report include:

1. Were there significant but offsetting variances in raw materials?
2. Which workers were not efficient?
3. Were the new workers being paid a lower than budget wage rate until they became proficient?
4. Is the training program for new workers effective?
5. How does the manufacturing overhead variance affect the validity of the predetermined overhead application rate used to apply overhead to production?

A method for answering these questions, and others, and for preparing a performance report that is useful for the cost controlling efforts of operating managers and supervisors will be discussed in Chapter 15.

Reporting for Segments of an Organization

A **segment** of an organization is a division, product line, sales territory, or other organizational unit. Management frequently wants to report company results by segment in such a way that the total income for each segment equals the total company net income. For example, assume that Cruisers, Inc., has three divisions: Sailboats, Motorboats, and Repair Parts. The following income statement might be prepared:

CRUISERS, INC.
Segmented Income Statement
Quarter Ended July 31, 1992

	Total Company	Sailboat Division	Motorboat Division	Repair Parts Division
Sales	$560,000	$320,000	$160,000	$80,000
Variable expenses .	240,000	128,000	72,000	40,000
Contribution margin	$320,000	$192,000	$ 88,000	$40,000
Fixed expenses. . .	282,000	164,000	72,000	46,000
Operating income. .	$ 38,000	$ 28,000	$ 16,000	$ (6,000)

From an analysis of this segment income statement management might decide to eliminate the Repair Parts Division because it is operating at a loss. In fact, you might think that operating income would increase by $6,000 if this division were eliminated.

Now suppose that, as a result of a detailed analysis of the fixed expenses, you learn that the fixed expenses assigned to each division represent the sum of the fixed expenses incurred in each division **(direct fixed expenses)** plus an allocated share of the corporate fixed expenses **(common fixed expenses)** that would continue to be incurred even if one of the divisions were to be closed. (Would the president's salary—a common fixed expense—be reduced if one of the divisions were closed?) Your analysis of fixed expenses shows:

	Total Company	Sailboat Division	Motorboat Division	Repair Parts Division
Direct fixed expenses	$170,000	$100,000	$40,000	$30,000
Common fixed expenses allocated in proportion to sales	112,000	64,000	32,000	16,000
Total fixed expenses	$282,000	$164,000	$72,000	$46,000

Some thought about the behavior of common fixed expenses, which will continue to be incurred even if the Repair Parts Division is closed, reveals that Cruisers, Inc., would be worse off by $10,000 because that division's contribution to common fixed expenses and profits would be eliminated. This is illustrated clearly in a more appropriately designed segment income statement:

CRUISERS, INC.
Segmented Income Statement
Quarter Ended July 31, 1992

	Total Company	Sailboat Division	Motorboat Division	Repair Parts Division
Sales	$560,000	$320,000	$160,000	$80,000
Variable expenses .	240,000	128,000	72,000	40,000
Contribution margin	$320,000	$192,000	$ 88,000	$40,000
Direct fixed expenses	170,000	100,000	40,000	30,000
Segment margin . .	$150,000	$ 92,000	$ 48,000	$10,000
Common fixed expenses	112,000			
Operating income. .	$ 38,000			

The key feature of the corrected segmented income statement is that common fixed expenses have not been *arbitrarily allocated* to the segments. The corrected statement reflects the contribution of each segment to the common fixed expenses and company profit. Using this approach should avoid analytical errors like the one that would have resulted in closing the Repair Parts Division.

The same statement format separating direct and common fixed expenses should be used whenever both classifications of fixed expenses exist. For example, if the Sailboat Division's segment margin of $92,000 were to be broken down by sales territory, that division's $100,000 of direct fixed expenses would be analyzed, and the portion that is direct to each territory would be subtracted from the territory contribution margin to arrive at the territory's **segment margin.** The division's fixed expenses that are common from a territory perspective *would not* be allocated to the territories; they would be subtracted as a single amount from the total territory segment margin to arrive at the division's segment margin of $92,000.

Sometimes the segments of an organization are referred to as *responsibility centers, cost centers, profit centers,* or *investment centers.* A **responsibility center** is an element of the organization over which a manager has been assigned responsibility and authority, and for which performance is evaluated. A **cost center** does not directly generate any revenue for the organization. For example, the Industrial Engineering Department would be a cost center. An organization segment that is responsible for selling a product, like the Sailboat Division of Cruisers, Inc., could be either a **profit center** or an **investment center.** The method of evaluating the performance of each kind of center (or segment) is summarized in Exhibit 14–7.

Because individuals would like to think of their efforts in terms of profits rather than costs, sometimes an effort is made to convert

EXHIBIT 14–7   Methods of Evaluating Responsibility Centers (Segments)

Segment	How Performance Is Evaluated
Cost center	Actual costs incurred compared to budgeted costs
Profit center	Actual segment margin compared to budged segment margin
Investment center	Comparison of actual and budgeted return on investment (ROI) based on segment margin and assets used by or under control of the segment

cost centers to profit centers or investment centers by establishing a **transfer price** at which products, components, or services are "sold" from one segment of the organization to another. Since the revenue of one segment becomes the cost of another segment, it is difficult to establish a transfer price that is considered fair by all concerned. This issue, plus the increased bookkeeping costs, means that there have to be significant behavioral and other qualitative benefits expected to warrant transfer pricing at the cost center level of the organization. Transfer pricing is applied to intersegment transactions between major divisions of a company and affiliates organized as separate legal entities. These transfer prices can influence bonuses, source of supply decisions, and state and national income tax obligations. The determination of an appropriate transfer price in these situations is usually very complex.

The Flexible Budget

Consider the following partial performance report for the hull manufacturing department of Cruisers, Inc., for the month of March:

Activity	Budget Amount	Actual Amount	Variance	Explanation
Raw materials . .	$ 64,056	$ 69,212	$ 5,156 U	Produced more boats than planned.
Direct labor . . .	48,720	54,992	6,272 U	Same as above.
Manufacturing overhead:				
Variable . . .	10,880	12,438	1,558 U	Same as above.
Fixed.	36,720	37,320	600 U	Immaterial.
Totals	$160,376	$173,962	$13,586 U	

Now suppose that you find out that the budget amount was based on the expectation that 100 hulls would be built during March, but that actually 110 hulls had been built. Your first inclination is to recalculate the budget amount columns by increasing each of the variable cost items by 10 percent to determine how much cost should have been incurred for the activity actually performed. (Why isn't the fixed overhead budget amount also increased 10 percent?) Adjusting the original budget so it reflects budgeted amounts for actual activity is called *flexing the budget*.

The performance report using the **flexible budget** would be:

Activity	Budget Amount	Actual Amount	Variance	Explanation
Raw materials.	$ 70,462	$ 69,212	$1,250 F	Immaterial
Direct labor.	53,592	54,992	1,400 U	Immaterial
Manufacturing overhead:				
Variable	11,968	12,438	470 U	Immaterial
Fixed.	36,720	37,320	600 U	Immaterial
Totals	$172,742	$173,962	$1,220 U	

The variances are now relatively insignificant, and the initial conclusion made from this report is the correct one—the production manager is performing according to plan for the number of hulls that were actually produced.

Of course, there is a question about why 110 hulls were produced when the original budget called for production of 100 hulls. The answer to that question, however, is not relevant to controlling costs for the number of hulls actually made.

Flexible budgeting does not affect the predetermined overhead application rate used to apply overhead to production. To the extent that the actual level of production differs from the activity estimate used in developing the predetermined overhead application rate, fixed manufacturing overhead will be overapplied or underapplied. However, this is not a cost control issue. It is an accounting issue, usually resolved by closing the amount of overapplied or underapplied overhead to cost of goods sold.

Flexible budgeting means that *the budget allowance for variable costs should be flexed to show the costs that should have been incurred for the level of activity actually experienced.* The variance in the level of activity should be investigated and explained so that improvements in activity forecasting accuracy can be achieved, but this is a separate and distinct issue from cost performance evaluation.

SUMMARY

A budget is a financial plan. Many organizations have a policy to require budgets because budgets force planning, provide a benchmark against which to compare performance, and require coordination between the functional areas of the organization. Performance reporting involves comparing planned results with actual results.

To a large extent the budgeting process is influenced by behavioral considerations. How the budget is used by management will influence the validity of the budget as a planning and controlling tool. In most instances an interactive, participative approach to budget preparation, together with an attitude that the budget is a plan, results in a most useful budget document.

Budgets can be prepared for a single period, or on a multiperiod, rolling basis. Which is most appropriate for any activity depends on the degree of control over the activity and the rapidity with which the environment of the activity changes. Different activities may have different budget time frames.

An operating budget is made up of several budgets. The sales forecast (or revenue budget) is the starting point for all of the other budgets that are prepared and that become components of the operating budget. There is a hierarchy of budgets, and the results of one budget will provide input for another budget.

The purchases or production budget is prepared once the sales forecast has been determined and an inventory policy has been established. Ending inventory is expressed as a function of the expected sales or usage of the subsequent period. One period's ending inventory is the next period's beginning inventory.

There is a natural tendency for operating managers to build slack into their budget estimates. When budget managers combine departmental budgets into an overall organizational budget, the cumulative slack can cause the overall budget to lose significance. Budget managers must be aware of the slack issue; they deal with it in different ways.

The operating expense budget is a function of the sales forecast, cost behavior patterns, and planned changes from past levels of advertising, administrative, and other activities.

A budgeted income statement shows planned operating results for the entity as a whole. If top management is not satisfied with budgeted net income, changes in operations may be planned and/or various elements of the operating budget may be returned to operating managers for revision.

Once the income statement budget has been settled, a cash budget can be prepared. Cash flows from operating activities are forecast by adjusting net income for noncash items included in the income statement, as well as expectations about cash receipts and disbursements related to revenues and expenses. Cash flows from investing and financing activities are estimated, and the estimated cash balance at the end of the fiscal period is determined. Cash in excess of a minimum operating balance is available for investment. A deficiency in cash means that plans should be made to liquidate temporary investments or borrow money, or that cash payment assumptions must be revised.

The budgeted balance sheet uses data from all of the other budgets. Management uses this budget to evaluate the entity's projected financial position. If the result is not satisfactory, appropriate operating, investing, and financing plans will be revised.

The challenge to accurate budgeting is having an accurate estimate of activity and assumptions and policies that reflect what is likely to happen in the future. Computer spreadsheet models can make the budget calculation a relatively easy process that can be repeated many times to determine the impact of changes in estimates and assumptions.

Part of the payoff of the budgeting process involves comparing planned results with actual results. This is done in a performance report. The variance shown in the performance report is the difference between the budget and actual amounts. Management by exception involves focusing attention on those activities that have a significant variance. The objective of this analysis is to understand why the variance occurred and, if appropriate, to take action to eliminate unfavorable variances and capture favorable variances.

Segment reporting for an organization involves assigning revenues and expenses to divisions, product lines, geographic areas, or other responsibility centers. In this process costs that are common to a group of segments should not be arbitrarily allocated to individual segments in that group.

Flexible budgeting recognizes cost behavior patterns. The original budget amount for variable items based on planned activity is adjusted by calculating a budget allowance based on actual activity for the period. This results in a variable cost variance that is meaningful because the effect of a difference between budgeted and actual volume of activity is removed from the variance. Only variable cost budgets are flexed.

KEY TERMS AND CONCEPTS

budget *(p. 424)* A financial plan.

budget slack *(p. 436)* Allowances for contingencies built into a budget. Sometimes called *padding* or *cushion*.

common fixed expense *(p. 445)* An expense that is not assigned to an organization segment in a segmented income statement because the expense would be incurred even if the segment were eliminated.

continuous budget *(p. 427)* A budget that is prepared for several periods in the future, and that is revised several times prior to the budget period. Sometimes called a *rolling budget*.

cost center *(p. 446)* A responsibility center for which performance is evaluated by comparing budgeted cost with actual cost.

direct fixed expense *(p. 445)* An expense assigned to an organization segment in a segmented income statement that would not be incurred if the segment were eliminated.

favorable variance *(p. 441)* The excess of actual revenue over budgeted revenue or budgeted cost over actual cost.

flexible budget *(p. 447)* A budget that has been adjusted to reflect a budget allowance based on actual level of activity, rather than the planned level of activity used to establish the original budget.

investment center *(p. 446)* A responsibility center for which performance is evaluated by comparing budgeted return on investment with actual return on investment.

management by exception *(p. 442)* A management concept that involves thorough planning, and then exerting corrective effort only in those areas that do not show results consistent with the plan.

operating budget *(p. 428)* An operating plan comprising the sales budget (or sales forecast), the purchases/production budget, the operating expense budget, the income statement budget, the cash budget, and the budgeted balance sheet.

participative budgeting *(p. 426)* A budgeting process that involves input and negotiation of several layers of management.

performance report *(p. 441)* A report comparing planned and actual activity or costs.

profit center *(p. 446)* A responsibility center for which performance is evaluated by comparing budgeted profit with actual profit.

responsibility center *(p. 446)* An element of the organization over which a manager has been assigned responsibility and authority.

responsibility reporting *(p. 442)* A system of performance reporting that involves successive degrees of summarization as the number of management responsibility levels being reported about increases.

rolling budget *(p. 427)* A budget that is prepared for several periods in the future, and that is revised several times prior to the budget period. Sometimes called a *continuous budget.*

sales forecast *(p. 429)* Expected sales for future periods; a key to the budgeting process.

segment *(p. 444)* A unit of an organization, such as a product line, sales territory, or group of related activities.

segment margin *(p. 446)* The contribution of a segment of an organization to the common fixed expenses and operating income of the organization.

single-period budget *(p. 427)* A budget that has been prepared only once prior to the budget period. This contrasts with a "continuous budget."

top-down budgeting *(p. 426)* A budgeting approach that implies little or no input from lower levels of management.

transfer price *(p. 447)* A price established for the "sale" of goods or services from one segment of the organization to another segment of the organization.

unfavorable variance *(p. 442)* The excess of budgeted revenue over actual revenue or actual cost over budgeted cost.

variance *(p. 441)* The difference between budget and actual; variances are labeled as "favorable" or "unfavorable," usually on the basis of the arithmetic difference between budget and actual.

zero-based budgeting *(p. 426)* A budgeting process that involves justifying resource requirements based on an analysis and prioritization of unit objectives without reference to prior period budget allowances.

EXERCISES AND PROBLEMS

14–1. Western Manufacturing Co. has a policy that requires that 20 percent of the expected sales of its product for any month be on hand at the end of the prior month. Forecasted sales, in units, for the months of May through August are as follows:

May.	30,000 units
June.	40,000 units
July	60,000 units
August.	50,000 units

Required:
    a. Calculate the number of units planned for ending inventory for May, June, and July.
    b. Calculate the number of units that will be budgeted to be produced in July.

14–2. Wee Tot Day Care Center's experience was that four disposable diapers were used each day for each infant enrolled. The desired inventory at the end of each month was the diaper requirements for the first five days of the next month. Forecast infant enrollment, as well as the number of days infants would be served, for the next four months follows:

	Forecast Enrollment	Number of Service Days in Month
April	42	22
May	46	21
June	37	22
July	33	23

Assume that the diaper inventory at the end of March equaled the desired inventory.

Required:
    a. Calculate the desired ending inventory and projected usage of diapers for the months of April, May, and June.
    b. Calculate the number of diapers to be purchased during the months of April, May, and June.
    c. Assume that diapers are packaged in cases that hold five dozen and

that the day care center gets a price break if purchases are made 10 cases at a time. How does this information affect the purchases budget?

14–3. Recognition, Inc., makes award medallions that are attached to ribbons. Each medallion requires 24 inches of ribbon. The sales forecast for February is 2,000 medallions. Estimated beginning inventories and desired ending inventories for February are the following:

	Estimated Beginning Inventory	*Desired Ending Inventory*
Medallions	1,000	800
Ribbon (yards)	50	20

Required:

a. Calculate the number of medallions to be made in February.
b. Calculate the number of yards of ribbon to be purchased in February.

14–4. Walman Co. is forecasting sales of 30,000 units of product Y for March. To make one unit of finished product, two pounds of raw material B are required. Actual beginning and desired ending inventories of raw material B and product Y are:

	March 1 Actual	*March 31 Desired*
Raw material B	19,000 pounds	16,000 pounds
Product Y	8,000 units	10,000 units

Required:

a. Calculate the number of units of product Y to be produced during March.
b. Calculate the number of pounds of raw material B to be purchased during March.

14–5. Two ounces of x-scent are required for each gallon of Bracer, a popular after-shave lotion. Budgeted *production* of Bracer for the first three quarters of 1993, in gallons is:

Quarter I	10,000 gallons
Quarter II	18,000 gallons
Quarter III	11,000 gallons

Management's policy is to have on hand at the end of every quarter enough x-scent inventory to meet 25 percent of the next quarter's production needs. 5,000 ounces of x-scent were on hand at the beginning of Quarter I.

Required:

a. Calculate the number of ounces of x-scent to be purchased in each of the first two quarters of 1993.
b. Explain why management plans for an ending inventory instead of

planning to purchase each quarter the amount of raw material needed for that quarter's production.

14–6. Threeputt Co. had actual sales for July and August, and forecast sales for September, October, November, and December as follows:

Actual:	July	3,020 units
	August	3,233 units
Forecast:	September.	3,400 units
	October	3,800 units
	November	3,600 units
	December	3,100 units

Required:

a. The firm's policy is to have finished goods inventory on hand at the end of each month that is equal to one-half of the next month's sales. It is currently estimated that there will be 1,780 units on hand at the end of August. Calculate the number of units to be produced in each of the months of September, October, and November.

b. Each unit of finished product requires 6 pounds of raw material A. The firm's policy is to have raw material inventory on hand at the end of each month that is equal to the next month's estimated usage. It is currently estimated that 20,000 pounds of raw material A will be on hand at the end of August. Calculate the number of pounds of raw material A to be purchased in each of the months of September and October.

14–7. B-Mart is a bargain retailer. The firm's average gross profit ratio is 22 percent. The sales forecast for the next four months follows:

July	$192,000
August	215,000
September	230,000
October	206,000

Management's inventory policy is to have ending inventory equal to 1.5 times the cost of sales for the subsequent month, although it is estimated that the cost of inventory at June 30 will be $235,000.

Required:

Calculate the purchases budget, in dollars, for the months of July and August.

14–8. Bluestone Co. is a retail jeweler. Most of the firm's business is in jewelry and watches. The firm's average percentage markup on cost for jewelry is 90 percent, and for watches is 40 percent. The sales forecast for the next two months for each product category is as follows:

	Jewelry	Watches
May	$85,000	$22,000
June	96,000	20,000

Bluestone's policy, which is expected to be achieved at the end of April, is to have ending inventory equal to 50 percent of the cost of the next month's sales.

Required:

a. Calculate the cost of goods sold for jewelry and watches for May and June.

b. Calculate a purchases budget, in dollars, for each product for the month of May.

14–9. Lynn Company's sales are all made on account. The firm's collection experience has been that 20 percent of a month's sales is collected in the month the sale is made, 70 percent is collected in the month following the sale, and 9 percent is collected in the second month following the sale. The sales forecast for the months of May through August is:

May	$200,000
June	300,000
July	350,000
August	250,000

Required:

Calculate the cash collections that would be included in the cash budgets for July and August.

14–10. Threeputt Co. had actual sales for July and August, and forecast sales for September, October, November, and December as follows:

Actual:	July	$126,848
	August	135,792
Forecast:	September.	144,000
	October	160,000
	November.	152,000
	December	130,000

Based on an analysis of accounts receivable made near the end of August, it was estimated that collections of August 31 accounts receivable will amount to $84,000 in September and $21,000 in October. Based on past experience, it is estimated that 30 percent of a month's sales is collected in the month of sale, 50 percent is collected in the month following the sale, and 18 percent is collected in the second month following the sale.

Required:

Calculate the estimated cash receipts for September, October, and November.

14–11. QB Sportswear is a custom imprinter that began operations six months ago. Sales have exceeded management's most optimistic projections. Sales are made on account; half of one month's sales are collected in the month following the month of sale, and 45 percent are collected in the second month following the month of sale. Merchandise purchases and operating expenses are paid as follows:

In the month during which the merchandise is pur-
chased or the cost is incurred   75%
In the subsequent month   25%

QB Sportswear's income statement budget for each of the next four
months, newly revised to reflect the success of the firm, follows:

	September	*October*	*November*	*December*
Sales	$42,000	$54,000	$68,000	$59,000
Cost of goods sold:				
Beginning inventory	$ 6,000	$14,400	$20,600	$21,900
Purchases	37,800	44,000	48,900	33,100
Cost of goods available for sale	$43,800	$58,400	$69,500	$55,000
Less: Ending Inventory	(14,400)	(20,600)	(21,900)	(20,000)
Cost of goods sold	$29,400	$37,800	$47,600	$35,000
Gross profit	$12,600	$16,200	$20,400	$24,000
Operating expenses	10,500	12,800	14,300	16,100
Operating income	$ 2,100	$ 3,400	$ 6,100	$ 7,900

Cash on hand August 31 is estimated to be $40,000. Collections of August
31 accounts receivable were estimated to be $20,000 in September and
$15,000 in October. Payments of August 31 accounts payable and accrued
expenses in September were estimated to be $24,000.

Required:
a. Prepare a cash budget for September.
b. What is your advice to management of QB Sportswear?

14–12. Refer to the QB Sportswear data presented in Problem 14–11.

Required:
a. Prepare a cash budget for October and November. What are the prospects for this company if its sales growth continues at a similar rate?
b. Assume now that QB Sportswear is a mature firm, and that the September–November data represent a seasonal peak in business. Prepare
a cash budget for December, January, and February assuming that the
income statements for January and February are the same as December's. Explain how the cash budget would be used to support a request
to a bank for a seasonal loan.

14–13. The president of Bookston, Inc., attended a seminar about the contribution margin model idea and returned to her company full of enthusiasm
about it. She requested that last year's traditional model income statement be revised, and she received the following report:

	Total Company	Division A	Division B	Division C
Sales	$100,000	$40,000	$25,000	$35,000
Variable expenses . .	60,000	26,000	15,000	19,000
Contribution margin . . .	$ 40,000	$14,000	$10,000	$16,000
Fixed expenses . .	30,000	10,000	11,000	9,000
Net income (loss)	$ 10,000	$ 4,000	$(1,000)	$ 7,000

The president was told that the fixed expenses of $30,000 included $21,000 that had been split evenly between divisions because they were general corporate expenses. After looking at the statement, the president exclaimed, "I knew it! Division B is a drag on the whole company. Close it down!"

Required:

a. Evaluate the president's remark.

b. Calculate what the company's net income would be if Division B were closed down.

c. Write a policy statement related to the allocation of fixed expenses.

14–14. Murphey Co. produces three models of calculators. The following table summarizes data about each model:

	Business	Math	Student
Selling per unit	$ 28	$ 32	$ 10
Contribution margin per unit	14	15	2
Units sold per month . .	2,000	1,500	4,500
Total contribution margin	$28,000	$22,500	$ 9,000
Direct fixed expenses . .	15,000	12,000	6,000
Segment margin.	$13,000	$10,500	$ 3,000
Allocated company fixed expenses	4,000	4,000	4,000
Operating income (loss)	$ 9,000	$ 6,500	$(1,000)

Required:

a. Criticize the above presentation.

b. Calculate the effect on total company net income if the student model were discontinued.

c. Calculate the contribution margin ratio for each model.

d. If an advertising campaign focusing on a single model were to result in an increase of 5,000 units in the quantity of units sold, which model should be advertised? Explain your answer.

e. If an advertising campaign focusing on a single model were to result in an increase of $15,000 in revenues, which model should be advertised? Explain your answer.

14–15. Forum Co. manufactures a single product. The original budget for April was based on expected production of 10,000 units; actual production for March was 11,000 units. The original budget and actual costs incurred for the manufacturing department are shown below:

	Original Budget	*Actual Costs*
Direct materials.	$ 30,000	$ 32,000
Direct labor	42,000	47,000
Variable overhead. . . .	18,000	20,000
Fixed overhead	33,000	34,000
Total	$123,000	$133,000

Required:

Prepare an appropriate performance report for the manufacturing department. Provide an Explanation column in the report, but leave the column blank.

14–16. The chair of the Biology Department of Science University has a budget for laboratory supplies. Supplies have a variable cost behavior pattern that is a function of the number of students enrolled in laboratory courses. For planning purposes when the budget was prepared in March 1993, it was estimated that there would be 200 students enrolled in laboratory courses during the Fall 1993 Semester. Actual enrollment for the fall semester was 212 students.

Required:

a. Explain what action should be taken with respect to the supplies budget when the actual enrollment is known.

b. Would your answer to *(a)* be any different if the actual enrollment turned out to be 182 students? Explain your answer.

14–17. The cost formula for the maintenance department of the Sutol Co. is $3,800 per month plus $2.70 per machine hour used by the production department.

Required:

a. Calculate the maintenance cost that would be budgeted for a month in which 3,700 machine hours are planned to be used.

b. Calculate the flexed budget amount that would be shown as the budget in the performance report if 3,580 machine hours were actually used in the month.

14–18. One of the significant costs for a nonpublic college or university is student aid in the form of gifts and grants awarded to students because of academic potential or performance, and/or financial need. Gifts and grants are only a part of a financial aid package, usually accounting for no more than 20 percent of the total package. Federal and state grants, other scholarships, loans, and income from work constitute the rest of financial aid, but these funds are not provided by the institution. Assume that for the 1993–1994 academic year, Wonder College had a gift and grant budget of $900,000, and that all of these funds had been committed to students by June 15, 1993. The college had capacity to enroll up to 200 additional students.

Required: *1*   Explain why and how flexible budgeting should be applied by the management of Wonder College in administering its gift and grant awards budget.

Chapter 15

Standard Costs and Variance Analysis

A **standard cost** is a unit budget allowance for a component—material, labor, or overhead—of a product or service. Standard costs are used in the planning and control processes of manufacturing and service firms that perform repetitive operations in the production of goods or performance of services. Although usually associated with manufacturing, standards costs are being used with greater frequency in financial and consumer service companies.

This chapter will review the various methods of establishing standards, and will then explain how variances can be analyzed so that supervisors and managers can identify why they occurred, can plan action to eliminate those variances that are unfavorable, and can capture or preserve those that are favorable.

LEARNING OBJECTIVES

After studying this chapter you should understand:

- Why and how standards are useful in the planning and control process.
- How standard costs are used in the cost accounting system.
- The different approaches to developing a standard.
- How the standard cost of a product is developed.
- How and why the two components of a standard cost variance are calculated.
- The specific names assigned to variances for different product inputs.

- How the control and analysis of fixed overhead variances differs from the control and analysis of variable cost variances.
- The alternative methods of accounting for variances.

STANDARD COSTS

Using Standard Costs

Standard costs are used in the planning and control phases of the management process and are used in financial accounting to value the inventory of a manufacturing firm. There are two elements of a standard cost: the quantity of input and the cost per unit of input. The quantity of input could be weight or volume of raw materials, hours of labor, kilowatt hours of electricity, number of welding rods, or any other measure of physical input use. Standard cost systems are traditionally and most extensively used in the manufacturing environment, but their use in the service sector of the economy is growing rapidly.

Because the standard represents a unit budget (i.e., the expected quantity and cost of the resources required to produce a unit of product or provide a unit of service), standards are used extensively in the budget preparation process. Once the sales forecast has been developed and expressed in units, standards are used to plan for the inputs that will need to be provided to make the product or provide the service.

As the budget period proceeds, actual inputs used can be compared to the standard inputs that should have been used to make or service the actual output achieved, and, based on these performance reports, managers can determine where to focus their efforts so goals will be achieved.

In many situations control focuses on the quantity dimensions of the standard cost, rather than the dollar amount of the standard cost (the product of quantity multiplied by unit cost) because the supervisor responsible can relate more easily to the physical quantity than to the dollar cost. For example, the supervisor responsible for raw material usage and the supervisor responsible for order-processing activity probably relate more easily to pounds used and number of orders processed per employee, respectively, than they would to the costs of those inputs used during a reporting period.

Standard costs that have been appropriately developed (see discussion below) can be used in the cost accounting system described in Chapter 12. This results in a cost system that is easier to use than one involving actual costs, especially when it comes to valuing the inventory because the standard costs have been developed prior to or early in the accounting period, whereas actual costs aren't known until after the accounting period has been completed.

Developing Standards

Because standards are unit budgets, all of the management philosophy and individual behavior considerations identified in the discussion of the budgeting process in Chapter 13 apply also to standards. Three classifications of the approach to developing standards are:

Ideal, or engineered, standards.

Attainable standards.

Past experience standards.

An **ideal standard** is one that assumes that operating conditions will be ideal, and that material and labor inputs will be provided at maximum levels of efficiency at all times. One of the work measurement techniques used by industrial engineers is called *motion and time study*. This technique involves a very detailed analysis of the activities involved in performing a task, with the objective of designing workstation layout and operator movements so that the task can be performed most efficiently. Industrial engineers recognize that individual fatigue and other factors will result in actual performance over a period of time that will be less than 100 percent efficient, as defined by motion and time study analysis, but these factors are ignored when an ideal standard is established. The principal disadvantage of ideal standards is that unfavorable variances will almost certainly be generated, and, as a result, supervisors and employees will not use the standard as a performance target.

An **attainable standard** is one that recognizes that there will be some operating inefficiencies relative to ideal conditions. Actual performance will result in both favorable and unfavorable variances. Employees are more likely to try to achieve this kind of standard than an ideal standard because of the sense of accomplishment that comes from meeting a legitimate goal. There may be varying degrees of "tightness" or "looseness" in an attainable standard, depending upon management philosophy and operating circumstances. For example, some firms create a highly competitive work environment and establish tight standards that require considerable effort to achieve. Once an attainable standard is established, it is not set forever. Changes in worker efficiency and/or changes in the work environment may call for changes in the standard.

A **past experience standard** has the disadvantage of including all of the inefficiencies that have crept into the operation over the years. Such a standard does not contain any challenge, and performance is not likely to improve over time. Such a standard reflects current performance but is not likely to provide incentive for improvement.

Establishing performance standards for an organization that has not had them before is a significant management challenge. It is only natural for workers to be uncomfortable with the idea that someone will now be measuring and watching their efficiency. The usefulness of standards for planning and control purposes will increase over time as those affected by them learn and become accustomed to how supervisors and managers use the resulting performance reports. Many organizations have experienced productivity and profitability increases, and workers have experienced increases in job satisfaction and compensation as a result of well-designed and carefully implemented standard cost systems.

Costing Products with Standard Costs

The process of establishing a standard cost for a product involves aggregating the individual standard costs for each of the inputs to the product: raw materials, direct labor, and manufacturing overhead. Once the standard quantities allowed have been developed, as explained in the prior section, a standard cost for each unit of input is developed, and the standard cost for a unit of product is determined.

Developing the standard cost for each unit of input involves estimating costs for the budget period. The purchasing agent will provide input for raw material costs, the personnel department will be involved in establishing standard labor rates, and the production, purchasing, and personnel departments will provide data for estimating overhead component costs. Because of the necessity to recognize cost behavior patterns for planning and control purposes, overhead costs will be classified as variable or fixed. Variable overhead will usually be expressed in terms of direct labor hours, machine hours, or some other physical measure that reflects the causes of overhead expenditures. Fixed overhead is expressed as a total cost per accounting period for planning and control purposes, but for product costing purposes it is allocated to individual products. The allocation is made by developing a fixed overhead application rate that is established by dividing the total fixed overhead budget amount by an estimated total volume of activity such as direct labor hours, machine hours, or some other meaure of activity. This is similar to the process used for variable overhead, but because fixed overhead does not behave on a per unit basis, this approach is not valid for planning and controlling fixed overhead; it is used only to allocate fixed overhead to individual products for product costing purposes.

The result of this process is a standard cost calculation that might look like this for a Model 21 sailboat hull manufactured by Cruisers, Inc.:

Variable costs:
  Raw materials:

218 yds. of fiberglass cloth @ $2.10/yd.	$ 457.80
55 gal. of epoxy resin @ $.92/gal.	50.60
1 purchased keel plate @ $132.16	132.16
Total raw materials	$ 640.56

Direct labor:

26 hours of "build-up" labor @ $12.80/hr.	$ 332.80
8 hours of finishing labor @ $19.30/hr..	154.40
Total direct labor	$ 487.20

Variable overhead (based on total direct labor hours):

34 hours @ $3.20/hr.	$ 108.80
Total standard variable cost per unit.	$1,236.56

Fixed costs:
  Fixed overhead (the $10.80 rate is based on total budgeted
    fixed overhead for the year divided by total estimated direct
    labor hours to be incurred during the year):

34 hours @ $10.80/hr	$ 367.20
Total standard cost per unit	$1,603.76

Note: For consistency purposes the total variable and fixed manufacturing overhead cost totals $14 per direct labor hour, as shown in Exhibit 12–4. This is the predetermined overhead application rate used for cost accounting purposes. The fixed overhead component of that rate is determined as explained in Exhibit 12–4; the variable component is developed by building a standard based on the relationship between the elements of variable overhead (e.g., utilities and maintenance) and the chosen activity base. In this example that activity base is direct labor hours, but it can be any other physical measure that has a causal relationship with the cost.

In a similar fashion the standard cost of every component of the boat would be developed. The standard cost of the Model 21 is the sum of the standard cost for each component. The standard cost of all other models would be compiled in the same way. There is a great deal of effort and cost involved in implementing a standard cost system, but the benefit/cost ratio is positive because of the planning, control, and product costing uses of the system. Many firms revise standard quantities allowed when necessary because of performance and operating changes, and they revise standard costs per unit of input on an annual basis. However, some large firms with many products involving hundreds of raw material and direct labor inputs have adopted a different strategy. They may review and revise standards on a cyclical basis over a two- or three-year period, or they may retain standards for several years, anticipating and accepting variances that result from quantity or price changes. Managers of any firm using standards must weigh the trade-offs involved in keeping the standards current compared to revising them periodically.

Other Uses of Standards

In addition to being used for product costing in a manufacturing environment, standards can be developed and used for planning and control of period costs and qualitative goals in both manufacturing and service organizations. For example, a day care center could develop a standard cost for the food provided to its clients and/or a standard for the number of staff required for a given number of clients of a given age.

Both manufacturing firms and service organizations are seeking to respond to increased competitive pressures by becoming more efficient. One result of this has been the development of goals, which can be expressed as standards, for such activities as these:

Quality control, including total quality management programs and statistical quality control measures.

Inventory control, including just-in-time inventory management systems and flexible manufacturing systems.

Machine usage, including downtime for setup, preventative maintenance, and unscheduled repairs.

Service levels, including customer/client response times, out-of-stock frequencies, and delivery times.

Few of these standards are expressed in terms of dollars per unit of product; they need not be expressed in dollars to be useful for management planning and control.

VARIANCE ANALYSIS

Analysis of Variable Cost Variances

To achieve the control advantages associated with a standard cost system, performance reports, similar to those described in Chapter 14, must be provided to individuals responsible for incurring costs.

However, the total variance for any particular cost component, the **budget variance,** as it is usually called because it is the difference between budgeted cost and actual cost, is due to two factors: the difference between the standard and actual *quantity* of the input, and the difference between the standard and actual *unit cost* of the input. Even if the same individual were responsible for both quantity and price, it would be desirable to break the budget variance into the **quantity variance** and the **cost per unit of input variance.** Because different managers are usually responsible for each component of the total variance, it is essential to separate the two components so that each manager can take the appropriate action to eliminate an unfavorable variance or capture a favorable one.

As is the case with much of managerial and financial accounting, different organizations use different terms for these variances. In the discussion that follows *quantity variance* will be referred to as a *usage* or *efficiency* variance, and the *cost per unit of input variance* will be referred to as a *price, rate,* or *spending* variance. These terms are generally, but not exclusively, used in practice. In addition, variances will be referred to here as *favorable* or *unfavorable.* In some organizations, a favorable variance is shown as a positive, but otherwise unlabeled, amount, and an unfavorable variance is shown as a negative amount. Whether a variance is favorable or unfavorable is determined in the context of the item being evaluated, and the goals of the organization. Thus spending less for raw materials because lower than specified quality materials were purchased may give rise to an arithmetically favorable variance (actual cost was less than standard cost) that is not desirable because of the negative impact on product quality.

To illustrate the two components of the budget variance, we shall focus on the "build-up" labor of the Model 21 hull for which the standard cost was summarized earlier. Assume that 100 hulls were made last month. The actual and standard labor hours and hourly rates for "buildup" labor inputs for the 100 hulls, and the variances (F is favorable, U is unfavorable) are summarized below:

Actual	2,580 hours @ $12.85/hr.		$33,153
Standard	2,600 hours @ $12.80/hr.		33,280
Budget variance	20 F	$ .05 U	$ 127 F

The analysis of the budget variance into the portion caused by the difference between actual and standard hours (the quantity variance), and the portion caused by the difference between the actual and standard hourly pay rate (the cost per unit of input variance) is:

Variance due to hours difference:
   20 hours × $12.80 (standard rate) $256 F
Variance due to rate difference:
   $.05/hr. × 2,580 hours (actual hours) $129 U
      Budget variance $127 F

The quantity variance due to the difference between standard hours allowed and the actual hours incurred is called the **direct labor efficiency variance** because it relates to the efficiency with which labor was used. The cost per unit of input variance due to the difference between the actual and standard hourly pay rates is the **direct labor rate variance.** Part of the budget variance is really a joint variance due to the fact that there was a difference between both standard and actual hours and the standard and actual rate per hour. However, rather than report three variances, the joint variance is included with the rate variance. This keeps the efficiency variance "pure," which is appropriate because efficiency is usually more subject to control than are pay rates.

The efficiency variance would be reported to the supervisor responsible for direct labor inputs to the product. The rate variance would be reported to the personnel manager or other individual who is responsible for pay rates. Management-by-exception procedures are appropriate, and, if a variance is significant, the reasons for it will be determined so that appropriate action can be taken to eliminate unfavorable variances and capture favorable ones.

The variances are labeled favorable or unfavorable based on the arithmetic difference between standard and actual, but these labels are not necessarily synonymous with "good" and "bad," respectively. This example illustrates a trade-off that can frequently be made. Even though the workers were paid more than the standard rate, the work was performed in a length of time that was short enough to more than make up for the unfavorable rate variance. If this occurred because of a conscious decision by the production supervisor, a permanent change in the way the work is done and a change in the standards could be appropriate. Alternatively, achieving a favorable rate variance by using less skilled employees may result in a more than offsetting unfavorable efficiency variance.

The budget variance for raw materials and variable overhead can be analyzed and separated into two components just as the direct labor variance is. The label assigned to each of the components varies from input to input, but the calculations are similar. The labels generally used are **raw materials usage variance, raw materials price variance, variable overhead efficiency variance,** and **vari-**

able overhead spending variance. These variances are summarized here:

		Variance Due to Difference between Standard and Actual
Input	*Quantity*	*Cost per Unit of Input*
Raw materials	Usage	Price
Direct labor	Efficiency	Rate
Variable overhead	Efficiency	Spending

The terms *usage* and *efficiency* refer to quantity of input; from the perspective of direct labor, efficiency relates to the quantity of hours actually used relative to the quantity for which the standard calls. The variable overhead quantity variance is called the *efficiency variance* because variable overhead is, in most cases, assumed to be related to direct labor hours. The terms used for cost per unit of input variances are consistent with the way costs are usually referred to: price for raw materials and rate for employee wages. "Spending" is used for variable overhead because of the number of different costs that go into overhead, and although an overall rate is calculated, the cost per unit of input variance reflects the fact that the amount spent for elements of overhead differs from the spending that was anticipated when the rate was established.

The general model for calculating each variance is:

$$
\begin{array}{lll}
\text{Quantity} & \text{(Standard} & \text{Actual)} & \text{Standard} \\
\text{variance} = & \text{(quantity} - & \text{quantity)} \times & \text{cost per} \\
& \text{(allowed} & \text{used)} & \text{unit}
\end{array}
$$

$$
\begin{array}{lll}
\text{Cost per unit} & \text{(Standard} & \text{Actual)} & \text{Actual} \\
\text{of input} = & \text{(cost per} - & \text{cost per)} \times & \text{quantity} \\
\text{variance} & \text{(unit} & \text{unit)} & \text{used}
\end{array}
$$

The arithmetic sign of the variance calculated using the above formulas indicates whether the variance is favorable (+) or unfavorable (−). Variance calculation examples for some of the Model 21 hull costs are illustrated in Exhibit 15–1.

Note that although the total budget variance of $234 F calculated in Exhibit 15–1 is easily considered immaterial, some of the individual variances are much more significant. It just happens that they are largely offsetting. This emphasizes the need to analyze the variances for each standard. Thus, although not illustrated in Ex-

---

EXHIBIT 15–1   Calculation of Standard Cost Variances

I. Assumptions:

The following performance report summarizes budget and actual usage and costs for the items shown for a month in which 100 Model 21 hulls were made.

	Budget	*Actual*	*Variance*
Raw materials:			
Glass fiber cloth:	$45,780	$46,125	$345 U
Budget: Standard/hull of 218 yds.			
@ $2.10/yd. × 100 hulls			
Actual: 22,500 yds. @ $2.05/yd.			
Direct labor:			
"Build-up" labor:	33,280	32,893	387 F
Budget: Standard/hull of 26 hrs.			
@ $12.80/hr. × 100 hulls			
Actual: 2,540 hrs. @ $12.95/hr.			
Variable overhead:			
Related to "build-up" labor:	8,320	8,128	192 F
Budget: Standard/hull of 26 hrs.			
@ $3.20/hr. × 100 hulls			
Actual: 2,540 hrs. @ $3.20/hr.			
Totals	$87,380	$87,146	$234 F

II. Required:

Analyze the budget variance for each item by calculating the quantity and cost per unit of input variances.

III. Solution:

$$\text{Quantity variance} = \begin{pmatrix} \text{Standard} \\ \text{quantity} \\ \text{(allowed)} \end{pmatrix} - \begin{pmatrix} \text{Actual} \\ \text{quantity} \\ \text{used)} \end{pmatrix} \times \begin{pmatrix} \text{Standard} \\ \text{cost per} \\ \text{unit} \end{pmatrix}$$

Raw material
usage variance = ((218 yds. × 100 hulls) − 22,500 yds.) × $2.10
           = $1,470 U

Direct labor
efficiency variance = ((26 hrs. × 100 hulls) − 2,540 hrs.) × $12.80
            = $768 F

Variable overhead
efficiency variance = ((26 hrs. × 100 hulls) − 2,540 hrs.) × $3.20
            = $192 F

(continued)

EXHIBIT 15–1   *(concluded)*

Cost per unit of input variance	=	(Standard cost per unit)	−	Actual cost per unit)	×	Actual quantity used

Raw material
price variance
  = ($2.10/yd. − $2.05/yd.) × 22,500 yds.
  = $1,125 F

Direct labor
rate variance
  = ($12.80/hr. − $12.95/hr.) × 2,540 hrs.
  = $381 U

Variable overhead
spending variance = ($3.20/hr. − $3.20/hr.) × 2,540 hrs.
  = 0

Recap of variances:

	Usage/ Efficiency	Price/Rate/ Spending	Total
Raw materials	$1,470 U	$1,125 F	$345 U
Direct labor	768 F	381 U	387 F
Variable overhead	192 F	0	192 F
Totals	$ 510 U	$ 744 F	$234 F

---

hibit 15–1, variances for the other raw material, direct labor, and variable overhead components of the Model 21 hulls would also be computed.

What use will be made of the information in Exhibit 15–1? Remember that the objectives of variance analysis are to highlight deviations from plan, to capture favorable variances, and to eliminate unfavorable variances. With respect to raw materials, it is possible that the favorable price variance of $1,125 was caused by buying lower-quality fiberglass that resulted in the unfavorable usage variance of $1,470. As a result of the performance report, there should be communication between the purchasing agent and the raw materials supervisor to resolve the issue. Without this analysis and communication, the purchasing agent, not being aware that the price savings were more than offset by higher usage, might continue to buy lower-quality material. The favorable labor efficiency variance of $762 might be the result of using more experienced and higher-paid employees this month, which in turn caused a $381 unfavorable rate variance. After analysis and discussion the direct labor supervisor, the production superintendent, and the personnel manager might decide to continue this trade-off. Variance analysis information should result in actions to maintain or increase the profitability of the company. If the benefit of calculating variances is not greater than the cost of doing so, there isn't much sense in making the calculations.

As is the case with any performance reporting, variances should be communicated to the individuals responsible as promptly as feasible after activity has occurred so that the causes of the variances can be easily remembered and appropriate action can be taken. All variances need not be reported with the same frequency. In most organizations the usage of raw materials and the efficiency of direct labor are most subject to short-term control, and so these variances will be reported more frequently than the cost per unit of input variances. In many situations it is appropriate to report raw material usage variances and direct labor efficiency variances in physical terms because the supervisors involved are more accustomed to thinking in pounds and square feet or direct labor hours than in dollars. For example, using the data in Exhibit 15–1, and eliminating standard cost per unit from the model, the quantity variances would be calculated and expressed as follows:

$$\begin{array}{cccc} \text{Quantity} & \text{(Standard} & \text{Actual)} \\ \text{variance} = & \text{(quantity} & - & \text{quantity)} \\ & \text{(allowed} & & \text{used)} \end{array}$$

Raw material
usage variance = (218 yds. $\times$ 100 hulls) − 22,500 yds.
= 700 yds. U

Direct labor
efficiency variance = (26 hrs. $\times$ 100 hulls) − 2,540 hrs.
= 60 hrs. F

Some organizations calculate and report the raw materials price variance at the time materials are purchased rather than when they are used. This variance is called the **raw materials purchase price variance.** This is especially appropriate if raw materials inventories are maintained, as opposed to having materials put directly into production, because it shows the purchasing manager any price variance soon after the purchase is made rather than later when the material is used. For example, if 4,000 pounds of raw material A were purchased at a cost of $3.64 per pound, and the standard cost was $3.60 per pound, the purchase price variance would be calculated as follows:

General model:

Cost per unit   (Standard   Actual)   Actual
     of input   = (cost per   −   cost per) × quantity
     variance   (unit   unit)   used

Modification for purchase price variance:

Cost per unit   (Standard   Actual)   Actual
     of input   = (cost per   −   cost per) × quantity
     variance   (unit   unit)   *purchased*

$$= (\$3.60 - \$3.64) \times 4{,}000 \text{ lbs.}$$

$$= \$160 \text{ U}$$

Analysis of Fixed Overhead Variance

The analysis of the fixed overhead variance differs from the analysis of variable cost variances because of the different cost behavior pattern. For control purposes the focus is on the difference between the fixed overhead that was budgeted for the period and actual fixed overhead expenditures. This difference is labeled a *budget variance* (the same term used to identify the difference between budgeted and actual variable costs). A variance also arises if the number of units of product made differs from planned production. The reason for this is that fixed overhead is applied to production using a predetermined application rate (see Exhibit 12–1) based on planned activity. If actual activity is different, the amount of fixed overhead applied to production will be different from that planned to be applied. This variance is called a **volume variance.**

It is not appropriate to make any per unit fixed overhead variance calculations because fixed costs do not behave on a per unit basis.

To illustrate the calculation of fixed overhead variances, we return to the production of Model 21 sailboats by Cruisers, Inc. The predetermined fixed overhead application rate shown in the standard cost calculation on page 464 is $10.80 per direct labor hour. To recap from Chapter 12, this rate would have been determined as follows:

Total estimated (budgeted) fixed manufacturing overhead for the year	$648,000
Total estimated (budgeted) direct labor hours for the year	60,000 hours
Predetermined fixed overhead application rate ($648,000/60,000 hours)	$10.80/direct labor

Now assume that the actual fixed manufacturing overhead for the year totaled $661,500, and that standard direct labor hours allowed for actual production during the year totaled 61,300 hours. The fixed manufacturing overhead account would appear as follows:

Fixed Manufacturing Overhead

Actual costs incurred	661,500	Fixed manufacturing overhead applied to production (61,300 direct labor hours × $10.80/direct labor hr.)	662,040
		Balance (overapplied overhead)	540

The overapplied overhead is made up of a budget variance and a volume variance, as follows:

Budget variance:		
Budgeted fixed manufacturing overhead . .		$648,000
Actual fixed manufacturing overhead		661,500
Budget variance		$ 13,500 U
Volume variance:		
Budgeted direct labor hours for year	60,000 hrs.	
Standard direct labor hours allowed for actual production during year	61,300 hrs.	
Excess of standard hours allowed for volume of production actually achieved over estimated hours	1,300 hrs.	
Predetermined fixed overhead application rate	× $10.80/hr.	
Volume variance		14,040 F
Net variance (overapplied overhead)		$ 540 F

This is another situation in which although the net variance is small, it results from larger offsetting variances that may deserve investigation.

The above illustration uses annual data; in practice the analysis is likely to be made monthly, or with a frequency that leads to effective control of fixed overhead. As stated earlier, by its very nature fixed overhead is difficult to control on a short-term basis, but for many firms it has become a significant cost that may be greater than all of the variable costs combined, so it does receive much management attention.

Accounting for Variances

Some interesting issues arise in connection with the accounting for variances. Usually, if the net total of all of the favorable and unfavorable variances is not significant relative to the total of all production costs incurred during the period, the net variance will be included with cost of goods sold in the income statement. Since standard costs were used in valuing inventories during the period, standard costs were also released to cost of goods sold; classifying the net variance with this amount has the effect of reporting cost of goods sold at the actual cost of making those items. If the net variance is significant relative to total production costs, it may be allocated between inventories and cost of goods sold in proportion to the standard costs included in these accounts. On the other hand, if the standards represent currently attainable targets, then a net unfavorable variance can be interpreted as the cost of production inefficiencies that should be recognized as a cost of the current period. If this is the case, none of the net variance should be assigned to inventory because doing so results in postponing the income statement recognition of the inefficiencies until the product is sold. A net variance that is favorable would indicate that the standards were too loose, and so it would be appropriate to allocate the variance between inventory and cost of goods sold. In any event the financial statements and explanatory notes are not likely to contain any reference to the standard cost system or accounting for variances because disclosures about these details of the accounting system do not increase the usefulness of the statements as a whole.

SUMMARY

A standard cost is a unit budget for a component of a product or service. As such, standards are used like any budget in planning and controlling. Standards can also facilitate calculation of a product cost for inventory valuation purposes.

Because a standard is a unit budget, it can be used in the process of building the various component budgets of the operating budget. Standards also provide a benchmark for evaluating performance. Standards are usually expressed in monetary terms ($/unit) but can also be useful when expressed in physical quantities (lbs./unit).

Standards are usually established on the basis of engineering studies. A standard should be attainable if it is to be a positive motivator. Ideal standards and past experience standards are less useful.

The standard cost for a product is the sum of the standard costs for raw materials, direct labor, and manufacturing overhead used in making the product. A fixed manufacturing overhead standard is a unitized fixed expense, and therefore must be used carefully because fixed expenses do not behave on a per unit basis.

Standards are useful for the entire range of planning and control activities; they are not restricted to use in product costing. Thus many service organizations and manufacturing firms have developed standards for period costs. Standards can also be developed for qualitative goals that may not be expressed in financial terms.

Variances from standard can be caused by a difference between standard and actual quantity, and by a difference between standard and actual costs per unit of input. Variance analysis breaks the total variance into a part caused by each difference. This is done because different managers are responsible for each component of the total variance. The objective of reporting variances is to have the appropriate manager take action to eliminate unfavorable variances, or capture favorable variances. Communication between managers is essential to achieve this objective.

Variances can be labeled in many ways, but a generally used classification is the following:

	Variance Due to Difference between Standard and Actual	
Input	*Quantity*	*Cost per Unit of Input*
Raw materials	Usage	Price
Direct labor	Efficiency	Rate
Variable overhead	Efficiency	Spending

Quantity variances for raw materials and direct labor are frequently expressed by quantity as well as dollar amount, because the manager responsible for controlling the variance usually thinks in quantity terms.

Fixed manufacturing overhead variances are analyzed differently from variable cost variances because of the cost behavior pattern difference. The fixed overhead budget variance is the difference between total budgeted and total actual fixed overhead. The fixed overhead volume variance arises because the actual level of activity differed from that used in calculating the fixed overhead application rate.

The accounting for variances can become quite complex. In

most standard cost systems standard costs are recorded in work in process inventory (and finished goods inventory), and variances are taken directly to the income statement in the fiscal period in which they arise as an adjustment of cost of goods sold.

KEY TERMS AND CONCEPTS

attainable standard *(p. 462)*   A standard cost or production standard that is achievable under actual operating conditions.

budget variance *(p. 466)*   The difference between budgeted amount and actual amount.

cost per unit of input variance *(p. 466)*   That part of a variable cost budget variance due to a difference between the standard and actual cost per unit of input. See also *raw materials price variance, direct labor rate variance,* and *variable overhead spending variance.*

direct labor efficiency variance *(p. 467)*   That part of the direct labor budget variance due to the difference between actual hours required and standard hours allowed for the work done.

direct labor rate variance *(p. 467)*   That part of the direct labor budget variance due to the difference between the actual hourly wage rate paid and the standard rate.

ideal standard *(p. 462)*   A standard cost or a production standard that assumes ideal operating conditions and maximum efficiency at all times.

past experience standard *(p. 463)*   A standard cost or production standard that is based on historical data.

quantity variance *(p. 466)*   That part of a variable cost budget variance due to a difference between the standard and actual quantity of inputs. See also *raw materials usage variance, direct labor efficiency variance,* and *variable overhead efficiency variance.*

raw materials price variance *(p. 467)*   That part of the total raw materials budget variance due to the difference between standard cost and actual cost of raw materials *used.*

raw materials purchase price variance *(p. 471)*   That part of the total raw materials budget variance due to the difference between standard cost and actual cost of raw materials *purchased.*

raw materials usage variance *(p. 467)*   That part of the total raw materials budget variance due to the difference between standard usage and actual usage of raw materials.

standard cost *(p. 460)*   A unit budget allowance for a cost component of a product or an activity.

variable overhead efficiency variance *(p. 467)*   That part of the variable overhead budget variance due to the difference between actual hours required and standard hours allowed for the work done.

variable overhead spending variance *(p. 468)* That part of the variable overhead budget variance due to the difference between actual variable overhead cost and the standard cost for the actual inputs (direct labor hours, for example) used.

volume variance *(p. 472)* A fixed manufacturing overhead variance caused by actual activity being different from the estimated activity used in calculating the predetermined overhead application rate.

EXERCISES AND PROBLEMS

15–1. Natway Mfg. Co. manufactures and sells household cleaning products. The company's research department has developed a new cleaner for which a standard cost must be determined. The new cleaner is made by mixing 11 quarts of triphate solution and 4 pounds of sobase granules and boiling the mixture for several minutes. After the solution has cooled 2 ounces of methage are added. This "recipe" produces 10 quarts of the cleaner, which is then packaged in one-quart plastic dispenser bottles. Raw material costs are:

Triphate solution.	$ .30 per quart
Sobase granules	.74 per pound
Methage.	1.20 per ounce
Bottle.	.12 each

Required:

a. Using the above data, calculate the raw material cost for one bottle of the new cleaner.

b. Assume that the above costs are the current best estimates of the costs at which required quantities of the raw materials can be purchased. Would you recommend that any other factors be considered in establishing the raw material cost standard for the new cleaner?

c. Explain the process that would be used to develop the direct labor cost standard for the new product.

15–2. Wood Turning Co. makes decorative candle pedestals. An industrial engineer consultant developed ideal time standards for one unit of the model 2C pedestal. The standards are given below, along with the cost accountant's determination of current labor pay rates:

Worktype 1.	.15 hours @ $12.30 per hour
Worktype 2.	.30 hours @ $10.90 per hour
Worktype 3.	.60 hours @ $19.50 per hour

Required:

a. Using the above data, calculate the direct labor cost for a model 2C pedestal.

b. Would it be appropriate to use the cost calculated in (*a*) as a standard cost for evaluating direct labor performance and valuing inventory? Explain your answer.

15–3. Starchy Co. processes corn into corn starch and corn syrup. The company's productivity and cost standards follow:

From every bushel of corn processed, 12 pounds of starch and 3 pounds of syrup should be produced.

Standard direct labor and variable overhead totals $.42 per bushel of corn processed.

Standard fixed overhead (the predetermined fixed overhead application rate) is $.35 per bushel processed.

Required:

a. Calculate the standard absorption cost per pound for the starch and syrup produced from the processing of 15,000 bushels of corn that have an average cost of $2.83 per bushel.

b. Evaluate the usefulness of this cost for management planning and control purposes.

15–4. A cost analyst for Stamper Mfg. Co. has assembled the following data about the Model 24 stamp pad:

The piece of sheet metal from which eight pad cases can be made costs $.14. This amount is based on the number of sheets in a 3,000-pound bundle of sheet metal, which is the usual purchase quantity.

The foam pad that is put in the case costs $.02, based on the number of pads that can be cut from a large roll of foam.

Production standards, based on an engineering analysis recognizing attainable performance, provide for the manufacture of 1,800 pads by two workers in an eight-hour shift. The standard direct labor pay rate is $11 per hour.

Manufacturing overhead is applied to units produced using a predetermined overhead application rate of $16 per direct labor hour of which $7 per hour is fixed manufacturing overhead.

Required:

a. Calculate the standard absorption cost of a package of 12 stamp pads.

b. Stamper Mfg. Co.'s management is considering a special promotion that would result in increased sales of 2,000 packages of 12 pads per package. Calculate the cost per package that is relevant for this analysis.

15–5. The standards for one case of Springfever Tonic are:

Direct materials	4 lbs. @ $ 5.00/lb. = $20
Direct labor	3 hrs. @ $13.00/hr. = 39
Variable overhead (based on direct labor hours)	3 hrs. @ $ 6.00/hr. = 18

During the week ended April 25, the following activity took place:

7,400 lbs. of raw materials were purchased for inventory at a cost of $4.95 per pound.

2,000 cases of finished product were produced, and:
  8,300 lbs. of raw material were used.
  5,800 direct labor hours were worked at a total cost of $78,300.
  $35,670 of actual variable overhead costs were incurred.

Required:

Calculate each of the following variances:
a. Price variance for raw materials purchased.
b. Raw materials usage variance.
c. Direct labor rate variance.
d. Direct labor efficiency variance.
e. Variable overhead spending variance.
f. Variable overhead efficiency variance.

15–6. The standards for one case of Fallscent are:

Direct materials	3 lbs. @ $ 7.00/lb. = $21
Direct labor	2 hrs. @ $12.00/hr. = 24
Variable overhead (based on	
direct labor hours	2 hrs. @ $ 5.00/hr. = 10

During the week ended October 8 the following activity took place:

7,000 lbs. of raw materials were purchased for inventory at a cost of $6.80 per pound.

1,800 cases of finished product were produced, and:
  6,000 lbs. of raw material were used.
  3,900 direct labor hours were worked at a total cost of $47,190.
  $19,890 of actual variable overhead costs were incurred.

Required:

Calculate each of the following variances:
a. Price variance for raw materials purchased.
b. Raw materials usage variance.
c. Direct labor efficiency variance.
d. Direct labor rate variance.
e. Variable overhead efficiency variance.
f. Variable overhead spending variance.

15–7. Goodwrench's Garage uses standards to plan and control labor time and expense. The standard time for an engine tune-up is 3.5 hours, and the standard labor rate is $15 per hour. Last week 24 tune-ups were completed. The labor efficiency variance was six hours unfavorable, and the labor rate variance totaled $81 favorable.

Required:

a. Calculate the actual direct labor hourly rate paid for tune-up work last week. .
b. Calculate the dollar amount of the labor efficiency variance.
c. What is the most likely explanation for these two variances? Is this a good trade-off for the management of the garage to make?

15–8. Sam's Tailor Shop uses standards to plan and control labor time and expense. The standard time for trouser alterations is 45 minutes to adjust cuffs and 30 minutes to adjust the waist. The standard labor rate for a tailor is $9.50 per hour. Last week 40 cuff alterations and 22 waist alterations were performed. The labor efficiency variance was 3 hours favorable, and the labor rate variance totaled $20 unfavorable.

Required:

a. Calculate the actual direct labor hourly rate paid to the tailor last week.
b. Calculate the dollar amount of the labor efficiency variance.
c. What is a likely explanation of these two variances? Is this a good trade-off for management of the tailor shop to make?

15–9. Presented below is a partially completed performance report for a recent week for direct labor for the binding department of a book publisher.

	Original Budget	Flexed Budget	Actual	Variance
Direct labor	$1,800		$1,888	

The original budget is based on the expectation that 3,000 books would be bound; the standard is 20 books per hour at a pay rate of $12 per hour. During the week 2,860 books were actually bound. Employees worked 160 hours at an actual total cost of $1,888.

Required:

a. Calculate the flexed budget amount against which actual performance should be evaluated, and then calculate the variance.
b. Calculate the direct labor efficiency variance in terms of hours.
c. Calculate the direct labor rate variance.

15–10. For the Stamping Department of a manufacturing firm, the standard cost for direct labor is $12 per hour, and the production standard calls for 2,000 stampings per hour. During February 121 hours were required for actual production of 230,000 stampings. Actual direct labor cost for the Stamping Department for February was $1,573.

Required:

a. Complete the following performance report for February.

	Flexed Budget	Actual	Budget Variance
Direct labor			

b. Analyze the budget variance by calculating the direct labor efficiency and rate variances for February.
c. What alternatives to the above monthly report could result in improved control over the Stamping Department's direct labor?

15–11. If a company uses a standard cost system, should all variances be calculated with the same frequency (e.g., monthly) and should they be expressed in dollar amounts? Explain your answer, and include in it the reason for calculating variances.

15–12. Assume that you are the production manager of a small branch plant of a large manufacturing firm. The central accounting control department sends you monthly performance reports showing the flexed budget amount, actual cost and variance for raw materials, direct labor, variable overhead (which is expressed on a direct labor-hour basis), and fixed overhead. The variable cost budget variances are separated into quantity and cost per unit of input variances, and the fixed overhead budget and volume variances are shown. All variances are expressed in dollars.

Required:

a. Rank the eight variances in descending order of their usefulness to you for planning and controlling purposes. Explain your ranking.
b. Given the usefulness ranking in part (*a*), explain how the frequency of reporting and the units in which the variance is reported might make the performance reports more useful.

15–13. During the year ended May 31, 1993, Teller Register Co. reported favorable raw material usage and direct labor and variable overhead efficiency variances that totaled $285,800. Price and rate variances were negligible. Total standard cost of goods produced during the year was $1,905,340.

Required:

a. Comment about the effectiveness of the company's standards for controlling material and labor usage.
b. If standard costs are used for valuing finished goods inventory, will the ending inventory valuation be higher or lower than if actual costs were used? Explain your answer.
c. Assume that the ending inventory of finished goods valued at standard cost is $158,780. Calculate the adjustment to finished goods inventory that would be appropriate because of the erroneous standards.

15–14. York Co. uses a standard cost system. When raw materials are purchased, the standard cost of the raw materials purchased is recorded as the increase in the Raw Materials Inventory account. When raw materials are used, the standard cost of the materials allowed for the units produced is recorded as an increase in the Work in Process Inventory account. Likewise, the standard cost of direct labor and variable manufacturing overhead is recorded as an increase in Work in Process Inventory.

Required:

a. Explain where in the financial statements the difference between the actual and standard cost of raw materials purchased will be recorded.
b. In the above system, under what circumstances will the increases and decreases in the Finished Goods Inventory account, due to production and sales, respectively, represent the actual cost of products made and sold?
c. How does the accounting for overapplied or underapplied overhead, originally discussed in Chapter 12, differ from York Co.'s cost accounting system?

15–15. An insurance company developed standard times for processing claims. When a claim was received at the processing center, it was first reviewed and classified as simple or complex. The standard time for processing was:

| Simple claim | 45 minutes |
| Complex claim | 2.5 hours |

Employees were expected to be productive 7.5 hours per day. Compensation costs were $90 per day per employee. During April, which had 20 working days, the following number of claims were processed:

| Simple claims | 3,000 processed |
| Complex claims | 600 processed |

Required:

a. Calculate the number of workers that should have been available to process April claims.

b. Assume that 27 workers were actually available throughout the month of April. Calculate a labor efficiency variance, expressed as both a number of workers and a dollar amount for the month.

15–16. A bank developed a standard for teller staffing that provided for one teller to handle 12 customers per hour. During June the bank averaged 50 customers per hour and had five tellers on duty at all times. (Relief tellers filled in during lunch and rest breaks.) The teller compensation cost is $12 per hour. The bank is open eight hours a day, and there were 21 working days during June.

Required:

a. Calculate the teller efficiency variance during June expressed in terms of number of tellers and cost per hour.

b. Now assume that during June, during the 11:00 A.M. to 1:00 P.M. period every day, the bank served 80 customers per hour. During the other six hours of the day, 40 customers per hour were served.

   1. Calculate a teller efficiency variance for the 11:00 to 1:00 period expressed in terms of number of tellers per hour and total cost for the month.

   2. Calculate a teller efficiency variance for the other six hours of the day expressed in terms of number of tellers per hour and total cost for the month.

   3. As teller supervisor, explain the significance of the variances calculated in 1 and 2 above, and explain how you might respond to the uneven work flow during each day.

15–17. Revco's production budget for October called for making 40,000 units of a single product. The firm's production standards allow one-half of a machine hour per unit produced. The fixed overhead budget for October was $36,000. Revco uses an absorption cost sytem. Actual activity and costs for October were:

| Units produced | 39,000 |
| Fixed overhead costs incurred | $37,000 |

Required:

a. Calculate the predetermined fixed overhead application rate that would be used in October.

b. Calculate the number of machine hours that would be allowed for actual October production.

    c. Calculate the fixed overhead applied to work in process during October.

    d. Calculate the over- or underapplied fixed overhead for October.

    e. Calculate the fixed overhead budget and volume variances for October.

15–18. Presented below are the original overhead budget and the actual costs incurred for April for Compo, Inc. Compo's managers relate overhead to direct labor hours for planning, control, and product costing purposes. The original budget is based on budgeted production of 15,000 units in 5,000 standard direct labor hours. Actual production of 16,200 units required 5,600 actual direct labor hours.

	Original Budget	*Actual Costs*
Variable overhead	$21,000	$23,600
Fixed overhead	32,000	33,200

Required:

    a. Calculate the flexed budget allowances for variable and fixed overhead for April.

    b. Calculate the direct labor efficiency variance for April expressed in terms of direct labor hours.

    c. Calculate the predetermined overhead application rate for both variable and fixed overhead for April.

    d. Calculate the fixed and variable overhead applied to production during April if overhead is applied on the basis of standard hours allowed for actual production achieved.

    e. Calculate the fixed overhead budget and volume variances for April.

    f. Calculate the over- or underapplied fixed overhead for April.

Chapter 16

Capital Budgeting

Capital Budgeting is the process of analyzing proposed capital expenditures—investments in plant, equipment, new products, and so on—to determine whether or not the proposed investment will generate, over time, a large enough return on investment (ROI) to contribute to the organization's overall ROI objectives.

Capital budgeting differs from operational budgeting in the time frame being considered. Capital budgeting concerns investments and returns that are spread over a number of years. Operational budgeting involves planning for a period that is usually not longer than one year. (Even in multiyear operational budgeting, there is an opportunity to rebudget for periods beyond the current year.)

Capital budgeting is an activity that involves most of the functional areas of the organization. The managerial accountant may make the mathematical calculations, but the departments affected by the proposed capital expenditure will have significant input to the process.

LEARNING OBJECTIVES

After studying this chapter you should understand:

- The attributes of capital budgeting that make it a significantly different activity from operational budgeting.
- Why present value analysis is appropriate in capital budgeting.
- Why not all management decisions are made strictly on the basis of quantitative analysis techniques.
- The concept of cost of capital, and why it is used in capital budgeting.

- That the term *discount rate* means the interest rate used in a present value calculation.
- How the net present value technique is used.
- Why the present value ratio is used to assign a profitability ranking to alternative capital expenditure projects.
- How the internal rate of return technique differs from the net present value approach of evaluating capital expenditure projects.
- How issues concerning estimates, cash flows in the distant future, the timing of cash flows within the year, and investments made over a period of time are treated in the capital budgeting process.
- How the payback period of a capital expenditure project is calculated, and the advantages and disadvantages of this method of evaluating proposed capital expenditure projects.
- Why the accounting rate of return of a project is calculated, and how it can most appropriately be used.
- How capital budgeting relates to operational budgeting.

INVESTMENT ANALYSIS

Investment Decision Special Considerations

Investment decisions involve committing financial resources now in anticipation of a return that will be realized over an extended period of time. This extended time frame, which can be many years, adds complexity to the analysis of whether or not to make the investment because of compound interest/present value considerations. The time value of money can be ignored for most operating expenditure decisions because the benefit of an expenditure will be received soon after the expenditure is made, and a simple benefit/cost relationship can be determined. This is not so for capital expenditures because the benefits of the expenditure will be received over several years, and $100 of benefit to be received five years from now is not the same as $100 of benefit to be received one year from now.

The concept of present value was explained in Business Procedure Capsule 11 in Chapter 6. It would be appropriate for you to review that explanation now unless you have a full understanding of the present value idea.

Most business firms and other organizations have more investment opportunities than resources available for investment. Thus a method to select which investments should be made must be used. Capital budgeting procedures, especially those applying present value analysis techniques, are useful in helping management identify the alternatives that will contribute most to the future profitability of the firm. However, as is the case with most quantitative techniques, the quantitative "answer" will not dictate management's decision. The quantitative result will be considered along with qualitative factors in the decision-making process. Examples of qualitative factors include willingness to assume the competitive risks associated with expanding (or not expanding) into a new market area, the implications for keeping control of a board of directors if more stock must be sold to raise funds for the expansion, and top management's personal goals for the organization. Because capital budgeting involves projections into the future, top management attitudes about the risk of forecasting errors have a major impact on investment decisions.

Most firms involve the board of directors in capital budgeting by having the board approve all capital expenditures above a minimum amount. Depending on the company and its financial circumstances, this amount may range from $5,000 to $100,000. This high-level approval is required because the capital expenditure represents a major commitment of company resources, and it involves a multiyear period of time.

Cost of Capital

The principal financial objective of a firm organized for profit is to earn a return on the assets invested that will permit payment of all borrowing costs (interest) and provide the owners a return on their investment (ROE — return on equity) that compensates them fairly for the financial risks being taken. To meet the requirements of these resource providers, whose claims are shown on the right-hand side of the balance sheet, attention must be focused on the assets that are reported on the left-hand side of the balance sheet. Thus return on assets (ROI — return on investment) becomes a primary concern of financial managers who evaluate proposed capital expenditures.

The **cost of capital** is the rate of return on assets that must be earned to permit the firm to meet its interest obligations and provide the expected return to the owners. Determining the cost of capital of a company is a complex process. Suffice to say here that cost of capital is a composite of borrowing costs and share owner dividend and earnings' growth rate expectations. The most useful result of the cost of capital calculation is as a "worry point" guide to management (i.e., an indication of an approximate minimum ROI that creditors and owners are expecting). Most firms set a cost of capital rate for investment analysis and evaluation purposes that is somewhat greater than the calculated rate to allow for estimation errors in the calculation, and to provide some cushion for estimation errors in the data used in the investment analysis itself. The cost of capital used for analyzing proposed capital expenditures is also influenced by the perceived riskiness of the proposal being evaluated. More risky proposals (e.g., new product development or expansion into a new activity) will be required to earn a higher rate of return than less risky proposals (e.g., equipment replacement or expansion of an existing activity). This risk difference is related to the uncertainties associated with operating in a somewhat different environment than that in which the firm is experienced. For most firms, the cost of capital is probably in the range of 15 percent to 25 percent.

In the present value calculations made in the capital budgeting process, the cost of capital is the discount rate (i.e., the interest rate at which the future period cash flows are discounted) used to determine the present value of the future **cash flows** expected from the investment proposal being analyzed.

In the capital budgeting illustrations presented in this chapter the cost of capital rate will be a given. You should recognize that in practice the development of the cost of capital rate is both complex and time-consuming.

Capital Budgeting Techniques

There are four capital budgeting techniques generally recognized. Two of them involve using present value analysis, and two do not. Because money does have value over time, the two methods that recognize this fact are clearly superior, at least conceptually, to the two that ignore time value of money. The methods are:

Methods that use present value analysis:
   Net present value (NPV) method.
   Internal rate of return (IRR) method.
Methods that do not use present value analysis:
   Payback method.
   Accounting rate of return method.

Each of the methods uses the amount to be invested in the capital project. The NPV, IRR, and **payback methods** use the amount of *cash* generated by the investment each year. The **accounting rate of return method** uses accrual accounting net income resulting from the investment. For most investment projects the difference between the cash generated each year and accrual accounting net income is depreciation expense — a noncash item that reduces accrual accounting net income. Again, because of their focus on cash flows and recognition of the time value of money, the NPV and IRR methods are much more appropriate methods than either payback or accounting rate of return.

Net Present Value.   The **net present value method** involves calculating the present value of the expected cash flows from the project using the cost of capital as the discount rate, and comparing the total present value of the cash flows to the amount of investment required. If the present value of the cash flows is greater than the investment, the net present value is positive, and it can be concluded that the rate of return of the project is greater than the cost of capital. If the present value of the cash flows is less than the investment, the net present value is negative, and it can be concluded that the rate of return of the project is less than the cost of capital. If the present value of the cash flows equals the investment, then the net present value is zero, and the rate of return of the project is equal to the cost of capital. The net present value method is illustrated in Exhibit 16–1.

When alternative projects involving different investment amounts are being considered, the NPV approach must be carried one step further. Projects should not be assigned a profitability ranking on the basis of the dollar amount of the net present value because of disparities in the investment amounts. The ratio of the present value of the cash flows to the investment, the **present value ratio** (or **profitability index**), does provide a ranking mechanism. For example, assume the following data for the projects indicated:

Project	Present Value of Cash Flows	Investment	Net Present Value	Present Value Ratio
A	$ 22,800	$ 20,000	$2,800	1.14
B	104,000	100,000	4,000	1.04

Even though project B has the greater net present value, it is clear from looking at the present value ratios that project A has the higher rate of return and is thus a more desirable investment. When the NPV approach to investment analysis is used, it is appropriate to take the second step and calculate the present value ratio, especially when a selection must be made from several projects, all of which have a positive net present value.

Internal Rate of Return.   The difference between the net present value method and the **internal rate of return method** is that the

EXHIBIT 16–1   Net Present Value Analysis of a Proposed Investment

I. Assumptions:
   A. A new packaging machine costing $100,000 installed has an estimated useful life of five years, and an estimated salvage value of $6,000 after five years. The new machine will be purchased at the end of 1993.
   B. Installation of the machine will result in labor savings during each of the next five years as follows:

1994	$26,000
1995	27,000
1996	31,000
1997	35,000
1998	38,000

   C. The firm's cost of capital is 16%.

II. Time-Line Presentation of Cash Flows from the Investment:

	12/31/93	1994	1995	1996	1997	1998
Cash flows from investment:						
Savings.		26,000	27,000	31,000	35,000	38,000
Salvage.						6,000
Total.		26,000	27,000	31,000	35,000	44,000

III. Net Present Value Calculation:

	12/31/93	1994	1995	1996	1997	1998
Present value factor (Table 6–1, 16%)		0.8621	0.7432	0.6407	0.5523	0.4761
Present value of cash flows from investment.		22,415	20,066	19,862	19,331	20,948

Total present value of cash flows
from investment . . . . $102,622 ←
Investment . . . . (100,000)
Net present value . . . . $ 2,622

IV. Conclusion from Analysis:
   The net present value is positive; therefore the projected rate or return on this investment is greater than the 16 percent cost of capital. Based on this quantitative analysis, the investment should be made.

discount (interest) rate—the cost of capital—is a given in the NPV approach, whereas the IRR approach solves for the actual rate of return that will be earned by the proposed investment. This is the discount (interest) rate at which the present value of the cash flows from the project will equal the investment. Thus the IRR method may require several calculations using different discount rates. Once the project's internal rate of return is known, a conclusion about the suitability of the investment is made by comparing the IRR to the cost of capital. If the IRR is greater than the cost of capital, the investment will be recommended. If the IRR is less than the cost of capital, the investment will not be recommended.

With respect to the investment proposal illustrated in Exhibit 16–1, the IRR can be seen to be greater than 16 percent. Determination of the actual IRR requires another set of present value calculations using a higher discount rate, and then interpolation to determine the actual discount rate at which the present value of the cash flows would equal the investment (i.e., the discount rate at which the net present value equals zero). The IRR method is illustrated in Exhibit 16–2.

There are some theoretical advantages to the NPV approach to evaluate proposed capital expenditures, but many managers use both approaches because they are more comfortable knowing the actual rate of return. Computer programs make the actual calculation easy; estimating the future cash flows associated with a proposal is the most challenging part of the process.

Some Analytical Considerations.   *Estimates.*   The validity of the present value calculation result will be a function of the accuracy with which future cash flows can be estimated. A great deal of effort will be expended in making estimates. When the project involves a replacement machine, the estimates of future cash flows (inflows from expense savings, outflows for maintenance—both preventative and periodic) can be made relatively easily. When the project is a new product, or a major capacity expansion, the most important, and hardest, data to estimate are revenues. Most firms will require a **post-audit** of the project to determine whether or not the anticipated benefits are actually being realized. While it may be too late to affect a project already completed, knowledge about past estimating errors should permit analysts to improve future estimates. An understanding of the significance of various estimates on the results of the calculations can be obtained by changing the estimates. This process is a form of sensitivity analysis that helps identify the most significant estimates.

Cash Flows Far in the Future.   Given the challenges of estimating, many capital budgeting analysts will not consider probable cash flows that will be more than 10 years in the future. In essence their position is that if the project will not have a satisfactory return considering the cash flows in the first 10 years, then the project is too risky to accept even if later cash flows will give it a satisfactory rate of return. The present value of $100 to be received in 11 years, at a discount rate of 20 percent, is $13.46, so far-distant cash flows

EXHIBIT 16–2 Internal Rate of Return (IRR) Analysis of a Proposed Investment

I. Assumptions:
Same as in Exhibit 16–1.
The NPV of the proposed investment at a discount rate of 16% is $2,622 (from Exhibit 16–1).

II. NPV calculation of proposed investment at a discount rate of 18%:

	12/31/93	1994	1995	1996	1997	1998
Cash flows from investment:						
Savings.		26,000	27,000	31,000	35,000	38,000
Salvage.						6,000
Total		26,000	27,000	31,000	35,000	44,000

III. Net present value calculation:

	12/31/93	1994	1995	1996	1997	1998
Present value factor (Table 6–1, 18%)		0.8475	0.7182	0.6086	0.5158	0.4371
Present value of cash flows from investment.		22,035	19,391	18,867	18,053	19,232
Total present value of cash flows from investment	$ 97,578 ←					
Investment	(100,000)					
Net present value	$ (2,422)					

IV. Interpolation:

Discount rate	16%	17%	18%
Net Present value	$2,622	0	$(2,422)

The discount rate at a NPV of 0 is almost exactly 17%.

V. Conclusion from analysis:
The internal rate of return of the project is the discount rate at which the NPV = 0, so the IRR is 17 percent. The expected IRR is more than the firm's 16 percent cost of capital. Based on this quantitative analysis, the investment should be made.

will not add significantly to the total present value of the cash flows.

Timing of Cash Flows within the Year. The present value factors in Tables 6–1 and 6–2 assume that all of the cash flow each year is received at the end of the year. It is more likely that the cash flows will be received fairly evenly throughout the year, and although present value can be calculated using that assumption, it is not uncommon for the end-of-the-year assumption to be used because it results in a slightly lower, more conservative present value amount.

Investment Made over a Period of Time. Capital expenditure projects involving new products, new plants, and capacity expansion usually require expenditures made over a period of time. For example, payments are usually made to a building contractor every month during construction, and for a major project, construction may extend over several years. When this is going to occur, the investment amount used in the present value analysis should be determined as of the point at which the project is expected to be put into service. This means that interest on cash disbursements made during the construction, or preoperating, period should be considered so that the investment amount will include the time value of money invested during that period.

Income Tax Effect of Cash Flows from the Project.   The cash flows identified with a proposed capital expenditure should include all of the associated inflows and outflows, including income taxes. The model for making this calculation is essentially the same as that used in the statement of cash flows to determine cash generated from operations. For example: assume that a capital expenditure proposal for a new product reflects the following makeup of operating income, income taxes, and net income for the first year the product is sold:

Revenues	$240,000
Variable expenses	100,000
Contribution margin.	$140,000
Direct fixed expenses:	
Requiring cash disbursements	85,000
Depreciation of equipment.	20,000
Operating income.	$ 35,000
Income taxes @ 40%	14,000
Net income	$ 21,000

To calculate the amount of cash flow from this product, it is necessary to add back the depreciation expense to net income. Remember that depreciation is a deduction for income tax purposes but is not a cash expenditure. Therefore, the cash flow during the first year for this new product would be:

Net income	$21,000
Add: Depreciation expense	20,000
Cash flow from the product	$41,000

Similarly, the cash flow from the new product for each year to be used in the NPV or IRR calculation would be calculated by adding depreciation expense to the projected net income after taxes. In addition, any other differences between accrual basis earnings and cash flows would be recognized.

Working Capital Investment. Capital expenditure proposals that involve new products or capacity expansion will usually require a working capital increase because accounts receivable and inventories will increase. The working capital increase required is treated as additional investment (i.e., it is a cash outflow at the beginning of the project or later if working capital needs will be greater then). If the new product or capacity expansion has a definite life, the investment in working capital will be recovered (it will be a cash inflow) after the product is discontinued or the expansion is reversed.

Least Cost Projects. Not all capital expenditures are made to reduce costs or increase revenues. Some expenditures required by law — environmental controls, for example — will increase operating costs. (The "benefit" may be the avoidance of a fine or the ability to continue in business.) Alternative expenditures in this category should also be evaluated using present value analysis; however, instead of seeking a positive NPV or IRR, the objective is to have the lowest negative result. However, even though the present value ratio will be less than 1.0, the most desirable alternative is still the one with the highest present value ratio.

Payback. The payback method to evaluate proposed capital expenditures answers the question: How many years will it take to recover the amount of the investment? The answer to this question is determined by adding up the cash flows, beginning with the cash flows of the first year, until the total cash flows equal the investment, and then counting the number of years of cash flow required. For example, using the data from Exhibit 16–1, for a machine costing $100,000, the annual and cumulative cash flows were:

Year	Cash Flow	Cumulative Cash Flow
1991 (1st year).	$26,000	$ 26,000
1992 (2nd year)	27,000	53,000
1993 (3rd year)	31,000	84,000
1994 (4th year)	35,000	119,000
1995 (5th year)	44,000	163,000

The investment is recovered during the fourth year, after $16,000 of that year's $35,000 has been realized. Expressed as a decimal, 16/35 is 0.46; the project's payback period would be expressed as 3.46 years.

The obvious advantage of the payback method is its simplicity. Present value analysis is confusing to some people, but anyone can understand payback period. There are two major disadvantages to the payback method. First, it does not consider the time value of money, and this is a fatal flaw. Secondly, it does not consider cash flows that continue after the investment has been recovered. Thus a project having a payback period of three years and no subsequent cash flow at all would appear to be more desirable than a project that has a payback period of four years and cash flows that continue for five more years. The payback method, as traditionally used, does not consider cash flows after the investment has been recovered.

In spite of its flaws, the payback method is used by many firms, especially in connection with equipment replacement decisions. The widespread use of the payback method is due to its ease of understanding and the fact that in a rapidly changing technological environment, the speed with which an investment is recovered is

---

EXHIBIT 16–3   Accounting Rate of Return Analysis of a Proposed Investment

I. Assumptions:
   Same as in Exhibit 16–1.

II. Calculation:

$$\frac{\text{Accounting}}{\text{rate of return}} = \frac{\text{Operating income}}{\text{Average investment}}$$

$$= \frac{\text{Savings} - \text{Depreciation expense}}{\text{Average investment}}$$

For 1994:

$$= \frac{26,000 - 18,800^*}{(100,000 + (100,000 - 18,800))/2^\dagger}$$

$$= \frac{7,200}{90,600}$$

$$= 7.9\%$$

* Straight-line depreciation expense:
   (Cost − Salvage value)/Estimated life
   (100,000 − 6,000)/5 years = 18,800
† Net book value at end of 1991:
   Cost − Accumulated depreciation
   100,000 − 18,800 = 81,200

important. Some firms require early and significant cash flows from an investment in new plant and equipment because they don't have the financial capacity to finance their activities while waiting for the payoff from an investment to begin. Some analysts report the payback period along with NPV (or present value ratio) and IRR just to answer the "How long until the investment is recovered?" question.

Accounting Rate of Return. The accounting rate of return method to evaluate proposed capital expenditures focuses on the impact of the project on the financial statements. Accounting operating income (or net income) is related to the effect of the investment on the balance sheet. This is done on a year-by-year basis. The calculation for 1994, using data from Exhibit 16–1, is illustrated in Exhibit 16–3.

The fatal flaw of the accounting rate of return approach is that the time value of money is not considered. Some financial managers will make the accounting rate of return calculation, not for investment evaluation purposes, but so they can anticipate the effect that the investment will have on the financial statements. Large start-up costs for a new product line, or new production facility, may adversely affect reported results for a year or two. Management should be aware of this so that stockholders can be put on notice in advance in order to minimize the impact of the start-up costs on the market price of the firm's common stock.

The Investment Decision

As is the case with virtually every management decision, both quantitative and qualitative factors are considered. After the results of the quantitative models just illustrated have been obtained, the project with the highest time-adjusted rate of return may not be selected. Overriding qualitative factors could include the following:

Commitment to a segment of the business that requires capital investment to achieve or regain competitiveness even though that segment does not have as great an ROI as others.

Regulations that mandate investment to meet safety, environmental, or access requirements. Fines and other enforcement incentives aside, management's citizenship goals for the organization may result in a high priority for these investments.

Technological developments within the industry may require new facilities to maintain customers or market share at the cost of lower ROI for a period of time.

The organization may have limited resources to invest in capital projects, and, as a result of the capital rationing process less ambitious, lower ROI projects may be approved instead of large-scale, higher ROI projects for which resources cannot be obtained.

In addition to considering issues such as these, managements' judgments about the accuracy of the estimates used in the capital budgeting model may result in selection of projects for which the estimates are believed to be more accurate.

The important point to be remembered here is that although the use of appropriate quantitative models (whether they involve time value of money calculations, use of cost behavior pattern information, analysis of variances, or other applications you have learned) can significantly improve the value of the factors that management considers in any decision, most decisions are significantly influenced by top managements' values and experiences—qualitative factors. This is one reason top managers receive top salaries and why their job is at risk if they make the wrong decision.

Integration of Capital Budget with Operating Budgets

Several aspects of the capital budget interact with the development of the operating budget. Contribution margin increases and cost savings from anticipated capital expenditure projects must be built into the expenditure and income statement budgets. Cash disbursements for capital projects must be included in the cash budget. The impact of capital expenditures on the balance sheet forecast must be considered. Thus the development of the capital budget is an integral part of the overall budgeting process.

SUMMARY

Capital budgeting has a much longer-term time frame than operational budgeting. Capital expenditure analysis, which leads to the capital budget, attempts to determine the impact of a proposed capital expenditure on the organization's ROI.

Capital budgeting procedures should involve use of present value analysis because an investment is made today in expectation of returns far into the future. The time value of money must be recognized if appropriate capital expenditure decisions are to be made.

In addition to evaluating the results of numerical analysis, decision makers consider qualitative factors related to the proposed investment. Most qualitative factors relate to the risks associated with the investment, or with the numbers used to support the investment decision.

Cost of capital is the ROI that should be earned on the proposed investment. The risk associated with the proposal will affect the cost of capital, or desired ROI, used to evaluate the investment.

Net present value and internal rate of return are two investment analysis methods that recognize the time value of money. The net present value approach uses the cost of capital as the discount rate and results in calculating a difference between the present value of the future cash flows from the investment, and the amount invested. If the net present value is zero or positive, the proposed investment's ROI is equal to or greater than the cost of capital, and the investment is an appropriate one to make. The internal rate of return approach solves for the proposal's ROI, which is then compared to cost of capital. The investment is an appropriate one to make if the ROI of the proposed investment equals or exceeds the cost of capital.

The present value ratio, or profitability index, provides a means to rank alternative proposals.

Some analytical considerations related to capital budgeting include estimating accuracy, timing of cash flows during a year, and investments made over a period of time. Many firms require the post-audit of a capital project to evaluate the estimates made in the initial analysis. Some projects will require an increase in working capital, which is considered part of the investment.

Payback and accounting rate of return are two investment analysis methods that do not recognize the time value of money and are thus not appropriate analytical techniques. Nevertheless, many analysts and managers use the results of these methods along with the results of the NPV and IRR methods.

In addition to considering the results of the various quantitative models used to evaluate investment proposals, management also identifies and considers qualitative factors when deciding whether or not to proceed with an investment. These qualitative factors are frequently more significant than the quantitative model results.

The capital budget is integrated into the operating budget. Production capacity, depreciation expense, and cash outflows for purchases of new plant and equipment are directly affected by the capital budget.

KEY TERMS AND CONCEPTS

accounting rate of return method *(p. 487)*   A capital budgeting analytical technique that calculates the rate of return on the investment based on the financial statement impacts of the investment.

capital budgeting *(p. 484)*   The process of analyzing proposed investments in plant and equipment and other long-lived assets.

cash flows *(p. 487)*   In capital budgeting, the cash receipts and disbursements associated with a capital expenditure over its life.

cost of capital *(p. 486)*   The ROI that must be earned to permit the firm to meet its interest obligations and provide the owners their expected return; the discount rate used in the present value calculations of capital budgeting.

internal rate of return (IRR) method *(p. 488)*   A capital budgeting analytical technique that solves for the time-adjusted rate of return on an investment over its life.

net present value (NPV) method *(p. 488)*   A capital budgeting analytical technique that relates the present value of the returns from an investment to the present value of the investment, given a cost of capital.

payback method *(p. 487)*   A capital budgeting analytical technique that calculates the length of time for the cash flows from an investment to equal the investment.

post-audit *(p. 490)*   The process of comparing the assumptions used in a capital budgeting analysis with the actual results of the investment.

present value ratio *(p. 488)*   The ratio of the present value of the cash flows from an investment to the investment. See *profitability index*.

profitability index *(p. 488)*   The ratio of the present value of the cash flows from an investment to the investment; used for ranking proposed capital expenditures by profitability.

EXERCISES AND PROBLEMS

16–1. An investor has asked for your help with the following time value of money applications. Use the appropriate factors from Table 6–1 or Table 6–2 to answer the following questions.

Required:

a. What is the present value of $36,000 to be received in three years using a discount rate of 16 percent?

b. How much should be invested today at a return on investment of 16 percent compounded annually to have $36,000 in three years?

c. If the return on investment was greater than 16 percent compounded annually, would the amount to be invested today to have $36,000 in three years be more or less than the answer to part (*b*)? Explain your answer.

16–2. Time value of money concepts have many applications. Use the appropriate factors from Table 6–1 or Table 6–2 to answer the following questions.

Required:

a. Blue Co.'s common stock is expected to have a cash dividend of $2 per share for each of the next five years, and it is estimated that the market value per share will be $50 at the end of five years. If an investor requires a return on investment of 12 percent, what is the maximum price the investor would be willing to pay for a share of Blue Co. common stock today?

b. Sadvester bought a bond with a face amount of $1,000, a stated interest rate of 8 percent, and a maturity date 20 years in the future for $980. Two years later, market interest rates were 10 percent.

   1. Why was Sadvester able to purchase the bond for less than its face amount two years ago?

   2. What is the market value of the bond today, two years after it was purchased?

c. Jill purchased a U.S. Series EE savings bond for $75, and six years later received $106.38 when the bond was redeemed. What average annual return on investment did Jill earn over the six years?

16–3. Capital budgeting analysis involves the use of many estimates.

Required:

For each of the following estimating errors, state whether the net present value of the project will be too high or too low.

a. The investment is too high.

b. The cost of capital is too low.

c. The cash flows from the project are too high.

d. The number of years over which the project will generate cash flows is too low.

16–4. Beck Equipment Co. is evaluating the cost of capital to use in its capital budgeting process. Over the recent past the company has averaged a return on equity of 15 percent and a return on assets of 12 percent. The company can currently borrow short-term money for 9 percent.

Required:

a. Which of the above rates is most relevant to deciding the cost of capital to use? Explain your answer.

b. Without prejudice to your answer to (*a*), explain why the company might choose to use a cost of capital of 16 percent to evaluate capital expenditure opportunities.

16–5. Exerco is considering the investment of $28,000 in a new machine. The machine will generate cash flow of $7,000 per year for each year of its six-year life and will have a salvage value of $5,000 at the end of its life. Exerco's cost of capital is 16 percent.

Required:

a. Calculate the net present value of the proposed investment. (Ignore income taxes.)

b. What will the internal rate of return on this investment be relative to the cost of capital? Explain your answer.

16–6. A capital budgeting analyst for Cornpro Corp. is evaluating a proposed investment associated with a new product. The following data estimates have been obtained from members of the task force created to study the new product:

Investment in machinery and equipment required to produce the product	$384,000
Net increase in working capital (accounts receivable and inventories, less increase in accounts payable) associated with the new product. It can be assumed that this investment will be recovered at the end of the product's life.	82,000
Net cash flow from operations for the product, for years	
1	114,000
2	142,000
3	133,000
4	130,000
5	132,000
6	118,000
7	64,000
Salvage value of the machinery and equipment, at the end of the product's life	15,000
Cost of capital	20%

Required:

a. Calculate the net present value of the proposed investment.

b. What will the internal rate of return on this investment be relative to the cost of capital? Explain your answer.

c. Differences between estimates made by the task force and actual results would have an effect on the actual rate of return on the project. Identify the significant estimates made by the task force, and state the effect on the actual rate of return on the investment if the estimated amount turns out to be less than the actual amount finally achieved.

16–7. Sanders Company is considering the investment of $28,000 in a new machine. It is estimated that the new machine will generate additional cash flow of $7,000 per year for each year of its six-year life and will have a salvage value of $5,000 at the end of its life. Sanders Company financial managers estimate that the firm's cost of capital is 16 percent.

Required:

a. Calculate the net present value of the investment.

b. Calculate the profitability index of the investment.

c. What is the internal rate of return of this investment, relative to the cost of capital?

d. Calculate the payback period of the investment.

16–8. Capper Co. is evaluating the purchase of another sewing machine that will be used to manufacture sport caps. The invoice price of the machine is $113,000. In addition, delivery and installation costs will total $3,500. The machine has the capacity to produce 10,000 dozen caps per year. Sales are forecast to increase gradually, and production volumes for each of the seven years of the machine's life are expected to be:

1993	3,000 dozen
1994	4,700 dozen
1995	7,100 dozen
1996	9,400 dozen
1997	10,000 dozen
1998	10,000 dozen
1999	10,000 dozen

The caps have a contribution margin of $4.20 per dozen. Fixed costs associated with the additional production (other than depreciation expense) will be negligible. Salvage value and the investment in working capital should be ignored. Capper Co.'s cost of capital for this capacity expansion has been set at 16 percent.

Required:

a. Calculate the net present value of the proposed investment in the new sewing machine.
b. Calculate the profitability index of the investment.
c. What is the internal rate of return of this investment relative to the cost of capital?
d. Calculate the payback period of the investment.

16–9. The Goodwrench Garage is considering investing in a new tune-up computer. The cost of the computer is $24,000. A cost analyst has calculated the discounted present value of the expected cash flows from the computer, based on the firm's cost of capital of 20 percent, to be $26,220.

Required:

a. What is the expected return on investment of the machine, relative to 20 percent?
b. The payback period of the investment in the machine is expected to be 4.6 years. How much weight should this measurement carry in the decision about whether or not to invest in the machine? Explain your answer.

16–10. City Hospital is considering the acquisition of a new diagnostic scanning machine. The investment required to get the machine operational will be $2,466,840. The machine will be capable of performing 7,500 scanning procedures per year, but based on the experience of other hospitals, management estimates that the machine will be used at 80 percent of its capacity. The hospital's cost of capital is 12 percent; the machine has an estimated useful life of six years and no salvage value.

Required:

a. Assuming a constant cash flow every year, calculate the annual net cash flow required from the scanner if the IRR of the investment is to equal 12 percent. (*Hint: The annual cash flow requirement is an annuity.*)
b. If the direct cash costs of operating the scanner equal 50 percent of the net cash flow requirement, what price should the hospital charge per scanning procedure in order to achieve a 12 percent ROI?

16–11. Information about four investment proposals is summarized below:

Proposal	Investment Required	Net Present Value
1	$50,000	$30,000
2	60,000	24,000
3	30,000	15,000
4	45,000	9,000

Required: Calculate the profitability index of each proposal, and indicate which proposal is the most desirable investment.

16–12. Management of Blue Co. is considering an investment in an expansion of the company's product line. It is estimated that the investment required will be $250,000, and that the investment will be made at the beginning of 1993. The estimated cash returns from the new product are summarized in the following table; it may be assumed that the returns will be received in a lump sum at the end of each of the years.

Year	Amount of Cash Return
1993	$35,000
1994	52,000
1995	91,000
1996	95,000
1997	93,000
1998	82,000

The cost of capital used in Blue Co.'s capital budgeting analysis is 16 percent.

Required:
  a. Calculate the present value of the cash returns.
  b. Calculate the net present value of the investment.
  c. Calculate the present value ratio (or profitability index) of the investment.
  d. Estimate the approximate internal rate of return of the product line expansion. Do not calculate the internal rate of return.
  e. Calculate the payback period of the investment.
  f. Based on the above quantitative analyses, would you recommend that the product-line expansion project be undertaken? Explain your answer.
  g. Identify some qualitative factors that you would want to have considered with respect to this project before management proceeds with the investment.

16–13. Spiffy Co. uses the accounting rate of return method to evaluate proposed capital investments. The company's desired rate of return (its cost of capital) is 18 percent. The project being evaluated involves a new product that will have a three-year life. The investment required is $100,000, which consists of an $80,000 machine and inventories and accounts receivable totaling $20,000. The machine will have a useful life of three years and a salvage value of $50,000. The salvage value will be received during the fourth year, and the inventories and accounts receivable related to the product will also be converted back to cash in the fourth year. Accrual accounting net income from the product will be $29,000 a year, before depreciation expense, for each of the three years. Because of the time lag between selling the product and collecting the accounts receivable, cash flows from the product will be:

1st year.	$14,000
2nd year	24,000
3rd year	29,000
4th year	20,000

Required:

a. Calculate the accounting rate of return for the first year of the product. Assume straight-line depreciation. Based on this analysis, would the investment be made? Explain your answer.

b. Calculate the net present value of the product using a cost of capital of 18 percent and assuming that cash flows occur at the end of the respective years. Based on this analysis, would the investment be made? Explain your answer.

c. Which analytical approach is the most appropriate to use? Explain your answer.

16–14. Oldweigh Corp. evaluates capital expenditure proposals using the accounting rate of return method. A recent proposal involved a $50,000 investment in a machine that had an estimated useful life of five years and an estimated salvage value of $10,000. The machine was expected to increase net income (and cash flows) before depreciation expense by $15,000 a year. The criteria for approving a new investment are that it have a rate of return of 16 percent and a payback period of three years or less.

Required:

a. Calculate the accounting rate of return on this investment for the first year. Assume straight-line depreciation. Based on this analysis would the investment be made? Explain your answer.

b. Calculate the payback period for this investment. Based on this analysis, would the investment be made? Explain your answer.

c. Calculate the net present value of this investment using a cost of capital of 16 percent. Based on this analysis, would the investment be made? Explain your answer.

d. What recommendation would you make to the management of Oldweigh Corp. about evaluating capital expenditure proposals? Support your recommendation with the appropriate rationale.

Appendix A

This appendix is the 1991 Annual Report of Armstrong World Industries, Inc.

As discussed in the text, financial statement disclosures and accounting methods are continually evolving. The presentations in this document reflect generally accepted principles of accounting as of the date of their publication. Subsequent changes in accounting principles and reporting standards will be reflected in subsequent years' reports.

ABOUT THE COVER:
The bedroom shown was created in a
cooperative venture by interior
designers of Armstrong, *Country
Home* magazine and GEAR, home
furnishings design and licensing
specialists. The room was one of 11
interior spaces in a country classic
designer showhouse sponsored as a
charity event by the Junior Women's
Club of Doylestown, Pennsylvania. It
will appear on the cover of the June
issue of *Country Home.* Products
featured are a pencil post canopy
bed by Thomasville Furniture
Industries, Inc., and Components
Tile flooring by Armstrong.

A RMSTRONG IS PRIMARILY A MANUFACTURER AND MARKETER OF

INTERIOR FURNISHINGS. ITS PRODUCTS INCLUDE FLOOR COVERINGS

(RESILIENT FLOORING AND ALL CERAMIC TILE), BUILDING PRODUCTS

AND FURNITURE. ARMSTRONG PEOPLE ALSO MAKE AND MARKET A

VARIETY OF SPECIALTY PRODUCTS FOR THE BUILDING, AUTOMOTIVE,

TEXTILE AND OTHER INDUSTRIES—IMPORTANT PARTS OF ARMSTRONG

BUSINESSES. THE COMPANY'S ACTIVITIES EXTEND WORLDWIDE.

FINANCIAL HIGHLIGHTS

(millions except for per-share data)	1991	1990*	1989*
Net sales	$2,439.3	$2,518.8	$2,488.7
Earnings from continuing businesses before income taxes	$ 100.3	$ 223.1	$ 243.6
Earnings from continuing businesses	60.6	146.4	157.7
Return on sales	2.5%	5.8%	6.3%
Net earnings	48.2	141.0	187.6
Return on average common shareholders' equity	3.3%	13.0%	17.9%
Total shareholders' equity	$ 885.5	$ 899.2	$ 976.5
Common shareholders' equity	873.8	892.7	973.8
Average number of common shares outstanding:			
Primary	37.2	38.9	45.4
Fully diluted	43.1	44.7	48.6
Purchases of property, plant, and equipment	$ 133.8	$ 195.1	$ 231.0
Aggregate cost of acquisitions	$ —	$ 16.1	$ —
Per share of common stock:			
Earnings from continuing businesses:			
Primary	$1.11	$3.26	$3.26
Fully diluted	1.11	2.99	3.11
Net earnings:			
Primary	.77	3.12	3.92
Fully diluted	.77	2.86	3.72
Dividends paid	1.19	1.135	1.045

* Certain amounts have been restated to exclude discontinued businesses.

Looking outward to customers—Members of Armstrong's President's Office, (from left) William W. Adams, Chairman and President, and Executive Vice-Presidents E. Allen Deaver and George A. Lorch keep abreast of changing customer needs through frequent visits to retailers, distributors, contractors and professional product specifiers and in meetings with customers at the company's headquarters in Lancaster, Pennsylvania.

To the shareholder:

Above all else, we want to be forthright and realistic in these annual letters and in all our communications to you, our shareholder.

Looking at the numbers alone, 1991 was certainly not a good year for Armstrong. And at this writing, we really can't promise any substantial improvement in the first half of this year.

Even the most cursory look at the financial highlights shown on the inside cover reveals that the year was subpar by Armstrong standards. We finished 1991 behind the previous year's results in just about all measurements of importance to investors. The specific results are summarized in the charts on page 17 (glimpses of our performance in key categories over a five-year period), and they are examined in all the usual detail in the narrative and tables on pages 18 through 38.

Whether it comes as a result of a quick glance or a thorough study, a question that logically follows is, "How does this year look?" We cannot make a clear forecast. While some signs are encouraging, it appears that the stalled U.S. economy is not going to experience any sudden turnaround. Nor are our most important end-use market segments, most of which are dependent to varying degrees on the state of that economy, likely to show any sort of pronounced, renewed vigor.

What we accomplish this year may largely be the product of our own internal ignition. Look inside Armstrong, and you will see our people focused on the six basic elements of better performance: sales growth, sales productivity, manufacturing productivity, service productivity, cost and expense management, and asset management. This year, sales growth is the most important of these six. Process improvement drives the other five.

Despite the disappointing earnings, we made as much progress in process improvement—all across the company, all around the world—as we have in any other single year! More than simply corrective action, this higher level of improvement stretches us to make permanent the best ways to make products,

the best ways to sell them and the best ways for our staff organizations to provide critically important support.

A glimpse at process improvement

We speak of process improvement in some depth later in this report. But a few examples stand out. First, our emphasis on process improvement generated a major evolutionary step in our global business management. From what began in January 1990 with the formation of five worldwide strategic management teams, we successfully moved at midyear 1991 to entirely reengineered international business teams that bring North America, Europe and the Pacific area much closer together. These teams are sure to help business unit managers to "think globally, act locally," bringing to each geographic market the best that Armstrong has to offer in products and systems.

A second example deals with an important subsidiary, The W. W. Henry Company, our major producer of grouts, mortars and adhesives used in the installation of vinyl floors, carpets and ceramic tile surfaces. Its success in 1991, in large measure, came through its ability to better serve its own customers and those of Armstrong and American Olean. Expansions at two plants allow regionalized manufacturing and service from more customer-oriented strategic points in the United States.

Third, in the field of manufacturing, at two important plant locations we converted to focused-factory operations where efficiency and service are improved through concentration on specific families of products. One of these facilities is at Lancaster, Pennsylvania, where our largest single plant became four focused

1

THE PRESIDENT'S LETTER

factories, each producing its own type of resilient flooring. The other is at Braintree, Massachusetts, where one factory became two for the production of different types of industrial products. These major changes—and so many more throughout all of Armstrong—are the results of painstaking process improvements, payoffs of our continuing emphasis on quality management.

Last June, we developed with our senior management an overall view that describes and unifies what Armstrong is attempting to do and how we plan to heighten our success. We want to share our thoughts on this with you and our other investors.

One performance measure we like comes to us from author Peter Drucker, who says that a company is successful when it increases its capacity to create wealth, to create value, for its owners and for all who have an economic relationship to the company. (Each of our several constituencies, in addition to shareholders, has these economic relationships, of course.)

We like the simplicity and truth of what Mr. Drucker said. We believe that our reason for being is *to increase the value of this company.*

The Armstrong Value Chain

And how will we do that? We must forge and strengthen what we have called the Armstrong Value Chain, a sequence of linked corporate achievements that both create and define our success.

The chain begins, not surprisingly, with *customer satisfaction.* That yields *market position,* which results in *financial performance,* which, in turn, gives us *increased value.* (It may help you understand the chain if you glance at the diagram below.)

Looking at the links one by one, we turn first to the end of the chain, at the point of greatest interest to our shareholders—increased value. Investors use various measures to determine the underlying value of a company. Most marry a calculation of the shareowner's equity in the company to an expectation of the company's ability to increase and reinvest its future earnings. Armstrong must create such value with a sound balance sheet, reflecting a reasonable cost of capital and a properly balanced ratio of debt to total capital. (We aim to bring that ratio down to a range of 35 to 37 percent from the current 47 percent.)

Financial performance goals

Increased value is a product of financial performance, which has

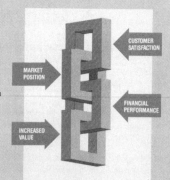

twin components: growth and profitability. We need to grow at 8 to 10 percent per year, on average over time, to sustain a dynamic approach to the business, creating new customers and generating new cash flows to invest in our future. Central to financial performance is our goal of annual returns on common shareholder's equity (ROE) of from 15 to 20 percent. Our return on equity is a function of our return on assets (ROA) multiplied by our financial leverage. To illustrate, if we achieve an ROA of 8 percent, our financial leverage (that is, the relationship between our assets and our equity) should yield 15 to 20 percent ROE.

Reaching our internal goal of an 8 percent return on assets requires, simply, better operating profits on each sales dollar and fewer assets to generate that sales dollar. The profit anatomy of a number of Armstrong businesses is quite good. The profit anatomy of *all* Armstrong businesses must be satisfactory if we are to return to where we have been: at or above a corporate ROA of 8 percent.

These are our financial targets. In themselves, however, they don't give us direction on what we need to do to reach them. We cannot achieve good financial performance without good market position. Market position has three central elements: product coverage (What part of the end-use market segments can we serve with our products?), product presence (How often are Armstrong products present where consumers make their buying decisions?) and sales success rates (How often do the customers select Armstrong rather than the product of a competitor?). On all three counts—coverage, presence, success rates—we operate from positions of strength in all our businesses. That will not change, regardless of U.S. and worldwide economic conditions.

The vital link

And that takes us to the vital link in the Armstrong Value Chain: customer satisfaction. As we said earlier, this is where the Armstrong Value Chain really begins. It starts with what we offer and to whom—and a clear proposition of why what we offer is a better value than the consumers' or the buyers' other choices. But it goes much further, to the deployment of a total quality improvement process—to assure complete conformance to what our customers expect, to their satisfaction and to their delight.

The pages that follow this letter present a sampling of what Armstrong is doing these days to ensure total satisfaction among customers of our products and services. Armstrong's emphasis on customer satisfaction has never been greater.

It is the mainspring of the successes we have enjoyed from our quality management process, now in its ninth year.

Four years ago, we set forth a new point of corporate strategy. It called on all of us "To look outward to our markets and customers using the Quality Management Process to continuously improve the value of our products and services."

There's nothing optional about that strategy at Armstrong. It is a requirement imposed by a demanding marketplace and a challenge requiring imagination, discipline and a love of change. It is a requirement and a challenge that we accept willingly, eagerly. This is what we are good at doing—and what we are doing better every day, every quarter, every year.

Changes to the Board of Directors

William M. Ellinghaus, a much-valued member of the Board for eight years, retired on March 1, 1991. Mr. Ellinghaus brought to the Board a keen understanding of organizational dynamics and of the practice of successful management techniques. We thank him for his years of splendid service.

Elected to the Board at the Annual Meeting of Shareholders on April 29, 1991, was Van C. Campbell, Vice Chairman for Finance and Administration, Corning Incorporated.

Barbara Hackman Franklin was sworn in today as the new Secretary of Commerce of the United States and has resigned from the Board. Miss Franklin, who joined the board in October 1989, had a short but distinguished career as an Armstrong director. We are sorry to lose her from the Board but are pleased to see her move to this important national post.

Mary Joan Glynn retired from the Board, effective February 25, after 17 years as an Armstrong director. Mrs. Glynn's valuable service on the Board spanned the period of the company's greatest growth and some of its most difficult challenges. We will miss her counsel and contributions.

Frank Breeze decided last year that it would not be his intention to stand for reelection to the Board when his term expires in April 1992. First elected to the Board in April 1983, Mr. Breeze was diligent and thoughtful in his many contributions to the work of the Board and its committees. We wish him well in his retirement.

The Board has reduced the number of directors from 13 to an anticipated 11 as of the end of April. We hope to add a director to the Board by the end of 1992.

Dividends increased in 1991

During 1991, total dividends paid on the common stock of the company amounted to $1.19 per share. This is 4.8 percent greater than the total dividends of $1.135 per share paid in 1990.

Meeting on January 27, the directors declared a first-quarter dividend of 30 cents per share of common stock, payable February 29 to shareholders of record as of February 7, 1992.

The outlook

We can't add to all that has been said in the business media about the limping economies of North America and parts of Europe. What we have to assume is that there will be no dramatic turns in the short term to make things easier for Armstrong. What successes we realize this year, of necessity, will be propelled from within by Armstrong people throughout the world.

On this point—the prospects for internally driven success—we can assure the shareholders of this company that Armstrong people will exert still greater pressures in those areas of activity that have produced the successes we have enjoyed in this period of economic uncertainty. In summary, Armstrong will:

- Be energetic in new product development and in all forms of sales promotion
- Continue to reach new levels of manufacturing efficiency and productivity in each of our 89 plants
- Apply the expected disciplines on cost and expense control in all quarters of the company
- Allocate near-term investments to focus on areas promising the greatest near-term returns without sacrificing long-term opportunities
- Maintain prudent cash management and healthy cash flows

Beyond these, investors can be sure that we will adhere to the principles of quality management, will continue to improve our processes and, by all means, will maintain our focus on satisfying our customers in all our businesses everywhere. These forge the chain of value for shareholders and for all who have an economic relationship with Armstrong.

Respectfully submitted,

William W. Adams
Chairman and President
February 28, 1992

■ Retailers of the Armstrong do-it-yourself assortment of floor tiles reacted with enthusiasm to the introduction of Statement Solarian Tile, an entirely new line of floors designed to appeal to consumers at the upper reaches of the interior fashions ladder. The tiles offer a mix of design options to owners wanting to create unusually distinctive looks in the "show areas" of their homes. Retailer purchases of Statement Solarian Tile during the introductory period more than doubled Armstrong expectations.

■ In Japan, professional specifiers such as architects and designers of commercial interiors found their Armstrong flooring choices broadened substantially with the introduction of more than 100 new designs, patterns and colors by the Japanese distributor, ABC Trading Company. The offerings represent a broad mix of commercial-grade tile and sheet flooring materials produced in the United States, Canada, Australia and the United Kingdom.

■ In its first full year of national distribution, Armstrong's new Visions Solarian no-wax flooring met with a level of customer satisfaction that far outstripped Armstrong expectations—tripling the levels of planned sales in both dollars and total yardage. Most of the customer reaction was based on the floor's positioning in the "Best" family of Armstrong's "Good-Better-Best" sequence of floor product maintenance and performance ratings. It is merchandised as having the Armstrong CleanSweep finish.

■ Armstrong vinyl floors with the company's CleanSweep wear layer earned the Good Housekeeping Seal, now appearing on CleanSweep floors promotional and merchandising materials. The Seal reinforces protection for the ultimate consumer and confidence in Armstrong. The CleanSweep guarantee calls attention to these Armstrong flooring materials as "easiest to clean of any vinyl sheet floor" and says the floors "will not permanently stain from household or traffic stains." The guarantee offers a replacement floor for any consumer "not satisfied that these floors are the easiest to clean."

■ More than 2,000 retailer customers are merchandising the new line of Armstrong Ceramic Tile in the wake of the company's successful introduction in 1991. In addition to finding clear advantages in expanding their offerings beyond traditional Armstrong vinyl floors, the retailers praised the point of sale displays and other merchandising aids developed to facilitate buying decisions of homeowners. Retailers

Extensive customer research with retailers and consumers preceded the design of Armstrong Ceramic Tile displays and other selling aids.

participated as members of the Armstrong teams that planned and implemented all phases of the ceramic tile launch.

■ An extensive program of market and customer research led to the introduction of a new commercial-grade resilient flooring named Companion Square Tile in

October. The product captures some of the popular visual effects in the Armstrong Suffield line of sheet flooring and can be combined with other tile materials to create overall floor designs that are highly customized—a growing requirement among specifiers and owners.

■ Owners, managers and officials of health-care facilities who have called for new decorating options with durable, easy-to-maintain sheet flooring reacted positively to a score of new colors and patterns in Armstrong's Classic Corlon flooring line. They were introduced at the industry's National Symposium on Health Care Design in Boston last November.

■ Armstrong's ceramic tile subsidiary, American Olean Tile Company, responded to the growing need for ceramic surfaces with improved slip retardance through the introduction of a new line named Sure-Step. This quarry tile features a raised pattern to increase protection from slippage—of special importance in areas used for food preparation, hospitality and fast-food service.

The raised surface that gives American Olean's new Sure-Step quarry tile its slip retardance characteristic also adds to its design appeal.

New Companion Square Tile's aesthetic and performance benefits make it especially appropriate for health care, mercantile and school settings.

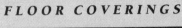

FLOOR COVERINGS

Nearly 1,700 elite SMART retailers of Armstrong floors visited the company's corporate headquarters in Lancaster, Pennsylvania, during the September-through-November period to learn, among other things, more about Armstrong and how they might be of greater service to their customers. ("SMART" is an acronym identifying an Armstrong program for these retailers focusing on sales, merchandising, advertising, retail support and tactics for servicing consumers.) The program of visits was one of the largest of its type ever hosted in Lancaster. Sherry Qualls (at left center), Armstrong residential floors advertising manager, is shown in a new product presentation.

■ Residential ceiling customers—both the retail home improvement centers that sell the ceilings and the consumers who buy from them—reacted enthusiastically to the company's introduction of Cascade ceiling materials, a new line of 2' x 2' panels offered in white and four colors. The panels have a special "stepped-edge" design inspired by fine molding treatments. These help create distinctive effects, especially when used with Armstrong's color-matching metal grid suspension systems.

■ Continuous monitoring of ceiling contractor requirements in France is assured through a system in which updated information on contractor needs is fed to a central data base, then retrieved through the personal computers of marketing representatives.

Personal computers provide important customer-need information in France.

■ Customers of Armstrong ceilings have added assurance that their shipments from company plants will arrive right on schedule and in perfect condition as a result of Armstrong's installation of a new warehouse management system at plants in St. Helens, Oregon, and Pensacola, Florida, in 1991. The first of these installations was put in place at Armstrong's plant in Macon, Georgia, in 1990. Plants at Marietta, Pennsylvania; Mobile, Alabama, and Gatineau, Quebec, Canada, are scheduled to go on-line with the system. The system substantially enhances inventory accuracy and materials handling.

■ In a major development geared to ease inventory maintenance by key customers, Armstrong established a full-service distribution center for all commercial ceiling products at its plant in St. Helens. The plant will offer services in the western United States, the western provinces of Canada and Pacific Rim countries. St. Helens joins the company's other commercial ceiling centers that service areas in the remainder of the United States: in Marietta, Pensacola, Macon and Mobile. These full-service centers, in addition to offering major inventory control benefits, also provide quicker delivery to customers. In 1992, St. Helens will join the Macon and Marietta plants in offering full services for both residential and commercial products.

■ For speedier and more efficient handling of customer claims on the rare occasions when Armstrong products or business practices (such as billing) don't meet expectations, the company implemented major improvements in claims resolution in North America. Typically, claims that used to take about three and one-half months are now resolved in two to 13 working days.

■ The company is enhancing its brand recognition in Western Europe through highly visible promotion ventures such as sponsorship of a prestigious art exhibit in Milan, Italy. To link Armstrong ceiling designs with art, a series of contemporary artists displayed works on contemporary commercial and institutional design themes for professionals who influence the specification of ceilings. This enhanced brand recognition is adding to the appeal of the company's ceiling products in Europe. Specifications of Armstrong ceilings are exceeding earlier projections there.

■ Conformance to customer requirements resulted in the specification of the Armstrong Second Look Series ceilings—more than one million square feet of the product together with Armstrong's color-matching Prelude suspension system—in an eight-store Sears, Roebuck project in Mexico. Customer satisfaction with on-time manufacturing and delivery schedules resulted in the award of the business for Ypasa S.A. de C.V., Armstrong's acoustical contractor in Mexico City.

■ Customers of Armstrong ceilings in Asia are substantially increasing their order levels—the result of process improvements directed at meeting changing marketplace needs. For the past several years, manufacturing, sales, marketing and logistics members of the Building Products global team traveled throughout Asia to identify specialized customer needs in Korea, Taiwan, Hong Kong, the People's Republic of China, Singapore, Thailand, Malaysia and Indonesia. In these countries, Armstrong salespeople not only identified the special customer needs but also helped implement the plans to meet them. Armstrong accelerated product development and process improvements to get new products to the marketplace more quickly. Reports Dave Boomer, St. Helens plant manager, "Pacific customers provide our greatest opportunity." In 1991, a major portion of St. Helens' output was shipped across the Pacific without a single customer complaint.

BUILDING PRODUCTS

Specifiers such as architects, designers and building owners have new opportunities for selecting deep dimensional ceilings that create "boxed" (also known as "coffered") effects within 2' x 2' or 4' x 4' modules with Metaphors ceiling materials, one of Armstrong's more popular 1991 product launches. The professionals can specify from a choice of three designs, each with special mitered moldings that interface with Armstrong suspension systems and Armstrong ceiling panels to permit design options that are virtually unlimited.

THE VITAL LINK IN THE VALUE CHAIN: *TOTAL SATISFACTION FOR CUSTOMERS OF OUR*

■ Coincident with the European Community 1992 and all that it means to the company's insulation business, Armstrong transferred the responsibility for managing this worldwide business to Europe—to be closer to key customers and to better enable the company to enhance its customer services. Armstrong has major European plants producing insulation materials in Münster and Friesenhofen, Germany; Oldham, England; Rothrist, Switzerland; Palafrugell, Spain, and Trezzano Rosa, Italy. Significant expansion of production facilities in Spain is planned this year.

■ More than 300 professionals from Hungary who specialize in the specification of plumbing and heating insulations visited an exhibit at the "Aqua-Therm" program, the first event of its kind in that country. Armstrong and the company's national distributor in Hungary jointly sponsored the exhibit to inform wholesalers, architects, contractors and installers of the properties of Armstrong insulation products.

■ Following 18 months of preparation, Armstrong World Industries, G.m.b.H., in Germany, implemented an advanced customer order management system to continuously monitor all key elements of customer requirements in the insulation business. These elements include order entry, inventory, production planning and customer schedules. Plans call for the system's implementation throughout Europe in the next several years.

■ With the promise of heightened customer satisfaction providing the key motivation, Armstrong's plant in

Braintree, Massachusetts, completed a major transition to become two separate focused-factory operations. One factory concentrates on the production of textile cots and aprons, cork-and-rubber gasket materials and specialty rubber products. The second produces Armaflex insulation and related foam products. The emphasis at both operations is on improved customer service and process effectiveness. Among these improvements is the reduction of cycle time—the amount of time required by a process, from beginning to end, to meet a customer need.

■ Armstrong became the first company in the Federated Republic of Germany to be certified by the North Rhine-Westphalia State Materials Testing Institute as a producer of insulation materials, meeting the requirements of stringent European manufacturing standards. The company's quality assurance system, as certified by the Institute, offers specifiers and end-users optimum confidence and complies with regulations relating to the free traffic of products within Europe as part of the European Community 1992.

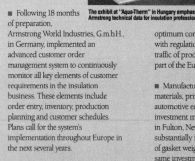
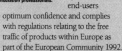
The exhibit at "Aqua-Therm" in Hungary emphasized Armstrong technical data for insulation professionals.

■ Manufacturers who purchase gasket materials, primarily for use in automotive equipment, found that an investment made at Armstrong's plant in Fulton, New York, resulted in substantially improved quality in terms of gasket weight and thickness. This same investment allowed Armstrong to meet customer requirements calling for increased gasketing material thickness in a single step without "layering."

Further, the investment permits reduced turnaround time between the placement of an order and delivery—always of critical importance to customers.

■ Two major German companies that provide gaskets for that country's largest automakers conducted audits of the suppliers of materials from which the gaskets are produced. They declared Armstrong's quality processes as best, helping the company to increase its penetration in that important geographic market. Also in Europe, Armstrong successfully established a three-day delivery capability from its Münster warehouse—considered by customers to be the quickest delivery service in Europe.

■ The 1990 negotiation of a joint venture in the People's Republic of China to facilitate production and delivery of textile mill supplies in China and to export the products throughout southeastern Asia came to fruition at midyear. Known as Armstrong Textile Rubber Products Company Shanghai Ltd., the venture began production in May, two days after the factory closed operations as a Chinese state-owned enterprise.

■ Each of the five customer service representatives at Armstrong's textile mill supplies facility in Greenville, South Carolina, is now assigned specific customers to service rather than responding to requests from the entire spectrum of accounts. The move is helping to cement stronger Armstrong-customer relationships and generate more intimate knowledge of specialized customer requirements.

INDUSTRY PRODUCTS

In a highly successful step that enhances the importance of Armstrong to purchasers of gasket materials, the company is performing some of the testing that traditionally has been done by automobile manufacturers. For example, specialists at Armstrong's Research and Development Center test gaskets for up to 500 hours in actual engines provided by the automakers, then return those engines completely sealed for the manufacturers' evaluations. The company also performed testing for the U.S.-produced Honda lawn mower. Here, an engine with Armstrong gasketing materials is being tested for a major European automaker by John Berdiner, gasket performance analyst.

9

■ The cycle time between a retailer's order of custom-made Thomasville upholstered products and the time of shipment was reduced from about six weeks to an average of four weeks. This strengthens the value of the line to consumers for whom extended cycle times are negatives in making purchase decisions. Thomasville Upholstery pieces were advertised nationally for the first time, further adding to their consumer appeal and retailer merchandising benefit.

■ Thomasville wood furniture offered significant additions to its lines for retail customers to broaden their assortments. Among them were six patterns in the First Impressions line of youth furniture, the company's entry in the youth bedroom segment of the market; a reintroduction of the American Oak Collection

The Montrachet collection armoire in Vineyard Finish.

in two finishes; Montrachet, a new rural French motif collection in two finishes and 65 pieces; Stone Creek, a set of accent pieces priced at Thomasville's lowest price point; and Thomasville Home Theater, a new video concept in which the company joined with a major consumer electronics firm to coordinate entertainment centers with a 52-inch rear-screen television projection and audio equipment.

■ Key retailers joined the Armstrong Furniture Retail Division product development team in 1991 to help bring

about the introduction of 16 new products. This was double the number normally introduced during a year's time. Made possible through substantial reductions in developmental cycle time, the introductions significantly enhance the choices available to prospective purchasers of Armstrong Retail furniture.

■ A network of 38 quality improvement facilitators will lead all Thomasville plant and office locations in motivating and training their colleagues in the principles and implementation of customer satisfaction and process improvement measures throughout the company.

■ For specialty store retailers seeking assembled furniture as American-made alternatives to higher-priced European imports, the Armstrong Furniture Retail Division introduced several polyester-finished product lines. Armstrong's RTA (ready-to-assemble) Division polyester-finished products offered large mass merchandisers exceptional value at the more profitable ends of their furniture lines.

■ Thomasville Furniture Industries, Inc., successfully completed a pilot test of a customer satisfaction survey

Customers complete questionnaires in the Thomasville survey program. The results are summarized in Customer Satisfaction Improvement (CSI) scores for the stores that participate.

program with a sampling of five of its Thomasville Home Furnishing Stores and Gallery retailers. In the test, 2,500 Gallery customers received survey forms to evaluate Thomasville and the retailers in critically important areas such as product quality, availability of helpful product information, promptness of service, sales assistance skills, care in handling and length of time from purchase to delivery (cycle time). A total of 130 Thomasville Home Furnishing Stores and Gallery locations signed up for the program to monitor their customer satisfaction levels on an ongoing basis.

■ Customer service coordinators at the Appomattox, Virginia, facility of Armstrong Furniture Division cut the time needed to process orders—from receipt through shipment—from a minimum of five days to a single day. This is a result of a major business information systems undertaking that spanned four years of development. The 1992 plans call for the system to be expanded to the Thomasville Wood Division.

■ Process improvements in the delivery of Thomasville Upholstery's Advantage Express Line of sofas, loveseats, sectionals and sleepers are resulting in shipments of 55 percent of orders in three weeks or less and 97 percent of orders in four weeks—rare in custom order furniture businesses where the order-to-shipment time frames are usually expressed in terms of months rather than weeks.

FURNITURE PRODUCTS

A Thomasville Furniture process improvement team reduced the cycle time for the production of chair seats from 48 to less than seven hours—taking the seat department a significant step closer to meeting its long-range goal in the companywide "Eighty in Five" effort. The reduction of cycle time, one of two thrusts of "Eighty in Five" (see page 12), is a major contributor to increased levels of customer satisfaction in the furniture business. Roger Burkhart (second from left), Thomasville plant facilitator, is shown reviewing an improved work flow diagram with seat department associates.

11

In last year's Annual Report, Armstrong shared with its investors an announcement that changed the shape of the company in 1991. Presented to approximately 25,000 employees in November 1990, the announcement centered on a corporate stretch goal program named "Eighty in Five."

Its ultimate goal: *total* customer satisfaction.

As the main thrust of this effort, every Armstrong business unit is called on to meet a demanding goal: to reduce by 80 percent in five years or less the nonconformances that inhibit customer satisfaction—and to accomplish this goal *everywhere*, both inside and outside the organization. (In corporate activity, one intracompany group is a customer of at least one other.) A second emphasis of "Eighty in Five" is to achieve this nonconformance reduction by trimming cycle time—the amount of time required by a process, from beginning to end, to meet a customer requirement (such as development of a new product to meet a homeowner's or professional specifier's need).

Process improvement is central to the progress reported as part of "Eighty in Five." Virtually all of the examples of developments that have heightened the levels of customer satisfaction in each of the four business segments explained on pages 4-11 are results of the improvements of processes through which things get done.

As this report goes to the printer, more than 1,100 process improvement teams are at work within the company.

All set their focus on improving the way Armstrong people do things—most important, in the eyes of customers. And those customers are *internal* (example: Armstrong marketing representatives benefit from agreements negotiated with automobile leasing companies) as well as *external* (example: customers outside the United States gain from decreased complexities and increased efficiencies made possible through Armstrong's new methods of processing orders for product shipments abroad; see opposite page).

The company is using the demanding criteria of the Malcolm Baldrige National Quality Award for its own internal award—the Armstrong Quality Achievement Award. The criteria serve as guideposts for achieving substantial improvements in Armstrong's ability to compete favorably in the United States and abroad. The Armstrong award will serve to recognize organizations who have done the best in fostering internal improvements.

Armstrong people first employed the National Quality Award criteria in 1990, when they formed a matrix for self-assessments involving more than 800 people and 55 Armstrong organizations worldwide. Based on these assessments, they formalized organizational quality plans and put them into action as precise directions for bringing about improvement.

The Baldrige examinations provided other benefits, including an underscoring of the importance of:
—*An understanding of the requirements for achieving quality excellence*
—*The role quality improvement plays in sustaining global leadership*
—*The integration of quality plans with business unit plans to support Armstrong's corporate goal of achieving total customer satisfaction*

Beyond these 1990 experiences, the Corporate Quality Council and the Armstrong Planning Committee (corporate officers) agreed that the Armstrong Quality Achievement Award will help provide an ongoing impetus to accomplish the following:
—*Knowing where Armstrong stands in comparison with other organizations and companies*
—*Measuring progress over time*
—*Promoting awareness, understanding, ownership and involvement*
—*Recognizing quality achievement*
—*Encouraging healthy competition*
—*Preparing Armstrong's candidacy for the Malcolm Baldrige National Quality Award*

The company's Floor Products Operations was the inaugural winner of the Armstrong Quality Achievement Award. In its report that led to the award, the organization underscored its emphasis on prevention-based quality systems as foundations for achieving significantly increased levels of customer satisfaction. Two Malcolm Baldrige National Quality Award examiners were among the members of the evaluation team that studied the works of 12 Armstrong organizations applying for the company award.

Armstrong introduced its Corporate Quality Policy (see inside back cover) in 1983 to employees around the world. Armstrong people today have never been more confident in the potential of the company's quality management process.

The company's Floor Products Operations won the first Armstrong Quality Achievement Award.

An 11-member process improvement team enhanced the quality of service to export customers of Armstrong ceilings, virtually reengineering the entire order-to-delivery process. Redundant steps in the process were eliminated, cycle time was cut by more than one-half, and pricing and invoicing systems were streamlined to provide increased efficiencies for customers and Armstrong. The team's 1992 efforts focus on improving the process for documenting transactions with U.S. Customs and automating shipment status information while products are en route to destinations. An ongoing goal is to improve communications between customers and the company's export order services organization.

13

ENVIRONMENTAL STEWARDSHIP

In the context of Armstrong's policy on the environment (see opposite page), we are pleased with our continuing progress on environmental issues. At the same time, we know that there is much more to be done. We are committed to continuous improvement.

Employee awareness

One of the initiatives of our environmental affairs organization is a newsletter, *Environmental Releases*, distributed to employees around the world. It exchanges environmental information and shares success stories.

That organization also conducted two-day pollutant reduction seminars attended by key Armstrong employees from 26 of our North American business units. At three U.S. locations, company managers from North American organizations attended managers' environmental briefings. The seminars and briefings focused on how to meet corporate environmental goals through pollution reduction measures, with seminar leaders also reviewing pertinent regulatory issues.

Pollution reduction

Each operating facility is required to examine environmental issues as it plans capital projects, develops new products and improves manufacturing processes. Project engineers always address pollutant abatement measures prior to seeking approval for capital expenditures. As part of Armstrong's "Eighty in Five" stretch-goal program (see page 12), engineers pursue processes designed to meet strict "lowest achievable emission rates"— not merely to comply with regulations.

Likewise, people at Armstrong's Research and Development organization integrate environmental requirements in developing new products and processes. They use the life-cycle analysis framework to assess the total environmental impact of products, from the origin of their raw materials to their final disposal. The company is fostering partner relation-

ships with key suppliers in a cooperative effort to reduce environmental impact.

Manufacturing plants identify and quantify pollutants, then establish goals for their reduction and elimination as integral parts of process improvement. Some examples:

Abatement. To improve air quality, seven additional pollution control devices were placed into service in 1991 at our Macon, Georgia, ceiling plant and our flooring plants in Lancaster, Pennsylvania; Montreal, Quebec, Canada, and Teesside, England.

Process modification. While control devices abate existing pollutants, it is generally more desirable to reduce or eliminate pollutants altogether through process modification and material substitution.

During 1991, the company's plant in Montreal converted its rotogravure sheet flooring press operation from organic-solvent inks to water-based inks. This change significantly reduces emissions of volatile organic compounds (VOCs). Another rotogravure operation, at the Armstrong plant in Beech Creek, Pennsylvania, reduced nitrous oxide emissions by more than 90 percent and VOCs by a small amount—both the results of process modification. The W. W. Henry Company, an Armstrong subsidiary, successfully developed and introduced a new line of adhesives (known as "Next Generation") used in flooring installations. These adhesives reduce VOC emissions well below existing and proposed regulatory levels.

In Armstrong's insulation business, the worldwide objective of replacing chlorofluorocarbons (CFCs) with more ozone-friendly hydrochlorofluorocarbons (HCFCs) in the production of polyethylene pipe insulation will be met during the second quarter of 1992 with the conversion at our plant near Atlanta, Georgia. This conversion to HCFCs has already been completed at company plants in Rothrist, Switzerland; Oldham, England, and

Palafrugell, Spain. This is well ahead of the schedule of the Montreal Protocol, an agreement signed by 72 countries addressing substances that deplete stratospheric ozone.

Armstrong's newest ceiling plant, at St. Helens, Oregon, employs a water-jet cutter that replaces dry saws traditionally used in this operation, eliminating dust and reducing noise.

Post-consumer-use recycling. In a major 1991 development, Armstrong joined AGPR, a European consortium of flooring manufacturers and polyvinyl chloride (PVC) producers whose goals are to recover used flooring and to convert the PVC into raw materials for new floors. An AGPR recycling facility in Grossheim, Germany, began operation in December 1990. Here, old floors are converted to formulated PVC material and returned to consortium members for reuse.

Reduction of toxic chemical releases. The Emergency Planning and Community Right-to-Know Act of 1986 requires U.S. manufacturers to report annually the environmental releases and off-site transfers of more than 300 toxic chemicals and chemical compounds. The Environmental Protection Agency (EPA) established a Toxics Release Inventory (TRI) of these releases and transfers. With a base year of 1988, the TRI for Armstrong shows that the total releases and transfers of toxic chemicals from our facilities were reduced by one-fourth in 1989 and by more than one-third in 1990. (1991 data will be reported at midyear 1992.)

As an example, Armstrong is finding successful alternatives to methyl chloroform (also known as 1,1,1-trichloroethane), a cleanup solvent widely used because of its low levels of flammability and toxicity. As with CFCs, methyl chloroform is considered injurious to the earth's protective ozone layer. From a base year of 1988, emissions were reduced by one-half in 1989 and by nearly three-fourths in 1990. Amended work practices and material substitutions account for the reductions and are expected to generate still further improvement in 1991. The corporate objective is to completely eliminate use of the solvent.

Environmental auditing

Armstrong entered the fifth year of environmental audits at its plants in the United States and Canada. The purposes of the audit process are to (1) identify and address facility compliance issues, (2) recommend how plant personnel can better manage environmental issues to minimize liability potential and (3) determine how well a facility incorporates pollutant reduction processes in meeting overall company environmental goals.

Energy conservation

A new Armstrong team conducted energy surveys at eight parent company and domestic subsidiary plants, identifying 80 specific energy conservation opportunities. Some of these opportunities involve replacement of electrical and mechanical equipment, with a potential for electrical power savings of more than 6.5 million kWh annually. Energy efficiency is a requirement when specifying these replacements and in the design for future equipment. The surveys are continuing in 1992.

Armstrong's continuing goal is to ensure that our activities as a corporation do not harm the natural world around us. On all counts, progress is underway everywhere the company conducts its businesses.

Corporate policy on the environment

Armstrong recognizes the importance of protecting the environment and using resources intelligently. We are committed to exercising environmental stewardship in our dealings with customers, employees, community neighbors and government in meeting an obligation to future generations. A responsible approach to environmental concerns is in harmony with the fourth of our corporate operating principles: *"To serve fairly and in proper balance the interests of all groups associated with the business—customers, stockholders, employees, suppliers, community neighbors, government and the general public."*

Our overall goal is to make sure that our activities as a corporation do not harm the natural world around us. Specifically, our policy on the environment embodies these aims:

■ To exercise care in the selection, use and conservation of energy and raw materials, especially natural resources, to assure that we are not wasting such resources.

■ To make use of research and production technology to provide for environmental safety in workplaces and communities; to seek to reduce risks to the earth, its waters and atmosphere.

■ To be prepared for emergencies and to act promptly and responsibly to protect people and the environment should accidents or incidents occur.

■ To make only products that are environmentally safe in their intended use by our customers and consumers, and to accompany them with adequate information for their proper use, maintenance and disposal.

■ To reduce waste, to make use of recycling in all our operations and to take care that we are disposing of unneeded materials in an environmentally safe manner.

DIVIDENDS AND PRIMARY NET EARNINGS PER SHARE

The 1981-91 period was one of rising dividends paid to investors, even during those years in which the company's primary earnings per share declined.

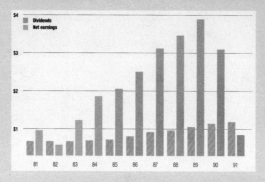

1991 ESTIMATED SALES BY MARKET SEGMENTS

The Armstrong products sold to each end-use market segment shown at right include the following:

Residential Building and Improvement:
Resilient Flooring
Ceramic Tile
Ceiling Systems
Insulation Materials
Furniture
Adhesives

Nonresidential Building and Improvement:
Resilient Flooring
Ceramic Tile
Ceiling and Wall Systems
Insulation Materials
Furniture
Custom Architectural Products
Adhesives

Industrial Specialty Markets:
Gasket and Friction Materials
Insulation Materials
Textile Mill Supplies
Adhesives

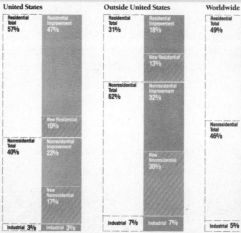

United States
Residential Total 57% — Residential Improvement 47%
New Residential 10%
Nonresidential Total 40% — Nonresidential Improvement 23%
New Nonresidential 17%
Industrial 3% — Industrial 3%

Outside United States
Residential Total 31% — Residential Improvement 18%
New Residential 13%
Nonresidential Total 62% — Nonresidential Improvement 32%
New Nonresidential 30%
Industrial 7% — Industrial 7%

Worldwide
Residential Total 49% — Residential Improvement 38%
New Residential 11%
Nonresidential Total 46% — Nonresidential Improvement 25%
New Nonresidential 21%
Industrial 5% — Industrial 5%

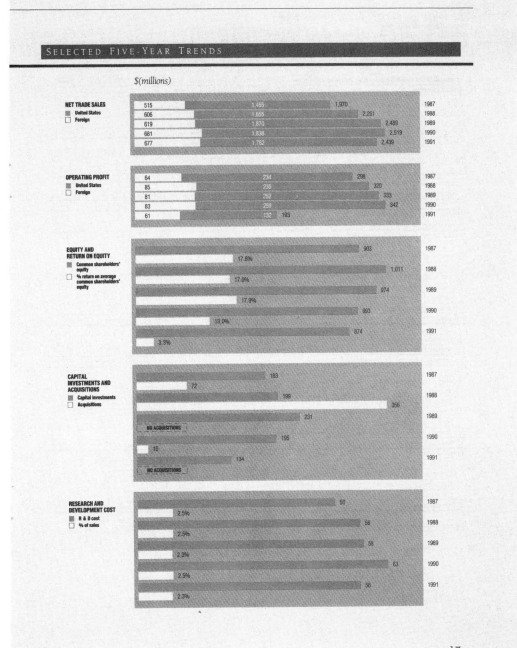

SELECTED FIVE-YEAR TRENDS

$(millions)

NET TRADE SALES
United States
Foreign

	US	Foreign	Total	Year
	515	1,455	1,970	1987
	606	1,655	2,261	1988
	619	1,870	2,489	1989
	681	1,838	2,519	1990
	677	1,762	2,439	1991

OPERATING PROFIT
United States
Foreign

	US	Foreign	Total	Year
	64	234	298	1987
	85	235	320	1988
	81	252	333	1989
	83	259	342	1990
	61	132	193	1991

EQUITY AND RETURN ON EQUITY
Common shareholders' equity
% return on average common shareholders' equity

Equity	% return	Year
903	17.6%	1987
1,011	17.0%	1988
974	17.9%	1989
893	13.0%	1990
874	3.3%	1991

CAPITAL INVESTMENTS AND ACQUISITIONS
Capital investments
Acquisitions

Capital investments	Acquisitions	Year
183	72	1987
199	356	1988
231	NO ACQUISITIONS	1989
195	16	1990
134	NO ACQUISITIONS	1991

RESEARCH AND DEVELOPMENT COST
R & D cost
% of sales

R & D cost	% of sales	Year
50	2.5%	1987
56	2.5%	1988
58	2.3%	1989
63	2.5%	1990
58	2.3%	1991

17

ARMSTRONG WORLD INDUSTRIES, INC., AND SUBSIDIARIES

Financial Statements and Review

The Financial Review, pages 21-31, is an integral part of these statements.

CONSOLIDATED STATEMENTS OF EARNINGS

Years ended December 31 (millions except for per-share data)	1991	1990*	1989*
Current earnings			
Net sales	$2,439.3	$2,518.8	$2,488.7
Cost of goods sold	1,801.1	1,816.6	1,764.0
Gross profit	638.2	702.2	724.7
Selling and administrative expense	468.3	462.6	436.6
Earnings from continuing businesses before other			
income (expense) and income taxes	169.9	239.6	288.1
Other income (expense):			
Interest expense	(45.8)	(37.5)	(40.5)
Gain on sale of woodlands	–	60.4	9.5
Miscellaneous income (expense)	(23.8)	(39.4)	(13.5)
	(69.6)	(16.5)	(44.5)
Earnings from continuing businesses before income taxes	100.3	223.1	243.6
Income taxes	39.7	76.7	85.9
Earnings from continuing businesses	60.6	146.4	157.7
Discontinued businesses:			
Earnings (losses), net of income tax benefit of $1.9 in 1991, and $2.2 in 1990,			
and tax expense of $6.1 in 1989	(3.8)	(4.3)	8.2
Provision for (loss) gain on disposition of discontinued businesses, net of income tax			
benefit of $4.6 in 1991, and $3.8 in 1990 and tax expense of $8.0 in 1989	(8.6)	(9.1)	21.7
Cumulative effect of change in accounting for income taxes	–	8.0	–
Net earnings	$ 48.2	$ 141.0	$ 187.6
Dividends paid on $3.75 preferred stock	$ –	$ –	$ .2
Dividends paid on Series A convertible preferred stock	19.4	19.5	9.5
Net earnings applicable to common stock	$ 28.8	$ 121.5	$ 177.9
Per share of common stock:			
Primary:			
Earnings from continuing businesses	$ 1.11	$ 3.26	$ 3.26
Earnings (losses) from discontinued businesses	(.11)	(.11)	.18
Provision for (loss) gain on disposition of discontinued businesses	(.23)	(.23)	.48
Cumulative effect of change in accounting for income taxes	–	.20	–
Net earnings	$ .77	$ 3.12	$ 3.92
Fully diluted:			
Earnings from continuing businesses	$ 1.11	$ 2.99	$ 3.11
Earnings (losses) from discontinued businesses	(.11)	(.11)	.16
Provision for (loss) gain on disposition of discontinued businesses	(.23)	(.20)	.45
Cumulative effect of change in accounting for income taxes	–	.18	–
Net earnings	$ .77	$ 2.86	$ 3.72

*Restated for the results of discontinued businesses.

ARMSTRONG WORLD INDUSTRIES, INC., AND SUBSIDIARIES
Financial Statements and Review
The Financial Review, pages 21-31, is an integral part of these statements.

CONSOLIDATED BALANCE SHEETS

As of December 31 (millions except for numbers of shares and per-share data)	1991	1990
Assets		
Current assets:		
Cash and cash equivalents	$ 8.2	$ 24.6
Accounts and notes receivable		
(less allowance for discounts and losses: 1991—$30.1; 1990—$32.8)	305.3	302.7
Inventories	336.4	349.2
Other current assets	68.9	50.1
Total current assets	718.8	726.6
Property, plant, and equipment		
(less accumulated depreciation and amortization: 1991—$881.6; 1990—$820.4)	1,152.9	1,147.4
Other noncurrent assets	278.2	272.3
	$2,149.9	$2,146.3
Liabilities and shareholders' equity		
Current liabilities:		
Short-term debt	$ 204.2	$ 251.8
Current installments of long-term debt	11.9	3.3
Accounts payable and accrued expenses	249.1	271.1
Income taxes	14.7	18.6
Total current liabilities	479.9	544.8
Long-term debt	301.4	233.2
Employee Stock Ownership Plan loan guarantee	264.7	267.6
Deferred income taxes	164.6	167.5
Other long-term liabilities	43.4	26.5
Minority interest in subsidiaries	10.4	7.5
Total noncurrent liabilities	784.5	702.3
Shareholders' equity:		
Class A preferred stock. Authorized 20 million shares;		
issued 5,654,450 shares of Series A convertible preferred stock;		
outstanding: 1991—5,605,557 shares; 1990—5,618,289 shares;		
retired: 1991—48,893 shares; 1990—36,161 shares	267.7	268.3
Common stock, $1 par value per share.		
Authorized 200 million shares; issued 51,878,910 shares	51.9	51.9
Capital in excess of par value	25.8	25.7
Reduction for ESOP loan guarantee	(256.0)	(261.8)
Retained earnings	1,208.7	1,224.1
Foreign currency translation	44.7	48.3
	1,342.8	1,356.5
Less common stock in treasury, at cost: 1991—14,776,338 shares; 1990—14,787,008 shares	457.3	457.3
Total shareholders' equity	885.5	899.2
	$2,149.9	$2,146.3

19

ARMSTRONG WORLD INDUSTRIES, INC., AND SUBSIDIARIES
Financial Statements and Review
The Financial Review, pages 21-31, is an integral part of these statements.

CONSOLIDATED STATEMENTS OF CASH FLOWS

Years ended December 31 (millions)	1991	1990	1989
Cash flows from operating activities:			
Net earnings	$48.2	$141.0	$187.6
Adjustments to reconcile net earnings to net cash			
provided by operating activities:			
Depreciation and amortization	135.7	130.1	134.0
Deferred income taxes	(1.6)	16.1	(10.6)
Gain from cumulative effect of change in accounting for income taxes	—	(8.0)	—
(Gain) loss on sale of discontinued businesses	8.6	9.1	(21.7)
Gain from sale of woodlands	—	(60.4)	(9.5)
Changes in operating assets and liabilities net of			
effect from dispositions and acquisitions:			
(Increase) decrease in receivables	(3.9)	22.8	(9.2)
(Increase) decrease in inventories	7.9	(5.6)	(3.2)
(Increase) decrease in other current assets	(17.1)	.9	(7.3)
(Increase) in other noncurrent assets	(23.2)	(22.2)	(28.8)
Increase (decrease) in accounts payable and accrued expenses	(25.8)	(14.0)	12.0
Increase (decrease) in income taxes payable	(4.4)	(17.8)	3.5
Increase (decrease) in other long-term liabilities	15.1	(3.6)	14.3
Other, net	10.9	11.8	(.7)
Net cash provided by operating activities	150.4	200.2	260.4
Cash flows from investing activities:			
Purchases of property, plant, and equipment	(133.4)	(194.9)	(231.0)
Proceeds from sale of land, facilities, and discontinued businesses	3.0	72.5	194.7
Acquisitions	—	(16.1)	—
Net cash used for investing activities	(130.4)	(138.5)	(36.3)
Cash flows from financing activities:			
Increase (decrease) in short-term debt	(47.6)	150.4	(283.4)
Issuance of long-term debt	83.2	42.0	.2
Reduction of long-term debt	(5.2)	(3.7)	(10.7)
Sale of convertible preferred stock	—	—	270.0
Redemption of $3.75 cumulative preferred stock	—	—	(10.6)
Purchase of treasury stock	—	(185.2)	(167.1)
Cash dividends paid	(63.6)	(63.8)	(57.2)
Other, net	(3.7)	.9	(15.8)
Net cash used for financing activities	(36.9)	(59.4)	(274.6)
Effect of exchange rate changes on cash and cash equivalents	.5	5.2	(2.1)
Net increase (decrease) in cash and cash equivalents	$(16.4)	$ 7.5	$ (52.6)
Cash and cash equivalents at beginning of year	$ 24.6	$ 17.1	$ 69.7
Cash and cash equivalents at end of year	$ 8.2	$ 24.6	$ 17.1
Supplemental cash flow information			
Interest paid	$ 45.0	$ 37.7	$ 42.9
Income taxes paid	$ 53.5	$ 67.7	$ 87.6

ARMSTRONG WORLD INDUSTRIES, INC., AND SUBSIDIARIES

FINANCIAL REVIEW

The consolidated financial statements and the accompanying data in this report include the accounts of the parent Armstrong World Industries, Inc., and its domestic and foreign subsidiaries. All significant intercompany transactions have been eliminated from the consolidated statements.

To assist in understanding this financial review, the accounting policies and principles used are printed in *italics*.

OPERATING STATEMENT ITEMS

Discontinued businesses included in the financial statements reflect the disposition of certain of the company's noncore businesses in 1991, industrial specialties businesses in 1990, and most assets of its carpet businesses and the company's subsidiary, Applied Color Systems, Inc., in 1989.

Net sales in 1991 for the noncore businesses were $12.2 million and for the years 1990 and 1989 were $12.5 million and $15.0 million, respectively.

Operating statement categories, except where otherwise indicated, have been restated to exclude the effects of these discontinued businesses.

Net sales in 1991 totaled $2,439.3 million, 3.2% below the 1990 total of $2,518.8 million. 1990 sales were 1.2% above the 1989 total of $2,488.7 million.

The amounts reported as net sales are the total sales billed during the year less the sales value of goods returned, trade discounts and customers' allowances, and freight costs incurred in delivering products to customers.

Earnings from continuing businesses were $60.6 million in 1991, compared with $146.4 million in 1990 and $157.7 million in 1989.

Net earnings of $48.2 million for 1991 were 65.8% below the $141.0 million reported for 1990. Net earnings for 1990 were 24.8% below the $187.6 million reported for 1989.

Earnings per common share are presented on the Consolidated Statements of Earnings on page 18.

Primary earnings per share, for "earnings from continuing businesses" and "net earnings," are determined by dividing the earnings, after deducting preferred dividends, by the average number of common shares outstanding and shares issuable under stock options.

Fully diluted earnings per share include the shares of common stock outstanding and the adjustments to common shares and earnings required to portray the convertible preferred shares on an "if converted" basis unless the effect is antidilutive.

Research and development costs were $55.6 million in 1991, $63.3 million in 1990, and $57.8 million in 1989.

Advertising costs were $42.9 million in 1991, $40.6 million in 1990, and $47.0 million in 1989.

Maintenance and repair costs were $138.1 million in 1991, $136.9 million in 1990, and $126.4 million in 1989.

Depreciation and amortization amounted to $135.3 million in 1991, $129.1 million in 1990, and $123.5 million in 1989. These amounts include amortization of intangible assets of $18.0 million in 1991, $16.7 million in 1990, and $15.8 million in 1989.

Depreciation charges for financial reporting purposes are determined generally on the straight-line basis at rates calculated to provide for the retirement of assets at the end of their useful lives. Accelerated depreciation is generally used for tax purposes. When assets are disposed of or retired, their costs and related depreciation are removed from the books, and any resulting gains or losses are reflected in "Miscellaneous income (expense)." Intangibles are amortized over periods ranging from three to 40 years.

Details of miscellaneous income (expense) *(millions)*	1991	1990	1989
Interest and dividend income	$ 5.3	$ 5.6	$ 6.8
Proxy contest, litigation and settlement expense	—	(15.4)	(3.6)
Restructuring costs	(12.8)	(6.8)	(5.9)
Foreign exchange, net gain (loss)	5.9	(.1)	(1.0)
Accrual for costs associated with litigation involving residual claims for a previously owned facility	—	(5.0)	—
Amortization of intangibles and other net gain (loss)	(20.1)	(15.4)	(6.8)
Subtotal	(21.7)	(37.1)	(10.5)
Less minority interest	2.1	2.3	3.0
Total	$(23.8)	$(39.4)	$(13.5)

Employee compensation cost summary *(millions)*	1991	1990	1989
Wages and salaries	$704.1	$713.1	$679.5
Payroll taxes	69.6	68.1	63.0
Pension costs (credits)	.2	(4.3)	(7.4)
Insurance and other benefit costs	62.7	62.5	54.5
Total	$836.6	$839.4	$789.6

Average total employment of 24,066 in 1991 compares with 25,014 in 1990 and 25,349 in 1989. The decrease in 1991 occurred in the U.S. operations resulting from reduced activity and various early retirement opportunity programs.

Pension costs

The company and a number of its subsidiaries have pension plans covering substantially all employees. Benefits from the principal plan are based on the employee's compensation and years of service.

Generally, the company's practice is to fund the actuarially determined current service costs and the amounts necessary to amortize prior service obligations over periods ranging up to 30 years, but not in excess of the full funding limitation.

21

ARMSTRONG WORLD INDUSTRIES, INC., AND SUBSIDIARIES

FINANCIAL REVIEW

Pension costs (continued)

Funding requirements are determined independently of expense, using an expected long-term rate of return on assets of 8.67%. The company's principal plan is subject to the full funding limitation in 1991, 1990, and 1989, and the company made no contribution to that plan in any of these years. Contributions of $.3 million in 1991, $.3 million in 1990, and $.8 million in 1989 were made to defined-benefit plans of company subsidiaries.

Pension costs from all plans reflect a net cost of $.2 million in 1991, and net credits of $4.3 million in 1990 and $7.4 million in 1989.

Net credit for U.S. defined-benefit pension plans (millions)	1991	1990	1989
Actual (return) loss on assets	$(210.6)	$ 5.0	$(165.6)
Less amount deferred	140.2	(73.7)	105.4
Expected return on assets	(70.4)	(68.7)	(60.2)
Net amortization and other	(4.5)	(7.5)	(5.9)
Service cost—benefits earned during the year	16.2	16.3	15.3
Interest on the projected benefit obligation	45.7	43.0	40.0
Net pension credit	$ (13.0)	$ (16.9)	$ (10.8)

In 1991, early retirement benefits were offered to participants of the principal pension plan at a cost of $1.1 million. In 1989, other credits from the plan included $7.9 million from the termination of the contributory portion of the plan and $2.0 million from settlement of the pension obligation for a portion of the employees who elected the early retirement opportunity in the autumn of 1988.

The funded status of the company's U.S. defined-benefit pension plans is presented in the table below.

The plan assets at each December 31 are based on measurements from October 31 to December 31. Stated at fair value, they are primarily listed stocks, bonds, and investments with a major insurance company.

Funded status of U.S. defined-benefit pension plans (millions)	1991	1990
Actuarial present value of benefit obligations: Vested benefit obligation	$ (534.0)	$(465.1)
Accumulated benefit obligation	$ (567.4)	$(490.9)
Projected benefit obligation for services rendered to date	$ (674.1)	$(597.1)
Plan assets at fair value	1,010.6	839.5
Plan assets in excess of projected benefit obligation	336.5	242.4
Unrecognized transition asset	(65.7)	(72.0)
Unrecognized prior service cost	85.2	87.6
Unrecognized net gain—experience different from assumptions	(262.8)	(177.0)
Prepaid pension cost	$ 93.2	$ 81.0

Note: Rates used in determining the actuarial present value of the projected benefit obligation at the end of 1991 and 1990 are: (1) the

discount rate or the assumed rate at which the pension benefits could be effectively settled, 7.25% in 1991 and 7.75% in 1990; and (2) the compensation rate or the long-term rate at which compensation is expected to increase as a result of inflation, promotions, seniority, and other factors, 5.75% in all years. The expected long-term rate of return on assets was 8.75% in 1991 and 1990.

The company has pension plans covering employees in a number of foreign countries which utilize assumptions that are consistent, but not identical, with those of the U.S. plans.

Net cost for non-U.S. defined-benefit pension plans (millions)	1991	1990	1989
Actual (return) loss on assets	$ (8.7)	$ 4.0	$ (8.9)
Less amount deferred	2.4	(9.2)	4.7
Expected return on assets	(6.3)	(5.2)	(4.2)
Net amortization and other	.1	—	.2
Service cost—benefits earned during the year	4.4	4.2	4.0
Interest on the projected benefit obligation	5.8	5.1	4.2
Net pension cost	$ 4.0	$ 4.1	$ 4.2

The following table presents the funded status of the non-U.S. defined-benefit pension plans at December 31.

Funded status of non-U.S. defined-benefit pension plans (millions)	1991	1990
Actuarial present value of benefit obligations: Vested benefit obligation	$(68.9)	$(57.8)
Accumulated benefit obligation	$(72.4)	$(60.5)
Projected benefit obligation for services rendered to date	$(83.1)	$(74.8)
Plan assets at fair value	81.9	72.4
Projected benefit obligation greater than plan assets	(1.2)	(2.4)
Unrecognized transition obligation	3.3	2.1
Unrecognized prior service cost	2.4	—
Unrecognized net gain—experience different from assumptions	(6.3)	(2.4)
Adjustment required to recognize minimum liability	(1.2)	(.5)
Accrued pension cost	$ (3.0)	$ (3.2)

The company has defined-contribution pension plans for eligible employees at certain of its U.S. subsidiaries, such as the Employee Stock Ownership Plan (ESOP) described on page 23. Beginning in 1989, company contributions and accrued compensation expense related to the ESOP are included with other plans' contributions and costs, based on the compensation of each eligible employee. The costs of such plans totaled $5.3 million in 1991, $5.7 million in 1990, and $5.7 million in 1989.

Various other funded and unfunded pension benefit costs that were charged to earnings amounted to $2.8 million in 1991, $2.8 million in 1990, and $3.4 million in 1989.

Employee Stock Ownership Plan (ESOP)

In 1989, Armstrong established an ESOP that borrowed $270 million from banks and insurance companies, repayable over 15 years and guaranteed by the company. The ESOP used the monies to purchase 5,654,450 shares of a new series of convertible preferred stock issued by the company. Through December 31, 1991, the ESOP has allocated to participants 675,314 shares and retired 48,893 shares. The preferred stock has a minimum conversion value of $47.75 per share with an annual dividend of $3.462.

The ESOP currently covers parent company non-union employees, some union employees, and those employees of major domestic subsidiaries who wish to participate in the voluntary contribution portion of the plan.

Armstrong used the proceeds from the 1989 sale of preferred stock to repurchase common stock in 1989 and 1990 for the company treasury.

The company's guarantee of the ESOP loan has been recorded as a long-term obligation and as a reduction of shareholders' equity on its consolidated balance sheet.

During 1991, 1990 and 1989, the company paid preferred stock dividends to the ESOP totaling $19.4 million, $19.5 million and $9.5 million, respectively. Employee contributions were $6.0 million in 1991, $5.3 million in 1990 and $1.8 million in 1989. Company contributions were $.7 million in 1991 and $1.0 million in 1989; none were required in 1990. The ESOP trustee made debt service payments in 1991 of $26.1 million, in 1990 of $24.8 million and in 1989 of $12.3 million, primarily for interest charges.

The company recorded costs for the ESOP, utilizing the 80 percent of the shares allocated method, of $3.6 million in 1991, $4.0 million in 1990, and $5.6 million in 1989, consisting primarily of accrued compensation expenses plus company contributions and one-time setup costs in 1989. Costs for all years continue to be offset by savings from changes to company-sponsored health-care benefits and elimination of a contribution-matching feature in the company-sponsored voluntary retirement savings plan.

Other postretirement costs

Certain of the company's employees, both domestic and foreign, become eligible for company-sponsored health-care and life insurance benefits when they retire from active service.

The company announced in 1989 a 15-year phaseout of Armstrong-sponsored health-care benefits for parent company non-union employees and in 1990 for some union employees. Shares of ESOP convertible preferred stock are scheduled to be allocated to these employees, based on employee age and years to expected retirement. In addition, they may enroll in a voluntary portion of the ESOP to purchase additional shares.

The cost of health-care and life insurance benefits for retirees is expensed as incurred. For 1991, health-care costs totaled $11.0 million and life insurance premiums were $1.7 million. These amounts were $9.7 million and $1.5 million respectively in 1990, and $8.4 million and $1.6 million respectively in 1989.

The Statement of Financial Accounting Standards No. 106, "Employers' Accounting for Postretirement Benefits Other Than Pensions," is effective for fiscal years beginning after December 15, 1992. Under FAS No. 106, the cost of postretirement benefits other than pensions must be recognized on an accrual basis as employees perform services to earn the benefits. The company is currently evaluating the impact of this standard and the method and timing of its adoption. The estimated present value of earned postretirement benefits ranges from $250 million to $350 million. The increase in expense before tax created by this accounting change is estimated at $10 million to $13 million annually if the transition obligation is recognized immediately, or $23 million to $31 million if it is amortized over 20 years. These expenses represent future, not present, cash outflows.

Taxes totaled $126.4 million in 1991, $161.4 million in 1990, and $164.8 million in 1989.

Details of taxes *(millions)*	1991	1990	1989
Earnings from continuing businesses before income taxes:			
Domestic	$100.5	$186.8	$231.0
Foreign	58.7	85.3	86.3
Eliminations	(58.9)	(49.0)	(73.7)
Total	$100.3	$223.1	$243.6
Income taxes:			
Payable:			
Federal	$ 13.0	$ 26.0	$ 55.8
Foreign	27.8	32.5	30.0
State	.1	1.5	9.2
	40.9	60.0	95.0
Deferred:			
Federal	(5.7)	10.5	(9.3)
Foreign	.9	1.3	.8
State	3.6	4.9	(.6)
	(1.2)	16.7	(9.1)
Total income taxes	39.7	76.7	85.9
Payroll taxes	69.6	68.1	63.0
Property, franchise, and capital stock taxes	17.1	16.6	15.9
Total taxes	$126.4	$161.4	$164.8
Components of deferred tax (benefit) expense:			
Difference between book and tax depreciation	$ 12.5	$ 18.7	$ (4.7)
Purchased tax benefits	(2.5)	1.5	(1.2)
Prefunding for medical benefits	—	.5	(2.7)
Pension plan	5.4	6.9	8.7
Alternative minimum tax	(10.6)	(7.9)	—
Other items	(6.0)	(3.0)	(9.2)
Total deferred tax (benefit) expense	$ (1.2)	$ 16.7	$ (9.1)

Effective January 1, 1990, the company adopted Statement of Financial Accounting Standards No. 96, "Accounting for Income Taxes." Under its provisions, deferred tax assets and liabilities are based on tax rates and laws in effect as of the balance sheet date rather than the historical tax rates. The cumulative effect of

ARMSTRONG WORLD INDUSTRIES, INC., AND SUBSIDIARIES

FINANCIAL REVIEW

Taxes (continued)

the change on prior years was an $8.0 million gain, excluded from the preceding table on page 23. 1989 amounts have not been restated. A 1991 deferred income tax charge of $3.7 million reflecting increases in state income tax rates, primarily Pennsylvania's, as required by FAS No. 96 is included in the preceding table.

At December 31, 1991, unremitted earnings of subsidiaries outside the United States were $108.5 million at current balance sheet exchange rates on which no U.S. taxes have been provided. If such earnings were to be remitted without offsetting tax credits in the United States, withholding taxes would be $14.6 million. The company's intention, however, is to permanently reinvest those earnings or to repatriate them only when it is tax effective to do so.

Reconciliation to U.S. statutory tax rate	1991	1990	1989
Effective tax rates	39.6%	34.4%	35.3%
State income taxes	(2.4)	(2.0)	(2.4)
Benefit on ESOP dividend	6.6	3.0	1.4
Taxes on foreign income	(7.3)	(1.8)	(.9)
Other items	(2.5)	.4	.6
Statutory tax rate	34.0%	34.0%	34.0%

In February 1992, Financial Accounting Standard No. 109, "Accounting for Income Taxes," was issued, superseding FAS No. 96. Armstrong can elect to adopt FAS No. 109 in either 1992 or 1993. This standard requires recognition in shareholders' equity of the tax benefit from dividends paid on unallocated shares held by the Employee Stock Ownership Plan. Under FAS No. 96, this tax benefit was recognized in the statement of earnings for years 1991, 1990, and 1989 amounting to approximately $7.0 million, $7.4 million, and $3.7 million, respectively. Accounting for the tax benefits from the ESOP dividend under FAS No. 109 will not affect the comparability of the earnings per-share data.

For 1989, the difference between the effective tax rate and the statutory tax rate for earnings from discontinued businesses was primarily due to state income taxes. The tax rate related to the provision for gain or loss on discontinued businesses reflects the nondeductibility of certain intangible assets in 1990 and the removal of deferred tax liabilities in excess of taxes paid in 1989.

BALANCE SHEET ITEMS

Cash and cash equivalents decreased to $8.2 million at the end of 1991 from $24.6 million at the end of 1990. Operating and other factors associated with the decrease in cash and cash equivalents are detailed in the Consolidated Statements of Cash Flows on page 20.

Short-term investments, substantially all of which have maturities of three months or less when purchased, are considered to be cash equivalents and are carried at cost or less, generally approximating market value.

Accounts and notes receivable (millions)	1991	1990
Customers' receivables	$289.5	$297.3
Customers' notes	30.9	28.2
Miscellaneous receivables	15.0	10.0
	335.4	335.5
Less allowance for discounts and losses	30.1	32.8
Net	$305.3	$302.7

Generally, the company sells its products to select, preapproved groups of customers that include: flooring and building material distributors, ceiling systems contractors, regional and national mass merchandisers and home centers, original equipment manufacturers, and large furniture retailers. The businesses of these customers are directly affected by changes in economic and market conditions. The company considers these factors and the financial condition of each customer when establishing its allowance for losses from doubtful accounts.

Trade receivables are recorded in gross billed amounts as of date of shipment. Provision is made for estimated applicable discounts and losses.

Inventories were $12.8 million lower at the end of 1991, primarily as a result of lower sales. The ratio of inventories to net sales at December 31 was 13.8% for both years.

Approximately 47% in 1991 and 45% in 1990 of the company's total inventory is valued on a LIFO (last-in, first-out) basis. Such inventory values were lower than would have been reported on a total FIFO (first-in, first-out) basis, by $104.3 million at the end of 1991 and $101.6 million at year-end 1990.

Inventories (millions)	1991	1990
Finished goods	$210.9	$216.7
Goods in process	40.3	41.1
Raw materials and supplies	85.2	91.4
Total	$336.4	$349.2

Inventories are valued at the lower of cost or market. Approximately two-thirds of 1991's domestic inventories are valued using the LIFO method. Other inventories are generally determined on a FIFO method.

Other current assets were $68.9 million at the end of 1991, an increase of $18.8 million over the $50.1 million at year-end 1990. The principal reason for this increase was the result of higher deferred income tax benefits, increasing to $35.1 million at year-end 1991 from $24.1 million at the end of 1990.

Property, plant, and equipment (millions)	1991	1990
Land	$ 34.9	$ 36.1
Buildings	498.5	472.6
Machinery and equipment	1,432.1	1,360.2
Construction in progress	69.0	98.9
	2,034.5	1,967.8
Less accumulated depreciation and amortization	881.6	820.4
Net book value	$1,152.9	$1,147.4

The change in fixed assets from $1,967.8 million to $2,034.5 million resulted from capital additions and capitalized leases of $133.8 million, reduced by $67.1 million from sales, retirements, disposals, and other changes.

Because of translating foreign currency property, plant, and equipment into U.S. dollars at lower exchange rates, net book value was decreased by $3.6 million in 1991.

The unexpended cost of approved capital appropriations amounted to $62.9 million at December 31, 1991, substantially all of which is scheduled to be expended during 1992.

Property, plant, and equipment values are stated at acquisition cost, with accumulated depreciation and amortization deducted to arrive at net book value.

Other noncurrent assets were $278.2 million in 1991 and $272.3 million in 1990. The principal reason for the increase is the addition to prepaid pension costs. This increase is partially offset by amortization of intangibles and by the write-off of licenses, patents, and goodwill of certain of Armstrong's noncore businesses in 1991. Other noncurrent assets include zero coupon municipal bonds that mature between the years 2012 and 2015 and have a face value of $13.7 million. Proceeds from these matured bonds may be used to repay part of an $18.6 million installment note that becomes due in the year 2013, as discussed on page 26.

Noncurrent assets are carried at cost or less or under the equity method of accounting. See also the comments on page 26, referring to parallel-loan agreements and interest rate/currency swaps.

Accounts payable and accrued expenses (millions)	1991	1990
Trade payables	$103.0	$119.6
Other payables	41.2	34.8
Payroll and related taxes	42.1	63.7
Other	62.8	53.0
Total	$249.1	$271.1

Income taxes (millions)	1991	1990
Payable—current	$12.3	$18.3
Deferred—current	2.4	.3
Total	$14.7	$18.6

As previously stated, effective January 1, 1990, the company adopted the liability method of accounting for income taxes in conformance to Statement of Financial Accounting Standards No. 96, "Accounting for Income Taxes." The tax effects of principal temporary differences between the carrying amounts of assets and liabilities and their tax bases are summarized below.

Deferred income taxes (millions)	1991	1990
Provisions for expenses	$ 17.2	$ 33.7
Accumulated depreciation	128.9	111.8
Liabilities related to pensions	37.2	31.2
Other—net	(18.7)	(9.2)
Net deferred tax liability	$164.6	$167.5

Debt (millions)	1991	Average year-end interest %	1990	Average year-end interest %
Short-term debt:				
Payable to banks:				
Foreign	$ 27.6	9.16	$ 20.8	8.93
Domestic	—	—	17.5	8.35
Commercial paper	176.6	5.02	213.5	8.07
Total short-term debt	$204.2	—	$251.8	—
Long-term debt:				
9¼% debentures due 2008	$125.0	9.75	$125.0	9.75
Medium-term notes	125.0	8.68	41.9	8.72
8% sinking-fund debentures due 1996	8.6	8.00	10.6	8.00
Capitalized leases	1.1	12.46	2.5	8.79
Mortgages, notes, and other	53.6	8.61	56.5	8.57
Total long-term debt	313.3	—	236.5	—
Less current installments	11.9	—	3.3	—
Net long-term debt	$301.4	9.12	$233.2	9.26

In March 1988, the company filed a registration statement with the Securities and Exchange Commission to offer up to $250 million of debt securities. The following month a public offering of $125 million of 9¼% debentures due in the year 2008 was completed. During October 1990 the company established a medium-term note program in the amount of $125 million. These notes were issued at varying rates and varying maturities ranging from three years to 10 years. From December 1990 through April 1991, the company issued fixed rate notes ranging from 8% to 9% due no later than April 17, 2001. The debentures and notes are not redeemable by the company until maturity and there are no sinking-fund requirements. Proceeds from these offerings were used to reduce short-term borrowings.

The 8% sinking-fund debentures are redeemable at the company's option at 100% until maturity at May 15, 1996. Sinking-fund payments sufficient to retire $2.5 million principal amount of the debentures are due annually. Debentures held in anticipation of future sinking-fund requirements totaled $4.0 million at December 31, 1991, compared with $4.4 million at December 31, 1990.

All obligations related to long-term debt have been satisfied through 1991.

Scheduled amortization of long-term debt (millions)			
1993	$10.5	1996	$42.6
1994	15.0	1997	13.7
1995	23.7		

Under a parallel-loan agreement, Armstrong borrowed £6.0 million in 1978 from the pension funds of an unrelated British company, and Armstrong loaned $11.0 million (the approximate

ARMSTRONG WORLD INDUSTRIES, INC., AND SUBSIDIARIES

FINANCIAL REVIEW

Debt (continued)

equivalent of £6.0 million on the original date) to the same pension funds, with a net annual interest cost of 1⅜%. Each loan is to be repaid in equal installments, with a right to prepay without premium. Installments were paid in 1986 and 1988 with the last payment paid in 1990.

For reporting purposes, the assets and liabilities of the parallel loans are offset because the agreement provides for a right of offset.

In 1983, the company purchased an £11.0 million note of a United Kingdom financial institution through the issuance of a noninterest-bearing installment note and made the first of two required payments. The proceeds from the £11.0 million note were received in 1985. The second installment payment of $18.6 million is due in December 2013, and the $1.2 million present value of this payment is recorded in other long-term debt. (See comments under "Other noncurrent assets" on page 25 for possible offset to this future payment.)

Armstrong currently has unused domestic short-term lines of credit of approximately $245 million from eight banks. In addition, the company's foreign subsidiaries have approximately $99 million of unused short-term lines of credit available from numerous banks that serve them. Most of the credit lines are extended on a fee basis.

The company borrows from its banks generally at rates approximating the lowest available to commercial borrowers and can issue short-term commercial notes supported by the lines of credit.

Financial instruments with off-balance-sheet risks

The company includes foreign currency options, forward contracts, interest-rate swaps, and foreign currency swaps in its selective hedging of foreign currency and interest rate risk exposures. Realized and unrealized gains and losses on those contracts which hedge expected future cash flows are recognized in other income and expense. Realized and unrealized gains and losses on those contracts which hedge net investment in foreign subsidiaries are recognized in shareholders' equity.

At December 31, 1991, foreign currency options and forward contracts hedging anticipated transactions totaled approximately U.S. $20 million in denominations of Belgian francs, Canadian dollars, and German marks. An unrealized net loss of approximately $1 million was deferred as of December 31 for these hedging activities. The maximum number of years in which anticipated transactions are hedged is three years.

At December 31, 1991, foreign currency options and forward contracts hedging foreign investment positions totaled approximately U.S. $85 million in denominations of French francs, German marks, and Netherland guilders.

In 1987, the company entered into an interest-rate swap agreement with financial institutions to manage its exposure to short-term interest rates. These swaps total $64.1 million, expire in 1992 and 1994, and provide for the company to pay interest at the 30-day U.S. commercial paper rate and to receive interest at an average fixed annual rate of 9.71%.

In 1987, Armstrong, to hedge certain foreign investments, entered into medium-term interest-rate or currency swap agreements with third parties whereby the company swapped U.S. $86.3 million for an equivalent amount of certain foreign currencies in denominations of Belgian francs, French francs, and German marks. Of the original amounts exchanged under these agreements, $49.1 million is repayable in 1992 and the balance in 1994. At the end of 1991, the net balance owed under these swaps was $16.8 million. The agreements provide for the company to make average fixed-interest payments of approximately 6.8% while receiving interest at the 30-day commercial paper rate.

The counterparts to these instruments comprise a limited number of major international financial institutions, and the company continually monitors its position and the credit ratings of its counterparts. It does not anticipate any losses because of credit exposure with the counterparts.

For reporting purposes, the assets and liabilities of the foreign currency options and forward contracts, interest-rate swaps, and interest-rate or currency swaps are offset because the agreements provide for a right of offset.

Additionally, at December 31, 1991, the company had $26.6 million in standby letters of credit and financial guarantees. Generally, the company's policy does not require collateral or other security to support these financial instruments with credit risk.

Other long-term liabilities include amounts for deferred compensation, workers' compensation, unfunded retirement benefits, vacation accrual, and a reserve for the estimated potential liability primarily associated with claims pending in the company's asbestos-related litigation.

Based upon the company's experience with this litigation—as well as the Wellington Agreement, other settlement agreements with certain of the company's insurance carriers, and an earlier interim agreement with several primary carriers—this reserve is intended to cover potential liability and settlement costs, legal and administrative costs not covered under the agreements, and certain other factors which have been involved in the litigation about which uncertainties exist. Future costs of litigation against the company's insurance carriers and other legal costs indirectly related to the litigation, expected to be modest, will be expensed outside the reserve. Amounts, primarily insurance litigation costs, estimated to be payable within one year are included under current liabilities. .

Although the company does not know how many claims will be filed against it in the future, nor the details thereof or of pending suits not fully reviewed, nor the expense and any liability that may ultimately result therefrom, based upon its experience and other factors referred to in the "Litigation" note on pages 29 and 30, the company believes that it is probable that such charges to expense associated with the suits and claims should be minimal.

Geographic areas

United States net trade sales include export sales to non-affiliated customers of $29.3 million in 1991, $28.2 million in 1990, and $26.4 million in 1989.

"Europe" includes operations located primarily in Belgium, England, France, Germany, Italy, the Netherlands, Spain, and Switzerland. Operations in Australia, Canada, China, Hong Kong, Indonesia, Japan, Singapore, and Thailand are in "Other foreign."

Transfers between geographic areas and commissions paid to affiliates marketing exported products are accounted for by methods that approximate arm's-length transactions, after considering the costs incurred by the selling company and the return on assets employed of both the selling unit and the purchasing unit. Operating profits of a geographic area include profits accruing from sales to affiliates.

Geographic areas at December 31 *(millions)*	1991	1990	1989
Net trade sales:			
United States	$1,761.7	$1,838.1	$1,869.7
Europe	508.5	506.2	425.8
Other foreign	169.1	174.5	193.2
Total foreign	677.6	680.7	619.0
Inter-area transfers:			
United States	65.5	56.9	60.5
Europe	3.9	5.1	8.9
Other foreign	9.9	8.5	6.7
Eliminations	(79.3)	(70.5)	(76.1)
Total net sales	$2,439.3	$2,518.8	$2,488.7
Operating profit:			
United States	$ 131.5	$ 258.8	$ 252.4
Europe	51.8	72.2	60.7
Other foreign	9.3	10.7	20.3
Total foreign	$ 61.1	$ 82.9	$ 81.0
Total operating profit	$ 192.6	$ 341.7	$ 333.4
Identifiable assets (Note):			
United States	$1,435.5	$1,462.2	$1,453.7
Europe	398.5	387.2	316.8
Other foreign	74.9	73.6	78.3
Corporate	250.5	235.0	194.4
Eliminations	(9.5)	(11.7)	(18.8)
Discontinued businesses	—	—	8.6
Total assets	$2,149.9	$2,146.3	$2,033.0

Reconciliation *(millions)*	1991	1990	1989
Operating profit	$192.6	$341.7	$333.4
Corporate expense, net	(46.5)	(81.1)	(49.3)
Interest expense	(45.8)	(37.5)	(40.5)
Earnings from continuing businesses before income taxes	$100.3	$223.1	$243.6

Note: Identifiable assets for geographic areas and industry segments exclude cash, marketable securities, and assets of a corporate nature. Capital additions for industry segments include property, plant, and equipment from acquisitions.

Industry segments

The company operates worldwide in four reportable segments: floor coverings, building products, furniture, and industry products. Floor coverings sales include sales of resilient floors, ceramic tile, and accessories.

Industry segments at December 31 *(millions)*	1991	1990	1989
Net trade sales:			
Floor coverings	$1,058.0	$1,095.9	$1,113.9
Building products	676.3	711.1	695.4
Furniture	417.9	436.4	438.3
Industry products	287.1	275.4	241.1
Total net sales	$2,439.3	$2,518.8	$2,488.7
Operating profit:			
Floor coverings	$ 84.6	$ 131.2	$ 137.7
Building products	46.7	142.9	126.8
Furniture	18.2	19.6	28.4
Industry products	43.1	48.0	40.5
Total operating profit	$ 192.6	$ 341.7	$ 333.4
Depreciation and amortization:			
Floor coverings	$ 62.8	$ 63.8	$ 68.8
Building products	35.1	29.1	25.9
Furniture	13.7	13.6	12.4
Industry products	10.5	10.3	9.4
Corporate	13.2	12.3	7.0
Total depreciation and amortization	$ 135.3	$ 129.1	$ 123.5
Capital additions (Note):			
Floor coverings	$ 61.6	$ 82.9	$ 93.5
Building products	39.1	57.1	81.1
Furniture	6.7	10.9	16.0
Industry products	21.1	26.2	10.8
Corporate	5.2	17.4	12.3
Total capital additions	$ 133.7	$ 194.5	$ 213.7
Identifiable assets (Note):			
Floor coverings	$ 915.1	$ 940.7	$ 906.2
Building products	556.0	556.7	507.1
Furniture	239.7	242.7	260.5
Industry products	188.6	171.2	156.1
Corporate	250.5	235.0	194.5
Discontinued businesses	—	—	8.6
Total assets	$2,149.9	$2,146.3	$2,033.0

27

ARMSTRONG WORLD INDUSTRIES, INC., AND SUBSIDIARIES

FINANCIAL REVIEW

Stock options—Under the Long-Term Stock Option Plan for Key Employees, 403,525 shares of company common stock were reserved for future options at December 31, 1991, compared with 693,775 shares reserved at December 31, 1990. The option prices are not less than the closing market price of the shares on the dates the options were granted. There are both nonstatutory and incentive stock options; some include provision for full or partial stock appreciation rights, and all expire 10 years from the date of grant.

The average share price of all options exercised was $13.20 in 1991 and $14.03 in 1990.

Changes in option shares outstanding

(thousands except for share price)	1991	1990
Option shares outstanding at beginning of year	1,179.8	944.3
Options granted	311.8	300.0
	1,491.6	1,244.3
Less: Option shares exercised	10.9	34.8
Stock appreciation rights exercised	.6	6.4
Options canceled	21.6	23.3
	33.1	64.5
Option shares outstanding at end of year	1,458.5	1,179.8
Average share price of options outstanding	$33.21	$34.28
Option shares exercisable at end of year	1,150.7	879.7

Treasury share changes for 1991, 1990, and 1989 are as follows:

Years ended December 31

(thousands)	1991	1990	1989
Common shares			
Balance at beginning of year	14,787.0	9,621.5	5,621.6
Stock purchased	.1	5,205.6	4,101.1
Stock issuance activity, net	(10.8)	(40.1)	(101.2)
Balance at end of year	14,776.3	14,787.0	9,621.5
Preferred shares			
$3.75 cumulative, no par value			
Balance at beginning of year	—	—	58.2
Shares purchased	—	—	103.3
Stock retired	—	—	(161.5)
Balance at end of year	—	—	—

Shareholders' equity changes for 1991, 1990, and 1989 are summarized below:

Years ended December 31

(millions except for per-share data)	1991	1990	1989
Series A convertible preferred stock:			
Balance at beginning of year	$ 268.3	$ 270.0	$ —
Shares issued	—	—	270.0
Shares redeemed	.6	1.7	—
Balance at end of year	$ 267.7	$ 268.3	$ 270.0
Common stock, $1 par value:			
Balance at beginning and end of year	$ 51.9	$ 51.9	$ 51.9
Capital in excess of par value:			
Balance at beginning of year	$ 25.7	$ 25.5	$ 22.1
Retirement of preferred stock	—	—	1.3
Stock issuances	.1	.2	2.1
Balance at end of year	$ 25.8	$ 25.7	$ 25.5
Reduction for ESOP loan guarantee:			
Initial amount	$ (261.8)	$ (267.3)	$ (270.0)
Principal paid	2.9	1.5	.9
Accrued compensation	2.9	4.0	1.8
Balance at end of year	$ (256.0)	$ (261.8)	$ (267.3)
Retained earnings:			
Balance at beginning of year	$1,224.1	$1,146.9	$1,016.5
Net earnings for year	48.2	141.0	187.6
Total	$1,272.3	$1,287.9	$1,204.1
Less dividends:			
Preferred stock			
$3.75 per share	$ —	$ —	$ .2
$3.462 per share	19.4	19.5	9.5
Common stock			
$1.19 per share in 1991;			
$1.135 per share in 1990;			
$1.045 per share in 1989	44.2	44.3	47.5
Total dividends	$ 63.6	$ 63.8	$ 57.2
Balance at end of year	$1,208.7	$1,224.1	$1,146.9
Foreign currency translation:			
Balance at beginning of year	$ 48.3	$ 21.9	$ 24.1
Translation adjustments and hedging activities	(2.4)	21.2	(2.9)
Allocated income taxes	(1.2)	5.2	.7
Balance at end of year	$ 44.7	$ 48.3	$ 21.9
Treasury stock at cost:			
Preferred stock, $3.75 cumulative:			
Balance at beginning of year	$ —	$ —	$ 4.7
Stock purchased	—	—	10.6
Stock retired	—	—	(15.3)
Balance at end of year	$ —	$ —	$ —
Common stock:			
Balance at beginning of year	$ 457.3	$ 272.4	$ 104.7
Stock purchases	—	185.2	167.1
Stock issuance activity, net	—	(.3)	.6
Balance at end of year	$ 457.3	$ 457.3	$ 272.4
Total shareholders' equity	$ 885.5	$ 899.2	$ 976.5

Preferred stock purchase rights plan

In 1986, the Board of Directors declared a distribution of one right for each share of the company's common stock outstanding on and after March 21, 1986. Following the two-for-one stock split later in 1986, one-half of one right attaches to each share of common stock outstanding. In general, the rights become exercisable at $175 per right for a fractional share of a new series of Class A preferred stock (which will differ from the Series A Convertible Preferred Stock issued to the Employee Stock Ownership Plan described on page 23) 10 days after a person or group either acquires beneficial ownership of shares representing 20% or more of the voting power of the company or announces a tender or exchange offer that could result in such person or group beneficially owning shares representing 28% or more of the voting power of the company. If thereafter any person or group becomes the beneficial owner of 28% or more of the voting power of the company or if the company is the surviving company in a merger with a person or group that owns 20% or more of the voting power of the company, then each owner of a right (other than such 20% stockholder) would be entitled to purchase shares of common stock having a value equal to twice the exercise price of the right. Should the company be acquired in a merger or other business combination, or sell 50% or more of its assets or earnings power, each right would entitle the holder to purchase, at the exercise price, common shares of the acquirer having a value of twice the exercise price of the right. The exercise price was determined on the basis of the Board's view of the long-term value of the company's common stock. The rights have no voting power nor do they entitle a holder to receive dividends. At the company's option, the rights are redeemable prior to becoming exercisable at 5 cents per right. The rights expire on March 21, 1996.

Litigation

The company is one of many defendants in pending lawsuits and claims involving, as of December 31, 1991, approximately 71,250 individuals alleging personal injury from exposure to asbestos-containing products. A total of about 22,375 lawsuits and claims were received by the company in 1991, compared with 19,410 in 1990. Nearly all the personal injury suits and claims seek compensatory and punitive damages arising from alleged exposure to asbestos-containing insulation products used, manufactured, or sold by the company. The company discontinued the sale of all asbestos-containing insulation products in 1969. A significant number of suits in which the company believes it should not be involved were filed in 1991 by persons engaged in the vehicle tire production, construction, and steel industries. Although a large number of suits and claims pending in prior years have been resolved, neither the rate of future dispositions nor the number of future potential unasserted claims can be reasonably predicted.

Attention continues to be given by various judges to finding a comprehensive solution to the large number of pending as well as potential future asbestos-related personal injury claims, and the Judicial Panel for Multi-district Litigation ordered the transfer of all federal cases not in trial to a single court for pretrial purposes. It is not known whether those efforts will result in a fair and comprehensive resolution of the asbestos-related personal injury litigation. A few state judges have been undertaking to consolidate numbers of asbestos personal injury cases for trial. The company generally opposes these actions as being unfair. Approximately 8,500 cases have been consolidated for a multiphase trial which is expected to begin in February 1992 in a state court in Baltimore, Maryland. The company is one of 14 defendants in this multiphase trial.

The pending personal injury lawsuits and claims against the company are being paid by insurance proceeds under the 1985 Agreement Concerning Asbestos-Related Claims, the "Wellington Agreement." A new claims handling organization, known as the Center for Claims Resolution, was created in October 1988 by Armstrong and 20 other companies to replace the Wellington Asbestos Claims Facility, which became inactive. Except for eliminating the future availability of an insurer-paid special defense fund linked to the existence of the Facility, the dissolution of the Facility does not essentially affect the company's overall Wellington insurance settlement which provides for a final settlement of nearly all disputes concerning insurance for personal injury claims as between the company and three of its primary insurers and eight of its excess insurers. The one primary carrier that did not sign the Wellington Agreement paid into the Wellington Facility and settled with the company in March 1989 all outstanding issues relating to insurance coverage for personal injury and property damage claims. In addition, one of the company's large excess-insurance carriers entered into a settlement agreement in 1986 with the company under which payments for personal injury claims were made through the Wellington Facility, and this carrier continues to make payments for such claims through the Center for Claims Resolution. Other excess-insurance carriers also have entered into settlement agreements with the company which complement Wellington. ACandS, Inc., a former subsidiary of the company, which for certain insurance periods has coverage rights under some company insurance policies, subscribed to the Wellington Agreement but did not become a member of the Center for Claims Resolution.

One excess carrier and certain companies in an excess carrier's block of coverage have become insolvent. Certain carriers providing excess level coverage solely for property damage claims also have become insolvent. However, it is not expected that the insolvency of these carriers will affect the company's ability to have insurance available to pay asbestos-related claims. ACandS, Inc., filed a lawsuit against the company to have a certain amount of insurance from the joint policies reserved solely for its use in the payment of the costs associated with the asbestos-related personal injury and property damage claims, and the companies have reached a tentative settlement of their dispute.

ARMSTRONG WORLD INDUSTRIES, INC., AND SUBSIDIARIES

Litigation (continued)

The Center for Claims Resolution operates under a concept of allocated shares of liability payments and defense costs for its members based primarily on historical experience, and it defends the members' interests and addresses pending and future claims in a manner consistent with the prompt, fair resolution of meritorious claims. In late 1991, the Center sharing formula was revised to provide that members will pay only on claims in which the member is a named defendant. This change will cause a slight increase in the company's share, but should enhance the company's case management focus. Although the Center members and their participating insurers were not obligated beyond one year, the insurance companies have committed to the continuous operation of the Center for a fourth year and to the funding of the Center's operating expenses. No forecast can be made for future years regarding either the rate of claims resolution by the Center or the rate of utilization of company insurance.

The company is also one of many defendants in a total of 105 pending lawsuits and claims, including class actions, as of December 31, 1991, brought by public and private entities, including public school districts, states' attorneys general, and private property owners. These lawsuits and claims include allegations of property damage to buildings caused by asbestos-containing products and generally claim compensatory and punitive damages and equitable relief, including reimbursement of expenditures, or removal and replacement of such products. These suits and claims appear to be aimed at friable (easily crumbled) asbestos-containing products although allegations in some suits encompass other asbestos-containing products, including allegations with respect to asbestos-containing resilient floor tile. The company vigorously denies the validity of the allegations against it contained in these suits and claims. Increasing defense costs, paid by the company's insurance carriers either under reservation or settlement arrangement, will be incurred. These suits and claims are not encompassed within the Wellington Agreement nor are they being handled by the Center for Claims Resolution.

In 1989, Armstrong concluded the trial phase of a lawsuit in California state court to resolve disputes concerning certain of its insurance carriers' obligations with respect to personal injury and property damage liability coverage, including defense costs, for alleged personal injury and property damage asbestos-related lawsuits and claims. As indicated earlier, the company reached a settlement agreement after the conclusion of the trial phase with one of its primary carriers which is also an excess carrier. The Court has issued final decisions and the carriers have appealed. Based upon the trial court's favorable final decisions in important phases of the trial relating to coverage for personal injury and property damage lawsuits and claims, and a review of the coverage issues by its counsel, the company believes it has a substantial legal basis for sustaining on appeal its right to defense

and indemnification. For the same reasons, the company also believes that it is probable that claims by the several primary carriers for recoupment of defense expenses in the property damage litigation, which the carriers have also appealed, will ultimately not be successful.

Although the company does not know how many claims will be filed against it in the future, nor the details thereof or of pending suits not fully reviewed, nor the expense and any liability that may ultimately result therefrom, based upon its experience and other factors, the company believes that it is probable that nearly all of the expenses and any liability payments associated therewith will be paid—in the case of the personal injury claims, by agreed-to coverage under the Wellington Agreement and supplemented by payments by nonsubscribing insurers that entered into settlement agreements with the company and additional insurance coverage reasonably anticipated from the outcome of the insurance litigation—and in the case of the property damage claims, under an existing interim agreement, by insurance coverage settlement agreements and through additional coverage reasonably anticipated from the outcome of the insurance litigation. Thus, the company has not recorded any liability for any defense costs or indemnity relating to these lawsuits other than as described in the "Other long-term liabilities" section regarding the reserve on page 26.

Even though uncertainties still remain as to the potential number of unasserted claims, the liability resulting therefrom, and the ultimate scope of its insurance coverage, after consideration of the factors involved, including the Wellington Agreement, the settlements with other insurance carriers, the remaining reserve, the establishment of the Center for Claims Resolution, and its experience, the company believes that this litigation will not have a material adverse effect on its earnings, liquidity, or financial position.

In June 1991, in *Fineman and The Industry Network System v. Armstrong*, the Federal District Court in Newark, New Jersey, overturned an earlier jury verdict awarding antitrust and tort and punitive damages of about $238 million against Armstrong. Furthermore, the Court ruled that, in the event of a successful appeal restoring the jury's verdict, the company would be entitled to a new trial on the matter. The plaintiffs have appealed the Court's ruling to the Third Circuit Federal Court of Appeals, and oral argument is scheduled for early March. The company believes that the Court's order awarding judgment to the company will be sustained on appeal, and that even if the jury's verdict is restored on appeal, it is unlikely that the Court's order for a new trial will be overturned. However, in the unlikely event that the jury's verdict were to be reinstated and no new trial were permitted, the resulting liability would have a material adverse effect on the company's earnings and financial position.

Management's statement of responsibility

The management of Armstrong World Industries, Inc., is responsible for the integrity of the financial statements of the company and for ascertaining that these statements accurately reflect Armstrong's financial position and results of operations. The company's financial statements are prepared in accordance with generally accepted accounting principles and include management estimates and judgments, where appropriate. In the opinion of management, the financial statements set forth a fair presentation of the consolidated financial condition of the company at December 31, 1991 and 1990 and the consolidated results of its operations and cash flows for the years ended December 31, 1991, 1990, and 1989.

Armstrong has an accounting system and related internal controls that, in the opinion of the management, provide reasonable assurance that the company's assets are safeguarded and that the company's records reflect the transactions of the company accurately, fairly, and in reasonable detail. The internal control system provides for the careful selection and training of personnel, the delegation of management authority and responsibility, the dissemination of management and control policies and procedures, and an extensive internal audit program. The Internal Audit Department is staffed to perform periodic audits covering all parent company and subsidiary locations. A review of controls and practices to assure compliance with corporate ethical policy is performed as a part of each audit. The auditing procedures of the Internal Audit Department are coordinated with those of the independent auditors.

The company's independent auditors, KPMG Peat Marwick, provide an objective review of management's reporting of operating results and financial condition. Working with our internal auditors and conducting tests as appropriate, KPMG Peat Marwick have audited the financial statements included in this Annual Report, and their opinion concerning these statements appears below.

An Audit Committee comprising five nonemployee directors is appointed by the company's Board of Directors. This committee meets periodically with management, internal auditors, and independent auditors of the company to discuss the scope and results of the internal and independent audits, financial and operating results, internal controls, company policies, and other significant matters, including the financial statements in this Annual Report. Both the internal and independent auditors have unrestricted access to the Audit Committee.

Chairman and President
(chief executive officer)

Controller
(chief accounting officer)

Senior Vice-President, Finance,
and Treasurer
(chief financial officer)

Independent auditors' report

The Board of Directors and Shareholders,
Armstrong World Industries, Inc.:

We have audited the consolidated balance sheets of Armstrong World Industries, Inc., and subsidiaries as of December 31, 1991 and 1990, and the related consolidated statements of earnings and cash flows for each of the years in the three-year period ended December 31, 1991. These consolidated financial statements are the responsibility of the company's management. Our responsibility is to express an opinion on these consolidated financial statements based on our audits.

We conducted our audits in accordance with generally accepted auditing standards. Those standards require that we plan and perform the audit to obtain reasonable assurance about whether the financial statements are free of material misstatements. An audit includes examining, on a test basis, evidence supporting the amounts and disclosures in the financial statements. An audit also includes assessing the accounting principles used and significant estimates made by management, as well as evaluating the overall financial statement presentation. We believe that our audits provide a reasonable basis for our opinion.

In our opinion, the consolidated financial statements referred to above present fairly, in all material respects, the financial position of Armstrong World Industries, Inc., and subsidiaries at December 31, 1991 and 1990, and the results of their operations and their cash flows for each of the years in the three-year period ended December 31, 1991, in conformity with generally accepted accounting principles.

KPMG PEAT MARWICK

Philadelphia, Pa.
February 17, 1992

ARMSTRONG WORLD INDUSTRIES, INC., AND SUBSIDIARIES

Quarterly financial information *(millions except for per-share data)*	First	Second	Third	Fourth	Total year
			1991*		
Net sales	$596.1	$627.8	$632.4	$583.0	$2,439.3
Gross profit	151.1	173.3	172.6	141.2	638.2
Earnings (losses) from continuing businesses	15.8	24.4	23.0	(2.6)	60.6
Net earnings (losses)	14.8	23.4	22.0	(12.0)	48.2
Per share of common stock:***					
Primary:					
Earnings (losses) from continuing businesses	.30	.53	.49	(.20)	1.11
Net earnings (losses)	.27	.50	.46	(.45)	.77
Fully diluted:					
Earnings (losses) from continuing businesses	.30	.50	.47	(.20)	1.11
Net earnings (losses)	.27	.47	.44	(.45)	.77
Dividends per share of common stock	.29	.30	.30	.30	1.19
Price range of common stock—low	22⅞	25⅛	27⅜	23½	22⅞
Price range of common stock—high	31	30½	33¾	34½	34½
			1990**		
Net sales	$635.1	$649.0	$636.1	$598.6	$2,518.8
Gross profit	192.4	190.2	171.5	148.1	702.2
Earnings from continuing businesses	58.5	51.9	29.0	7.0	146.4
Net earnings	65.2	44.8	26.3	4.7	141.0
Per share of common stock:***					
Primary:					
Earnings from continuing businesses	1.29	1.18	.65	.06	3.26
Net earnings	1.45	1.01	.58	—	3.12
Fully diluted:					
Earnings from continuing businesses	1.16	1.08	.60	.06	2.99
Net earnings	1.31	.92	.54	—	2.86
Dividends per share of common stock	.265	.29	.29	.29	1.135
Price range of common stock—low	31¾	32⅜	23½	18	18
Price range of common stock—high	38¾	37⅞	37	27⅜	38¾

*First, second, and third quarters for 1991 restated for the results of discontinued businesses and to conform to total year expense classifications.
**Restated for the results of discontinued businesses.
***Quarterly earnings (losses) per-share data do not equal the total year amounts due to changes in the average shares outstanding and, for fully diluted data, the exclusion of the antidilutive effect in certain quarters and for the total year.

Fourth quarter 1991 compared with fourth quarter 1990

Fourth-quarter 1991 sales from continuing businesses of $583.0 million declined 2.6% from the 1990 level of $598.6 million.

The net loss for the fourth quarter 1991 was $12.0 million, or 45 cents per share of common stock, on both a primary and fully diluted basis. Included in these figures were costs of $9.4 million after tax, or 25 cents per share, resulting from the discontinuation of three noncore businesses, and $4.8 million after tax, or 13 cents per share, of losses related to restructuring charges.

The company's net earnings in the fourth quarter of 1990 were $4.7 million, but there were no earnings per share after providing for preferred dividends. These earnings also included after-tax charges associated with discontinued businesses of $2.3 million, or 6 cents per share; restructuring charges of $2.2 million, or 6 cents per share, related to the closing of a Toronto manufacturing facility and severance pay associated with personnel reductions; and an accrual of $2.7 million, or 7 cents per share, for costs associated with litigation involving residual claims in connection with a plant formerly owned by Armstrong.

The company reported a fourth-quarter 1991 loss from continuing businesses of $2.6 million, or 20 cents per share, compared with earnings from continuing businesses of $7.0 million, or 6 cents per share, in the 1990 quarter.

The restructuring charges previously mentioned for 1991 are almost equal in amount to charges in 1990 for restructuring and for costs associated with litigation involving residual claims. The decline in earnings from continuing businesses reflects lower sales, a slight increase in cost of goods sold, and increases in selling and administrative expenses related to inflationary cost increases and start-up costs associated with selling residential ceramic tile through resilient flooring distributors.

Two of Armstrong's four industry segments—furniture and industry products—showed fourth-quarter increases in sales. The other two segments—floor coverings (which includes ceramic tile) and building products—declined year-to-year. Only the furniture segment improved its operating profit when compared with fourth quarter 1990. The furniture segment reported higher operating profits because of an increase in sales and a lower level of promotional activity. Floor coverings' operating profits reflect the lower sales level, primarily because of reduced commercial-institutional market opportunity, start-up costs associated with the new Armstrong ceramic business, restructuring costs and write-down of certain manufacturing assets. The building products segment was affected by lower sales, price competitiveness, a shift to lower-margin products, and some restructuring costs. The industry products segment, while recording improved sales and profitability in its European insulation business, was adversely affected by restructuring costs in its North American businesses.

Management's discussion and analysis of financial condition and results of operations

1991 compared with 1990

Financial condition

As shown on the Consolidated Statements of Cash Flows, net cash provided by operating activities in 1991 was $150.4 million or approximately three-fourths of the funds necessary to cover investments in property, plant, and equipment and dividends. The balance of cash required was financed by increased borrowings and reduced cash and cash equivalents.

In the fourth quarter of 1990, the company established a medium-term note program utilizing the remaining $125 million on its registration statement filed in 1988 with the Securities and Exchange Commission. These notes were issued at varying rates and varying maturities ranging from three years to 10 years. During the first quarter 1991, the company issued $56 million of such medium-term notes. Another $27 million of notes were issued in the second quarter, completing this $125 million program. Proceeds from the medium-term note program were used to reduce the company's short-term debt. The company has filed a registration statement with the Securities and Exchange Commission (which has not yet been declared effective) to potentially offer up to $250 million of debt securities.

Inventories were reduced by $12.8 million reflecting first-half reductions for lower sales levels and to conserve cash. Other current assets increased $18.8 million, principally because of additions to deferred income tax benefits and investments in foreign currency options. Other noncurrent assets moved higher by $5.9 million due to an increase in prepaid pension costs, which was offset in part by amortization of intangibles.

The company's year-end ratio of current assets to current liabilities was improved to approximately 1.5 to 1 from the 1.3 to 1 ratio reported in 1990. The factors contributing to this improvement included the reduction in short-term debt resulting from the issuance of medium-term notes, and decreased accounts payable and accrued expenses caused by lower activity levels in the fourth quarter.

The company is involved in significant litigation which is described more fully in the "Litigation" note to the financial statements on pages 29 and 30 and which should be read in connection with this discussion and analysis. Although the company does not know how many claims will be filed against it in the future, nor the details thereof or of pending suits not fully reviewed, nor the expense and any liability that may ultimately result therefrom, based upon its experience and other factors referred to in the "Litigation" note, the company believes that it is probable that nearly all of the expenses and any liability payments associated therewith will be paid—in the case of the personal injury claims, by agreed-to coverage under the Wellington Agreement and supplemented by payments by nonsubscribing insurers that entered into settlement agreements with the company and additional insurance coverage reasonably anticipated from the outcome of the insurance litigation—and in the case of the property damage claims, under an existing interim agreement, by insurance coverage settlement agreements and through additional coverage reasonably anticipated from the outcome of the insurance litigation. To the extent that costs of the property damage litigation are being paid by the company's insurance carriers under reservation of rights, the company believes that it is probable that such payments will not be subjected to recoupment. Thus, the company has not recorded any liability for any defense costs or indemnity relating to these lawsuits other than as described in the "Other long-term liabilities" note regarding the reserve on page 26. Even though uncertainties still remain as to the potential number of unasserted claims, the liability resulting therefrom, and the ultimate scope of its insurance coverage, after consideration of the factors involved, including the Wellington Agreement, the settlements with other insurance carriers, the remaining reserve, the establishment of the Center for Claims Resolution, and its experience, the company believes that this litigation will not have a material adverse effect on its earnings, liquidity, or financial position.

As of year-end 1991, long-term debt represented 34% of shareholders' equity, an increase from the 26% reported in 1990. Long-term debt does not include the company's guarantee of the ESOP loan, which has been recorded both as a long-term obligation and as a reduction of shareholders' equity. Early in 1991, the company's long-term debt rating was reduced by Standard & Poor's to A+ and Moody's to A2. Should a need develop for additional financing, it is management's opinion that the company has sufficient financial strength to warrant the required support from lending institutions and financial markets.

Consolidated results

Net sales in 1991 of $2.44 billion declined 3.2% from 1990 sales of $2.52 billion. This is the fourth consecutive year in which the company's markets have reflected declining opportunity. The major countries throughout the world in which Armstrong does business are generally in recession and experiencing reduced demands for the company's products. A review of 1991 shows a weak first quarter that was attributed to the lagging economy and the Mideast war. The company's business strengthened in the second and third quarters as

ARMSTRONG WORLD INDUSTRIES, INC., AND SUBSIDIARIES

consumer confidence improved, but then declined later in the year. The fourth quarter, particularly in the U.S., declined significantly, and opportunity fell below that of 1990.

Net earnings in 1991 were $48.2 million, a decrease of 66% from the $141.0 million reported for the previous year. Included in the 1991 earnings was a $12.4 million after-tax provision for the expected losses associated with the disposition of three noncore businesses as well as their 1991 operating losses. The 1990 net earnings included a charge of $13.4 million related to discontinued businesses. Also included in 1990 results was a gain of $8.0 million resulting from the company's implementation of the Financial Accounting Standard (FAS) No. 96, "Accounting for Income Taxes."

Net earnings per share of common stock for 1991 were 77 cents on both a primary and fully diluted basis as compared with 1990 net earnings of $3.12 and $2.86, respectively.

Return on common shareholders' equity for 1991 was 3.3%, compared with 13.0% in 1990.

Earnings from continuing businesses were $60.6 million; compared with $146.4 million the previous year—a decline of 59%. Earnings per share of common stock from continuing businesses were $1.11 on both a primary and fully diluted basis, compared with 1990 levels of $3.26 and $2.99, respectively.

Included in the net earnings for 1991 was an increase in the effective tax rate to 39.6% from 34.4% in the previous year. The increase in the effective tax rate is caused by an increased share of the company's total earnings coming from foreign countries with higher tax rates and by a $3.7 million deferred income tax charge reflecting increases in state income tax rates as required by FAS No. 96, "Accounting for Income Taxes."

The earnings from continuing businesses before income taxes were $100.3 million, a 55% decline from 1990's $223.1 million.

Significant items included in the 1991 earnings from continuing businesses before tax included restructuring charges of $12.8 million related to severance pay and early retirement incentives, higher interest expense of $8.3 million caused mainly by the settlement of prior year tax returns in the first quarter of 1991, and higher average debt levels as a result of the repurchase of Armstrong common stock in 1990.

The 1990 earnings from continuing businesses before tax included the sale of woodlands, $60.4 million, partially offset by costs and expenses associated with the proxy contest and Armstrong's response to a takeover threat, $15.4 million; restructuring costs including severance pay, a provision for the write-down of assets, and costs and expenses associated with a plant closing that totaled $6.8 million; and an accrual for costs associated with litigation involving residual claims for a previously owned facility of $5.0 million.

The cost of goods sold for 1991, when expressed as a percent of sales, was 73.8% as compared to 1990's 72.1%. This higher cost relationship is the result of spreading fixed costs over a lower sales volume; severe competitive pricing pressures in some businesses; higher raw material costs in most businesses; a lower margin product mix; and manufacturing inefficiencies

caused by production schedule reductions needed to meet lower demand and to reduce inventories.

Geographic area results *(see page 27)*

United States—Sales and operating profits for 1991 fell below 1990 levels by 4% and 49%, respectively. These results reflect the recessionary environment in the United States and the lower opportunity afforded by the markets for the company's products. Nonresidential construction, which was weak at the beginning of the year, continued a sharp decline throughout the year. New housing starts and sales of existing homes, while lower on a year-to-year comparison, started to show signs of slow improvement in the second half of the year. Sales of consumer household durable goods declined in 1991 when compared to 1990.

Lower unit sales volume, coupled with manufacturing inefficiencies related to reduced production schedules to meet the lower demand, as well as competitive and promotional sales pricing and movement towards a lower margin product mix, adversely affected operating results. The company's continued concentration on its quality management process and emphasis on cost control was successful in offsetting a portion of the negative factors previously mentioned. The 1991 results include the start-up costs related to Armstrong's marketing of ceramic tile as well as restructuring costs at several of its facilities.

Export trade sales of Armstrong products in 1991 from the U.S. improved 4% when compared with 1990.

Europe—During 1991, the economic environment in Europe weakened in both the commercial and residential markets, especially in the United Kingdom. Net sales increased nearly 1%, while operating profits declined by 28%. The building products business was impacted by reduced opportunity, especially in its British markets, a movement towards lower margin product mix, and severe competitive pricing. The European flooring business continued to reflect the declines which started in 1990 and continued throughout 1991. Restructuring costs also adversely affected both building products' and floorings' operating results. The insulation materials market ran contrary to the trend and continued to reflect sales and profit growth.

Other foreign—Both sales and operating profits in 1991 declined from those of 1990 by 3% and 13%, respectively. The Australian economy remained in a major recession resulting in reduced sales and profitability. In contrast, sales improvement was noted in the Southeast Asian area.

The operating profit reduction reflects the reduced sales opportunity along with continued competitive pricing pressures.

Industry segment results *(see page 27)*

Floor coverings—For the second consecutive year, sales and operating profits of this segment have been lower than those of the prior year. During 1991, sales and operating profits declined 4% and 36%, respectively. Worldwide end-use markets continue to offer less opportunity in most sectors, reflecting economic recessions in many of the major countries where the company does business—United States, Canada, England, and Australia. The commercial-institutional construction and renovation markets in these countries were significantly depressed. Most notably affected were sales of ceramic tile in the United States. Resilient flooring sales fell modestly in the United States mainly because of lower sales of new and existing homes. This decline occurred despite several new product introductions, including Visions Solarian, and a year-to-year sales improvement in the do-it-yourself sector.

Factors related to the lower profitability were: lower unit volume, strong competitive pricing, somewhat higher raw material prices, and normal inflationary factors. In addition, manufacturing efficiencies declined as production schedules were scaled back to accommodate both the lower demand and the decision to reduce inventory levels. Also, start-up costs associated with the new marketing program to sell residential ceramic tile through resilient flooring distributors, restructuring costs of $3.0 million, and a write-down of a ceramic tile dryer accounted for nearly a quarter of the year-to-year profit decline. The 1990 results included $2.1 million related to a provision for the write-down of assets of one of the company's small floor covering businesses. Also affecting profitability in both years were costs of increased capacity installed during that time period.

Capital investments were lower than those of 1990 and were directed towards product development, cycle time reduction, and improving manufacturing processes. Capital expenditures in 1990 included a $21 million project to modernize American Olean's plant in Lansdale, Pennsylvania.

Building products—The commercial construction markets in North America continued to decline throughout 1991 while those of many of the European countries joined the decline during the second quarter. As a result, worldwide competitive pricing pressures became severe, and sales of this segment fell 5% with operating profits dropping 67%.

The lower operating profit in 1991 was primarily the result of: lower unit volume, severe competitive pricing, a swing towards lower margin products, the impact of capacity added over the past couple of years, and normal inflationary pressures. The 1991 results also included restructuring costs, primarily severance pay and retirement incentives, that accounted for $4.5 million of the decline. The 1990 results included a $60.4 million gain from the sale of woodlands, offset to a small extent by a $1.6 million charge for costs related to the closing of the wall panel manufacturing facility in Toronto, Canada.

Furniture—In 1991, even though sales of the U.S. consumer household durable goods industry declined, this segment recorded an improved operating profit for each quarter when compared with the preceding quarter throughout the year. The last six months of 1991, as compared with the similar period in 1990, reflected sales increases of 2.4% and operating profit improvement of 140%. However, for the total year, sales and operating profits declined 4% and 7%, respectively, when compared to last year. The upholstery and ready-to-assemble furniture businesses were the subsegments providing sales and operating profit improvement.

During 1991, Thomasville management continued to control costs and moved aggressively to obtain what business there was

available. As in 1990, promotional pricing was a factor in obtaining the business that was achieved. The lower unit sales volume and manufacturing inefficiencies created by a reduced production schedule had an adverse effect on profitability.

Capital expenditures in 1991 were below 1990 levels. In 1991, the businesses concentrated on improving customer satisfaction through new product introductions, reduction of cycle time for manufacturing, and processing of customer orders.

Industry products—The operating results for this segment were mixed, with 1991 sales increasing by 4% from those of 1990, but operating profits declining by 10%. The insulation products business remained extremely strong during 1991, particularly in Europe, and recorded improved sales and operating profits.

Major capital appropriations were approved in late 1991 to expand the European insulation manufacturing at several locations. The fiber products and textile mill supplies businesses operated in weak end-use market segments worldwide. Lower sales volume, competitive pricing, and higher operating expenses were the key factors that adversely affected these businesses.

1990 compared with 1989

Financial condition

As shown on the Consolidated Statements of Cash Flows, cash provided by operating activities in 1990 was $200.2 million or approximately three-fourths of the funds necessary to cover investments in property, plant, and equipment and increased dividends. Another $72.5 million of cash was provided during 1990 from the sale of woodlands and other miscellaneous assets.

Other uses of cash during 1990 included the purchase of common stock for the treasury. In May, First City Financial Corporation and its affiliates sold their block of approximately 4.8 million shares of the company's common stock. Following the First City sale, Armstrong repurchased approximately 3.7 million shares, through its investment banker, as part of a previous Board authorization. A substantial portion of that purchase completed the authorization for the company's Employee Stock Ownership Plan. An agreement was reached with First City resolving all litigation between the parties; the agreement also restricted future company stock purchases by First City for a 10-year period, addressed confidential treatment of certain information, and provided for the payment to the company of $.6 million and by the company of $5.0 million to First City. Earlier in 1990, the company purchased 1.5 million shares of its common stock in the open market or in negotiated transactions. Funds of $185.2 million, required for purchasing the treasury stock, were obtained by issuing short-term debt.

Receivables were lowered by $12.8 million during 1990 primarily as a result of lower sales in the fourth quarter. Inventories were $15.1 million higher with most of the increase caused by translation of foreign currency inventories to U.S. dollars at higher exchange rates. Other current assets decreased $7.5 million, principally because assets of the discontinued businesses remaining at the end of 1989 were collected. Other noncurrent assets increased $22.8 million due to prepaid

35

ARMSTRONG WORLD INDUSTRIES, INC., AND SUBSIDIARIES

pension costs and an investment in a Mexican manufacturer of ceramic tile, with a partial offset resulting from amortization of intangibles and from the write-off of licenses, patents, and goodwill of certain of the company's industrial specialties businesses.

The company's year-end ratio of current assets to current liabilities was approximately 1.3 to 1 as compared to 1.8 to 1 reported in 1989. The contributing factor to this decline was an increase in the short-term debt as previously mentioned.

As of year-end 1990, long-term debt represented 26% of shareholders' equity, an increase from the 19% reported in 1989. Long-term debt does not include the company's guarantee of the ESOP loan, which has been recorded both as a long-term obligation and as a reduction of shareholders' equity.

Consolidated results

Net sales for 1990 were $2.52 billion, an increase of 1% over the 1989 figure of $2.49 billion. Excluding the benefit from translating foreign currency sales to U.S. dollars at higher exchange rates, 1990 sales would have declined by 1%. Although the real market potential for the company declined throughout 1990, sales exceeded those of the prior year in each of the first three quarters. The decline accelerated in the fourth quarter putting increased pressure on operating margins and negatively impacting 1990 results. In North America, further reduction of expenses and curtailment of production schedules occurred in late 1990. On a positive note, the opportunity in Europe remained encouraging.

Net earnings in 1990 were $141.0 million, compared with $187.6 million in 1989—a 25% decrease. Net earnings per common share were $3.12 on a primary basis and $2.86 on a fully diluted basis compared with $3.92 and $3.72, respectively, for 1989. The return on average common shareholders' equity in 1990 was 13.0% compared with 17.9% in 1989.

Net earnings included operating losses from discontinued businesses and losses on the provision for disposition of discontinued businesses totaling $13.4 million in 1990 compared with earnings and gains from discontinued businesses of $29.9 million in 1989. (These 1990 losses reflected the provisions for disposition of three noncore businesses in 1991, certain industrial specialty businesses in 1990, and additional provisions for costs and expenses related to the businesses sold in 1989. In late 1989, the company sold its carpet businesses and its subsidiary, Applied Color Systems, Inc.)

Effective January 1, 1990, the company implemented Financial Accounting Standard No. 96, "Accounting for Income Taxes," which provided a gain from the cumulative effect of change in accounting for income taxes of $8.0 million.

Earnings after tax from continuing businesses in 1990 were $146.4 million compared with $157.7 million in 1989. Earnings per share of common stock from continuing businesses in 1990 were $3.26 on a primary basis and $2.99 on a fully diluted basis, compared with 1989 levels of $3.26 on a primary basis and $3.11 on a fully diluted basis. Earnings from continuing businesses for 1990 reflected a decline in the company's effective tax rate to 34.4% compared with 35.3% in 1989.

The earnings from continuing businesses before income taxes were $223.1 million, an 8% decrease from 1989's $243.6 million. The gain from the sale of woodlands in 1990 of $60.4 million as compared to 1989's gain on sale of woodlands of $9.5 million helped to minimize the decline in profitability. Items that partially offset this benefit included: costs and expenses associated with the proxy contest, legal and financial advice, litigation costs related to Armstrong's response to a corporate takeover threat, and the First City settlement totaling $15.4 million in 1990 and $3.6 million in 1989; the 1990 expenses of $2.1 million related to provisions for the write-down of assets of one of the company's small floor covering business units; accrued severance pay of $3.1 million in 1990 and $5.9 million in 1989 related to personnel reduction and restructuring; the costs and expenses of $1.6 million associated with the closing of Armstrong's wall panel manufacturing facility in Toronto, Canada; and costs of $5.0 million associated with litigation involving residual claims in connection with a manufacturing facility that Armstrong once owned. 1989 included a gain of $4.4 million from the asbestos-related insurance settlement.

Earnings from continuing businesses before other income (expense) and income taxes were $239.6 million in 1990, a 17% decrease from the $288.1 million in 1989. Competitive pricing pressures and promotional pricing negatively impacted net sales, but a combination of lower raw material costs and manufacturing productivity improvements more than offset pricing pressures. Lower unit volumes in many businesses, in combination with higher costs associated with new manufacturing capacity added over the past couple of years, and the effects of inflation on nonmanufacturing expenses adversely affected profits. The translation of foreign currency expenses to U.S. dollars at higher exchange rates accounts for half of the year-to-year nonmanufacturing expense increase. The 1989 results included the termination of the contributory annuity portion of an employee retirement plan, which reduced costs by $8.0 million. Also, 1989 included $5.0 million of charges for obsolescence of machinery and other costs associated with the modernization program at the Lansdale, Pennsylvania, plant of American Olean Tile Company, Inc., a company subsidiary.

Geographic area results (see page 27)

United States—Sales decreased 2% while operating profits increased 3% when compared with 1989. The U.S. end-use markets, while soft at the beginning of 1990, weakened rapidly in the latter part of the year. Reduced opportunity was noted in nonresidential construction, new housing starts, sales of existing homes, and consumer household durable goods.

Sales and margins were positively affected by higher sales prices in some businesses, generally lower raw material prices that began to increase in late 1990, improved manufacturing processes, a continued emphasis on cost control, the positive influences of the company's quality management process, and accentuation on serving the customer and on employee involvement. These factors were more than sufficient to offset generally lower unit sales volumes, competitive and promotional sales pricing that was needed to obtain the volume that was available, and higher costs resulting from normal inflationary pressures as well as from capacity added over the past couple of years. The 1990 results also included a provision for the write-down of the assets of one of the company's small floor covering businesses, while 1989 results included a charge for obsolescence of machinery and other costs associated with the modernization of the Lansdale Plant of American Olean.

Export trade sales of Armstrong products in 1990 from the U.S. improved 7% when compared with 1989.

Europe—The markets for the company's building and insulation products businesses remained strong for 1990. However, the European flooring business continued to be affected by the weakness in the British economy. Total Europe sales and operating profits increased 19%. Translation of foreign currency sales into U.S. dollars at higher exchange rates accounted for approximately two-thirds of the year-to-year improvement in both sales and operating profits.

The principal reasons for the year-to-year improvement in profit were the effects of foreign currency translation mentioned previously, higher unit sales volume, higher sales prices in some businesses, and generally lower raw material prices.

Capital investments increased in 1990 because of expenditures to expand capacity and modernize manufacturing facilities, primarily in the ceilings and industry products areas.

Other foreign—Sales and operating profits in 1990 declined from those of 1989 by 10% and 47%, respectively. The Canadian and Australian economies were in a recession, and the market opportunity for the company's products was significantly reduced. In contrast, improved results were recorded in Southeast Asia.

The principal reasons for the operating profit reduction were lower unit sales volume, competitive pricing pressures, and a provision for costs associated with the closing of Armstrong's wall panel manufacturing facility in Toronto during 1990.

Industry segment results (see page 27)

Floor coverings—During 1990, sales and operating profits for this segment declined 2% and 5%, respectively. Weak market conditions, most pronounced in the English-speaking countries outside the United States, and reduced commercial opportunities in North America adversely affected results. Resilient flooring in North America remained relatively strong when compared with other parts of the floor covering segment.

Factors related to the lower profitability were: a decline in unit volume in some portions of the segment, increased fixed costs associated with manufacturing capacity added over the past couple of years, normal inflationary factors, and the write-down of assets of one of the company's small floor coverings business units. The 1989 operating profit included a charge of $5.0 million for obsolescence of machinery and other costs associated with the modernization project at the Lansdale Plant of the company's subsidiary, American Olean Tile Company, Inc. Providing some offsets to these negative factors were: higher sales prices; margin improvements resulting from the introduction of a wide variety of new products; lower raw material prices, which began to move higher toward the end of 1990; and improved manufacturing efficiencies.

Capital investments in the floor coverings segment, while lower than those of previous years, continued at high levels. In 1990, American Olean completed the $21 million project to modernize its plant in Lansdale. This project substantially expanded capacity, improved yields, increased manufacturing flexibility, and reduced costs. Other capital investments were made to obtain process and quality improvements, cost and cycle time reductions, and new product capabilities.

Building products—Worldwide sales grew by 2% with strong growth noted in Europe and Southeast Asia. However, much of this growth was offset by the continuing decline in the North American commercial construction markets and competitive pricing for projects in progress.

Operating profits improved 13%, but both years included gains from the sale of woodlands. These gains amounted to $60.4 million in 1990 and $9.5 million in 1989. Adverse factors affecting the 1990 results included lower unit volume in North America; worldwide competitive pricing pressures; the start-up of the new St. Helens, Oregon, manufacturing facility; higher manufacturing costs; and the closing of the wall panel manufacturing facility in Toronto.

Capital investments, while lower than the previous year, reflect capacity additions in Europe and completion and start-up of the new St. Helens facility. During 1990, the company continued to invest in computerized logistic systems, manufacturing control systems, and warehouse management systems in order to improve customer service.

Furniture—Although this segment reported higher sales during the first half of 1990, the weakening economy and lower consumer confidence resulted in a sales decline during the second half. Total 1990 sales fell short of 1989 results by less than 1% with operating profits declining 31%.

Operating profit improvement in the first two quarters of 1990 was more than offset by the declines recorded during the last two quarters. Operating profits were adversely affected by weakening economic conditions and consumer confidence, promotional pricing needed to obtain the volume that was available, and costs associated with capacity added over the past couple of years.

Capital investments in 1990 included the purchase of an idle manufacturing facility in High Point, North Carolina, from another furniture company.

Industry products—Worldwide 1990 net sales increased 14% with operating profits increasing 19% when compared with 1989. Results for the worldwide insulation business set new records due to strong demand for these products on the European continent. The worldwide gasket materials business also provided improved results when compared with 1989.

Translation of foreign currency into U.S. dollars at higher exchange rates accounted for about half of the sales improvement and profit increase.

During 1990, ground was broken in Münster, Germany, for a new European development center for industry products. In addition, construction began on a new pipe insulation manufacturing facility in the Atlanta area.

ARMSTRONG WORLD INDUSTRIES, INC., AND SUBSIDIARIES

SIX-YEAR SUMMARY

For year		1991	1990	1989	1988	1987	1986
Net sales	$(millions)	2,439.3	2,518.8	2,488.7	2,261.2	1,969.6	1,602.3
Cost of goods sold	$(millions)	1,801.1	1,816.6	1,764.0	1,611.0	1,383.6	1,117.5
Selling and administrative expense	$(millions)	468.3	462.6	436.6	392.0	339.0	286.2
Interest expense	$(millions)	45.8	37.5	40.5	25.8	11.5	5.4
Gain on sale of woodlands	$(millions)	—	60.4	9.5	1.9	—	—
Miscellaneous income (expense)	$(millions)	(23.8)	(39.4)	(13.5)	11.7	3.0	1.6
Earnings from continuing businesses before tax	$(millions)	100.3	223.1	243.6	246.0	238.5	194.8
Income taxes	$(millions)	39.7	76.7	85.9	92.4	97.4	82.6
Earnings from continuing businesses	$(millions)	60.6	146.4	157.7	153.6	141.1	112.2
As a percentage of sales		2.5%	5.8%	6.3%	6.8%	7.2%	7.0%
As a percentage of average monthly assets		2.9%	7.1%	8.3%	10.2%	11.6%	11.3%
Earnings from continuing businesses applicable to common stock (a)	$(millions)	41.2	126.9	148.0	153.2	140.7	111.8
Per common share—primary	$	1.11	3.26	3.26	3.31	2.98	2.33
Per common share—fully diluted (b)	$	1.11	2.99	3.11	3.31	2.98	2.33
Net earnings	$(millions)	48.2	141.0	187.6	162.7	150.4	122.4
As a percentage of sales		2.0%	5.6%	7.5%	7.2%	7.6%	7.6%
Net earnings applicable to common stock (a)	$(millions)	28.8	121.5	177.9	162.3	150.0	122.0
As a percentage of average shareholders' equity		3.3%	13.0%	17.9%	17.0%	17.6%	16.0%
Per common share—primary	$	.77	3.12	3.92	3.51	3.18	2.54
Per common share—fully diluted (b)	$	.77	2.86	3.72	3.51	3.18	2.54
Dividends declared per share of common stock	$	1.19	1.135	1.045	.975	.885	.7325
Purchases of property, plant, and equipment	$(millions)	133.8	195.1	231.0	198.7	183.0	139.8
Aggregate cost of acquisitions	$(millions)	—	16.1	—	355.8	71.5	53.1
Total depreciation and amortization	$(millions)	135.7	130.1	134.0	109.2	91.4	74.3
Average number of employees— continuing businesses		24,066	25,014	25,349	22,801	21,020	18,916
Average number of common shares outstanding	(millions)	37.1	38.8	45.4	46.2	47.2	48.1
YEAR-END POSITION							
Working capital	$(millions)	238.9	181.8	323.5	139.0	255.3	327.7
Net property, plant, and equipment	$(millions)	1,152.9	1,147.4	1,059.2	1,040.2	760.7	603.0
Total assets	$(millions)	2,149.9	2,146.3	2,033.0	2,097.7	1,602.5	1,298.2
Long-term debt	$(millions)	301.4	233.2	181.3	185.9	67.7	58.8
Total debt as a percentage of total capital (c)		46.9%	45.7%	36.1%	35.9%	22.8%	16.9%
Shareholders' equity	$(millions)	885.5	899.2	976.5	1,021.8	913.8	813.0
Book value per share of common stock	$	23.55	24.07	23.04	21.86	19.53	16.85
Number of shareholders (d) (e)		8,896	9,110	9,322	10,355	9,418	9,621
Common shares outstanding	(millions)	37.1	37.1	42.3	46.3	46.2	47.5
Market value per common share	$	29¼	25	37¼	35	32¼	29⅞

Notes:
(a) After deducting preferred dividend requirements.
(b) See italicized definition of fully diluted earnings per share on page 21.
(c) Total debt includes short-term debt, current installments of long-term debt, long-term debt, and ESOP loan guarantee. Total capital includes total debt and total shareholders' equity.
(d) Includes one trustee who is the shareholder of record on behalf of approximately 4,600 employees in 1991, 4,500 employees in 1990, 4,700 employees in 1989, and 4,400 employees in 1988 who have beneficial ownership through the company's retirement savings plans.
(e) Includes, for 1987 and 1986, a trustee who was the shareholder of record on behalf of approximately 11,000 employees who obtained beneficial ownership through the Armstrong Stock Ownership Plan, which was terminated at the end of 1987.

THE BOARD OF DIRECTORS
(as of January 1992)†

Wm. Wallace Abbott
Senior Advisor
to the Administrator
United Nations
Development Programme
(technical assistance to
developing countries)
Former Senior Vice President
The Procter & Gamble
Company
(cleaning, food and beverage,
personal care, and health-care
products)

William W. Adams
Chairman of the Board
and President
Armstrong World Industries, Inc.

Francis V. Breeze*
Former Vice Chairman and
Chief Administrative Officer
PPG Industries, Inc.
(flat glass, chemicals, coatings,
and fiber glass)

Van C. Campbell*
Vice Chairman for
Finance and Administration
Corning Incorporated
(glass and ceramic products)
(elected effective March 1, 1991)

E. Allen Deaver
Executive Vice-President
Armstrong World Industries, Inc.

Barbara Hackman Franklin*
President
Franklin Associates
(management consulting)

Mary Joan Glynn
Senior Vice-President
BBDO
(advertising agency)

Michael C. Jensen
Edsel Bryant Ford Professor of
Business Administration
Harvard Business School

Joseph L. Jones
Former Chairman of the Board
and President
Armstrong World Industries, Inc.

George A. Lorch
Executive Vice-President
Armstrong World Industries, Inc.

James E. Marley*
President
and Chief Operating Officer
AMP Incorporated
(electrical/electronic connection
devices)

Robert F. Patton*
Chairman
Bank Consulting Associates
(financial institution consulting)

J. Phillip Samper
Former Vice Chairman
and Executive Officer
Eastman Kodak Company
(photographic, chemical, and
health-care products)
Former President
and Chief Executive Officer
Kinder-Care Learning
Centers, Inc.
(child day-care centers)

---

† *Retiring from the Board of
Directors on March 1, 1991, was
William M. Ellinghaus, former
Executive Vice Chairman, New York
Stock Exchange, Inc., and former
President, American Telephone and
Telegraph Company
(telecommunications).*

*Member of the Audit Committee

OFFICERS
(as of January 1992)

William W. Adams*
Chairman of the Board
and President

E. Allen Deaver*
Executive Vice-President

George A. Lorch*
Executive Vice-President

Henry A. Bradshaw*
Group Vice-President,
Building Products Operations

Dennis M. Draeger*
Group Vice-President,
Floor Products Operations

William W. Locke*
Group Vice-President,
International and Industry
Products Operations

L. A. Pulkrabek*
Senior Vice-President, Secretary
and General Counsel

William J. Wimer*
Senior Vice-President, Finance,
and Treasurer

Forbes H. Burgess
Vice-President and Director,
Business Information Services
and Manufacturing Science

Wendy W. Claussen
Vice-President and Director,
Product Styling and Design

Joseph E. Hennessey
Vice-President and Director,
Research and Development

John N. Jordin
Vice-President and Director,
Human Resources and
Government Affairs

E. Jürgen Philipp
Vice-President,
European Operations

Fredric A. Stoner
Vice-President and Director,
Advertising and Marketing
Services

Louis C. Varljen
Vice-President and Director,
Engineering

John C. Wylie
Vice-President,
Operations and Quality Management

Bruce A. Leech, Jr.*
Controller

Alan L. Brayman
Assistant Treasurer

Louis L. Davenport
Assistant Treasurer

Warren M. Posey
Assistant Treasurer

Claude L. Beaudoin
Assistant Secretary and
Associate General Counsel,
Patent and Trademark Affairs

John H. Miller, Jr.
Assistant Secretary and
Associate General Counsel,
Legal Affairs

Robert A. Sills
Director, Taxes

**An executive officer, as defined by the
Securities and Exchange Commission, as
are Frederick B. Starr, President,
Thomasville Furniture Industries, Inc., and
William L. Snyder, President, American
Olean Tile Company, Inc.*

CORPORATE DATA

Corporate Address

Armstrong
World Industries, Inc.
313 West Liberty Street
P.O. Box 3001
Lancaster, Pa. 17604
717 397-0611

Transfer Agent and Registrar for Common Stock

First Chicago Trust
Company of New York
30 West Broadway
New York, N.Y. 10007

Dividends on Common and Preferred Stock

Disbursed directly by
Armstrong World Industries,
Inc., Lancaster, Pa.

Trustee for Debentures and Notes

The First National Bank
of Chicago
Mail Suite 0126
One First National Plaza
Chicago, Ill. 60670-0126

Trustee for Employee Stock Ownership Plan

Mellon Bank, N.A.
One Mellon Bank Center
Pittsburgh, Pa. 15258-0001

Stock Exchange Listings

(Symbol: ACK)
New York Stock
Exchange, Inc.
Philadelphia Stock
Exchange, Inc.
Pacific Stock Exchange, Inc.

Annual Meeting

The Annual Meeting of the
Armstrong Shareholders will
be held at 10 a.m., April 27,
1992, at the company's
general offices (Armstrong
House North) in Lancaster.

Investor Relations

Shareholders, security
analysts, portfolio managers,
and other representatives of
the investment community
who have questions about
Armstrong should address
them to:

Warren M. Posey
Assistant Treasurer
Armstrong
World Industries, Inc.
313 West Liberty Street
P.O. Box 3001
Lancaster, PA 17604
Phone: 717 396-2216

You may obtain, without cost, a copy of Armstrong's Annual
Report on Form 10-K by writing to the Secretary's Office at the
corporate address. For inquiries concerning shareholder records
or for ordering printed reports, call:

Shareholder records
717 396-2810
Report ordering
717 396-2436

Subsidiaries and Affiliates in the United States
(as of January 1992)

American Olean Tile
Company, Inc.
Lansdale, Pa.

Armstrong Cork Finance
Corporation
Wilmington, Del.

IWF, Inc.
Reno, Nev.

Armstrong
Realty Group, Inc.
Lancaster, Pa.

Armstrong Ventures, Inc.
Wilmington, Del.

ArmStar
(50-percent-owned
unincorporated affiliate)
Lenoir City, Tenn.

Armstrong World
Industries
(Delaware) Inc.
Wilmington, Del.

AWI (Nevada), Inc.
Reno, Nev.

BEGA/FS, Inc.
(60 percent owned)
Carpinteria, Calif.

Charleswater
Products, Inc.
Lancaster, Pa.

Chemline Industries, Inc.
Lancaster, Pa.

Design Ideas Incorporated
Lancaster, Pa.

Thomasville Furniture
Industries, Inc.
Thomasville, N.C.

Fayette Enterprises, Inc.
Fayette, Miss.

Gordon's, Inc.
Johnson City, Tenn.

*Thomasville
Upholstery, Inc.*
Statesville, N.C.

The W. W. Henry
Company
Huntington Park, Calif.

Subsidiaries and Affiliates Outside the United States
(as of January 1992)

Armstrong—ABC Co., Ltd.
(50 percent owned)
Tokyo, Japan

ISA Co., Ltd.
(50 percent owned)
Shizuoka City, Japan

Armstrong FSC, Ltd.
Hamilton, Bermuda

Armstrong (Japan) K.K.
Tokyo, Japan

Armstrong-Nylex Pty. Ltd.
(51 percent owned)
Melbourne, Australia

Armstrong (Singapore)
Pte. Ltd.
Singapore, Republic
of Singapore

Armstrong Textile Rubber
Products Company
Shanghai Ltd.
(51 percent owned)
Shanghai, People's Republic
of China

Armstrong World
Industries Canada Ltd.
Montreal, Quebec, Canada

Armstrong World
Industries—France, S.A.
Montrouge, France

Armstrong World
Industries, G.m.b.H.
Münster, Germany

Armstrong World
Industries (H.K.) Limited
Hong Kong

Armstrong World
Industries Italia S.r.l.
Varese, Italy

Armstrong World
Industries Ltd.
London, England

*Armstrong Cork (Ireland)
Limited*
Dublin, Ireland

*Armstrong Europe
Services*
London, England

Inarco Limited
(40 percent owned)
Bombay, India

Armstrong World
Industries Pty. Ltd.
Sydney, New South Wales,
Australia

Armstrong World
Industries, S.A.
Palafrugell, Spain

Armstrong World
Industries (Schweiz) A.G.
Rothrist, Switzerland

Armstrong
World Industries
(Thailand) Ltd.
Bangkok, Thailand

ISO Holding, A.G.
Schwyz, Switzerland

*Armstrong World
Industries—A.C.I. B.V.*
Hoogezand, Netherlands

*Armstrong
World Industries
Netherlands B.V.*
Hoogezand, Netherlands

*Armstrong World
Industries—Belgium S.A.*
Ghlin, Belgium

*Armstrong World
Industries—Pontarlier S.A.*
Pontarlier, France

Liberty Commercial
Services Ltd.
Hamilton, Bermuda

Recubrimientos
Interceramic S.A. de C.V.
(49 percent owned)
Chihuahua, Mexico

Plants (total: 89)
(as of January 1992)

Armstrong
World Industries, Inc.,
plants (22)
Atlanta, Ga.
Beaver Falls, Pa.
Beech Creek, Pa.
Braintree, Mass.
Carpinteria, Calif.
El Monte, Calif.
Franklin Park, Ill.
Fulton, N.Y.
Greenville, S.C.
Hilliard, Ohio
Jackson, Miss.
Kankakee, Ill.
Lancaster, Pa.
Macon, Ga.
Marietta, Pa.
Mobile, Ala.
Pensacola, Fla.
St. Helens, Ore.
South Gate, Calif.
Sparrows Point, Md.
Stillwater, Okla.
Tampa, Fla.

American Olean Tile
Company, Inc.,
plants (6)
Fayette, Ala.
Jackson, Tenn.
Lansdale, Pa.
Lewisport, Ky.
Olean, N.Y.
Quakertown, Pa.

ArmStar plant (1)
Lenoir City, Tenn.

BEGA/FS, Inc., plant (1)
Carpinteria, Calif.

Thomasville Furniture
Industries, Inc.,
plants (23)
Appomattox, Va.
Brookneal, Va.
Carysbrook, Va.
Lenoir, N.C.
Pleasant Garden, N.C.
Sawmills, N.C.
Thomasville, N.C. (15)
West Jefferson, N.C.
Winston-Salem, N.C.

*Fayette Enterprises, Inc.,
plant (1)*
Fayette, Miss.

Gordon's, Inc., plant (1)
Johnson City, Tenn.

*Thomasville Upholstery,
Inc., plants (4)*
Conover, N.C.
Hickory, N.C.
Statesville, N.C.
Troutman, N.C.

The W. W. Henry
Company plants (7)
Arlington, Tex.
Chicago, Ill.
Dallas, Ga.
Dover, Ohio
Maywood, Calif.
Orange, Calif.
South River, N.J.

Plants of subsidiaries and
affiliates outside the
United States (23)
Australia
Braeside, Victoria
Thomastown, Victoria
Belgium
Ghlin
Canada
Gatineau, Quebec
Montreal, Quebec
China, People's Republic of
Shanghai
England
Oldham
Tanfield Lea
Team Valley, Gateshead
Teesside, Thornaby,
Stockton-on-Tees
France
Pontarlier
Germany
Friesenhofen
Münster
India
Baroda
Bhavnagar
Coimbatore
Thana
Italy
Trezzano Rosa
Mexico
Chihuahua
Netherlands
Hoogezand
Spain
Palafrugell (2)
Switzerland
Rothrist

ARMSTRONG OPERATING PRINCIPLES

- To respect the dignity and inherent rights of the individual human being in all dealings with people.

- To maintain high moral and ethical standards and to reflect honesty, integrity, reliability and forthrightness in all relationships.

- To reflect the tenets of good taste and common courtesy in all attitudes, words and deeds.

- To serve fairly and in proper balance the interests of all groups associated with the business—customers, stockholders, employees, suppliers, community neighbors, government and the general public.

CORPORATE QUALITY POLICY

- We are committed to quality performance.

- As an organization—and as individuals—we will continually seek out the specific needs of those who depend upon us.

- We will then consistently satisfy those needs by doing everything *right the first time*.

This entire Annual Report is printed on paper stock that is both *recycled* and *recyclable*. For more information on Armstrong's response to environmental concerns, see pages 14 and 15.

Appendix B—Assignment Material Solutions

CHAPTER 2

2–1.

	Category	Financial Statement(s)
Cash	A	BS
Accounts payable	L	BS
Common stock	OE	BS, SOE
Depreciation expense	E	IS, SCF
Net sales	R	IS
Income tax expense	E	IS
Short-term investments	A	BS
Gain on sale of land	G	IS
Retained earnings	OE	BS, SOE
Dividends payable	L	BS
Accounts receivable	A	BS
Short-term debt	L	BS

2–3. Prepare the retained earnings portion of a statement of change in owners' equity for the year ended December 31, 1993:

Retained earnings, December 31, 1992	$318,000
Add: Net income for the year	97,000
Less: Dividends for the year	(43,000)
Retained earnings, December 31, 1993	$372,000

2–5. Set up the accounting equation and show the effects of the asset sale and payment of liabilities. Since total assets must equal total liabilities and owners' equity, the amount of the other assets is calculated by subtracting the cash amount given from the total of liabilities and owners' equity.

	A	=	L		OE
	Cash +	Other assets =	Lia- bilities +		Owners' equity
Data given	8,000 +	? =	20,000 +		5,000
Calculate other assets to make equation balance		17,000			
	8,000 +	17,000 =	20,000 +		5,000
Sale of other assets	+12,500	−17,000 =			−4,500 {loss on sale
Pay liabilities	−20,000		= −20,000		
Balance	500 +	0 =	0 +		500

2–7. Set up the accounting equation at the beginning of the year; enter given changes during the year; enter given end-of-the-year data; solve for the unknown. Remember that net assets is another term for owners' equity.

	A	=	L	+	OE	
Beginning of year	12	=	7	+	5	
Changes during year			−1	+	+3	(net income)
					?	(dividends)
End of year	?	=	?	+	6	

By looking at the OE column, you can see that dividends must have been $2. Also by looking at the model, you can see that year-end liabilities are $6 and that therefore year-end assets must be $12; thus total assets did not change during the year.

2–9. *a.* Financial highlights on the inside of the front cover (the first page of the report that is reproduced in Appendix A), and six-year summary on page 38.

b. On page 31, that the ". . . financial statements referred to above present fairly, in all material respects, the financial position of Armstrong World Industries, Inc. and subsidiaries at December 31, 1991 and 1990 and the results of their operations and their cash flows for each of the years in the three-year period ended December 31, 1991, in conformity with generally accepted accounting principles."

2–11. Amounts in the balance sheet reflect the following use of the data given:

a. An asset should have a "probable future economic benefit"; therefore the accounts receivable are stated at the amount expected to be collected from customers.

b. Assets are reported at original cost, not current "worth." Depreciation in accounting reflects the spreading of the cost of an asset over its estimated useful life.

c. Assets are reported at original cost, not an assessed or appraised value.

d. The amount of the note payable is calculated using the accounting equation of A = L + OE. Total assets can be determined based on items *a*, *b*, and *c*; total owners' equity is known after considering item *e*; and the note payable is the difference between total liabilities and the accounts payable.

e. Retained earnings is the difference between cumulative net income and cumulative dividends.

Assets		Liabilities	
Cash	$ 700	Note payable . .	$ 2,200
Accounts receivable	3,400	Accounts payable	3,400
Land	7,000	Total liabilities. .	$ 5,600
Automobile	9,000	Owners' equity:	
Less:		Capital stock . .	$ 8,000
Accumulated		Retained earnings	3,500
depreciation . . .	(3,000)	Total owners'	
		equity . . .	$11,500
		Total liabilities +	
Total assets	$17,100	owners' equity.	$17,100

2–13. The strategy is to enter the amount of the change in the amount of each asset, liability, and owners' equity item between the two dates. This change amount is then used in the statement of cash flows. Note that because the retained earnings section of the balance sheet is an analysis of the change in retained earnings for the month, the net income and dividend amounts for the month are shown in the change column, not the differences between the January and February net income and dividend amounts.

MILLCO INC.
Balance Sheets
January 31 and February 28, 1994

	February 28	January 31	*Change (000 omitted)*
Assets			
Cash	$ 42,000	$ 37,000	+ 5
Accounts receivable . .	64,000	53,000	+11
Merchandise inventory.	81,000	94,000	−13
Total current assets	$187,000	$184,000	
Plant and equipment:			
Production equipment	166,000	152,000	+14

(continued)

	February 28	January 31	Change (000 omitted)
Less: Accumulated depreciation . . .	(24,000)	(21,000)	(+ 3)
Total assets.	$329,000	$315,000	
Liabilities			
Short-term debt	$ 44,000	$ 44,000	—
Accounts payable . . .	37,000	41,000	− 4
Other accrued liabilities	21,000	24,000	− 3
Total current liabilities . . .	$102,000	$109,000	− 7
Long-term debt	33,000	46,000	−13
Total liabilities	$135,000	$155,000	
Owners' Equity			
Common stock, no par value, 40,000 shares authorized, 30,000 and 28,000 shares issued, respectively .	$104,000	$ 96,000	+ 8
Retained earnings:			
Beginning balance . .	$ 64,000	$ 43,000	
Net income for month	36,000	29,000	+36*
Dividends	(10,000)	(8,000)	−10*
Ending balance . . .	$ 90,000	$ 64,000	
Total owners' equity.	$194,000	$160,000	
Total liabilities and owners' equity . . .	$329,000	$315,000	

* for the month

The statement of cash flows uses the change amounts from the two month-end balance sheets, as follows:

MILLCO, INC.
Statement of Cash Flows
For the Month Ended February 28, 1994

Cash flows from operating activities:

Net income	$ 36,000
Add (Deduct) items not affecting cash	
Depreciation expense (Increase in accumulated depreciation)	3,000
Increase in accounts receivable	(11,000)
Decrease in merchandise inventory	13,000
Decrease in current liabilities	(7,000)
Net cash provided by operating activities.	$ 34,000

Cash flows from investing activities:

Purchased production equipment	$(14,000)

Cash flows from financing activities:

Paid long-term debt	(13,000)
Cash received from sale of common stock	8,000
Dividends paid	(10,000)
Net cash used for financing activities	$(15,000)
Net increase in cash for the month.	$ 5,000

Notice that the statement of cash flows has explained the change in cash during the month (it increased $5,000) by using the change in every other balance sheet item.

2–15.

Balance Sheet
December 31, 1990

Assets

Cash	$ 24.6
All other assets	2,121.7
Total assets	$2,146.3

Liabilities and Owners' Equity

Liabilities	$1,247.1
Owners' equity:	
Retained earnings	1,224.1
All other OE	(324.9)
Total OE	$ 899.2
Total L + OE	$2,146.3

Income Statement
For the Year Ended
December 31, 1991

Revenues	$2,439.3
Expenses	2,391.1
Net income	$ 48.2

Statement of
Cash Flows
For the Year Ended
Dec. 31, 1991

Cash provided by operating activities	$ 150.4
Cash used for investing activities	(130.4)
Cash used for financing activities	(36.9)
Effect of exchange rate changes	.5
Cash at the beginning of the year	24.6
Cash at the end of the year	$ 8.2

Statement of Changes in
Owners' Equity
For the Year Ended
December 31, 1991

Retained earnings:		
Balance, Dec. 31, 1990	$1,224.1	
Net Income	48.2	
Dividends	(63.6)	
Balance, Dec. 31, 1991	$1,208.7	
All other owners' equity:		
Balance, Dec. 31, 1990	$ (324.9)	
Changes	1.7	
Balance, Dec. 31, 1991	$ (323.2)	

Balance Sheet
December 31, 1991

Assets

Cash	$ 8.2
All other assets	2,141.7
Total assets	$2,149.9

Liabilities and Owners' Equity

Liabilities	$1,264.4
Owners' equity:	
Retained earnings	1,208.7
All other OE	(323.2)
Total OE	$ 885.5
Total L + OE	$2,149.9

CHAPTER 3

3–1. Calculate the return from each investment.

    a. $\text{ROI} = \dfrac{\text{Amount of return}}{\text{Amount invested}}$ Julie: $\dfrac{50}{560} = 8.93\%$

                                                                  Sam: $\dfrac{53}{620} = 8.55\%$

Julie's investment is preferred because it has the higher ROI.
b. Risk is a principal factor to be considered.

3–3. Calculate the amount of return from each alternative, and then calculate the ROI of the additional return from the higher-paying investment relative to the $50 that must be invested to get the higher return.

$$\text{ROI} \times \text{Amount invested} = \text{Amount of return}$$

        Alternative 1 $0.10 \times \$500 = \$50$

        Alternative 2 $0.105 \times \$550 = \$57.75$

The extra amount of return of $7.75 on an additional investment of $50 is an ROI of 15.5 percent. ($7.75/$50 = 0.155). Therefore do not pay an interest rate of more than 15.5 percent to borrow the additional $50 needed for investment alternative 2.

3–5. ROI = Margin × Turnover

              = (Profits/Sales) × (Sales/Average assets)

a. $0.18 = 0.12 \times (600{,}000/?)$? (Average assets) = $400,000

b. Turnover = Sales/Average assets

        $1.3 = ?/950{,}000$? (Sales) = 1,235,000

        ROI = (Profits/Sales) × Turnover

              = $(78{,}000/1{,}235{,}000) \times 1.3$

              = 8.21%

c.   ROI = Margin × Turnover

      $7.37\% = ? \times 2.1$? = 3.5%

3–7. Remember that net assets is the same as owners' equity.

Beginning net assets =	346,800
Add net income	42,300
Less dividends	(12,000)
Ending net assets =	377,100

$$\text{ROE} = \text{Net income/Average owners' equity}$$
$$= 42,300/((346,800 + 377,100)/2)$$
$$= 11.7\%$$

3–9. *a.* ROI = Margin × Turnover

$$= 0.32 \times 0.4$$
$$= 12.8\%$$

Turnover = Sales/Average assets

$$0.4 = ?/800,000 \qquad\qquad ? \text{ (Sales)} = 320,000$$

b. ROI = Margin × Turnover

$$.128 = 0.15 \times ? \qquad\qquad ? \text{ (Turnover)} = 0.85333$$

Turnover = Sales/Average assets

$$0.85333 = ?/800,000 \qquad\qquad ? \text{ (Sales)} = \$682,664$$

3–11. *a.* ROI = Margin × Turnover

$$= (48.2/2,439.3) \times 2,439.3/((2,149.9 + 2,146.3)/2)$$
$$= 0.020 \times 1.14$$
$$= 2.3\%$$

b. ROE = Net income/Average owners' equity

$$= 48.2/((885.5 + 899.2)/2)$$
$$= 5.4\%$$

c. Working capital = Current assets − Current liabilities

	12/31/91	12/31/90
Current assets	$718.8	$726.6
− Current liabilities	479.9	544.8
= Working capital	$238.9	$181.8

d. Current ratio = Current assets/Current liabilities

12/31/91	718.8/479.9 = 1.50
12/31/90	726.6/544.8 = 1.33

e. Acid-test ratio = (Cash and cash equivalents
+ Accounts and notes receivable)/Current liabilities

	12/31/91	12/31/90
Cash and cash equivalents	$ 8.2	$ 24.6
Accounts and notes receivable	305.3	302.7
Total	$313.5	$327.3
Current liabilities	$479.9	$544.8
Acid-test ratio	0.65	0.60

3–13. *a.*

	1/31/93	1/31/92
Working capital:		
Current assets	$14	$18
Current liabilities	9	6
Working capital	$ 5	$12
Current ratio	14/9 = 1.56	18/6 = 3.0

b. Even though the firm has more cash at January 31, 1993, it is less liquid based on measures of working capital and current ratio.

c. Accounts receivable were collected, inventories were reduced, and current liabilities increased. These changes and the increase in cash are all possible because changes in a firm's cash position and its profitability are not directly related.

3–15. *a.*

	Do Not Prepay Accounts Payable	Prepay Accounts Payable
Working capital:		
Current assets	$12,639	$8,789
Current liabilities	7,480	3,630
Working capital	$ 5,159	$5,159
Current ratio	1.7	2.4

Early payment of the accounts payable does not affect working capital but does improve the current ratio. Is this balance sheet "window dressing" worth the opportunity cost of not being able to invest the cash?

b.

	Without Loan	With Loan
Working capital:		
Current assets	$12,639	$17,639
Current liabilities	7,480	12,480
Working capital	$ 5,159	$ 5,159
Current ratio	1.7	1.4

If the loan is taken after the end of the fiscal year, the current ratio on the year-end balance sheet will be higher than if the loan is taken before the end of the year. Working capital is not affected.

3–17. A constant rate of growth plots as a straight line when a logarithmic scale is used. This makes it easier to reach an appropriate conclusion from the data.

CHAPTER 4

4–1.

Trans-action	Cash +	Accounts Receivable +	Merchandise Inventory +	Equipment =	Note Payable +	Accounts Payable +	Paid-In Capital +	Retained Earnings +	Revenue −	Expenses
			Assets		=	*Liabilities* +		*Owners' equity*		
a.	+ 180						+ 180			
b.	+ 100				+ 100					
c.	− 75			+ 75						
d.	− 40									− 40
e.	− 90		+ 150			+ 60				
f.	+ 65		− 40						+ 65	− 40
g.						+ 20				− 20
h.	− 120		+ 400			+ 280				
i.	+ 130	+ 320	− 300						+ 450	− 300
j.						+ 35				− 35
Totals	150 +	320 +	210 +	75 =	100 +	395 +	180	+	515 −	435

Month-end totals:	Assets	$755	
		Liabilities	$495
		Owners' equity	260
		Total	$755

Net income for the month:	Revenues	$515
	Expenses	435
	Net income	$ 80

4–3. *a.* Dr. Cash   180
Cr.   Paid-In Capital   180
b. Dr. Cash   100
Cr.   Note Payable   100
c. Dr. Equipment   75
Cr.   Cash   75
d. Dr. Rent Expense   40
Cr.   Cash   40
e. Dr. Merchandise Inventory   150
Cr.   Cash   90
Cr.   Accounts Payable   60
f. Dr. Cash   65
Cr.   Sales Revenue   65
Dr. Cost of Goods Sold   40
Cr.   Merchandise Inventory   40
g. Dr. Advertising Expense   20
Cr.   Accounts Payable   20
h. Dr. Merchandise Inventory   400
Cr.   Cash   120
Cr.   Accounts Payable   280

i. Dr. Cash   130
    Dr. Accounts Receivable   320
        Cr. Sales Revenue   450
    Dr. Cost of Goods Sold   300
        Cr. Merchandise Inventory   300
j. Dr. Wages Expense   35
        Cr. Accounts Payable   35

4–5. Prepare an analysis of the change in retained earnings for the month:

Balance, February 1, 1993		$630,000
Net income (loss):		
Revenues	$123,000	
Expenses	131,000	
Loss		(8,000)
Dividends		(12,000)
Balance, February 28, 1993		$610,000

4–7. *a.* 4/1/93

    Cr. Note Receivable   6,000
        Cr. Accounts Receivable   6,000

b. 12/31/93

    Dr. Interest Receivable   675
        Cr. Interest Revenue   675
    (0.15 × 6,000 × 9/12)

c. 3/31/94

    Dr. Cash   6,900
        Cr. Note Receivable   6,000
        Cr. Interest Receivable   675
        Cr. Interest Revenue   225

In *c*, only $675 of the total interest of $900 had been accrued, so the interest receivable is reduced by the $675 that had been accrued in 1993; the other $225 that is received is recorded as interest revenue for 1994, the year in which it was earned.

Horizontal model alternative to journal entries.

a. Receipt of note on April 1, 1993:

Balance Sheet	Income Statement
Assets = Liabilities + Owners' equity ← Net income = Revenues − Expenses	
Note Receivable	
+6,000	
Account Receivable	
−6,000	

b. Accrual of 9 month's interest at December 31, 1993:

Balance Sheet	Income Statement
Assets = Liabilities + Owners' equity ← Net income = Revenues − Expenses	
Interest Receivable	Interest Revenue
+675	+675

c. Collection of note and interest at March 31, 1994 (only $675 of the interest revenue had been accrued in *b*, so the other $225 is recorded as revenue in 1994, the year it was earned and received):

Balance Sheet	Income Statement
Assets = Liabilities + Owners' equity ← Net income = Revenues − Expensesp	
Cash	Interest Revenue
+6,900	+225
Note Receivable	
−6,000	
Interest Receivable	
−675	

4–9. *a.* 1/10/93

Dr. Paper Napkin Expense	4,800	
(or Supplies Expense)		
Cr. Cash		4,800

To record as an expense the cost of paper napkins purchased for cash.

b. 1/31/93

Dr. Paper Napkins on Hand	3,850	
(or Supplies)		
Cr. Paper Napkin Expense		3,850
(or Supplies Expense)		

To remove from the expense account and set up as an asset the cost of paper napkins on hand January 31.

c. 1/10/93

Dr. Paper Napkins on Hand	4,800	
(or Supplies)		
Cr. Cash		4,800

To set up as an asset the cost of paper napkins purchased for cash.

d. 1/31/93

Dr. Paper Napkin Expense 950
(or Supplies Expense)
    Cr. Paper Napkins on Hand 950
To record the cost of paper napkins used in January.

e. Each approach results in the same expense for January and the same asset amount on the January 31 balance sheet.

Horizontal model alternative to journal entries.

a. 1/10/93 Record as an expense the cost of paper napkins purchased for cash.

Balance Sheet	Income Statement
Assets = Liabilities + Owners' equity ←	Net income = Revenues − Expenses
Cash −4,800	Supplies Expense −4,800

b. 1/31/93 Remove from the expense account and set up as an asset the cost of the paper napkins on hand January 31.

Balance Sheet	Income Statement
Assets = Liabilities + Owners' equity ←	Net income = Revenues − Expenses
Supplies +3,850	Supplies Expense +3,850 (a reduction in Supplies Expense)

c. 1/10/93 Set up as an asset the cost of paper napkins purchased for cash.

Balance Sheet	Income Statement
Assets = Liabilities + Owners' equity ←	Net income = Revenues − Expenses
Supplies +4,800 Cash −4,800	

d. 1/31/93 Record the cost of paper napkins used in January.

Balance Sheet	Income Statement
Assets = Liabilities + Owners' equity ←	Net income = Revenues − Expenses
Supplies −950	Supplies Expense −950

e. Each approach results in the same expense for January and the same asset amount on the January 31 balance sheet.

4–11.

Big Blue Rental Corp. Income Statement Month of August 1993	Preliminary	Adjustments/ Corrections Debit	Credit	Final
Commision revenue . . .	$ 4,500	$	a. $200	$ 4,700
Interest revenue	850		f. 140	990
Total revenues.	$ 5,350	$	$340	$ 5,690
Rent expense	$ 510	$	e. $340	$ 170
Wages expense	1,190	d. 130		1,320
Supplies expense.	—	b. 180		180
Interest expense	—	c. 20		20
Total expenses.	$ 1,700	$330	$340	$ 1,690
Net income	$ 3,650	$330	$680	$ 4,000

Big Blue Rental Corp. Balance Sheet August 31, 1993	Preliminary	Debit	Credit	Final
Cash	$ 400	$	$	$ 400
Notes receivable	13,000			13,000
Commissions receivable	—	a. 200		200
Interest receivable	—	f. 140		140
Prepaid rent	—	d. 340		340
Supplies.	650		b. 180	470
Total assets	$14,050	$680	$180	$14,550
Accounts payable	$ 120	$	$	$ 120
Note payable	2,400			2,400
Interest payable	40		c. 20	60
Wages payable.	—		d. 130	130
Dividend payable	—		g. 1400	1,400
Total liabilities.	$ 2,560	$	$ 1,550	$ 4,110
Paid-in capital	$ 2,400	$	$	$ 2,400
Retained earnings:				
Balance, August 1 . . .	$ 5,440	$	$	$ 5,440
Net income	3,650	330	680	4,000*
Dividends	—	g. 1400		(1,400)
Balance, August 31	$ 9,090	$ 1,730	$ 680	$ 8,040
Total owners' equity . .	$11,490	$ 1,730	$ 680	$10,440
Total liabilities and owners' equity	$14,050	$ 1,730	$ 2,230	$14,550

* This line is the same as the bottom line of the income statement. Remember that net income is an increase in retained earnings, and net income is the link between the income statement and balance sheet.

4–13. *a.*   **Accounts Receivable**

Beginning balance	1,200	
February sales		February collections from
revenue	12,000	customers ?
Ending balance	900	

Solution: 1,200 + 12,000 − ? = 900

            12,300 =   ?   = Collections in February

Journal entries:

Dr. Accounts Receivable   12,000
     Cr. Sales Revenue   12,000
     Revenue from credit sales.

Cr. Cash   12,300
     Cr. Accounts Receivable   12,300
     Collections from customers.

a. Horizontal model alternative approach:

Balance Sheet	Income Statement

Assets = Liabilities + Owners' equity ← Net income = Revenues − Expenses

Beg. bal. Accounts Receivable
          1,200

Sales: Accounts Receivable   Sales Revenue
          +12,000   +12,000

Collect: Cash
          + ?

          Accounts Receivable
          − ?

End. bal. Accounts Receivable
          900

Amount of accounts receivable collected in cash:

Beg. bal. + Increase − Decrease   = End. bal.
            from   from
            sales   collections
   1,200 + 12,000 −   ?   =   900
                          12,300 = ? (collections)

b.   **Supplies on Hand**

Beginning balance	540	
Cost of supplies		Cost of supplies
purchased	?	used 2,340
Ending balance	730	

Solution: $540 + ? - 2,340 = 730$

$\qquad\qquad\qquad ? = 2,530 =$ Supplies purchased

Journal entries:

Dr. Supplies Expense. 2,340
    Dr. Supplies on Hand. 2,340
    Supplies used during month.

Dr. Supplies on Hand. 2,530
    Cr. Cash or Accounts Payable 2,530
    Supplies purchased during month.

b. Horizontal model alternative approach:

	Balance Sheet	Income Statement
	Assets = Liabilities + Owners' equity ← Net income = Revenues − Expenses	
Beg. bal.	Supplies on Hand 540	
Supplies used:	Supplies on Hand −2,340	Supplies Expense −2,340
Supplies purchased:	Cash − ?	*or* Accounts Payable + ?
	Supplies on Hand + ?	
End. bal.	Supplies on Hand 730	

Cost of supplies purchased in February:

Beg. bal. + Supplies − Supplies = End. bal.
$\qquad\qquad$ purchased $\quad$ used

$\quad$ 540 $\quad + \quad$? $\quad - \quad$ 2,340 $\quad = \quad$ 730

$\qquad$? (supplies purchased) = 2,530

c.

Wages Payable

Wages paid	3,800	Beginning balance	410
		Wages accrued	4,100
		Ending balance	?

Solution: $410 + 4,100 - 3,800 = ?$

$\qquad\qquad\qquad 710 = ? =$ Ending balance

Journal entries:

Dr. Wages Payable 3,800
    Cr. Cash. 3,800
    Wages paid during month.

> Dr. Wages Expense. 4,100
> Cr. Wages Payable 4,100
> Wage expense accrued during month.

    c. Horizontal model alternative approach:

	Balance Sheet		Income Statement	
	Assets = Liabilities + Owners' equity ← Net income = Revenues − Expenses			
Beg. bal.		Wages Payable 410		
Paid wages:	Cash −3,800	Wages Payable −3,800		
Wages accrued:		Wages Payable +4,100		Wages Expense −4,100
End. bal.		Wages Payable ?		

Ending balance of wages payable:

$$\text{Beg. bal.} + \text{Wages Accured} - \text{Wages paid} = \text{End. bal.}$$
$$410 + 4{,}100 - 3{,}800 = ?$$
$$710 = ?$$

4–15.

Transaction/Situation	Assets	Liabilities	Owners' Equity	Net Income
1. Paid on insurance premium of $360 for the coming year. An asset, Prepaid Insurance, was debited	+ 360 − 360			
2. Recognized insurance for one month from the above premium via a reclassification adjusting entry	− 30			− 30
3. Paid $800 of wages accrued at the end of the prior month	− 800	−800		
4. Paid $2,600 of wages for the current month	−2,600			−2,600
5. Accrued $600 of wages at the end of the current month		+600		− 600
6. Received cash of $1,500 on accounts receivable accured at the end of the prior month	+1,500 −1,500			

4–17. *a.* and *b.*

	Balance Sheet			Income Statement	
	Assets = Liabilities + Owners' equity	←	Net income = Revenues − Expenses		
	Cash	Retained Earnings			
Beg. bal.		$1,224.1			
Net earnings		48.2			
Dividends	−63.6	−63.6			
End. bal.		$1,208.7			

c. The dividend amount also appears as cash dividends paid in the "Cash flows from financing activities" section of the statement of cash flows.

4–19. *a.* If the payment of the premium on a fire insurance policy was recorded as insurance expense when the payment was made, and some or all of the premium was applied to the subsequent accounting period, it would be necessary to reclassify the amount of the premium applicable to the subsequent period from Insurance Expense to an asset account such as Prepaid Insurance in order to have a more accurate income statement and balance sheet at the end of the current period. This reclassification would achieve a better matching of revenues and expenses, because only the expense applicable to the current fiscal period would be subtracted from current period revenues to arrive at current period net income.

b. If insurance expense for the current period had been incurred, but the premium had not been paid by the end of the current period, it would be necessary to accrue the insurance expense and liability to the insurance company to achieve the matching referred to in *a*.

CHAPTER 5

5–1.

Balance per bank		$373	Balance per books		$844
Timing differences:			Timing difference:		
Less: Outstanding checks			Less: NSF check		(75)
No. 462	$13				
No. 483	50	(63)	Error:		
			No. 471 recorded as		
Add: Deposit in transit		450	$56 (should be $65)		(9)
Reconciled balance		$760	Reconciled balance		$760

5–3. *a.* Adjusting entries should be made for the book balance reconciling items:

For NSF check:

Dr. Accounts Receivable   75
    Cr. Cash   75

For error:

Dr. Liability or Expense account originally debited . . .   9
    Cr. Cash   9

Balance Sheet	Income Statement
Assets = Liabilities + Owners' equity ← Net income = Revenues − Expenses	

NSF check: Cash
−75

Accounts Receivable
+75

Error: Cash Liability or Expense account affected
                by $56 instead of $65
       −9   −9   or −9

b. The cash amount to be shown on the balance sheet is $760.

5–5. The balance sheet of Marco Sales Co. should show all of the firm's cash. This includes:

Reconciled cash balance of Denver office	$ 1,500
Reconciled cash balance of Chicago office	12,535
Cash in transit from Denver to Chicago	4,390
Total cash to be reported on balance sheet.	$18,425

5–7. If the total market value of all the securities were less than cost, the market value would be reported. (See text page 130.) The comment that cost approximates market value communicates the fact that there is no significant unrealized gain, or appreciation, in the carrying value of the securities.

5–9. *a.*

Allowance for Bad Debts

		1/1/93 Balance	13,400
January to November write-offs	?	January to November expense	21,462
(13,400 + 21,462 − ? = 9763)		(Dr. was to Bad Debts expense)	
	? = 25,099		
		11/30/93 Balance	9,763
Adjustment required	?		
b. (9,763 − ? = 9,500)			
	? = 263		
		12/31/93 Balance	9,500

Adjusting journal entry:

Dr. Allowance for Bad Debts   263
    Cr. Bad Debts Expense.   263
To adjust allowance account to appropriate balance, and
correct overstatement of expense recorded in January to
November period.

Horizontal model alternative to journal entry:

Balance Sheet	Income Statement
Assets = Liabilities + Owners' equity $\leftarrow$	Net income = Revenues − Expenses
Allowance for Bad Debts +263	Bad Debts Expense +263

c. The write-off will not have any effect on 1993 net income because the
   write-off affects both the accounts receivable asset and the allowance
   account contra asset. Net income was affected when the expense was
   recognized.

5–11. Selection and training relate to the efficiency with which a firm's operations
are carried out. Also having qualified and trained personnel should result in
more accuracy of the firm's record-keeping than having unqualified, un-
trained personnel.

5–13. *a.* 0.02 × $340,000,000 × 0.90 = $6.12 million
   b. Sales during last 10 days = 340,000,000/365 × 10 = 9,315,000. Discount
       expected = 0.02 × 9,315,000 × 0.9 = $167,670; this should be the
       balance in the allowance for cash discounts.
   c. By paying within 10 days instead of 30 days, the customer is "invest-
       ing" funds for 20 days, and receiving slightly more than a 2 percent
       return (for a $100 obligation, the return is $2 on an investment of $98) on
       that investment. But ROI is expressed as an annual percentage rate, and
       there are slightly more than 18 twenty-day periods in a year. Thus the
       annual ROI is a little greater than 36 percent.

5–15.

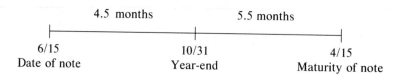

	4.5 months		5.5 months	
6/15		10/31		4/15
Date of note		Year-end		Maturity of note

a. Interest earned = 4,500 × 0.138 × 4.5/12 = 232.88
   Entry to accrue interest earned:

Dr. Interest Receivable. 232.88
    Cr. Interest Revenue. 232.88

Balance Sheet	Income Statement
Assets = Liabilities + Owners' equity ← Net income = Revenues − Expenses	

Interest accrual: Interest
Receivable
+232.88

Interest
Revenue
+ 232.88

b. What accounts are affected, and how are they affected?

Cash is being received for note principal and 10 month's interest.

Notes Receivable is reduced because note is being paid off.

Interest Receivable accrued at 10/31 is being collected.

Interest revenue for 5.5 months from 10/31 to 4/15 has been earned.

Dr. Cash	5,017.50	$(4,500 + (4,500 \times 0.138 \times 10/12))$
Cr. Note Receivable	4,500.00	
Cr. Interest Receivable.	232.88	(accrued at 10/31)
Cr. Interest Revenue	284.62	$(4,500 \times 0.138 \times 5.5/12)$

Balance Sheet	Income Statement
Assets = Liabilities + Owners' equity ← Net income = Revenues − Expenses	

Cash
+ 5,017.50
Note Receivable
− 4,500.00
Interest Receivable
− 232.88

Interest
Revenue
+ 284.62

5–17. *a.* Ending inventory:

	FIFO		*LIFO*	
Blowers	10 of 11/7 @ 200 =	$2,000	10 of 1/21 @ 200 =	$2,000
Mowers	20 of 9/20 @ 210 =	$4,200	20 of 4/6 @ 210 =	$4,200
	5 of 8/15 @ 215 =	1,075	5 of 5/22 @ 215 =	1,075
		$5,275		$5,275

There is no difference between ending inventories; therefore there will be no difference between cost of goods sold under either alternative because the amount of goods available for sale (the sum of the beginning inventory and purchases amounts) in this problem is not affected by the inventory cost-flow assumption.

b. Probably LIFO because the higher cost of the most recent (last-in) purchase will become part of the cost of goods sold, thus increasing cost, decreasing profits, and *decreasing income taxes.*

5–19. The older, relatively lower cost of inventory reductions is going to cost of goods sold. Revenues reflect current price levels. Thus inventory reductions result in profit increases because old, low costs are subtracted from current selling prices.

Inventory reductions of FIFO firms may also cause profit increases because the cost of inventory reductions may also be less than current cost, but the profit effect will not be so great as for a firm that uses LIFO.

5–21. ROI = Net income/Average assets.

		FIFO	*LIFO*
a.	Net income	$120	$100
	Average assets	600	580
	ROI	20%	17.2%
b.	Net income	$130	$140
	Average assets	650	620
	ROI	20%	22.6%

5–23. To result in better matching of revenues and expenses, and a more meaningful net income amount. Although the expenditure of cash has been made, the item relates to the earning of revenue in a subsequent accounting period.

5–25.

	Current Assets	*Current Liabilities*	*Owners' Equity*	*Net Income*
a. Accrued interest income of $15 on a note receivable	Interest Receivable +15			Interest Income +15
1. Determined that the Allowance for Doubtful Accounts Balance should be increased by $2,200.	Allowance for Doubtful Accounts −2,200			Bad Debts Expense −2,200
2. Recognized bank service charges of $30 for the month.	Cash −30			Service Charge Expense −30
3. Received $25 cash for interest receivable that had been accrued in a prior month.	Cash +25 Interest Receivable −25			
4. Purchased five units of a new item of inventory on account at a cost of $35 each.	Inventory +175	Accounts Payable +175		
5. Purchased 10 more units of the above item at a cost of $38 each.	Inventory +380	Accounts Payable +380		

(continued)

	Current Assets	Current Liabilities	Owners' Equity	Net Income
6. Sold eight of the items purchased in items 4 and 5 above, and recognized the cost of goods sold using the FIFO cost-flow assumption.	Inventory −289 (5 units @ $35) (3 units @ $38)			Cost of Goods sold −289

CHAPTER 6

6–1. *a.* Allocate purchase cost in proportion to appraised values.

$$\text{Cost of land} = (80,000/(80,000 + 20,000)) \times 90,000$$
$$= 72,000$$

b. Cost of land is amount paid plus cost of razing building.

$$\text{Cost of land} = 90,000 + 10,000 = 100,000$$

6–3. No. Cost of repairing damage is a loss due to carelessness. There is no future benefit from the repair cost; therefore it should not be capitalized as an asset.

6–5. *a.* Repair costs capitalized in error, $20,000.
Depreciation expense in current year on above amount:

To be depreciated	$20,000
Remaining life	5 years
Depreciation expense in current year	$4,000
Increase in repair expense	$ 20,000
Decrease in depreciation expense	(4,000)
Net increase in expenses	$ 16,000
Operating income originally reported	160,000
Corrected operating income	$144,000

b. ROI for current year based on original data:

$$\text{ROI} = \text{Operating income/Average total assets}$$

$$= 160,000/((940,000 + 1,020,000)/2)$$

$$= 16.3\%$$

ROI for current year based on corrected data:

Year-end assets originally reported		$1,020,000
Less net book value of mistakenly capitalized repair expense		
Cost	$20,000	
Less accumulated depreciation	(4,000)	(16,000)
Corrected year-end assets		$1,004,000

$$\text{ROI} = \text{Operating income/Average total assets}$$

$$= 144,000/((960,000 + 1,004,000)/2)$$

$$= 14.7\%$$

c. In subsequent years, depreciation expense will be too high, net income will be too low, and average assets will be too high. Thus ROI will be too low.

6–7. *a.*

$$\text{Amount to be depreciated} = \text{Cost} - \text{Salvage value}$$

$$\text{Annual depreciation expense} = \text{Amount to be depreciated/Life}$$

$$\text{Annual depreciation expense} = (80,000 - 8,000)/8 = \$9,000/\text{year}$$

After five years' accumulated depreciation = $9,000 \times 5 = \$45,000$

b. Straight-line rate = 1/8 = 12.5%; double the rate = 25%

			At End of Year	
Year	*Net Book Value at Beginning of Year*	*Depreciation Expense*	*Accumulated Depreciation*	*Net Book Value*
1	80,000	80,000 × 0.25 = 20,000	20,000	60,000
2	60,000	60,000 × 0.25 = 15,000	35,000	45,000
3	45,000	45,000 × 0.25 = 11,250	46,250	33,750

c.   Sum of digits 1 thru 8 = 36

Amount to be depreciated = Cost − Salvage = 72,000

For years 1 thru 5, depreciation expense
$$= (8 + 7 + 6 + 5 + 4)/36 \times \text{amount to be depreciated}$$
$$= 30/36 \times 72,000 = \$60,000$$

Under sum-of-the-years' digits depreciation, accumulated depreciation after five years is $60,000, compared to $45,000 under straight-line depreciation.

d.   Net book value = Cost − Accumulated depreciation

After eight years under each method the asset will have been depreciated to salvage value of 8,000; accumulated depreciation will be $72,000, and net book value will be $8,000.

6–9.

Cost of machine	$9,600
Estimated salvage value	1,200
Amount to be depreciated	$8,400
Estimated life	7 years

1. Straight-line depreciation:

Straight-line depreciation expense per year	$1,200
Depreciation expense for 1993 (9 months)	$900
Depreciation expense for 1994 (12 months)	$1,200

2. Sum-of-the-years' digits depreciation:

Sum of digits 1 through 7   28

Depreciation expense first year = 7/28 × $8,400 = $2,100

Depreciation expense second year = 6/28 × $8,400 = $1800

Depreciation expense for 1993 = 9/12 of first year = $1,575

Depreciation expense for 1994:

3/12 of first year expense =	$ 525
9/12 of second year expense =	1,350
Depreciation expense for 1994	$1,875

6–11. Straight-line depreciation is used for financial reporting purposes because depreciation expense will be lower than under accelerated depreciation. Accelerated depreciation is used for tax purposes so taxes will be minimized.

6–13. Alpha should have a higher ROI than Beta. Alpha's plant is older and will be depreciated to a greater extent than Beta's. Thus Alpha's asset base will be lower, so its ROI will be higher. The implication for Beta is that because of its lower ROI, its ability to raise capital will be reduced unless it has production/technological advantages or efficiencies.

6–15. *a.*

List price of new computer	$110,000
Less: Trade-in allowance	12,000
Cash to be paid	$ 98,000

Net book value = Cost − Accumulated depreciation

$$21,000 = 85,000 - ?$$

$$64,000 = ? = \text{Accumulated depreciation}$$

Cost of new asset in a trade-in transaction:

Net book value of old asset	$ 21,000
Cash paid "to boot"	98,000
Cost of new computer	$119,000

b.

Balance Sheet	Income Statement

Assets = Liabilities + Owners' equity ← Net income = Revenues − Expenses

Computer Equipment (old)
−85,000

Accumulated Depreciation—Computer Equipment (old)
+64,000

Cash
−98,000

Computer Equipment (new)
+ ?

Cost of new computer equipment is the amount needed to keep the equation in balance:

$$-85,000 + 64,000 - 98,000 + ? = 0$$

$$? = 119,000$$

Journal entry:

Dr. New Computer Cost.	?	? = 119,000
Dr. Accumulated Depreciation—		to balance
Old Computer	64,000	entry
Cr. Cash		98,000
Cr. Old Computer Cost		85,000

6–17. The list price of the new asset must be considered, because the amount of cash paid is the difference between the list price and the trade-in allowance.

6–19. ROI would be higher for a firm using capital leases that were not reflected on the balance sheet than for a firm that purchased assets because the firm that leased would have a lower asset investment on the balance sheet. Costs associated with using assets are about the same whether leased or purchased with borrowed funds.

6–21. *a.*

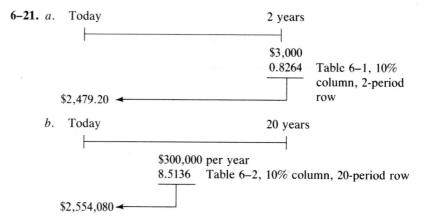

a. Today _____ 2 years

$3,000
0.8264   Table 6–1, 10% column, 2-period row

$2,479.20 ←

b. Today _____ 20 years

$300,000 per year
8.5136   Table 6–2, 10% column, 20-period row

$2,554,080 ←

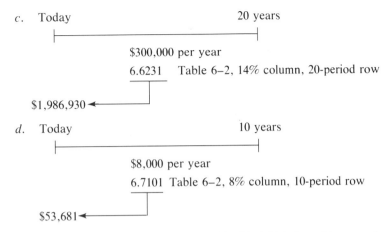

c. Today ⊢──────────────── 20 years

$300,000 per year

6.6231 Table 6–2, 14% column, 20-period row

$1,986,930 ◄─────

d. Today ⊢──────────────── 10 years

$8,000 per year

6.7101 Table 6–2, 8% column, 10-period row

$53,681 ◄─────

6–23. *a.* Yes, because I would still earn a 15% ROI, which I would expect from an investment in this type of business.

b. $40,000 would be recorded as goodwill.

CHAPTER 7

7–1. Discount basis means interest is paid in advance.

    a. Proceeds = Face amount of note − Interest

$$= 300{,}000 - (300{,}000 \times 9\% \times 6/12)$$
$$= 300{,}000 - 13{,}500$$
$$= 286{,}500$$

    b. Note is dated April 15; to June 30 is 2.5 months.

$$\text{Interest} = 300{,}000 \times 0.09 \times 2.5/12$$
$$= 5{,}625$$

    c. Current liability = Face amount less discount balance

$$= 300{,}000 - (13{,}500 - 5{,}625)$$
$$= 300{,}000 - 7{,}875$$
$$= 292{,}125$$

7–3. *a.* At 3/31/93

Balance Sheet	Income Statement
Assets = Liabilities + Owners' equity ←	Net income = Revenues − Expenses
Payroll Taxes Payable +4,800	Payroll Tax Expense −4,800

Journal entry:

```
Dr.  Payroll Tax Expense . . . . . . . . . . .      4,800
     Cr.  Payroll Taxes Payable . . . . . . . .              4,800
```

b. Failure to make the accrual resulted in an understatement of expense and an overstatement of net income. On the March 31, 1993, balance sheet, current liabilities are understated, and retained earnings is overstated.

c.   3/31/93   3/31/94

|———|

Paid taxes of prior year, recognized expense this year $4,800

Should have recognized expense this year $5,000

Effect on net income for year ended March 31, 1994:

Expense is too high by amount applicable to prior year: $4,800.

Expense is too low by accrual not made this year: $5,000.

Net effect is that expense this year is $200 too low, and profits this year are $200 too high.

On March 31, 1994, balance sheet, current liabilities are $5,000 understated, and retained earnings is $5,000 overstated.

7–5. As of December 31 the amount of the accrual is $2,700,000 × 60% × 5%.

Balance Sheet	Income Statement
Assets = Liabilities + Owners' equity ←	Net income = Revenues − Expenses
Estimated Liability for Advertising Allowance + 81,000	Advertising Expense −81,000

Journal entry:

```
Dr.  Advertising Expense . . . . . . . . . . .      81,000
     Cr.  Estimated Liability for Advertising Al-
     lowance. . . . . . . . . . . . . . . . . .              81,000
```

7–7. a. Keg deposits are a current liability on the balance sheet.

b.

Balance Sheet	Income Statement
Assets = Liabilities + Owners' equity ←	Net income = Revenues − Expenses
Cash Keg Deposits −15 −15	

Journal entry:

```
Dr.  Keg Deposits . . . . . . . . . . . . . . .      15
     Cr.  Cash . . . . . . . . . . . . . . . . .              15
```

c. The deposit liability for the 200 kegs (200 × \$15 = \$3,000) should be eliminated; an income statement account associated with keg expense should be credited.

d. The cost of kegs purchased would be capitalized in a long-lived asset account and then be depreciated over the kegs' estimated useful life. The net book value of kegs removed from service or lost (as in *c*) would be removed from the asset and recorded as an expense.

7–9. *a.* The market interest rate is higher than the stated interest rate so the bonds will sell for less than their face amount.

b.

Balance Sheet	Income Statement
Assets = Liabilities + Owners' equity ← Net income = Revenues − Expenses	

Cash	Bonds Payable
+1,080,000	+1,000,000
	Premium on
	Bonds Payable
	+80,000

Journal entry:

```
Dr.  Cash  . . . . . . . . . . . . .   1,080,000
     Cr.  Bonds Payable . . . . . . .               1,000,000
     Cr.  Premium on Bonds Payable . .                  80,000
```

c.

```
        |———————————————————————————————|
   4/1/90              6 months          10/31/90
 Bonds issued
```

Interest to be paid (1,000,000 × 11% × 0.5)	\$55,000
Premium amortization (80,000/20 yrs × 0.5 yr)	2,000
Interest expense for 6 months	\$53,000

Effect of interest payment on financial statements:

Balance Sheet	Income Statement
Assets = Liabilities + Owners' equity ← Net income = Revenues − Expenses	

Cash	Premium on		Interest
−55,000	Bonds Payable		Expense
	−2,000		−53,000

Journal entry:

```
Dr.  Interest expense . . . . . . . . . . .    53,000
Dr.  Premium on bonds payable . . . . . .       2,000
     Cr.  Cash . . . . . . . . . . . . . . .               55,000
```

7–11. *a.* If interest rates have dropped enough so the cost of a new borrowing to pay off the old bonds at a premium will be less than the cost of continuing to pay the 15% interest rate on the old bonds.

b. It would be shown as a decrease in cash from financing activities.

7–13. The principal risk associated with financial leverage is that a decrease in the entity's operating income could result in a decrease in cash flows and an inability to make interest and required principal payments on the debt. A second risk is that as the amount of debt increases, lenders require a higher interest rate to compensate for the additional risk they are taking.

7–15. *a.*
$$\frac{\text{Deferred income taxes, } 12/31/91 \quad \$164.6}{\text{Total stockholders' equity, } 12/31/91 \quad \$885.5} = 18.6\%$$

Yes, the deferred income taxes are material in relation to stockholders' equity.

b. Deferred income tax expense due to difference between book and tax depreciation (in millions):

1991	$12.5
1990	18.7
1989	(4.7)

The increase is due to capital additions, which result in greater tax depreciation than book depreciation. Purchases of property, plant, and equipment from the six-year summary on page 38:

1991	$133.8 million
1990	195.1 million
1989	231.0 million

c. The deferred tax liability is sometimes considered part of owners' equity because as long as the company maintains or expands its plant and equipment investment, the increase in the deferred tax liability account from each year's additions will be more than the decrease each year from prior years' acquisitions for which tax depreciation is now less than book depreciation expense. Because the liability keeps increasing over time, it appears that the liability is never being paid and thus can be considered part of owners' equity.

7–17.

Transaction/ Adjustment	Current Assets	Current Liabilities	Long-term Debt	Net Income
a.		+ 867		− 867
b.		+ 170		− 170
c.		+1,700		−1,700
d.		+1,500		−1,500

7–19.

Transaction/ Adjustment	Current Assets	Long-lived Assets	Current Liabilities	Long-term Liabilities	Owners' Equity	Net Income
a.			Income Taxes Payable +500	Deferred Income Taxes +200		Income Tax Expense −700

(continued)

Transaction/ Adjustment	Current Assets	Long-lived Assets	Current Liabilities	Long-term Liabilities	Owners' Equity	Net Income
b.	Cash +4,950			Bonds Payable +5,000 Discount on Bonds Payable −50		
c.	Cash −3,000	Land +3,000				
d.	Inventory −64		Estimated Liability for Warranty Claims −64			

CHAPTER 8

8–1. *a.* Balance sheet amount equals number of shares issued × par value.

1,400,000 shares × $5 = $7,000,000

b. Cash dividends are paid on shares outstanding.

1,250,000 shares × $.15 = $187,500

c. Treasury stock accounts for the difference between shares issued and shares outstanding.

8–3. *a.*

Number of shares issued	161,522
Less: Number of shares in treasury	(43,373)
Number of shares outstanding	118,149
× Dividend requirement per share	$3.75
Total annual dividends required to be paid	$443,058.75

b.

Dividend per share is 6% × Par value = 6% × $40 = $2.40

× Number of shares outstanding	73,621
Total annual dividends required to be paid	$176,690.40

c. Dividend per share:

11.4% × Stated value = 11.4% × $100 = $11.40

× Number of shares outstanding	37,600
Total annual dividends required to be paid	$428,640

8–5. Preferred dividends for 1991, 1992, and 1993 would have to be paid before a dividend on the common stock could be paid.

$$\text{Annual dividend} = \$6.50 \times 22{,}000 \text{ shares} = \$143{,}000$$

$$\text{Dividends for 3 years} = 3 \times 143{,}000 = \$429{,}000$$

8–7. *a.* February 21 is the declaration date. Because this is a regular dividend of the same amount as prior dividends, the stock price would not be significantly affected.

b. March 8 is the ex-dividend date. On this date the market price of the stock is likely to fall by the amount of the dividend because purchasers will not receive the dividend.

c. March 15 is the record date. The market price of the stock should not be affected because for a publicly traded stock the ex-dividend date affects who receives the dividend.

d. March 30 is the payment date. The market price of the stock should not be affected because the corporation is merely paying a liability (dividends payable).

8–9. To declare a dividend, the firm must have retained earnings and enough cash to pay the dividend. Of course, the board must approve a dividend.

8–11. If the company can reinvest its retained earnings at a higher ROI than I could earn on the money paid to me in dividends, I would prefer that the company not pay a cash dividend. If I needed current income from my investment, I would want cash dividends.

I don't really care whether the company issues a stock dividend because a stock dividend doesn't change my equity in the company, the total market value of my investment, or the company's ability to earn a return on investment.

8–13. *a.* A 2-for-1 split means that the stockholder will own two shares for every share now owned. Thus I will own 200 shares.

b. Because there are now twice as many shares of stock outstanding, and the financial condition of the company hasn't changed, the market price per share will be half of what it was. The total market value of my investment will not have changed.

8–15. *a.*

Balance Sheet		Income Statement
Assets = Liabilities + Owners' equity ←		Net income = Revenues − Expenses

1. Purchase of 800 shares of treasury stock @ $18.25/share:

Cash	Treasury Stock
−14,600	−14,600

Journal entry:

Dr. Treasury stock.   14,600
    Cr.   Cash   14,600

2. Sale of 600 of above shares @ $19.50/share:

Cash	Treasury Stock
+11,700	+10,950
	Additional Paid-In Capital
	+750

Journal entry:

Dr. Cash 11,700
    Cr. Treasury stock.   10,950
    Cr. Additional paid-in capital   750

b.   36,200 shares outstanding prior to treasury stock purchase
     −   800 shares of treasury stock purchased

     35,400 shares outstanding in June
     × \$0.35 cash dividend per share

     \$12,390 total cash dividend

8–17.

Trans-action	Cash	Other Assets	Liabil-ities	Paid-In Capital	Retained Earnings	Treasury Stock	Net Income
a.	+			+			
b.			+		−		
c.	−						−
d.				+	−		
e.		+		+			

8–19. *a.* Annual dividend per share = 12% × \$60 = \$ 7.20
    Number of shares outstanding   1,500
    Annual dividend requirement   \$10,800

b. Balance sheet amount = Par value × Number of shares issued
                                = \$60 × 1,500 = \$90,000

c. Number of shares issued = Balance sheet amount/Par value
                                              (or stated value)
                            = \$240,000/\$8 =30,000 shares

$$\frac{\text{Number of shares}}{\text{outstanding}} = \frac{\text{Number of}}{\text{shares issued}} - \frac{\text{Number of}}{\text{treasury shares}}$$

                            = 30,000 − 2,000 = 28,000 shares

d.

	Common Stock	Additional Paid-In Capital
November 30, 1993	\$240,000	\$540,000
January 1, 1993	210,000	468,750
Increase	\$ 30,000	\$ 71,250

$$\frac{\text{Number of}}{\text{shares sold}} = \text{Increase in common stock amount/Par value}$$

                = 30,000/\$8 = 3,750 shares

$$\text{Selling price} \atop \text{per share} = \text{(Increase in common stock + Increase in additional} \atop \text{paid-in capital)/No. of shares sold}$$

$$= (\$30,000 + \$71,250)/3,750 \text{ shares}$$

$$= \$27 \text{ per share}$$

e. Treasury stock was resold at a price higher than its cost.

f. Retained earnings:

Balance, January 1, 1993	$90,300	
Add: Net income	24,000	
Less: Preferred dividend	(10,800)	From *a*
Common dividend	?	
Balance, November 30, 1993.	$97,000	

$$90,300 + 24,000 - 10,800 - ? = 97,000$$

$$? = (6,500)$$

CHAPTER 9

9–1.

6/9	21 days	6/30	28 days	7/28

a. In the year ended June 30, recognize 21/49 of summer school tuition because that proportion of the summer session is in the year ended June 30. Summer session expenses will be accrued or deferred (i.e., recognized as incurred) so an appropriate matching of revenue and expense will occur in each fiscal year.

Amount of revenue for the year ended 6/30 is:

$$21/49 \times \$112,000 = \$48,000$$

b. No. Revenues and expenses would still be allocated to each fiscal period to achieve matching, as well as more meaningful financial statements, for each period.

9–3. A sale could be billed before the product is shipped. Internal controls would involve a policy of not billing until after shipment, and procedures that required a copy of the shipping record be received in the billing department before the sales invoice could be mailed to the customer.

9–5. Strategy is to use the cost of goods sold model with hypothetical data that are the same except for the item in error.

	"Correct"	*"Error"*
Beginning inventory	$100,000	$100,000
Add: Purchases	300,000	300,000

(continued)

	"Correct"	*"Error"*
Goods available for sale	$400,000	$400,000
Less: Ending inventory.	(75,000)	(125,000)
Cost of goods sold	$325,000	$275,000

The overstatement of ending inventory causes cost of goods sold to be too low so gross profit and operating income are too high, or overstated, by $50,000.

9–7. *a.*

	(in millions)		
	1991	*1990*	*1989*
Net sales.	$2,439.3	$2,518.8	$2,488.7
Cost of goods sold	1,801.1	1,816.6	1,764.0
Gross profit	$ 638.2	$ 702.2	$ 724.7
Gross profit ratio	26.2%	27.9%	29.1%

b. Use an estimated gross profit ratio for 1992 of 27%.

Net sales ($ millions)	$845
Cost of goods sold (73%)	617
Gross profit (27%)	$228

9–9. I would prefer to have operating income data because they describe how well management has done operating the business. Net income is important but includes nonoperating items like discontinued operations, other income and expense, extraordinary items, and so on.

9–11. Strategy: Use the income statement model. Operating expenses include general and administrative expenses, selling expenses, and research and development expenses, if separately disclosed.

Net sales.	$784
Cost of goods sold	
Gross profit	$305
General and asministrative expenses	98
Advertising expense.	62
Other selling expenses.	51
Operating income	$ 94

9–13. Strategy is to calculate ending inventory in the cost of goods sold model for different gross profit ratios so that the ratio that gives the highest ending inventory is selected.

	Gross Profit Ratio		Calculation
	33%	*30%*	*Sequence*
Sales	$142,680	$142,680	Given
Cost of goods sold:			
Beginning inventory	$ 63,590	$ 63,590	Given
Add: Purchases	118,652	118,652	Given
Goods available for sale . .	$182,242	$182,242	
Less: Ending inventory. . .	(86,646)	(82,366)	Calc 3rd
Cost of goods sold	$ 95,596	$ 99,876	Calc 2nd
Gross profit	$ 47,084	$ 42,804	Calc 1st (Gross profit × Sales)

Kiwi management would argue for using a 33 percent gross profit ratio for 1993 to the date of the tornado because the higher the gross profit ratio, the higher the estimated ending inventory lost in the storm, and the higher the insurance claim.

9–15.

Net income	$473,700
Less: Dividends required on preferred stock ($4.50 × 38,000 shares)	171,000
Net income available for common stockholders	$302,700
Number of common share outstanding	105,200
Earnings per share (302,700/105,200)	$2.88

9–17. Armstrong uses the multiple-step format. The multiple-step format seems easier to read and interpret because of the intermediate captions and sub-totals.

9–19. *a.* The two most significant sources of cash from operating activities were:

Net earnings	$141.0 million
Depreciation and amortization	130.1 million

b. The cash flows from investing activities were:

Purchase of property, plant and equipment	$194.9 million
Proceeds from sale of land, facilities, and discontinued businesses	72.5 million
Acquisitions	16.1 million

c. The two most significant financing activities were:

Increase in short-term debt	150.4 million
Purchase of treasury stock.	185.2 million

d. Dividends totaled $63.8 million.

e.

ARMSTRONG WORLD INDUSTRIES, INC.
Condensed Statement of Cash Flows
For the Year-Ended December 31, 1990
($ millions)

Cash flows from operating activities:	
Net earnings.	$ 141.0
Adjustments to reconcile net earnings to net cash provided by operating activities:	
Depreciation and amortization.	130.1
All other (net)	(70.9)
Net cash provided by operating activities	200.2
Cash flows from investing activities:	
Purchases of property, plant and equipment.	$(194.9)
Proceeds from sale of land, facilities, and discontinued businesses.	72.5
Acquisitions.	(16.1)
Net cash used for investing activities.	$(138.5)
Cash flows from financing activities:	
Increase in short-term debt	$ 150.4
Purchase of treasury stock	(185.2)
Cash dividends paid	(63.8)
All other financing activities (net)	44.4
Net cash provided from financing activities	$ (54.2)
Increase in cash	$ 7.5

9–21. Cash and cash equivalents increased $7.5 million from $17.1 million at the beginning of the year to $24.6 million at the end of the year. Cash of $200.2 million provided by operating activities was more than cash used for investing activities and cash used for financing activities. This is good. Purchases of property, plant and equipment of $194.9 million were more than the $72.5 million proceeds from the sales of land, facilities, and discontinued businesses. The principal uses of cash for financing activities were for purchase of treasury stock ($185.2 million) and payment of dividends ($63.8 million). Short- and long-term debt increased $192.4 million. In summary, the company's cash flows are strong. Cash generated from operating activities covered net investment requirements and dividends; borrowing was needed to finance the purchase of treasury stock.

CHAPTER 10

10–3. *a* and *b*

ARMSTRONG WORLD INDUSTRIES, INC.
ROI and Funds Generated from Operations by Segments

ROI	1991	1990	1989	Statement of Cash Flows	1991	1990	1989
Floor coverings:							
Sales	$1,058.0	$1,095.9	$1,113.9	Operating profit	$84.6	$131.2	$137.7
Operating profit	84.6	131.2	137.7	Add: Depreciation &			
Identifiable assets	915.1	940.7	906.2	amortization	62.8	63.8	68.8
				Less: Capital additions	−61.6	−82.9	−93.5
Margin	0.08	0.12	0.12	Net cash flows from			
Turnover	1.16	1.16	1.23	operating and in-			
ROI	0.09	0.14	0.15	vesting activities	$85.8	$112.1	$113.0
Industry products:							
Sales	$287.1	$275.4	$241.1	Operating profit	$43.1	$48.0	$40.5
Operating profit	43.1	48.0	40.5	Add: Depreciation &			
Identifiable assets	188.6	171.2	156.1	amortization	10.5	10.3	9.4
				Less: Capital additions	−21.1	−26.2	−10.8
Margin	0.15	0.17	0.17	Net cash flows from			
Turnover	1.52	1.61	1.54	operating and			
ROI	0.23	0.27	0.26	investing activities	$32.5	$32.1	$39.1

---

    c. The downward trend in ROI of the Floor Coverings segment probably reflects the impact of the recession and reduced housing starts and home remodeling. The higher ROI for the Industry Products segment, relative to Floor Coverings, may reflect less price competition in that segment. The decline in 1991 ROI for the Industry Products segment probably also reflects the recession. Both segments are generating positive cash flows, which is significant and important.

10–5. *a.* Original earnings per share are $3.12; to reflect a 3-for-1 stock split, divide by 3; adjusted earnings per share = $1.04.

    b. For 1994, 1992 earnings per share as adjusted in 1993 will have to be adjusted again by dividing by 2; adjusted earnings per share for 1992, to be reported in 1994, = $1.04/2 = $.52

    c. To reflect a 10 percent stock dividend, divide unadjusted earnings per share by 1.1. Adjusted earnings per share = $3.12/1.1 = $2.84

10–7. Earnings as restated: $.60
        Multiply by 2 to reflect 2-for-1 stock split $1.20
        Multiply by 1.05 to reflect 5% stock dividend $1.26

Proof:

Original earnings per share	$1.26
Adjust for stock split (divide by 2)	$.63
Adjust for 5% stock dividend (divide by 1.05)	$.60

10–9. The auditor's opinion is that the identified financial statements present fairly, **in all material respects** (emphasis added), financial position, results of operations, and cash flows in conformity with generally accepted accounting principles.

CHAPTER 11

11–1. *a.* ROI = Margin * Turnover

$$= \frac{\text{Operating income}}{\text{Net sales}} \times \frac{\text{Net sales}}{\text{Average total assets}}$$

$$= 498/8{,}251 \times 8{,}251/((4{,}873 + 2{,}758) + (4{,}289 + 2{,}472)/2)$$

$$= .06 \times 1.15$$

Current liabilities

Total assets less Curr. liab.

$$= 6.9\%$$

ROE = Net income/Average owners' equity

$$= 350/((3{,}565 + 3{,}149)/2)$$

$$= 10.4\%$$

b. Number of days' sales in accounts receivable
= Accounts receivable/Average day's sales (1)

$$= 2{,}174/22.6 = 96.2 \text{ days}$$

1. Average number of day's sales = Annual sales/365

$$= 8{,}251/365 = 22.6$$

Inventory turnover = Cost of goods sold/Average inventory

$$= 6{,}253/((1{,}323 + 1{,}211)/2) = 4.9 \text{ times}$$

Plant and equipment turnover = Net sales/Average plant and equipment

$$= 8{,}251/((2{,}563 + 2{,}528)/2)$$

$$= 3.24 \text{ times}$$

c. Leverage ratios:
Debt/equity ratio:
(Long-term debt/Owners' equity)
1,287/3,565 = 36.1%

Debt ratio:
(Long-term debt/(Long-term debt + Owners' equity)
1,287/4,852 = 26.5%

Times interest earned:
(Earnings before interest and taxes/Interest expense)
498/209 = 2.4 times

d. Market price per share	$42.00	
Earnings per share	$ 3.51	
Price/earnings ratio	12.0	
Dividends per share	$ .50	
Dividend payout ratio (Dividend/earnings)	14.2%	
Dividend yield (Dividend/market price)	1.2%	

11–3. Key data would be the recent (three-to-five year) *trend* in earnings per share, cash dividends per share, market price, and P/E ratio. These data would be in tabular and graphic format.

Market price would be noted weekly. Quarterly and annual data to note are earnings and dividend trends.

The sell/hold/buy decision is based on stock price performance relative to the price objective established from analysis of the above data.

11–5. ───────────────────────────

ARMSTRONG WORLD INDUSTRIES, INC., AND SUBSIDIARIES
Common Size Balance Sheet
December 31, 1990

Total current assets	33.8%
Property, plant and equipment (net)	53.5
Other noncurrent assets	12.7
Total assets	100.0%
Total current liabilities	25.4%
Total noncurrent liabilities	32.7
Total shareholders' equity	41.9
Total liabilities and shareholders' equity	100.0%

CHAPTER 12

12–1.

	Product Direct	Indirect	Period	Variable	Fixed
Raw materials	X	───	───	X	───
Staples used to secure packed boxes of product. . .	X	───	───	X	───

	Product				
	Direct	*Indirect*	*Period*	*Variable*	*Fixed*
Plant janitors' wages . . .	___	X	___	X	X
Order process- ing clerks' wages . . .	___	___	X	X	___
Advertising expenses . .	___	___	X	___	X
Production workers' wages . . .	X	___	___	X	___
Supervisors' salaries . . .	X	___	___	___	X
Salesforce commissions	___	___	X	X	___
Maintenance supplies used	___	X	___	X	___
President's salary . . .	___	___	X	___	X
Electricity cost	___	X	X	X	X
Real estate taxes for: Factory. . .	___	X	___	___	X
Office build- ing	___	___	X	___	X

Note: Janitors' wages and electricity probably have a mixed cost behavior pattern. Electricity for administrative areas would be a period cost.

12–3. *a.* Differential cost: What costs will differ if a friend comes along?

b. Allocated cost: How to allocate? Based on number of people, weight, number of suitcases, or what?

c. Sunk cost: What costs have been and will be incurred, even if you don't make the trip?

d. Opportunity cost: What are other opportunities for you to earn some revenue, or cost of alternative travel for classmate?

12–5. *a.*   Overhead application rate $= \dfrac{\text{Estimated total overhead for year}}{\text{Estimated total activity for year}}$

$= \$118,000/36,875$ direct labor hours

$= \$3.20/$Direct labor hour

b. Total costs for 800 bowls:

Raw materials	$1,440
Direct labor (140 hrs. @ $9.20).	1,288
Overhead (140 direct labor hrs. @ $3.20)	448
Total cost	$3,176

Cost per bowl = Total cost/Number of bowls made

= $3,176/800

= $3.97 each

Cost of bowls sold = 550 × $3.97 = $2,183.50

Cost of bowls in inventory = 250 × $3.97 = $992.50

12–7. *a.* Predetermined overhead application rate
= Estimated overhead dollars/Estimated activity

$9.70 per machine hour = ?/8,400 machine hours

? = $81,480

b.
Actual overhead incurred		81,480
Overhead applied = 8,200 hours @ $9.70		$79,540
Overhead was underapplied by		$ 1,940

c. The overapplied or underapplied overhead for the year will be transferred to cost of goods sold in the income statement because most of it would have ended up there anyway even if the "correct" overhead application rate had been used because most products made during the year are sold during the same year.

12–9. Total cost for 250 ties:

a. Raw materials	$ 820.00
b. Direct labor (32 direct labor hrs.)	208.00
Overhead:	
Based on raw materials: 215% × $820	1,763.00
Based on direct labor: 32 hrs. × $3.10	99.20
Total cost.	$2,890.20

Cost per tie = $2,890.20/250 = $11.5608 each

12–11.

Cost Element	Probable Cost Behavior Pattern	Estimated Cost for 3,000 units	4,500 units
Raw materials	Variable	$12,000	$18,000
Factory depreciation expense	Fixed	9,000	9,000
Direct labor	Variable	21,000	31,500

(continued)

12–11.

Cost Element	Probable Cost Behavior Pattern	Estimated Cost for 3,000 units	4,500 units
Factory manager's salary	Fixed	5,000	5,000
Computer rent expense	Fixed	4,800	4,800
Equipment repair expense	Variable	2,100	3,150

12–13. *a.* Variable manufacturing costs:

Raw materials	$25,720
Direct labor	18,930
Variable manufacturing overhead	14,570
Total variable costs	$59,220
Fixed manufacturing overhead	10,320
Total manufacturing costs	$69,540

Direct (or variable cost) per spatula = $59,220/20,000 = $2.961 each

Absorption cost per spatula   = $69,540/20,000 = $3.477 each

b. The fixed cost per spatula is $3.477 − $2.961 = $.516
The total fixed cost associated with 3,800 spatulas in inventory is:

$$3,800 \times \$.516 = \$1,960.80$$

Under absorption costing this amount would be in inventory; under direct or variable costing this amount would be in cost of goods sold. Thus under direct or variable costing gross profit would be $1,960.80 less than under absorption costing.

c. Total cost = $10,320 + ($2.961 × the number of spatulas made)

The cost of making 100 more spatulas would be $296.10.

12–15. *a.* Total cost of goods manufactured:

Manufacturing costs:	
Raw material	$ 36,800
Direct labor	79,300
Manufacturing overhead	47,200
Total	$163,300
Number of units made	3,800

Average cost per unit: $163,300/3,800 = $42.9737 each

b. Cost of goods sold: 3,500 units @ $42.9737 = $150,408
c. Difference between total manufacturing cost and cost of goods sold is in inventory in the balance sheet.

12–17. Use T-accounts, enter the beginning and ending balance amounts and the debits that are given, and then solve for the credits; raw materials used, cost of goods manufactured, and cost of goods sold.

Raw Materials

Beginning balance	45,790		
Purchases	217,580		
		Used	209,940
Ending balance	53,430		

Work in Process

Beginning balance	18,930	Cost of goods manufactured	774,930
Raw materials	209,940		
Direct labor	392,100		
Manufacturing overhead	169,300		
Ending balance	15,340		

Finished Goods

Beginning balance	63,650	Cost of goods sold	770,300
Cost of goods manufactured	774,930		
Ending balance	68,280		

CHAPTER 13

13–1. *a.* Strategy: First, calculate variable cost per unit in February and use same per unit cost for April. Second, fixed cost will be the same for each month. Third, knowing total cost for April, and variable and fixed cost for April, solve for mixed cost for April.

	February	*April*
Activity	*5,000 units*	*7,000 units*
Costs:		
Variable	$10,000/5,000 units = $2/unit	$14,000
Mixed	20,000	?
Fixed	30,000	30,000
Total	$60,000	$68,000

Mixed cost for April: $14,000 + ? + 30,000 = 68,000$

$? = 24,000$

b.   Variable rate = (High $ − Low $)/(High units − Low units)

= (24,000 − 20,000)/(7,000 − 5,000)

= $2.00/unit

$$\text{Total mixed cost} = \text{Fixed cost} + \text{Variable cost}$$
$$24,000 = ? + (2.00 \times 7,000 \text{ units})$$
$$10,000 = ?$$

$$\text{Cost formula} = \text{Fixed cost} + \text{Variable cost}$$
$$= \$10,000 + \$2.00/\text{unit}$$

$$\text{Proof at 5,000 units: Mixed cost} = \$10,000 + (2.00 \times 5,000)$$
$$= \$20,000$$

13–3. *a.*

Revenues (8,000 units × \$4.)	\$32,000
Variable expenses:	
Cost of goods sold (8,000 units × \$2.10)	\$16,800
Selling expenses (8,000 units × \$.10)	800
Administrative expenses (8,000 units × \$.20)	1,600
Total variable expenses	\$19,200
Contribution margin	\$12,800
Fixed expenses:	
Cost of goods sold.	\$ 6,000
Selling expenses.	1,200
Administrative expenses	4,000
Total fixed expenses	\$11,200
Operating income	\$ 1,600

b.

$$\text{Contribution margin/unit} = \text{Total contribution margin/Volume}$$
$$= \$12,800/8,000 \text{ units}$$
$$= \$1.60/\text{unit}$$

or:

$$\text{Contribution margin/unit} = \text{Selling price/unit} - \text{Variable expense/unit}$$
$$= \$4.00 - \$2.40$$
$$= \$1.60$$

$$\text{Contribution margin ratio} = \text{Contribution margin/Revenues}$$
$$= \$12,800/\$32,000 = 40\%$$

or:
$$\text{Contribution margin unit/Selling price per unit} = \$1.60/\$4.00$$
$$= 40\%$$

c. 1. Volume of 12,000 units:

	Per unit	×	*Volume*	=	*Total*	%
Revenue	4.00					100%
Variable expenses	2.40					60
Contribution margin	1.60	×	12,000	=	19,200	40%

(*continued*)

	Per unit × *Volume* =	*Total*	*%*
Fixed expenses		11,200	
Operating income		8,000	

or:

4,000 more units sold @ $1.60 contribution margin/unit = $6,400 increase in contribution margin and operating income. Present operating income is $1,600 so new operating income will be $8,000.

2. Volume of 4,000 units:

Total contribution margin = 4,000 × $1.60 =	$ 6,400
Fixed expenses (no change)	11,200
Operating loss	$(4,800)

or:

Operating income decreases 4,000 units × $1.60 = $6,400 from present operating income of $1,600, causing an operating loss of $4,800.

d. Use contribution margin ratio of 40%.

1. Revenue increase of $12,000 causes a 40% × 12,000 or $4,800 increase in contribution margin and operating income. Operating income = $6,400.
2. Revenue decrease of $7,000 causes a 40% × 7,000 or $2,800 decrease in contribution margin and operating income. Operating income changes to a loss of $1,200.

13–5. *a.*

	Per unit ×	*Volume* =	*Total*
Revenue	15		
Variable expenses.	9		
Contribution margin.	6 ×	5,400 =	32,400
Fixed expenses			27,000
Operating income			5,400

b.

	Per unit ×	*Volume* =	*Total*
Revenue	13		
Variable expenses.	9		
Contribution margin.	4 ×	8,400 =	33,600
Fixed expenses			27,000
Operating income			6,600

c. Does increase in volume move fixed expenses into a new relevant range? Are variable expenses really linear?

d.

	Per unit ×	*Volume* =	*Total*
Revenue	16		
Variable expenses.	9		

(continued)

	Per unit	×	Volume	=	Total
Contribution margin	7	×	5,400	=	37,800
Fixed expenses					33,000
Operating income					4,800

e. 1. Volume of 5,400 units per month:

	Per unit	×	Volume	=	Total
Revenue	15.00				
Variable expenses . .	9.80				
Contribution margin .	5.20	×	5,400	=	28,080
Fixed expenses					22,800
Operating income . . .					5,280

Current fixed expenses = 27,000
−2 salaries @ 2,500 = (5,000)
+2 salaries @ 400 = 800
22,800

2. Volume of 6,000 units per month:

	Per unit	×	Volume	=	Total
Revenue	15.00				
Variable expenses	9.80				
Contribution margin	5.20	×	6,000	=	31,200
Fixed expenses					22,800
Operating income					8,400

f.

	Per unit	×	Volume	=	Total
Revenue	15				
Variable expenses . .	9				
Contribution margin .	6	×	6,000	=	36,000
Fixed expenses . . .					28,000
Operating income . .					8,000

(Original 27,000 + 1,000 advertising increase.)

The sales force compensation plan change results in a $400 greater increase in operating income.

g.

	Per unit	×	Volume	=	Total
Revenue	15				
Variable expenses	9				
Contribution margin	6	×	?	=	27,000
Fixed expenses					27,000
Operating income					0

At the break-even point total contribution margin must equal total fixed expenses.

Break-even volume: $\$6 \times ? = \$27,000$

$? = 4,500$ units

Total revenue $= 4,500$ units $\times \$15.00 = \$67,500$

13–7. *a.* Current operation

	Luxury	Economy	Total
Revenues	$20 \times 10,000 = 200,000$	$12 \times 20,000 = 240,000$	440,000
Variable expenses	9	7	
Contribution margin	$11 \times 10,000 = \overline{110,000}$	$5 \times 20,000 = \overline{100,000}$	210,000
Fixed expenses			70,000
Operating income			140,000

Contribution margin ratio $= \$210,000/\$440,000 = 47.7\%$

b.

Break-even point revenues $=$ Fixed expenses/Contribution margin ratio

$= \$70,000/0.477$

$= \$146,751$

c. Because sales mix might change. For example, if the break-even point sales dollars were all to come from the economy model, total contribution margin would be the economy model contribution margin ratio ($\$5/\$12 = 0.4167$) multiplied by sales of $\$146,751$, which equals $\$61,146$—less than fixed expenses!

d. Proposed operation

	Luxury	Economy	Value	Total
Revenues	20	12	15	
Variable expenses	9	7	8	
Contribution margin	$11 \times 6,000 = 66,000$	$5 \times 17,000 = 85,000$	$7 \times 8,000 = 56,000$	207,000
Fixed expenses				84,000
Operating income				123,000

e. Based on these data, adding the value model would result in a lower operating income.

f. 2,000 more units of the Value model would increase contribution margin and operating income by $\$14,000$ (2,000 units @ $\$7.00$ contribution margin per unit). Operating income rises to $\$137,000$, but this is still less than under the current operation.

13–9. *a.* Use the model, enter the known data, and solve for the unknown.

	Per unit	$\times$	Volume	$=$	Total	%
Revenue.	?					100%
Variable expenses	7.80					
Contribution margin . . .	?	$\times$	_____	$=$	_____	35%

Variable expenses = 65% of selling price

Selling price = $7.80/0.65

= $12

b.

	Per unit	×	Volume	=	Total	%
Revenue.	12.00					100%
Variable expenses	7.80					
Contribution margin . . .	4.20	×	?	=		35%
Fixed expenses					15,000	
Operating income					6,000	

Total contribution margin must be $21,000. Divide that by the contribution margin per unit of $4.20, which gives 5,000 units of the new product that must be sold.

13–11. a.

	Per unit	×	Volume	=	Total	%
Revenue.	1.25					100%
Variable expenses	.35					
Contribution margin . . .	.90	×	400	=	360	72%
Fixed expenses					120	
Operating income from increased volume					240	
Variable expenses of 600 cones given away, @ .35					210	
Net increase in operating income					30	

b. Not only does the promotion itself result in increased operating income, but also it is likely that customers will purchase some other products (e.g., beverages) on which additional contribution margin will be earned.

13–13. a.

	Per unit	×	Volume	=	Total	%
Revenue	32.00					100%
Variable expenses . . .	20.00					
Contribution margin . .	12.00	×	4,100	=	49,200	37.5%
Fixed expenses					43,200	
Operating income					6,000	

b.

	Per unit	×	Volume	=	Total	%
Revenue	32.00					100%
Variable expenses . . .	20.00					
Contribution margin . .	12.00	×	?	=	43,200	37.5%

(continued)

b.

	Per unit	×	Volume	=	Total	%
Fixed expenses					43,200	
Operating income					0	

Break-even volume = $43,200/$12 = 3,600 units

Break-even revenues = 3,600 units × $32 = $115,200

c. 1.

	Per unit	×	Volume	=	Total	%
Revenue	32.00					100%
Variable expenses	14.00					
Contribution margin	18.00	×	4,100	=	73,800	56.25%
Fixed expenses					67,800	
Operating income					6,000	

2.

	Per unit	×	Volume	=	Total	%
Revenue	32.00					100%
Variable expenses	14.00					
Contribution margin	18.00	×	?	=	67,800	56.25%
Fixed expenses					67,800	
Operating income					0	

Break-even volume = $67,800/$18 = 3,767 units

Break-even revenues = 3,767 units × $32 = $120,544

3. As sales volume moves above the break-even point, contribution margin and operating income will increase by a larger amount per unit sold than under the other cost structure.
4. The new cost structure has much more risk, because if sales volume declines, the impact on contribution margin and operating income will be greater than under the other cost structure.

13–15. *a.*

Raw materials per unit	$1.50
Direct labor per unit	1.50
Variable overhead per unit	2.00
Fixed overhead per unit.	2.00*
Total cost per unit	$7.00

* The fixed overhead per unit is based on the total fixed overhead for the year ($100,000 divided by the current output of 50,000 units per year).

b. The above calculation includes an inappropriate unitization of fixed expenses because unless the additional production of 30,000 units results in movement to a new relevant range, total fixed expenses will not change.

   c. The offer should be accepted because there is a contribution margin of $1 per unit (revenue of $6 per unit less variable cost of $5 per unit).

13–17. Pros:

1. The sale will still generate a positive contribution margin ratio of 5 percent.
2. Saturn Candy Company will achieve goodwill with the customer.
3. The candy given to the children will increase brand awareness and could lead to higher sales in the future.
4. The Substance Abuse Awareness Club is a positive moral force in the community.

Cons:

1. Saturn Candy Company incurs the opportunity cost equal to the lost contribution margin if the candy could have been sold at the regular price.
2. When other customers learn of the discounted sale, they may ask for the same special price for other "worthy causes." Unless Saturn Candy Company develops a policy with some limits for this type of special pricing, the company could lose control of the cost.

Appropriate policy safeguards should be developed, and the candy should be sold at the special price.

CHAPTER 14

14–1.

	May	*June*	*July*	*August*
Sales forecast in units	30,000	40,000	60,000	50,000
Beginning inventory .			12,000	
Production			?	
Goods available for sale			70,000	
a. Less: Ending inventory*	(8,000)	(12,000)	(10,000)	
Number of units sold			60,000	

* 20% of next month's unit sales.

   b. July production:

$$12,000 + ? - 10,000 = 60,000$$
$$? = 58,000$$

14–3. *a.* Use the cost of goods sold model, and work from the bottom up and the top down to calculate production:

Beginning inventory	1,000 medallions
Production	? medallions
Goods available for sale	?
Less: Ending inventory	(800) medallions
Number sold	2,000 medallions

Goods available for sale = 2,000 + 800 = 2,800 medallions

Production = 2,800 − 1,000 = 1,800 medallions

b. Use the same approach, but notice that quantity used is a function of quantity produced from the production budget. Each medallion requires ⅔ yard of ribbon.

Begininng inventory	50 yds.
Purchases	? yds.
Material available for use	? yds.
Less: Ending inventory	(20) yds.
Used in production	1,200 yds. (⅔ × 1,800 medallions)

Material available for use = 1,200 + 20 = 1,220 yds.

Purchases = 1,220 − 50 = 1,170 yds.

14–5.

	Quarter I	Quarter II
Raw material inventory/usage model:		
Beginning inventory	5,000	9,000
a. Purchases	?	?
Goods available for use		
Less: Ending inventory*	(9,000)	(5,500)
Usage (2 oz. × number of gallons of product to be produced).	20,000	36,000

* 25% × next quarter usage.

Beginning inventory + Purchases − Ending Inventory = Usage

Quarter I   5,000 + ? − 9,000 = 20,000   Purchases = 24,000 oz.

Quarter II 9,000 + ? − 5,500 = 36,000   Purchases = 32,500 oz.

b. Inventory provides a "cushion" for delivery delays or production needs in excess of the production forecast.

14–7.

	July	August	September
Sales forecast	$192,000	$215,000	$230,000
Cost of sales @ 78%	149,760	167,700	179,400

(continued)

14–7.

	July	August	September
Purchases budget:			
Beginning inventory	235,000	149,760	
Purchases	?	?	
Cost of merchandise available for sale	?	?	
Less: Ending inventory (1.5 × next month's cost of goods sold)	(251,550)	(269,100)	
Cost of goods sold	149,760	167,700	
Cost of merchandise available for sale (Cost of goods sold + Ending inventory)	$401,310	$436,800	
Purchases (Cost of merchandise available for sale − Beginning inventory)	$166,310	$287,040	

14–9.

	May	June	July	August
Sales forecast	$200,000	$300,000	$350,000	$250,000
Cash collections:				
20% of current month sales			$ 70,000	$ 50,000
70% of prior month sales			210,000	245,000
9% of second prior month sales . . .			18,000	27,000
Total cash collections budget			$298,000	$322,000

14–11. *a.*

	September	October
Sales forecast	$42,000	$54,000
Purchases budget	37,800	44,000
Operating expense budget	10,500	12,800
Beginning cash	40,000	
Cash receipts:		
Of Aug. 31 accounts receivable	20,000	
From September sales	–0–	
Total cash receipts	20,000	
Cash disbursements:		
Of Aug. 31 accounts payable and accrued expenses	24,000	
For September purchases (0.75 × $37,800)	28,350	
For September operating expenses (0.75 × $10,500)	7,875	
Total cash disbursements	60,225	
Ending cash	(225)	

b. QB Sportswear's management should try to accelerate the collection of accounts receivable, slow down the payment of accounts payable and accrued expenses, and/or negotiate a bank loan. If sales growth continues at a very high rate, the company probably will need to secure some permanent financing through sale of bonds or stock.

14–13. *a.* The president's remark ignores the misleading result of arbitrarily allocated fixed expenses.

    b.

Current net income of company		$10,000
Less: Lost contribution margin of Division B		(10,000)
Add: Division B direct fixed expenses that would be eliminated:		
Total division's fixed expenses per report	$11,000	
Less: Allocated corporate	(7,000)	4,000
Company net income without Division B		$ 4,000

    c. Never arbitrarily allocate fixed expenses!

14–15.

Item	Original Budget (10,000 units)	Flexed Budget (11,000 units)	Actual Cost	Variance
Direct materials . .	$ 30,000	$ 33,000	$ 32,000	$1,000 Favorable
Direct labor	42,000	46,200	47,000	800 Unfavorable
Variable overhead .	18,000	19,800	20,000	200 Unfavorable
Fixed overhead . .	33,000	33,000	34,000	1,000 Unfavorable
Total	$123,000	$132,000	$133,000	$1,000 Unfavorable

Note: Flexed budget for variable expenses is 11,000/10,000 multiplied by original budget. Fixed expenses do not change as activity changes.

14–17. *a.*

$$\text{Cost formula} = \$3,800 + \$2.70/\text{machine hour}$$
$$\text{Budget} = 3,800 + (2.70 \times 3,700)$$
$$= \$13,790$$

    b.

$$\text{Flexed budget} = 3,800 + (2.70 \times 3,580)$$
$$= \$13,466$$

CHAPTER 15

15–1. *a.* Costs for a "batch" 10 quarts:

Triphate solution 11 qts. @ $.30/qt.	$3.30
Sobase granules 4 lbs. @ $.74/lb.	2.96
Methage 2 oz. @ $1.20/oz.	2.40
Bottles 10 @ $.12 ea.	1.20
Total cost for 10 quarts	$9.86
Cost per quart	$.986

b. Other factors to be considered:

Possible cost increases during coming year.
Spillage/spoilage/waste in manufacturing process.

c. Expected labor costs for an economical or most likely production quantity would be determined and then be expressed on a per unit basis.

15–3. *a.*

Raw material cost	$2.83 per bushel
Direct labor and variable overhead	.42 per bushel
Fixed overhead	.35 per bushel
Total absorption cost	$3.60 per bushel

Each bushel yields 15 pounds of product.
The cost per pound = $3.60/15 = $.24

b. This cost per pound is not very useful for management planning and control because it includes unitized fixed expenses, which do not behave on a per unit basis.

15–5. *a.* Purchase price variance:

(Standard price − Actual price) × Quantity purchased

($5.00 − $4.95) × 7,400 lbs. = $370 Favorable

b. Raw material usage variance:

(Standard usage − Actual usage) × Standard price
((2,000 cases × 4 lbs.) − 8,300 lbs.) × $5.00/lb. = $1,500 Unfavorable

c. Direct labor rate variance:

(Standard rate − Actual rate) × Actual hours

($13.00 − $13.50*) × 5,800 hours = $2,900 Unfavorable

* Actual rate: $78,300/5,800 hours = $13.50

d. Direct labor efficiency variance:

(Standard hours − Actual hours) × Standard rate

((2,000 cases × 3 hrs.) − 5,800) × $13.00 = $2,600 Favorable

e. Variable overhead spending variance:

(Standard rate − Actual rate) × Actual hours

($6.00 − $6.15*) × 5,800 hours = $870 Unfavorable

* Actual rate: $35,670/5,800 hours = $6.15

    f. Variable overhead efficiency variance:

$$\text{(Standard hours} - \text{Actual hours)} \times \text{Standard rate}$$

$$((2,000 \text{ cases} \times 3 \text{ hrs.}) - 5,800) \times \$6.00 = \$1,200 \text{ Favorable}$$

15–7. *a.* Standard hours allowed = 3.5 hours × 24 tune-ups = 84 hours. Efficiency variance was 6 hours unfavorable; therefore actual hours = 84 + 6 = 90 hours.

Standard labor cost allowed:

$15/hr × 3.5 hrs. × 24 tune-ups =	$1,260
Labor rate variance was favorable	81
Actual total labor cost	$1,179

Actual labor rate/hour = $1,179/90 hrs. = $13.10/hr.

    b. Direct labor efficiency variance:

$$\text{(Standard hours} - \text{Actual hours)} \times \text{Standard rate}$$

$$(84 - 90) \times \$15 = \$90 \text{ Unfavorable}$$

    c. Less skilled, lower-paid workers took longer than standard workers to get the work done. Net variance is $9 unfavorable ($90 U − $81 F). This was not a good trade-off based on the variance. From a qualitative viewpoint less skilled workers may not do as good a job.

15–9. *a.*

	Original Budget	*Flexed Budget*	*Actual*	*Variance*
Direct labor	$1,800	$1,716*	$1,888	$172 U

* 2,860 books/20 = 143 standard hours allowed.
  143 standard hours × $12/hr. = $1,716 flexed budget

    b. Direct labor efficiency variance = Standard hours − Actual hours

$$= 143 - 160$$
$$= 17 \text{ hours U}$$

    c. Direct labor rate variance = (Standard rate − Actual rate) × Actual hours

$$= (\$12 - (\$1,888/160 \text{ hrs.})) \times 160 \text{ hrs.}$$
$$= (\$12 - \$11.80) \times 160$$
$$= \$32 \text{ F}$$

15–11. No. For example, Goodwrench Garage management might be able to control results better if the efficiency variance is reported daily in hours. The rate variance might be reported only weekly or monthly. The reason for calculating variances is to permit action to eliminate unfavorable variances and capture favorable variances; the reason is *not* to assess blame.

15–13. *a.* Raw material usage and direct labor efficiency variances are in the aggregate about 15 percent of the total standard cost of goods produced. This indicates that the standards are not a very effective tool for controlling those costs.

b. The variances were favorable, so the standards are higher than actual costs incurred. Therefore, ending inventory values will be higher than actual cost.

c. Use the 15 percent difference between standard and actual. Ending inventory should be reduced to 85 percent of its standard cost to state it at actual. $85\% \times \$158,780 = \$134,963$. The adjustment would be a $15\% \times \$158,780 = \$23,817$ reduction in the ending inventory.

15–15.

	Simple Claims	*Complex Claims*
Standard processing time . .	.75 hrs.	2.5 hrs.
Work hours per day	7.5	7.5
Standard number of claims that should be processed per day per worker	10	3
Number of days in month . .	20	20
Standard number of claims to be processed in the month.	200	60
Claims processed.	3,000	600
Standard number of workers for month	15	10

a. Total workers required . . . 25
Actual number of workers. . 27

b. Efficiency variance, in number of workers . . . . . . 2 Unfavorable

Efficiency variance, in dollars   2 workers $\times$ \$90/day $\times$ 20 days
                                                    = \$3,600 Unfavorable

15–17. *a.*

$$\frac{\text{Predetermined overhead}}{\text{application rate}} = \frac{\text{Estimated \$ overhead}}{\text{Estimated activity}}$$

$$= \frac{\$36,000}{40,000 \text{ units} \times 0.5 \text{ hr./unit}}$$

$$= \$1.80/\text{machine hour}$$

b. 39,000 units produced $\times$ 0.5 machine hr./unit

= 19,500 machine hours allowed

c.   Applied overhead = \$1.80 $\times$ 19,500 hrs. = \$35,100

d.

Actual overhead incurred	\$37,000
Overhead applied	35,100
Underapplied overhead	\$ 1,900

e. Budget variance:

Budgeted overhead	$36,000	
Actual overhead	37,000	
Budget variance	$ 1,000	Unfavorable

Volume variance:

Budgeted hours	20,000	
Hours allowed for work done	19,500	
Difference	500	
× Predetermined application rate	$ 1.80	
Volume variance	$ 900	Unfavorable

CHAPTER 16

6–1. *a.*

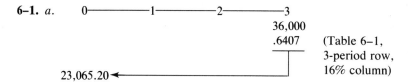

0—————1—————2—————3
36,000
.6407   (Table 6–1,
3-period row,
16% column)
23,065.20◄

b. This is a future value problem, the opposite of present value. As shown in the diagram, $23,065.20 invested today at 16 percent interest compounded annually would grow to $36,000 in three years.

c. Less could be invested today because at a higher interest rate there would be more interest earned. This can be seen by calculating the present value of $36,000 in three years at an interest rate higher than 16 percent. As can be seen in Table 6–1, the present value factors are smaller as interest rates get higher.

16–3. *a.* If the investment is too high, the net present value will be too low.

b. If the cost of capital is too low, the net present value will be too high.

c. If the cash flows from the project are too high, the net present value will be too high.

d. If the number of years over which the project will generate cash flows is too low, the net present value will be too low.

16–5. *a.*

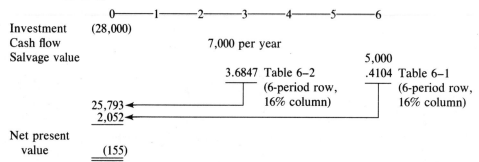

0———1———2———3———4———5———6
Investment   (28,000)
Cash flow   7,000 per year
Salvage value   5,000
                    3.6847 Table 6–2   .4104 Table 6–1
                    (6-period row,   (6-period row,
                    16% column)   16% column)
            25,793◄
            2,052◄

Net present
value   (155)

b. Because the net present value is negative, the internal rate of return on this project will be lower than the cost of capital.

16–7. *a.*

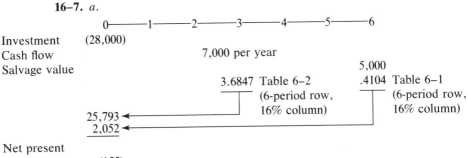

Net present
value   (155)

b.   Profitability index = PV of inflows/invstment
                                      = (25,793 + 2,052)/28,000
                                      = .99

c. Internal rate of return (actual rate of return) is less than cost of capital of 16 percent because Net PV is negative and because the profitability index < 1. IRR is not much less than 16 percent, however.

d. Payback period = 4 years.

Investment		$28,000
Return in year 1	$ 7,000	
Return in year 2	7,000	
Return in year 3	7,000	
Return in year 4	7,000	
Total return in 4 years	$28,000	

16–9. *a.* The net present value is positive $2,220 (present value of inflows of $26,220 less the investment of $24,000). Therefore the return on investment is higher than 20 percent.

b. The payback period should not carry much weight at all because it does not recognize the time value of money.

16–11.

Proposal	Investment	Net PV	PV of Inflows (Investment + Net PV)	Profitability Index (PV of Inflows/Investment)
1	$50,000	$30,000	$80,000	80/50 = 1.6
2	60,000	24,000	84,000	84/60 = 1.4
3	30,000	15,000	45,000	45/30 = 1.5
4	45,000	9,000	54,000	54/45 = 1.2

Proposal 1 has the highest profitability index and so is the most desirable investment.

16–13. *a.*

$$\text{Accounting rate of return} = \frac{\text{Net income}}{\text{Average investment}}$$

$$= \frac{29{,}000 - 10{,}000^*}{(100{,}000 + 90{,}000)/2^\dagger}$$

$$= 20\%$$

* Depreciation expense = (Cost − Salvage)/Life
= (80,000 − 50,000)/3
= 10,000

$\dagger$ Investment at end of year = Investment at beginning of year − Accumulated depreciation
= 100,000 − 10,000
= 90,000

Based on this analysis, the investment would be made because the rate of return of 20% is more than the cost of capital of 18%.

b.

	Year 1 January 1	Year 1 Full Year	Year 2	Year 3	Year 4
Investment:					
Machine	(80,000)				
Working capital	(20,000)				
Cash return:					
Operations		14,000	24,000	29,000	20,000
Salvage					50,000
Working capital					20,000
Totals	(100,000)	14,000	24,000	29,000	90,000
PV factor for 18%		0.8475	0.7182	0.6086	0.5158
Present value		11,865	17,237	17,649	46,422
Sum of PVs	93,173 ←				
Net PV	(6,827)				

Based on this analysis, the investment would not be made because the net present value is negative, indicating that the rate of return on the project is less than the discount rate of 18%.

c. The net present value analytical approach is the best one to use because it recognizes the time value of money.

Index